Collins
School
Dictionary

Collins *gem*

HarperCollins Publishers
Westerhill Road
Bishopbriggs
Glasgow
G64 2QT
Great Britain

Third Edition 2007

Reprint 10 9 8 7 6 5 4

© HarperCollins Publishers 2005,
2006, 2007

ISBN 978-0-00-726103-1

Collins Gem® is a registered
trademark of HarperCollins
Publishers Limited

www.collinslanguage.com

A catalogue record for this book is
available from the British Library

Computing Support
Thomas Callan

Typeset by Wordcraft

Printed in Italy by
LEGO Spa, Lavis (Trento), ITALY

Acknowledgements
We would like to thank those authors
and publishers who kindly gave
permission for copyright material
to be used in the Collins Word Web.
We would also like to thank Times
Newspapers Ltd for providing
valuable data.

When you buy Collins Gem School
Dictionary and register on
www.collinslanguage.com for the
free online and digital services, you
will not be charged by
HarperCollins for access to Collins
free Online Thesaurus and Collins
free Online Dictionary content on
that website. However, your
operator's charges for using the
internet on your computer will
apply. Costs vary from operator to
operator. HarperCollins is not
responsible for any charges levied
by online service providers for
accessing Collins Online Thesaurus
or Collins Online Dictionary on
www.collinslanguage.com using
these services.

HarperCollins does not warrant
that the functions contained in
www.collinslanguage.com
content will be error free, or that
defects will be corrected, or that
www.collinslanguage.com or the
server that makes it available
are free of viruses or bugs.

HarperCollins is not responsible for
any access difficulties that may be
experienced due to problems with
network, web, online or mobile
phone connections.

CONTENTS

EDITORIAL STAFF

EDITORS
Jamie Flockhart
Cordelia Lilly
Elspeth Summers

FOR THE PUBLISHERS
Morven Dooner
Elaine Higgleton

Being able to read, understand and write good English are vital and fundamental skills that underpin success in exams and, ultimately, success in the world beyond school. A dictionary is an essential tool for all students who want to do well in exams, because if you know how to use a dictionary effectively you can improve your performance in all subjects, not just English. This is why literacy strategies all over the world set ambitious targets for students to acquire dictionary skills at every stage of their education.

Collins Gem School Dictionary has been carefully researched with teachers and students to ensure that it includes the information on language that students need, to allow them to improve their performance in all other school subjects, and to achieve exam success. It provides:

Essential information on what words mean, how they are used, spelling, grammar and punctuation, so that students can use language well, communicate with others and express their ideas effectively.

Comprehensive coverage of core vocabulary from a wide range of curriculum subjects, such as Science, Information Technology, History, Geography and RE, to help with success in *all* subjects.

Collins Gem School Dictionary is very straightforward, with an accessible layout that's easy on the eye, guiding students quickly to what they want. It's relevant to school work in all subjects, accessible and student-friendly, and offers essential help on the route to success.

USING THIS DICTIONARY

Main Entry Words printed in large bold type:

> **abbey**
>
> All main entry words, including abbreviations, prefixes and suffixes, in alphabetical order:
>
> **abbot**
> **abbreviate**

Variant spellings shown in full, eg

> **adrenalin** or **adrenaline**

Parts of Speech shown in italics

> **athlete** *noun*

When a word can be used as more than one part of speech, the change of part of speech is shown after a triangle:

> **blight** *noun* **1** something that damages or spoils other things …
> ▷ *verb* **3** to harm

Parts of speech may be combined for some words:

> **alone** *adjective, adverb* without anyone or any thing else; on your own

Cross References	shown in bold type:

began *verb* past tense of **begin**

Irregular Parts or confusing forms of verb, nouns, adjectives, and adverbs shown in bold type:

go goes going went gone
mushy mushier mushiest

Meanings shown in separate categories

electric *adjective*
1 powered or produced by electricity **2** exciting or tense

Related Words	shown in the same paragraph as the main entry word:

abduct *verb* to take (someone) away by force >
abduction *noun: the abduction of a boy* >
abductor *noun*

Note: where the meaning of a related word is not given, it may be understood from the main entry word, or from an example.

ABBREVIATIONS USED IN THIS DICTIONARY

AD	anno Domini
Aust	Australia(n)
BC	before Christ
Brit	British
C *of* E	Church of England
E	East
eg	for example
esp	especially
etc	et cetera
fem	feminine
N	North
NZ	New Zealand
orig	originally
ŭ	trademark
RC	Roman Catholic
S	South
S *Afr*	South Africa(n)
Scot	Scottish
US	United States
usu	usually
W	West

a

a **an** *indefinite article* (before a vowel sound *an*) used before a noun being mentioned for the first time: *a tractor; an apple*

- *prefix* **1** (before a vowel *an-*) not, without or opposite to: *amoral* **2** towards or in the state of: *aback; asleep*

ardvark *noun* S African anteater with long ears and snout

back *adverb* **taken aback** startled or very surprised

bacus abacuses *noun* beads on a wire frame, used for doing calculations

alone *noun* edible sea creature with a shell lined with mother of pearl

andon *verb* **1** to desert or leave someone or something) **2** to ive up (something) completely *noun* **3** lack of inhibition: *e began to laugh with abandon* **abandoned** *adjective* **1** deserted **2** uninhibited > **abandonment** *oun*

ate *verb* to make or become ss strong

attoir *noun* place where imals are killed for meat

bey *noun* church with buildings tached to it in which monks or ns live or lived

bot *noun* head of an abbey of onks

reviate *verb* to shorten (a rd) by leaving out some letters

reviation shortened

form of a word or words

abdicate *verb* to give up (the throne or a responsibility) > **abdication** *noun*

abdomen *noun* part of the body containing the stomach and intestines > **abdominal** *adjective* relating to the stomach and intestines

abduct *verb* to take (someone) away by force > **abduction** *noun: the abduction of a boy* > **abductor** *noun*

aberration *noun* **1** sudden change from what is normal, accurate or correct **2** brief lapse in control of your thoughts or feelings

abet abets abetting abetted *verb* to help (someone) do something criminal or wrong

abhor abhors abhorring abhorred *verb formal* to hate (something) > **abhorrence** *noun: their abhorrence of racism* > **abhorrent** *adjective* hateful, loathsome

abide abides abiding abided *verb* **1** to bear or stand: *I can't abide that song* **2 abide by** to act in accordance with (a rule or decision) > **abiding** *adjective* lasting

ability abilities *noun* intelligence or skill needed to do something

abject *adjective* **1** very bad: *abject failure* **2** lacking all self-respect > **abjectly** *adverb*

ablaze *adjective* burning fiercely

able abler ablest *adjective* capable or competent

-able *suffix* (forming adjectives) **1** capable of or susceptible to (an action): *enjoyable; breakable* **2** causing (something):

comfortable

ably *adverb* skilfully and successfully

abnormal *adjective* not normal or usual > **abnormality** *noun* something that is not normal or usual > **abnormally** *adverb*

aboard *adverb, preposition* on, in, onto or into (a ship, train or plane)

abode *noun* old-fashioned home

abolish *verb* to do away with > **abolition** *noun: the abolition of slavery*

abominable *adjective* detestable or very bad > **abominably** *adverb*

Aboriginal *noun* someone descended from the people who lived in Australia before Europeans arrived > **Aboriginal** *adjective*

abort *verb* **1** to cause (a fetus) to be deliberately expelled from the womb ending the pregnancy prematurely so that the baby does not survive **2** to end (a plan or process) before completion

abortion *noun* operation or medical procedure to end a pregnancy

abortive *adjective* unsuccessful

abound *verb* to exist in large numbers

about *preposition* **1** concerning or on the subject of **2** in or near (a place) ▷ *adverb* **3** nearly, approximately **4** nearby **5** about to shortly going to **6** not about to determined not to

above *adverb, preposition* **1** over or higher (than) **2** greater (than) **3** superior (to)

above board *adjective* completely open and legal

abrasion *noun* scraped area on the skin

abrasive *adjective* **1** unpleasant and rude **2** rough and able to be used to clean or polish hard surfaces

abreast *adjective* **1** alongside and facing in the same direction **2** abreast of up to date with: *He will be keeping abreast of the news*

abroad *adverb* to or in a foreign country

abrupt *adjective* **1** sudden and unexpected **2** not friendly or polite > **abruptly** *adverb* > **abruptness** *noun*

abscess *noun* painful swelling containing pus

abseiling *noun* sport of going down a cliff or a tall building by sliding down ropes

absent *adjective* **1** not present **2** lacking **3** inattentive ▷ *verb* **4** absent yourself *formal* to stay away > **absence** *noun*

absentee *noun* person who shou[ld] be present but is not

absent-minded *adjective* inattentive or forgetful > **absen[t]-mindedly** *adverb* > **absent-mindedness** *noun* forgetfulnes[s]

absolute *adjective* **1** complete o[r] perfect: *absolute honesty* **2** not limited, unconditional: *the absolute ruler* **3** pure: *absolute alcohol* > **absolutely** *adverb* **1** completely ▷ *interjection* **2** certainly, yes

absolve *verb* to declare (someon[e]) to be free from blame or sin

absorb *verb* **1** to soak up (a liqu[id]) **2** to deal with or cope with (a shock, change or effect)

absorbent *adjective* able to abs[orb] liquid

absorption noun 1 soaking up of a liquid 2 great interest in something

abstain verb 1 to choose not to do or have (something) 2 to choose not to vote > **abstainer** noun 1 person who does not drink alcohol 2 person who chooses not to vote > **abstention** noun abstaining, especially from voting

abstinence noun state or practice of choosing not to take or do something, especially not to drink alcohol

abstract adjective 1 existing as a quality or idea rather than objects or events 2 Art using patterns of shapes and colours rather than realistic likenesses 3 (of nouns) referring to qualities or ideas rather than to physical objects: happiness; a question ▷ noun 4 summary 5 abstract work of art ▷ verb 6 to summarize 7 to remove or extract

absurd adjective 1 ridiculous and stupid 2 obviously senseless and illogical > **absurdity** noun: the absurdity of the situation > **absurdly** adverb

abundance noun 1 great amount or large number > **abundant** adjective present in great amounts or large numbers > **abundantly** adverb

abuse verb 1 to use (something) wrongly 2 to ill-treat (someone) violently 3 to speak harshly and rudely to (someone) ▷ noun 4 prolonged ill-treatment 5 harsh and vulgar comments 6 wrong use of something > **abuser** noun: convicted child abuser

abusive adjective 1 cruel and violent 2 (of language) very rude

and insulting > **abusively** adverb

abysmal adjective very bad indeed > **abysmally** adverb

abyss noun very deep hole or chasm

acacia noun type of thorny shrub with small yellow or white flowers

academic adjective 1 of an academy or university 2 of theoretical interest only ▷ noun 3 lecturer or researcher at a university > **academically** adverb

academy academies noun 1 organization of scientists, artists, writers or musicians 2 institution for training in a particular skill: a military academy 3 Scot secondary school

accelerate verb to move or cause to move more quickly

acceleration noun rate at which the speed of something is increasing

accelerator noun pedal in a motor vehicle, which is pressed to increase speed

accent noun 1 distinctive style of pronunciation of a local, national or social group: She had an Australian accent 2 mark over a letter to show how it is pronounced 3 an emphasis on something: The accent is on action and special effects

accentuate verb to stress or emphasize (something)

accept verb 1 to receive (something) willingly 2 to tolerate (a situation) 3 to consider (something) to be true 4 to receive (someone) into a community or group > **acceptable** adjective 1 tolerable

A

2 satisfactory > **acceptably** adverb **acceptance** noun **1** act of accepting something **2** favourable reception **3** belief or agreement

access noun **1** right or opportunity to enter a place or to use something ▷ verb **2** to obtain (data) from a computer

accessible adjective **1** easy to reach **2** easily understood or used > **accessibility** noun

accession noun taking up of an office or position: *her accession to the throne*

accessory accessories noun **1** an extra part **2** person involved in a crime although not present when it is committed

accident noun **1** mishap, often causing injury or death **2** event that happens by chance

accidental adjective happening by chance or unintentionally > **accidentally** adverb

accolade noun formal great praise or an award given to someone

accommodate verb **1** to provide (someone) with lodgings **2** to have room for **3** to oblige or do a favour for

accommodating adjective willing to help and to adjust to new situations

accommodation noun house or room for living in

accompaniment noun **1** something that accompanies: *Melon is a good accompaniment to cold meats* **2** Music supporting part that goes with a solo

accompany accompanies accompanying accompanied verb **1** to go with **2** to occur

at the same time as or as a result of **3** to provide a musical accompaniment for

accomplice noun person who helps another to commit a crime

accomplish verb to succeed in doing (something)

accomplished adjective very talented at something

accomplishment noun **1** completion of something **2** personal ability or skill

accord noun **1** agreement or harmony **2** of your own accord willingly ▷ verb **3** to grant (something to someone) **4** accord with formal to fit in with or be consistent with

accordance noun in accordance with conforming to or according to

according to preposition **1** as stated by **2** in conformity with > **accordingly** adverb **1** in an appropriate manner **2** consequently

accordion noun portable musical instrument played by moving the two sides apart and together and pressing a keyboard or buttons to produce the notes

accost verb to approach, stop and speak to (someone)

account noun **1** report or description **2** business arrangement making credit available **3** record of money received and paid out with the resulting balance **4** person's money held in a bank **5** on account of because of **6** of no account of no importance or value > **account for** verb **1** to give reasons for; explain **2** to b particular amount or proportion of (something): *The brain accounts for 3% of body weight*

accountable *adjective* responsible to someone or for something: *The committee is accountable to Parliament* ▷ **accountability** *noun*: *In a democracy there is accountability for error* ▷ **accountably** *adverb*

accountancy *noun* job of keeping or inspecting financial accounts

accountant *noun* person whose job is to keep or inspect financial accounts

accounting *noun* keeping and checking of financial accounts

accrue *accrues accruing accrued verb* (of money or interest) to increase gradually

accumulate *verb* to gather together in increasing quantity ▷ **accumulation** *noun* something that has been collected

accurate *adjective* completely correct or precise ▷ **accurately** *verb*

accuse *verb* to charge (someone) with wrongdoing ▷ **accused** *noun* defendant appearing on a criminal charge ▷ **accuser** *noun*

accustom *verb* **accustom yourself to** to become familiar with or used to (something) from habit or experience

accustomed *adjective* **1** usual **2 accustomed to a** used to (something) **b** in the habit of (doing something)

... *noun* **1** playing card with one symbol on it **2** *informal* expert ▷ *adjective* **3** *informal* good or skilful

...**bic** *adjective formal* harsh or bitter

ache *noun* **1** dull continuous pain ▷ *verb* **2** to be in or cause continuous dull pain

achieve *verb* to gain by hard work or ability

achievement *noun* something accomplished

acid *noun* **1** *Chemistry* one of a class of compounds, corrosive and sour when dissolved in water, that combine with a base to form a salt **2** *informal* the drug LSD ▷ *adjective* **3** containing acid **4** sour-tasting ▷ **acidic** *adjective* ▷ **acidity** *noun*

acid rain *noun* rain polluted by acid in the atmosphere which has come from factories

acknowledge *verb* **1** to recognize or admit the truth or reality of **2** to show recognition of a person by a greeting or glance **3** to let someone know that you have received (their letter or message) ▷ **acknowledgment** or **acknowledgement** *noun* **1** act of acknowledging something or someone **2** something done or given as an expression of gratitude

acne *noun* lumpy spots that cover someone's face

acorn *noun* fruit of the oak tree, consisting of a pale oval nut in a cup-shaped base

acoustic *adjective* **1** relating to sound and hearing **2** (of a musical instrument) not electronically amplified

acoustics *noun* **1** science of sounds ▷ *plural* **2** features of a room or building determining how sound is heard within it

acquaintance *noun* person known slightly but not well

acquire *verb* to obtain (something), usually permanently

acquisition *noun* **1** thing acquired **2** act of getting

acquit **acquits** **acquitting** **acquitted** *verb* **1** to pronounce (someone) innocent **2** **acquit yourself** to behave or perform in a particular way: *The French team acquitted themselves well*

acre *noun* unit for measuring areas of land. One acre equals 4840 square yards (4046.86 square metres)

acrid *adjective* sharp and bitter: *the acrid smell of burning*

acrimony *noun* formal bitterness and anger >**acrimonious** *adjective* (of a dispute or argument) bitter and angry

acrobat *noun* person skilled in gymnastic feats requiring agility and balance >**acrobatic** *adjective* involving agility and balance >**acrobatics** *plural noun* acrobatic feats

acronym *noun* word formed from the initial letters of other words, such as 'NASA' and 'NATO'

across *adverb, preposition* **1** from side to side (of) **2** on or to the other side (of)

acrylic *noun* **1** type of man-made cloth **2** kind of artists' paint which can be used like oil paint or thinned down with water

act *noun* **1** single thing done: *It was an act of disloyalty to the King* **2** law or decree **3** section of a play or opera **4** one of several short performances in a show **5** pretended attitude ▷ *verb* **6** to do something: *It would be irresponsible not to act swiftly* **7** to behave in a particular way **8** to perform in a play, film, etc

acting *noun* **1** art of an actor ▷ *adjective* **2** temporarily performing the duties of: *the acting manager*

action *noun* **1** process of doing something **2** thing done **3** legal proceeding: *a libel action* **4** operating mechanism **5** fighting in a war or battle: *255 men killed in action*

activate *verb* to make active or capable of working >**activation** *noun*: *A computer controls the activation of the air bag*

active *adjective* **1** moving or working **2** busy and energetic **3** *Grammar* (of a verb) in a form indicating that the subject is performing the action, e.g. *threw* in *Kim threw the ball* >**actively** *adverb*

activist *noun* person who works energetically to achieve political or social goals

activity activities *noun* **1** situation in which a lot of things are happening or being done **2** something you spend time doing

actor *noun* person who acts in a play, film, etc

actress *noun* woman who acts in a play, film, etc

actual *adjective* real, rather than imaginary or guessed at >**actually** *adverb* really, indeed

acumen *noun* ability to make good judgments: *business acumen*

acupuncture *noun* treatment of illness or pain involving the insertion of needles at various points on the body

cute adjective **1** severe or intense: an acute shortage of beds **2** very intelligent **3** sensitive or keen **4** (of an angle) less than 90° ▷ noun **5** accent (´) over a letter to indicate the quality or length of its sound, as in café ▷ **acutely** adverb

D abbreviation anno Domini: used n dates to indicate the number of years after the birth of Jesus Christ: 70 AD

d- prefix near or next to: adjoining

age noun wise saying

amant adjective unshakable n determination or purpose ▷ **adamantly** adverb

dam's apple noun a lump at the ront of the neck which is more obvious in men than in women or oung boys

apt verb **1** to adjust (something r yourself) to new conditions to change (something) to suit new purpose ▷ **adaptability** oun: adaptability to a changing vironment ▷ **adaptable** adjective le to adjust to new conditions

aptor or **adapter** noun device r connecting several electrical pliances to a single socket

d verb **1** to combine (numbers or antities) **2** to join (something omething else) **3** to say or ite (something more)

er noun small poisonous snake

ict noun **1** person who is able to stop taking drugs formal person devoted to nething ▷ **addicted** adjective ependent on a drug **2** devoted omething ▷ **addiction** noun

ctive adjective causing

addiction

addition noun **1** process of adding numbers together **2** thing added **3** in addition besides, as well

additional adjective extra or more: the decision to take on additional staff ▷ **additionally** adverb

additive noun something added, especially to a foodstuff, to improve it or prevent deterioration

address addresses addressing addressed noun **1** place where a person lives **2** destination or sender's location written on a letter, etc **3** location **4** formal public speech ▷ verb **5** to mark the destination on (an envelope, parcel, etc) **6** to attend to (a problem, task, etc) **7** to talk to (someone)

adept adjective very skilful at doing something: adept at motivating others

adequate adjective enough in amount or good enough for a purpose ▷ **adequately** adverb

adhere verb **1** to stick (to) **2** to act according (to a rule or agreement) **3** to continue to support or hold (an opinion or belief) ▷ **adherence** noun: strict adherence to the rules

adhesive noun **1** substance used to stick things together ▷ adjective **2** able to stick to things

adjacent adjective **1** near or next (to): a hotel adjacent to the beach **2** Maths (of angles) sharing one side and having the same point opposite their bases

adjective noun word that adds information about a noun or pronoun ▷ **adjectival** adjective of

a
b
c
d
e
f
g
h
i
j
k
l
m
n
o
p
q
r
s
t
u
v
w
x
y
z

or relating to an adjective

adjoining *adjective* next to and joined onto: *adjoining rooms*

adjourn *verb* **1** to stop (a trial or meeting) temporarily; suspend **2** (of a court, parliament, meeting) to come to a stop with a temporary suspension of activities **3** to go (to another place): *We adjourned to the lounge*

adjust *verb* **1** to adapt to new conditions **2** to alter (something) slightly to improve its suitability or effectiveness > **adjustable** *adjective* able to be adapted or altered: *adjustable seats* > **adjustment** *noun* slight alteration

ad-lib *ad-libs ad-libbing ad-libbed verb* **1** to improvise a speech etc without preparation: *I ad-lib on radio but use a script on TV* ▷ *noun* **2** comment that has not been prepared beforehand

administer *verb* **1** to manage (business affairs) **2** to organize and put into practice **3** to give (medicine or treatment)

administration *noun* **1** management of an organization **2** people who manage an organization **3** government: *the Bush administration*

admirable *adjective* very good and deserving to be admired > **admirably** *adverb*

admiral *noun* highest naval rank

admire *verb* to respect and approve of (a person or thing) > **admiration** *noun* respect and approval > **admirer** *noun* > **admiring** *adjective: an admiring glance* > **admiringly** *adverb*

admission *noun* **1** permission

to enter **2** entrance fee **3** confession: *an admission of guilt*

admit *admits admitting admitted verb* **1** to confess or acknowledge (a crime or mistake) **2** to concede (the truth of something) **3** to allow (someone) to enter **4** to make (someone) an in-patient in a hospital: *He was admitted to hospital with chest pain*

admittedly *adverb* it must be said

adolescent *noun* person between puberty and adulthood > **adolescence** *noun* period between puberty and adulthood

adopt *verb* **1** to take (someone else's child) as your own **2** to take up (a plan or principle) > **adoption** *noun* **1** taking up of a plan or principle **2** process of adopting a child

adorable *adjective* sweet and attractive

adore *verb* **1** to love intensely or deeply **2** *informal* to like very much: *I adore being in the countryside*

adorn *verb* to decorate or embellish > **adornment** *noun* decoration

adrenalin or **adrenaline** *noun* hormone produced by the body when a person is angry, nervous or excited, making the heart beat faster and giving the body more energy

adrift *adjective, adverb* **1** drifting **2** without a clear purpose

adulation *noun* uncritical admiration > **adulatory** *adjective: adulatory reviews*

adult *adjective* **1** fully grown; mature ▷ *noun* **2** adult person or animal

adultery adulteries noun sexual intercourse between a married person and someone he or she is not married to ▷ **adulterer** noun person who commits adultery ▷ **adulterous** adjective of or relating to adultery

adulthood noun time when a person is an adult

advance verb **1** to go or bring forward **2** to further (a cause) **3** to propose (an idea) **4** to lend (a sum of money) ▷ noun **5** forward movement **6** improvement: scientific advance **7** loan **8** in advance ahead ▷ adjective **9** done or happening before an event

advantage noun **1** more favourable position or state **2** benefit or profit **3** Tennis point scored after deuce **4** take advantage of a to use (a person) unfairly **b** to use (an opportunity)

advantageous adjective likely to bring benefits ▷ **advantageously** adverb

advent noun **1** arrival or coming into existence **2** Advent season of four weeks before Christmas in the Christian calendar

adventure noun exciting and risky undertaking or exploit

adventurer noun **1** person who enjoys doing dangerous and exciting things **2** person who unscrupulously seeks money or power

adventurous adjective willing to take risks and do new and exciting things ▷ **adventurously** adverb

adverb noun word that adds information about a verb, adjective or other adverb

▷ **adverbial** adjective

adversary adversaries noun opponent or enemy

adverse adjective unfavourable to your interests ▷ **adversely** adverb

adversity adversities noun time of danger or difficulty

advert noun informal advertisement

advertise verb **1** to present or praise (goods or services) to the public in order to encourage sales **2** to make (a vacancy, event, etc) known publicly ▷ **advertiser** noun person or company that pays for something to be advertised ▷ **advertising** noun: He works in advertising

advertisement noun public announcement to sell goods or publicize an event

advice noun recommendation as to what to do

- The noun advice is spelt with a c and the verb advise with an s

advisable adjective prudent, sensible ▷ **advisability** noun: doubts about the advisability of surgery

advise verb **1** to offer advice to **2** formal to inform or notify: We advised them of our decision

- The verb advise is spelt with an s and the noun advice is spelt with a c

adviser or **advisor** noun person who offers advice, for example on careers

advocate verb **1** to propose or recommend ▷ noun **2** person who publicly supports a cause **3** Scot, SAfr barrister ▷ **advocacy** noun public support of a cause

aerial *adjective* **1** in, from or operating in the air: *aerial combat* ▷ *noun* **2** metal pole, wire, etc. for receiving or transmitting radio or TV signals

aerial top dressing *noun* spreading of fertilizer from an aeroplane onto remote areas

aero- *prefix* involving the air, the atmosphere or aircraft: *aerobatics*

aerobics *noun* exercises designed to increase the amount of oxygen in the blood ▷ **aerobic** *adjective* designed for or relating to aerobics

aerodynamic *adjective* having a streamlined shape that moves easily through the air

aeroplane *noun* powered flying vehicle with fixed wings

aerosol *noun* pressurized can from which a substance can be dispensed as a fine spray

aerospace *noun* **1** earth's atmosphere and space beyond ▷ *adjective* **2** involved in making and designing aeroplanes and spacecraft

aesthetic *adjective formal* relating to the appreciation of art and beauty ▷ **aesthetically** *adverb*

afar *adverb literary* **from afar** from or at a great distance

affable *adjective* friendly and easy to talk to ▷ **affably** *adverb*

affair *noun* **1** event or happening **2** sexual relationship outside marriage **3** thing to be done or attended to: *My wife's career is her own affair* **4 affairs a** personal or business interests **b** matters of public interest

affect *verb* **1** to influence (someone or something): *the difficult conditions continued to affect our performance* **2** to move (someone) emotionally **3** to put on a show of: *He affects ignorance*

- Do not confuse the spelling of the verb *affect* with the noun *effect*. Something that *affects* you has an *effect* on you

affectation *noun* attitude or manner put on to impress

affection *noun* **1** fondness or love **2 affections** feelings of love for someone

affectionate *adjective* full of fondness for someone; loving ▷ **affectionately** *adverb*

affiliate *verb* **1** (of a group) to link up with a larger group ▷ *noun* **2** organization which has a close link with another, larger group ▷ **affiliation** *noun*: *The group has no affiliation to any political party*

affinity affinities *noun* close similarity or understanding between two things or people

affirm *verb* **1** to declare to be true **2** to indicate support or confirmation of (an idea or belief) ▷ **affirmation** *noun*: *His work is an affirmation of life*

affirmative *adjective* meaning or indicating yes

afflict *verb* to cause someone unhappiness or suffering ▷ **affliction** *noun* **1** something that causes unhappiness or suffering **2** condition of great distress or suffering

affluent *adjective* having plenty of money ▷ **affluence** *noun* wealth

afford *verb* **1** to have enough money to buy **2** to be able to spare (the time etc) **3** to give or supply > **affordable** adjective: an affordable small car

affray noun Brit, Aust, NZ law noisy fight; brawl

affront verb **1** to offend the pride or dignity of ▷ noun **2** insult: Our prisons are an affront to civilized society

afield adverb **far afield** far away

afloat adverb, adjective **1** floating on water **2** at sea or aboard ship **3** successful and making enough money: Companies are struggling hard to stay afloat

afoot adverb, adjective happening; in operation: Plans are afoot to build a new museum

afraid adjective **1** frightened **2** regretful: I'm afraid I lost my temper

afresh adverb again and in a new way

Africa noun second largest continent, which is surrounded by sea, with the Atlantic on its west side, the Mediterranean to the north and the Indian Ocean and the Red Sea to the east

African adjective **1** belonging or relating to Africa ▷ noun **2** someone, especially a Black person, from Africa

African-American noun American whose ancestors came from Africa

Afrikaans noun language used in S Africa, descended from Dutch

Afrikaner noun White South African whose mother tongue is Afrikaans

aft adverb at or towards the rear of a ship or aircraft

after preposition **1** following in time or place **2** in pursuit of:

He was after my mother's jewellery **3** concerning: He asked after Laura **4** considering: You seem all right after what happened last night **5** next in excellence or importance to **6** with the same name as: The building is named after the architect ▷ conjunction **7** at a later time than the time when: She arrived after the reading had begun ▷ adverb **8** at a later time

afterlife noun life after death

aftermath noun results of an event considered together

afternoon noun time between noon and evening

aftershave noun pleasant-smelling liquid men put on their faces after shaving

afterthought noun **1** idea occurring later **2** something added later

afterwards or **afterward** adverb later

again adverb **1** happening one more time: He looked forward to becoming a father again **2** returning to the same state or place as before: there and back again **3** in addition to an amount that has already been mentioned: I could eat twice as much again

against preposition **1** in opposition or contrast to: the Test match against England **2** touching and leaning on: He leaned against the wall **3** as a protection from: precautions against fire **4** in comparison with: The euro is now at its highest rate against the dollar

age ages ageing or **aging aged** noun **1** length of time a person or thing has existed: What age was he when he died? **2** time of life: He should know better at his age

3 state of being old or the process of becoming older: *The fabric was showing signs of age* **4** period of history: *the Iron Age* **5 ages** *informal* long time: *He's been talking for ages* **6 come of age** to become legally responsible for your actions (usually at 18) ▷ *verb* **7** to make or grow old

aged *adjective* **1** old: *an aged invalid* **2** being at the age of: *people aged 16 to 24*

agency agencies *noun* organization providing a particular service

agenda *noun* list of things to be dealt with, especially at a meeting

agent *noun* **1** person acting on behalf of another **2** person who works for a country's secret service **3** person or thing producing an effect: *bleaching agents*

aggravate *verb* **1** to make (a disease, situation or problem) worse **2** *informal* to annoy ▷ **aggravating** *adjective* ▷ **aggravation** *noun*

- Some people think that using *aggravate* to mean 'annoy' is wrong

aggregate *noun* **1** total made up of several smaller amounts **2** rock consisting of a mixture of minerals **3** sand or gravel used to make concrete ▷ *adjective* **4** gathered into a mass **5** total or final

aggression *noun* violent and hostile behaviour

aggressive *adjective* **1** full of hostility and violence **2** determined and eager to succeed: *aggressive sales*

techniques ▷ **aggressively** *adverb* ▷ **aggressiveness** *noun*: *a breed of dog with a reputation for aggressiveness*

aggressor *noun* person or country that starts a fight or a war

aggrieved *adjective* upset and angry

aghast *adjective* overcome with amazement or horror

agile *adjective* **1** able to move quickly and easily **2** mentally quick ▷ **agilely** *adverb* ▷ **agility** *noun* ability to move or think quickly

agitate *verb* **1** to disturb or excite **2** to stir or shake (a liquid) **3** to stir up public opinion for or against something ▷ **agitation** *noun* **1** state of disturbance or excitement **2** act of stirring or shaking something **3** stirring up of public opinion for or against something ▷ **agitator** *noun*: *a political agitator*

agnostic *noun* **1** person who believes that it is impossible to know whether God exists or not ▷ *adjective* **2** of agnostics ▷ **agnosticism** *noun* belief that it is impossible to know whether God exists or not

ago *adverb* in the past

agog *adjective* excited and eager to know more about something

agonizing or **agonising** *adjective* extremely painful, either physically or mentally

agony agonies *noun* extreme physical or mental pain

agoraphobia *noun* fear of open spaces ▷ **agoraphobic** *adjective* suffering from agoraphobia

agrarian *adjective* *formal* of land

agriculture: *agrarian economies*

agree *verb* **agreeing agreed**
verb **1** to be of the same opinion
2 to consent: *She agreed to go* **3** to
reach a joint decision **4** to be
similar or consistent **5 agree
with** to be good for (someone): *I
don't think milk agrees with me*

agreeable *adjective* **1** pleasant and
enjoyable **2** prepared to consent
to something > **agreeably** *adverb*

agreement *noun* **1** decision that
has been reached by two or more
people **2** legal contract

agriculture *noun* raising of crops
and livestock > **agricultural**
adjective of or relating to
agriculture

aground *adverb* onto the bottom
of shallow water

ahead *adverb* **1** in front; *He looked
ahead* **2** more advanced than
someone or something else:
*We are five years ahead of the
competition* **3** in the future

aid *noun* **1** money, equipment
or services provided for people
in need **2** help or support
something that makes a task
easier > *verb* **4** to help or assist

aide *noun* assistant to an
important person, especially in
the government or the army

AIDS *abbreviation* acquired
immunodeficiency syndrome:
a viral disease that destroys the
body's ability to fight infection

ailing *adjective* **1** sick or ill, and
not getting better **2** getting
into difficulties, especially with
money: *an ailing company*

ailment *noun* minor illness

aim *verb* **1** to point (a weapon
or missile) or direct (a blow

or remark) at someone or
something **2** to propose or intend
> *noun* **3** intention or purpose;
goal **4** aiming

aimless *adjective* having no
purpose > **aimlessly** *adverb*

air *noun* **1** mixture of gases
forming the earth's atmosphere
2 space above the ground or sky
3 breeze **4** quality or manner: *an
air of defiance* **5** simple tune **6 on
the air** in the act of broadcasting
on radio or television **7 airs**
manners put on to impress
people: *We never put on airs* > *verb*
8 to make known publicly **9** to
expose to air to dry or ventilate

airborne *adjective* **1** carried by air
2 (of aircraft) flying

air-conditioning *noun* system
that controls the temperature
and humidity of the air in a
building > **air-conditioned**
adjective: *an air-conditioned hotel*

aircraft *noun* any machine that
flies, such as an aeroplane
- The plural of *aircraft* is
  aircraft

airfield *noun* place where aircraft
can land and take off

air force *noun* branch of the armed
forces responsible for air warfare

air gun *noun* gun fired by
compressed air

air hostess *noun* female flight
attendant

airless *adjective* stuffy

airlift *noun* **1** transport of troops
or cargo by aircraft when other
routes are blocked > *verb* **2** to
transport by airlift

airline *noun* company which
provides air travel

airliner *noun* large passenger

aircraft

airmail noun **1** system of sending mail by aircraft **2** mail sent in this way

airman airmen noun man who serves in his country's air force

airport noun airfield for civilian aircraft, with facilities for aircraft maintenance and passengers

air raid noun attack by aircraft, in which bombs are dropped

airship noun large aircraft, consisting of a rigid balloon filled with gas and powered by an engine, with a passenger compartment underneath

airstrip noun cleared area where aircraft can take off and land

airtight adjective sealed so that air cannot enter

airy airier airiest adjective **1** full of fresh air and light **2** light-hearted and casual: *an airy wave of his hand* > **airily** adverb

aisle noun passageway separating the seating areas in a church, theatre, etc, or the rows of shelves in a supermarket

ajar adjective, adverb (of a door) partly open

akin adjective **akin to** similar, related: *The taste is akin to veal*

alabaster noun type of smooth white stone used for making ornaments

alacrity noun **with alacrity** quickly and eagerly

alarm noun **1** sudden fear caused by awareness of danger **2** warning sound **3** device that gives this **4** alarm clock > verb **5** to fill with fear > **alarming** adjective: *The disease has spread at an alarming rate*

alas adverb unfortunately, regrettably

albatross noun **1** large white sea bird with very long wings **2** a commitment that causes a great deal of difficulty

albeit conjunction formal even though: *He was making progress, albeit slowly*

albino albinos noun person or animal with white skin and hair and pink eyes

album noun **1** CD, cassette or record with a number of songs on it **2** book with blank pages for keeping photographs or stamps in

alchemy noun medieval form of chemistry concerned with trying to turn base metals into gold and to find the elixir of life > **alchemist** noun medieval scientist who tried to turn base metals into gold

alcheringa noun same as **Dreamtime**

alcohol noun **1** colourless flammable liquid present in intoxicating drinks **2** intoxicating drinks generally

alcoholic adjective **1** of alcohol: *alcoholic drinks* > noun **2** person addicted to alcohol > **alcoholism** noun addiction to alcohol

alcopop noun Brit, Aust, S Afr informal alcoholic drink that tastes like a soft drink

alcove noun recess in the wall of a room

ale noun kind of beer

alert adjective **1** paying full attention to what is happening: *The criminal was spotted by an alert member of the public* > noun

2 warning of danger **3 on the alert** watchful ▷ *verb* **4** to warn of danger >**alertness** *noun*: mental alertness

A level *noun* an advanced exam taken by students in many British schools and colleges, usually following GCSEs

algae *plural noun* plants which live in or near water and have no true stems, leaves or roots

algebra *noun* branch of mathematics in which symbols and letters are used instead of numbers to express relationships between quantities >**algebraic** *adjective*: *algebraic equations*

Algerian *adjective* **1** belonging or relating to Algeria ▷ *noun* **2** someone from Algeria

alias *aliases adverb* **1** also known as ▷ *noun* **2** false name

alibi *alibis noun* **1** plea of being somewhere else when a crime was committed **2** *informal* excuse

alien *adjective* **1** foreign **2** strange and outside your normal experience; different **3** from another world ▷ *noun* **4** foreigner **5** being from another world

alienate *verb* to cause (someone) to become hostile

alight *verb* **1** *formal* to step out (of a vehicle): *We alighted at Lenzie Station* **2** to land: *thirty finches alighting on a ledge* ▷ *adjective* **3** on fire

align *verb* **1** to bring (a person or group) into agreement with the policy of another **2** to place (two objects) in a straight line >**alignment** *noun*

alike *adjective* **1** like or similar ▷ *adverb* **2** in the same way

alimony *noun* allowance paid under a court order to a separated or divorced spouse

alive *adjective* **1** living; not dead **2** lively and active

alkali *noun* substance with a pH value of more than 7 >**alkaline** *adjective*: *Some soils are too alkaline for certain plant life*

all *adjective, pronoun* **1** whole quantity or number (of): *90% of all households; all our belongings; That was all I had* ▷ *adverb* **2** wholly, entirely **3** (in the score of games) each: *The final score was six points all* **4 give your all** to make the greatest possible effort

Allah *noun* name of God in Islam

allay *verb* to reduce (someone's fears or doubts)

allege *verb* to state without proof: *It is alleged that she was poisoned* >**alleged** *adjective*: *an alleged beating* >**allegedly** *adverb*

allegiance *noun* loyalty to a person, country or cause

allegory *allegories noun* story with an underlying meaning as well as the literal one. For example, George Orwell's novel *Animal Farm* is an allegory in that the animals who revolt in the farmyard are symbols of the political leaders in the Russian Revolution >**allegorical** *adjective*: *an allegorical novel*

allergy *allergies noun* extreme sensitivity to a substance, which causes the body to react to it >**allergic** *adjective* having or caused by an allergy

alleviate *verb* to lessen (pain or suffering): *measures to alleviate poverty* >**alleviation** *noun*: *the*

A

alleviation of pain

alley *noun* **1** narrow street or path **2** long narrow enclosure in which tenpin bowling or skittles is played

alliance *noun* **1** state of being allied **2** formal relationship between countries or groups for a shared purpose

alligator *noun* reptile of the crocodile family, found in the southern US and China

alliteration *noun literary* use of the same sound at the start of words occurring together, e.g. *moody music* > **alliterative** *adjective* relating to or connected with alliteration

allocate *verb* to assign (something) to someone or for a particular purpose > **allocation** *noun: the allocation of funding*

allot allots allotting allotted *verb* to assign as a share or for a particular purpose: *Space was allotted for visitors' cars*

allotment *noun* **1** *Brit* small piece of public land rented to grow vegetables on **2** share of something

allow *verb* **1** to permit (someone to do something) **2** to set aside **3 allow for** to take into account > **allowable** *adjective* able to be accepted or admitted

allowance *noun* **1** amount of money given at regular intervals **2** amount permitted **3 make allowances for a** to treat or judge (someone) less severely because he or she has special problems **b** to take (something) into account

alloy *noun* mixture of two or more metals

all right *adjective* **1** adequate or satisfactory **2** unharmed ▷ *interjection* **3** expression of approval or agreement

allude *verb* **allude to** to refer indirectly to

- You *allude to* something. Do not confuse *allude* with *elude*

allure *noun* attractiveness: *the allure of foreign travel* > **alluring** *adjective: the most alluring city in South-East Asia*

allusion *noun* indirect reference: *English literature is full of classical allusions*

ally allies allying allied *noun* **1** country, person or group with an agreement to support another ▷ *verb* **2 ally yourself with** to join as an ally

almanac *noun* **1** yearly calendar with detailed information on anniversaries, phases of the moon, etc **2** book published every year giving information about a particular subject

almighty *adjective* **1** having absolute power **2** *informal* very great ▷ *noun* **3 the Almighty** C

almond *noun* edible brown oval shaped nut which grows on a small tree

almost *adverb* very nearly

alms *plural noun* old-fashioned gifts of money, food or clothing to poor people

aloft *adverb* up in the air or in a high position

alone *adjective, adverb* without anyone or anything else; on your own

along *preposition* **1** over part or the length of ▷ *adverb* **2** moving forward: *We marched along, singing as we went* **3** in company with others: *Why not take her along?* **4 all along** from the beginning of a period of time right up to now: *You've known that all along*

alongside *preposition, adverb* beside (something)

aloof *adjective* distant or haughty in manner

aloud *adverb* spoken in a voice that can be heard

alphabet *noun* set of letters used in writing a language
> **alphabetical** *adjective* in the conventional order of the letters of an alphabet > **alphabetically** *adverb*

alpine *adjective* existing in or relating to high mountains

already *adverb* **1** before the present time **2** sooner than expected

alright *adjective, interjection* all right
- Some people think that *all right* is the only correct spelling and that *alright* is wrong

alsatian *noun* large wolflike dog

also *adverb* in addition, too

altar *noun* **1** table used for Communion in Christian churches **2** raised structure on which sacrifices are offered and religious rites are performed

alter *verb* to make or become different > **alteration** *noun*: *simple alterations to your diet*
- Do not confuse the spellings of *alter* and *altar*

altercation *noun* formal heated argument

alternate *verb* **1** to occur or to

cause (something) to occur by turns > *adjective* **2** occurring by turns **3** every second (one) of a series **4** (of two angles) on opposite sides of a line that crosses two other lines > **alternately** *adverb*
> **alternation** *noun*: *The alternation of sun and snow continued all week*

alternating current *noun* electric current that reverses direction at frequent regular intervals

alternative *noun* **1** something you can do or have instead of something else: *alternatives to prison such as community service* > *adjective* **2** able to be done or used instead of something else **3** (of medicine, lifestyle, etc) not conventional > **alternatively** *adverb*

although *conjunction* despite the fact that

altitude *noun* height above sea level: *an altitude of 1330 metres*

altogether *adverb* **1** entirely **2** on the whole **3** in total

aluminium *noun* light silvery-white metal that does not rust

always *adverb* **1** at all times **2** for ever

am *verb* see **be**

a.m. *abbreviation Latin* ante meridiem: before noon: *We got up at 6 a.m.*

amalgamate *verb* to combine or unite > **amalgamation** *noun*: *an amalgamation of two organizations*

amandla *noun S Afr* political slogan calling for power to the Black population

amass *verb* to collect or accumulate: *He amassed a huge*

a
b
c
d
e
f
g
h
i
j
k
l
m
n
o
p
q
r
s
t
u
v
w
x
y
z

A

fortune

amateur noun 1 person who engages in a sport or activity as a pastime rather than as a profession 2 person unskilled in something ▷ adjective 3 not professional

amateurish adjective lacking skill ▷ **amateurishly** adverb

amaze verb to surprise greatly; astound ▷ **amazed** adjective: You'd be amazed at the mess people leave ▷ **amazement** noun: I stared at her in amazement ▷ **amazing** adjective very surprising or remarkable ▷ **amazingly** adverb

ambassador noun senior diplomat who represents his or her country in another country

amber noun 1 clear yellowish fossil resin ▷ adjective 2 brownish-yellow

ambi- prefix both: ambidextrous

ambidextrous adjective able to use both hands with equal ease

ambience noun formal atmosphere of a place

ambient adjective surrounding: low ambient temperatures

ambiguous adjective having more than one possible meaning ▷ **ambiguity** noun: considerable ambiguity about the meaning of the agreement ▷ **ambiguously** adverb

ambition noun 1 desire for success: He's talented and full of ambition 2 something so desired; goal: His ambition is to be an actor

ambitious adjective 1 having a strong desire for success 2 requiring great effort or ability: an ambitious rebuilding schedule ▷ **ambitiously** adverb

ambivalent adjective having

or showing two conflicting attitudes or emotions ▷ **ambivalence** noun: her ambivalence about getting married again

amble verb 1 to walk at a leisurely pace ▷ noun 2 leisurely walk or pace

ambulance noun motor vehicle designed to carry sick or injured people

ambush noun 1 act of waiting in a concealed position to make a surprise attack 2 attack from a concealed position ▷ verb 3 to attack suddenly from a concealed position

amen interjection so be it: used at the end of a prayer

amenable adjective likely or willing to cooperate: Both brothers were amenable to the arrangement

amend verb to make small changes to correct or improve (something) ▷ **amendment** noun improvement or correction

amenity amenities noun useful or enjoyable feature available for the public to use

America noun 1 the whole of North, South and Central America 2 the United States

American adjective 1 of the United States of America or the American continent ▷ noun 2 someone from America or the American continent

amethyst noun bluish-violet variety of quartz used as a gemstone

amiable adjective friendly, pleasant-natured: The hotel staff were very amiable ▷ **amiability** noun: I found his amiability charm

> **amiably** adverb

amicable adjective fairly friendly: *an amicable divorce* > **amicably** adverb

amid or **amidst** preposition formal in the middle of; among

amiss adverb **1** wrongly, badly **2 take something amiss** to be offended by something ▷ adjective **3** wrong or faulty

ammonia noun strong-smelling alkaline gas containing hydrogen and nitrogen, used in household cleaning materials, explosives and fertilizers

ammunition noun **1** bullets, bombs and shells that can be fired from or as a weapon **2** facts that can be used in an argument

amnesia noun loss of memory

amnesty amnesties noun general pardon for offences against a government

amoeba amoebae or **amoebas** noun smallest kind of living creature, consisting of one cell. Amoebas reproduce by dividing into two

amok adverb **run amok** to run about in a violent frenzy

among or **amongst** preposition **1** surrounded by **2** in the company of **3** to each of: *Divide it among ourselves*

- If there are more than two things, you should use *among*. If there are only two things you should use *between*.

amoral adjective without moral standards

- Do not confuse *amoral* and *immoral*. You use *amoral* to talk about people with no

moral standards, but *immoral* for people who are aware of moral standards but go against them

amorous adjective feeling, showing or relating to sexual love: *an amorous relationship* > **amorously** adverb

amount noun **1** extent or quantity ▷ verb **2 amount to** to be equal or add up to

amp noun **1** ampere **2** informal amplifier

ampere noun basic unit of electric current

ampersand noun the character (&), meaning *and*

amphetamine noun drug used as a stimulant

amphibian noun animal that lives on land but breeds in water

amphibious adjective **1** (of an animal) living partly on land and partly in the water **2** (of a military operation) using boats to land soldiers on an enemy shore **3** (of a vehicle) able to move on both land and water

amphitheatre noun large, semicircular open area with sloping sides covered with rows of seats

ample adjective **1** more than sufficient **2** large > **amply** adverb

amplifier noun piece of equipment in a radio or stereo system which causes sounds or signals to become louder

amplify amplifies amplifying amplified verb **1** to increase the strength of (a current or sound signal) **2** to explain in more detail **3** to increase the size or effect of > **amplification** noun: *a voice that* needed no amplification

amplitude noun Physics the amplitude of a wave is how far its curve moves away from its normal position

amputate verb to cut off (a limb or part of a limb) for medical reasons > **amputation** noun: the amputation of his left leg

Amrit noun **1** mixture of sugar and water used in rituals of the Sikh religion **2** ceremony during which someone is accepted as a full member of the Sikh community

amuse verb **1** to cause to laugh or smile **2** to entertain or keep interested > **amused** adjective: an amused look on her face > **amusing** adjective funny or entertaining

amusement noun **1** state of being amused **2** something that amuses or entertains someone

an adjective form of **a** used before vowel sounds

-an suffix -an comes at the end of nouns and adjectives which show where or what someone or something comes from or belongs to: American; Victorian; Christian

anachronism noun person or thing placed in the wrong historical period or seeming to belong to another time: The President regarded the Church as an anachronism > **anachronistic** adjective: Many of its practices seem anachronistic

anaemia noun deficiency in the number of red blood cells, resulting in tiredness and a pale complexion > **anaemic** adjective

anaesthetic noun **1** substance causing loss of bodily feeling ⊳ adjective **2** causing loss of bodily feeling

anaesthetist noun doctor trained to administer anaesthetics

anaesthetize verb to cause to feel no pain by administering an anaesthetic

anagram noun word or phrase made by rearranging the letters of another word or phrase

anal adjective relating to the anus

analgesic adjective **1** pain-relieving ⊳ noun **2** substance that relieves pain

analogy analogies noun comparison made to show a similarity > **analogous** adjective similar in some respects

analyse verb **1** to examine (something) in detail in order to discover its meaning or essential features **2** to break (something) down into its components **3** to psychoanalyse (someone)

analysis analyses noun separation of a whole into its parts for study and interpretation **2** short for **psychoanalysis**

analyst noun person skilled in analysis

analytical or **analytic** adjective using logical reasoning > **analytically** adverb

anarchy noun lawlessness and disorder > **anarchic** adjective: anarchic attitudes and complete disrespect for authority

anatomy anatomies noun **1** science of the structure of the body **2** physical structure **3** person's body > **anatomical** adjective: anatomical details > **anatomically** adverb

ANC abbreviation African Nation

Congress

ancestor noun 1 person from whom you are descended 2 forerunner > **ancestral** adjective: the family's ancestral home

ancestry ancestries noun 1 family descent: of Japanese ancestry 2 origin or roots

anchor noun 1 heavy hooked device attached to a boat by a cable and dropped overboard to fasten the ship to the sea bottom > verb 2 to fasten with or as if with an anchor

anchorage noun place where boats can be anchored

anchovy anchovies noun small strong-tasting fish

ancient adjective 1 dating from very long ago: ancient Greece 2 very old or having a long history

ancillary adjective 1 supporting the main work of an organization: hospital ancillary workers 2 used as an extra or supplement

and conjunction 1 in addition to 2 as a consequence 3 then or afterwards

androgynous adjective formal having both male and female characteristics

android noun robot resembling a human

anecdote noun short amusing account of an incident

anecdotal adjective based on individual accounts rather than on reliable research and statistics: anecdotal evidence

anemone noun plant with white, purple or red flowers

anew adverb 1 once more 2 in a different way

angel noun 1 spiritual being

believed to be an attendant or messenger of God 2 person who is kind, pure or beautiful > **angelic** adjective 1 of or relating to angels 2 very kind, pure or beautiful > **angelically** adverb

anger noun 1 fierce displeasure or extreme annoyance > verb 2 to make (someone) angry

angina noun (also **angina pectoris**) heart disorder causing sudden severe chest pains

angle noun 1 space between or shape formed by two lines or surfaces that meet 2 distance between two lines or surfaces at the point where they meet, measured in degrees 3 corner 4 point of view: the same story from a German angle > verb 5 to bend or place (something) at an angle 6 to fish with a hook and line > **angle for** verb to try to get (something) by hinting

angler noun person who fishes with a hook and line > **angling** noun sport of fishing with a hook and line

Anglican noun 1 member of the Church of England > adjective 2 of the Church of England

Anglo-Saxon noun 1 member of any of the West Germanic tribes that settled in England from the fifth century AD 2 language of the Anglo-Saxons > adjective 3 of the Anglo-Saxons or their language

Angolan adjective 1 belonging or relating to Angola > noun 2 someone from Angola

angora noun 1 variety of goat, cat or rabbit with long silky hair 2 hair of the angora goat or rabbit 3 cloth made from this hair

angry angrier angriest adjective

a
b
c
d
e
f
g
h
i
j
k
l
m
n
o
p
q
r
s
t
u
v
w
x
y
z

A

1 full of anger **2** inflamed
> **angrily** adverb

anguish noun great mental
pain > **anguished** adjective: an
anguished cry

angular adjective **1** (of a person)
lean and bony **2** having straight
lines and sharp points

animal noun **1** living being except
a plant or any mammal except
a human being ▷ adjective **2** of
animals **3** of physical needs or
desires

animate verb **1** to give life to
2 to make lively **3** to produce (a
story) as an animated cartoon
▷ adjective **4** having life

animated adjective **1** lively
and interesting: an animated
conversation **2** (of a film) made
using animation: an animated
cartoon > **animatedly** adverb

animation noun **1** technique of
making cartoon films **2** liveliness
and enthusiasm: The crowd showed
no sign of animation > **animator**
noun person who makes animated
cartoons

animosity animosities noun
feeling of strong dislike and anger
towards someone

aniseed noun liquorice-flavoured
seeds of the anise plant

ankle noun joint between the foot
and leg

annex verb **1** to seize (territory)
2 to take (something) without
permission **3** to join or add
(something) to something larger
> **annexation** noun: Indonesia's
annexation of East Timor

annihilate verb to destroy (a place
or a group of people) completely
> **annihilation** noun

anniversary anniversaries
noun **1** date on which something
occurred in a previous year
2 celebration of this

announce verb to make known
publicly > **announcement** noun
public statement

announcer noun person who
introduces radio or television
programmes

annoy verb to irritate or displease
> **annoyance** noun: a long list of
annoyances; To her annoyance the
stranger did not go away > **annoyed**
adjective displeased by something
or someone > **annoying** adjective
irritating

annual adjective **1** happening
once a year: their annual conference
2 lasting for a year: the United
States' annual budget for national
defence ▷ noun **3** plant that
completes its life cycle in a year
4 book published once every year
> **annually** adverb

annuity annuities noun fixed sum
paid every year

annul annuls annulling annulled
verb to declare (something,
especially a marriage) officially
invalid > **annulment** noun official
declaration that something is
invalid

anoint verb to smear with
oil as a sign of consecration
> **anointment** noun act of
anointing someone

anomaly anomalies noun
something that deviates from
the normal: a statistical anomaly
> **anomalous** adjective: This
anomalous behaviour has baffled
scientists

anon. abbreviation anonymous

a

anonymous *adjective* by someone whose name is unknown or withheld >**anonymity** *noun*: *the anonymity of the voting booth* >**anonymously** *adverb*

anorak *noun* light waterproof hooded jacket

anorexia *noun* (also **anorexia nervosa**) psychological disorder characterized by fear of becoming fat and refusal to eat >**anorexic** *adjective* **1** suffering from anorexia ▷ *noun* **2** person suffering from anorexia

another *adjective, pronoun* **1** one more **2** different (one)

answer *noun* **1** reply to a question, request, letter, etc **2** solution to a problem **3** reaction or response ▷ *verb* **4** to give an answer (to) **5** to be responsible to (a person) **6** to respond or react: *a dog that answers to the name of Pugg*

answerable *adjective* **answerable for or to** responsible for or accountable to

answering machine *noun* device for answering a telephone automatically and recording messages

ant *noun* small insect living in large colonies

-ant *suffix* used to form adjectives and nouns: *important; deodorant*

antagonism *noun* open opposition or hostility

antagonist *noun* opponent or adversary

antagonistic *adjective* in active opposition >**antagonistically** *adverb*

antagonize *verb* to arouse hostility in

Antarctic *noun* **1** the Antarctic area around the South Pole ▷ *adjective* **2** of this region

Antarctic Circle *noun* imaginary circle around the southernmost part of the earth

ante- *prefix* before in time or position: *antedate; antechamber*

antecedent *noun* **1** event or circumstance happening or existing before another ▷ *adjective* **2** preceding, prior

antelope *noun* deerlike mammal with long legs and horns

antenatal *adjective* concerned with the care of pregnant women and their unborn children

antenna antennae antennas *noun* **1** long thin feeler, of which there are two, attached to an insect's head **2** *Austr, NZ, US* radio or television aerial

● Note that the plural of sense 1 is *antennae* and the plural of sense 2 is *antennas*

anthem *noun* **1** song of loyalty, especially to a country **2** piece of choral music, usually set to words from the Bible

anther *noun* part of a flower's stamen containing pollen

anthology anthologies *noun* collection of poems or other literary pieces by various authors

anthropo- *prefix* involving or to do with human beings: *anthropology*

anthropology *noun* study of human origins, institutions and beliefs >**anthropological** *adjective*: *anthropological theories* >**anthropologist** *noun* person who studies or is an expert in anthropology

anti- *prefix* **1** against or opposed to: *anti-war* **2** opposite to:

b
c
d
e
f
g
h
i
j
k
l
m
n
o
p
q
r
s
t
u
v
w
x
y
z

anticlimax **3** counteracting: antifreeze

antibiotic noun **1** chemical substance capable of destroying bacteria ▷ adjective **2** of antibiotics

antibody antibodies noun protein produced in the blood, which destroys bacteria

anticipate verb to foresee and act in advance of > **anticipation** noun: smiling in happy anticipation

anticlimax noun something that does not live up to expectations or is disappointing, especially in contrast to what has gone before

anticlockwise adverb, adjective in the opposite direction to the rotation of the hands of a clock

antics plural noun funny or silly ways of behaving

antidote noun substance that acts against the effect of a poison

antihistamine noun drug used to treat allergies

antipathy noun strong feeling of dislike or hostility towards something or someone

antiperspirant noun substance used to reduce or prevent sweating

antipodes plural noun **1** any two places diametrically opposite one another on the earth's surface **2 the Antipodes** Brit Australia and New Zealand > **antipodean** adjective: our antipodean visitors

antiquarian adjective of or relating to antiquities or rare books: antiquarian books

antiquated adjective out-of-date

antique noun **1** object of an earlier period, valued for its beauty, workmanship or age ▷ adjective

2 from or concerning the past **3** old-fashioned

antiquity antiquities noun **1** great age **2** distant past, especially the time of the ancient Egyptians, Greeks and Romans **3** antiquities objects dating from ancient times

anti-Semitism noun hatred of or discrimination against Jews > **anti-Semite** noun person who hates or discriminates against Jews > **anti-Semitic** adjective: anti-Semitic literature

antiseptic adjective **1** preventing infection by killing germs ▷ noun **2** antiseptic substance

antisocial adjective **1** avoiding the company of other people **2** (of behaviour) harmful to society

antithesis antitheses noun formal **1** exact opposite: Work is the antithesis of leisure **2** literary placing together of contrasting ideas or words to produce an effect of balance

antivenene noun substance which reduces the effect of a venom, especially a snake venom

antivirus adjective (usually of computer software) protecting computers from viruses

antler noun branched horn of male deer

antonym noun word that means the opposite of another

anus noun hole between the buttocks through which bodily wastes are excreted

anvil noun heavy iron block on which metals are hammered into particular shapes

anxiety anxieties noun nervousness or worry

anxious adjective 1 worried and tense 2 intensely desiring: She was anxious to have children ▷ **anxiously** adverb

any adjective, pronoun 1 one, some or no matter which ▷ adverb 2 at all: it isn't any worse

anybody pronoun any person

anyhow adverb 1 in any case 2 in a careless way

anyone pronoun 1 any person 2 person of any importance

anything pronoun any object, event, situation or action

anyway adverb 1 at any rate, nevertheless 2 in any manner

anywhere adverb in, at or to any place

Anzac noun 1 (in World War 1) a soldier serving with the Australian and New Zealand Army Corps 2 Australian or New Zealand soldier

aorta noun main artery of the body, carrying oxygen-rich blood from the heart

apart adverb 1 to or in pieces 2 to or at a distance 3 individual, distinct

apartheid noun (in South Africa until its abolition in 1994) former official government policy of keeping people of different races apart

apartment noun 1 room in a building 2 flat

apathetic adjective not interested in anything

apathy noun lack of interest or enthusiasm

ape noun 1 tailless monkey such as the chimpanzee or gorilla 2 stupid, clumsy or ugly man ▷ verb 3 to imitate

aphid noun small insect which sucks the sap from plants

aphrodisiac noun 1 substance that arouses sexual desire ▷ adjective 2 arousing sexual desire

apiece adverb each

aplomb noun relaxed confidence

apocalypse noun 1 end of the world 2 event of great destruction 3 **the Apocalypse** book of Revelation, the last book of the New Testament ▷ **apocalyptic** adjective: an apocalyptic vision

apocryphal adjective (of a story) generally believed not to have really happened

apolitical adjective not interested in politics

apologetic adjective showing or expressing regret ▷ **apologetically** adverb

apologize verb to make an apology

apology apologies noun 1 expression of regret for wrongdoing 2 **apology for** poor example (of)

apostle noun 1 ardent supporter of a cause or movement 2 **Apostle** one of the twelve disciples chosen by Christ to preach his gospel

apostrophe noun punctuation mark (') showing the omission of a letter or letters in a word, e.g. don't or forming the possessive, e.g. Jill's car

appal appals appalling appalled verb to fill with horror

appalling adjective so bad as to be shocking

apparatus noun equipment for a

a
b
c
d
e
f
g
h
i
j
k
l
m
n
o
p
q
r
s
t
u
v
w
x
y
z

particular purpose

apparent *adjective* **1** readily seen; obvious **2** seeming as opposed to real > **apparently** *adverb*

apparition *noun* figure, especially a ghostlike one

appeal *verb* **1** to make an earnest request **2** to attract, please or interest **3** *Law* to apply to a higher court to review (a case or issue decided by a lower court) > *noun* **4** earnest request: *an appeal for peace* **5** attractiveness **6** *Law* request for a review of a lower court's decision by a higher court > **appealing** *adjective*: *It was a very appealing idea*

appear *verb* **1** to become visible or present **2** to seem: *He appeared to be searching for something* **3** to be seen in public

appearance *noun* **1** sudden or unexpected arrival of someone or something at a place **2** an act or instance of appearing **3** introduction or invention of something **4** way a person or thing looks

appease *verb* **1** to pacify (a person) by yielding to his or her demands **2** to satisfy or relieve (a feeling) > **appeasement** *noun* pacification of a person by yielding to his or her demands

appendage *noun* less important part attached to a main part

appendicitis *noun* painful illness in which a person's appendix becomes infected

appendix **appendices** or **appendixes** *noun* **1** separate additional material at the end of a book **2** *Anatomy* short closed tube attached to the large intestine

● The plural of the extra
● section in a book is
● *appendices*. The plural of the
● body part is *appendixes*.

appetite *noun* **1** desire for food or drink **2** liking or willingness

appetizing or **appetising** *adjective* (of food) looking and smelling delicious and stimulating the appetite

applaud *verb* **1** to show approval of (something) by clapping your hands **2** to approve strongly of

applause *noun* approval shown by clapping your hands

apple *noun* round firm fleshy fruit that grows on trees

appliance *noun* device with a specific function: *kitchen appliances*

applicable *adjective* relevant or appropriate

applicant *noun* person who applies for something

application *noun* **1** formal request **2** act of applying something to a particular use **3** diligent effort **4** act of putting something, such as a lotion or paint, onto a surface

apply **applies** **applying** **applied** *verb* **1** to make a formal request **2** to put to practical use: *He applied his mind to the problem* **3** to put onto a surface: *She applied lipstick to her mouth* **4** to be relevant or appropriate: *The legislation applies only to people living in England and Wales* **5** **apply yourself** to concentrate on doing something or thinking about it

appoint *verb* **1** to assign (someone) to a job or position **2** to fix or decide (a time or place for something)

appointment noun
1 arrangement to meet a person
2 act of placing someone in a job 3 the job itself; position
4 **appointments** fixtures or fittings

apposite adjective appropriate and relevant: This year her theme was particularly apposite

appraise verb to estimate the value or quality of

appreciable adjective large enough to be noticed: an appreciable difference
> **appreciably** adverb

appreciate verb 1 to value highly
2 to be aware of and understand
3 to be grateful for 4 to rise in value

appreciative adjective
1 understanding and enthusiastic
2 thankful and grateful
> **appreciatively** adverb

apprehend verb formal 1 to arrest and take into custody 2 to understand (something) fully

apprehensive adjective fearful or anxious about a future event
> **apprehension** noun 1 dread, anxiety 2 arrest 3 understanding
> **apprehensively** adverb

apprentice noun 1 someone working for a skilled person for a fixed period in order to learn his or her trade > verb 2 to take or place (someone) as an apprentice
> **apprenticeship** noun period of learning a trade from a skilled worker

approach verb 1 to come near or nearer (to): As autumn approached, the trees began to change colour 2 to make a proposal or suggestion to

3 to begin to deal with (a matter)
> noun 4 act of coming close or closer: the approach of spring
5 suggestion or proposal made to someone 6 road or path that leads to a place 7 approximation

appropriate adjective 1 suitable or fitting He didn't think jeans were appropriate for a vice-president > verb 2 formal to take (something) for yourself 3 formal to put (money) aside for a particular purpose: The cash has already been appropriated for the youth club > **appropriately** adverb
> **appropriation** noun

approval noun 1 agreement given to a plan or request 2 favourable opinion 3 **on approval** (of goods) with an option to be returned without payment if unsatisfactory

approve verb 1 to consider good or right 2 to authorize; agree to
> **approved** adjective: an approved method > **approving** adjective: an approving look

approximate adjective 1 almost but not quite exact > verb
approximate to 2 to come close to 3 to be almost the same as
> **approximately** adverb

apricot noun 1 yellowish-orange juicy fruit like a small peach
> adjective 2 yellowish-orange

April noun 1 fourth month of the year 2 **April fool** victim of a practical joke played on April 1 (**April Fools' Day**)

apron noun 1 garment worn over the front of the body to protect the clothes 2 area at an airport or hangar for manoeuvring and loading aircraft 3 part of a stage in front of the curtain

apse noun arched or domed recess, especially in a church

apt adjective **1** having a specified tendency: *They are apt to jump to the wrong conclusions* **2** suitable: *a very apt description* **3** quick to learn: *an apt pupil* ▷ **aptly** adverb

aptitude noun natural ability

aqua- prefix of or relating to water: *aquatic*

aquarium aquariums or **aquaria** noun **1** tank in which fish and other underwater creatures are kept **2** building containing such tanks

Aquarius noun eleventh sign of the zodiac, represented by a person carrying water

aquatic adjective **1** living in or near water **2** done in or on water: *aquatic sports*

aqueduct noun long bridge with many arches carrying a water supply over a valley

Arab noun **1** member of a group of people who used to live in Arabia but who now live throughout the Middle East and North Africa ▷ adjective **2** of the Arabs

Arabic noun **1** language of the Arabs ▷ adjective **2** of Arabic, Arabs or Arabia

arable adjective suitable for growing crops on

arbiter noun person empowered to judge in a dispute

arbitrary adjective based on personal choice or chance, rather than reason > **arbitrarily** adverb

arbitrate verb to settle a dispute by acting as an impartial referee

arc noun **1** part of a circle or other curve ▷ verb **2** to form an arc

- Do not confuse the spellings
- of *arc* and *ark*

arcade noun **1** covered passageway lined with shops **2** set of arches and their supporting columns

arcane adjective mysterious and secret

arch noun **1** curved structure supporting a bridge or roof **2** something curved **3** curved lower part of the foot ▷ verb **4** to (cause to) form an arch ▷ adjective **5** superior or knowing **6** coyly playful: *an arch smile*

arch- prefix chief, principal: *archenemy*

archaeology or **archeology** noun study of ancient cultures from their physical remains > **archaeological** adjective: *an archaeological dig* > **archaeologist** noun person who studies the physical remains of ancient cultures

archaic adjective **1** ancient **2** out-of-date

archangel noun chief angel

archbishop noun chief bishop

archdeacon noun Anglican priest ranking just below a bishop

archer noun person who shoots with a bow and arrow

archery noun sport in which people shoot at a target with a bow and arrow

archipelago archipelagos noun group of islands

architect noun person qualified to design and supervise the construction of buildings

architecture noun **1** style in which a building is designed and built **2** designing and construction of buildings > **architectural** *adjective: a unique architectural style*

archive *noun* (often plural) **1** collection of records or documents **2** place where these are kept ▷ *verb* **3** to store (something) in an archive

Arctic *noun* **1** **the Arctic** area around the North Pole ▷ *adjective* **2** of this region **3** **arctic** *informal* very cold

Arctic Circle *noun* imaginary circle around the northernmost part of the world

ardent *adjective* full of enthusiasm and passion > **ardently** *adverb*

ardour *noun* strong and passionate feeling of love or enthusiasm

arduous *adjective* hard to accomplish and requiring much effort

are *verb* see **be**

area *noun* **1** particular part of a place, country or the world **2** size of a two-dimensional surface **3** subject field

arena *noun* **1** seated enclosure for sports events **2** area of a Roman amphitheatre where gladiators fought **3** sphere of activity: *the political arena*

Argentinian *adjective* **1** belonging or relating to Argentina ▷ *noun* **2** someone from Argentina

arguable *adjective* (of an idea or point) not necessarily true or correct and therefore worth questioning > **arguably** *adverb*

argue *argues arguing argued* *verb* **1** to try to prove by giving reasons: *She argued that her client*

had been wrongly accused **2** to debate **3** to quarrel

argument *noun* **1** quarrel **2** discussion **3** point presented for or against something

argumentative *adjective* always disagreeing with other people

aria *noun* elaborate song for solo voice, especially one from an opera

arid *adjective* **1** parched, dry **2** uninteresting

Aries *noun* first sign of the zodiac, represented by a ram

arise *arises arising arose arisen* *verb* **1** to come about **2** to come into notice **3** *formal* to get up from a sitting, kneeling or lying position

aristocracy *aristocracies* *noun* highest social class

aristocrat *noun* member of the aristocracy > **aristocratic** *adjective: a wealthy, aristocratic family*

arithmetic *noun* **1** calculation by or of numbers ▷ *adjective* **2** of arithmetic > **arithmetical** *adjective* of arithmetic > **arithmetically** *adverb*

ark *noun* *Old Testament* boat built by Noah, which survived the Flood **Ark**

● Do not confuse the spellings of *arc* and *ark*

arm *noun* **1** either of the upper limbs from the shoulder to the wrist **2** sleeve of a garment **3** side of a chair **4** section of an organization: *the political arm of the armed forces* **arms a** weapons used in a war **b** heraldic symbols of a family or country ▷ *verb* **5** to supply with weapons **6** to prepare (a bomb etc) for use

armada noun large number of warships

armadillo armadillos noun small South American mammal covered in strong bony plates

Armageddon noun **1** New Testament final battle between good and evil at the end of the world **2** catastrophic conflict

armament noun **1** military weapons **2** preparation for war

armchair noun upholstered chair with side supports for the arms

armed adjective **1** carrying a weapon or weapons **2** (of an explosive device) prepared for use

armistice noun agreed suspension of fighting

armour noun **1** metal clothing formerly worn to protect the body in battle **2** metal plating of tanks, warships, etc

armoured adjective covered with thick steel for protection from gunfire and other missiles: *an armoured car*

armoury armouries noun place where weapons are stored

armpit noun hollow under the arm at the shoulder

army armies noun military land forces of a nation

aroma noun pleasant smell > **aromatic** adjective having a distinctive pleasant smell

aromatherapy noun massage with fragrant oils to relieve tension

around preposition, adverb **1** on all sides (of) **2** from place to place (in) **3** somewhere in or near **4** (at) approximately

arouse verb **1** to stimulate; stir

up **2** to awaken > **arousal** noun: *Thinking angry thoughts can provoke strong physical arousal*

arrange verb **1** to plan **2** to agree **3** to put in order: *He started to arrange the books in piles* **4** to adapt (music) for performance in a certain way > **arrangement** noun: *travel arrangements; flower arrangement*

array noun **1** impressive display or collection ▷ verb **2** to arrange in order

arrears plural noun **1** money owed: *mortgage arrears* **2** in arrears late in paying a debt

arrest verb **1** to take (a person) into custody **2** to stop the movement or development of **3** to catch and hold (the attention) ▷ noun **4** act of taking a person into custody **5** slowing or stopping > **arresting** adjective attracting attention, striking

arrival noun **1** the act or time of arriving **2** person or thing that has just arrived

arrive verb **1** to reach a place or destination **2** to happen or come **3** informal to attain success

arrogant adjective proud and overbearing > **arrogance** noun: *the arrogance of those in power* > **arrogantly** adverb

arrow noun **1** pointed shaft shot from a bow **2** arrow-shaped sign or symbol used to show direction

arsenal noun place where arms and ammunition are made or stored

arsenic noun highly poisonous substance

arson noun crime of intentional setting property on fire

> **arsonist** *noun* person who sets property on fire intentionally

art *noun* **1** creation of works of beauty, especially paintings or sculpture **2** works of art collectively **3** skill **4 arts** literature, music, painting and sculpture, considered together

artefact *noun* something made by human beings

artery arteries *noun* **1** one of the tubes carrying blood from the heart **2** major road or means of communication

artful *adjective* cunning, wily
> **artfully** *adverb*

arthritis *noun* painful inflammation of a joint or joints
> **arthritic** *adjective* affected by arthritis

artichoke *noun* flower head of a thistle-like plant, cooked as a vegetable

article *noun* **1** written piece in a magazine or newspaper **2** item or object: *an article of clothing* **3** clause in a document **4** *Grammar* any of the words *the a* or *an*

articulate *adjective* **1** able to express yourself clearly and coherently ▷ *verb* **2** to speak or express (something) clearly and coherently > **articulately** *adverb*

articulation *noun* **1** expressing of an idea in words **2** process of articulating a speech sound

artificial *adjective* **1** not occurring naturally; man-made: *artificial flouring* **2** made in imitation of something natural **3** not sincere: *an artificial smile* > **artificially** *adverb*

artillery *noun* **1** large, powerful guns **2** branch of the army who

use these

artist *noun* **1** person who produces works of art, especially paintings or sculpture **2** person skilled at something

artiste *noun* professional entertainer such as a singer or dancer

artistic *adjective* **1** able to create good paintings, sculpture or other works of art **2** concerning or involving art or artists
> **artistically** *adverb*

artistry *noun* artistic skill: *his artistry as a cellist*

arty artier artiest *adjective* *informal* interest in painting, sculpture and other works of art

as *conjunction* **1** while or when **2** in the way that **3** that which: *do as you are told* **4** since or seeing that **5** for instance ▷ *adverb, conjunction* **6** used to indicate amount or extent in comparisons: *He is as tall as you (are)* ▷ *preposition* **7** in the role of; being: *As a mother, I am concerned*

asbestos *noun* fibrous mineral which does not burn

ascend *verb* *formal* to go or move up

ascendancy *noun* *formal* condition of being dominant

ascendant *adjective* **1** dominant or influential ▷ *noun* **2 in the ascendant** increasing in power or influence

ascent *noun* upward journey

ascertain *verb* *formal* to find (something) out definitely

ascribe *verb* **1** to attribute or put (something) down (to): *His stomach pains were ascribed to his intake of pork* **2** to attribute (a

A

B

C

D

E

F

G

H

I

J

K

L

M

N

O

P

Q

R

S

T

U

V

W

X

Y

Z

particular quality to someone or something)

ash noun **1** powdery substance left when something is burnt **2** tree with grey bark **3 ashes** remains after burning, especially of a human body after cremation

ashamed adjective feeling shame

ashen adjective grey or pale

ashore adverb towards or on land

ashtray noun receptacle for tobacco ash and cigarette butts

Asia noun largest continent, with Europe on its western side, the Arctic to the north, the Pacific to the east, and the Indian Ocean to the south. Asia includes several island groups, including Japan, Indonesia and the Philippines

Asian adjective **1** of the continent of Asia or any of its peoples or languages ▷ noun **2** someone from Asia or a descendant of one

aside adverb **1** to one side **2** out of other people's hearing ▷ noun **3** remark not meant to be heard by everyone present

ask verb **1** to say or write (something) in a form that requires an answer **2** to make a request or demand **3** to invite **4 asking for trouble** doing something that will cause problems

askew adverb, adjective to one side; crooked

asleep adjective **1** not awake; sleeping **2** (of limbs) numb

asparagus noun plant whose shoots are cooked as a vegetable

aspect noun **1** feature or element **2** position facing a particular direction: *The southern aspect of the cottage faces over fields*

3 appearance or look

asphalt noun black hard tarlike substance used for road surfaces etc

aspiration noun strong desire or aim

aspire verb **aspire to** to yearn for: *He aspires to public office* ▷ **aspiring** adjective: *an aspiring actor*

aspirin noun **1** drug used to relieve pain and fever **2** tablet of this

ass noun **1** donkey **2** informal stupid person

assailant noun someone who attacks another person

assassin noun person who murders a prominent person

assassinate verb to murder (a political or religious leader) ▷ **assassination** noun: *the assassination of Martin Luther King*

assault noun **1** violent attack ▷ verb **2** to attack violently

assegai noun slender spear used in S Africa

assemble verb **1** to collect or congregate **2** to put together the parts of (a machine)

assembly assemblies noun **1** assembled group **2** assembling

assent noun **1** agreement or consent ▷ verb **2** to agree

assert verb **1** to declare forcefully **2** to insist upon (your rights etc) **3 assert yourself** to put yourself forward forcefully

assertion noun firm statement, usually made without evidence

assertive adjective confident and direct in dealing with others ▷ **assertively** adverb ▷ **assertiveness** noun: *his lack of assertiveness*

assess verb **1** to judge the worth

importance of **2** to estimate the value of (income or property) for taxation purposes > **assessment** *noun* evaluation of someone or something

assessor *noun* person whose job is to assess the value of something

asset *noun* **1** valuable or useful person or thing **2 assets** property that a person or firm can sell, especially to pay debts

assign *verb* **1** to appoint (someone) to a job or task **2** to give a task or duty (to someone) **3** to set apart (a place or time) for a particular event

assignation *noun literary* secret meeting with someone, especially a lover

assignment *noun* **1** job someone is given to do **2** act of assigning

assimilate *verb* **1** to learn and understand (information) **2** to absorb or be absorbed > **assimilation** *noun: assimilation of knowledge; assimilation of minority ethnic groups*

assist *verb* to give help or support > **assistance** *noun* help or support

assistant *noun* **1** helper ▷ *adjective* **2** junior or deputy: *an assistant teacher*

associate *verb* **1** to connect in the mind **2** to mix socially ▷ *noun* **3** partner in business **4** friend or companion ▷ *adjective* **5** having partial rights or subordinate status: *associate member*

association *noun* **1** society or club **2** act of associating **3** friendship: *Their association had to remain a secret* **4** mental connection of ideas or feelings

assonance *noun* rhyming of vowel

sounds but not consonants, as in *time* and *light*

assorted *adjective* consisting of various types mixed together: *assorted swimsuits*

assortment *noun* group of similar things that are different sizes and colours

assume *verb* **1** to take to be true without proof: *I assumed that he would turn up* **2** to take (something) upon yourself: *He assumed command* **3** to pretend: *I assumed indifference*

assumption *noun* **1** belief that something is true, without thinking about it **2** taking of power or responsibility: *their assumption of power in 1997*

assurance *noun* **1** something said which is intended to make people less worried **2** confidence **3** insurance that provides for events that are certain to happen, such as death

assure *verb* **1** to promise or guarantee **2** to convince **3** to make (something) certain **4** to insure against loss of life

asterisk *noun* **1** star-shaped symbol (*) used in printing or writing to indicate a footnote etc ▷ *verb* **2** to mark with an asterisk

astern *adverb* **1** at or towards the stern of a ship **2** backwards

asteroid *noun* any of the small planets that orbit the sun between Mars and Jupiter

asthma *noun* illness causing difficulty in breathing > **asthmatic** *adjective* suffering from asthma

astonish *verb* to surprise greatly > **astonished** *adjective* greatly surprised >**astonishing** adjective: an astonishing display of physical strength >**astonishingly** adverb >**astonishment** noun: We won, much to our astonishment

astound verb to overwhelm with amazement >**astounded** adjective: I was astounded by its beauty >**astounding** adjective: The results are quite astounding

astray adverb off the right path

astride adjective 1 with a leg on either side 2 with legs far apart ▷ preposition 3 with a leg on either side of

astringent adjective 1 causing contraction of body tissue 2 checking the flow of blood from a cut 3 severe or harsh ▷ noun 4 astringent substance

astro- prefix involving the stars and planets: astronomy; astronaut

astrology noun study of the alleged influence of the stars, planets and moon on human affairs >**astrologer** noun person who studies astrology >**astrological** adjective: astrological predictions

astronaut noun person trained for travelling in space

astronomical adjective 1 involved with or relating to astronomy 2 extremely large in amount >**astronomically** adverb

astronomy noun scientific study of stars and planets

Astroturf® noun artificial grass

astute adjective perceptive or shrewd: an astute diplomat >**astutely** adverb >**astuteness** noun: the astuteness of his observations

asunder adverb literary into parts or pieces

asylum noun 1 refuge or sanctuary 2 old-fashioned mental hospital

asymmetrical or **asymmetric** adjective unbalanced or with one half not exactly the same as the other half >**asymmetry** noun lack of symmetry

at preposition 1 indicating location or position: She met us at the airport 2 towards or in the direction of: She was staring at the wall behind him 3 indicating position in time: We arrived at 2.30 4 engaged in: children at play 5 during the passing of: She works at night as a nurse's aide 6 for or in exchange for: Crude oil is selling at its highest price for 14 years 7 indicating the object of an emotion: I'm angry at you because you were rude to me

atheist noun someone who believes there is no God >**atheism** noun belief that there is no God >**atheistic** adjective: atheistic philosophers

athlete noun person trained in or good at athletics

athletic adjective 1 physically fit or strong 2 relating to an athlete or athletics >**athletically** adverb

athletics plural noun track-and-field sports such as running, jumping, throwing, etc

Atlantic noun ocean separating North and South America from Europe and Africa

atlas atlases noun book of maps

atmosphere noun 1 mass of gases surrounding a heavenly body, especially the earth 2 air in a particular place: a musty atmosphere 3 prevailing tone or mood (of a place etc): *a relaxed atmosphere* **4** mood created by the writer of a novel or play > **atmospheric** *adjective* **1** relating to the atmosphere of a planet **2** (of a place or a piece of music) having a quality which is interesting or exciting and which evokes an emotion

atom *noun* **1** smallest unit of matter which can take part in a chemical reaction **2** very small amount

atomic *adjective* **1** relating to or using atomic bombs or atomic energy **2** relating to atoms

atomic bomb *noun* bomb in which the energy is provided by nuclear fission

atone *verb formal* to make amends (for sin or wrongdoing) > **atonement** *noun* a gesture of atonement

atrocious *adjective* **1** extremely cruel or wicked **2** horrifying or shocking **3** *informal* very bad > **atrociously** *adverb*

atrocity atrocities *noun* act of cruelty

attach *verb* **1** to join, fasten or connect **2** to attribute or ascribe: *He attaches particular importance to the proposed sale*

attaché *noun* specialist attached to a diplomatic mission: *the Russian Cultural Attaché*

attached *adjective* **1** married, engaged or in an exclusive sexual relationship **2** **attached to** fond of

attachment *noun* **1** affection or regard for **2** piece of equipment attached to a tool or machine to do a particular job **3** *Computing*

file attached to an e-mail message

attack *verb* **1** to launch a physical assault (against): *He attacked the government's economic policies* **2** to criticize **3** to set about (a job or problem) with vigour **4** to affect adversely: *fungal diseases that attack crops* **5** to take the initiative in a game or sport ▷ *noun* **6** act of attacking **7** sudden bout of illness > **attacker** *noun* person who attacks someone

attain *verb formal* to achieve, accomplish or reach: *He eventually attained the rank of major* > **attainable** *adjective*: *an attainable goal* > **attainment** *noun* accomplishment

attempt *verb* **1** to try, make an effort: *They attempted to escape* ▷ *noun* **2** effort or endeavour: *He made no attempt to go for the ball*

attend *verb* **1** to be present at **2** to go regularly to a school, college, etc **3** to look after: *They were attended by numerous servants* **4** **attend to** to apply yourself to (something) > **attendance** *noun* **1** attending **2** number attending

attendant *noun* **1** person who assists, guides or provides a service ▷ *adjective* **2** accompanying: *increasing road traffic and its attendant pollution*

attention *noun* **1** concentrated direction of the mind **2** consideration **3** care **4** alert position in military drill

attentive *adjective* **1** giving attention: *an attentive audience* **2** considerately helpful > **attentively** *adverb* > **attentiveness** *noun* **1** alertness **2** thoughtfulness

a b c d e f g h i j k l m n o p q r s t u v w x y z

attest verb (often followed by to) to affirm or prove the truth of

attic noun space or room within the roof of a house

attire noun formal clothing

attitude noun 1 way of thinking and behaving 2 way of sitting, standing or lying

attorney noun 1 person legally appointed to act for another 2 US, SAfr lawyer

attract verb 1 to arouse the interest or admiration of 2 (of a magnet) to draw (something) closer by exerting a force on it

attraction noun 1 act or quality of attracting 2 object or place people visit for interest or pleasure 3 quality that attracts someone or something

attractive adjective 1 pleasant to look at or be with: 2 interesting and possibly advantageous: an attractive proposition > **attractively** adverb > **attractiveness** noun: his attractiveness to women

attribute verb 1 attribute something to to regard something as belonging to or produced by: a play attributed to Shakespeare > noun 2 quality or feature representative of a person or thing > **attributable** adjective: deaths attributable to smoking > **attribution** noun act of attributing

attrition noun constant wearing down to weaken or destroy

attuned adjective accustomed or well adjusted (to something)

aubergine noun Brit dark purple tropical fruit, cooked and eaten as a vegetable. It is also called an eggplant

auburn adjective (of hair) reddish-brown

auction noun 1 public sale in which articles are sold to the highest bidder > verb 2 to sell (something) by auction

auctioneer noun person who conducts an auction

audacious adjective recklessly bold or daring: an audacious escape from jail > **audaciously** adverb > **audacity** noun audacious behaviour

audi- prefix involving hearing or sound: audible; auditorium

audible adjective loud enough to be heard: She spoke in a barely audible whisper > **audibly** adverb

audience noun 1 group of spectators or listeners 2 private or formal meeting with an important person: an audience with the Queen

audio adjective 1 of sound or hearing 2 of or for the transmission or reproduction of sound

audit noun 1 official examination of business accounts > verb 2 to examine (business accounts) officially > **auditor** noun person qualified to audit accounts

audition noun 1 test of a performer's ability for a particular role or job > verb 2 to test (someone) or be tested in an audition

auditorium noun, pl **auditoriums** or **auditoria** noun area of a concert hall or theatre where the audience sits

augment verb formal to increase or enlarge

August noun eighth month of the year

aunt noun 1 father's or mother's sister 2 uncle's wife

au pair noun young foreign person who does housework in return for board and lodging

aura noun distinctive air or quality of a person or thing

aural adjective relating to or done through the sense of hearing

auspices plural noun formal **under the auspices of** with the support and approval of

auspicious adjective formal showing signs of future success: *It was an auspicious start to the month* > **auspiciously** adverb

austere adjective 1 stern or severe 2 without luxuries 3 severely simple or plain > **austerely** adverb

Australasia noun Australia, New Zealand and neighbouring islands in the Pacific > **Australasian** adjective

Australia noun smallest continent and the largest island in the world, situated between the Indian Ocean and the Pacific

Austrian adjective 1 belonging or relating to Austria ▷ noun 2 someone from Austria

authentic adjective known to be real; genuine > **authentically** adverb > **authenticity** noun: *doubts cast on the painting's authenticity*

author noun 1 writer of a book etc 2 originator or creator

- Use *author* to talk about both men and women writers, as *authoress* is now felt to be insulting

authoritarian adjective insisting on strict obedience to authority: *thirty years of authoritarian government* > **authoritarianism** noun 1 state of being authoritarian 2 belief that the state has a right to control its citizens' lives

authoritative adjective 1 recognized as being reliable 2 possessing authority > **authoritatively** adverb

authority authorities noun 1 power to command or control others: *the authority of the state* 2 Brit local government department: *local health authorities* 3 expert in a particular field: *the world's leading authority on fashion* 4 the people with the power to make decisions: *A third escapee turned himself in to the authorities*

authorize verb 1 to give authority to 2 to give permission for > **authorization** noun: *authorization to use military force*

auto- prefix self-: *autobiography*

autobiography autobiographies noun account of a person's life written by that person > **autobiographical** adjective (of a piece of writing) relating to events in the life of the author

autograph noun 1 handwritten signature of a (famous) person ▷ verb 2 to write your signature on or in

automatic adjective 1 (of a device) operating mechanically by itself 2 (of a process) performed by automatic equipment 3 done without conscious thought 4 (of a firearm) self-loading 5 occurring as a necessary consequence: *The penalty for murder is an automatic life sentence* ▷ noun **6** self-loading firearm **7** vehicle in which the gears change automatically as the vehicle's speed changes > **automatically** adverb

automobile noun US motor car

autonomous adjective **1** having self-government **2** independent of others > **autonomy** noun self-government

autopsy autopsies noun examination of a corpse to determine the cause of death

autumn noun season between summer and winter ▷ **autumnal** adjective: *the autumnal colour of the trees*

auxiliary auxiliaries adjective **1** secondary or supplementary: *auxiliary fuel tanks* **2** supporting ▷ noun **3** person or thing that supplements or supports: *nursing auxiliaries*

auxiliary verb noun verb used to form the tense, voice or mood of another, such as *will* in *I will go*

avail verb **1** to be of use or advantage (to) **2 avail yourself of** to make use of ▷ noun **3** use or advantage: *to no avail*

available adjective **1** obtainable or accessible **2** ready for work or free for people to talk to > **availability** noun: *the easy availability of guns*

avalanche noun **1** mass of snow or ice falling down a mountain **2** sudden overwhelming quantity of anything

avant-garde noun **1** group of innovators, especially in the arts ▷ adjective **2** innovative and progressive

avarice noun formal greed for wealth and possessions > **avaricious** adjective greedy for wealth and possessions

avenge verb to take revenge in retaliation for (harm done) or on behalf of (a person harmed) > **avenger** noun

avenue noun **1** wide street **2** road between two rows of trees **3** means of doing something: *We are exploring a number of avenues*

average noun **1** typical or normal amount or quality **2** result obtained by adding quantities together and dividing the total by the number of quantities **3** or **average** usually or typically: *Men are, on average, taller than women* ▷ adjective **4** usual or typical: *the average American citizen* **5** calculated as an average ▷ verb **6** to calculate the average of **7** to amount to as an average: *Monthly sales averaged more than 110,000*

averse adjective **averse to** disinclined or unwilling: *He's not averse to publicity*

aversion noun **1** strong dislike **2** person or thing disliked

avert verb **1** to turn away: *He had to avert his eyes* **2** to ward off: *a final attempt to avert war*

avian adjective relating to birds > **avian flu** same as **bird flu**

aviary aviaries noun large cage or enclosure for birds

aviation noun art or science of flying aircraft

aviator noun old-fashioned pilot of an aircraft

avid adjective **1** keen or enthusiastic **2** greedy (for) > **avidly** adverb

avocado avocados noun pear-shaped tropical fruit with a leathery green skin and yellowish-green flesh

avoid verb 1 to prevent from happening 2 to refrain from doing 3 to keep away from > **avoidable** adjective: This accident was avoidable > **avoidance** noun: the avoidance of stress

avowed adjective formal 1 openly declared: an avowed supporter of vegetarianism 2 (of a belief or aim) strongly held: the council's avowed intention to stamp out racism > **avowedly** adverb

avuncular adjective friendly and helpful in manner towards younger people, rather like an uncle

await verb 1 to wait for 2 to be in store for

awake awakes awaking awoke **awoken** verb 1 to emerge or rouse from sleep 2 to become or cause to become alert ▷ adjective 3 not sleeping 4 alert

awaken verb 1 to awake 2 to cause (someone) to be aware of

award verb 1 to give (something, such as a prize) formally ▷ noun 2 something awarded, such as a prize

aware adjective having knowledge, informed > **awareness** noun: an awareness of green issues

awash adverb, adjective washed over by water

away adverb 1 from a place: go away 2 to another place: put that away 3 out of existence: fade away 4 continuously: laughing away 5 adjective 5 not present or distant: two miles away 7 Sport

played on an opponent's ground

awe formal noun wonder and respect mixed with dread

awesome adjective 1 inspiring awe 2 informal excellent or outstanding

awful adjective 1 very bad or unpleasant 2 informal very great: It took an awful lot of courage > **awfully** adverb 1 in an unpleasant way 2 informal very

awkward adjective 1 clumsy or ungainly 2 embarrassed 3 difficult 4 inconvenient > **awkwardly** adverb > **awkwardness** noun 1 shyness 2 clumsiness

awning noun canvas roof supported by a frame to give protection against the weather

awry adverb, adjective 1 with a twist to one side; askew 2 wrong or not as planned: Why had their plans gone so badly awry?

axe axes axing axed noun 1 tool with a sharp blade for felling trees or chopping wood 2 informal dismissal from employment etc ▷ verb 3 informal to dismiss (employees), restrict (expenditure) or terminate (a project)

axiom noun 1 generally accepted principle 2 self-evident statement > **axiomatic** adjective self-evident

axis axes noun 1 (imaginary) line round which a body can rotate or about which an object or geometrical figure is symmetrical 2 one of two fixed lines on a graph, against which quantities or positions are measured

axle noun shaft on which a wheel

A
B
C
D
E
F
G
H
I
J
K
L
M
N
O
P
Q
R
S
T
U
V
W
X
Y
Z

or pair of wheels turns

ayatollah *noun* Islamic religious leader in Iran

azure *literary noun* **1** deep blue colour of a clear blue sky ▷ *adjective* **2** deep blue

b

babble *verb* to talk excitedly or foolishly

baboon *noun* large monkey with a pointed face and a long tail

baby babies *noun* **1** very young infant; infant **2** *informal* sweetheart ▷ *adjective* **3** comparatively small of its type > **babyhood** *noun* period of being a baby > **babyish** *adjective* immature

baby-sit baby-sits baby-sitting baby-sat *verb* to take care of a child while the parents are out > **baby-sitter** *noun* person who baby-sits > **baby-sitting** *noun* taking care of a child while the parents are out

baccalaureate *noun* internationally recognized course of study made up of several different subjects, offered by some schools as an alternative to A levels

bach *NZ noun* **1** small holiday cottage ▷ *verb* **2** to look after oneself when one's spouse is away

bachelor *noun* unmarried man

back *noun* **1** rear part of the human body, from the neck to the pelvis; also the corresponding part of an animal's body **2** part or side of an object opposite the front **3** *Ball games* defensive player or position > *verb* **4** to move (a car) backwards **5** to provide money for (a person or organization) **6** to bet on the success of (a competitor) **7 back onto** to have the back facing towards (something) ▷ *adjective* **8** at, to or towards the rear ▷ *adverb* **9** at, to or towards the rear **10** to or towards the original starting point or condition > **back up** *verb* to support (someone)

backbone *noun* **1** spinal column **2** strength of character

backdate *verb* to make (a document or arrangement) valid from an earlier date than the one on which it is completed

backdrop *noun* the background to a situation or event

backer *noun* person who gives (someone or something) financial support

backfire *verb* **1** (of a plan) to have the opposite result to the one intended; fail **2** (of an engine) to make a loud noise like an explosion

background *noun* **1** events or circumstances that help to explain something **2** person's social circumstances, education and experience **3** part of a scene or picture furthest from the viewer

backing *noun* **1** support or help **2** music that accompanies a pop song

backlash *noun* sudden and hos

reaction

backlog noun accumulation of things still to be done

backpack noun large bag carried on the back

backside noun informal buttocks

backward adjective **1** directed towards the back **2** (of a country or society) not having modern industries or technology **3** (of a child) unable to learn as quickly as other children > adverb **4** the same as **backwards** > **backwardness** noun being backward

backwards adverb **1** in reverse **2** in the reverse direction **3** behind

bacon noun salted or smoked pig meat

bacteria plural noun very tiny organisms which can cause disease > **bacterial** adjective: a bacterial infection

- The word bacteria is plural.
- The singular form is bacterium

bad worse worst adjective **1** of poor quality **2** lacking skill or talent **3** harmful **4** immoral or evil **5** rotten or decayed **6** unpleasant > **badly** adverb: they have behaved badly > **badness** noun being bad

bade verb a past tense of **bid**

badge noun piece of metal, plastic or cloth worn to show membership of an organization, support for a cause, etc

badger noun **1** burrowing animal of Europe, Asia and North America with a black and white head > verb **2** to pester or harass

badminton noun game played with rackets and a shuttlecock, which is hit back and forth over a high net

Bafana bafana plural noun S Afr South African national soccer team

baffle verb to perplex or puzzle > **baffled** adjective: The police are baffled > **baffling** adjective perplexing or puzzling

bag noun container for carrying things in

baggage noun suitcases packed for a journey

baggy baggier baggiest adjective (of clothes) hanging loosely

bagpipes plural noun musical wind instrument with reed pipes and an inflatable bag

bail noun **1** Law money deposited with a court as security for a person's reappearance in court **2** Cricket either of two wooden bars across the tops of the stumps > **bail out** verb **1** to remove (water) from a boat **2** to make an emergency parachute jump from an aircraft

bailiff noun **1** law officer who makes sure that the decisions of a court are obeyed **2** landlord's agent

Baisakhi noun Sikh festival celebrated every April

bait noun **1** piece of food put on a hook or in a trap in order to catch fish or animals > verb **2** to put a piece of food on or in (a hook or trap) **3** to persecute or tease

baize noun woollen fabric, usually green, used to cover billiard and card tables

bake verb **1** to cook (food) by dry heat, as in an oven **2** to heat (earth or clay) until it hardens

baker noun person whose business is to make or sell bread, cakes, etc >**bakery** noun place where bread, cakes, etc are baked or sold

bakkie noun SAfr small truck

balance noun 1 state in which a weight or amount is evenly distributed 2 amount that remains: *the balance of what you owe* 3 difference between the credits and debits of an account ▷ verb 4 to remain steady 5 to equalize the money going into and coming out of (an account)

balcony balconies noun 1 platform on the outside of a building with a rail along the outer edge 2 area of upstairs seats in a theatre or cinema

bald adjective 1 having little or no hair on the scalp 2 plain or blunt >**baldly** adverb plainly or bluntly >**baldness** noun being bald

bale noun large bundle of hay or paper tightly bound together >**bale out** verb same as **bail out**

balk or **baulk** verb (followed by at) to object to and refuse to do (something)

ball noun 1 round or nearly round object, especially one used in games 2 large formal social event at which people dance

ballad noun 1 long song or poem that tells a story 2 slow romantic pop song

ballast noun substance, such as sand, used to stabilize a ship when it is not carrying cargo

ballerina noun female ballet dancer

ballet noun 1 classical style of expressive dancing based on

conventional steps 2 theatrical performance of this

balloon noun 1 inflatable rubber bag used as a plaything or decoration 2 large bag inflated with air or gas, that travels through the air with passengers in a basket underneath

ballot noun 1 method of voting in which other people do not see how you vote 2 actual vote or paper indicating a person's choice ▷ verb 3 to ask for a vote from (people)

ballpoint or **ballpoint pen** noun pen with a tiny ball bearing as a writing point

ballroom noun very large room used for dancing or formal balls

balm noun sweet-smelling soothing ointment

balmy balmier balmiest adjective (of weather) mild and pleasant

balsa noun very light wood from a tropical American tree

balustrade noun railing or wall or a balcony or staircase

bamboo noun tall tropical plant with hard hollow stems used for making furniture

ban bans banning banned verb 1 to prohibit or forbid (something officially) ▷ noun 2 official prohibition

banal adjective ordinary and unoriginal >**banality** noun being ordinary and unoriginal

banana noun long curved fruit with a yellow skin

band noun 1 group of musicians playing together 2 group of people with a common purpose 3 strip of some material, used to hold objects 4 Physics range of frequencies or wavelengths between two limits > **band together** verb to unite

bandage noun **1** piece of material used to cover a wound or wrap an injured limb > verb **2** to cover (a wound) with a bandage

bandit noun robber, especially a member of an armed gang

bandstand noun roofed outdoor platform for a band

bandwagon noun **jump on the bandwagon** to become involved in something that seems assured of success

bandy bandies bandying bandied verb **1** to exchange (words) in a heated manner **2** to use (a name, term, etc) frequently

bane noun person or thing that causes misery or distress

bang noun **1** short loud explosive noise **2** hard blow or loud knock > verb **3** to hit or knock (something), especially with a loud noise **4** to close (a door) noisily

Bangladeshi adjective **1** belonging or relating to Bangladesh > noun **2** person from Bangladesh

bangle noun decorative ring worn round the arm or the ankle

banish verb **1** to send (someone) into exile **2** to get rid of (something) > **banishment** noun being banished

banisters plural noun railing supported by posts on a staircase

banjo banjos or **banjoes** noun guitar-like musical instrument with a circular body

bank noun **1** business that looks

after people's money **2** any supply, store or reserve **3** sloping side of an area of raised ground **4** sloping ground at the side of a river **5** long row or mass of something > verb **6** to deposit (cash or cheques) in a bank **7** (of an aircraft) to tip to one side on turning > **banker** noun manager or owner of a bank > **banking** noun business activity of banks > **bank on** verb to rely on (something happening)

bank holiday noun public holiday, when banks are officially closed

banknote noun piece of paper money

bankrupt noun **1** person declared by a court to be unable to pay his or her debts > adjective **2** financially ruined > verb **3** to make (someone) bankrupt > **bankruptcy** noun bankrupt state

banksia noun aust Australian evergreen tree or shrub

banner noun **1** long strip of cloth with a message or slogan on it **2** placard carried in a demonstration or procession **3** advertisement that extends across the top of a web page

banquet noun grand formal dinner

banter noun teasing or joking conversation

baobab noun small fruit tree that grows in Africa and northern Australia

baptism noun ceremony in which someone is baptized > **baptismal** adjective

Baptist noun member of a Protestant church that believes in adult baptism by immersion

baptize verb to sprinkle water on (someone) or immerse (someone) in water, as a sign that he or she has become a Christian

bar bars barring barred noun **1** counter or room where alcoholic drinks are served **2** long straight piece of metal, wood, etc **3** solid, usually rectangular block, of any material: *a bar of soap* **4** Music one of the many very short sections into which any piece of music is divided. Each bar in a piece usually contains the same set number of beats **5** unit of atmospheric pressure **6** the Bar profession of a barrister ▷ verb **7** to secure (a door) with a bar **8** to obstruct (the way) **9** to ban or forbid (someone or something) ▷ preposition **10** (also **barring**) except for

barb noun point facing in the opposite direction to the main point of a fish-hook etc

barbarian noun member of a wild or uncivilized people

barbaric adjective cruel or brutal > **barbarity** noun state of being barbaric

barbecue barbecues barbecuing barbecued noun **1** grill on which food is cooked over hot charcoal, usually outdoors **2** outdoor party at which barbecued food is served ▷ verb **3** to cook (food) on a barbecue

barbed adjective unkind or spiteful remark that appears innocent

barbed wire noun strong wire with protruding sharp points

barber noun person who cuts men's hair and shaves beards

bar code noun arrangement of numbers and lines on a package, which can be electronically scanned at a checkout to give the price of the goods

bard noun literary poet

bare adjective **1** unclothed or naked **2** without the natural or usual covering **3** empty **4** plain, simple and unadorned **5** just sufficient ▷ verb **6** to uncover (something)

barefoot adjective, adverb not wearing anything on the feet

barely adverb only just

bargain noun **1** agreement establishing what each party will give, receive or perform in a matter that involves them both **2** something bought or offered at a low price ▷ verb **3** to negotiate the terms of an agreement > **bargain for** verb to anticipate (something) or take (something) into account

barge noun **1** flat-bottomed boat used to transport freight ▷ verb **2** informal to push violently

bark noun **1** loud harsh cry of a do **2** tough outer layer of a tree > ve **3** (of a dog) to make its typical cry **4** to shout (something) in an angry tone

barley noun tall grasslike plant grown for grain

bar mitzvah noun ceremony tha takes place on a Jewish boy's 13th birthday, after which he is regarded as an adult

barmy barmier barmiest adjecta informal insane

barn noun large building on a far used for storing grain

barnacle noun shellfish that live attached to rocks, ship bottoms etc

barometer *noun* instrument that measures air pressure and shows when the weather is changing

baron *noun* member of the lowest rank of nobility > **baronial** *adjective* of or relating to a baron

baroness *noun* woman who has the rank of baron or who is the wife of a baron

barracks *plural noun* building where soldiers live

barracuda *noun* large tropical sea fish with sharp teeth

barrage *noun* 1 continuous delivery of questions, complaints, etc 2 continuous artillery fire 3 artificial barrier across a river to control the water level

barrel *noun* 1 cylindrical container with rounded sides and flat ends 2 tube-shaped part of a gun through which bullets are fired

barren *adjective* 1 (of a woman or female animal) incapable of having babies or young; infertile 2 (of land) unable to support the growth of crops, fruit, etc **barrenness** *noun* being barren

barricade *noun* 1 barrier, especially one put up hastily or defence > *verb* 2 to put up a barricade across (an entrance)

barrier *noun* anything that prevents access, progress or agreement

barrister *noun* Brit, Aust, NZ lawyer qualified to plead in a higher court

barrow *noun* 1 wheelbarrow 2 movable stall used by street traders

barter *verb* 1 to trade (goods) in exchange for other goods > *noun*

2 trade by the exchange of goods

base *noun* 1 bottom or supporting part of anything 2 centre of operations, organization or supply 3 *Chemistry* compound that reacts with an acid to form a salt > *verb* 4 **base something on** or **upon** to make up the basic elements of something using 5 (followed by *at*, *in*) to position or place (someone) somewhere > *adjective* 6 dishonourable or immoral 7 of inferior quality or value

baseball *noun* team game in which runs are scored by hitting a ball with a bat then running round four bases

basement *noun* partly or wholly underground storey of a building

bases *noun* the plural of **basis**

bash *informal verb* 1 to hit (someone) violently or forcefully > *noun* 2 heavy blow

bashful *adjective* shy or modest

basic *adjective* 1 of or forming a base or basis 2 elementary or simple > **basically** *adverb*: *it's basically a vegan diet* > **basics** *plural noun* essential main principles, facts, etc

basilica *noun* rectangular church with a rounded end and two aisles

basin *noun* 1 round open container 2 sink for washing the hands and face 3 bowl of land from which water runs into the river

basis bases *noun* essential main principle from which something is started or developed

bask *verb* to lie in or be exposed to something, especially pleasant warmth

basket *noun* container made

of thin strips of cane woven together

basketball noun team game in which points are scored by throwing the ball through a high horizontal hoop

bass¹ noun **1** man with a very deep singing voice **2** musical instrument that provides the rhythm and lowest part in the harmonies

bass² or **basses** noun edible sea fish

basset hound noun smooth-haired dog with short legs and long ears

bassoon noun low-pitched woodwind instrument

bastard noun **1** offensive despicable person **2** old-fashioned person whose parents were not married when he or she was born

baste verb to moisten (meat) during cooking with hot fat

bastion noun something that protects a system or way of life

bat bats batting batted noun **1** any of various types of club used to hit the ball in certain sports **2** mouselike flying animal, active at night ▷ verb **3** to strike (the ball) with or as if with a bat

batch noun group of people or things dealt with at the same time

bated adjective **with bated breath** in suspense or fear

bath noun **1** large container in which to wash the body **2** act of washing in such a container **3** baths public swimming pool ▷ verb **4** to wash in a bath

bathe verb **1** to swim in open water for pleasure **2** to apply liquid to (the skin or a wound) in order to cleanse or soothe **3** (followed by in) to fill (a place) with something: bathed in sunlight ▷ **bather** noun person who swims ▷ **bathing** noun swimming or washing

bathroom noun room with a bath or shower, washbasin and, usually, a toilet

baton noun **1** thin stick used by the conductor of an orchestra **2** short stick passed from one runner to another in a relay race **3** police officer's truncheon

batsman batsmen noun Cricket person who bats or specializes in batting

battalion noun army unit consisting of three or more companies

batten noun strip of wood fixed to something, especially to hold it in place ▷ **batten down** verb to secure (something) with battens

batter verb **1** to hit (someone) repeatedly ▷ noun **2** mixture of flour, eggs and milk, used in cooking ▷ **battering** noun beating or defeat

battery batteries noun **1** device that produces electricity in a torch, radio, etc **2** group of heavy guns operating as a single unit ▷ adjective **3** (of hens) kept in small cages for the mass production of eggs

battle noun **1** fight between large armed forces **2** conflict or struggle ▷ verb **3** to struggle

battlefield noun place where a battle is fought

battlement noun wall with gaps along the top for firing guns or

battleship noun large heavily armoured warship

batty battier battiest adjective informal eccentric or crazy

bauble noun trinket of little value

bawdy bawdier bawdiest adjective (of writing etc) containing humorous references to sex

bawl verb to shout or weep noisily

bay noun **1** stretch of coastline that curves inwards; inlet **2** area set aside for a particular purpose: *loading bay* **3** Mediterranean laurel tree **4** reddish-brown horse ▷ adjective **5** (of a horse) reddish-brown ▷ verb **6** to make a deep howling noise

bayonet noun sharp blade that can be fixed to the end of a rifle

bazaar noun **1** sale in aid of charity **2** market area, especially in Eastern countries

BC abbreviation before Christ

be verb **1** to exist or live **2** used to link the subject of a sentence and its complement: *John is a musician* **3** used to form continuous tenses: *the man is running* **4** used to form the passive voice: *He was brought up by his grandparents*

be- prefix (forming verbs from nouns) to treat as to *befriend*

beach noun area of sand or pebbles on a shore

beacon noun fire or light on a hill or tower, used as a warning

bead noun **1** small piece of plastic, wood, etc, pierced for threading on a string to form a necklace etc **2** small drop of moisture

beady adjective (of eyes) small, round and glittering

beagle noun small hound with short legs and drooping ears

beak noun **1** projecting horny jaws of a bird **2** informal nose

beaker noun **1** large drinking cup **2** glass container with a lip that is used in laboratories

beam noun **1** broad smile **2** ray of light **3** long thick piece of wood, metal, etc, used in building ▷ verb **4** to smile broadly

bean noun seed or pod of various plants, eaten as a vegetable or used to make coffee etc

bear bears bearing bore borne verb **1** to support (something) or hold (something) up **2 born** to give birth to (a baby) **3** to tolerate or endure (someone or something) **4** to hold (something) in the mind ▷ noun **5** large strong wild animal with a shaggy coat > **bearable** adjective able to be tolerated > **bearer** noun person who carries or presents something > **bear out** verb to show (what someone says) to be truthful

beard noun hair growing on the lower parts of a man's face > **bearded** adjective having a beard

bearing noun **1** relevance **2** way in which a person moves or stands

beast noun **1** large wild animal **2** brutal or uncivilized person

beastly beastlier beastliest adjective unpleasant or disagreeable

beat beats beating beat beaten verb **1** to hit (someone or something) hard and repeatedly **2** to move (wings) up and down **3** (of a heart) to pump blood with a regular rhythm **4** to stir or mix (eggs, cream or butter) vigorously **5** to overcome or defeat ▷ *noun* **6** regular pumping action of the heart **7** area patrolled by a particular police officer **8** main rhythm of a piece of music ▷ **beater** *noun* tool for beating eggs, cream or butter ▷ **beating** *noun* hitting someone hard and repeatedly ▷ **beat up** *verb* to injure (someone) by repeated blows or kicks

beaut *noun Aust, NZ informal* **1** outstanding person or thing ▷ *adjective* **2** good, excellent

beautiful *adjective* very attractive or pleasant ▷ **beautifully** *adverb*

beauty beauties *noun* **1** combination of all the qualities of a person or thing that delight the senses and mind **2** very attractive woman **3** *informal* something outstanding of its kind

beaver *noun* animal with a big flat tail and webbed hind feet

because *conjunction* **1** on account of the fact that **2 because of** on account of

beck *noun* **at someone's beck and call** having to be constantly available to do as someone asks

beckon *verb* (followed by *to*) to summon (someone) with a gesture

become becomes becoming became become *verb* **1** to come to be (something) **2** to suit (someone) **3 become of** to happen to (someone or something)

bed beds bedding bedded *noun* **1** piece of furniture for sleeping on **2** area of ground in which plants are grown **3** bottom of a river,

lake or sea **4** layer of rock ▷ **bed down** *verb* to sleep somewhere for the night

bedclothes *plural noun* sheets and covers that are used on a bed

bedding *noun* sheets and covers that are used on a bed

bedlam *noun* noisy confused situation

bedpan *noun* container used as a toilet by people too ill to get out of bed

bedraggled *adjective* untidy, wet or dirty

bedridden *adjective* confined to bed because of illness or old age

bedrock *noun* **1** solid rock beneath the surface soil **2** basic facts or principles

bedroom *noun* room used for sleeping in

bedspread *noun* cover put over a bed, on top of the sheets and blankets

bedstead *noun* metal or wooden frame of an old-fashioned bed

bee *noun* winged insect that makes wax and honey

beech *noun* tree with a smooth greyish bark

beef *noun* flesh of a cow, bull or ox

beefy beefier beefiest *adjective* **1** like beef **2** *informal* strong and muscular

beehive *noun* structure in which bees live

beeline *noun* **make a beeline for** *informal* to go to (a place) as quickly and directly as possible

been *verb* past participle of **be**

beer *noun* alcoholic drink brewed from malt and hops

beetle *noun* insect with a hard

wing cover on its back

beetroot noun type of beet plant with a dark red root

befall befalls befalling befell befallen verb old-fashioned to happen to (someone)

before conjunction, preposition, adverb **1** earlier than or prior to: before I go; before the war **2** previously: I'd never been there before **3** in front of They stopped before a large white villa **4** in preference to or rather than death before dishonour

beforehand adverb in advance

befriend verb to become friends with (someone)

beg begs begging begged verb **1** to ask for money or food, especially in the street **2** to ask (someone) anxiously to do something

beggar noun person who lives by begging

begin begins beginning began begun verb to start or commence > beginner noun person who has just started learning to do something > beginning noun first part of something or the time when something starts

egonia noun tropical plant with brightly coloured flowers

egrudge verb to be envious of (someone) for something that he or she possesses

ehalf noun on behalf of in the interest of or for the benefit of

ehave verb **1** to act in a particular way **2** to conduct (oneself) properly

ehaviour noun manner of behaving

ehead verb to cut off the head of

beheld verb past of **behold**

behind preposition **1** at the back of: behind the wall **2** not as far advanced as: behind schedule **3** responsible for or causing: the reasons behind her departure **4** supporting: The whole country was behind him ▷ adverb **5** remaining after other people have gone: He stayed behind to clear up **6** not up to date: He's behind with his rent ▷ noun **7** informal buttocks

behold beholds beholding beheld verb old-fashioned to look at

beige adjective pale creamy-brown

being noun **1** state or fact of existing **2** something that exists or is thought to exist **3** human being ▷ verb **4** present participle of **be**

belated adjective late or too late > **belatedly** adverb

belch verb **1** to expel wind from the stomach noisily through the mouth **2** (of smoke or fire) to come out in large amounts: smoke belched from the factory ▷ noun **3** act of belching

beleaguered adjective **1** struggling against difficulties or criticism **2** besieged by an enemy

belfry belfries noun part of a tower where bells are hung

Belgian adjective **1** belonging or relating to Belgium ▷ noun **2** person from Belgium

belief noun **1** faith or confidence **2** opinion **3** principle accepted as true, often without proof

believe verb **1** to accept (something) as true or real **2** to think, assume or suppose (something) > **believable**

adjective: *The book is full of believable characters* **believe in** verb to be convinced of the truth or existence of (something or someone) >**believer** noun: *a great believer in herbal medicines*

belittle verb to treat (someone) as having little value or importance

bell noun 1 hollow, usually metal, cup-shaped or round instrument with a swinging piece inside that causes a ringing sound when it strikes against the sides as the bell is moved 2 device that rings or buzzes as a signal

bellbird noun Aust, NZ Australian or New Zealand bird that makes a sound like a bell

belligerent adjective aggressive and keen to start a fight or an argument >**belligerence** noun aggressiveness >**belligerently** adverb

bellow verb 1 to make a low deep cry like that of a bull 2 to shout (something) in anger ▷ noun 3 loud deep roar

belly bellies noun 1 part of the body that contains the intestines 2 stomach 3 front, lower or inner part of something

belong verb 1 (followed by *to*) to be the property of (someone) 2 (usually followed by *to*) to be a part or member of (something) 3 to have a rightful place; go: *It belongs in the kitchen* >**belongings** plural noun personal possessions

beloved adjective dearly loved

below preposition, adverb at or to a position lower (than); underneath

belt noun 1 band of cloth, leather, etc, usually worn round the waist 2 long narrow area: *a belt of trees* 3 circular strip of rubber that drives moving parts in a machine ▷ verb 4 informal to hit (someone) very hard 5 informal to move very fast

bemused adjective puzzled or confused

bench noun 1 long seat 2 long narrow work table 3 **the bench** judge or magistrate sitting in court, or judges and magistrates collectively

bend bends bending bent verb 1 to form a curve or cause (something) to form a curve 2 (often followed by *down, forward etc*) to move the head and shoulders forwards and downwards ▷ noun 3 curved part

bene- prefix meaning good or well beneficial

beneath adverb 1 below ▷ preposition 2 below 3 not worthy of

benefactor noun person who supports a person or institution by giving money

beneficial adjective helpful or advantageous >**beneficially** adverb helpfully or advantageously

beneficiary beneficiaries noun person who gains or benefits from something

benefit noun 1 something that improves or promotes 2 advantage or sake: *I'm doing this for your benefit* 3 money given by the government to people who are unemployed or ill ▷ verb 4 (followed by *from*) to gain an advantage or help from

(something)

• benefit is spelt with two *es* not two *is*

benevolence noun kindness and helpfulness > **benevolent** adjective kind and helpful > **benevolently** adverb: smiling benevolently

benign adjective **1** showing kindliness **2** (of a tumour) not threatening to life > **benignly** adverb kindly

bent verb **1** past of bend ▷ adjective **2** curved **3** informal dishonest or corrupt **4** bent on determined to do (something)

bequeath verb to leave (money or property) to someone in a will

bequest noun legal gift of money or property by someone who has died

berate verb to scold (someone) harshly

bereaved adjective having recently lost a close friend or relative through death > **bereavement** noun: those who have suffered a bereavement

bereft adjective (followed by of) deprived (of something): bereft of ideas

beret noun round flat close-fitting brimless cap

berm noun NZ narrow grass strip between the road and the footpath in a residential area

berry berries noun small soft stoneless fruit

berserk adjective go berserk to become violent or destructive

berth noun **1** bunk in a ship or train **2** space in a harbour where a ship stays while being loaded or unloaded ▷ verb **3** to dock (a ship)

beseech beseeches beseeching beseeched or **besought** verb to ask (someone) earnestly for something > **beseeching** adjective: She gave him a beseeching look

beset besets besetting beset verb to trouble or harass (someone) constantly

beside preposition **1** at, by or to the side of **2** as compared with **3** beside yourself overwhelmed or overwrought

besiege verb **1** to surround (a place) with military forces **2** to overwhelm (someone), as with requests

besought verb a past of **beseech**

best adjective **1** most excellent of a particular group etc ▷ adverb **2** in a manner that is better than all others ▷ noun **3** most outstanding or excellent person, thing or group in a category

best man noun groom's attendant at a wedding

bestow verb (followed by on) to give (something) to someone

bet bets betting bet noun **1** the act of staking a sum of money on the outcome of an event **2** sum of money risked on the outcome of an event ▷ verb **3** to make or place a bet **4** informal to predict (something) > **betting** noun: a fine for illegal betting

betray verb **1** to do something that harms (someone who trusts you), such as helping his or her enemies **2** to reveal (your feelings or thoughts) unintentionally > **betrayal** noun act of betraying someone or something > **betrayer** noun person who betrays someone

betrothed *adjective old-fashioned* engaged to be married
> **betrothal** *noun* engagement to be married

better *adjective* **1** more excellent than others; superior **2** improved or fully recovered in health
▷ *adverb* **3** in a more excellent manner **4** in or to a greater degree

between *preposition, adverb* indicating position in the middle, alternatives, etc

- If there are two things, you should use *between*. If there are more than two things you should use *among*

beverage *noun* drink

bevy *bevies noun* flock or group

beware *verb* (usually followed by *of*) to be on your guard (against)

bewilder *verb* to confuse (someone) utterly > **bewildered** *adjective* greatly confused > **bewildering** *adjective* very confusing > **bewilderment** *noun* great confusion

bewitch *verb* **1** to attract and fascinate (someone) **2** to cast a spell over (someone) > **bewitched** *adjective* > **bewitching** *adjective*: *bewitching brown eyes*

beyond *preposition* **1** at or to a point on the other side of **2** outside the limits or scope of ▷ *adverb* **3** at or to the far side of something

bi- *prefix* two or twice: *bifocal; biweekly*

bias *biases* or **biasses** *biasing* or **biassing** *biased* or **biassed** *noun* **1** mental tendency, especially prejudice ▷ *verb* **2** to cause (someone) to have a bias > **biased**

or **biassed** *adjective* prejudiced

bib *noun* **1** piece of cloth or plastic worn to protect a very young child's clothes when eating **2** upper front part of dungarees etc

Bible *noun* **1** sacred writings of the Christian religion > **biblical** *adjective* of or relating to the Bible

bicentenary *bicentenaries noun* 200th anniversary

biceps *noun* large muscle in the upper part of your arm

- The plural of *biceps* is *biceps*

bicker *verb* to argue over petty matters

bicycle *noun* vehicle with two wheels, one behind the other, pedalled by the rider

bid *bids bidding bade* or *bid bidden verb* **1** *bid* to offer (a sum) in an attempt to buy something **2** *old-fashioned* to give (a greeting) to (someone) ▷ *noun* **3** offer to buy something for a specified amount **4** attempt to do something ▷ *noun* command

- When *bid* means 'offer a certain sum' (sense 1), the past tense and past participle are *bid*. When *bid* means 'give a greeting' (sense 2), the past tense is *bade* and the past participle is *bidden*

biddy-bid or **biddy-biddy** *noun* NZ prickly low-growing plant found in New Zealand

bide *bides biding bided verb* **bide your time** to wait patiently for an opportunity

bidet *noun* low basin for washing the genital area

big *bigger biggest adjective*

large or important > **biggish** *adjective* fairly big > **bigness** *noun* largeness

bigamy *noun* crime of marrying a person while still legally married to someone else > **bigamist** *noun* person who commits bigamy

bigot *noun* person with strong, unreasonable prejudices, especially regarding religion or race > **bigoted** *adjective* extremely prejudiced in an unreasonable way, especially regarding religion or race > **bigotry** *noun: religious bigotry*

bike *noun informal* bicycle or motorcycle

bikini bikinis *noun* woman's brief two-piece swimming costume

bilateral *adjective* (of an agreement) made between two groups or countries

bile *noun* bitter yellow fluid produced by the liver

bilge *noun* the lowest part of a ship, where dirty water collects

bilingual *adjective* involving or using two languages

bill *noun* 1 statement of money owed for goods or services supplied 2 formal statement of a proposed new law 3 poster 4 *chiefly US & Canadian* piece of paper money 5 list of events, such as a theatre programme ● bird's beak

billabong *noun Aust* lagoon or pool formed from part of a river

billboard *noun* large board on which advertisements are displayed

billet *verb* 1 to assign a lodging to (a soldier) ▷ *noun* 2 building for housing soldiers

billiards *noun* game played on a table with balls and a cue

billion *adjective, noun* 1 one thousand million (1,000,000,000) 2 formerly, one million million (1,000,000,000,000) 3 **billions** large but unspecified number; lots > **billionth** *adjective, noun*

- As the meaning of *billion* has
- changed from one million
- million to one thousand
- million, a writer may mean
- either of these things when
- using it, depending on when
- the book or article was
- written

billow *noun* 1 large sea wave ▷ *verb* 2 to rise up or swell out

billy billies; also spelt **billycan** *noun Aust* metal pot for boiling water over a camp fire

bin *noun* container, especially one for rubbish

binary *adjective* 1 composed of two parts 2 *Maths, computers* of or in a counting system with only two digits, 0 and 1

bind binds binding bound *verb* 1 to make (something) secure with or as if with a rope 2 to place (someone) under an obligation 3 to enclose and fasten (the pages of a book) between covers ▷ *noun* 4 *informal* annoying situation

bindi-eye *noun Aust* small Australian plant with prickly fruits

binding *noun* 1 anything that binds or fastens 2 book cover

binge *noun informal* wild bout of drinking or eating too much

bingo *noun* gambling game in which numbers are called out and covered by the players on their individual cards

binoculars *plural noun* instrument with lenses for each eye through which you look in order to see distant objects or people

bio- *prefix* life or living things: *biology*

bioactive *adjective* having an effect on living tissue

biochemistry *noun* study of the chemistry of living things > **biochemical** *adjective* relating to chemical processes that happen in living things > **biochemist** *noun*

biodegradable *adjective* capable of being decomposed by natural means

biofuel *noun* any biological substance used as fuel

biography biographies *noun* account of a person's life by another person

biology *noun* study of living things > **biological** *adjective* of or relating to biology > **biologically** *adverb*: *Much of our behaviour is biologically determined* > **biologist** *noun*

biometric *adjective* (of any automated system) using physiological or behavioural traits as a means of identification: *biometric fingerprinting*

bionic *adjective* having a part of the body that is operated electronically

biopsy biopsies *noun* examination of tissue from a living body

birch *noun* tree with thin peeling bark

bird *noun* creature with feathers and wings, most types of which can fly

birth *noun* 1 process of bearing young; childbirth 2 act of being born 3 beginning of something 4 **give birth to** to bear (a baby)

birthday *noun* anniversary of the day of your birth

birthmark *noun* mark on the skin formed before birth

biscuit *noun* small flat dry sweet or plain cake

bisect *verb* to divide (a line or area) into two equal parts

bisexual *adjective* sexually attracted to both men and women

bishop *noun* 1 high-ranking clergyman in some Christian Churches 2 chessman which is moved diagonally

bison *noun* large hairy animal of the cattle family, native to North America and Europe

bistro bistros *noun* small restaurant

bit *noun* 1 small piece, portion or quantity 2 metal mouthpiece on a horse's bridle 3 cutting or drilling part of a tool 4 *Computer* smallest unit of information held in a computer's memory, either 0 or 1 5 **a bit** rather, somewhat 6 **bit by bit** gradually ▷ *verb* 7 past tense of **bite**

bitch *noun* 1 female dog, fox or wolf 2 *offensive* spiteful woman > **bitchy** *adjective* spiteful

bite bites biting bit bitten *verb* 1 to cut into (something or someone) with your teeth ▷ *noun* 2 act of biting 3 wound or sting inflicted by biting 4 snack

bitter *adjective* 1 having a sharp unpleasant taste; sour

2 showing or caused by hostility or resentment **3** extremely cold > **bitterly** adverb: They bitterly resented their loss of power > **bitterness** noun e.g.; the bitterness of the dispute

bivouac noun temporary camp in the open air

bizarre adjective odd or unusual

blab blabs blabbing blabbed verb to reveal (secrets) indiscreetly

black adjective **1** of the darkest colour, like coal **2** Black dark-skinned **3** (of a situation) without hope **4** angry or resentful: black looks **5** involving jokes about death or suffering: black comedy > noun **6** darkest colour **7** Black member of a dark-skinned race **8** complete darkness > **blackness** noun being very dark > **black out** verb to lose consciousness

● When you are writing about
● a person or people, Black
● should start with a capital
● letter

blackberry blackberries noun small blackish edible fruit

BlackBerry® noun hand-held wireless device incorporating e-mail, browser, and mobile-phone functions

blackbird noun common European bird, the male of which has black feathers

blackboard noun hard black surface used by teachers for writing on with chalk

black box noun an electronic device in an aircraft which collects and stores information during flights

blackcurrant noun very small blackish edible fruit that grows in bunches

blacken verb **1** to make (something) black **2** blacken **someone's name** to say bad things about someone

blackhead noun very small black spot on the skin caused by a pore being blocked with dirt

blacklist noun **1** list of people or organizations considered untrustworthy etc > verb **2** to put (someone) on a blacklist

blackmail noun **1** act of attempting to obtain money from someone by threatening to reveal information > verb **2** to attempt to obtain money from (someone) by blackmail > **blackmailer** noun person who blackmails someone

black market noun illegal trade in goods or currencies

blackout noun temporary loss of consciousness

blacksmith noun person who makes things out of iron, such as horseshoes

bladder noun part of the body where urine is held until it leaves the body

blade noun **1** cutting edge of a weapon or tool **2** thin flattish part of a propeller, oar, etc **3** leaf of grass

blame verb **1** to consider (someone) responsible for something that is wrong > noun **2** responsibility for something that is wrong

blameless adjective not responsible for something that is wrong

blanch verb **1** to become white or pale **2** to prepare (vegetables etc) by plunging them in boiling water

bland adjective dull and uninteresting > **blandly** adverb: She smiled blandly

blank adjective 1 not written on 2 showing no interest or expression

blanket noun 1 large thick cloth used as covering for a bed 2 thick covering of something, such as snow

blare verb 1 to make a loud harsh noise > noun 2 loud harsh noise

blaspheme verb to speak disrespectfully of God or religion > **blasphemer** noun person who blasphemes > **blasphemous** adjective speaking disrespectfully of God or religion > **blasphemy** noun speech that shows disrespect for God or religion

blast noun 1 explosion 2 sudden strong gust of air or wind 3 sudden loud sound, as of a trumpet > verb 4 to blow up (a rock etc) with explosives

blatant adjective extremely obvious

blaze noun 1 strong fire or flame 2 very bright light > verb 3 to burn or shine brightly

blazer noun lightweight jacket, often in the colours of a school etc

bleach verb 1 to make (material or hair) white or pale > noun 2 chemical used to make material or hair white or to disinfect

bleak adjective 1 exposed and barren 2 offering little hope

bleary adjective (of eyes) red and watery, through tiredness

bleat verb 1 (of a sheep or goat) to utter its characteristic high-pitched cry > noun 2 cry of sheep and goats

bleed bleeds bleeding bled verb to lose blood from a wound

bleep noun short high-pitched sound made by an electrical device

blemish noun 1 mark that spoils the appearance of something > verb 2 to spoil (someone's reputation)

blend verb 1 to mix (parts or ingredients) 2 to look good together > noun 3 mixture

blender noun machine for mixing liquids and foods at high speed

bless blesses blessing blessed or **blest** verb to ask God to protect (someone or something) > **blessed** adjective (followed by with) having (a particular quality or talent) > **blessing** noun 1 something good that you are thankful for 2 with someone's blessing with someone's approval

blew verb past tense of **blow**

blight noun 1 something that damages or spoils other things 2 disease that makes plants wither > verb 3 to harm (something) seriously

blind adjective 1 unable to see 2 (followed by to) unable or unwilling to understand (something) 3 not determined by reason: blind hatred > verb 4 to deprive (someone) of sight 5 to deprive (someone) of good sense, reason or judgment 6 covering for a window > **blind** adverb: She groped blindly for the glass > **blindness** noun: inability to see

blindfold verb 1 to prevent (someone) from seeing by covering the eyes > noun 2 piec of cloth used to cover the eyes

blinding *adjective* (of a light) so bright that it hurts your eyes ▷ **blindingly** *adverb* **blindingly obvious** *informal* very obvious indeed

blink *verb* to close and immediately reopen (the eyes)

blinkers *plural noun* leather flaps on a horse's bridle to prevent sideways vision

bliss *noun* perfect happiness ▷ **blissful** *adjective*: We spent a blissful week together ▷ **blissfully** *adverb*: blissfully happy

blister *noun* **1** small bubble on the skin containing watery liquid, caused by a burn or rubbing ▷ *verb* **2** (of the skin) to develop a blister ▷ **blistering** *adjective* **1** (of weather) very hot **2** (of criticism) extremely harsh

blithe *adjective* casual and indifferent ▷ **blithely** *adverb* casually and indifferently

blitz *noun* **1** bombing attack by enemy aircraft on a city ▷ *verb* **2** to make a bombing attack on (a city)

blizzard *noun* heavy snowstorm with strong winds

bloated *verb* larger than normal, often because of the liquid or gas inside

blob *noun* **1** soft mass or drop **2** indistinct or shapeless form

bloc *noun* people or countries combined by a common interest

block *noun* **1** large solid piece of wood, stone, etc **2** large building of offices, flats, etc **3** area of land in a town that has streets on all its sides **4** obstruction or hindrance

5 *informal* person's head ▷ *verb* **6** to obstruct (something) by introducing an obstacle

blockade *noun* **1** action that prevents goods from reaching a place ▷ *verb* **2** to prevent supplies from reaching (a place)

blockage *noun* something that blocks a pipe or tunnel

blog *noun* person's online journal; (also **weblog**)

blogger *noun* person who keeps a blog

blogosphere *noun* *informal* blogs on the internet as a whole

bloke *noun informal* man

blonde or **blond** *adjective, noun* fair-haired (person)

blood *noun* **1** red fluid that flows around the body **2** race or ancestors **3** **in cold blood** deliberately

bloodless *adjective* **1** (of face, skin) very pale **2** (of coup, revolution) without casualties

blood pressure *noun* measure of how forcefully your blood is being pumped round your body

bloodshed *noun* slaughter or killing

bloodshot *adjective* (of an eye) inflamed

bloodstream *noun* flow of blood round the body

bloodthirsty *adjective* taking pleasure in violence

blood transfusion *noun* process in which blood is injected into the body of someone who has lost a lot of blood

blood vessel *noun* narrow tubes in the body through which the blood flows

bloody bloodier bloodiest

adjective **1** covered with blood **2** marked by much killing

bloom noun **1** blossom on a flowering plant **2** youthful or healthy glow ▷ verb **3** to bear flowers **4** to be in a healthy glowing condition

blossom noun **1** growth of flowers that appears on a tree before the fruit ▷ verb **2** (of a tree) to produce blossom

blot blots blotting blotted noun **1** drop of ink spilled on a surface **2** something that spoils something, such as someone's reputation >**blot out** verb to be in front of (something) and hide (it) completely

blotch noun discoloured area or stain >**blotchy** adjective having discoloured areas or stains

blouse noun woman's shirtlike item of clothing

blow blows blowing blew blown verb **1** (of air, the wind, etc) to move **2** to move or be carried as if by the wind **3** to expel (air etc) through the mouth or nose **4** to cause (a musical instrument) to sound by forcing air into it **5** informal to spend (money) freely ▷ noun **6** hard hit **7** sudden setback >**blow up** verb **1** to destroy (something) with an explosion **2** to fill (a balloon or tyre) with air **3** informal to enlarge (a photograph)

blubber noun fat of whales, seals, etc

bludge Aust, NZ informal verb **1** to avoid work **2** to scrounge ▷ noun **3** easy task

bludgeon noun **1** short thick club ▷ verb **2** to hit (someone) with a bludgeon **3** to force or bully

(someone) into doing something

blue bluer bluest; blues noun **1** colour of a clear unclouded sky **2 out of the blue** unexpectedly ▷ adjective **3** of the colour blue >**bluish** or **blueish** adjective slightly blue

bluebell noun flower with blue bell-shaped flowers

bluebottle noun **1** large fly with a dark-blue body **2** Aust, NZ small stinging jellyfish

blue-collar adjective denoting manual industrial workers

blueprint noun description of how a plan is expected to work

blues plural noun **the blues 1** feeling of depression **2** type of folk music of Black American origin

Bluetooth® noun technology allowing short-range wireless communication

bluff verb **1** to pretend to be confident in order to influence (someone) ▷ noun **2** act of bluffing **3** steep cliff or bank ▷ adjective **4** good-naturedly frank and hearty

blunder noun **1** clumsy mistake ▷ verb **2** to make a blunder **3** to act clumsily

blunt adjective **1** not having a sharp edge or point **2** (of people, speech, etc) straightforward or uncomplicated

blur blurs blurring blurred verb **1** to become vague or less distinct or to make (something) vague or less distinct ▷ noun **2** something vague, hazy or indistinct >**blurred** adjective: blurred vision

blurt out verb to say (something) suddenly after trying to keep it a secret

blush verb 1 to become red in the face, especially from embarrassment or shame ▷ noun 2 reddening of the face

bluster verb 1 to speak loudly or in a bullying way ▷ noun 2 empty threats or protests > **blustery** adjective (of weather) rough and windy

boa noun 1 any of various large snakes that kill by crushing 2 long scarf of fur or feathers

boar noun 1 male pig used for breeding 2 wild pig

board noun 1 long flat piece of sawn timber 2 smaller flat piece of rigid material for a specific purpose: ironing board; chess board 3 group of people who run a company, trust, etc 4 meals provided for money 5 **on board** on or in a ship, aeroplane, etc ▷ verb 6 to go aboard (a train, aeroplane, etc) 7 to cover (something) with boards 8 to receive meals and lodgings in return for money

boarder noun Brit pupil who lives at school during the school term

boarding school noun school where the pupils live during the term

boardroom noun room where the board of a company meets

boast verb 1 to speak too proudly about your talents, etc; brag 2 to possess (something to be proud of) ▷ noun 3 bragging statement > **boastful** adjective speaking too proudly about your talents, etc

boat noun small vehicle for travelling across water

b bobs bobbing bobbed verb

1 to move up and down repeatedly 2 to cut (the hair) in a bob ▷ noun 3 short abrupt movement 4 hairstyle in which the hair is cut short evenly all round the head

bobbin noun reel on which thread is wound

bode verb to be an omen of (good or ill)

bodice noun upper part of a dress

bodily adjective 1 relating to the body ▷ adverb 2 by taking hold of the body

body bodies noun 1 entire physical structure of an animal or human 2 trunk or torso 3 corpse 4 organized group of people 5 main part of anything 6 woman's one-piece undergarment

bodyguard noun person or group of people employed to protect someone

bodywork noun outer shell of a motor vehicle

boer noun (in South Africa) a white farmer, especially one of Dutch descent

boerewors noun S Afr spiced sausage

bog noun 1 wet spongy ground 2 informal toilet

boggle verb to be surprised, confused or alarmed

bogus adjective not genuine

bohemian adjective leading an unconventional life

boil verb 1 to change from a liquid to a vapour or cause (a liquid) to change to a vapour so quickly that bubbles are formed 2 to cook (food) by the process of boiling ▷ noun 3 state or action of boiling 4 painful red swelling on the skin

boiler noun piece of equipment that provides hot water

boiling adjective informal very hot

boisterous adjective noisy and lively

bold adjective **1** confident and fearless **2** immodest or impudent **3** clear and noticeable: bold colours > **boldly** adverb in a bold manner > **boldness** noun being bold

bollard noun short thick post used to prevent the passage of motor vehicles

bolster verb to support or strengthen (something)

bolt noun **1** sliding metal bar for fastening a door etc **2** metal pin that screws into a nut **3** flash (of lightning) **4 bolt upright** stiff and rigid > verb **5** to run away suddenly **6** to fasten (a door) with a bolt **7** to eat (food) hurriedly

bomb noun **1** container fitted with explosive material **2** informal large amount of money **3 the bomb** nuclear bomb > verb **4** to attack (a place) with bombs **5** to move very quickly > **bomber** noun **1** aircraft that drops bombs **2** person who throws or puts a bomb in a particular place

bombard verb **1** to attack (a place) with heavy gunfire or bombs **2** to attack (someone) verbally, especially with questions > **bombardment** noun: The capital is under constant bombardment

bombshell noun shocking or unwelcome surprise

bona fide adjective genuine

bond noun **1** something that binds, fastens or holds things together **2** something that unites people; link **3** written or spoken agreement **4** Finance certificate of debt issued to raise funds **5 bonds** chains or ropes used to restrain or imprison > verb **6** to link or attach (things)

bondage noun slavery

bone noun **1** any of the hard parts in the body that form the skeleton > verb **2** to remove the bones from (meat for cooking etc) > **boneless** adjective without bones

bonfire noun large outdoor fire

bonnet noun **1** metal cover over a vehicle's engine **2** hat that ties under the chin

bonny bonnier bonniest adjective Scot beautiful

bonus noun something given, paid or received above what is due or expected

bony bonier boniest adjective very thin

boo interjection **1** shout of disapproval > verb **2** to shout 'boo' to show disapproval of (someone or something)

book noun **1** number of pages bound together between covers **2** long written work **3** number of tickets, stamps, etc fastened together > verb **4** to reserve (a hotel room, travel, etc) in advance **5** to record the name of (a person who has committed an offence)

bookcase noun piece of furniture with shelves for books

booking noun arrangement to book something such as a hotel room

book-keeping noun recording of the money spent and received by a business

booklet noun small book with a paper cover

bookmaker noun person whose occupation is taking bets

bookmark noun piece of card put between the pages of a book to mark your place

boom verb 1 to make a loud deep echoing sound 2 to increase rapidly ▷ noun 3 loud deep echoing sound 4 rapid increase in something

boomerang noun curved wooden missile that can be made to return to the thrower

boon noun something helpful or beneficial

boost noun 1 encouragement or help ▷ verb 3 to cause (something) to improve or increase

boot noun 1 outer covering for the foot that extends above the ankle 2 space in a car for luggage 3 to boot in addition ▷ verb 4 informal to kick (someone or something) 5 to start up (a computer)

booth noun 1 small partly enclosed cubicle 2 stall at a fair or market

booty noun valuable articles obtained as plunder

booze verb, noun informal (to consume) alcoholic drink ▷ **boozer** noun informal 1 person who is fond of drinking alcohol 2 Brit, Aust, NZ pub ▷ **boozy** adjective fond of drinking alcohol

border noun 1 dividing line between political or geographical regions 2 band around or along the edge of something ▷ verb 3 to provide (something) with a border 4 (followed by on) to be nearly the same as (something): resentment that borders on hatred

borderline adjective only just

acceptable as a member of a class or group: a borderline case

bore verb 1 to make (a hole) with a drill etc 2 to make (someone) weary by being dull and uninteresting 3 past tense of **bear** ▷ noun 4 dull or repetitious person or thing ▷ **bored** adjective tired and impatient; fed up ▷ **boredom** noun being bored ▷ **boring** adjective dull and uninteresting

● You can say that you are bored
● with or bored by someone or
● something, but you should
● not say bored of

born verb 1 be born to come out of your mother's womb at birth ▷ adjective 2 possessing certain qualities from birth: a born musician

borne verb a past participle of **bear**

borough noun Chiefly Brit town or district with its own council

borrow verb 1 to obtain (something) temporarily 2 to adopt (ideas etc) from another source ▷ **borrower** noun person who borrows something

● You borrow something from
● a person, not off them. Do
● not confuse borrow and lend.
● If you borrow something,
● you get it from another
● person for a while; if you lend
● something, someone gets it
● from you for a while

Bosnian adjective 1 belonging to or relating to Bosnia ▷ noun 2 person from Bosnia

bosom noun 1 chest of a person, especially the female breasts ▷ adjective 2 very dear: a bosom friend

boss bosses bossing bossed noun person in charge of or employing others > **boss around** verb to keep telling (someone) what to do

bossy bossier bossiest adjective enjoying telling other people what to do > **bossiness** noun: They resent what they see as bossiness

botany noun study of plants > **botanic** or **botanical** adjective: an area of great botanical interest > **botanist** noun

botch verb to spoil (something) through clumsiness

both adjective, pronoun two considered together

● You can use of after both, but it is not essential. Both the boys means the same as both of the boys

bother verb 1 to take the time or trouble (to do something) 2 to give annoyance or trouble to (someone) 3 to pester (someone) ▷ noun 4 trouble, fuss or difficulty > **bothersome** adjective causing annoyance or trouble

bottle noun 1 container for holding liquids 2 Brit informal courage ▷ verb 3 to put (something) in a bottle > **bottle up** verb to restrain (strong feelings)

bottleneck noun narrow stretch of road where traffic is held up

bottle store noun SAfr shop licensed to resell alcohol for drinking elsewhere

bottom noun 1 lowest, deepest or farthest removed part of a thing 2 buttocks ▷ adjective 3 lowest or last > **bottomless** adjective having no bottom or seeming to have no bottom

bough noun large branch of a tree

bought verb past of **buy**

● Do not confuse bought and brought. Bought comes from buy and brought comes from bring

boulder noun large rounded rock

boulevard noun wide, usually tree-lined, street

bounce verb 1 (of a ball etc) to rebound from an impact 2 informal (of a cheque) to be returned uncashed owing to a lack of funds in the account ▷ noun 3 act of rebounding 4 springiness 5 informal vitality or vigour

bouncy bouncier bounciest adjective 1 lively and enthusiastic 2 capable of bouncing

bound verb 1 past of **bind** 2 to move forwards by jumps 3 to form a boundary of (something) ▷ noun 4 jump upwards or forwards 5 bounds limits ▷ adjective 6 destined or certain (to do something) 7 compelled or obliged (to do something) 8 going or intending to go towards: homeward bound

boundary boundaries noun dividing line that indicates the farthest limit

boundless adjective without end or limit

bountiful adjective freely available in large amounts

bounty noun 1 generosity 2 generous gift or reward

bouquet noun 1 bunch of flowers 2 aroma of wine

bourgeois adjective (used expressing disapproval) typical of fairly rich middle-class people

> **bourgeoisie** *noun* fairly rich middle-class people in a society

bout *noun* 1 period of activity or illness 2 boxing or wrestling match

boutique *noun* small clothes shop

bovine *adjective* 1 relating to cattle 2 rather slow and stupid

bow¹ *verb* 1 to lower (one's head) or bend (one's knee or body) as a sign of respect or shame 2 (followed by *to*) to comply with or accept (something) ▷ *noun* 3 movement made when bowing 4 front end of a ship

bow² *noun* 1 knot with two loops and loose ends 2 weapon for shooting arrows 3 long stick stretched with horsehair for playing stringed instruments

bowel *noun* 1 intestine, especially the large intestine 2 **bowels** innermost part

bowerbird *noun* Aust bird found in Australia, the male of which builds a shelter during courtship

bowl *noun* 1 round container with an open top 2 hollow part of an object 3 large heavy ball ▷ *verb* 4 Cricket to send (a ball) towards the batsman ▷ **bowling** *noun* game in which bowls are rolled at group of pins

bowls *noun* game played on smooth grass with wooden bowls

bow tie *noun* man's tie in the form of a bow, often worn at formal occasions

box *noun* 1 container with a firm flat base and sides 2 separate compartment in a theatre, table, etc 3 evergreen tree with shiny leaves 4 **the box** *Informal* television ▷ *verb* 5 to put

(something) into a box 6 to fight (an opponent) in a boxing match

boxer *noun* 1 person who participates in the sport of boxing 2 medium-sized dog with smooth hair and a short nose

boxing *noun* sport of fighting with the fists, wearing padded gloves

box office *noun* place where tickets are sold in a theatre or cinema

boy *noun* male child ▷ **boyhood** *noun* period of being a boy ▷ **boyish** *adjective: a boyish grin*

boycott *verb* 1 to refuse to deal with (an organization or country) ▷ *noun* 2 instance of boycotting

boyfriend *noun* male friend with whom a person is romantically involved

bra *noun* woman's undergarment for supporting the breasts

braaivleis or **braai** or **braais** S Afr *noun* 1 grill on which food is cooked over hot charcoal, usually outdoors 2 outdoor party at which food is cooked in this way

brace *noun* 1 object fastened to something to straighten or support it 2 pair, especially of game birds ▷ *verb* 3 to steady or prepare (yourself) for something unpleasant 4 to strengthen or fit (something) with a brace

bracelet *noun* ornamental chain or band for the wrist

bracing *adjective* refreshing and invigorating

bracken *noun* large fern

bracket *noun* 1 pair of characters used to enclose a section of writing 2 group that falls within certain defined limits 3 support fixed to a wall ▷ *verb* 4 to put (words or letters) in brackets **5** to class (people or things) together

brag brags bragging bragged verb to speak arrogantly and boastfully ▷ noun person who brags

Brahma noun Hindu god, one of the Trimurti

Brahman noun in the Hindu religion, the ultimate and impersonal divine reality of the universe

brahmin noun member of the highest caste in Hindu society

braid verb **1** to plait (hair, thread, etc) ▷ noun **2** length of hair etc that has been plaited **3** narrow ornamental tape of woven silk etc

brain noun **1** soft mass of nervous tissue in the head that controls the body and enables thinking and feeling **2** intellectual ability

brainchild noun idea produced by creative thought

brainwash verb to cause (a person) to alter his or her beliefs, especially by methods based on isolation, sleeplessness, etc ▷ **brainwashing** noun

brainwave noun sudden clever idea

brainy brainier brainiest adjective informal clever

braise verb to cook (food) slowly in a covered pan with a little liquid

brake noun **1** device for slowing or stopping a vehicle ▷ verb **2** to slow down or stop a vehicle by using a brake

- Do not confuse the spellings of brake and break, or braking and breaking

bramble noun prickly shrub that produces blackberries

bran noun husks of cereal grain

branch noun **1** part of a tree that grows out from its trunk **2** one of the offices or shops that are part of an organization **3** one of the areas of study or activity that are part of a subject ▷ verb **4** (of stems, roots, etc) to divide, then develop in different directions > **branch out** verb to try something different

brand noun **1** particular product **2** particular kind or variety **3** identifying mark burnt onto the skin of an animal ▷ verb **4** to mark (an animal) with a brand **5** to give (someone) a reputation for being as specifed: I was branded as a rebel

brandish verb to wave (a weapon etc) in a threatening way

brand-new adjective absolutely new

brandy noun alcoholic spirit distilled from wine

brash adjective offensively loud, showy or self-confident > **brashness** noun being brash

brass noun **1** alloy of copper and zinc **2** family of wind instruments made of brass **3** N English dialect money

brassiere noun bra

brat noun unruly child

bravado noun showy display of self-confidence

brave adjective **1** having or showing courage and daring ▷ noun **2** Native American warrior ▷ verb **3** to confront (an unpleasant or dangerous situation) with courage > **bravely** adverb > **bravery** noun brave behaviour

bravo interjection well done!

brawl noun **1** noisy fight ▷ verb **2** to fight noisily

brawn noun **1** physical strength > **brawny** adjective strong and muscular

bray verb **1** (of a donkey) to utter its loud harsh sound ▷ noun **2** donkey's loud harsh sound

brazen adjective shameless and bold > **brazenly** adverb in a shameless and bold manner

brazier noun portable container for burning charcoal or coal

Brazilian adjective **1** belonging or relating to Brazil ▷ noun **2** person from Brazil

breach noun **1** breaking of a promise, obligation, etc **2** gap or break ▷ verb **3** to break (a promise, law, etc) **4** to make a gap in (a barrier)

bread noun **1** food made by baking a mixture of flour and water or milk **2** informal money

breadth noun extent of something from side to side

breadwinner noun person whose earnings support a family

break breaks breaking broke broken verb **1** to separate (something) into two or more pieces or become separated into two or more pieces **2** to damage (something) or become damaged so as to be unusable **3** to fail to observe (an agreement etc) **4** to end: *The good weather broke at last* **5** to weaken or be weakened, as in spirit **6** (of a boy's voice) to become permanently deeper **7 break even** to make neither a profit nor a loss ▷ noun **8** act or result of breaking **9** gap or interruption in continuity

> **breakable** adjective > **break down** verb **1** to stop working **2** to start crying > **break up** verb **1** to come to an end **2** (of a school) to close for the holidays

● Do not confuse the spellings ● of *break* and *brake*, or *breaking* ● and *braking*.

breakage noun act of breaking something or a thing that has been broken

breakaway adjective (of a group) separated from a larger group

breakdown noun **1** act or instance of breaking down **2** nervous breakdown **3** details relating to the separate elements of something

breaker noun large wave

breakfast noun first meal of the day

break-in noun illegal entering of a building, especially by a burglar

breakneck adjective fast and dangerous

breakthrough noun important development or discovery

breakwater noun wall that extends into the sea to protect a coast from the force of the waves

bream noun **1** freshwater fish with silvery scales **2** food fish of European seas

breast noun **1** either of the two soft fleshy milk-secreting glands on a woman's chest **2** chest

breath noun **1** taking in and letting out of air during breathing **2** air taken in and let out during breathing

breathe verb to take air into the lungs and let it out again

breathless adjective breathing fast or with difficulty > **breathlessly**

adverb in a breathless manner >**breathlessness** *noun*

breathtaking *adjective* very beautiful or exciting

bred *verb* past of **breed**

breeches *plural noun* trousers reaching to just below the knee

breed breeds breeding bred *verb* 1 to keep (animals or plants) in order to produce more animals or plants with particular qualities 2 to mate and produce offspring; reproduce ▷ *noun* 3 group of animals or plants within a species that have particular qualities

breeze *noun* gentle wind

brevity *noun* shortness

brew *verb* 1 to make (beer) by boiling and fermenting malt 2 to make (tea or coffee) in a pot by pouring hot water over it 3 to be about to happen ▷ *noun* 4 beverage produced by brewing >**brewer** *noun* person or company that brews beer

brewery breweries *noun* place where beer is brewed

briar *noun* same as **brier**

bribe *verb* 1 to offer or give something to (someone) to gain favour, influence, etc ▷ *noun* 2 something given or offered as a bribe >**bribery** *noun* practice of bribing

bric-a-brac *noun* small ornaments or pieces of furniture of no great value

brick *noun* rectangular block of baked clay used in building

bricklayer *noun* person who builds with bricks

bride *noun* woman who has just been or is about to be married >**bridal** *adjective*: *a bridal gown*

bridegroom *noun* man who has just been or is about to be married

bridesmaid *noun* girl or woman who attends a bride at her wedding

bridge *noun* 1 structure for crossing a river etc 2 platform from which a ship is steered or controlled 3 upper part of the nose 4 piece of wood supporting the strings of a violin etc 5 card game based on whist, played between two pairs

bridle *noun* headgear for controlling a horse

brief *adjective* 1 lasting a short time ▷ *noun* 2 (also **briefing**) set of instructions ▷ *verb* 3 to give information and instructions to >**briefly** *adverb*

briefcase *noun* small flat case for carrying papers, books, etc

briefing ▷ *noun* meeting at which information and instructions are given

brier or **briar** *noun* wild rose with long thorny stems

brigade *noun* army unit smaller than a division

brigadier *noun* high-ranking army officer

brigalow *noun* Aust type of acacia tree

bright *adjective* 1 giving out or reflecting a lot of light; brilliant 2 (of colours) intense or vivid 3 clever >**brightly** *adverb* >**brightness** *noun*

brighten *verb* 1 to become brighter 2 to look suddenly happier >**brighten up** *verb* to make (something) more attractive and cheerful

brilliant *adjective* 1 shining with

light 2 splendid **3** extremely clever > **brilliance** noun > **brilliantly** adverb

brim noun **1** upper rim of a cup etc **2** wide part of a hat that sticks outwards at the bottom

brine noun salt water

bring brings bringing brought verb **1** to carry, convey or take (something or someone) to a particular place or person **2** to cause (something) to happen > **bring about** verb to cause (something) to happen > **bring off** verb to succeed in achieving (something) > **bring out** verb to produce (a new product) and offer it for sale > **bring up** verb **1** to rear (a child) **2** to mention (a subject) **3** to vomit (food)

brink noun edge of a steep place

brisk adjective lively and quick > **briskly** adverb > **briskness** noun

bristle noun **1** short stiff hair > verb **2** (of hair on an animal's body) to stand up like bristles > **bristly** adjective (of hair) thick and rough

British adjective belonging or relating to the United Kingdom of Great Britain and Northern Ireland

Briton noun person from the United Kingdom of Great Britain and Northern Ireland

brittle adjective hard but easily broken

broach verb to introduce (a topic) or discussion

broad adjective **1** having great breadth or width **2** not detailed having many different aspects or concerning many different people: broad support **4** strongly marked: a broad American accent > **broadly** adverb to a large extent or in most cases

broadband noun telecommunication transmission technique using a wide range of frequencies

broad bean noun thick flat edible bean

broadcast broadcasts broadcasting broadcast noun **1** programme or announcement on radio or television > verb **2** to transmit (a programme or announcement) on radio or television **3** to make (information) widely known > **broadcaster** noun person who broadcasts radio or television programmes > **broadcasting** noun transmission of radio or television programmes

broaden verb **1** to become wider **2** to cause (something) to involve more things or concern more people

broad-minded adjective tolerant or open-minded

broadsheet noun newspaper with large pages and long news stories

brocade noun rich fabric woven with a raised design

broccoli noun green vegetable, similar to cauliflower

brochure noun booklet that contains information about a product or service

brogue noun **1** sturdy walking shoe **2** strong accent, especially Irish

broke verb past tense of **break** > adjective **2** informal having no money

broker noun person whose job is

to buy and sell shares for other people

brolga noun large grey Australian crane with a trumpeting call; also called **native companion**

brolly brollies noun informal umbrella

bronchitis noun inflammation of the bronchi

brontosaurus noun very large plant-eating four-footed dinosaur

bronze noun 1 alloy of copper and tin 2 statue, medal, etc made of bronze ▷ adjective 3 made of, or coloured like, bronze

brooch noun ornament with a pin, worn fastened to clothes

brood noun 1 number of birds produced at one hatching ▷ verb 2 to think long and unhappily

brook noun small stream

broom noun 1 long-handled sweeping brush 2 yellow-flowered shrub

broth noun soup, usually containing vegetables

brother noun 1 boy or man with the same parents as another person 2 member of a male religious order ▷ **brotherly** adjective: a brotherly kiss

brotherhood noun 1 affection and loyalty between brothers or close male friends 2 association, such as a trade union

brother-in-law brothers-in-law noun 1 brother of your husband or wife 2 husband of your sister

brought verb past of **bring**

- Do not confuse brought and bought. Brought comes from bring and bought comes from buy

brow noun 1 part of the face from the eyes to the hairline 2 eyebrow 3 top of a hill

brown noun 1 colour of earth or wood ▷ adjective 2 of the colour brown

Brownie Guide or **Brownie** noun junior Guide

browse verb 1 to look through (a book or articles for sale) in a casual manner 2 Computers to look for information on the Internet 3 to nibble on young shoots or leaves ▷ noun 4 instance of browsing

browser noun Computers software package that enables a user to read hypertext on the Internet

bruise noun 1 discoloured area on the skin caused by an injury ▷ verb 2 to cause a bruise on (a part of the body)

brumby brumbies noun Aust wild horse

brunette noun girl or woman with dark brown hair

brunt noun main force or shock of blow, attack, etc

brush noun 1 device made of bristles, wires, etc used for cleaning, painting, etc ▷ verb 2 to clean or scrub (something) with a brush 3 to touch (something) lightly and briefly ▷ **brush off** verb informal to dismiss or ignore (someone) ▷ **brush up** verb to refresh your knowledge of (a subject)

brusque adjective blunt or curt in manner or speech ▷ **brusquely** adverb ▷ **brusqueness** noun

Brussels sprout noun vegetable like a tiny cabbage

brutal adjective cruel and violent ▷ **brutality** noun ▷ **brutally** adverb

brute noun 1 brutal person 2 large animal ▷ adjective 3 wholly instinctive or physical, like an animal 4 without reason > **brutish** adjective of or like an animal

bubble noun 1 ball of air in a liquid or solid ▷ verb 2 to form bubbles 3 to move or flow with a gurgling sound > **bubble over** verb to express an emotion freely > **bubbly** adjective 1 excited and lively 2 full of bubbles

buck noun 1 male of the goat, hare, kangaroo, rabbit and reindeer 2 **pass the buck** informal to shift blame or responsibility onto someone else ▷ verb 3 (of a horse etc) to jump with legs stiff and back arched > **buck up** verb to become more cheerful

bucket noun deep open-topped container with a handle; pail

buckle noun 1 clasp for fastening a belt or strap ▷ verb 2 to fasten (a belt or strap) with a buckle 3 to bend out of shape through pressure or heat

bud buds budding budded noun 1 swelling on a tree or plant that develops into a leaf or flower ▷ verb 2 to produce buds > **budding** adjective just beginning to develop

Buddha noun Indian religious teacher and founder of Buddhism

Buddhism noun eastern religion founded by Buddha > **Buddhist** noun 1 person who believes in Buddhism ▷ adjective 2 of or relating to Buddhism

budge verb to move slightly

budgerigar noun small cage bird bred in many different-coloured varieties

budget noun 1 financial plan for a period of time 2 money allocated for a specific purpose ▷ verb 3 to plan the spending of money or time ▷ adjective 4 cheap > **budgetary** adjective of or relating to a financial plan

budgie noun informal short for **budgerigar**

buff adjective dull yellowish-brown

buffalo buffaloes noun 1 wild animal like a large cow with long curved horns 2 US bison

buffer noun something that lessens shock or protects from damaging impact, circumstances, etc

buffet¹ noun 1 café at a station 2 meal at which people serve themselves

buffet² verb (of wind or sea) to strike (a place or person) violently and repeatedly

bug bugs bugging bugged noun 1 small insect 2 informal minor illness 3 small mistake in a computer program 4 concealed microphone ▷ verb 5 informal to irritate (someone) 6 to conceal a microphone in (a room or telephone)

bugle noun instrument like a small trumpet > **bugler** noun person who plays a bugle

build builds building built verb 1 to make, construct or form (something) by joining parts or materials ▷ noun 2 shape of the body

building noun structure with walls and a roof

building society noun organization where money can be borrowed or invested

bulb noun **1** same as **light bulb**
2 onion-shaped root which grows
into a flower or plant

Bulgarian adjective **1** belonging
or relating to Bulgaria ▷ noun
2 person from Bulgaria
3 language spoken in Bulgaria

bulge noun **1** swelling on an
otherwise flat or smooth surface
▷ verb **2** to swell outwards

bulk noun **1** size or volume,
especially when great **2** main
part **3 in bulk** in large quantities

bulky bulkier bulkiest adjective
large and heavy

bull noun male of some animals,
such as cattle, elephants and
whales

bulldog noun squat dog with a
broad head and a muscular body

bulldozer noun powerful tractor
for moving earth

bullet noun small piece of metal
fired from a gun

bulletin noun short official report
or announcement

bullion noun gold or silver in the
form of bars

bullock noun young castrated bull

bullroarer noun Aust wooden
slat attached to a string that
is whirled round to make a
roaring noise, used by Australian
Aborigines in religious
ceremonies

bully bullies bullying bullied
noun **1** person who uses strength
or power to hurt or frighten
other people ▷ verb **2** to make
(someone) do something by using
force or threats

bump verb **1** (often followed
by into) to knock or strike
(something or someone) with

a jolt ▷ noun **2** soft or dull noise
made by something knocking
into something else **3** raised
uneven part; lump > **bump off**
verb informal to murder > **bumpy**
adjective

bumper noun **1** bar on the front
or back of a vehicle to protect
against damage ▷ adjective
2 unusually large or abundant

bun noun **1** small sweet bread roll
or cake **2** hair gathered into a ball
shape at the back of the head

bunch noun **1** number of things
growing, fastened or grouped
together ▷ verb **2** to group
(things) together or be grouped
together in a bunch

bundle noun **1** number of things
gathered loosely together
▷ verb **2** to push (someone or
something) somewhere quickly
and roughly

bung noun **1** stopper for a cask
etc ▷ verb **2** Brit informal to throw
(something) somewhere in a
careless manner > **bung up** verb
informal to block (a hole)

bungalow noun one-storey house

bungle verb to spoil (something)
through incompetence

bunion noun painful lump on the
big toe

bunk noun **1** narrow shelflike bed
2 do a bunk Brit informal to leave a
place without telling anyone

bunker noun **1** sand-filled hollow
forming an obstacle on a golf
course **2** underground shelter
3 large storage container for
coal etc

bunting noun decorative flags

bunyip noun Aust legendary
monster said to live in swamps

and lakes

buoy noun floating object anchored in the sea to warn of danger

buoyant adjective **1** able to float **2** lively and cheerful > **buoyancy** noun

burden noun **1** heavy load **2** something difficult to cope with; worry > **burdensome** adjective: a burdensome debt

bureau bureaux noun **1** office that provides a service **2** writing desk with shelves and drawers

bureaucracy noun complex system of rules and procedures that operates in government departments > **bureaucratic** adjective involving complicated rules and procedures

bureaucrat noun person who works in a government department, especially one who follows rules and procedures strictly

burgeoning adjective growing or developing rapidly

burglar noun thief who breaks into a building > **burglary** noun: arrested for burglary

burgle verb to break into someone's house) and steal things

burial noun burying of a dead body

burly burlier burliest adjective (of a person) broad and strong

burn burns burning burned or burnt verb **1** to be on fire or set (something) on fire **2** to destroy (something) by fire or be destroyed by fire **3** to damage, injure or mark (someone or something) by heat **4** to feel strong emotion **5** to record

data on (a compact disc) ▷ noun **6** injury or mark caused by fire or exposure to heat

● You can write either burned or burnt as the past form of burn

burp informal verb **1** to belch ▷ noun **2** belch

burrow noun **1** hole dug in the ground by a rabbit etc ▷ verb **2** to dig holes in the ground

bursary bursaries noun sum of money given to someone to help fund their education

burst bursts bursting burst verb **1** to break open or apart noisily and suddenly **2** to come or go somewhere suddenly and forcibly **3** to be full to the point of breaking open ▷ noun **4** instance of breaking open suddenly **5** sudden outbreak or occurrence > **burst into** to be overcome by (tears or an emotion) suddenly

bury buries burying buried verb **1** to place (a dead body) in a grave **2** to place (something) in the earth and cover it with soil **3** to conceal or hide (something)

bus buses noun large motor vehicle for carrying passengers

bush noun **1** dense woody plant, smaller than a tree **2** wild uncultivated part of a country

bushman bushmen noun **1** Aust, NZ person who lives or travels in the bush **2** NZ person whose job is to clear the bush for farming

Bushman Bushmen noun S Afr member of a group of people in southern Africa who live by hunting and gathering food

bushranger noun Aust, NZ in the past, an outlaw living in the bush

bushy bushier bushiest adjective

(of hair) thick and shaggy

business noun 1 purchase and sale of goods and services 2 commercial establishment; company 3 trade or profession 4 proper concern or responsibility 5 affair: *it's a dreadful business*

businesslike adjective efficient and methodical

busker noun street entertainer

bust busts busting bust or **busted** noun 1 woman's bosom 2 sculpture of the head and shoulders ▷ verb informal 3 to burst or break 4 (of the police) to raid (a place) or arrest (someone) ▷ adjective informal 5 broken 6 **go bust** to become bankrupt

bustle verb 1 to hurry with a show of activity or energy ▷ noun 2 energetic and noisy activity

busy busier busiest; busies busying busied adjective 1 occupied doing something 2 crowded or full of activity ▷ verb 3 to keep (yourself) busy > **busily** adverb very actively

but conjunction 1 contrary to expectation 2 in contrast 3 other than 4 without it happening ▷ preposition 5 except ▷ adverb 6 only 7 **but for** if it had not been for

butcher noun shopkeeper who sells meat

butler noun chief male servant

butt noun 1 thicker end of something 2 unused end of a cigar or cigarette 3 person or thing that is the target of ridicule 4 large barrel ▷ verb 5 to strike (something or someone) with the head or horns > **butt in** to interrupt a conversation

butter noun 1 soft fatty food made from cream, often eaten spread on bread or used in cooking ▷ verb 2 to put butter on (bread, etc)

buttercup noun small yellow wild flower

butterfly butterflies noun insect with brightly coloured wings

buttock noun either half of the human bottom

button noun 1 small disc or knob sewn onto clothing, which can be passed through a slit in another piece of fabric to fasten it 2 knob that operates a piece of equipment when pressed ▷ verb 3 to fasten (a garment) with buttons

buttonhole noun 1 slit in a garment through which a button is passed 2 flower worn on a lapel

buxom adjective (of a woman) large, healthy and attractive

buy buys buying bought verb 1 to acquire (something) by paying money for it ▷ noun 2 thing acquired through payment > **buyer** noun 1 customer 2 person employed to buy merchandise

buzz noun 1 rapidly vibrating humming sound 2 informal sense of excitement ▷ verb 3 to make a humming sound 4 to be filled with an air of excitement > **buzz around** verb to move around quickly and busily

buzzard noun bird of prey of the hawk family

buzzer noun device that makes a buzzing sound

by preposition 1 indicating the doer of an action: *bitten by a dog* 2 indicating the manner or mea

of something: *travelling by train;*
He frightened her by hiding in the
bushes **3** beside or next to: *down by*
the river **4** past: *driving by the school*
5 at or before: *in bed by midnight*
▷ *adverb* **6** past **7** by and by
eventually **8** by and large in
general

-election *noun* election held
to choose a new member of
parliament after the previous
member has resigned or died

gone *adjective* past or former

pass bypasses *noun* main road
built to avoid a city

stander *noun* person present
but not involved

te *noun* Computers group of bits
processed as one unit of data

C

noun 1 taxi **2** enclosed driver's
compartment on a train, truck,

aret *noun* dancing and singing
how in a nightclub

bage *noun* vegetable with a
ge head of green leaves

bage tree *noun* NZ a palm-like
e found in New Zealand with
all bare trunk and big bunches
spiky leaves; also a similar tree
nd in eastern Australia

n *noun* **1** room in a ship or boat
ere a passenger sleeps **2** area
ere the passengers or the crew
n a plane **3** small wooden hut,

usually in the country

cabinet *noun* **1** piece of furniture
with drawers or shelves
2 Cabinet committee of senior
government ministers

cable *noun* **1** strong thick rope
2 bundle of wires that carries
electricity or electronic signals
3 telegram sent abroad ▷ *verb*
4 to send (someone) a message
by cable

cable car *noun* vehicle pulled up a
steep slope by a moving cable

cable television *noun* television
service people can subscribe
to and which is received from
underground wires which carry
the signals

cacao *noun* tropical tree with seed
pods from which chocolate and
cocoa are made

cache *noun* hidden store of
weapons or treasure: *a cache*
of guns

cachet *noun formal* status and
respect something has

cackle *verb* **1** to laugh harshly
▷ *noun* **2** harsh laugh

cacophony *noun formal* harsh
discordant sound

cactus cacti or **cactuses** *noun*
fleshy desert plant with spines
but no leaves

cad *noun old-fashioned* man who
behaves dishonourably

caddie or **caddy** *noun* **1** person
who carries a golfer's clubs ▷ *verb*
2 to act as a golf caddie

cadence *noun* rise and fall in the
pitch of the voice

cadet *noun* young person training
for the armed forces or police

cadge *verb informal* to get
(something) by taking advantage

Caesarean or **Caesarian** noun (also **Caesarean section**) surgical operation in which a pregnant woman's baby is delivered through a cut in its mother's abdomen

café noun **1** small or inexpensive restaurant serving light refreshments **2** S Afr corner shop or grocer

cafeteria noun self-service restaurant

caffeine noun stimulant found in tea and coffee

cage noun **1** enclosure of bars or wires, for keeping animals or birds **2** enclosed platform of a lift in a mine > **caged** adjective kept in a cage

cagey cagier cagiest adjective informal reluctant to go into details

cagoule noun Brit lightweight hooded waterproof jacket

cahoots plural noun **in cahoots** informal conspiring together

cairn noun mound of stones erected as a memorial or marker

cajole verb to persuade by flattery: He allowed himself to be cajoled into staying on

cake noun **1** sweet food baked from a mixture of flour, eggs, etc **2** flat compact mass of something, such as soap > verb **3** to form into a hardened mass or crust

calamity calamities noun event that causes disaster or distress > **calamitous** adjective resulting in or from disaster

calcium noun Chemistry silvery-white metallic element found in bones, teeth, limestone and chal

calculate verb **1** to work out by a mathematical procedure or by reasoning **2** to plan deliberately; intend

calculating adjective selfishly scheming: a calculating man

calculator noun small electronic device for making calculations

calculus noun branch of mathematics dealing with infinitesimal changes to a variable number or quantity

calendar noun **1** chart showing a year divided up into months, weeks and days **2** system for determining the beginning, length and division of years: the Jewish calendar **3** schedule of events or appointments

calf calves noun **1** young cow, bu elephant, whale or seal **2** leathe made from calf skin **3** back of th leg between the ankle and knee

calibre noun **1** person's ability or worth: a player of her calibre **2** diameter of the bore of a gun of a shell or bullet

call verb **1** to name **2** to shout to attract attention **3** to telephor **4** to summon **5** (often followe by on) to visit **6** to arrange (a meeting, strike, etc) > noun **7** or shout **8** animal's or bird's cr **9** telephone communication **10** short visit **11** summons or invitation **12** need or demand > **call for** verb **1** to require **2** to come and fetch > **call off** verb to cancel > **call up** verb **1** to sum to serve in the armed forces **2** to cause you to remember (something)

call box noun kiosk for a public telephone

call centre noun office where staff deal with customers' orders or questions over the telephone

calling noun 1 profession or career, especially a caring one 2 strong urge to follow a particular career or profession, especially a caring one

callous adjective showing no concern for other people's feelings ▷ **callously** adverb ▷ **callousness** noun: the callousness of his attacker

calm adjective 1 not agitated or excited 2 (of sea or weather) not affected by the wind ▷ noun 3 peaceful state ▷ verb 4 to calm down ▷ **calm down** verb to make (someone) calm or become calm ▷ **calmly** adverb ▷ **calmness** noun

calorie noun 1 unit of measurement for the energy value of food 2 unit of heat equal to about 4.187 joules ▷ **calorific** adjective of calories or heat

calves the plural of **calf**

calypso calypsos noun West Indian song with improvised topical lyrics

calyx calyxes or **calyces** noun botany outer leaves that protect a flower bud

camaraderie noun feeling of trust and friendship between a group of people

camber noun slight upward curve towards the centre of a road

camel noun humped mammal that can survive long periods without food or water in desert regions

cameo cameos noun 1 small part in a film or play performed by a well-known actor or actress 2 brooch or ring with a carving on it, typically of a head in profile, in a different coloured stone from the background

camera noun 1 apparatus used for taking photographs or pictures for television or cinema 2 mobile phone incorporating a camera 3 **in camera** in private session

camomile or **chamomile** noun plant with a strong smell and daisy-like flowers which are used to make herbal tea

camouflage noun 1 use of natural surroundings or artificial aids to conceal or disguise something ▷ verb 2 to conceal by camouflage

camp noun 1 (place for) temporary lodgings consisting of tents, huts or cabins 2 group supporting a particular idea or belief: the pro-government camp ▷ verb 3 to stay in a camp ▷ adjective 4 informal effeminate or homosexual 5 informal consciously artificial or affected ▷ **camper** noun person who stays temporarily in a tent, hut or cabin ▷ **camping** noun activity of staying in tents, huts or cabins by holidaymakers, travellers, etc

campaign noun 1 series of coordinated activities designed to achieve a goal ▷ verb 2 to take part in a campaign ▷ **campaigner** noun person who campaigns to achieve a goal

camp-drafting noun Aust competition in which men on horseback select cattle or sheep from a herd or flock

campus campuses noun area of land and the buildings that make up a university or college

can¹ could verb 1 to be able to: I can speak Italian 2 to be allowed to: You can go to the cinema

can² cans canning canned
noun **1** metal container for
food or liquids ▷ verb **2** to put
(something) into a can

Canadian adjective **1** belonging
or relating to Canada ▷ noun
2 someone from Canada

canal noun **1** artificial waterway
2 passage in the body

canary canaries noun small
yellow songbird often kept as
a pet

can-can noun lively high-kicking
dance performed by a female
group

cancel cancels cancelling
cancelled verb **1** to stop
(something that has been
arranged) from taking place **2** to
mark (a cheque or stamp) with
an official stamp to prevent
further use **3** cancel out to be
ineffective by having the opposite
effect: *Their opening goal was
cancelled out just before half-time*
> **cancellation** noun

cancer noun **1** serious disease
resulting from a malignant
growth or tumour **2** malignant
growth or tumour > **cancerous**
adjective resulting from cancer

candelabra or **candelabrum**
noun large branched candle holder

candid adjective honest and
straightforward > **candidly**
adverb

candidate noun **1** person seeking
a job or position **2** person taking
an examination > **candidacy** or
candidature noun position of
being a candidate in an election

candied adjective covered or
cooked in sugar

candle noun stick of wax enclosing

a wick, which is burned to
produce light

candlestick noun holder for a
candle

candy candies noun US sweet or
sweets

cane noun **1** stem of the bamboo
or similar plant **2** flexible rod
used to beat someone **3** slender
walking stick ▷ verb **4** to beat
with a cane

canine adjective **1** of or like a dog
▷ noun **2** sharp pointed tooth
between the incisors and the
molars

canister noun metal container

cannabis noun drug obtained
from the dried leaves and flowers
of the hemp plant

canned adjective **1** preserved in a
can **2** (of music or laughter on a
television or radio show) recorded
beforehand

cannibal noun **1** person who
eats human flesh **2** animal
that eats others of its own kind
> **cannibalism** noun practice of
eating the flesh of one's own kind

cannon cannons cannoning
cannoned noun large wheeled
gun formerly used in battles to
fire heavy metal balls

cannot verb can not: *She cannot
come home yet*

canny cannier canniest adjective
clever and cautious > **cannily**
adverb

canoe noun light narrow open
boat propelled by a paddle or
paddles > **canoeing** noun sport
of rowing in a canoe > **canoeist**
noun person who rows a canoe

canon noun **1** priest serving in
a cathedral **2** Church decree

regulating morals or religious practices **3** general rule or standard: *the first canon of nursing*

anopy canopies *noun* **1** covering above a bed, door, etc **2** any large or wide covering: *the thick forest canopy*

antankerous *adjective* quarrelsome or bad-tempered

anteen *noun* **1** restaurant attached to a workplace or school **2** box containing a set of cutlery

anter *noun* **1** movement of a horse at a speed between a trot and a gallop ▷ *verb* **2** to move at a canter

antilever *noun* beam or girder fixed at one end only

anton *noun* political and administrative region of a country, especially Switzerland

anvas *noun* **1** heavy coarse cloth used for sails and tents **2** piece of canvas or similar material on which you can paint with oils **3** oil painting on canvas

anvass *verb* **1** to try to get votes or support for a particular person or political party: *a woman who canvassed for the Conservatives* **2** to find out the opinions of (people) **3** conducting a survey ▷ *noun* activity of canvassing

ayon *noun* deep narrow valley

caps capping capped *noun* soft, flat hat, often with a peak at the front **2** small lid **3** small explosive device used in a toy gun **4** upper financial limit ▷ *verb* **5** to cover or top with something **6** to select (a player) for a national team **7** to impose an upper limit on (a tax) **8** to outdo or excel: *capping anecdote with anecdote*

capable *adjective* **1** **capable of** able to do something: *a man capable of extreme violence* **2** skilful or talented > **capably** *adverb*

capacity capacities *noun* **1** ability to contain, absorb or hold **2** maximum amount or number that can be contained or produced: *a seating capacity of eleven thousand* **3** physical or mental ability: *people's creative capacities* **4** position or role: *in his capacity as councillor*

cape *noun* **1** short cloak with no sleeves **2** large piece of land that juts out into the sea

caper *noun* **1** a light-hearted practical joke ▷ *verb* **2** to skip about playfully

capillary capillaries *noun* very fine blood vessel ▷ *adjective*

capital *noun* **1** chief city of a country **2** amount of money or property owned or used by a business **3** sum of money saved or invested in order to gain interest **4** large letter, as used at the beginning of a name or sentence **5** top part of a stone column, often decorated ▷ *adjective* **6** *law* involving or punishable by death: *a capital offence*

capitalism *noun* economic system based on the private ownership of industry > **capitalist** *adjective* **1** of capitalists or capitalism **2** supporting capitalism ▷ *noun* **3** supporter of capitalism **4** person who owns a business

capitalize *verb* **1** to write or print (words) in capitals **2** to convert into or provide with capital **3** **capitalize on** to take advantage of (a situation)

capital punishment *noun* legal

a
b
c
d
e
f
g
h
i
j
k
l
m
n
o
p
q
r
s
t
u
v
w
x
y
z

killing used as a punishment for certain crimes

capitulate verb to surrender on agreed terms > **capitulation** noun surrender under agreed conditions

cappuccino cappuccinos noun coffee with steamed milk, sprinkled with powdered chocolate

capricious adjective often changing unexpectedly

Capricorn noun tenth sign of the zodiac, represented by a goat

capsize verb (of a boat) to overturn accidentally

capsule noun **1** soluble gelatine case containing a dose of medicine **2** plant's seed case **3** detachable crew compartment of a spacecraft

captain noun **1** commander of a ship or civil aircraft **2** middle-ranking naval officer **3** junior officer in the army **4** leader of a team or group > verb **5** to be captain of > **captaincy** noun position of being captaincy

caption noun **1** title or explanation accompanying an illustration > verb **2** to provide with a caption

captivate verb to attract and hold the attention of: I was captivated by her > **captivating** adjective: her captivating smile

captive noun **1** person kept in confinement > adjective **2** kept in confinement: a captive bird **3** (of an audience) unable to leave > **captivity** noun state of being kept in confinement

captor noun person who captures

a person or animal

capture verb **1** to take by force **2** to succeed in representing (a quality or mood): Today's newspapers capture the mood of the nation ▷ noun **3** capturing: the fift anniversary of his capture

car noun **1** motor vehicle designe to carry a small number of people **2** passenger compartment of a cable car, lift, etc **3** US railway carriage

carafe noun glass bottle for servir water or wine

caramel noun **1** chewy sweet made from sugar and milk **2** burnt sugar, used for colourin and flavouring food

carat noun **1** unit of weight of precious stones **2** measure of th purity of gold in an alloy

caravan noun **1** large enclosed vehicle for living in, designed to be towed by a car **2** group travelling together in Eastern countries

carb noun short for **carbohydrat carburettor**

carbohydrate noun any of a large group of energy-producir compounds in food, such as sugars and starches

carbon noun non-metallic elem occurring as charcoal, graphit and diamond, found in all orga matter

carbonated adjective (of a drink) containing carbon dioxide

carbon dioxide noun colourles gas breathed out by people and animals, and used in fire extinguishers and in making fizzy drinks

arbon footprint noun measure of the carbon dioxide produced by an individual or company

arbon offset noun act which compensates for carbon emissions of an individual or company

arburettor noun device which mixes petrol and air in an internal-combustion engine

arcass noun dead body of an animal

rd noun 1 piece of thick stiff paper or cardboard used for identification, reference or sending greetings or messages: a birthday card 2 one of a set of cards with a printed pattern, used for playing games 3 small rectangle of stiff plastic with identifying numbers for use as a credit card, cheque card or charge card > **cards** any card game, or card games in general 5 **on the cards** very likely to happen

rdboard noun thin stiff board made from paper pulp

diac adjective relating to the heart

digan noun knitted jacket that fastens up the front

dinal noun 1 any of the high-ranking clergymen of the RC Church who elect the Pope and act as his counsellors > adjective fundamentally important

e verb 1 to be concerned about 2 to like (to do something) > noun 3 careful attention or caution: Treat with extreme care 4 protection or charge: The children are now in the care of an orphanage 5 trouble or worry: money cares 6 **in care** (of a child) cared for by the state 7 **care of** at the address

of > **care for** verb 1 to like or be fond of 2 to look after

career noun 1 series of jobs in a profession or occupation that a person has through their life 2 part of a person's life spent in a particular occupation > verb 3 to rush in an uncontrolled way

carefree adjective having no worries or responsibilities

careful adjective 1 acting sensibly and with care: Be careful what you say to him 2 complete and well done: It needs very careful planning > **carefully** adverb

careless adjective 1 done badly without enough attention: careless driving 2 relaxed and unconcerned: careless laughter > **carelessly** adverb > **carelessness** noun: drivers who kill through carelessness

caress noun 1 gentle affectionate touch or embrace > verb 2 to touch gently and affectionately

caretaker noun 1 person employed to look after a place > adjective 2 temporarily in charge until a new leader or government is appointed; acting: O'Leary was named caretaker manager

cargo cargoes noun goods carried by a ship, aircraft, etc

caricature noun 1 drawing or description of a person that exaggerates features for comic effect > verb 2 to make a caricature of

carnage noun violent killing of large numbers of people

carnal adjective formal of a sexual or sensual nature

carnation noun cultivated plant

with fragrant white, pink or red flowers

carnival *noun* festive period with processions, music and dancing in the street

carnivore *noun* meat-eating animal > **carnivorous** *adjective* meat-eating

carol *noun* joyful religious song sung at Christmas time

carousel *noun* **1** revolving conveyor belt for luggage or photographic slides **2** US merry-go-round

carp *noun* **1** large freshwater fish ▷ *verb* **2** to complain or find fault

carpel *noun* seed-bearing female part of a flowering plant

carpenter *noun* person who makes or repairs wooden structures > **carpentry** *noun* skill or work of a carpenter

carpet *noun* **1** heavy fabric for covering floors ▷ *verb* **2** to cover with a carpet

carriage *noun* **1** one of the sections of a train for passengers **2** four-wheeled horse-drawn vehicle **3** moving part of a machine that supports and shifts another part: *a typewriter carriage* **4** charge made for conveying goods **5** way a person holds their head and body when they move

carriageway *noun* **1** Brit part of a road along which traffic passes in one direction **2** NZ part of a road used by vehicles

carrier *noun* **1** person or thing that carries something: *a troop carrier* **2** person or animal that does not suffer from a disease but can transmit it to others

carrier bag *noun* bag made of plastic or paper, used for carrying shopping

carrion *noun* dead and rotting flesh

carrot *noun* **1** long tapering orange root vegetable **2** something offered as an incentive

carry carries carrying carried *verb* **1** to take (something) from one place to another **2** to have (something) with you habitually in your pocket etc **3** to be capable of transmitting (a disease) **4** to have as a factor or result: *The charge carries a maximum penalty of twenty years* **5** to secure the adoption of (a bill or motion) **6** (of sound) to travel a certain distance > **carry away** *verb* **be carried away, get carried away** to behave hastily or foolishly through excitement > **carry on** *verb* **1** to continue **2** *informal* to cause a fuss > **carry out** *verb* **1** to follow (an order or instruction) **2** to accomplish (a task)

cart *noun* **1** vehicle with wheels used to carry goods and often pulled by horses, donkeys or ox ▷ *verb* **2** to carry, usually with some effort

cartilage *noun* strong flexible tissue forming part of the skeleton

carton *noun* container made of cardboard or waxed paper

cartoon *noun* **1** humorous or satirical drawing **2** sequence these telling a story **3** film ma by photographing a series of drawings which give the illus of movement when projected > **cartoonist** *noun* person who draws cartoons

cartridge noun 1 casing containing an explosive charge and bullet for a gun 2 part of the pick-up of a record player that converts the movements of the stylus into electrical signals 3 sealed container of film, tape, etc

cartwheel noun acrobatic movement in which you turn over sideways in a wheel-like motion with your weight supported in turns by your hands and feet

carve verb 1 to cut (something) to form an object 2 to form (an object or design) by cutting 3 to slice (cooked meat)

carving noun carved object

cascade noun 1 waterfall or group of waterfalls 2 something flowing or falling like a waterfall ▷ verb 3 to flow or fall in a cascade

case noun 1 particular situation, event or example: *a clear case of mistaken identity* 2 condition or state of affairs 3 set of arguments supporting an action or cause 4 person or problem dealt with by a doctor, social worker, solicitor or police officer 5 container 6 protective covering 6 trial or lawsuit 7 *Grammar* form of a noun, pronoun or adjective showing its relation to other words in the sentence: *the accusative case* 8 **in case** allowing for the possibility that: *I didn't want to shout in case I startled you*

casement noun window that is hinged on one side

cash cashes cashing cashed noun 1 banknotes and coins ▷ verb 2 to obtain cash for 3 **cash in on** *informal* to gain profit or advantage from

cashew noun edible kidney-shaped nut

cash flow noun money that a business makes and spends

cashier noun 1 person responsible for handling cash in a bank, shop, etc 2 ▷ verb to dismiss (someone) with dishonour from the armed forces

cashmere noun fine soft wool obtained from goats

cash register noun till that displays and adds the prices of the goods sold

casing noun protective case, covering

casino casinos noun public building or room where gambling games are played

cask noun 1 barrel used to hold alcoholic drink 2 *Aust* cubic carton containing wine, with a tap for dispensing

casket noun 1 small box for valuables 2 *US* coffin

casserole noun 1 covered dish in which food is cooked slowly, usually in an oven 2 dish cooked in this way ▷ verb 3 to cook in a casserole

cassette noun plastic case containing a reel of film or magnetic tape

cassette recorder noun machine used for recording and playing cassettes

cassock noun long tunic, usually black, worn by priests

cassowary cassowaries noun large flightless bird of Australia and New Guinea

cast casts casting cast noun 1 actors in a play or film collectively 2 object shaped by a mould while molten **3** mould used to shape such an object **4** rigid plaster-of-Paris casing for immobilizing broken bones while they heal ▷ *verb* **5** to select (an actor) to play a part in a play or film **6** to give or deposit (a vote) **7** to throw (a fishing line) into the water **8** to shape (an object) by pouring molten material into a mould: *An image of him has been cast in bronze* **9** to throw with force **10** to direct (a glance)

castanets *plural noun* musical instrument, used by Spanish dancers, consisting of curved pieces of wood clicked together in the hand

castaway *noun* shipwrecked person

caste *noun* **1** any of the four hereditary classes into which Hindu society is divided **2** system of social classes decided according to family, wealth and position

caster sugar or **castor sugar** *noun* finely ground white sugar

castigate *verb formal* to reprimand (a person) harshly

cast-iron *adjective* **1** made of a hard but brittle type of iron **2** definite or unchallengeable

castle *noun* **1** large fortified building, often built as a ruler's residence **2** rook in chess

cast-off *noun* discarded person or thing

castor or **caster** *noun* small swivelling wheel fixed to the bottom of a piece of furniture for easy moving

castor oil *noun* oil obtained from an Indian plant, used as a lubricant and laxative

castrate *verb* to remove the testicles of > **castration** *noun* removal of the testicles from a male animal

casual *adjective* **1** careless or without interest: *a casual glance over his shoulder* **2** (of work or workers) occasional or not permanent: *casual labour in the farm industry* **3** for informal wear **4** happening by chance: *a casual remark* > **casually** *adverb*

casualty casualties *noun* **1** person killed or injured in an accident or war **2** person or thing that has suffered as the result of something

casuarina *noun* Australian tree with jointed green branches

cat *noun* **1** small domesticated furry mammal **2** related wild mammal, such as the lion or tiger **3** **let the cat out the bag** reveal a secret

catacombs *plural noun* underground burial place consisting of tunnels with recesses for tombs

catalogue catalogues cataloguing catalogued *noun* **1** book containing details of items for sale **2** systematic list of items ▷ *verb* **3** to make a systematic list of

catalyst *noun* **1** substance that speeds up a chemical reaction without itself changing **2** something that causes a change to happen: *the catalyst which provoked civil war*

catamaran *noun* boat with two parallel hulls connected to each other

catapult noun **1** Y-shaped device with a loop of elastic, used by children for firing stones ▷ verb **2** to shoot forwards or upwards violently **3** to cause (someone) suddenly to be in a particular situation: catapulted to stardom

cataract noun **1** area of the lens of someone's eye that has become opaque instead of clear, preventing them from seeing properly **2** large waterfall

catarrh noun condition in which you get a lot of mucus in your nose and throat

catastrophe noun great and sudden disaster ▷ **catastrophic** adjective disastrous

catch catches catching caught verb **1** to seize and hold **2** to capture (a person or animal): I caught ten fish **3** to surprise in an act: two boys were caught stealing **4** to hit unexpectedly: His shoe caught me in the belly **5** to be in time for (a bus, train, etc) **6** to see or hear **7** to become infected with (an illness) **8** to entangle or become entangled: The white fibres caught on the mesh **9** to understand or make out: I didn't quite catch his meaning **10** catch informal to be punished ▷ noun **11** device for fastening a door, window, etc **12** informal concealed or unforeseen drawback > **catch** verb informal **1** to become popular **2** to understand **catch out** verb informal to trap (someone) in an error or lie **catch up** verb **1** (often followed by with) to reach the same place or level (as someone): She ran to catch up with him **2** (often followed by on, with) to do

something in order to get up to date (with something): He had a lot of paperwork to catch up on **3** be caught up in to be unwillingly or accidentally involved in

catching adjective infectious

catchy catchier catchiest adjective (of a tune) pleasant and easily remembered

catechism noun instruction on the doctrine of a Christian Church in a series of questions and answers

categorical adjective absolutely clear and certain: a categorical denial > **categorically** adverb

categorize verb to put in a category

category categories noun set of things with a particular characteristic in common: Occupations can be divided into four categories

cater verb to provide what is needed or wanted, especially food or services

caterer noun person or business that provides food for parties and groups

caterpillar noun wormlike larva of a moth or butterfly

catharsis catharses noun formal relief of strong suppressed emotions, for example through drama or psychoanalysis > **cathartic** adjective causing catharsis: His laughter was cathartic

cathedral noun important church with a bishop in charge of it

cattle plural noun domesticated cows and bulls

catty cattier cattiest adjective informal unpleasant and spiteful

> cattiness noun

catwalk noun narrow pathway or platform that people walk along, for example over a stage

Caucasian adjective **1** of the race of people with light-coloured skin ▷ noun **2** person belonging to this race

caught verb past of **catch**

cauldron noun large pot used for boiling

cauliflower noun vegetable with a large head of white flower buds surrounded by green leaves

cause noun **1** something that produces a particular effect **2 cause for** reason or motive **3** aim or principle supported by a person or group: *dedication to the cause of peace* ▷ verb **4** to be the cause of

causeway noun raised path or road across water or marshland

caustic adjective **1** capable of burning by chemical action **2** bitter and sarcastic

caution noun **1** care, especially in the face of danger **2** warning ▷ verb **3** to warn or advise: *He cautioned against an abrupt turnaround* **> cautionary** adjective warning

cautious adjective acting with or involving great care in order to avoid danger or risk **> cautiously** adverb

cavalcade noun procession of people on horseback or in cars

cavalier adjective **1** arrogant and behaving without sensitivity ▷ noun **2 Cavalier** supporter of Charles I in the English Civil War

cavalry noun **cavalries** part of the army originally on horseback, but now using fast armoured vehicles

cave noun hollow in the side of a hill or cliff **> cave in** verb **1** to collapse inwards **2** *informal* to give way under pressure

caveman **cavemen** noun prehistoric cave dweller

cavern noun large cave

cavernous adjective large, deep and hollow

caviar or **caviare** noun tiny salted eggs of the sturgeon, regarded as a delicacy

cavity **cavities** noun **1** hollow space **2** decayed area on a tooth

cavort verb to jump around excitedly

caw noun **1** cry of a crow, rook or raven ▷ verb **2** to make this cry

cc abbreviation **1** cubic centimetre **2** carbon copy

CD abbreviation compact disc

CD-ROM abbreviation compact disc read-only memory

cease verb to bring or come to an end

ceaseless adjective going on without stopping **> ceaselessly** adverb

cedar noun **1** evergreen coniferous tree **2** its wood

cede verb to surrender (territory or legal rights): *Haiti was ceded to France in 1697*

ceiling noun **1** inner upper surface of a room **2** upper limit set on something: *a ceiling on prices*

celebrate verb **1** to hold festivities to mark (a happy event, anniversary, etc): *a party to celebrate the end of the exams* **2** to perform (a religious ceremony) **> celebration** noun: *a celebration of his life* **> celebratory** adjective *celebratory meal*

celebrated *adjective* well known

celebrity celebrities *noun*
1 famous person **2** state of being
famous

celery *noun* vegetable with long
green crisp edible stalks

celestial *adjective formal*
1 heavenly or divine **2** of the sky:
*celestial planets and other celestial
objects*

celibate *adjective* **1** unmarried
and abstaining from sex ▷ *noun*
2 celibate person > **celibacy** *noun*
state of being celibate

cell *noun* **1** smallest unit of an
organism that is able to function
independently **2** small room for
a prisoner, monk or nun **3** small
compartment of a honeycomb
etc **4** small group operating as
the core of a larger organization
5 device that produces electrical
energy by chemical reaction

cellar *noun* **1** underground room
for storage **2** stock of wine

cello cellos *noun* large low-pitched
instrument of the violin family
> **cellist** *noun* person who plays
the cello

cellophane® *noun* thin
transparent cellulose sheeting
used as wrapping

cellphone *noun* a small portable
telephone

cellular *adjective* relating to the
cells of animals or plants

cellular phone *noun* same as
cellphone

celluloid *noun* kind of plastic
used to make toys and, formerly,
photographic film

Celsius *noun* temperature scale
on which water freezes at 0° and

boils at 100°

Celtic *noun* **1** group of languages
including Gaelic and Welsh
▷ *adjective* **2** of the Celts or the
Celtic languages

cement *noun* **1** fine grey powder
mixed with water and sand
to make mortar or concrete
2 something that unites, binds
or joins **3** material used to fill
teeth ▷ *verb* **4** to join, bind or
cover with cement **5** to make (a
relationship) stronger

cemetery cemeteries *noun* place
where dead people are buried

cenotaph *noun* monument
honouring soldiers who died
in a war

censor *noun* **1** person authorized
to examine films, books, etc, to
ban or cut anything considered
obscene or objectionable ▷ *verb*
2 to ban or cut parts of (a film,
book, etc) > **censorship** *noun*
practice or policy of censoring
films, publications, etc

censure *noun* **1** severe disapproval
▷ *verb* **2** to criticize (someone or
something) severely

census censuses *noun* official
count of a population

cent *noun* hundredth part of a
monetary unit such as the dollar
or euro

centaur *noun* Greek mythological
creature with the head, arms and
torso of a man, and the lower
body and legs of a horse

centenary centenaries *noun*
Chiefly Brit 100th anniversary or its
celebration

centi- *prefix* one hundredth:
centimetre

centigrade *adjective* same as

Celsius
- Scientists say and write *Celsius* rather than *Centigrade*

centilitre *noun* one hundredth of a litre

centime *noun* unit of currency used in Switzerland and some other countries, and formerly used in France and Belgium

centimetre *noun* one hundredth of a metre

centipede *noun* small wormlike creature with many legs

central *adjective* 1 of, at or forming the centre 2 main or most important > **centrally** *adverb*

Central America *noun* another name for the Isthmus of Panama, the area of land joining North America to South America

central heating *noun* system of heating a building in which water or air is heated in a tank and travels round the building through pipes and radiators round the building

centralize *verb* to bring (a country or an organization) under central control > **centralization** *noun* process of bringing under central control

centre *noun* 1 middle point or part 2 place for a specified activity: *a health centre* 3 political party or group favouring moderation 4 *Sport* player who plays in the middle of the field > *verb* 5 to put in the centre of something 6 **centre on** to have as a centre or main theme

centrifugal *adjective* moving away from a centre

centripetal *adjective* moving towards a centre

centurion *noun* (in ancient Rome) officer commanding 100 men

century centuries *noun* 1 period of 100 years 2 cricket score of 100 runs by a batsman

ceramic *noun* 1 hard brittle material made by heating clay to a very high temperature 2 object made of this 3 **ceramics** art of producing ceramic objects > *adjective* 4 made of ceramic

cereal *noun* 1 grass plant with edible grain, such as oat or wheat 2 this grain 3 breakfast food made from this grain, eaten mixed with milk

cerebral *adjective formal* 1 of or relating to the brain 2 involving intelligence rather than emotion or instinct

cerebral palsy *noun* illness caused by damage to a baby's brain, which makes its muscles and limbs very weak

ceremonial *adjective* of or relating to ceremony or ritual: *ceremonial dress* > **ceremonially** *adverb*

ceremony ceremonies *noun* 1 set of formal actions performed at a special occasion or important public event: *his recent coronation ceremony* 2 very formal and polite behaviour: *He hung up the phone without ceremony* 3 **stand on ceremony** to insist on or act with excessive formality

certain *adjective* 1 sure: *He was certain we'd agree* 2 definite: *It's not certain it exists* 3 some but not much: *a certain resemblance*

certainly *adverb* 1 without doubt 2 of course

certainty certainties *noun* 1 state of being sure 2 something that is inevitable: *There are no* *certainties*

certificate noun official document stating the details of a birth, academic course, etc

certify certifies certifying certified verb 1 to confirm or attest to 2 to guarantee (that certain required standards have been met) 3 to declare legally insane

cervix cervixes or **cervices** noun technical entrance to the womb at the top of the vagina >**cervical** adjective relating to the cervix

cessation noun formal ending or pause: *a swift cessation of hostilities* compare

CFC abbreviation chlorofluorocarbon

chaff noun outer parts of grain separated from the seeds by eating

chaffinch noun small European songbird with black and white wings

chagrin noun formal feeling of annoyance or disappointment

chain noun 1 flexible length of connected metal links 2 series of connected facts or events 3 group of shops, hotels, etc owned by one firm ▷ verb 4 to restrict or fasten with or as if with a chain: *They had chained themselves to railings*

chain saw noun large saw with teeth fixed in a chain that is driven round by a motor

chain-smoke verb to smoke (cigarettes) continuously

chair noun 1 seat with a back, for one person 2 official position of authority 3 person holding this 4 professorship ▷ verb 5 to preside over (a meeting)

chair lift noun series of chairs suspended from a moving cable for carrying people up a slope

chairman chairmen noun person in charge of a company's board of directors or a meeting >**chairmanship** noun: *during his chairmanship* >**chairperson** noun >**chairwoman** noun

- Some people don't like to use
- *chairman* when talking about
- a woman. You can use *chair*
- or *chairperson* to talk about a
- man or a woman

chalet noun 1 kind of Swiss wooden house with a steeply sloping roof 2 similar house, used as a holiday home

chalice noun gold or silver cup used in churches to hold the Communion wine

chalk noun 1 soft white rock consisting of calcium carbonate 2 piece of chalk, often coloured, used for drawing and writing on blackboards ▷ verb 3 to draw or mark with chalk >**chalk up** verb to score or register (something): *He chalked up his first win* >**chalky** adjective containing or covered with chalk

challenge noun 1 testing situation: *a new challenge at the right time in my career* 2 call to take part in a contest or game 3 questioning of the rightness or value of something: *a challenge to authority* 4 demand by a sentry for identification or a password ▷ verb 5 to invite or call (someone) to take part in a contest, fight or argument: *She challenged me to a game* 6 to call (a decision or action) into question 7 to order (a person) to stop and be identified > **challenger** noun competitor who takes on a champion or leader > **challenging** adjective requiring great effort and determination

chamber noun 1 hall used for formal meetings 2 legislative or judicial assembly 3 old-fashioned bedroom 4 hollow place or compartment inside something, especially inside an animal's body or inside a gun 5 **chambers** judge's room for hearing private cases not taken in open court

chambermaid noun woman employed to clean bedrooms in a hotel

chameleon noun small lizard that changes colour to blend in with its surroundings

chamois leather noun soft leather cloth used for polishing

champagne noun sparkling white French wine

champion noun 1 overall winner of a competition 2 someone who defends a person or cause > verb 3 to support

championship noun competition to find the champion of a sport

chance noun 1 likelihood or probability 2 opportunity to do something 3 risk or gamble 4 unpredictable element that causes things to happen one way rather than another: I found out by chance > verb 5 to try (something) in spite of the risk

chancellor noun 1 head of government in some European countries 2 honorary head of a university

Chancellor of the Exchequer noun Brit cabinet minister

responsible for finance and taxes

chandelier noun ornamental light with branches and holders for several candles or bulbs

change noun 1 difference or alteration 2 variety or novelty 3 replacement of something by something else: a change of clothes 4 money returned to you if you pay for something with a larger sum than needed 5 coins of low value > verb 6 to make or become different 7 to exchange (something for something else) 8 to exchange (money) for smaller coins of the same total value or for a foreign currency 9 to put on other clothes 10 to leave one train, bus, etc and board another

changeable adjective changing often

changeover noun change from one system or activity to another

channel channels channelling channelled noun 1 wavelength used to receive programmes broadcast by a television or radio station; also the station itself 2 means of access or communication 3 broad strait connecting two areas of sea 4 bed or course of a river, stream or canal 5 groove > verb 6 to direct or convey through a channel or channels: a system set up to channel funds to poorer countries

chant verb 1 to repeat (a slogan, name, etc) over and over 2 to sing or recite (a psalm) > noun 3 group of words repeated over and over again 4 psalm that has a short simple melody with several words sung on one note

Chanukah another spelling of

Hanukkah

chaos noun complete disorder or confusion > **chaotic** adjective in a state of disorder or confusion > **chaotically** adverb

chap noun informal man or boy

chapel noun 1 section of a church or cathedral with its own altar 2 type of small church

chaperone noun 1 older person who accompanies and supervises a young person or young people on a social occasion ▷ verb 2 to act as a chaperone to

chaplain noun member of the Christian clergy who regularly works in a hospital, school or prison

chapter noun 1 division of a book 2 period in a life or history 3 branch of a society or club 4 group of Christian clergy who work in a cathedral

char chars charring charred verb to blacken by partial burning > **charred** adjective burnt

character noun 1 combination of qualities distinguishing a person, group or place 2 reputation, especially good reputation 3 unusual or interesting quality: a building of great character 4 person represented in a play, film or story 5 unusual or amusing person 6 letter, numeral or symbol used in writing or printing

characteristic noun 1 distinguishing feature or quality ▷ adjective 2 typical **characteristically** adverb

characterize verb 1 to be a characteristic of 2 **characterize** s to describe as

characterless adjective dull and uninteresting

charade noun ridiculous and unnecessary activity or pretence > **charades** noun game in which one team acts out a word or phrase, which the other team has to guess

charcoal noun black form of carbon made by burning wood without air, used as a fuel and also for drawing

charge verb 1 to ask (an amount of money) as a price 2 to enter a debit against a person's account for (a purchase) 3 (of the police) to accuse (someone) formally of a crime 4 to rush forward, often to attack 5 to fill (a battery) with electricity 6 formal to command or assign: The president has charged his foreign minister with trying to open talks ▷ noun 7 price charged for something 8 formal accusation of a crime in a court of law 9 onrush or attack 10 custody or guardianship: in the charge of the police 11 person or thing entrusted to someone's care 12 explosive put in a gun or other weapon 13 amount of electricity stored in a battery 14 **in charge of** in control of

charger noun 1 device for charging or recharging batteries 2 (in the Middle Ages) horse ridden into battle by a knight

chariot noun two-wheeled horse-drawn vehicle used in ancient times in wars and races

charisma noun person's power to attract or influence people > **charismatic** adjective having charisma

charity charities noun 1 organization that gives help,

such as money or food, to those in need **2** giving of help to those in need **3** help given to those in need **4** kindly attitude towards people > **charitable** adjective **1** kind or lenient in your attitude towards others **2** of or for charity: *charitable organizations* > **charitably** adverb

charlatan noun person who claims expertise that he or she does not have

charm noun **1** quality of attracting, fascinating or delighting people **2** trinket worn on a bracelet **3** magic spell ▷ verb **4** to attract, fascinate or delight **5** to influence by personal charm **6** to protect or influence as if by magic: *a charmed life*

charmer noun person who uses their charm to influence people

charming adjective very pleasant and attractive > **charmingly** adverb

chart noun **1** graph, table or diagram showing information **2** map of the sea or stars **3** the **charts** informal weekly lists of the best-selling pop records ▷ verb **4** to plot the course of **5** to make a chart of

charter noun **1** document granting or demanding certain rights **2** fundamental principles of an organization **3** hire of transport for private use ▷ verb **4** to hire by charter **5** to grant a charter to > **chartered** adjective officially qualified to practise a profession

chase verb **1** to pursue (a person or animal) persistently or quickly ▷ noun **2** act or an instance of chasing a person or animal

chasm noun **1** deep crack in the earth **2** very large difference between two things or groups of people; gulf: *the chasm between rich and poor*

chassis noun frame, wheels and mechanical parts of a vehicle

● She plural of *chassis* is also
● *chassis*

chaste adjective old-fashioned not having sex outside marriage or at all > **chastity** noun state of not having sex outside marriage or at all

chastise verb formal to scold severely

chat chats chatting chatted noun **1** informal conversation ▷ verb **2** to have an informal conversation > **chat up** verb informal to talk flirtatiously to (someone) with a view to starting a romantic or sexual relationship

chateau chateaux noun large country house or castle in France

chatroom noun site on the Internet where users have group discussions by e-mail

chatter verb **1** to speak quickly and continuously about unimportant things **2** (of the teeth) to rattle with cold or fear ▷ noun **3** unimportant talk

chatty chattier chattiest adjective talkative and friendly

chauffeur noun person employed to drive a car for someone

chauvinist noun person who believes that their own country, race, group or sex is superior > **chauvinistic** adjective characterised by chauvinism

cheap adjective **1** costing relatively little **2** of poor quality **3** not

valued highly: *cheap promises*
4 mean or despicable > **cheaply**
adverb

cheat *verb* **1** to act dishonestly to
gain profit or advantage ▷ *noun*
2 person who cheats

check *verb* **1** to examine or
investigate **2** to slow the growth
or progress of ▷ *noun* **3** test to
ensure accuracy or progress
4 break in progress **5** US cheque
6 pattern of squares or crossed
lines **7** Chess position of a king
under attack > **check in** *verb* **1** to
register your arrival at a hotel or
airport **2** to register the arrival
of (guests or passengers) at a
hotel or airport > **check out**
verb **1** to pay the bill and leave a
hotel **2** to examine or investigate
(something) **3** *informal* to have
a look at

heckmate *noun* Chess winning
position in which an opponent's
king is under attack and unable
to escape

heckout *noun* counter in a
supermarket, where customers
pay

heckpoint *noun* place where
traffic has to stop in order to be
checked

heckup *noun* thorough medical
examination

heek *noun* **1** either side of the
face below the eye **2** *informal*
mpudence, boldness or lack of
espect ▷ *verb* **3** Brit, Aust, NZ
nformal to speak impudently to

eeky **cheekier** **cheekiest**
adjective rather rude and
disrespectful > **cheekily** *adverb*

eer *verb* **1** to applaud or
ncourage with shouts
▷ *noun* **2** shout of applause or

encouragement > **cheer up** *verb*
to become or make (someone)
happy or hopeful

cheerful *adjective* **1** happy and
in good spirits **2** bright and
pleasant-looking > **cheerfully**
adverb > **cheerfulness** *noun*
happiness

cheerio *interjection informal*
goodbye

cheery **cheerier** **cheeriest**
adjective happy and cheerful

cheese *noun* hard or creamy food
made from milk

cheesecake *noun* dessert with a
biscuit-crumb base covered with
a sweet cream-cheese mixture

cheetah *noun* large fast-running
spotted African wild cat

chef *noun* cook in a restaurant

chemical *noun* **1** substance used
in or resulting from a reaction
involving changes to atoms or
molecules ▷ *adjective* **2** involved
in chemistry or using chemicals
> **chemically** *adverb*

chemist *noun* **1** shop selling
medicines and cosmetics
2 person who is qualified to
make up prescription medicines;
pharmacist **3** scientist who does
research in chemistry

chemistry *noun* science of the
composition, properties and
reactions of substances

chemotherapy *noun* treatment
of disease, often cancer, using
chemicals

cheque *noun* written order asking
your bank to pay money out of
your account to a person, shop or
organization

chequered *adjective* **1** marked by
varied fortunes: *a chequered career*

2 having a pattern of squares

cherish *verb* **1** to care deeply about (something) and look after it lovingly **2** to care for

cherry cherries *noun* **1** small red or black fruit with a stone **2** tree on which it grows ▷ *adjective* **3** deep red

cherub cherubs or **cherubim** *noun* angel, often represented as a winged child ▷ **cherubic** *adjective* (of a baby or child) attractive

chess *noun* game for two players with 16 pieces each, played on a chequered board of 64 squares

chessboard *noun* board divided into 64 squares of two alternating colours on which chess is played

chest *noun* **1** front of the body, from neck to waist **2** large strong box with a hinged lid

chestnut *noun* **1** reddish-brown edible nut **2** tree on which it grows **3** reddish-brown horse **4** *informal* old joke ▷ *adjective* **5** (of hair or a horse) reddish-brown

chest of drawers *noun* piece of furniture consisting of drawers in a frame

chew *verb* to grind (food) between the teeth ▷ **chewy** *adjective* requiring a lot of chewing

chewing gum *noun* flavoured gum to be chewed but not swallowed

chic *adjective* **1** stylish or elegant ▷ *noun* **2** stylishness or elegance

chick *noun* baby bird

chicken *noun* **1** domestic fowl **2** its flesh, eaten as food: *roast chicken* **3** *informal* coward ▷ *adjective* **4** *informal* cowardly ▷ **chicken out** *verb informal* (often followed by *of*) to fail to do something through cowardice

chickenpox *noun* infectious disease with an itchy rash

chicory *noun* **1** plant whose bitter leaves are used in salads **2** root of this plant, used as a coffee substitute

chide chides chiding chided *verb* *old-fashioned* to rebuke or scold

chief *noun* **1** head of a group of people ▷ *adjective* **2** most important: *the chief source of oil* > **chiefly** *adverb* **1** especially **2** mainly

chieftain *noun* leader of a tribe or clan

chiffon *noun* very thin lightweight cloth made of silk or nylon

chihuahua *noun* breed of very small dog with pointed ears

chilblain *noun* inflammation of the fingers or toes, caused by exposure to cold

child children *noun* **1** young human being, boy or girl **2** son or daughter

childbirth *noun* act of giving birth to a child

childhood *noun* time when a person is a child

childish *adjective* immature and foolish ▷ **childishly** *adverb* > **childishness** *noun* immature and foolish behaviour

- If you call someone *childish*, you think they are immature or foolish. If you call them *childlike*, you think they are innocent like a young child

childless *adjective* having no children

childlike *adjective* like a child in appearance or behaviour

childminder *noun* person who is

qualified and paid to look after other people's children while they are at work

Chilean adjective 1 belonging or relating to Chile ▷ noun 2 someone from Chile

chill noun 1 feverish cold 2 moderate coldness ▷ verb 3 to make (something) cool or cold 4 to cause (someone) to feel cold or frightened 5 informal to relax ▷ adjective 6 unpleasantly cold

chilli noun **chillies** noun 1 small red or green hot-tasting pepper, used in cooking 2 **chilli con carne** hot-tasting Mexican dish of meat, onions, beans and chilli powder

chilly **chillier** **chilliest** adjective 1 rather cold 2 unfriendly and without enthusiasm

chilly-bin noun NZ informal portable container for keeping food and drink cool

chime noun 1 musical ringing sound of a bell or clock 2 **chimes** set of bells or other objects which make ringing sounds ▷ verb 3 to make a musical ringing sound 4 to indicate (the time) by chiming

chimney noun hollow vertical structure for carrying away smoke from a fire

chimpanzee noun small ape with dark fur that lives in forests in Africa

chin noun part of the face below the mouth

china noun 1 fine earthenware or porcelain 2 dishes or ornaments made of this 3 Brit, Aust, NZ, S Afr informal friend

Chinese adjective 1 of China ▷ noun 2 person from China 3 any of the languages of China

- The plural of Chinese is also
- Chinese

chink noun 1 small narrow opening 2 short, light, ringing sound, like one made by glasses touching each other

chintz noun glazed cotton fabric usually decorated with flowery patterns

chip **chips** **chipping** **chipped** noun 1 strip of potato, fried in deep fat 2 tiny wafer of semiconductor material forming an integrated circuit 3 counter used to represent money in gambling games 4 small piece removed by chopping, breaking, etc 5 mark left where a small piece has been broken off something ▷ verb 6 to break small pieces from > **chip in** verb informal 1 to contribute (money) 2 to interrupt with a remark

chipboard noun thin board made of compressed wood particles

chipmunk noun small squirrel-like North American rodent with a striped back

chiropodist noun person who treats minor foot complaints > **chiropody** noun medical treatment of the feet

chirp verb 1 (of a bird or insect) to make a short high-pitched sound ▷ noun 2 chirping sound

chisel **chisels** **chiselling** **chiselled** noun 1 metal tool with a sharp end for shaping wood or stone ▷ verb 2 to carve or form with a chisel

chivalry noun 1 polite and helpful behaviour, especially by men towards women 2 medieval system and principles of knighthood > **chivalrous** *adjective* gallant or courteous

chives *plural noun* herb with a mild onion flavour

chlorine *noun* strong-smelling greenish-yellow gaseous element, used to disinfect water and to make bleach

chloroform *noun* strong-smelling liquid formerly used as an anaesthetic

chlorophyll *noun* green colouring matter of plants, which enables them to convert sunlight into energy

chock-a-block or **chock-full** *adjective* completely full

chocolate *noun* **1** sweet food made from cacao seeds **2** sweet or drink made from this > *adjective* **3** dark brown

choice *noun* **1** act of choosing or selecting **2** opportunity for choice or power of choosing: *parental choice* **3** person or thing chosen or that may be chosen: *You've made a good choice* **4** alternative action or possibility > *adjective* **5** of high quality: *choice food and drink*

choir *noun* **1** organized group of singers, especially in church **2** part of a church occupied by the choir

choke *verb* **1** to hinder or stop the breathing of (a person) by strangling or smothering **2** to have trouble in breathing **3** to block or clog up

choko chokos *noun* fruit that is shaped like a pear and used as a vegetable in Australia and New Zealand

cholera *noun* serious infectious disease causing severe vomiting and diarrhoea

cholesterol *noun* fatty substance found in animal tissue, an excess of which can cause heart disease

chook *noun Aust, NZ informal* hen or chicken

choose chooses choosing chose chosen *verb* **1** to select from a number of alternatives **2** to decide (to do something) because you want to

choosy choosier choosiest *adjective* fussy and difficult to satisfy

chop chops chopping chopped *verb* **1** to cut (something) with a blow from an axe or knife **2** to cut into pieces **3** *Boxing karate* to hit (an opponent) with a short sharp blow **4** **chop and change** to change your mind repeatedly > *noun* **5** cutting or sharp blow **6** slice of lamb or pork, usually with a rib

chopper *noun* **1** *informal* helicopter **2** small axe

choppy choppier choppiest *adjective* (of the sea) fairly rough

chopsticks *plural noun* pair of thin sticks used to eat Chinese or other East Asian food

choral *adjective* relating to singing by a choir: *choral music*

chore *noun* uninteresting job that has to be done

choreography *noun* art of composing dance steps and movements > **choreographer** *noun* person who composes dance steps and movements

chortle *verb* **1** to chuckle in amusement > *noun* **2** amused chuckle

Christ noun Jesus of Nazareth, regarded by Christians as the Messiah

christen verb **1** to give a Christian name to in baptism **2** to give a name to (a person or thing) >**christening** noun Christian ceremony in which a child is given a name and made a member of a church

Christian noun **1** person who believes in and follows Christ ▷ adjective **2** of Christ or Christianity **3** kind, good and considerate >**Christianity** noun religion based on the life and teachings of Christ

Christian name noun personal name given to Christians at baptism: loosely used to mean a person's first name

Christmas noun **1** annual festival on Dec. 25 commemorating the birth of Christ **2** period around this time

aromatic adjective **1** of colour or colours **2** Music (of a scale) proceeding by semitones

rome noun grey metallic element used in steel alloys and for electroplating

romosome noun microscopic gene-carrying body in the nucleus of a cell

ronic adjective **1** (of an illness) lasting a long time **2** habitual **3** Brit, Aust, NZ informal of poor quality >**chronically** adverb

ronicle noun **1** record of events in order of occurrence ▷ verb **2** to record in or as if in a chronicle

ronological adjective arranged in the order in which things

happened >**chronologically** adverb

chronology chronologies noun arrangement or list of events in order of occurrence

chrysalis chrysalises noun insect in the stage between larva and adult, when it is in a cocoon

chrysanthemum noun garden flower with a large head made up of thin petals

chubby chubbier chubbiest adjective plump and round: his chubby cheeks

chuck verb **1** informal to throw **2** informal to give up or reject

chuckle verb **1** to laugh softly ▷ noun **2** soft laugh

chug chugs chugging chugged noun **1** short dull sound like the noise of an engine ▷ verb **2** to operate or move with this sound

chum noun informal close friend

chunk noun **1** thick solid piece **2** considerable amount

chunky chunkier chunkiest adjective **1** (of a person) broad and heavy **2** (of an object) large and thick

church noun **1** building for public Christian worship **2** particular Christian denomination: the Catholic Church **3** Church institutional religion as a political or social force: conflict between Church and State

Church of England noun Anglican church in England, where it is the state church, with the King or Queen as its head

churchyard noun grounds round a church, used as a graveyard

churn noun **1** machine in which cream is shaken to make butter

▷ verb **2** to stir (cream) vigorously to make butter **3 churn out** *informal* to produce (things) rapidly in large numbers

chute *noun* steep slope down which things may be slid

chutney *noun* pickle made from fruit, vinegar, spices and sugar

cider *noun* alcoholic drink made from fermented apple juice

cigar *noun* roll of cured tobacco leaves for smoking

cigarette *noun* thin roll of shredded tobacco in thin paper, for smoking

cinder *noun* piece of material that will not burn, left after burning coal

cinema *noun* **1** place for showing films **2** business of making films

cinnamon *noun* spice obtained from the bark of an Asian tree

cipher or **cypher** *noun* **1** system of secret writing **2** unimportant person

circa *preposition* *formal* about or approximately; used especially before dates

circle *noun* **1** perfectly round geometric figure, line or shape **2** group of people sharing an interest or activity **3** *Theatre* section of seats above the main level of the auditorium ▷ *verb* **4** to move in a circle (round)

circuit *noun* **1** complete route or course, especially a circular one, for example a motor-racing track **2** complete path through which an electric current can flow

circular *adjective* **1** in the shape of a circle **2** moving in a circle ▷ *noun* **3** letter or advert sent to a lot of people at the same time

circulate *verb* to send, go or pass from place to place or person to person

circulation *noun* **1** flow of blood around the body **2** number of copies of a newspaper or magazine sold **3** sending or moving round: *traffic circulation* > **circulatory** *adjective* of or relating to circulation: *the human circulatory system*

circumcise *verb* to remove the foreskin of (a male) > **circumcision** *noun*

circumstance *noun* **1** condition, situation or event affecting or influencing a person or event **2** unplanned events and situations which cannot be controlled: *a victim of circumstance* **3 circumstances** person's position and conditions in life

circus circuses *noun* (performance given by) a travelling company of acrobats, clowns, performing animals, etc

cistern *noun* water tank, especially one that holds water for flushing a toilet

citadel *noun* fortress in or near a city

cite *verb* *formal* **1** to quote or refer to **2** to bring forward as proof **3** to summon to appear before a court of law

citizen *noun* **1** native or naturalized member of a state or nation **2** inhabitant of a city or town > **citizenship** *noun* **1** position or status of a citizen, with its rights and duties **2** person's conduct as a citizen

citrus fruit *noun* juicy sharp-tasting fruit such as an orange or lemon

city cities noun 1 large or important town 2 **the City** Brit part of London which contains the main British financial institutions such as the Stock Exchange

civic adjective of or relating to a city or citizens

civil adjective 1 relating to the citizens of a country 2 relating to people or things that are not connected with the armed forces: civil aviation 3 polite or courteous > **civility** noun polite or courteous behaviour > **civilly** adverb

civil engineering noun design and construction of roads, bridges and public buildings

civilian noun 1 person not belonging to the armed forces ▷ adjective 2 not relating to the armed forces or police

civilization noun 1 high level of human cultural and social development 2 particular society which has reached this level: the tale of a lost civilization

civilized or **civilised** adjective 1 (of a society) having a developed social organization and way of life 2 (of a person) polite and reasonable

civil servant noun member of the civil service

civil service noun government departments responsible for the administration of a country

civil war noun war between people of the same country

cl symbol centilitre

clad adjective literary (often followed by in) dressed or clothed (in)

claim verb 1 to assert as a fact

2 to demand (something) as a right ▷ noun 3 assertion that something is true 4 assertion of a right 5 something claimed as a right

claimant noun person who is making a claim, especially for money

clairvoyant adjective 1 able to know about things that will happen in the future ▷ noun 2 person who is, or claims to be, clairvoyant

clam clams clamming clammed noun edible shellfish with a hinged shell > **clam up** verb informal to stop talking, especially through nervousness

clamber verb to climb awkwardly, using hands and feet

clammy clammier clammiest adjective unpleasantly damp and sticky

clamour noun 1 loud protest 2 loud persistent noise or outcry ▷ verb 3 **clamour for** to demand noisily

clamp noun 1 tool with movable jaws for holding things together tightly ▷ verb 2 to fasten with a clamp > **clamp down** verb (often followed by on) to become stricter (about something) in order to stop or control it

clan noun 1 group of families with a common ancestor, especially among Scottish Highlanders 2 close group ▷ adjective

clandestine adjective secret and hidden

clang verb 1 to make a loud ringing metallic sound ▷ noun 2 ringing metallic sound

clank noun 1 harsh metallic sound

▷ *verb* **2** to make such a sound

clap *claps clapping clapped*
verb **1** to applaud by hitting the
palms of your hands sharply
together **2** to place or put quickly
or forcibly: *He should be clapped
in irons* ▷ *noun* **3** act or sound of
clapping **4** sudden loud noise: *a
clap of thunder*

clapper *noun* piece of metal inside
a bell, which causes it to sound
when struck against the side

claret *noun* dry red wine from the
Bordeaux region of France

clarify *clarifies clarifying
clarified verb* to make
(something) clear and easy to
understand > **clarification**
noun explanation that makes
something easier to understand

clarinet *noun* woodwind
instrument with a single reed

clarity *noun* clearness

clash *verb* **1** to come into conflict
2 (of events) to happen at the
same time **3** (of colours) to look
unattractive together **4** (of
objects) to make a loud harsh
sound by being hit together
▷ *noun* **5** a fight or argument
6 fact of two events happening at
the same time

clasp *noun* **1** device for fastening
things **2** firm grasp or embrace
▷ *verb* **3** to grasp or embrace
firmly

class *noun* **1** group of people
sharing a similar social position
2 system of dividing society into
such groups **3** group of people
or things sharing a common
characteristic **4** group of pupils
or students taught together
5 standard of quality **6** *informal*
elegance or excellence: *a touch*

of class ▷ *adjective* **7** *informal*
excellent, skilful or stylish: *a class
act* ▷ *verb* **8** to place in a class;
classify or categorize: *They are
officially classed as visitors*

classic *adjective* **1** being a typical
example of something: *a
classic symptom of iron deficiency*
2 of lasting interest because
of excellence: *a classic film*
3 attractive because of simplicity
of form: *the classic dinner suit*
▷ *noun* **4** something of the
highest quality **5** **classics** study
of ancient Greek and Roman
literature and culture

classical *adjective* **1** of or in a
restrained conservative style
2 denoting serious art music **3** of
or influenced by ancient Greek
and Roman culture > **classically**
adverb

classified *adjective* officially
declared secret by the
government

classify *classifies classifying
classified verb* to arrange
into groups with similar
characteristics > **classification**
noun **1** placing things
systematically in categories
2 division or category in a
classifying system

classroom *noun* a room in a schoo
where pupils have lessons

classy *classier classiest adjective*
informal stylish and elegant

clatter *verb* **1** to make a loud
rattling noise, as when hard
objects hit each other ▷ *noun*
2 loud rattling noise

clause *noun* **1** section of a legal
document **2** group of words wit
a subject and a verb, which may
be a complete sentence or one o

the parts of a sentence

claustrophobia noun abnormal fear of confined spaces > **claustrophobic** adjective **1** (of a person) uncomfortable in a confined space **2** (of a place) enclosed, overcrowded or restricting movement

claw noun **1** sharp hooked nail of a bird or beast **2** similar part, such as a crab's pincer ▷ verb **3** to tear with claws or nails

clay noun fine-grained earth, soft when moist and hardening when baked, used to make bricks and pottery

clean adjective **1** free from dirt or impurities **2** without anything in it or on it: a clean sheet of paper **3** morally acceptable or inoffensive: good clean fun **4** (of a reputation or record) free from corruption or dishonesty **5** complete: a clean break **6** simple and streamlined in design: the clean lines of the new model ▷ verb **7** to make (something) free from dirt **8 come clean** informal to reveal or admit something > **cleaner** noun person, device or substance that removes dirt > **cleanly** adverb

cleanliness noun state or degree of being clean

cleanse verb to remove dirt from > **cleanser** noun

clear adjective **1** free from doubt or confusion: It was clear that he did not want to talk **2** easy to see or hear **3** able to be seen through; transparent **4** free of obstruction **5** (of sky) free from clouds **6** (of skin) without blemish ▷ adverb **7** out of the way ▷ verb **8** to make or become clear **9** to pass

by or over (something) without contact **10** to prove (someone) innocent of a crime or mistake **11** to make as profit > **clearly** adverb > **clear out** verb **1** to remove and sort the contents of (a room or container) **2** Brit, Aust, NZ informal to go away > **clear up** verb **1** to put (a place or thing that is disordered) in order **2** to explain or solve (a problem or misunderstanding) **3** (of the weather) to become brighter **4** (of an illness) to become better

clearance noun **1** act of clearing: slum clearance **2** official permission

clearing noun area of bare ground in a forest

cleavage noun **1** division between a woman's breasts, as revealed by a low-cut dress **2** division or split

cleaver noun butcher's heavy knife with a square blade

cleft noun narrow opening or crack

clementine noun small orange citrus fruit

clench verb **1** to close or squeeze (your teeth or fist) tightly **2** to grasp firmly

clergy plural noun priests and ministers as a group

clergyman clergymen noun male member of the clergy

clerical adjective **1** of or relating to clerks or office work **2** of the clergy

clerk noun employee in an office, bank or court who keeps records, files and accounts

clever adjective **1** intelligent and quick to understand **2** very effective or skilful > **cleverly** adverb > **cleverness** noun

clianthus noun plant with clusters of scarlet flowers, found in Australia and New Zealand

cliché noun expression or idea that is no longer effective because of overuse ▷ **clichéd** adjective: The dialogue is clichéd and corny

click noun **1** short sharp sound ▷ verb **2** to make this sound **3** informal (of two people) to get on well together **4** informal to become suddenly clear **5** Computers to press and release a button on a mouse in order, for example, to select an option on the screen or highlight something **6** informal to be a success

client noun person who uses the services of a professional person or company

clientele noun customers or clients collectively

cliff noun steep rock face, especially along the sea shore

climate noun **1** typical weather conditions of an area **2** general attitude and opinion of people at a particular time: the American political climate ▷ **climatic** adjective: climatic changes

climax noun **1** most intense point of an experience, series of events, or story **2** same as orgasm ▷ **climactic** adjective: the film's climactic scene

climb verb **1** to go up or ascend (stairs, a mountain, etc) **2** to move or go with difficulty **3** to rise to a higher point or intensity ▷ noun **4** act or an instance of climbing **5** place or thing to be climbed, especially a route in mountaineering ▷ **climber** noun

clinch verb to settle (an argument or agreement) decisively: Peter

clinched the deal

cling clings clinging clung verb **1** (usually followed by to, onto) to hold (onto) tightly or stay closely attached (to) **2** (followed by to) to continue to do or believe in: still clinging to old-fashioned values

clingfilm® noun thin polythene material for wrapping food

clinic noun **1** building where outpatients receive medical treatment or advice **2** private or specialized hospital

clinical adjective **1** of or relating to the medical treatment of patients: clinical tests **2** logical and unemotional: the cold, clinical attitudes of his colleagues ▷ **clinically** adverb

clip clips clipping clipped verb **1** to cut with shears or scissors **2** to attach or hold together with a clip ▷ noun **3** short extract of a film **4** informal sharp blow **5** device for attaching or holding things together

clippers plural noun tool for clipping

clipping noun something cut out, especially an article from a newspaper

clique noun small group of people who stick together and do not mix with other people

clitoris noun small, highly sensitive organ near the opening of a woman's vagina

cloak noun **1** loose sleeveless outer garment ▷ verb **2** to cover or conceal

cloakroom noun room for coats or a room with toilets and washbasins in a public building

clock noun **1** instrument for

showing the time **2** device with a dial for recording or measuring ▷ verb **3** to record (time) with a stopwatch, especially in the calculation of a speed

clockwise adverb, adjective in the direction in which the hands of a clock rotate

clockwork noun **1** mechanism similar to that of a clock, used in wind-up toys **2 like clockwork** with complete regularity and precision

clog clogs clogging clogged verb **1** to block or obstruct ▷ noun **2** wooden or wooden-soled shoe

cloister noun covered pillared arcade, usually in a monastery

clone noun **1** animal or plant produced artificially from the cells of another animal or plant, and identical to the original **2** informal person who closely resembles another ▷ verb **3** to produce a clone

close¹ verb **1** to shut **2** to prevent access to **3** to finish business or stop operating **4** to end **5** to bring or come nearer together ▷ noun **6** end or conclusion

▷ **closed** adjective > **close down** verb to stop operating or working: *The factory closed down many years ago*

close² adjective **1** near: *a restaurant close to their home* **2** intimate: *close friends* **3** careful or thorough: *close scrutiny* **4** (of weather) oppressive or stifling ▷ adverb **5** near: *He walked close behind her* **6** closely or tightly: *She held him close* > **closely** adverb > **closeness** noun

closed shop noun place of work in which all workers must belong to a particular trade union

closet noun **1** US cupboard **2** small private room ▷ adjective **3** private or secret ▷ verb **4** to shut (oneself) away in private

close-up noun detailed close view of something, especially a photograph taken close to the subject

closure noun closing

clot clots clotting clotted noun **1** soft thick lump formed from liquid **2** Brit, Aust, NZ informal stupid person ▷ verb **3** to form soft thick lumps

cloth noun **1** woven fabric **2** piece of woven fabric

clothe clothes clothing clothed verb **1** to put clothes on **2** to provide with clothes

clothes plural noun things people wear to cover them and keep them warm

clothing noun clothes collectively

cloud noun **1** mass of condensed water vapour floating in the sky **2** floating mass of smoke, dust, etc ▷ verb **3** cloud over to become cloudy **4** to confuse: *His judgment was clouded by alcohol*

cloudy cloudier cloudiest adjective **1** having a lot of clouds **2** (of liquid) not clear

clout informal noun **1** hard blow **2** power or influence: *I don't have much clout round here* ▷ verb **3** to hit hard

clove noun **1** dried closed flower bud of a tropical tree, used as a spice **2** segment of a bulb of garlic

clover noun **1** plant with three-lobed leaves **2 in clover** informal in ease or luxury

clown noun **1** comic entertainer in a circus **2** amusing person

3 stupid person ▷ *verb* **4** to behave foolishly **5** to perform as a clown

cloying *adjective* unpleasantly sickly, sweet or sentimental

club clubs clubbing clubbed *noun* **1** association of people with common interests **2** building used by such a group **3** thick stick used as a weapon **4** stick with a curved end used to hit the ball in golf **5** playing card with black three-leaved symbols ▷ *verb* **6** to hit with a club **7 club together** to combine resources for a common purpose

cluck *noun* **1** low clicking noise made by a hen ▷ *verb* **2** to make this noise

clue *noun* **1** something that helps to solve a mystery or puzzle **2 not have a clue** to be completely baffled

clump *noun* **1** small group of things or people **2** dull heavy tread ▷ *verb* **3 clump about** to walk or tread with heavy footsteps

clumsy clumsier clumsiest *adjective* **1** lacking skill or physical coordination **2** said or done without thought or tact > **clumsily** *adverb* > **clumsiness** *noun*

cluster *noun* **1** small close group ▷ *verb* **2** to gather or be gathered in clusters

clutch *verb* **1** to grasp tightly **2 clutch at** to try to get hold of ▷ *noun* **3** foot pedal that the driver of a motor vehicle presses when changing gear **4 in someone's clutches** in someone's power or at the mercy of someone

clutter *verb* **1** to fill (a room, desk,

etc) with objects that take up space and cause mess ▷ *noun* **2** untidy mess

cm *symbol* centimetre

co- *prefix* together, joint or jointly: *coproduction*

coach *noun* **1** long-distance bus **2** railway carriage **3** large four-wheeled horse-drawn carriage **4** person who coaches a sport or a subject ▷ *verb* **5** to train or teach

coal *noun* **1** black rock consisting mainly of carbon, used as fuel **2** burning piece of coal

coalition *noun* temporary alliance especially between political parties forming a government

coarse *adjective* **1** rough in texture **2** rude or offensive > **coarsely** *adverb* > **coarseness** *noun*

coast *noun* **1** place where the land meets the sea ▷ *verb* **2** to move by momentum, without the use of power > **coastal** *adjective* in or near the coast

coastguard *noun* **1** organization that aids ships and swimmers in trouble and prevents smuggling **2** member of this

coastline *noun* outline of a coast: *a rugged coastline*

coat *noun* **1** outer garment with long sleeves **2** animal's fur or hair **3** covering layer: *a coat of paint* ▷ *verb* **4** to cover (something) with a layer > **coating** *noun* covering layer

coax *verb* **1** to persuade (someone) gently **2** to obtain (something) by persistent coaxing

cobalt *noun* Chemistry brittle silvery-white metallic element which is used for producing a blue dye

cobble noun 1 cobblestone
2 **cobble together** to put
together clumsily

cobbler noun shoe mender

cobra noun venomous hooded
snake of Asia and Africa

cobweb noun very thin net that a
spider spins for catching insects

cocaine noun addictive drug
used as a narcotic and as an
anaesthetic

cock noun 1 male bird, especially of
domestic fowl 2 stopcock ▷ verb
3 to draw back (the hammer of a
gun) to firing position 4 to lift
and turn (part of the body)

cockatoo cockatoos noun crested
parrot of Australia or the East
Indies

cockerel noun young domestic
cock

cockney noun 1 native of the East
End of London 2 London dialect

cockpit noun 1 pilot's
compartment in an aircraft
2 driver's compartment in a
racing car

cockroach noun large dark-
coloured insect often found in
dirty rooms

cocktail noun alcoholic drink
made from several ingredients

cocky cockier cockiest; cockies
informal adjective 1 cheeky or too
self-confident ▷ *noun* 2 *Aust*
cockatoo 3 *Aust, NZ informal*
farmer > **cockiness** noun

cocoa noun 1 powder made from
the seed of the cacao tree 2 drink
made from this powder

coconut noun 1 very large nut
with white flesh, milky juice and
a hard hairy shell 2 edible flesh
of this fruit

cocoon noun 1 silky protective
covering of a silkworm or other
insect larva, in which the pupa
develops 2 protective covering
▷ *verb* 3 to wrap up tightly for
protection

cod noun large food fish of the
North Atlantic

   ● The plural of **cod** is also **cod**

code noun 1 system of letters,
symbols or prearranged signals
by which messages can be
communicated secretly or
briefly 2 group of numbers and
letters which is used to identify
something 3 set of principles or
rules: *a code of practice* ▷ *verb* 4 to
put into code > **coded** *adjective*

coffee noun 1 drink made from
the roasted and ground seeds of a
tropical shrub 2 beanlike seeds of
this shrub ▷ *adjective* 3 medium-
brown

coffin noun box in which a dead
body is buried or cremated

cog noun 1 one of the teeth
on the rim of a gearwheel
2 unimportant person in a big
organization

cognac noun French brandy

coherent *adjective* 1 logical
and consistent 2 capable of
intelligible speech > **coherence**
noun logical or natural connection
or consistency

cohesive *adjective* sticking
together to form a whole

coil verb 1 to wind in loops 2 to
move in a winding course ▷ *noun*
3 something coiled 4 single loop
of this

coin noun 1 piece of metal money
2 metal currency collectively
▷ *verb* 3 to invent (a word or

phrase) **4 coin it in** *informal* to earn money quickly

coinage *noun* **1** coins collectively **2** currency of a country **3** newly invented word or phrase **4** act of coining

coincide *verb* **1** to happen at the same time **2** to agree or correspond exactly

coincidence *noun* **1** chance occurrence of simultaneous or apparently connected events: *I had moved to London, and by coincidence, Helen had too* **2** coinciding > **coincidental** *adjective* resulting from coincidence > **coincidentally** *adverb*

coke *noun* solid fuel left after gas has been distilled from coal

colander *noun* bowl-shaped container with holes in it for straining or rinsing food

cold *adjective* **1** lacking heat **2** lacking affection or enthusiasm **3** (of a colour) giving an impression of coldness ▷ *noun* **4** lack of heat **5** mild illness causing a runny nose, sneezing and coughing > **coldly** *adverb* > **coldness** *noun* lack of affection or enthusiasm

cold-blooded *adjective* **1** showing no pity **2** having a body temperature that varies according to the surrounding temperature

cold war *noun* political hostility between countries without actual warfare

coleslaw *noun* salad dish of shredded raw cabbage in a dressing

colic *noun* severe pains in the stomach and bowels

collaborate *verb* **1** to work with another on a project **2** to cooperate with an enemy invader > **collaboration** *noun* **1** act of working with others on a joint project **2** something created by working with others **3** act of helping the enemy occupiers of one's country > **collaborator** *noun*

collage *noun* **1** art form in which various materials or objects are glued onto a surface **2** picture made in this way

collapse *verb* **1** to fall down suddenly **2** to fail completely **3** to fold compactly, especially for storage ▷ *noun* **4** collapsing **5** sudden failure or breakdown

collapsible *adjective* able to be folded up for storage

collar *noun* **1** part of a garment round the neck **2** band put round an animal's neck **3** cut of meat from an animal's neck ▷ *verb* **4** *Brit, Aust, NZ informal* to seize or arrest **5** *informal* to catch in order to speak to

collateral *noun* money or property which is used as a guarantee that someone will repay a loan, and which the lender can take if the loan is not repaid

colleague *noun* fellow worker, especially in a profession

collect *verb* **1** to gather together: *collecting money for charity* **2** to accumulate (stamps, coins, etc) as a hobby **3** to go to a place to fetch (a person or thing); pick up

collected *adjective* calm and self-controlled

collection *noun* **1** things collected: *a collection of paintings*

2 collecting: *tax collection* **3** sum of money collected: *a collection for charity*

collective *adjective* **1** of or done by a group: *a collective decision* ▷ *noun* **2** group of people working together on an enterprise and sharing the benefits from it > **collectively** *adverb*

collective noun *noun* noun that refers to a single unit made up of a number of things: *flock; swarm*

college *noun* **1** place where students study after they have left school **2** name given to some secondary schools **3** one of the institutions into which some universities are divided **4** NZ teacher training college

collide *verb* to crash together violently

collie *noun* silky-haired dog used for rounding up sheep

colliery collieries *noun* coal mine

collision *noun* violent crash between moving objects

colloquial *adjective* suitable for informal speech or writing > **colloquialism** *noun* colloquial word or phrase > **colloquially** *adverb*

cologne *noun* mild perfume

colon *noun* **1** punctuation mark (:) **2** part of the large intestine connected to the rectum

colonel *noun* senior commissioned army or air-force officer

colonial *noun* **1** inhabitant of a colony ▷ *adjective* **2** relating to a colony **3** *Aust* of the period of Australian history before the Federation in 1901 > **colonialism** *noun* policy of acquiring and maintaining colonies

colonize *verb* **1** to establish a colony in (an area) **2** (of plants and animals) to become established in (a new environment) > **colonization** *noun*: *plans for the colonization of Mars*

colony colonies *noun* **1** group of people who settle in a new country but remain under the rule of their homeland **2** territory occupied by a colony **3** group of people or animals of the same kind living together

colossal *adjective* very large

colour *noun* **1** appearance of things as a result of reflecting light **2** substance that gives colour **3** skin complexion of a person **4** quality that makes something interesting or exciting: *bringing more culture and colour to the city* ▷ *verb* **5** to apply colour to **6** to influence (someone's judgment) > **colouring** *noun*

colour-blind *adjective* unable to distinguish between certain colours

colourful *adjective* **1** with bright or varied colours **2** vivid or distinctive in character: *a colourful personality* > **colourfully** *adverb*

colt *noun* young male horse

column *noun* **1** pillar **2** vertical division of a newspaper page **3** regular feature in a newspaper **4** vertical arrangement of numbers **5** narrow formation of troops

columnist *noun* journalist who writes a regular feature in a newspaper

coma noun state of deep unconsciousness

comb noun toothed implement for arranging the hair ▷ verb 1 to use a comb on 2 to search (a place) with great care

combat noun 1 fight or struggle: his first experience of combat ▷ verb 2 to fight or struggle against

combination noun 1 mixture 2 act of combining or state of being combined 3 set of numbers that opens a special lock

combine verb 1 to bring or mix (different things) together 2 to come together ▷ noun 3 association of people or firms for a common purpose 4 (also **combine harvester**) machine that reaps and threshes grain in one process

combustion noun process of burning

come comes coming came come verb 1 to move towards a place or arrive there 2 to occur 3 to reach a specified point or condition: The sea water came up to his waist 4 to be produced or be available: It also comes in other colours 5 **come from** to be or have been a native or resident of: My mother comes from Norway 6 to become: a dream come true > **come about** verb to happen: The discussion came about because of the proposed changes > **come across** verb 1 to meet or find by accident 2 **come across as** to give the impression of being > **come off** verb 1 to emerge from a situation in a certain position: The people who have come off worst are the poor 2 informal to have the intended effect: It was a gamble that didn't

come off > **come on** verb 1 to make progress 2 (of power or water) to start running or functioning 3 to begin: I think I've got a cold coming on > **come round** verb 1 to recover consciousness 2 to change your opinion > **come to** verb 1 to recover consciousness 2 to amount to (a total figure) > **come up** verb 1 to be mentioned 2 to be about to happen 3 **come up against** to come into conflict with 4 **come up with** to produce or propose: a knack for coming up with great ideas

comeback noun informal return to a former position or status: The sixties singing star is making a comeback

comedian noun 1 entertainer who tells jokes 2 person who performs in comedy

comedienne noun a female comedian

comedy comedies noun 1 humorous play, film or programme 2 such works as a genre

comet noun object that travels around the sun leaving a bright trail behind it

comfort noun 1 physical ease or wellbeing 2 something or someone that brings relief from worries or unhappiness 3 **comforts** things that make life easier or more pleasant ▷ verb 4 to soothe or console

comfortable adjective 1 providing comfort 2 physically relaxed 3 informal well-off financially > **comfortably** adverb

comic adjective 1 funny 2 of or relating to comedy ▷ noun 3 comedian 4 magazine containing strip cartoons

comical *adjective* amusing

comma *noun* punctuation mark (,)

command *verb* 1 to order 2 to have authority over 3 to deserve and get: *a public figure who commands respect* 4 to have (a view over something) ▷ *noun* 5 authoritative instruction that something must be done 6 authority to command 7 knowledge (of language) 8 military or naval unit with a specific function

commandant *noun* army officer in charge of a place or group of people

commander *noun* 1 military officer in command of a group or operation 2 middle-ranking naval officer

commandment *noun* one of ten rules of behaviour that, according to the Old Testament, people should obey

commando commandos or **commandoes** *noun* member of a military unit trained for swift raids in enemy territory

commemorate *verb* to honour or keep alive the memory of > **commemoration** *noun*: *a commemoration of the battle of Stalingrad* > **commemorative** *adjective*: *a commemorative plaque*

commence *verb formal* to begin > **commencement** *noun* beginning of something

commend *verb* 1 to praise 2 to recommend > **commendable** *adjective*: *a commendable achievement* > **commendation** *noun*: *a commendation from the judges*

comment *noun* 1 remark 2 talk or gossip 3 explanatory note ▷ *verb* 4 to make a comment

commentary commentaries *noun* 1 spoken accompaniment to a broadcast or film 2 explanatory notes

commentator *noun* someone who gives a radio or television commentary

commerce *noun* buying and selling of goods and services

commercial *adjective* 1 of commerce 2 (of television or radio) paid for by advertisers 3 having profit as the main aim ▷ *noun* 4 television or radio advertisement > **commercially** *adverb*

commission *noun* 1 piece of work that an artist is asked to do 2 duty or task 3 percentage paid to a salesperson for each sale made 4 group of people appointed to perform certain duties 5 committing of a crime 6 *Military* rank or authority officially given to an officer 7 out of commission not in working order ▷ *verb* 8 to place an order for 9 *Military* to give a commission to 10 to grant authority to

commit commits committing committed *verb* 1 to perform (a crime or error) 2 to pledge (yourself) to a course of action 3 to send (someone) to prison or hospital > **committal** *noun* sending someone to prison or hospital

commitment *noun* 1 dedication to a cause 2 engagement or obligation that: *business commitments*

committed *adjective* having strong beliefs; devout: *a committed feminist*

committee *noun* group of people appointed to perform a specified service or function

commodity commodities *noun formal* something that can be bought or sold

common *adjective* 1 occurring often 2 belonging to two or more people; shared 3 belonging to the whole community: *common property* 4 lacking in taste or manners ▷ *noun* 5 area of grassy land belonging to a community > **commonly** *adverb*

commoner *noun* person who does not belong to the nobility

commonplace *adjective* happening often

common sense *noun* ability to act or react sensibly, using good judgment

commotion *noun* noisy disturbance

communal *adjective* shared

commune *noun* 1 group of people who live together and share everything ▷ *verb* 2 **commune with** to feel very close to: *communing with nature*

communicate *verb* to make known or share (information, thoughts or feelings)

communication *noun* 1 process by which people or animals exchange information 2 thing communicated 3 *formal* letter or telephone call 4 **communications** means of travelling or sending messages

communicative *adjective* talking freely

communion *noun* 1 sharing of thoughts or feelings 2 **Communion** Christian ritual of sharing consecrated bread and wine 3 religious group with shared beliefs and practices

communism *noun* belief that all property and means of production should be shared by the community > **communist** *noun, adjective*

community communities *noun* 1 all the people living in one district 2 group with shared origins or interests

commute *verb* to travel daily to and from work

compact *adjective* 1 closely packed 2 taking up very little space 3 concise or brief ▷ *verb* 4 to pack closely together

compact disc *noun* plastic disc on which sound, images and data are or can be stored for use in CD players and computers

companion *noun* person who associates with or accompanies someone: *a travelling companion* > **companionship** *noun* relationship of friends or companions

company companies *noun* 1 business organization; firm 2 group of actors 3 having someone with you: *I enjoyed her company* 4 person or people with you

comparable *adjective* similar in size or quality: *The skill is comparable to playing the violin* > **comparably** *adverb*

comparative *adjective* 1 relative 2 involving comparison: *He studied comparative religion* 3 *Grammar* denoting the form of an adjective or adverb indicating *more* ▷ *noun* **4** *Grammar* comparative form of a word, such as *colder, faster, better* > **comparatively** *adverb*

compare *verb* **1** to examine (things) and point out the resemblances or differences **2 compare to** to liken (something) to **3** (often followed by *with*) to be worth in comparison: *How do they compare?*

comparison *noun* **1** analysis of the similarities and differences between things **2** comparing

compartment *noun* **1** section of a railway carriage **2** separate section

compass *noun* **1** instrument for showing direction, with a needle that points north **2** **compasses** hinged instrument for drawing circles; (also **pair of compasses**)

compassion *noun* pity or sympathy > **compassionate** *adjective* showing or having compassion

compatible *adjective* able to exist, work or be used together > **compatibility** *noun*

compatriot *noun* fellow countryman or countrywoman

compel *compels compelling compelled verb* to force (someone to be or do something)

compelling *adjective* **1** extremely interesting: *a compelling novel* **2** convincing: *compelling new evidence*

compensate *verb* **1** to make amends to (someone), especially for injury or loss **2 compensate for** to cancel out the effects of something): *The trip more than*

compensated for the hardship > **compensation** *noun* payment to make up for loss or injury > **compensatory** *adjective*: *compensatory payments*

compere *noun* **1** person who presents a stage, radio or television show ▷ *verb* **2** to be the compere of

compete *verb* **1** to try to be more successful or popular than other similar people or organizations **2** to take part in a competition

competent *adjective* able to carry out tasks satisfactorily > **competently** *adverb*

competition *noun* **1** act of competing **2** event in which people compete **3** people against whom you compete

competitive *adjective* **1** involving rivalry **2** showing the urge to compete **3** cheap enough to be successful when compared with similar commerical rivals > **competitively** *adverb*

competitor *noun* person, team or firm that competes

compile *verb* to collect and arrange (information), especially to make a book > **compilation** *noun*: *a compilation of his jazz works* > **compiler** *noun*

complacent *adjective* self-satisfied and unconcerned, and therefore not taking necessary action > **complacency** *noun*: *complacency about the risks of flooding* > **complacently** *adverb*

complain *verb* **1** to express resentment or displeasure **2 complain of** to say that you are suffering from (an illness) > **complaint** *noun*

1 complaining **2** mild illness

complement *noun* **1** thing that completes something **2** complete amount or number **3** *Grammar* word or words added to a verb to complete the meaning ▷ *verb* **4** to make complete ▷ **complementary** *adjective*: *two complementary strategies are necessary*

- Do not confuse *complement* and *compliment*. The *e* spelling is for senses that involve completion

complete *adjective* **1** thorough or absolute **2** finished **3** having all the necessary parts ▷ *verb* **4** to finish **5** to make whole or perfect ▷ **completely** *adverb* ▷ **completion** *noun* finishing

complex *adjective* **1** made up of parts **2** complicated ▷ *noun* **3** whole made up of parts **4** group of unconscious feelings that influences behaviour ▷ **complexity** *noun*: *the complexity of modern weapons systems*

complexion *noun* **1** skin of the face **2** character or nature

complicate *verb* to make or become complex or difficult to deal with

complicated *adjective* so complex as to be difficult to understand or deal with

complication *noun* something that makes a situation more difficult to deal with

compliment *noun* **1** expression of praise **2** **compliments** formal greetings ▷ *verb* **3** to praise

- Do not confuse *compliment* and *complement*.

complimentary *adjective* **1** expressing praise **2** free of charge

comply complies complying complied *verb* (followed by *with*) to act in accordance (with)

component *noun*, *adjective* (being) part of a whole

compose *verb* **1** to put together **2** to be the component parts of **3** to create (a piece of music or writing) **4** to calm (yourself) **5** to arrange artistically

composed *adjective* calm and in control of your feelings

composer *noun* person who writes music

composition *noun* **1** way that something is put together or arranged **2** work of art, especially a musical one **3** essay **4** composing

compost *noun* decayed plants used as a fertilizer

composure *noun* ability to stay calm

compound *noun* **1** thing, especially a chemical, made up of two or more combined parts or elements **2** fenced enclosure containing buildings ▷ *adjective* **3** made up of two or more combined parts or element ▷ *verb* **4** to combine or make by combining **5** to intensify or make worse

comprehend *verb formal* to understand ▷ **comprehension** *noun*: *This was beyond her comprehension*

comprehensible *adjective* able to be understood

comprehensive *adjective* **1** including everything

necessary or relevant ▷ noun
2 Brit comprehensive school
>**comprehensively** adverb

compress verb **1** to squeeze together **2** to make shorter ▷ noun **3** pad applied to stop bleeding or cool inflammation >**compression** noun

comprise verb formal to be made up of or to make up

compromise noun **1** settlement reached by concessions on each side ▷ verb **2** to settle a dispute by making concessions **3** to put (oneself or another person) in a dishonourable position >**compromising** adjective revealing an embarrassing or guilty secret about someone: *compromising photographs*

compulsion noun **1** irresistible urge **2** forcing by threats or violence

compulsive adjective **1** resulting from or acting from a compulsion **2** irresistible or absorbing: *compulsive viewing*

compulsory adjective required by rules or laws

computer noun electronic machine that stores and processes data

computer-aided design noun use of computers and computer graphics to help design things

computerize verb to adapt (a system or process) so that it can be handled by computer

computing noun use of computers and the writing of programs or them

comrade noun **1** fellow member of a union or socialist political party **2** fellow soldier >**comradeship**

noun friendship between a number of people doing the same job or sharing the same difficulties

con cons conning conned informal noun short for **confidence trick 2 pros and cons** see pro ▷ verb **3** to deceive or swindle

concave adjective curving inwards

conceal verb **1** to cover and hide **2** to keep secret >**concealment** noun: *concealment of weapons*

concede verb **1** to admit (something) as true or correct **2** to acknowledge defeat in (a contest or argument)

conceit noun **1** too high an opinion of yourself **2** far-fetched or clever comparison

conceited adjective having an excessively high opinion of yourself

conceivable adjective imaginable or possible >**conceivably** adverb

conceive verb **1** to imagine or think **2** to form in the mind **3** to become pregnant

concentrate verb **1** to fix your attention or efforts on something **2** to bring or come together in large numbers in one place **3** to make (a liquid) stronger by removing water from it ▷ noun **4** concentrated liquid >**concentration** noun **1** concentrating **2** proportion of a substance in a mixture or solution

concentrated adjective (of a liquid) made stronger by having water removed

concentration camp noun prison camp for civilian prisoners, especially in Nazi Germany

concept noun abstract or

a b c d e f g h i j k l m n o p q r s t u v w x y z

general idea > **conceptual** *adjective* of or based on concepts > **conceptually** *adverb*

conception *noun* 1 notion, idea or plan 2 process by which a woman becomes pregnant

concern *noun* 1 anxiety or worry 2 something that is of importance to someone 3 business or firm > *verb* 4 to worry (someone) 5 to involve (yourself) 6 to be relevant or important to

concerning *preposition* about or regarding

concert *noun* 1 musical entertainment 2 **in concert** a working together b (of musicians) performing live

concerted *adjective* done together

concerto concertos or concerti *noun* large-scale composition for a solo instrument and orchestra

concession *noun* 1 grant of rights, land or property 2 reduction in price for a specified category of people 3 conceding 4 thing conceded

conch conches *noun* 1 shellfish with a large spiral shell 2 its shell

concise *adjective* brief and to the point > **concisely** *adverb*

conclude *verb* 1 to decide by reasoning 2 to come or bring to an end 3 to arrange or settle finally > **concluding** *adjective*

conclusion *noun* 1 decision based on reasoning 2 ending 3 final arrangement or settlement

conclusive *adjective* ending doubt, convincing > **conclusively** *adverb*

concoct *verb* 1 to make up (a story or plan) 2 to make by combining ingredients > **concoction** *noun*: *a concoction of honey, yogurt and fruit*

concourse *noun* 1 large open public place where people can gather 2 large crowd

concrete *noun* 1 mixture of cement, sand, stone and water, used in building > *adjective* 2 made of concrete 3 definite, rather than general or vague 4 real or solid, not abstract

concubine *noun* History woman living in a man's house but not married to him and kept for his sexual pleasure

concur concurs concurring concurred *verb* formal to agree

concurrent *adjective* happening at the same time or place > **concurrently** *adverb* at the same time

concussion *noun* sickness or loss of consciousness caused by a blow to the head > **concussed** *adjective* having concussion

condemn *verb* 1 to express disapproval of 2 to sentence: *He was condemned to death* 3 to force into an unpleasant situation 4 to declare (something) unfit for use > **condemnation** *noun*: *widespread condemnation of Saturday's killings*

condensation *noun* coating of tiny drops formed on a surface by steam or vapour

condense *verb* 1 to make shorter 2 to turn from gas into liquid

condescending *adjective* behaving in a way that suggests you feel superior to someone; patronizing

condition *noun* 1 particular state of being 2 necessary requirement for something else to happen 3 restriction or qualification 4 state of health or physical

fitness **5** medical problem
6 conditions circumstances
7 on condition that only if ▷ *verb*
8 to train or influence to behave
in a particular way **9** to treat with
conditioner

conditional *adjective* depending
on circumstances

condolence *noun* **1** sympathy
2 condolences expression of
sympathy

condom *noun* rubber sheath worn
on the penis or in the vagina
during sexual intercourse to
prevent conception or infection

condominium *noun Aust,
US, Canadian* block of flats in
which each flat is owned by the
occupant

condone *verb* to overlook or
forgive (wrongdoing)

conducive *adjective* **conducive to**
likely to lead to

conduct *noun* **1** management of
an activity **2** behaviour ▷ *verb*
3 to carry out (a task) **4** *formal*
to behave (oneself) **5** to direct
(musicians) by moving your
hands or a baton **6** to lead or
guide **7** to transmit (heat or
electricity)

conductor *noun* **1** person who
conducts musicians **2** official
on a bus who collects fares
3 something that conducts heat
or electricity

cone *noun* **1** object with a circular
base, tapering to a point **2** cone-
shaped ice-cream wafer **3** *Brit,
Aust, NZ* plastic cone used as
a traffic marker on the roads
4 scaly fruit of a conifer tree

confectionery *noun* sweets

confederation *noun* organization

formed for business or political
purposes

confer **confers** **conferring**
conferred *verb* **1** to discuss
together **2** to grant or give

conference *noun* meeting for
discussion

confess *verb* **1** to admit (a fault or
crime) **2** to admit to be true **3** to
declare (your sins) to God or a
priest, in the hope of forgiveness

confession *noun* **1** something
confessed **2** confessing

confessional *noun* small stall in
which a priest hears confessions

confetti *noun* small pieces
of coloured paper thrown at
weddings

confidant *noun formal* person
confided in > **confidante** *noun*
woman or girl confided in

confide *verb* **1** to tell someone (a
secret) **2** to entrust

confidence *noun* **1** trust **2** self-
assurance **3** something confided
4 in confidence as a secret

confident *adjective* sure, especially
of yourself > **confidently** *adverb*

confidential *adjective* **1** private
or secret **2** entrusted with
someone's secret affairs
> **confidentially** *adverb*
> **confidentiality** *noun: the
confidentiality of the client-doctor
relationship*

confine *verb* **1** to keep within
bounds **2** to restrict the
free movement of ▷ *noun*
3 confines boundaries or limits
> **confinement** *noun* **1** being
confined **2** period of childbirth

confined *adjective* (of a space)
small and enclosed

confirm *verb* **1** to prove to be

a
b
c
d
e
f
g
h
i
j
k
l
m
n
o
p
q
r
s
t
u
v
w
x
y
z

true **2** to reaffirm or strengthen **3** *Christianity* to administer the rite of confirmation to

confirmed *adjective* firmly established in a habit or condition

confiscate *verb* to seize (property) by authority

conflict *noun* **1** disagreement **2** struggle or fight ▷ *verb* **3** to be incompatible

conform *verb* **1** to comply with accepted standards or customs **2 conform to, conform with** to be like or in accordance with ▷ **conformist** *noun, adjective* (person) complying with accepted standards or customs ▷ **conformity** *noun* compliance with accepted standards or customs

confront *verb* **1** to face **2** to come face to face with **3** (often followed by *about, with*) to tackle (someone) about something or presenting something as evidence

confrontation *noun* serious argument

confuse *verb* **1** to mix up **2** to perplex or disconcert **3** to make unclear ▷ **confused** *adjective*: *confused thinking* ▷ **confusing** *adjective*: *The statement is highly confusing* ▷ **confusion** *noun*: *confusion about the number of casualties*

congeal *verb* (of a liquid) to become thick and sticky

congenial *adjective* **1** pleasant or agreeable **2** having similar interests and attitudes

congenital *adjective Medicine* (of a condition) existing from birth

congested *adjective* crowded to excess ▷ **congestion** *noun*: *traffic congestion*

conglomerate *noun* **1** large corporation made up of many companies **2** thing made up of several different elements

congratulate *verb* to express pleasure to (someone) at his or her good fortune or success ▷ **congratulatory** *adjective*: *a congratulatory telegram*

congregate *verb* to gather together in a crowd

congregation *noun* people who attend a church

congress *noun* **1** formal meeting for discussion **2 Congress** federal parliament of the US

conical *adjective* cone-shaped

conifer *noun* cone-bearing tree, such as the fir or pine ▷ **coniferous** *adjective*

conjecture *noun* guesswork about something

conjugate *verb* to give the inflections of (a verb)

conjunction *noun* **1** combination **2** simultaneous occurrence of events **3** part of speech joining words, phrases or clauses, such as *and*, *but* or *because* **4** in **conjunction** done or used together

conjurer or **conjuror** *noun* someone who entertains people by doing magic tricks

conker *noun informal* nut of the horse chestnut

connect *verb* **1** to join together **2** to associate in the mind

connection or **connexion** *noun* **1** relationship or association **2** link or bond **3** opportunity to transfer from one public vehicle to another **4** influential acquaintance

connective *noun* word or short phrase that connects clauses, phrases or words

connoisseur *noun* person with special knowledge of the arts, food or drink

connotation *noun* associated idea conveyed by a word

conquer *verb* **1** to defeat **2** to overcome (a difficulty) **3** to take (a place) by force > **conqueror** *noun*

conquest *noun* **1** conquering of a country or group of people **2** lands captured by conquest

conscience *noun* sense of right or wrong as regards thoughts and actions

conscientious *adjective* painstaking > **conscientiously** *adverb*

conscious *adjective* **1** alert and awake **2** aware **3** deliberate or intentional > **consciously** *adverb* > **consciousness** *noun*: She hit her head and lost consciousness

consecrated *adjective* (of a building or place) officially declared to be holy

consecutive *adjective* in unbroken succession

consensus *noun* general agreement

consent *noun* **1** agreement or permission ▷ *verb* **2** (followed by *to*) to agree (to something)

consequence *noun* **1** result or effect **2** *formal* importance: *We paid little of consequence*

consequent *adjective* resulting > **consequently** *adverb* as a result;

therefore

conservation *noun* **1** protection of natural resources and the environment **2** conserving > **conservationist** *noun*

conservative *adjective* **1** opposing change **2** moderate or cautious **3** conventional in style **4** **Conservative** of the Conservative Party, the British right-wing political party which believes in private enterprise and capitalism ▷ *noun* **5** conservative person **6** **Conservative** supporter or member of the Conservative Party > **conservatism** *noun* > **conservatively** *adverb*

conservatory *conservatories noun* room with glass walls and a glass roof, attached to a house

conserve *verb* **1** to protect from harm, decay or loss **2** to preserve (fruit) with sugar ▷ *noun* **3** jam containing large pieces of fruit

consider *verb* **1** to regard as **2** to think about **3** to be considerate of **4** to discuss **5** to look at

considerable *adjective* large in amount or degree > **considerably** *adverb*

considerate *adjective* thoughtful towards others

consideration *noun* **1** careful thought **2** fact that should be considered **3** thoughtfulness **4** payment for a service

considered *adjective* presented or thought out with care

considering *preposition* taking (a specified fact) into account

consign *verb* **1** to put somewhere **2** to send (goods)

consignment *noun* shipment

of goods

consist *verb* **1 consist of** to be made up of **2 consist in** to have as its main or only feature

consistency consistencies *noun* **1** being consistent **2** degree of thickness or smoothness

consistent *adjective* **1** unchanging or constant **2 consistent with** in agreement with or tallying with ▷ **consistently** *adverb*

console *verb* **1** to comfort (someone) in distress ▷ *noun* **2** panel of controls for electronic equipment

consolidate *verb* **1** to make or become stronger or more stable **2** to combine into a whole ▷ **consolidation** *noun: the consolidation of power*

consonant *noun* **1** speech sound made by partially or completely blocking the breath stream, such as *b* or *f* **2** letter representing this

consort *verb* **1 consort with** to keep company (with) ▷ *noun* **2** husband or wife of a monarch

consortium consortia or **consortiums** *noun* association of business firms

conspicuous *adjective* **1** clearly visible **2** noteworthy or striking ▷ **conspicuously** *adverb*

conspiracy conspiracies *noun* **1** conspiring **2** plan made by conspiring

conspirator *noun* someone involved in a conspiracy

conspire *verb* **1** to plan a crime together in secret **2** *literary* to act together as if by design

constable *noun* police officer of the lowest rank

constabulary constabularies

noun police force of an area

constant *adjective* **1** continuous **2** unchanging **3** faithful ▷ *noun* **4** unvarying quantity **5** something that stays the same ▷ **constancy** *noun* ▷ **constantly** *adverb*

constellation *noun* group of stars

consternation *noun* anxiety or dismay

constipated *adjective* unable to empty your bowels ▷ **constipation** *noun* difficulty in emptying your bowels

constituency constituencies *noun* **1** area represented by a Member of Parliament **2** voters in such an area

constituent *noun* **1** member of a constituency **2** component part ▷ *adjective* **3** forming part of a whole

constitute *verb* to form or make up

constitution *noun* **1** principles on which a state is governed **2** physical condition **3** structure ▷ **constitutional** *adjective* **1** of a constitution **2** in accordance with a political constitution ▷ **constitutionally** *adverb*

constrained *adjective* compelled or forced (to do something)

constraint *noun* something that limits someone's freedom of action

constrict *verb* to make narrower by squeezing ▷ **constriction** *noun: severe constriction of the arteries*

construct *verb* to build or put together

construction *noun* **1** constructing **2** thing

constructed **3** interpretation **4** *Grammar* way in which words are arranged in a sentence, clause or phrase

constructive *adjective* (of advice, criticism, etc) useful and helpful > **constructively** *adverb*

consul *noun* official representing a state in a foreign country > **consular** *adjective*: *consular officials*

consulate *noun* workplace or position of a consul

consult *verb* to ask advice from or discuss matters with (someone)

consultancy *noun* **1** organization whose members give expert advice on a subject **2** work or position of a consultant

consultant *noun* **1** specialist doctor with a senior position in a hospital **2** specialist who gives professional advice

consultation *noun* **1** act of consulting **2** meeting for discussion or the seeking of advice > **consultative** *adjective* giving advice

consume *verb* **1** to eat or drink **2** to use up **3** to destroy **4** to obsess

consumer *noun* person who buys goods or uses services

consumerism *noun* belief that a country will have a strong economy if its people buy a lot of goods and spend a lot of money

consuming *adjective* (of passion, interest, etc) most important and very engrossing

consummate *verb* **1** to make (a marriage) legal by sexual intercourse **2** to complete or fulfil ▷ *adjective* **3** supremely skilled: *a*

consummate politician **4** complete or extreme: *consummate skill* > **consummation** *noun*: *the consummation of marriage*

consumption *noun* **1** amount consumed **2** consuming **3** old-fashioned tuberculosis

contact *noun* **1** communicating **2** touching **3** useful acquaintance **4** connection between two electrical conductors in a circuit ▷ *verb* **5** to get in touch with

contact lens *noun* lens placed on the eyeball to correct defective vision

contagious *adjective* spreading by contact

contain *verb* **1** to hold or be capable of holding **2** to consist of **3** to control or restrain > **containment** *noun* prevention of the spread of something harmful

container *noun* **1** object used to hold or store things in **2** large standard-sized box for transporting cargo by truck or ship

contaminate *verb* **1** to make impure or pollute **2** to make radioactive > **contamination** *noun*: *the contamination of the sea*

contemplate *verb* **1** to think deeply about **2** to consider as a possibility **3** to gaze at > **contemplation** *noun*: *He was deep in contemplation* > **contemplative** *adjective*: *a quiet, contemplative person*

contemporary contemporaries *adjective* **1** present-day or modern **2** living or occurring at the same time ▷ *noun* **3** person or thing living or occurring at the same time as another

a b c d e f g h i j k l m n o p q r s t u v w x y z

contempt noun 1 dislike and disregard for the authority of a court

contemptible adjective not worthy of any respect

contemptuous adjective showing contempt > **contemptuously** adverb

contend verb 1 contend with 2 to deal with 2 formal to state or assert 3 to compete

contented adjective happy and satisfied with your life > **contentedly** adverb > **contentment** noun: a strong feeling of contentment

contention noun formal 1 disagreement or dispute 2 point asserted in argument

contest noun 1 competition or struggle ▷ verb 2 to dispute or object to 3 to fight or compete for

contestant noun person who takes part in a contest

context noun 1 circumstances of an event or fact 2 words before and after a word or sentence that help make its meaning clear

continent noun 1 one of the earth's large masses of land 2 **the Continent** mainland of Europe > **continental** adjective: the continental crust

contingency contingencies noun something that may happen

contingent noun 1 group of people that represents or is part of a larger group ▷ adjective 2 **contingent on** dependent on (something uncertain)

continual adjective 1 constant 2 recurring frequently > **continually** adverb

continuation noun 1 continuing 2 part added

continue continues continuing continued verb 1 to (cause to) remain in a condition or place 2 to carry on (doing something) 3 to resume after an interruption

continuous adjective continuing uninterrupted > **continuously** adverb

contort verb to twist out of shape > **contorted** adjective: faces contorted with hatred

contour noun 1 outline 2 (also **contour line**) line on a map joining places of the same height

contra- prefix against or contrasting: contraflow

contraception noun prevention of pregnancy by artificial means

contraceptive noun 1 device used or pill taken to prevent pregnancy ▷ adjective 2 preventing pregnancy

contract noun 1 (document setting out) a formal agreement ▷ verb 2 to make a formal agreement (to do something) 3 to make or become smaller or shorter 4 to catch (an illness) > **contractual** adjective: contractual obligations

contractor noun firm that supplies materials or labour

contradict verb 1 to declare the opposite of (a statement) to be true 2 to be at variance with > **contradiction** noun: a contradiction of all that the Olympics is supposed to be > **contradictory** adjective: contradictory statements

contraption noun strange-looking device

contrary noun 1 complete opposite ▷ adjective 2 opposed

completely different **3** perverse or obstinate ▷ *adverb* **4** in opposition

contrast *noun* **1** obvious difference **2** person or thing very different from another ▷ *verb* **3** to compare in order to show differences **4 contrast with** to be very different from

contravene *verb formal* to break (a rule or law)

contribute *verb* **1** to give for a common purpose or fund **2 contribute to** to be partly responsible (for) > **contribution** *noun: charitable contributions* > **contributor** *noun: Old buses are major contributors to pollution* > **contributory** *adjective: contributory factors*

contrive *verb formal* **1** to make happen **2** to devise or construct

contrived *adjective* planned or artificial

control **controls** **controlling** **controlled** *noun* **1** power to direct something **2** a curb or check **3 controls** instruments used to operate a machine ▷ *verb* **4** to have power over **5** to limit or restrain **6** to regulate or operate > **controller** *noun*

controversial *adjective* causing controversy

controversy **controversies** *noun* fierce argument or debate

conundrum *noun formal* puzzling problem

convalesce *verb* to recover after an illness or operation

convection *noun* transmission of heat in liquids or gases by the circulation of currents

convene *verb formal* **1** to arrange or call (a meeting) **2** to gather for a formal meeting

convenience *noun* **1** quality of being convenient **2** useful object **3** *Brit formal* public toilet

convenient *adjective* **1** suitable or opportune **2** easy to use **3** nearby > **conveniently** *adverb*

convent *noun* **1** building where nuns live or lived **2** school run by nuns

convention *noun* **1** widely accepted view of proper behaviour **2** assembly or meeting **3** formal agreement

conventional *adjective* **1** (unthinkingly) following the accepted customs **2** customary **3** (of weapons or warfare) not nuclear, biological or chemical > **conventionally** *adverb*

converge *verb* to meet or join

conversation *noun* informal talk > **conversational** *adjective: conversational German* > **conversationalist** *noun: a witty conversationalist*

converse *verb* **1** *formal* to have a conversation ▷ *noun* **2** statement or idea that is the opposite of another ▷ *adjective* **3** reversed or opposite > **conversely** *adverb*

convert *verb* **1** to change in form, character or function **2** to cause to change in opinion or belief ▷ *noun* **3** person who has converted to a different belief or religion

convex *adjective* curving outwards

convey *verb* **1** to communicate (information) **2** to carry or transport

conveyor belt *noun* continuous moving belt for transporting things, especially in a factory

convict *verb* **1** to declare guilty ▷ *noun* **2** person serving a prison sentence

conviction *noun* **1** firm belief **2** instance of being convicted

convince *verb* to persuade by argument or evidence

convincing *adjective* believable > **convincingly** *adverb*

convoluted *adjective* **1** coiled or twisted **2** (of an argument or sentence) complex and hard to understand

convoy *noun* group of vehicles or ships travelling together

convulsion *noun* **1** violent muscular spasm **2 convulsions** uncontrollable laughter

coo coos cooing cooed *verb* (of a dove or pigeon) to make a soft murmuring sound

cook *verb* **1** to prepare (food) by heating **2** (of food) to be cooked **3 cook up** *informal* to devise (a story or scheme) ▷ *noun* **4** person who cooks food

cooker *noun Chiefly Brit* apparatus for cooking heated by gas or electricity

cookery *noun* art of cooking

cool *adjective* **1** moderately cold **2** calm and unemotional **3** indifferent or unfriendly **4** *informal* sophisticated or excellent ▷ *verb* **5** to make or become cool ▷ *noun* **6** coolness **7** *informal* calmness or composure > **coolly** *adverb* > **coolness** *noun*

coolabah *noun* Australian eucalypt that grows along rivers

coop[1] *noun* cage or pen for poultry

coop[2] *noun* Brit, US, Aust (shop run by) a cooperative society

cooperate *verb* to work or act together > **cooperation** *noun* cooperation between police and the public

cooperative *adjective* **1** willing to cooperate **2** (of an enterprise) owned and managed collectively ▷ *noun* **3** cooperative organization

cop cops copping copped *informal noun* **1** policeman ▷ *verb* **2** to take or seize

cope *verb* (often followed by *with*) to deal successfully (with something); manage

copious *adjective formal* abundant or plentiful

copper *noun* **1** soft reddish-brown metal **2** copper or bronze coin **3** *Brit informal* policeman

copse *noun* small group of trees growing close together

copulate *verb* to have sexual intercourse > **copulation** *noun*

copy copies copying copied *noun* **1** thing made to look exactly like another **2** single specimen of a book etc **3** material for printing ▷ *verb* **4** to make a copy of **5** to ape or try to be like > **copier** *noun*

copyright *noun* **1** exclusive legal right to reproduce and control a book, work of art, etc ▷ *verb* **2** to take out a copyright on ▷ *adjective* **3** protected by copyright

coral *noun* **1** hard substance formed from the skeletons of very small sea animals ▷ *adjective* **2** orange-pink

cord *noun* **1** thin rope or thick string **2** cordlike structure in the body **3** corduroy

cordial *adjective* **1** warm and friendly ▷ *noun* **2** drink with a fruit base

cordon noun **1** chain of police, soldiers, etc, guarding an area ▷ verb **2** **cordon off** to form a cordon round

corduroy noun cotton fabric with a velvety ribbed surface

core noun **1** central part of certain fruits, containing the seeds **2** central or essential part ▷ verb **3** to remove the core from

cork noun **1** thick light bark of a Mediterranean oak **2** piece of this used as a stopper ▷ verb **3** to seal with a cork

corkscrew noun spiral metal tool for pulling corks from bottles

cormorant noun large dark-coloured long-necked sea bird

corn noun **1** cereal plant such as wheat or oats **2** grain of such plants **3** US, Canadian, Aust, NZ maize **4** painful hard skin on the toe

cornea noun transparent membrane covering the eyeball

corner noun **1** area or angle where two converging lines or surfaces meet **2** place where two streets meet **3** remote place **4** Sport free kick or shot from the corner of the field ▷ verb **5** to force into a difficult or inescapable position **6** (of a vehicle) to turn a corner **7** to obtain a monopoly of

ornet noun **1** brass instrument similar to the trumpet **2** cone-shaped ice-cream wafer

ornflour noun **1** Chiefly Brit fine maize flour **2** NZ fine wheat flour

ornflower noun plant with blue flowers

ornice noun decorative moulding round the top of a wall

corny cornier corniest adjective informal very obvious or sentimental and not at all original: corny old love songs

coronary coronaries noun (also **coronary thrombosis**) condition in which the flow of blood to the heart is blocked by a blood clot

coronation noun ceremony of crowning a monarch

coroner noun Brit, Aust, NZ official responsible for the investigation of violent, sudden or suspicious deaths

coronet noun small crown

corporal noun **1** noncommissioned officer in an army ▷ adjective **2** of the body

corporal punishment noun physical punishment, such as caning

corporate adjective **1** of business corporations **2** shared by a group

corporation noun **1** large business or company **2** city or town council

corps noun **1** military unit with a specific function **2** organized body of people
   ● The plural of corps is also
   ● corps

corpse noun dead body

corpuscle noun red or white blood cell

correa noun Australian shrub with large green and white flowers

correct adjective **1** free from error or true **2** in accordance with accepted standards ▷ verb **3** to put right **4** to indicate the errors in **5** to rebuke or punish > **correctly** adverb > **correction** noun **1** correcting **2** alteration correcting something

>corrective adjective intended to put right something wrong

correlate verb to be closely connected or to have a mutually influential relationship: *Obesity correlates with increased risk of stroke and diabetes* **>correlation** noun: *the correlation between smoking and disease*

correspond verb 1 to be consistent or compatible (with) 2 to be the same or similar 3 to communicate by letter

correspondence noun 1 communication by letters 2 letters so exchanged 3 relationship or similarity

correspondent noun 1 person employed by a newspaper etc to report on a special subject or from a foreign country 2 letter writer

corresponding adjective resulting from a change to something else: *the rise in interest rates and corresponding fall in house values* **>correspondingly** adverb

corridor noun 1 passage in a building or train 2 strip of land or airspace providing access through foreign territory

corroboree noun Aust Aboriginal gathering or dance

corrode verb to eat or be eaten away by chemical action or rust **>corrosion** noun: *metal corrosion* **>corrosive** adjective: *Sodium is highly corrosive*

corrugated adjective folded into alternate grooves and ridges

corrupt adjective 1 open to or involving bribery 2 morally depraved 3 (of a text or data) unreliable through errors or alterations ▷ verb 4 to make

corrupt **>corruptible** adjective

corruption noun dishonesty and illegal behaviour by people in positions of power

corset noun women's close-fitting undergarment worn to provide support or make the wearer look slimmer

cosmetic noun 1 preparation used to improve the appearance of a person's skin ▷ adjective 2 improving the appearance only

cosmic adjective of the whole universe

cosmopolitan adjective 1 composed of people or elements from many countries 2 having lived and travelled in many countries

cosmos noun the universe

cosset verb to pamper

cost costs costing cost noun 1 amount of money, time, labour, etc, required for something 2 costs expenses of a lawsuit ▷ verb 3 to have as its cost 4 to involve the loss or sacrifice of 5 costed to estimate the cost of

costly costlier costliest adjective 1 expensive 2 involving great loss or sacrifice

costume noun 1 style of dress of a particular place or time, or for a particular activity 2 clothes worn by an actor or performer

cosy cosier cosiest; cosies adjective 1 warm and snug 2 intimate or friendly ▷ noun 3 cover for keeping things warm: *a tea cosy* **>cosily** adverb **>cosiness** noun

cot noun 1 baby's bed with high sides 2 small portable bed

cottage noun small house in the

country

cottage cheese noun soft mild white cheese

cotton noun 1 white downy fibre covering the seeds of a tropical plant 2 cloth or thread made from this ▷ verb 3 **cotton on (to)** informal to understand

cotton wool noun fluffy cotton used for surgical dressings etc

couch noun 1 piece of upholstered furniture for seating more than one person ▷ verb 2 to express in a particular way

cough verb 1 to expel air from the lungs abruptly and noisily ▷ noun 2 act or sound of coughing 3 illness which causes coughing

could verb past tense of **can¹**

coulomb noun SI unit of electric charge

council noun 1 group meeting for discussion or consultation 2 local governing body of a town or region ▷ adjective 3 of or by a council

councillor noun member of a council

counsel counsels counselling counselled noun 1 advice or guidance 2 barrister or barristers ▷ verb 3 to give guidance 4 to urge or recommend ▷ **counselling** noun: Victims were offered counselling ▷ **counsellor** noun: a marriage guidance counsellor

count verb 1 to say numbers in order 2 to find the total of 3 to be important 4 to regard as 5 to take into account ▷ noun 6 counting 7 number reached by counting 8 Law one of a number of charges 9 European nobleman ▷ **counting** preposition including:

nearly 4000 of us, not counting women and children ▷ **count on** verb to rely or depend on

countdown noun counting backwards to zero of the seconds before an event

countenance noun literary face or facial expression

counter verb 1 to oppose or retaliate against ▷ adverb 2 in the opposite direction 3 in direct contrast ▷ noun 4 opposing or retaliatory action 5 long flat surface in a bank or shop, on which business is transacted 6 small flat disc used in board games

counteract verb to act against or neutralize

counterfeit adjective 1 fake or forged ▷ noun 2 fake or forgery ▷ verb 3 to fake or forge

counterpart noun person or thing complementary to or corresponding to another

countess noun 1 woman holding the rank of count or earl 2 wife or widow of a count or earl

countless adjective too many to count

country countries noun 1 nation 2 nation's territory 3 nation's people 4 part of the land away from cities

countryman countrymen noun 1 person from your native land 2 Brit, Aust, NZ person who lives in the country ▷ **countrywoman** noun

countryside noun land away from cities

county counties noun (in some countries) division of a country

coup noun 1 successful action

2 coup d'état

couple noun **1** two people who are married or romantically involved **2** two partners in a dance or game **3 a couple of** a pair of ▷ verb **4** to connect or associate

couplet two consecutive lines of verse, usually rhyming and of the same metre

coupon noun **1** piece of paper entitling the holder to a discount or gift **2** detachable order form **3** football pools entry form

courage noun ability to face danger or pain without fear ▷ **courageous** adjective: a courageous decision ▷ **courageously** adverb

courgette noun type of small vegetable marrow

courier noun **1** person employed to look after holiday-makers **2** person employed to deliver urgent messages

course noun **1** series of lessons or medical treatment **2** route or direction taken **3** area where golf is played or a race is run **4** any of the successive parts of a meal **5** mode of conduct or action **6** natural development of events **7 of course a** (adverb) as expected, naturally **b** (interjection) certainly, definitely ▷ verb **8** (of liquid) to run swiftly

court noun **1** body which decides legal cases **2** place where it meets **3** marked area for playing a racket game **4** courtyard **5** residence, household or retinue of a sovereign ▷ verb **6** old-fashioned to try to gain the love of **7** to try to win the favour of **8** to invite: to court disaster

courteous adjective polite

courtesy courtesies noun **1** politeness or good manners **2** courteous act **3 (by) courtesy of** with the consent of

courtier noun attendant at a royal court

court-martial verb to try by court martial

courtship noun formal courting of an intended spouse or mate

courtyard noun paved space enclosed by buildings or walls

cousin noun child of your uncle or aunt

cove noun small bay or inlet

covenant noun **1** contract **2** Chiefly Brit formal agreement to make an annual (charitable) payment

cover verb **1** to place something over (something) to protect or conceal it **2** to extend over or lie on the surface of **3** to travel over **4** to insure against loss or risk **5** to include **6** to report (an event for a newspaper **7** to be enough to pay for ▷ noun **8** anything that covers **9** outside of a book or magazine **10** insurance **11** shelter or protection ▷ **cover up** verb **1** to cover completely **2** to conceal (a mistake or crime)

coverage noun amount or extent covered

covering noun layer of something which protects or conceals something else: A morning blizzard left a covering of snow

covert adjective concealed or secret ▷ **covertly** adverb

covet verb to long to possess (wh belongs to someone else)

cow noun mature female of cattle and of certain other mammals, such as the elephant or seal

coward noun person who lacks courage > **cowardly** adjective

cowboy noun (in the US) ranch worker who herds and tends cattle, usually on horseback

cower verb to cringe in fear

cox noun **1** person who steers a boat ▷ verb **2** to act as cox of (a boat)

coy adjective affectedly shy or modest > **coyly** adverb

coyote noun prairie wolf of N America

crab noun edible shellfish with ten legs, the first pair modified into pincers

crack verb **1** to split partially so that damage lines appear on the surface **2** to tell (a joke) **3** to solve (a code or problem) **4** to (cause to) make a sharp noise **5** to break down or yield under strain ▷ noun **6** line that appears on a surface caused by damage **7** narrow gap **8** sudden sharp noise **9** informal highly addictive form of cocaine ▷ adjective **10** informal first-rate; excellent: a crack shot

cracker noun **1** thin dry biscuit **2** decorated cardboard tube, pulled apart with a bang, containing a paper hat and a joke or toy **3** small explosive firework **4** informal outstanding thing or person

crackle verb **1** to make small sharp popping noises ▷ noun **2** crackling sound

cradle noun **1** baby's bed on rockers **2** supporting structure ▷ verb **3** to hold gently as if in a cradle

craft noun **1** activity such as

weaving, carving or pottery that requires skill with one's hands **2** skilful occupation **3** boat, plane or spacecraft

● When craft means 'a boat, plane or spacecraft' (sense 3), the plural is craft rather than crafts

craftsman craftsmen noun skilled worker > **craftsmanship** noun: the fine craftsmanship of his furniture > **craftswoman** noun

crafty craftier craftiest adjective skilled in deception

crag noun steep rugged rock

craggy craggier craggiest adjective (of a mountain or cliff) steep and rocky

cram crams cramming crammed verb **1** to force into too small a space **2** to fill too full **3** to study hard just before an examination

cramp noun **1** painful muscular contraction **2** clamp for holding masonry or timber together ▷ verb **3** to confine or restrict

cramped adjective (of a room or building) not large enough for the people or things in it

cranberry cranberries noun sour edible red berry

crane noun **1** machine for lifting and moving heavy weights **2** large wading bird with a long neck and legs ▷ verb **3** to stretch (your neck) to see something

crank noun **1** arm projecting at right angles from a shaft, for transmitting or converting motion **2** informal eccentric person ▷ verb **3** to start (an engine) with a crank

cranny crannies noun narrow opening

crash noun **1** collision involving a vehicle or vehicles **2** sudden loud smashing noise **3** financial collapse ▷ verb **4** to (cause to) collide violently with a vehicle, a stationary object or the ground **5** to (cause to) make a loud smashing noise **6** to (cause to) fall with a crash **7** to collapse or fail financially

crash helmet noun protective helmet worn by a motorcyclist

crate noun large wooden container for packing goods

crater noun very large hole in the ground or in the surface of a planet or moon

cravat noun man's scarf worn like a tie

crave verb **1** to desire intensely **2** to beg or plead for ▷ **craving** noun: a craving for chocolate

crawl verb **1** to move on your hands and knees **2** to move very slowly **3** informal to act in a servile manner ▷ noun **4** crawling motion or pace **5** overarm swimming stroke

crayfish crayfish or crayfishes noun edible shellfish like a lobster

crayon noun stick or pencil of coloured wax or clay

craze noun short-lived fashion or enthusiasm

crazy crazier craziest adjective **1** ridiculous **2** crazy about very fond of a person **3** insane ▷ **crazily** adverb ▷ **craziness** noun: the craziness of their last decision

creak verb **1** to make a harsh squeaking sound ▷ noun **2** harsh squeaking sound ▷ **creaky** adjective: a creaky door

cream noun **1** fatty part of milk **2** food or cosmetic resembling cream in consistency **3** best part (of something) ▷ adjective **4** yellowish-white ▷ verb **5** to beat to a creamy consistency ▷ **creamy** adjective: a creamy chocolate bar

crease noun **1** line made by folding or pressing **2** Cricket line marking the bowler's and batsman's positions ▷ verb **3** to make or become wrinkled or furrowed ▷ **creased** adjective: creased trousers

create verb **1** to make or cause to exist **2** to appoint to a new rank or position

creative adjective imaginative or inventive ▷ **creatively** adverb ▷ **creativity** noun

creature noun animal, person or other being

crèche noun place where small children are looked after while their parents are working, shopping, etc

credence noun belief in the truth or accuracy of a statement

credentials plural noun documents giving evidence of a person's identity or qualifications

credible adjective **1** believable **2** trustworthy ▷ **credibility** noun: The Minister has lost his credibility ▷ **credibly** adverb

credit noun **1** system of allowing customers to receive goods and pay later **2** reputation for trustworthiness in paying debts **3** money at your disposal in a bank account **4** side of an account book on which such sums are entered **5** (source or cause of) praise or approval **6** credits list of people responsible for the production of a film, programme or record ▷ *verb* **7** to enter as a credit in an account **8** (followed by *with*) to attribute (to) **9** to believe

creditable *adjective* praiseworthy

credit card *noun* card allowing a person to buy on credit

creditor *noun* person to whom money is owed

creed *noun* statement or system of (Christian) beliefs or principles

creek *noun* **1** narrow inlet or bay **2** *Aust, NZ, US, Canadian* small stream

creep creeps creeping crept *verb* **1** to move quietly and cautiously **2** to crawl with the body near to the ground **3** (of a plant) to grow along the ground or over rocks ▷ *noun* **4** *informal* obnoxious or servile person **5 give someone the creeps** *informal* to give someone a feeling of fear or disgust

creepy creepier creepiest *adjective informal* causing a feeling of fear or disgust

cremate *verb* to burn (a corpse) to ash > **cremation** *noun*

crematorium crematoriums or **crematoria** *noun* building where corpses are cremated

crepe *noun* **1** fabric or rubber with a crinkled texture **2** very thin pancake

crescendo crescendos *noun* gradual increase in loudness, especially in music

crescent *noun* **1** (curved shape of) the moon as seen in its first or last quarter **2** crescent-shaped street

cress *noun* plant with strong-tasting leaves, used in salads

crest *noun* **1** top of a mountain,

hill or wave **2** tuft or growth on a bird's or animal's head **3** heraldic design used on a coat of arms and elsewhere > **crested** *adjective*

crevice *noun* narrow crack or gap in rock

crew *noun* **1** people who work on a ship or aircraft **2** group of people working together **3** *informal* any group of people ▷ *verb* **4** to serve as a crew member (on)

crib cribs cribbing cribbed *noun* **1** baby's cradle ▷ *verb* **2** to copy (someone's work) dishonestly

crib-wall *noun* NZ retaining wall built against an earth bank

crick *noun* **1** muscle spasm or cramp in the back or neck ▷ *verb* **2** to cause a crick in

cricket *noun* **1** outdoor game played with bats, a ball and wickets by two teams of eleven **2** chirping insect like a grasshopper

crime *noun* **1** unlawful act **2** unlawful acts collectively

criminal *noun* **1** person guilty of a crime ▷ *adjective* **2** of crime > **criminally** *adverb*

criminology *noun* study of crime > **criminologist** *noun*

crimson *adjective* deep purplish-red

cringe *verb* to flinch or back away in fear or embarrassment

crinkle *verb* **1** to wrinkle, crease or fold ▷ *noun* **2** wrinkle, crease or fold

cripple *noun* **1** person who is lame or disabled ▷ *verb* **2** to make lame or disabled **3** to damage (something) > **crippled** *adjective* > **crippling** *adjective*

crisis crises *noun* **1** crucial stage,

turning point **2** time of extreme trouble

crisp *adjective* **1** fresh and firm **2** dry and brittle **3** clean and neat **4** (of weather) cold but invigorating **5** lively or brisk ▷ *noun* **6** *Brit* very thin slice of potato fried till crunchy

crispy crispier crispiest *adjective* hard and crunchy

criterion criteria *noun* standard of judgment

critic *noun* **1** professional judge of any of the arts **2** person who finds fault

critical *adjective* **1** very important or dangerous **2** fault-finding **3** able to examine and judge carefully **4** of or relating to a critic or criticism > **critically** *adverb*

criticism *noun* **1** fault-finding **2** analysis of a book, work of art, etc

criticize *verb* to find fault with

croak *verb* **1** (of a frog or crow) to give a low hoarse cry **2** to utter or speak with a croak ▷ *noun* **3** low hoarse sound

Croatian *adjective* **1** belonging to or relating to Croatia ▷ *noun* **2** person from Croatia **3** form of Serbo-Croat spoken in Croatia

crochet *verb* **1** to make by looping and intertwining yarn with a hooked needle ▷ *noun* **2** work made in this way

crockery *noun* dishes

crocodile *noun* **1** large amphibious tropical reptile **2** *Brit, Aust, NZ* line of people, especially schoolchildren, walking two by two

crocus crocuses *noun* small plant with yellow, white or purple

flowers in spring

croft *noun* small farm worked by one family in Scotland > **crofter** *noun*

croissant *noun* rich flaky crescent-shaped roll

crony cronies *noun* old-fashioned close friend

crook *noun* **1** *informal* criminal **2** bent or curved part **3** hooked pole ▷ *adjective* **4** *Aust, NZ informal* unwell, injured **5** go crook *Aust, NZ informal* to become angry

crooked *adjective* **1** bent or twisted **2** set at an angle **3** *informal* dishonest

croon *verb* to sing, hum or speak in a soft low tone

crop crops cropping cropped *noun* **1** cultivated plant **2** season's total yield of produce **3** group of things appearing at one time **4** (handle of) a whip ▷ *verb* **5** to cut very short **6** to produce or harvest as a crop **7** (of animals) to feed on (grass) > **crop up** *verb informal* to happen unexpectedly

croquet *noun* game played on a lawn in which balls are hit through hoops

cross *verb* **1** to move or go across (something) **2** to meet and pass **3** to place (one's arms or legs) crosswise ▷ *noun* **4** structure, symbol or mark of two intersecting lines **5** such a structure of wood as a means of execution **6** representation of the Cross as an emblem of Christianity **7** mixture of two things ▷ *adjective* **8** angry or annoyed > **crossly** *adverb* > **cross out** *verb* to delete with a cross or lines

crossbow *noun* weapon consisting of a bow fixed at the end of a piece of wood

cross-country *adjective, adverb* **1** by way of open country or fields ▷ *noun* **2** long race run over open ground

cross-eyed *adjective* with eyes looking towards each other

crossfire *noun* gunfire crossing another line of fire

crosshatching *noun* drawing an area of shade in a picture using two or more sets of parallel lines

crossing *noun* **1** place where a street may be crossed safely **2** place where one thing crosses another **3** journey across water

cross-legged *adjective* sitting with your knees pointing outwards and your feet tucked under them

cross section *noun* **1** (diagram of) a surface made by cutting across something **2** representative sample: *a cross section of society*

crossword *noun* (also **crossword puzzle**) puzzle in which you work out clues and write the answers letter by letter in the numbered blank squares that go across or down on a grid of black and white squares

crotch *noun* part of the body between the tops of the legs

crotchet *noun Music* musical note half the length of a minim

crouch *verb* **1** to bend low with the legs and body close ▷ *noun* **2** this position

crow *noun* **1** large black bird with a harsh call **2 as the crow flies** in a straight line ▷ *verb* **3** (of a cock) to make a shrill squawking sound

4 to boast or gloat

crowbar *noun* iron bar used as a lever

crowd *noun* **1** large group of people or things **2** particular group of people ▷ *verb* **3** to gather together in large numbers **4** to press together in a confined space **5** to fill or occupy fully

crowded *adjective* full of people

crown *noun* **1** monarch's headdress of gold and jewels **2** wreath for the head, given as an honour **3** top of the head or of a hill **4** artificial cover for a broken or decayed tooth ▷ *verb* **5** to put a crown on the head of (someone) to proclaim him or her monarch **6** to form or cause to form the top of **7** to put the finishing touch to (a series of events)

crucial *adjective* very important > **crucially** *adverb*

crucifix *noun* model of Christ on the Cross

crucify crucifies crucifying crucified *verb* to put to death by fastening to a cross

crude *adjective* **1** rough and simple **2** tasteless or vulgar **3** in a natural or unrefined state: *crude oil* > **crudely** *adverb* > **crudity** *noun*

cruel *adjective* **1** delighting in others' pain **2** causing pain or suffering > **cruelly** *adverb* > **cruelty** *noun*: *laws against cruelty to animals*

cruise *noun* **1** sail for pleasure ▷ *verb* **2** to sail from place to place for pleasure **3** (of a vehicle) to travel at a moderate and economical speed

cruiser *noun* **1** large, fast warship **2** motorboat with a cabin

crumb noun 1 small fragment of bread or other dry food 2 small amount

crumble verb 1 to break into fragments 2 to fall apart or decay ▷ noun 3 pudding of stewed fruit with a crumbly topping

crumbly adjective easily breaking into small pieces

crumpet noun round soft yeast cake, eaten buttered

crumple verb 1 to crush or crease 2 to collapse, especially from shock

crunch verb 1 to bite or chew with a noisy crushing sound 2 to make a crisp or brittle sound ▷ noun 3 crunching sound 4 informal critical moment

crunchy adjective (of food) pleasantly hard or crisp and making a noise when eaten

crusade noun 1 vigorous campaign in favour of a cause ▷ verb 2 to take part in a crusade

crush verb 1 to compress so as to injure, break or crumple 2 to break into small pieces 3 to defeat or humiliate utterly ▷ noun 4 dense crowd 5 informal infatuation: a teenage crush 6 drink made by crushing fruit

crust noun 1 hard outer part of something, especially bread ▷ verb 2 to cover with or form a crust

crusty crustier crustiest adjective 1 having a crust 2 impatient and irritable

crutch noun long sticklike support with a rest for the armpit, used by a lame person

crux cruxes noun crucial or decisive point

cry cries crying cried verb 1 to shed tears 2 to call or utter loudly ▷ noun 3 fit of weeping 4 loud utterance 5 urgent appeal: a cry for help > **cry off** verb informal to withdraw from an arrangement > **cry out for** verb to need urgently

crypt noun vault under a church, especially one used as a burial place

cryptic adjective obscure in meaning, secret

crystal noun 1 (single grain of) a symmetrically shaped solid formed naturally by some substances 2 very clear and brilliant glass, usually with the surface cut in many planes 3 tumblers, vases, etc, made of crystal ▷ adjective 4 bright and clear

crystallize verb 1 to make or become definite 2 to form into crystals

cub noun young wild animal such as a bear or fox

Cuban adjective 1 belonging or relating to Cuba ▷ noun 2 person from Cuba

cube noun 1 object with six equal square sides 2 number resulting from multiplying a number by itself twice ▷ verb 3 to cut into cubes 4 to find the cube of (a number)

cubic adjective 1 having three dimensions 2 cube-shaped

cubicle noun enclosed part of a large room, screened for privacy

cuckoo cuckoos noun migratory bird with a characteristic two-note call, which lays its eggs in the nests of other birds

cucumber noun long green-skinned fleshy fruit used in salads

cuddle verb 1 to hug ▷ noun 2 hug

cuddly adjective (of people, animals or toys) soft and pleasing

cue cues cueing cued noun 1 signal to an actor or musician to begin speaking or playing 2 signal or reminder 3 long tapering stick used in billiards, snooker or pool ▷ verb 4 to give a cue to 5 to hit (a ball) with a cue

cuff noun 1 end of a sleeve 2 **off the cuff** informal without preparation

cuff link noun one of a pair of decorative fastenings for shirt cuffs

cuisine noun style of cooking

cul-de-sac noun road with one end blocked off

culinary adjective of kitchens or cookery

cull verb 1 to choose or gather 2 to remove or kill (inferior or surplus animals) from a herd ▷ noun 3 culling

culminate verb to reach the highest point or climax > **culmination** noun: the culmination of four years of training

culprit noun person guilty of an offence or misdeed

cult noun 1 specific system of worship 2 devotion to a person, idea or activity 3 popular fashion

cultivate verb 1 to prepare (land) to grow crops 2 to grow (plants) 3 to develop or improve (something) 4 to try to develop a friendship with (someone) > **cultivation** noun: the cultivation of fruit

culture noun 1 ideas, customs and art of a particular society

2 particular society 3 developed understanding of the arts 4 cultivation of plants or rearing of animals 5 growth of bacteria for study > **cultural** adjective: our cultural heritage

cumulative adjective increasing steadily

cunjevoi noun very small Australian sea creature that lives on rocks

cunning adjective 1 clever at deceiving 2 ingenious ▷ noun 3 cleverness at deceiving 4 ingenuity > **cunningly** adverb

cup cups cupping cupped noun 1 small bowl-shaped drinking container with a handle 2 contents of a cup 3 (competition with) a cup-shaped trophy given as a prize ▷ verb 4 to put (your hands) together to form a shape like a cup 5 to hold in cupped hands

cupboard noun piece of furniture or alcove with a door, for storage

curable adjective (of disease) able to be cured

curate noun clergyman who assists a parish priest

curator noun person in charge of a museum or art gallery

curb noun 1 something that restrains ▷ verb 2 to control or restrain

curd noun coagulated milk, a thick white substance used to make cheese

curdle verb to turn into curd

cure verb 1 to get rid of (an illness or problem) 2 to make (someone) well again 3 to preserve by salting, smoking or drying ▷ noun 4 (treatment causing) curing of an illness or person **5** remedy or solution

curfew noun **1** law ordering people to stay inside their homes after a specific time at night **2** time set as a deadline by such a law

curiosity curiosities noun **1** eagerness to know or find out **2** rare or unusual object

curious adjective **1** eager to learn or know **2** eager to find out private details **3** unusual or peculiar: *a curious discovery* ▷ **curiously** adverb

curl noun **1** curved piece of hair **2** curved spiral shape ▷ verb **3** to make (hair) into curls or (of hair) grow in curls **4** to make into a curved spiral shape ▷ **curly** adjective: *naturally curly hair*

curler noun **1** small tube for curling hair **2** person who plays curling

curlew noun long-billed wading bird

currant noun **1** small dried grape **2** small round berry, such as a redcurrant

currawong noun Australian songbird

currency currencies noun **1** money in use in a particular country **2** general acceptance or use

current adjective **1** of the immediate present **2** most recent, up-to-date **3** commonly accepted ▷ noun **4** flow of water or air in one direction **5** flow of electricity **6** general trend ▷ **currently** adverb

current affairs plural noun political and social events discussed in newspapers and on television and radio

curriculum curriculums or curricula noun all the courses of study offered by a school or college

curriculum vitae noun outline of someone's educational and professional history, prepared for job applications; often abbreviated to CV

curry curries currying curried noun **1** Indian dish of meat or vegetables in a hot spicy sauce ▷ verb **2** to prepare (food) with curry powder **3** **curry favour** to ingratiate yourself with an important person ▷ **curried** adjective flavoured with hot spices

curse curses cursing cursed verb **1** to swear (at) **2** to ask a supernatural power to cause harm to ▷ noun **3** swearword **4** (result of) a call to a supernatural power to cause harm to someone **5** something causing trouble or harm ▷ **cursed** adjective: *The whole family seemed cursed*

cursor noun arrow or box on a computer monitor which indicates where the next letter or symbol is

cursory adjective quick and superficial

curt adjective brief and rather rude ▷ **curtly** adverb

curtail verb formal **1** to cut short **2** to restrict

curtain noun **1** piece of cloth hung at a window or used to form a screen **2** hanging cloth separating the audience and the stage in a theatre **3** opening or closing of the curtain at the theatre

curtsy curtsies curtsying

curtsied; also spelt **curtsey** *noun*
1 woman's gesture of respect
made by bending the knees and
bowing the head ▷ *verb* **2** to
make a curtsy

curve *noun* **1** continuously
bending line with no straight
parts ▷ *verb* **2** to form or move in
a curve > **curved** *adjective* > **curvy**
adjective

cushion *noun* **1** bag filled with
soft material, to make a seat
more comfortable **2** something
that provides comfort or absorbs
shock ▷ *verb* **3** to lessen the
effects of **4** to protect from injury
or shock

custard *noun* sweet yellow sauce
made from milk and eggs

custodian *noun* person in charge
of a public building

custody *noun* **1** protective care
2 imprisonment prior to being
tried > **custodial** *adjective: a
custodial sentence*

custom *noun* **1** long-established
activity or action **2** usual habit
3 *formal* regular use of a shop or
business

customary *adjective* **1** usual
2 established by custom
> **customarily** *adverb*

custom-built or **custom-
made** *adjective* made to the
specifications of an individual
customer

customer *noun* **1** person who
buys goods or services **2** *informal*
person with whom you have to
deal: *a tough customer*

cut *cuts cutting cut verb* **1** to
open up, penetrate, wound or
divide with a sharp instrument
2 to divide **3** to trim or shape by

cutting **4** to shorten or reduce
5 to suppress **6** to pretend not
to recognize ▷ *noun* **7** stroke
or incision made by cutting
8 piece cut off **9** reduction
10 deletion in a text, film or play
11 *informal* share, especially of
profits **12** style in which hair or
a garment is cut > **cut back** *verb*
1 to shorten by cutting **2** to make
a reduction > **cut down** *verb* **1** to
fell **2** to make a reduction > **cut
off** **1** to remove or separate
2 to stop the supply of
3 to interrupt (a person who
is speaking), especially during
a telephone conversation > **cut
out** *verb* **1** to shape by cutting
2 to delete or remove **3** *informal*
to stop doing something **4** (of
an engine) to cease to operate
suddenly

cute *adjective* **1** appealing or
attractive **2** *informal* clever or
shrewd

cuticle *noun* skin at the base of a
fingernail or toenail

cutlass *noun* curved one-edged
sword formerly used by sailors

cutlery *noun* knives, forks and
spoons

cutlet *noun* **1** small piece of meat
like a chop **2** flat croquette of
chopped meat or fish

cutting *noun* **1** article cut from a
newspaper or magazine **2** piece
cut from a plant from which to
grow a new plant **3** passage cut
through high ground for a road or
railway ▷ *adjective* **4** (of a remark)
hurtful

CV *abbreviation* curriculum vitae

cyanide *noun* extremely
poisonous chemical compound

cyber- *prefix* computers: *cyberspace*

cyberpet *noun* electronic toy that imitates the activities of a pet, and needs to be fed and entertained

cyberspace *noun* place said to contain all the data stored in computers

cycle *verb* 1 to ride a bicycle ▷ *noun* 2 *Brit, Aust, NZ* bicycle 3 *US* motorcycle 4 complete series of recurring events 5 time taken for one such series

cyclical or **cyclic** *adjective* occurring in cycles

cyclist *noun* person who rides a bicycle

cyclone *noun* violent wind moving round a central area

cygnet *noun* young swan

cylinder *noun* 1 solid or hollow body with straight sides and circular ends 2 chamber within which the piston moves in an internal-combustion engine > **cylindrical** *adjective*: *a cylindrical container*

cymbal *noun* percussion instrument consisting of a brass plate which is struck against another or hit with a stick

cynic *noun* person who believes that people always act selfishly

cynical *adjective* believing that people always act selfishly > **cynically** *adverb* > **cynicism** *noun*: *He viewed politicians with cynicism*

cypher *noun* same as **cipher**

cypress *noun* evergreen tree with dark green leaves

cyst *noun* (abnormal) sac in the body containing fluid or soft

matter

czar *noun* same as **tsar** > **czarina** another spelling of **tsarina**

Czech *adjective* 1 belonging or relating to the Czech Republic ▷ *noun* 2 person from the Czech Republic 3 language spoken in the Czech Republic

Czechoslovak *adjective* 1 belonging to or relating to the country that used to be Czechoslovakia ▷ *noun* 2 someone who came from the country that used to be Czechoslovakia

d

dab *dabs* *dabbing* *dabbed* *verb* 1 to pat lightly 2 to apply with short tapping strokes ▷ *noun* 3 small amount of something soft or moist 4 light stroke or tap 5 **dab hand** *informal* person who is particularly good at something

dabble *verb* 1 to be involved in something superficially 2 to splash about

dachshund *noun* dog with a long body and short legs

dad *noun* *informal* father

daddy-long-legs *noun* 1 *Brit* crane fly 2 *US, Canadian* small web-spinning spider with long legs

● The plural of *daddy-long-legs* is
● *daddy-long-legs*

daffodil noun yellow trumpet-shaped flower that blooms in spring

daft adjective informal foolish or crazy

dagga noun S Afr informal cannabis

dagger noun 1 short knifelike weapon with a pointed blade 2 **at daggers drawn** in a state of open hostility

dahlia noun brightly coloured

daily dailies adjective 1 occurring every day or every weekday ▷ adverb 2 every day ▷ noun 3 daily newspaper 4 Brit informal person who cleans other people's houses

dainty daintier daintiest adjective delicate or elegant > **daintily** adverb

dairy dairies noun 1 place for the processing or sale of milk and its products 2 NZ small shop selling groceries and milk often outside normal trading hours 3 food containing milk or its products: She can't eat dairy ▷ adjective 4 of milk or its products

dais noun raised platform in a hall, used by a speaker

daisy daisies noun small wild flower with a yellow centre and white petals

dale noun (esp. in N England) valley

Dalmatian noun large dog with a white coat and black spots

dam dams damming dammed noun 1 barrier built across a river to create a lake 2 lake created by this ▷ verb 3 to build a dam across a river)

damage verb 1 to harm or spoil ▷ noun 2 harm to a person or thing 3 **damages** money

awarded as compensation for injury or loss > **damaging** adjective

dame noun 1 Chiefly US & Canadian informal woman 2 **Dame** title of a woman who has been awarded the OBE or another order of chivalry

damn verb 1 to condemn as bad or worthless 2 (of God) to condemn to hell ▷ interjection 3 informal exclamation of annoyance ▷ adverb, adjective 4 informal extreme(ly)

damnation noun eternal punishment in Hell after death

damp adjective 1 slightly wet ▷ noun 2 slight wetness; moisture ▷ verb 3 to make damp **damp down** verb to reduce the intensity of (feelings or actions) > **damply** adverb > **dampness** noun: The smell of dampness was overpowering

dampen verb 1 to reduce the intensity of 2 to make damp

damper noun 1 movable plate to regulate the draught in a fire 2 pad in a piano that deadens the vibration of each string 3 **put a damper on** to have a depressing or inhibiting effect on

damson noun small blue-black plumlike fruit garden flower

dance verb 1 to move the feet and body rhythmically in time to music 2 to perform (a particular dance) 3 to skip or leap 4 to move rhythmically ▷ noun 5 series of steps and movements in time to music 6 social meeting arranged for dancing > **dancer** noun: a ballroom dancer > **dancing** noun: a meal followed by music and dancing

dandelion noun yellow-flowered wild plant

dandruff noun loose scales of dry dead skin shed from the scalp

D and T abbreviation design and technology

dandy dandies; dandier dandiest noun 1 old-fashioned man who is too concerned with the elegance of his appearance ▷ adjective 2 informal very good

Dane noun someone from Denmark

danger noun 1 possibility of being injured or killed 2 person or thing that may cause injury or harm 3 likelihood that something unpleasant will happen

dangerous adjective able to or likely to cause hurt or harm ▷ **dangerously** adverb

dangle verb 1 to hang loosely 2 to display as an enticement

Danish adjective 1 belonging or relating to Denmark ▷ noun 2 main language spoken in Denmark

dank adjective unpleasantly damp and chilly

dapper adjective (of a man) neat in appearance

dappled adjective marked with spots of a different colour

dare verb 1 to be courageous enough to try (to do something) 2 to challenge to do something risky ▷ noun 3 challenge to do something risky

daredevil noun recklessly bold person

daring adjective 1 willing to take risks ▷ noun 2 courage to do dangerous things

dark adjective 1 having little or no light 2 (of a colour) reflecting little light 3 (of hair or skin)

brown or black 4 gloomy or sad 5 sinister or evil ▷ noun 6 absence of light 7 night ▷ **darkly** adverb ▷ **darkness** noun: The room was plunged into darkness

darken verb to become or make (something) darker

darkroom noun darkened room for processing photographic film

darling noun 1 much-loved person 2 favourite ▷ adjective 3 much-loved

darn verb 1 to mend (a garment) with a series of interwoven stitches ▷ noun 2 patch of darned work

dart noun 1 small narrow pointed missile that is thrown or shot, especially in the game of darts 2 sudden quick movement 3 tapered tuck made in dressmaking 4 darts game in which darts are thrown at a circular numbered board ▷ verb 5 to move or direct quickly and suddenly

dash verb 1 to move quickly 2 to hurl or crash 3 to frustrate (someone's hopes) ▷ noun 4 sudden quick movement 5 small amount 6 mixture of style and courage 7 punctuation mark – indicating a change of subject 8 longer symbol used in Morse code

dashboard noun instrument panel in a vehicle

dashing adjective stylish and attractive

dasyure noun small marsupial that lives in Australia and eats meat

data noun 1 information consisting of observations,

measurements or facts
2 numbers, digits, etc, stored by a computer

database *noun* store of information that can be easily handled by a computer

date *noun* **1** specified day of the month **2** particular day or year when an event happened **3** *informal* appointment, especially with a person to whom you are sexually attracted **4** *informal* person with whom you have a date **5** dark-brown sweet-tasting fruit of the date palm ▷ *verb* **6** to mark with the date of **7** *informal* to go on a date (with) **8** to assign a date of occurrence to **9** to become old-fashioned **10** **date from** to originate from

dated *adjective* old-fashioned

datum *noun* singular form of **data**

daub *verb* to smear or spread quickly or clumsily

daughter *noun* **1** female child **2** woman who comes from a certain place or is connected with a certain thing

daughter-in-law **daughters-in-law** *noun* son's wife

daunt *verb* to make (someone) feel worried and intimidated about their prospects of success > **daunting** *adjective* worrying or intimidating

dawn *noun* **1** daybreak **2** beginning (of something) ▷ *verb* **3** to begin to grow light **4** to begin to develop or appear > **dawn on** *verb* to become apparent (to someone)

day *noun* **1** period of 24 hours **2** period of light between sunrise and sunset **3** part of a day

occupied with regular activity, especially work **4** period or point in time **5** time of success **6** **call it a day** to stop work or other activity

daybreak *noun* time in the morning when light first appears

daydream *noun* **1** pleasant fantasy indulged in while awake ▷ *verb* **2** to indulge in idle fantasy

daylight *noun* light from the sun

day-to-day *adjective* routine

day trip *noun* journey for pleasure to a place and back again on the same day

daze *noun* **in a daze** confused and bewildered

dazed *adjective* stunned and unable to think clearly

dazzle *verb* **1** to impress greatly **2** to blind temporarily by sudden excessive light ▷ *noun* **3** bright light that dazzles > **dazzling** *adjective: a dazzling smile*

de- *prefix* indicating: **1** removal: *dethrone* **2** reversal: *declassify* **3** departure: *decamp*

deacon *noun Christianity* **1** ordained minister ranking immediately below a priest **2** (in some Protestant churches) lay official who assists the minister > **deaconess** *noun*

dead *adjective* **1** no longer alive **2** no longer in use **3** numb: *My leg has gone dead* **4** complete, absolute: *dead silence* **5** *informal* very tired **6** (of a place) lacking activity ▷ *noun* **7** period during which coldness or darkness is most intense: *in the dead of night* ▷ *adverb* **8** extremely **9** suddenly: *I stopped dead*

dead end *noun* **1** road with one

end blocked off **2** situation in which further progress is impossible

deadline *noun* time or date before which something must be completed

deadlock *noun* point in a dispute at which no agreement can be reached

deadly deadlier deadliest *adjective* **1** likely to cause death **2** *informal* extremely boring ▷ *adverb* **3** extremely

deadpan *adjective, adverb* showing no emotion or expression

deaf *adjective* **1** unable to hear **2 deaf to** refusing to listen to or take notice of **>deafness** *noun* condition of being unable to hear

deafening *adjective* very loud

deal deals dealing dealt *noun* **1** agreement or transaction **2** kind of treatment: *a fair deal* **3 a great deal (of)** a large amount (of) ▷ *verb* **4** to inflict (a blow) on **5** *Cards* to give out (cards) to the players **>deal in** *verb* to buy or sell (goods) **>deal out** *verb* to distribute **>deal with** *verb* **1** to take action on **2** to be concerned with

dealer *noun* person or firm whose business involves buying or selling things

dealings *plural noun* transactions or business relations

dean *noun* **1** chief administrative official of a college or university faculty **2** chief administrator of a cathedral

dear *noun* **1** someone regarded with affection ▷ *adjective* **2** much-loved **3** costly **>dearly** *adverb*

dearth *noun* inadequate amount or scarcity

death *noun* **1** permanent end of life in a person or animal **2** instance of this **3** ending or destruction

debacle *noun formal* disastrous failure

debase *verb* to lower in value, quality or character

debatable *adjective* not absolutely certain

debate *noun* **1** discussion ▷ *verb* **2** to discuss formally **3** to consider (a course of action)

debilitating *adjective formal* causing weakness: *a debilitating illness*

debit *noun* **1** acknowledgment of a sum owing by entry on the left side of an account ▷ *verb* **2** to charge (an account) with a debit

debrief *verb* to receive a report from (a soldier, diplomat, etc) after an event **>debriefing** *noun*: *The mission was followed by a full debriefing*

debris *noun* fragments of something destroyed

debt *noun* something owed, especially money

debtor *noun* person who owes money

debut *noun* first public appearance of a performer

debutante *noun* young upper-class woman being formally presented to society

dec- or **deca-** *prefix* ten: *decathlon*

decade *noun* period of ten years

decadence *noun* deterioration in morality or culture **>decadent** *adjective*: *a decadent rock 'n' roll lifestyle*

decaffeinated *adjective* (of coffee

tea or cola) with caffeine removed

decanter noun stoppered bottle for wine or spirits

decapitate verb to behead

decathlon noun athletic contest with ten different events

decay verb 1 to become weaker or more corrupt 2 to rot ▷ noun 3 process of decaying 4 state brought about by this process

deceased formal adjective 1 dead ▷ noun 2 **the deceased** the dead person

deceit noun behaviour intended to deceive > **deceitful** adjective: a very deceitful little girl

deceive verb to mislead (someone) by lying

decelerate verb to slow down > **deceleration** noun: a deceleration in the rate of growth

December noun twelfth and last month of the year

decency noun behaviour that is respectable and follows accepted moral standards

decent adjective 1 (of a person) polite and morally acceptable 2 fitting or proper 3 conforming to conventions of sexual behaviour 4 informal kind > **decently** adverb

decentralize verb to reorganize into smaller local units > **decentralization** noun: the decentralization of health care

deception noun 1 deceiving 2 something that deceives, trick

deceptive adjective likely or designed to deceive > **deceptively** adverb

decibel noun unit for measuring the intensity of sound

decide verb 1 to (cause to) reach a

decision 2 to settle (a contest or question)

deciduous adjective (of a tree) shedding its leaves annually

decimal noun 1 fraction written in the form of a dot followed by one or more numbers ▷ adjective 2 relating to or using powers of ten 3 expressed as a decimal

decimate verb to destroy or kill a large proportion of

decipher verb to work out the meaning of (something illegible or in code)

decision noun 1 judgment, conclusion or resolution 2 act of making up your mind 3 firmness of purpose

decisive adjective 1 having a definite influence 2 having the ability to make quick decisions > **decisively** adverb > **decisiveness** noun

deck noun 1 area of a ship that forms a floor 2 similar area in a bus > **deck out** verb to make more attractive by decorating

deck chair noun light folding chair, made from canvas and wood and used outdoors

declaration noun firm, forceful statement, often an official announcement: a declaration of war

declare verb 1 to state firmly and forcefully 2 to announce officially 3 to acknowledge for tax purposes

decline verb 1 to become smaller, weaker or less important 2 to refuse politely to accept or do 3 Grammar to list the inflections of (a noun, pronoun or adjective) ▷ noun 4 gradual weakening or loss

a b c **d** e f g h i j k l m n o p q r s t u v w x y z

decode verb to convert from code into ordinary language

decommission verb to dismantle (a nuclear reactor, weapon, etc) which is no longer needed

decompose verb to be broken down through chemical or bacterial action > **decomposition** noun: the decomposition of plant tissue

decor noun style in which a room or house is decorated

decorate verb 1 to make more attractive by adding something ornamental 2 to paint or wallpaper 3 to award a (military) medal to

decoration noun 1 addition that makes something more attractive 2 way in which a room or building is decorated 3 official honour or medal awarded to someone

decorative adjective intended to look attractive

decorator noun person whose job is painting and putting up wallpaper in rooms and buildings

decorum noun formal polite and socially correct behaviour

decoy noun 1 person or thing used to lure someone into danger 2 dummy bird or animal, used to lure game within shooting range > verb 3 to lure away by means of a trick

decrease verb 1 to make or become less > noun 2 lessening or reduction 3 amount by which something has decreased > **decreasing** adjective: decreasing investment in training

decree decrees decreeing decreed noun 1 law made by someone in authority 2 court judgment > verb 3 to order by decree

dedicate verb 1 to commit (yourself or your time) wholly to a special purpose or cause 2 to inscribe or address (a book etc) to someone as a tribute

deduce verb to reach (a conclusion) by reasoning from evidence

deduct verb to subtract

deduction noun 1 deducting 2 something that is deducted 3 deducing 4 conclusion reached by deducing

deed noun 1 something that is done 2 legal document

deem verb to consider or judge

deep adjective 1 extending or situated far down, inwards, backwards, or sideways 2 of a specified dimension downwards, inwards or backwards 3 difficult to understand 4 of great intensity 5 **deep in** absorbed in (an activity) 6 (of a colour) strong or dark 7 Music low in pitch > noun 8 **the deep** poetic the sea > **deeply** adverb

deepen verb to make or become deeper or more intense

deer deer noun large wild animal, the male of which has antlers

● The plural of deer is deer

deface verb to deliberately spoil the appearance of

default noun 1 failure to do something 2 Computers instruction to a computer to select a particular option unless the user specifies otherwise 3 **by default** happening because something else has not happened 4 **in default of** in the absence of ▷ verb **5** to fail to fulfil an obligation

defeat verb **1** to win a victory over **2** to thwart or frustrate ▷ noun **3** defeating

defecate verb to discharge waste from the body through the anus

defect noun **1** imperfection or blemish ▷ verb **2** to desert one's cause or country to join the opposing forces > **defection** noun

defective adjective imperfect or faulty

defence noun **1** resistance against attack **2** argument in support of something **3** country's military resources **4** defendant's case in a court of law

defend verb **1** to protect from harm or danger **2** to support in the face of criticism **3** to represent (a defendant) in court

defendant noun person accused of a crime

defender noun **1** person who supports someone or something in the face of criticism **2** Sport player whose chief task is to stop the opposition scoring

defensible adjective capable of being defended because believed to be right

defensive adjective **1** intended for defence **2** overanxious to protect yourself against (threatened) criticism > **defensively** adverb > **defensiveness** noun: There was a note of defensiveness in her voice

defer verb deferring deferred verb **1** to delay (something) until a future time **2** defer to to comply with the wishes (of)

deference noun polite and respectful behaviour

> **deferential** adjective: He was always deferential to his elders
> **deferentially** adverb

defiance noun open resistance to authority or opposition > **defiant** adjective: The players are in defiant mood > **defiantly** adverb

deficiency deficiencies noun **1** state of being deficient **2** lack or shortage

deficient adjective **1** lacking some essential thing or quality **2** inadequate in quality or quantity

deficit noun amount by which a sum of money is too small

define verb **1** to state precisely the meaning of **2** to show clearly the outline of

definite adjective **1** firm, clear and precise **2** having precise limits **3** known for certain > **definitely** adverb

definition noun **1** statement of the meaning of a word or phrase **2** quality of being clear and distinct

definitive adjective **1** providing an unquestionable conclusion **2** being the best example of something > **definitively** adverb

deflate verb **1** to (cause to) collapse through the release of air **2** to take away the self-esteem or conceit from **3** Economics to cause deflation of (an economy)

deflect verb to (cause to) turn aside from a course > **deflection** noun: the deflection of light

deforestation noun destruction of all the trees in an area

deformed adjective disfigured or abnormally shaped

defraud verb to cheat out of

money, property, etc

defrost verb **1** to make or become free of ice **2** to thaw (frozen food) by removing it from a freezer

deft adjective quick and skilful in movement > **deftly** adverb

defunct adjective no longer existing or operative

defuse verb **1** to remove the fuse of (an explosive device) **2** to remove the tension from (a situation)

defy defies defying defied verb **1** to resist openly and boldly **2** to make impossible: The condition of the refugees defied description

degenerate adjective **1** having deteriorated to a lower mental, moral or physical level > noun **2** degenerate person > verb **3** to become degenerate > **degeneration** noun: the moral degeneracy of society

degradation noun **1** state of poverty and misery **2** state of humiliation or corruption

degrade verb **1** to reduce to dishonour or disgrace **2** to reduce in status or quality **3** Chemistry to decompose into smaller molecules

degree noun **1** stage in a scale of relative amount or intensity **2** academic award given by a university or college on successful completion of a course **3** unit of measurement for temperature, angles or latitude or longitude

dehydrated adjective weak through losing too much water from the body > **dehydration** noun: a runner suffering from dehydration

deign verb formal to agree (to do something), but as if doing

someone a favour

deity deities noun **1** god or goddess **2** state of being divine

déjà vu noun feeling of having experienced before something that is actually happening now

dejected adjective miserable and unhappy > **dejectedly** adverb > **dejection** noun: feelings of dejection and despair

delay verb **1** to put off to a later time **2** to slow up or cause to be late ▷ noun **3** act of delaying **4** interval of time between events

delectable adjective delightful, very attractive

delegate noun **1** person chosen to represent others, especially at a meeting > verb **2** to entrust (duties or powers) to someone **3** to appoint as a delegate

delegation noun **1** group chosen to represent others **2** delegating

delete verb to remove (something written or printed) > **deletion** noun: the deletion of superfluous words

deliberate adjective **1** done on purpose or planned in advance; intentional **2** careful and unhurried ▷ verb **3** to think something over > **deliberately** adverb

deliberation noun careful consideration of a subject

delicacy delicacies noun **1** fine, graceful or subtle in character **2** something particularly good to eat

delicate adjective **1** fine or subtle in quality or workmanship **2** having a fragile beauty **3** (of a taste etc) pleasantly subtle **4** easily damaged **5** requiring tac

> delicately adverb

delicatessen noun shop selling imported or unusual foods, often already cooked or prepared

delicious adjective very appealing to taste or smell **> deliciously** adverb

delight noun **1** (source of) great pleasure ▷ verb **2** to please greatly **3 delight in** to take great pleasure (in) **> delighted** adjective: I was delighted at the news

delightful adjective very pleasant and attractive **> delightfully** adverb

delinquent noun **1** someone, especially a young person, who repeatedly breaks the law ▷ adjective **2** repeatedly breaking the law **> delinquency** noun: He had no history of delinquency

delirious adjective **1** unable to speak or act in a rational way because of illness or fever **2** wildly excited and happy **> deliriously** adverb

deliver verb **1** to carry (goods etc) to a destination **2** to hand over **3** to aid in the birth of **4** to present (a lecture or speech) **5** to release or rescue **6** to strike (a blow)

delivery deliveries noun **1** delivering **2** something that is delivered **3** act of giving birth to a baby **4** style in public speaking

dell noun literary small wooded hollow

delta noun **1** fourth letter in the Greek alphabet **2** flat area at the mouth of some rivers where the main stream splits up into several branches

delude verb to make someone believe that something is not true

deluge noun **1** great flood **2** torrential rain **3** overwhelming number ▷ verb **4** to flood **5** to overwhelm

delusion noun **1** mistaken idea or belief **2** state of being deluded

de luxe adjective rich or sumptuous, superior in quality

delve verb to research deeply (for information)

demand verb **1** to request forcefully **2** to require as just, urgent, etc **3** to claim as a right ▷ noun **4** forceful request **5** Economics willingness and ability to purchase goods and services **6** something that requires special effort or sacrifice

demean verb **demean yourself** to do something unworthy of your status or character **> demeaning** adjective: demeaning sexist comments

demeanour noun way a person behaves

demented adjective mad

dementia noun state of serious mental deterioration

demi- prefix half

demise noun **1** eventual failure (of something successful) **2** formal death

demo demos noun informal demonstration, organized expression of public opinion

democracy democracies noun **1** government by the people or their elected representatives **2** state governed in this way

democrat noun **1** advocate of democracy **2 Democrat** member or supporter of the Democratic Party in the US

democratic adjective **1** of democracy **2** upholding democracy **3** Democratic of the Democratic Party, the more liberal of the two main political parties in the US > **democratically** adverb

demography noun study of population statistics, such as births and deaths > **demographic** adjective: demographic changes since World War II

demolish verb **1** to knock down or destroy (a building) **2** to disprove (an argument) > **demolition** noun

demon noun **1** evil spirit **2** person who does something with great energy or skill > **demonic** adjective: demonic forces

demonstrate verb **1** to show or prove by reasoning or evidence **2** to display and explain the workings of **3** to reveal the existence of **4** to show support or opposition by public parades or rallies

demonstration noun **1** organized expression of public opinion **2** explanation or display of how something works **3** proof

demote verb to reduce (someone) in status or rank > **demotion** noun: The team now faces demotion from the league

demure adjective quiet, reserved and rather shy > **demurely** adverb

den noun **1** home of a wild animal **2** small secluded room in a home **3** place where people indulge in criminal or immoral activities

denial noun **1** statement that something is not true **2** rejection of a request

denigrate verb formal to criticize (someone or something) unfairly

denim noun **1** hard-wearing cotton fabric, usually blue **2** denims jeans made of denim

denomination noun **1** group having a distinctive interpretation of a religious faith **2** unit in a system of weights, values or measures

denominator noun Maths number below the line in a fraction

denote verb **1** to be a sign of **2** to have as a literal meaning

denounce verb **1** to speak strongly against **2** to give information against

dense adjective **1** closely packed **2** difficult to see through **3** informal stupid > **densely** adverb

density densities noun **1** degree to which something is filled or occupied **2** measure of the compactness of a substance, expressed as its mass per unit volume

dent noun **1** hollow in the surface of something, made by hitting it ▷ verb **2** to make a dent in

dental adjective of teeth or dentistry

dentist noun person qualified to practise dentistry

dentistry noun branch of medicine concerned with the teeth and gums

dentures plural noun false teeth

denunciation noun severe public criticism (of someone or something)

deny denies denying denied verb **1** to declare (a statement) to be untrue **2** to refuse to give or allow **3** to refuse to acknowledge

deodorant noun substance

applied to the body to mask the smell of perspiration

depart verb to leave

department noun **1** specialized division of a large organization **2** major subdivision of the administration of a government > **departmental** adjective: departmental reorganization

depend verb **depend on 1** to put trust (in) **2** to be influenced or determined (by) **3** to rely (on) for income or support

dependable adjective reliable and trustworthy > **dependably** adverb

dependant noun person who depends on another for financial support

dependence noun state of being dependent

dependency dependencies noun **1** country controlled by another country **2** overreliance on another person or on a drug

dependent adjective depending on someone or something

depict verb **1** to produce a picture of **2** to describe in words

deplete verb **1** to use up (supplies or money) **2** to reduce in number > **depletion** noun: depletion of water supplies

deplorable adjective very bad or unpleasant

deplore verb to express or feel strong disapproval of

deploy verb to organize (troops or resources) into a position ready for immediate action > **deployment** noun: the deployment of troops

deport verb to remove (someone) forcibly from a country > **deportation** noun: thousands of migrants facing deportation

depose verb to remove (someone) from an office or position of power

deposit verb **1** to put (something) down **2** to entrust (something) for safekeeping, especially to a bank ▷ noun **3** sum of money paid into a bank account **4** money given in part payment for goods or services **5** accumulation of sediments, minerals, etc

depot noun **1** building where goods or vehicles are kept when not in use **2** NZ, US bus or railway station

depraved adjective morally bad > **depravity** noun: the depravity that can exist in war

depress verb **1** to make (someone) sad **2** to lower (prices or wages) > **depressing** adjective: a depressing lack of progress > **depressingly** adverb

depressant noun drug able to reduce nervous activity

depressed adjective **1** unhappy and gloomy **2** suffering from economic hardship: depressed industrial areas

depression noun **1** mental state in which a person has feelings of gloom and inadequacy **2** economic condition in which there is high unemployment and low output and investment **3** area of low air pressure **4** sunken place

deprive verb **deprive of** to prevent (someone) from (having or enjoying something) > **deprivation** noun: sleep deprivation

depth noun **1** distance

downwards, backwards or inwards **2** intensity of emotion **3** profundity of character or thought

deputation noun body of people appointed to represent others

deputy deputies noun person appointed to act on behalf of another

deranged adjective insane or uncontrolled

derby derbies noun **1** sporting event between teams from the same area ▷ noun **2 The Derby** horse race held annually at Epsom, named after the 12th Earl of Derby, who founded it in 1780

derelict adjective **1** unused and falling into ruins ▷ noun **2** formal social outcast or tramp

deride verb to treat with contempt or ridicule

derision noun attitude of contempt or scorn towards something or someone

derivation noun the origin of something, such as a word

derivative noun **1** word, idea, etc, derived from another ▷ adjective **2** not original, but based on or copied from something else

derive verb **derive from** to take or develop (from)

derogatory adjective intentionally offensive

descant noun Music tune played or sung above a basic melody

descend verb **1** to move down (a slope etc) **2** to move to a lower level, pitch, etc **3 descend to** to stoop to (unworthy behaviour) **4 descend on** to visit unexpectedly **5 be descended from** to be connected by a blood relationship to

descendant noun person or animal descended from an individual, race or species

descent noun **1** descending **2** downward slope **3** derivation from an ancestor

describe verb **1** to give an account of (something or someone) in words **2** to trace the outline of (a circle etc)

description noun **1** statement that describes something or someone **2** sort: *flowers of every description* >**descriptive** adjective: *his descriptive way of writing* >**descriptively** adverb

desert[1] noun region with little or no vegetation because of low rainfall

desert[2] verb **1** to abandon (a person or place) without intending to return **2** Military to leave (a post or duty) without no intention of returning >**desertion** noun: *the army's high rate of desertion*

deserter noun person who leaves the armed forces without permission

deserve verb to be entitled to or worthy of

deserving adjective worthy of help, praise or reward

design verb **1** to work out the structure or form of (something), by making a sketch or plans **2** to plan and make artistically **3** to intend for a specific purpose ▷ noun **4** preliminary drawing **5** arrangement or features of an artistic or decorative work **6** art of designing **7** intention: *by design*

designate verb 1 to give a name to 2 to select (someone) for an office or duty ▷ adjective 3 appointed but not yet in office

designation noun name

designing adjective cunning and scheming

desirable adjective 1 worth having 2 arousing sexual desire > **desirability** noun: *the desirability of a home in the country*

desire verb 1 to want very much ▷ noun 2 wish or longing 3 sexual appetite 4 person or thing desired

desist verb **desist from** to stop (doing something)

desk noun 1 piece of furniture with a writing surface and drawers 2 service counter in a public building

desktop adjective of a convenient size to be used on a desk or table

desolate adjective 1 uninhabited and bleak 2 very sad ▷ verb 3 to deprive of inhabitants 4 to make (someone) very sad > **desolation** noun: *a scene of desolation and ruin*

despair noun 1 total loss of hope ▷ verb 2 to lose hope > **despairing** adjective: *Tom made another despairing effort to win her round*

despatch verb, noun same as **dispatch**

desperate adjective 1 in despair and reckless 2 (of an action) undertaken as a last resort 3 having a strong need or desire > **desperately** adverb > **desperation** noun: *a feeling of desperation and helplessness*

despicable adjective deserving contempt > **despicably** adverb

despise verb to look down on with contempt

despite preposition in spite of

despondent adjective unhappy > **despondency** noun: *a mood of gloom and despondency*

dessert noun sweet course served at the end of a meal

destination noun place to which someone or something is going

destined adjective certain to be or to do something

destiny destinies noun 1 future marked out for a person or thing 2 the power that predetermines the course of events

destitute adjective having no money or possessions > **destitution** noun: *She ended her life in destitution*

destroy verb 1 to ruin or demolish 2 to put an end to 3 to kill (an animal)

destruction noun 1 destroying 2 cause of ruin

destructive adjective (capable of) causing destruction > **destructiveness** noun: *the destructiveness of their weapons*

desultory adjective 1 jumping from one thing to another; disconnected 2 random > **desultorily** adverb

detach verb to disengage and separate > **detachable** adjective

detached adjective 1 Brit, Aust, S Afr (of a house) not joined to another house 2 showing no emotional involvement

detachment noun 1 lack of emotional involvement 2 small group of soldiers

detail noun 1 individual piece of information 2 unimportant item 3 small individual features of something, considered collectively **4** Chiefly military (personnel assigned) a specific duty ▷ verb **5** to list fully > **detailed** adjective: a detailed list

detain verb **1** to delay (someone) **2** to hold (someone) in custody

detect verb **1** to notice **2** to discover or find > **detectable** adjective: The disease is not detectable at birth

detection noun **1** act of noticing, discovering or sensing something **2** work of investigating crime

detective noun policeman or private agent who investigates crime

detector noun instrument used to find something

detention noun **1** imprisonment **2** form of punishment in which a pupil is detained after school

deter deters deterring deterred verb to discourage (someone) from doing something by instilling fear or doubt

detergent noun chemical substance for washing clothes or dishes

deteriorate verb to become worse > **deterioration** noun: a deterioration in relations between the two men

determination noun condition of being determined or resolute

determine verb **1** to settle (an argument or a question) conclusively **2** to find out the facts about (something) **3** to make a firm decision (to do something)

determined adjective firmly decided, unable to be dissuaded > **determinedly** adverb

determiner noun Grammar word that determines the object to which a noun phrase refers: all

deterrent noun **1** something that deters **2** weapon, especially nuclear, intended to deter attack ▷ adjective **3** tending to deter > **deterrence** noun: nuclear deterrence

detest verb to dislike (someone or something) intensely

detonate verb to make (an explosive device) explode or (of an explosive device) to explode

detour noun route that is not the most direct one

detract verb **detract from** to make (something) seem less good

detriment noun disadvantage or damage > **detrimental** adjective: foods suspected of being detrimental to health

deuce noun **1** Tennis score of forty all **2** playing card with two symbols or dice with two spots

devalue devalues devaluing devalued verb **1** to reduce the exchange value of (a currency) **2** to reduce the value of (something or someone) > **devaluation** noun: devaluation of a number of currencies

devastate verb to damage (a place) severely or destroy it > **devastation** noun: A bomb blast brought chaos and devastation to the city

devastated adjective shocked and extremely upset

develop verb **1** to grow or bring to a later, more elaborate or more advanced stage **2** to come or bring into existence **3** to build houses or factories on (an area of land) **4** to produce (photographs) by making negatives or prints from a film

developer noun **1** person who develops property **2** chemical used to develop photographs or films

development noun **1** process of growing or developing **2** product of developing **3** event that changes a situation **4** area of land that has been developed > **developmental** adjective: the developmental needs of a child

deviant adjective **1** deviating from what is considered acceptable behaviour ▷ noun **2** deviant person

deviate verb **1** to differ from others in belief or thought **2** to depart from your previous behaviour > **deviation** noun: deviation from the norm

device noun **1** machine or tool used for a specific task **2** scheme or plan **3** **leave someone to his** or **her own devices** to leave someone alone to do as he or she wishes

devil noun **1 the Devil** (in Christianity and Islam) chief spirit of evil and enemy of God **2** evil spirit **3** evil person **4** person: poor devil **5** daring person: be a devil!

devious adjective **1** insincere and dishonest **2** indirect > **deviousness** noun: the deviousness of drug traffickers

devise verb to work out (something) in your mind

devoid adjective **devoid of** completely lacking (in)

devolution noun transfer of authority from a central government to regional governments

devote verb to apply or dedicate (one's time, money or effort) to a particular purpose

devoted adjective showing loyalty or devotion

devotee noun **1** person who is very enthusiastic about something **2** zealous follower of a religion

devotion noun **1** strong affection for or loyalty to someone or something **2** religious zeal **3 devotions** prayers > **devotional** adjective: devotional music

devour verb **1** to eat (something) greedily **2** (of an emotion) to engulf and destroy (someone) **3** to read (a book or magazine) eagerly

devout adjective deeply religious > **devoutly** adverb

dew noun drops of water that form on the ground at night from vapour in the air

dexterity noun **1** skill in using your hands **2** mental quickness > **dexterous** adjective: As people grow older they become less dexterous

dharma noun (in the Buddhist religion) ideal truth as set out in the teaching of the Buddha

diabetes noun disorder in which an abnormal amount of urine containing an excess of sugar is excreted > **diabetic** adjective, noun: diabetic patients; suitable for diabetics

diabolical adjective informal extremely bad

diagnose verb to determine by diagnosis > **diagnostic** adjective: X-rays and other diagnostic tools

a
b
c
d
e
f
g
h
i
j
k
l
m
n
o
p
q
r
s
t
u
v
w
x
y
z

diagnosis diagnoses noun discovery and identification of diseases from the examination of symptoms

diagonal adjective **1** from corner to corner **2** slanting ▷ noun **3** diagonal line > **diagonally** adverb

diagram noun sketch showing the form or workings of something

dial dials dialling dialled noun **1** face of a clock or watch **2** graduated disc on a measuring instrument **3** control on a radio or television set used to change the station **4** numbered disc on the front of some telephones ▷ verb **5** to operate the dial or buttons on a telephone in order to contact (a number)

dialect noun form of a language spoken in a particular area

dialogue noun **1** conversation between two people, especially in a book, film or play **2** discussion between representatives of two nations or groups

dialysis noun Medicine filtering of blood through a membrane to remove waste products

diameter noun Maths (length of) a straight line through the centre of a circle or sphere

diamond noun **1** exceptionally hard, usually colourless, precious stone **2** Geometry figure with four sides of equal length forming two acute and two obtuse angles **3** playing card marked with red diamond-shaped symbols ▷ adjective **4** (of an anniversary) sixtieth

diaphragm noun **1** muscular partition that separates the abdominal cavity and chest cavity

2 contraceptive device placed over the neck of the womb

diarrhoea noun condition in which the faeces are more liquid and frequently produced than usual

diary diaries noun (book for) a record of daily events, appointments or observations

dice noun **1** small cube each of whose sides has a different number of spots (1 to 6), used in games of chance ▷ verb **2** to cut (food) into small cubes > **diced** adjective: diced carrots

● The plural of dice is dice

dictate verb **1** to say aloud for someone else to write down **2 dictate to** to seek to impose your will on (other people) ▷ noun **3** authoritative command **4** guiding principle

dictator noun **1** ruler who has complete power **2** person in power who acts unfairly or cruelly > **dictatorship** noun: a military dictatorship

diction noun manner of pronouncing words and sounds

dictionary dictionaries noun **1** book consisting of an alphabetical list of words with their meanings or translations into another language **2** alphabetically ordered reference book of terms relating to a particular subject

didgeridoo noun Australian musical instrument made from a long hollow piece of wood

die dies dying died verb **1** (of a person, animal or plant) to cease all biological activity permanently **2** (of something inanimate) to cease to exist or function **3** be dying for or to do something informal to be eager for or to do something ▷ noun **4** dice **5** specially shaped or patterned block of metal used to cut or mould other metal

- The plural of die in sense **4** is dice

diesel noun **1** diesel engine **2** vehicle driven by a diesel engine **3** diesel oil

diet noun **1** food that a person or animal regularly eats **2** specific range of foods, to control weight or for health reasons **3** parliament of some countries ▷ verb **4** to follow a special diet so as to lose weight ▷ adjective **5** (of food) suitable for a weight-reduction diet > **dietary** adjective: dietary habits

dietician noun person trained to advise people about healthy eating

differ verb **1** to be unlike **2** to disagree

difference noun **1** state of being unlike **2** disagreement **3** remainder left after subtraction

different adjective **1** unlike **2** unusual > **differently** adverb

differentiate verb **1** to perceive or show the difference (between) **2** to make (one thing) distinct from such things > **differentiation** noun: the differentiation between the two product ranges will increase

difficult adjective **1** requiring effort or skill to do or understand **2** not easily pleased

difficulty difficulties noun **1** problem **2** fact or quality of

being difficult

diffident adjective lacking self-confidence > **diffidence** noun: he entered the room with a certain diffidence > **diffidently** adverb

diffract verb Physics (of rays of light or sound waves) to break up or change direction after hitting an obstacle > **diffraction** noun: the diffraction of light

diffuse verb **1** to spread over a wide area ▷ adjective **2** widely spread **3** lacking concision > **diffusion** noun: rates of diffusion of molecules

dig verb **1** to cut into, break up and turn over or remove (earth), esp. with a spade **2** dig up or out to find by effort or searching **3** dig in or into to thrust or jab ▷ noun **4** digging **5** archaeological excavation **6** thrust or poke **7** spiteful remark

digest verb **1** to subject to a process of digestion **2** to absorb mentally ▷ noun **3** shortened version of a book, report or article > **digestible** adjective: bananas are easily digestible

digestion noun (body's system for) breaking down food into easily absorbed substances

digger noun **1** machine used for digging **2** Austral friendly name to call a man

digicam noun digital camera

digit noun **1** finger or toe **2** Maths numeral from 0 to 9

digital adjective **1** displaying information as numbers rather than with hands and a dial: a digital clock **2** transmitting or receiving information in the form of thousands of very small signals:

digital radio > **digitally** *adverb*

dignified *adjective* full of dignity

dignitary dignitaries *noun* person of high official position

dignity dignities *noun* **1** serious, calm and controlled behaviour or manner **2** quality of being worthy of respect **3** sense of self-importance

digression *noun* departure from the main subject in speech or writing

dilapidated *adjective* (of a building) having fallen into ruin

dilate *verb* to make or become wider or larger > **dilated** *adjective*: *dilated pupils* > **dilation** *noun*: *dilation of the blood vessels*

dilemma *noun* situation offering a choice between two equally undesirable alternatives

diligent *adjective* **1** careful and persevering in carrying out duties **2** carried out with care and perseverance > **diligence** *noun*: *They are pursuing the matter with great diligence* > **diligently** *adverb*

dill *noun* sweet-smelling herb

dilly bag *noun* Austral small bag used to carry food

dilute *verb* **1** to make (a liquid) less concentrated, especially by adding water **2** to make (a quality etc) weaker in force > **dilution** *noun*: *a dilution of his powers*

dim dimmer dimmest; dims dimming dimmed *adjective* **1** badly lit **2** not clearly seen **3** unintelligent > *verb* **4** to become or make (something) dim **5** take a dim view of to disapprove of > **dimly** *adverb* > **dimness** *noun*: *the dimness of an early October evening*

dimension *noun* **1** measurement of the size of something in a particular direction **2** aspect or factor

diminish *verb* to become or make smaller, fewer or less

diminutive *adjective* **1** very small > *noun* **2** word or affix which implies smallness or lack of importance

dimmer *noun* device for dimming an electric light

dimple *noun* small natural dent, especially in the cheeks or chin

din *noun* loud unpleasant confused noise

dinar *noun* monetary unit of various Balkan, Middle Eastern and North African countries

dine *verb* formal to eat dinner

diner *noun* **1** person eating a meal **2** Chiefly US small cheap restaurant

dinghy dinghies *noun* small boat, powered by sails, oars or a motor

dingo dingoes *noun* Australian wild dog

dingy dingier dingiest *adjective* dull and drab

dinkum *adjective* Aust, NZ informal genuine or right

dinner *noun* main meal of the day, eaten either in the evening or at midday

dinosaur *noun* type of extinct prehistoric reptile, many of whic were of gigantic size

dint *noun* by dint of by means of

diocese *noun* district over which a bishop has control > **diocesan** *adjective*: *the diocesan synod*

dip dips dipping dipped *verb* **1** to plunge (something) quickly or briefly into a liquid **2** to slope downwards **3** to switch (car headlights) from the main to the lower beam **4** to lower briefly ▷ *noun* **5** dipping **6** brief swim **7** liquid chemical in which farm animals are dipped to rid them of insects **8** depression in a landscape **9** creamy mixture into which pieces of food are dipped before being eaten ▶ **dip into** *verb* to read passages at random from (a book or journal)

diploma *noun* qualification awarded by a college on successful completion of a course

diplomacy *noun* **1** conduct of the relations between nations by peaceful means **2** tact or skill in dealing with people

diplomat *noun* official engaged in diplomacy

dire *adjective* disastrous, urgent or terrible

direct *adjective* **1** (of a route) shortest or straight **2** without anyone or anything intervening **3** likely to have an immediate effect **4** honest, frank ▷ *adverb* **5** in a direct manner ▷ *verb* **6** to lead and organize **7** to tell (someone) to do something **8** to tell (someone) the way to a place **9** to address (a letter, package, remark, etc) **10** to provide guidance to (actors, cameramen, etc) in (a play or film)

direct current *noun* electric current that flows in one direction only

direction *noun* **1** course or line along which a person or thing moves, points or lies **2** management or guidance ▶ **directions** instructions for doing something or for reaching a place

directive *noun* instruction that must be obeyed

directly *adverb* **1** in a direct manner **2** at once ▷ *conjunction* **3** as soon as

director *noun* **1** person or thing that directs or controls **2** member of the governing board of a business etc **3** person responsible for the artistic and technical aspects of the making of a film etc ▷ **directorial** *adjective: her directorial debut*

directorate *noun* **1** board of directors **2** position of director

directory directories *noun* **1** book listing names, addresses and telephone numbers **2** *Computers* area of a disk containing the names and locations of the files it currently holds

direct speech *noun* the reporting of what someone has said by quoting the exact words

dirge *noun* slow sad song of mourning

dirt *noun* **1** unclean substance, filth **2** earth, soil **3** obscene speech or writing **4** *informal* harmful gossip

dirty dirtier dirtiest *adjective* **1** covered or marked with dirt **2** unfair or dishonest **3** obscene **4** displaying dislike or anger: *a dirty look* ▷ *verb* **5** to make (something) dirty

dis- *prefix* indicating: **1** reversal: *disconnect* **2** negation or lack: *dissimilar, disgrace* **3** removal or release: *disembowel*

disability disabilities *noun* **1** condition of being disabled **2** something that disables someone

disable verb to make ineffective, unfit or incapable > **disablement** noun: permanent total disablement

disabled adjective lacking a physical power, such as the ability to walk

disadvantage noun unfavourable or harmful circumstance

disaffected adjective having lost loyalty to or affection for someone or something

disagree disagrees disagreeing disagreed verb 1 to argue or have different opinions 2 to be different, conflict 3 disagree with to cause physical discomfort (to): Curry disagrees with me > **disagreement** noun: a minor disagreement

disagreeable adjective 1 unpleasant 2 (of a person) unfriendly or unhelpful

disappear verb 1 to cease to be visible 2 to cease to exist > **disappearance** noun: his wife's disappearance

disappoint verb to fail to meet the expectations or hopes of > **disappointed** adjective: I was disappointed that she was not there > **disappointing** adjective: a disappointing performance

disappointment noun 1 feeling of being disappointed 2 person or thing that disappoints

disapprove disapprove of to consider wrong or bad > **disapproval** noun: it was greeted with universal disapproval > **disapproving** adjective: a disapproving look

disarm verb 1 to deprive of weapons 2 to win the confidence or affection of 3 (of a country) to decrease the size of its armed forces

disarmament noun reducing or getting rid of military forces and weapons

disarray noun 1 confusion and lack of discipline 2 extreme untidiness

disassemble verb to take (something) to pieces

disaster noun 1 occurrence that causes great distress or destruction 2 something, such as a project, that fails > **disastrous** adjective: a disastrous military campaign > **disastrously** adverb

disband verb to (cause to) cease to function as a group

disc noun 1 flat circular object 2 compact disc or gramophone record 3 Anatomy circular flat structure in the body, especially between the vertebrae 4 Computers same as **disk**

discard verb to get rid of (something or someone) as useless or undesirable

discern verb formal to see or be aware of (something) clearly

discernible adjective able to be seen or recognized

discerning adjective having good judgment > **discernment** noun: his powers of discernment

discharge verb 1 to allow (a patient) to go 2 to dismiss (someone) from duty or employment 3 to fire (a gun) 4 to release or pour out (a substance or liquid) 5 formal to meet the demands of (a duty or responsibility) ▷ noun 6 substance that comes out from a place 7 discharging

disciple noun follower of the doctrines of a teacher, especially Jesus Christ

discipline noun 1 practice of imposing strict rules of behaviour 2 formal area of academic study ▷ verb 3 to attempt to improve the behaviour of (oneself or another) by training or rules 4 to punish ▷ **disciplinary** adjective: they took disciplinary action against him ▷ **disciplined** adjective able to behave and work in a controlled way

disc jockey noun person who introduces and plays pop records on a radio programme or at a disco

disclose verb to make (information) known ▷ **disclosure** noun: disclosure of information to the press

disco discos noun 1 nightclub where people dance to amplified pop records 2 occasion at which people dance to amplified pop records

discomfort noun inconvenience, distress or mild pain

disconcert verb to embarrass or upset ▷ **disconcerting** adjective: the unfamiliar layout was a little disconcerting

disconnect verb 1 to undo or break the connection between (two things) 2 to stop the supply of electricity or gas of

discontent noun lack of contentment ▷ **discontented** adjective: discontented workers

discontinue discontinues discontinuing discontinued verb to bring (something) to an end or come to an end

discord noun 1 lack of agreement or harmony between people 2 harsh confused sounds

discount verb 1 to take no account of (something) because it is considered to be unreliable, prejudiced or irrelevant 2 to deduct (an amount) from the price of something ▷ noun 3 deduction from the full price of something

discourage verb 1 to deprive (someone) of the will to persist in something 2 to oppose (something) by expressing disapproval ▷ **discouragement** noun: His shoulders drooped with exhaustion and discouragement ▷ **discouraging** adjective: a discouraging lack of interest

discourse noun formal 1 conversation 2 formal treatment of a subject in speech or writing ▷ verb 3 **discourse on** to speak or write (about something) at length

discover verb 1 to be the first to find or to find out about 2 to learn about for the first time 3 to find after study or search ▷ **discoverer** noun: the discoverer of penicillin

discredit verb 1 to damage the reputation of 2 to cause (an idea) to be disbelieved or distrusted ▷ noun 3 damage to someone's reputation

discreet adjective 1 careful to avoid embarrassment, especially by keeping confidences secret 2 unobtrusive ▷ **discreetly** adverb

discrepancy discrepancies noun conflict or variation between facts, figures or claims

discrete adjective formal separate and distinct

discretion noun 1 quality of behaving in a discreet way 2 freedom or authority to make judgments and decide what to do > **discretionary** adjective: judges were given wider discretionary powers

discriminate verb 1 **discriminate against** or **in favour of** to single out (a particular person or group) for worse or better treatment than others 2 **discriminate between** to recognize or understand the difference (between)

discus discuses noun heavy disc-shaped object thrown in sports competitions

discuss verb 1 to consider (something) by talking it over 2 to treat (a subject) in speech or writing

discussion noun conversation or piece of writing in which a subject is considered in detail

disdain noun 1 feeling of superiority and dislike > verb 2 to refuse with disdain > **disdainful** adjective: he was disdainful of his opponent's chances

disease noun unhealthy condition in people, animals or plants > **diseased** adjective: diseased lungs

disembark verb to get off a ship, aircraft or bus

disembodied adjective 1 lacking a body 2 seeming not to be attached to or coming from anyone

disenchanted adjective disappointed and disillusioned > **disenchantment** noun: growing disenchantment with the new regime

disfigure verb to spoil the appearance of

disgrace noun 1 condition of shame, loss of reputation or dishonour 2 shameful person or thing > verb 3 to bring shame upon (yourself or others)

disgraceful adjective shameful or scandalous > **disgracefully** adverb

disgruntled adjective sulky or discontented

disguise verb 1 to change the appearance or manner in order to conceal the identity of (someone or something) 2 to misrepresent (something) in order to obscure its actual nature or meaning > noun 3 mask, costume or manner that disguises 4 state of being disguised

disgust noun 1 great loathing or distaste > verb 2 to sicken or fill with loathing > **disgusted** adjective: I'm disgusted with the way he was treated > **disgusting** adjective: a disgusting habit

dish noun 1 shallow container used for holding or serving food 2 particular kind of food 3 short for **dish aerial** 4 informal attractive person > **dish out** verb informal to distribute > **dish up** verb informal to serve (food)

dishearten verb to weaken or destroy the hope, courage or enthusiasm of > **disheartened** adjective: She was disheartened by their hostile reaction > **disheartening** adjective: a frustrating and disheartening experience

dishevelled adjective (of a person's hair, clothes or general appearance) disordered and untidy

dishonest adjective not honest or fair > **dishonestly** adverb

dishonesty noun behaviour which is meant to deceive people, either by not telling the truth or by cheating

disillusion verb 1 to destroy the illusions or false ideas of ▷ noun 2 (also **disillusionment**) state of being disillusioned > **disillusioned** adjective: disillusioned with politics

disinfectant noun substance that destroys harmful germs

disintegrate verb (of an object) to break into fragments > **disintegration** noun: the violent disintegration of Yugoslavia

disinterest noun lack of personal involvement in a situation

disinterested adjective free from bias or involvement

disjointed adjective having no coherence; disconnected

disk noun Computers a circular storage device

dislike verb 1 to consider something or someone unpleasant or disagreeable ▷ noun 2 feeling of not liking something or someone

dislocate verb to displace (a bone or joint) from its normal position

dislodge verb to remove something or someone from a previously fixed position

dismal adjective 1 gloomy and depressing 2 informal of poor quality > **dismally** adverb

dismantle verb to take apart piece by piece

dismay verb 1 to fill with alarm or depression ▷ noun 2 alarm mixed with sadness

dismember verb formal 1 to remove the limbs of 2 to cut to pieces > **dismemberment** noun

dismiss verb 1 to remove (an employee) from a job 2 to allow (someone) to leave 3 to put (something) out of your mind 4 (of a judge) to state that (a case) will not be brought to trial > **dismissal** noun: Mr Low's dismissal from his post

dismissive adjective scornful or contemptuous

disobey verb to neglect or refuse to obey

disorder noun 1 state of untidiness and disorganization 2 public violence or rioting 3 illness

disorganized or **disorganised** adjective 1 confused and badly arranged 2 not good at planning work and activities efficiently

disown verb to deny any connection with (someone)

disparaging adjective critical and scornful: disparaging remarks

disparate adjective completely different > **disparity** noun: economic disparities between North and South

dispatch verb 1 to send off to a destination or to perform a task 2 to carry out (a duty or a task) with speed 3 old-fashioned to kill ▷ noun 4 official communication or report, sent in haste 5 report sent to a newspaper by a correspondent

dispel dispels dispelling **dispelled** verb to destroy or remove

dispensary dispensaries noun place where medicine is dispensed

dispense verb 1 to give out 2 to

prepare and distribute (medicine) ▷ verb **3 dispense with** to do away with or manage without

dispenser noun machine or container from which something is given out: *a cash dispenser*

disperse verb **1** to scatter over a wide area **2** to (cause to) leave a gathering ▷ **dispersion** or **dispersal** noun: *dispersion of their forces*

dispirited adjective depressed and having no enthusiasm for anything

dispiriting adjective causing loss of enthusiasm: *a dispiriting defeat*

displace verb **1** to move (something) from the usual location **2** to remove (someone) from office

displacement noun **1** removal of something from its usual or correct place or position **2** *Physics* weight or volume of liquid displaced by an object submerged or floating in it

display verb **1** to make visible or noticeable ▷ noun **2** displaying **3** something displayed **4** exhibition

displease verb to annoy or upset (someone) ▷ **displeasure** noun: *The train was late, much to my displeasure*

disposable adjective **1** designed to be thrown away after use **2** available for use: *disposable income*

disposal noun **1** getting rid of something **2 at your disposal** available for your use

dispose verb **1** to place in a certain order **2 dispose of a** to throw away **b** to give, sell or transfer to another **c** to deal with or settle **d** to kill

disprove verb to show (an assertion or claim) to be incorrect

dispute noun **1** disagreement, argument ▷ verb **2** to argue about (something) **3** to doubt the validity of **4** to fight over possession of

disqualify disqualifies disqualifying disqualified verb to stop (someone) officially from taking part in something for wrongdoing ▷ **disqualification** noun: *disqualification from the race*

disquiet noun **1** feeling of anxiety ▷ verb **2** to make (someone) anxious ▷ **disquieting** adjective: *He found her letter disquieting*

disregard verb **1** to give little or no attention to ▷ noun **2** lack of attention or respect

disrepair noun condition of being worn out or in poor working order

disrespect noun lack of respect ▷ **disrespectful** adjective: *accusations that he had been disrespectful to the Queen*

disrupt verb to interrupt the progress of ▷ **disruption** noun: *disruption to flights in Britain* ▷ **disruptive** adjective: *disruptive pupils*

dissatisfied adjective not pleased or contented ▷ **dissatisfaction** noun: *I want to express my dissatisfaction with the report*

dissect verb **1** to cut open (a corpse) to examine it **2** to examine critically and minutely ▷ **dissection** noun: *corpses needed for dissection*

dissent verb **1** to disagree ▷ noun **2** disagreement ▷ **dissenting**

adjective: dissenting voices

dissertation *noun* written thesis, usually required for a higher university degree

disservice *noun* harmful action

dissident *noun* **1** person who disagrees with and criticizes the government ▷ *adjective* **2** disagreeing with and criticizing the government

dissimilar *adjective* not alike; different

dissipate *verb* **1** to waste or squander **2** to scatter or disappear

dissipated *adjective* showing signs of overindulgence in alcohol and other physical pleasures

dissolve *verb* **1** to (cause to) become liquid **2** to break up or end officially **3** to break down emotionally: *she dissolved into tears*

dissuade *verb* to deter (someone) from doing something by persuasion

distance *noun* **1** space between two points **2** state of being apart **3** remoteness in manner **4 the distance** most distant part of the visible scene ▷ *verb* **5 distance yourself** *or* **be distanced from** to separate yourself or be separated mentally from

distant *adjective* **1** far apart separated by a specified distance **3** remote in manner **distantly** *adverb*

distaste *noun* dislike or disgust **distasteful** *adjective* unpleasant or offensive

distil *distils* **distilling** *distilled verb* **1** to subject to or obtain by distillation **2** to give off (a substance) in drops **3** to extract

the essence of ▷**distillation** *noun* process of evaporating a liquid and condensing its vapour

distillery *distilleries noun* place where spirit drinks are made

distinct *adjective* **1** not the same **2** easily sensed or understood **3** clear and definite ▷**distinctly** *adverb*

distinction *noun* **1** act of distinguishing **2** distinguishing feature **3** state of being different **4** special honour, recognition or fame

distinctive *adjective* easily recognizable ▷**distinctively** *adverb*

distinguish *verb* **1 distinguish between** to make, show or recognize a difference (between) **2** to be a distinctive feature of **3** to make out by hearing, seeing, etc ▷**distinguishable** *adjective: the brothers are not easily distinguishable* ▷**distinguished** *adjective* **1** dignified in appearance **2** highly respected ▷**distinguishing** *adjective: distinguishing features*

distort *verb* **1** to misrepresent (the truth or facts) **2** to twist out of shape ▷**distorted** *adjective: a distorted voice* ▷**distortion** *noun: audio signals transmitted without distortion*

distract *verb* **1** to draw the attention of (a person) away from something **2** to entertain ▷**distracted** *adjective* unable to concentrate, preoccupied ▷**distractedly** *adverb* ▷**distracting** *adjective: distracting noises*

distraction *noun* **1** something that diverts the attention

2 something that serves as an entertainment

distraught *adjective* extremely anxious or agitated

distress *noun* **1** extreme unhappiness **2** great physical pain **3** poverty ▷ *verb* **4** to upset badly

distressing *adjective* very worrying or upsetting

distribute *verb* **1** to hand out or deliver (leaflets, mail, etc) **2** to share (something) among the members of a particular group

distribution *noun* **1** distributing **2** arrangement or spread

distributor *noun* **1** wholesaler who distributes goods to retailers in a specific area **2** device in a petrol engine that sends the electric current to the spark plugs

district *noun* area of land regarded as an administrative or geographical unit

district nurse *noun* nurse who visits and treats people in their own homes

distrust *verb* **1** to regard as untrustworthy ▷ *noun* **2** feeling of suspicion or doubt > **distrustful** *adjective*: *I'm distrustful of all politicians*

disturb *verb* **1** to intrude on **2** to worry or make anxious **3** to change the position or shape of > **disturbing** *adjective*: *I found what she said about him disturbing*

disturbance *noun* **1** interruption or intrusion **2** unruly outburst in public

disuse *noun* state of being no longer used > **disused** *adjective*: *a disused coal mine*

ditch *noun* **1** narrow channel dug in the earth for drainage or irrigation ▷ *verb* **2** *informal* to abandon or discard

dither *verb* **1** to be uncertain or indecisive ▷ *noun* **2** state of indecision or agitation

ditto **dittos** *noun* **1** the same ▷ *adverb* **2** in the same way

ditty **ditties** *noun* old-fashioned short simple poem or song

diva *noun* distinguished female singer

dive **dives** **diving** **dived** *verb* **1** to plunge headfirst into water **2** (of a submarine or diver) to submerge under water **3** (of a bird or aircraft) to fly in a steep nose-down descending path **4** to move quickly in a specified direction **5** **dive in** or **into** to start doing (something) enthusiastically ▷ *noun* **6** diving **7** steep nose-down descent **8** *informal* disreputable bar or club

diverge *verb* **1** to separate and go in different directions **2** to deviate (from a prescribed course) > **divergence** *noun*: *a divergence of opinion* > **divergent** *adjective*: *divergent views*

diverse *adjective* **1** having variety, assorted **2** different in kind

diversify **diversifies** **diversifying** **diversified** *verb* **1** to create different forms of **2** (of an enterprise) to vary (products or operations) in order to expand or reduce the risk of loss > **diversification** *noun*: *diversification of agriculture*

diversion *noun* **1** official detour used by traffic when a main route is closed **2** something that distracts someone's attention **3** diverting **4** amusing pastime

divert verb 1 to change the direction of 2 to distract the attention of 3 to entertain or amuse

divide verb 1 to separate into parts 2 to share or be shared out in parts 3 to (cause to) disagree 4 to keep apart or be a boundary between 5 to calculate how many times (one number) can be contained in (another) ▷ noun 6 division or split

dividend noun 1 sum of money representing part of the profit made, paid by a company to its shareholders 2 extra benefit

divine adjective 1 of God or a god 2 godlike 3 informal splendid ▷ verb 4 to discover (something) by intuition or guessing > **divinely** adverb

divinity divinities noun 1 study of religion 2 god or goddess 3 state of being divine

division noun 1 dividing, sharing out 2 one of the parts into which something is divided 3 Maths process of dividing one number by another 4 difference of opinion

divisive adjective tending to cause disagreement

divisor noun number to be divided into another number

divorce noun 1 legal ending of a marriage 2 any separation, especially a permanent one ▷ verb 3 to legally end one's marriage (to) 4 to remove or separate > **divorced** adjective: he is divorced, with a young son

divulge verb to make (something) known

DIY abbreviation Brit, Aust, NZ do-it-yourself

dizzy dizzier dizziest adjective 1 having or causing a whirling sensation 2 mentally confused ▷ verb 3 to cause to feel giddy or confused > **dizziness** noun: his complaint causes dizziness

DNA abbreviation deoxyribonucleic acid: main constituent of the chromosomes of all living things

do does doing did done; dos verb 1 to perform or complete (a deed or action) 2 to be adequate: that one will do 3 to suit or improve: that style does nothing for you 4 to find the answer to (a problem or puzzle) 5 to cause or produce: it does no harm to think ahead 6 to give or grant: do me a favour 7 to work at, as a course of study or a job 8 used to form questions: how do you know? 9 used to intensify positive statements and commands: I do like port; do go on 10 used to form negative statements and commands: I do not know her well; do not get up 11 used to replace an earlier verb: he gets paid more than I do ▷ noun 12 informal party or celebration > **do away with** verb to get rid of > **do up** verb 1 to fasten 2 to decorate and repair > **do with** verb to find useful or benefit from: I could do with a rest > **do without** verb to manage without

docile adjective (of a person or animal) easily controlled

dock noun 1 enclosed area of water where ships are loaded, unloaded or repaired 2 enclosed space in a court of law where the accused person sits or stands 3 weed with broad leaves ▷ verb 4 to bring or be brought into dock 5 to link (two spacecraft) or (of two spacecraft) to be linked together in space **6** to deduct money from (a person's wages) **7** to remove part of (an animal's tail) by cutting through the bone

doctor noun **1** person licensed to practise medicine **2** person who has been awarded a doctorate ▷ verb **3** to alter in order to deceive **4** to poison or drug (food or drink) **5** informal to castrate (an animal)

doctorate noun highest academic degree in any field of knowledge > **doctoral** adjective: a doctoral thesis

doctrine noun **1** body of teachings of a religious, political or philosophical group **2** principle or body of principles that is taught or advocated > **doctrinal** adjective: doctrinal differences among religious leaders

document noun **1** piece of paper providing an official record of something **2** piece of text or graphics stored in a computer as a file that can be amended or altered by document processing software ▷ verb **3** to record or report (something) in detail **4** to support (a claim) with evidence

documentary documentaries noun **1** film or television programme presenting the facts about a particular subject ▷ adjective **2** (of evidence) based on documents

dodge verb **1** to avoid (a blow, being seen, etc) by moving suddenly **2** to evade by cleverness or trickery ▷ noun **3** cunning or deceitful trick

dodgy dodgier dodgiest adjective informal **1** dangerous or risky **2** untrustworthy

dodo dodos noun large flightless extinct bird

doe noun female deer, hare or rabbit

does verb third person singular of the present tense of **do**

dog dogs dogging dogged noun **1** domesticated four-legged mammal of many different breeds **2** related wild mammal, such as the dingo or coyote **3** male animal of the dog family **4** informal person: you lucky dog! **5 the dogs** informal greyhound racing **6 go to the dogs** informal to go to ruin physically or morally **7 let sleeping dogs lie** to leave things undisturbed ▷ verb **8** to follow (someone) closely **9** to trouble or plague

dog collar noun **1** collar for a dog **2** informal white collar fastened at the back, worn by members of the clergy

dog-eared adjective **1** (of a book) having pages folded down at the corner **2** shabby or worn

dogged adjective obstinately determined > **doggedly** adverb

dogma noun doctrine or system of doctrines proclaimed by authority as true

dogmatic adjective habitually stating your opinions forcefully c arrogantly > **dogmatism** noun

doldrums plural noun **1** depressed state of mind **2** state of inactivit

dole noun Brit, Aust, NZ informal money received from the state while unemployed ▷ **dole out** ve to distribute in small quantities

doll noun **1** small model of a huma being, used as a toy **2** informal pretty girl or young woman

dollar noun standard monetary unit of the USA, Australia, New Zealand, Canada and some other countries

dollop noun informal lump (of food)

dolphin noun sea mammal of the whale family, with a beaklike snout

domain noun 1 field of knowledge or activity 2 land under one ruler or government 3 Computers group of computers with the same name on the Internet 4 NZ public park

dome noun 1 rounded roof built on a circular base 2 something shaped like this > **domed** adjective: a domed roof

domestic adjective 1 of one's own country or a specific country 2 of the home or family 3 enjoying running a home 4 (of an animal) kept as a pet or to produce food > noun 5 person whose job is to do housework in someone else's house > **domestically** adverb

domesticate verb 1 to bring or keep (a wild animal or plant) under control or cultivation 2 to accustom (someone) to home life > **domesticated** adjective: domesticated animals

domesticity noun formal home life

dominance noun power or control

dominate verb 1 to control or govern 2 to tower above (surroundings) 3 to be very significant in > **dominating** adjective: dominating personalities > **domination** noun: centuries of domination by the Romans

domineering adjective forceful and arrogant

dominion noun 1 control or authority 2 land governed by one ruler or government 3 (formerly) self-governing division of the British Empire

domino dominoes noun 1 small rectangular block marked with dots, used in dominoes 2 **dominoes** game in which dominoes with matching halves are laid together

don dons donning donned verb 1 to put on (clothing) > noun 2 Brit member of the teaching staff at a university or college 3 Spanish gentleman or nobleman

donate verb to give, especially to a charity or organization

done verb past participle of **do**

donkey noun 1 long-eared member of the horse family 2 **donkey's years** informal long time

donor noun 1 Medicine person who provides blood or organs for use in the treatment of another person 2 person who makes a donation

doodle verb 1 to scribble or draw aimlessly > noun 2 shape or picture drawn aimlessly

doom noun 1 death or a terrible fate > verb 2 to destine or condemn to death or a terrible fate

doomed adjective certain to suffer an unpleasant or unhappy existence

doomsday noun the end of the world

door noun 1 hinged or sliding panel for closing the entrance to a building, room, etc 2 entrance

doorway noun opening into a building or room

dope noun 1 informal illegal drug,

usually cannabis **2** medicine or drug **3** *informal* stupid person ▷ *verb* **4** to give a drug to (a person or animal), especially in order to affect the outcome of a race

dormant *adjective* temporarily quiet, inactive or not being used

dormitory *dormitories noun* large room, especially at a school, containing several beds

dormouse *dormice noun* small mouselike rodent with a furry tail

dosage *noun* size of a dose

dose *noun* **1** specific quantity of a medicine taken at one time **2** *informal* something unpleasant to experience ▷ *verb* **3** to give a dose to (someone)

dossier *noun* collection of documents about a subject or person

dot *dots dotting dotted noun* **1** small round mark **2** shorter symbol used in Morse code **3** **on the dot** (referring to time) precisely or exactly ▷ *verb* **4** to mark with a dot **5** to scatter or spread around

dotcom or **dot.com** *noun* company that does most of its business on the Internet

dote *verb* **dote on** to love (someone) to an excessive degree ▷ **doting** *adjective*: doting parents

double *adjective* **1** as much again in number, amount, size, etc **2** composed of two equal or similar parts **3** designed for two users: *double room* **4** folded in two ▷ *adverb* **5** twice over ▷ *noun* **6** twice the number, amount, size, etc **7** person who looks almost exactly like another **8** **doubles** game between two pairs of

players **9** **at** or **on the double** quickly or immediately ▷ *verb* **10** to make or become twice as much or as many **11** to bend or fold (material etc) **12** to play two parts or serve two roles **13** to turn sharply ▷ **doubly** *adverb*

double bass *noun* stringed instrument, largest and lowest member of the violin family

double-cross *verb* **1** to cheat or betray ▷ *noun* **2** double-crossing

double-decker *noun* **1** bus with two passenger decks one on top of the other ▷ *adjective* **2** *informal* having two layers

double glazing *noun* two panes of glass in a window, fitted to reduce heat loss

doubt *noun* **1** uncertainty about the truth, facts or existence of something **2** unresolved difficulty or point ▷ *verb* **3** to question the truth of **4** to distrust or be suspicious of (someone)

doubtful *adjective* **1** unlikely **2** feeling doubt

dough *noun* **1** thick mixture of flour and water or milk, used for making bread etc **2** *informal* money

doughnut *noun* small cake of sweetened dough fried in deep fa

dour *adjective* sullen and unfriend

douse *verb* **1** to drench with wate or other liquid **2** to put out (a light)

dove *noun* bird with a heavy body, small head and short legs

dovetail *noun* **1** joint containing wedge-shaped tenons ▷ *verb* **2** t fit together neatly

dowager *noun* widow possessing property or a title obtained from her husband

dowdy dowdier dowdiest
adjective dull and old-fashioned

down preposition, adverb
1 indicating movement to or
position in a lower place ▷ adverb
2 indicating completion of an
action, lessening of intensity, etc:
calm down ▷ adjective 3 depressed,
unhappy ▷ verb 4 informal to drink
(something) quickly ▷ noun 5 soft
fine feathers

downcast adjective 1 sad and
dejected 2 (of the eyes) directed
downwards

downfall noun (cause of) a sudden
loss of position or reputation

downgrade verb to reduce
(something or someone) in
importance, status or value

downhill adjective 1 going or
sloping down 2 towards the
bottom of a hill

download verb 1 to transfer (data,
files, etc) from the memory of
one computer to that of another
▷ noun 2 file transferred in such
a way

downpour noun heavy fall of rain

downright adjective, adverb
extreme(ly)

downstairs adverb 1 to or on a
lower floor ▷ noun 2 lower or
ground floor

downstream adjective, adverb
in or towards the lower part of
a stream

down-to-earth adjective sensible
or practical

downtrodden adjective oppressed
and lacking the will to resist

downturn noun decline in the
economy or in the success of a
company or industry

downwards or **downward**
adverb 1 from a higher to a lower
level, condition or position
2 from an earlier time or source to
a later one

downwind adverb, adjective in the
same direction towards which
the wind is blowing

dowry dowries noun property
brought by a woman to her
husband at marriage

doze verb 1 to sleep lightly or
briefly 2 **doze off** to fall into a
light sleep ▷ noun 3 short sleep

dozen adjective, noun twelve

Dr abbreviation 1 Doctor 2 Drive

drab drabber drabbest adjective
dull and dreary > **drabness** noun:
the drabness of his office

draft noun 1 plan, sketch
or drawing of something
2 preliminary outline of a book,
speech, etc 3 written order
for payment of money by a
bank 4 US, Aust selection for
compulsory military service
▷ verb 5 to draw up an outline
or plan of 6 to send (people)
from one place to another to do
a specific job 7 US, Aust to select
for compulsory military service
8 Austral, NZ to select (cattle or
sheep) from a herd or flock

drag drags dragging dragged
verb 1 to pull with force, especially
along the ground 2 to trail on the
ground 3 to persuade or force
(oneself or someone else) to go
somewhere 4 **drag on** or **out** to
last or be prolonged tediously
5 to search (a river) with a dragnet
or hook 6 Computers to move (an
image) on the screen by use of the
mouse ▷ noun 7 person or thing
that slows up progress 8 informal

a b c d e f g h i j k l m n o p q r s t u v w x y z

tedious thing or person **9** *informal* women's clothes worn by a man

dragon *noun* mythical fire-breathing monster like a huge lizard

dragonfly dragonflies *noun* brightly coloured insect with a long slender body and two pairs of wings

dragoon *noun* **1** heavily armed cavalryman ▷ *verb* **2** to coerce or force

drain *noun* **1** pipe or channel that carries off water or sewage **2** cause of a continuous reduction in energy or resources ▷ *verb* **3** to draw off or remove liquid from **4** to flow away or filter off **5** to drink the entire contents of (a glass or cup) **6** to make constant demands on (energy or resources), exhaust

drainage *noun* **1** system of drains **2** process or method of draining

drake *noun* male duck

drama *noun* **1** serious play for theatre, television or radio **2** writing, producing or acting in plays **3** situation that is exciting or highly emotional

dramatic *adjective* **1** of or like drama **2** behaving flamboyantly > **dramatically** *adverb*

dramatist *noun* person who writes plays

drape *verb* **1** to cover with material, usually in folds **2** to place casually

drastic *adjective* strong and severe > **drastically** *adverb*

draught *noun* **1** current of cold air, especially in an enclosed space **2** portion of liquid to be drunk, especially medicine **3** gulp or swallow **4** one of the flat discs used in the game of draughts **5 draughts** game for two players using a chessboard and twelve draughts each ▷ *adjective* **6** (of an animal) used for pulling heavy loads **7** (of beer) served straight from barrels rather than in bottles

draughtsman draughtsmen *noun* person employed to prepare detailed scale drawings of machinery, buildings, etc

draughty draughtier draughtiest *adjective* exposed to draughts of air

draw draws drawing drew drawn *verb* **1** to sketch (a figure, picture, etc) with a pencil or pen **2** to pull (a person or thing) closer to or further away from a place **3** to move in a specified direction: *the car drew near* **4** to take from a source: *draw money from bank accounts* **5** to attract or interest **6** to formulate or decide *to draw conclusions* **7** (of two teams or contestants) to finish a game with an equal number of points ▷ *noun* **8** raffle or lottery **9** contest or game ending in a tie **10** event, act, etc, that attracts a large audience > **draw out** *verb* **1** to encourage (someone) to talk freely **2** to make (something) longer **3** (of a train) to leave a station > **draw up** *verb* **1** to prepare and write out (a contrac **2** (of a vehicle) to come to a stop

drawback *noun* disadvantage

drawbridge *noun* bridge that ca be raised or lowered preventing or giving access to a building su as a castle

drawer *noun* sliding box-shaped part of a piece of furniture, used for storage

drawing noun **1** picture or plan made by means of lines on a surface **2** art of making drawings

drawing room noun old-fashioned room where visitors are received and entertained

drawl verb **1** to speak slowly, with long vowel sounds ▷ noun **2** drawling manner of speech

drawn verb **1** past participle of **draw** ▷ adjective **2** haggard, tired or tense in appearance

dread verb **1** to anticipate with apprehension or fear ▷ noun **2** great fear >**dreaded** adjective: this dreaded disease

dreadful adjective **1** very disagreeable or shocking **2** extreme >**dreadfully** adverb

dream dreams dreaming dreamed or dreamt noun **1** imagined series of events experienced in the mind while asleep **2** cherished hope **3** informal wonderful person or thing ▷ verb **4** to see imaginary pictures in the mind while asleep **5** dream of or about to have an image (of) or fantasy (about) **6** dream of to consider the possibility of (something) ▷ adjective **7** ideal: a dream house

dreamtime noun (in Australian Aboriginal legends) the time when the world was being made and the first people were created

dreamy dreamier dreamiest adjective **1** vague or impractical **2** informal wonderful >**dreamily** adverb

dreary drearier dreariest adjective dull or boring

dregs plural noun **1** solid particles

that settle at the bottom of some liquids **2** most despised elements

drenched adjective soaking wet

dress noun **1** one-piece garment for a woman or girl, consisting of a skirt part and a top part and sometimes sleeves **2** complete style of clothing ▷ verb **3** to put your clothes on **4** to put formal clothes on **5** to put clothes on (a child, invalid, etc) **6** to apply a protective covering to (a wound) **7** to arrange or prepare (salad, meat, etc)

dresser noun **1** piece of furniture with shelves and with cupboards, for storing or displaying dishes **2** Theatre person employed to assist actors with their costumes

dressing gown noun coat-shaped garment worn over pyjamas or nightdress

dressing room noun room used for changing clothes, especially backstage in a theatre

dress rehearsal noun last rehearsal of a play or show, using costumes, lighting, etc

dribble verb **1** to (allow to) flow in drops **2** to allow saliva to trickle from the mouth **3** Sport to propel (a ball) by repeatedly tapping it with the foot, hand or a stick ▷ noun **4** small quantity of liquid falling in drops

drift verb **1** to be carried along by currents of air or water **2** to move aimlessly from one place or activity to another ▷ noun **3** something piled up by the wind or current, such as a snowdrift **4** general movement or development **5** point or meaning: catch my drift?

drill noun **1** tool or machine for

boring holes **2** strict and often repetitive training **3** *informal* correct procedure **4** machine for sowing seed in rows **5** small furrow for seed ▷ *verb* **6** to bore a hole in (something) with or as if with a drill **7** to teach by rigorous exercises or training

drink drinks drinking drank drunk *verb* **1** to swallow (a liquid) **2** to consume alcohol, especially to excess ▷ *noun* **3** (portion of) a liquid suitable for drinking **4** alcohol, or its habitual or excessive consumption > **drink in** *verb* to pay close attention to > **drink to** *verb* to drink a toast to > **drinker** *noun*: *I'm not much of a coffee drinker*

drip drips dripping dripped *verb* **1** to (let) fall in drops ▷ *noun* **2** falling of drops of liquid **3** sound made by falling drops **4** *informal* weak dull person **5** *Medicine* device by which a solution is passed in small drops through a tube into a vein

drive drives driving drove driven *verb* **1** to guide the movement of (a vehicle) **2** to transport in a vehicle **3** to force (someone) into a specified state **4** to push or propel **5** *Sport* to hit (a ball) very hard and straight ▷ *noun* **6** journey by car, van, etc **7** (also **driveway**) path for vehicles connecting a building to a public road **8** united effort towards a common goal **9** energy and ambition; *Psychology* **10** means by which power is transmitted in a mechanism > **drive at** *verb* *informal* to intend or mean: *what was he driving at?* > **driver** *noun* person who drives a vehicle

> **driving** *noun*

drive-in *adjective, noun* (denoting) a cinema, restaurant, etc, used by people in their cars

drivel *noun* foolish talk

drizzle *noun* **1** very light rain ▷ *verb* **2** to rain lightly > **drizzly** *adjective*: *drizzly rain*

dromedary dromedaries *noun* camel with a single hump

drone *verb* **1** to (make) a monotonous low dull sound ▷ *noun* **2** male bee > **drone on** *verb* to talk for a long time in a monotonous tone

drool *verb* to allow saliva to flow from the mouth

droop *verb* to hang downwards loosely

drop drops dropping dropped *verb* **1** to (allow to) fall vertically **2** to decrease in amount, strength or value **3** to mention (a hint or name) casually **4** to discontinue **5** **drop in** or **by** to pay someone a casual visit ▷ *noun* **6** small quantity of liquid forming a round shape **7** any small quantity of liquid **8** decrease in amount, strength or value **9** vertical distance that something may fall **10** **drops** liquid medication applied in small drops > **drop off** *verb* **1** *informal* to fall asleep **2** to grow smaller or less

droplet *noun* small drop

droppings *plural noun* faeces of certain animals, such as rabbits or birds

drought *noun* prolonged shortage of rainfall

drove *verb* **1** past tense of **drive** **2** to drive (sheep or cattle) over a long distance ▷ *noun* **3** herd of livestock being driven together

drown verb 1 to die or kill by immersion in liquid 2 to forget (one's sorrows) temporarily by drinking alcohol 3 to drench thoroughly 4 to make (a sound) inaudible by being louder

drowsy drowsier drowsiest adjective feeling sleepy > **drowsiness**

drudgery noun hard boring work

drug drugs drugging drugged noun 1 substance used in the treatment or prevention of disease 2 chemical substance, especially a narcotic, taken for the effects it produces > verb 3 to give a drug to (a person or animal) to cause sleepiness or unconsciousness 4 to mix a drug with (food or drink)

Druid noun member of an ancient order of Celtic priests

drum drums drumming drummed noun 1 percussion instrument sounded by striking a membrane stretched across the opening of a hollow cylinder 2 cylindrical object or container 3 **the drum** Austral information or advice > verb 4 to play (music) on a drum 5 to tap rhythmically or regularly > **drummer** noun person who plays a drum or drums

drumstick noun 1 stick used for playing a drum 2 lower joint of the leg of a cooked chicken etc

drunk verb 1 past participle of drink > adjective 2 intoxicated with alcohol to the extent of losing control over normal functions 3 overwhelmed by a strong influence or emotion > noun 4 person who is drunk or who frequently gets drunk

dry drier or dryer driest; dries drying dried adjective 1 lacking moisture 2 having little or no rainfall 3 informal thirsty 4 (of wine) not sweet 5 uninteresting 6 (of humour) subtle and sarcastic 7 prohibiting the sale of alcohol: a dry town > verb 8 to make or become dry 9 to preserve (food) by removing the moisture > **drily** or **dryly** adverb > **dryness** noun > **dry up** verb 1 to become completely dry 2 informal to forget what you were going to say or find that you have nothing left to say

dry-clean verb to clean (clothes etc) with chemicals rather than water

dryer or **drier** noun apparatus for removing moisture 2 comparative of dry

dual adjective having two parts, functions or aspects

dub dubs dubbing dubbed verb 1 to give (a person or place) a name or nickname 2 to provide (a film) with a new soundtrack, especially in a different language 3 to provide (a film or tape) with a soundtrack

dubious adjective feeling or causing doubt > **dubiously** adverb

duchess noun 1 woman who holds the rank of duke 2 wife or widow of a duke

duchy duchies noun territory of a duke or duchess

duck ducks ducking ducked noun 1 water bird with short legs, webbed feet and a broad blunt bill 2 its flesh, used as food 3 female of this bird 4 Cricket score of nothing > verb 5 to move (the head or body) quickly

a
b
c
d
e
f
g
h
i
j
k
l
m
n
o
p
q
r
s
t
u
v
w
x
y
z

downwards, to avoid being seen or to dodge a blow **6** to plunge suddenly under water **7** *informal* to dodge (a duty or responsibility)

duckling *noun* young duck

duct *noun* **1** tube, pipe or channel through which liquid or gas is conveyed **2** bodily passage conveying secretions or excretions

dud *informal noun* **1** ineffectual person or thing ▷ *adjective* **2** bad or useless

due *adjective* **1** expected or scheduled to be present or arrive **2** owed as a debt **3** fitting, proper **4 due to** attributable to or caused by ▷ *noun* **5** something that is owed or required **6 dues** charges for membership of a club or organization ▷ *adverb* **7** directly or exactly: *due south*

duel duels duelling duelled *noun* **1** formal fight with deadly weapons between two people, to settle a quarrel ▷ *verb* **2** to fight in a duel

duet *noun* piece of music for two performers

dug *verb* past of **dig** ▷ *noun*

dugong *noun* whalelike mammal of tropical waters

dugout *noun* **1** *Brit* (at a sports ground) covered bench where managers and substitutes sit **2** canoe made by hollowing out a log **3** *Military* covered excavation to provide shelter

duke *noun* **1** nobleman of the highest rank **2** prince or ruler of a small principality or duchy

dull *adjective* **1** not interesting **2** (of an ache) not acute **3** (of weather) not bright or clear

4 lacking in spirit **5** not very intelligent **6** (of a blade) not sharp ▷ *verb* **7** to make or become dull ▷ **dullness** *noun: the dullness of their routine* ▷ **dully** *adverb*

duly *adverb* **1** in a proper manner **2** at the proper time

dumb *adjective* **1** lacking the power to speak **2** silent **3** *informal* stupid

dumbfounded *adjective* speechless with astonishment

dummy dummies *noun* **1** figure representing the human form, used for displaying clothes etc **2** copy of an object, often lacking some essential feature of the original **3** rubber teat for a baby to suck **4** *informal* stupid person ▷ *adjective* **5** imitation or substitute

dump *verb* **1** to drop or let fall in a careless manner **2** *informal* to get rid of (someone or something no longer wanted) ▷ *noun* **3** place where waste materials are left **4** *informal* dirty unattractive place **5** *Military* place where weapons or supplies are stored

dumpling *noun* **1** small ball of dough cooked and served with stew **2** round pastry case filled with fruit

dunce *noun* person who is stupid or slow to learn

dune *noun* mound or ridge of drifted sand

dung *noun* faeces from animals such as cattle

dungarees *plural noun* trousers which have a bib covering the chest and straps over the shoulders

dungeon *noun* underground prison cell

dunk verb 1 to dip (a biscuit or bread) in a drink or soup before eating it 2 to put (something) in liquid

duo duos noun 1 pair of performers 2 informal pair of closely connected people

dupe verb 1 to deceive or cheat ▷ noun 2 person who is easily deceived

duplicate adjective 1 copied exactly from an original ▷ noun 2 exact copy ▷ verb 3 to make an exact copy of 4 to do again (something that has already been done) > **duplication** noun: unnecessary duplication of work

durable adjective long-lasting > **durability** noun: a material renowned for its durability

duration noun length of time that something lasts

duress noun compulsion by use of force or threats

during preposition throughout or within the limit of (a period of time)

dusk noun time just before nightfall, when it is almost dark

dust noun 1 small dry particles of earth, sand or dirt ▷ verb 2 to remove dust from (furniture) by wiping 3 to sprinkle (something) with a powdery substance

dustbin noun large container for household rubbish

duster noun cloth used for dusting

dustman dustmen noun Brit man whose job is to collect household rubbish

dusty dustier dustiest adjective covered with dust

Dutch adjective 1 of the Netherlands 2 ▷ noun main

language spoken in the Netherlands 3 **go Dutch** informal to share the expenses on an outing

dutiful adjective doing what is expected > **dutifully** adverb

duty duties noun 1 work or a task performed as part of your job 2 a task that a person feels morally bound to do 3 government tax on imports 4 **on duty** at work

duty-free adjective untaxed and therefore cheaper than normal: duty-free vodka

duvet noun kind of quilt used in bed instead of a top sheet and blankets

DVD abbreviation Digital Versatile (or Video) Disk

dwarf dwarfs or **dwarves**; dwarfs dwarfing dwarfed noun 1 person who is smaller than average 2 (in folklore) small ugly manlike creature, often possessing magical powers ▷ adjective 3 (of an animal or plant) much smaller than the usual size for the species ▷ verb 4 to cause (someone or something) to seem small by being much larger

dwell dwells dwelling dwelled or **dwelt** verb literary to live as a permanent resident > **dwell on** verb to think, speak or write at length about

dwelling noun place of residence

dwindle verb to grow less in size, strength or number

dye dyes dyeing dyed noun 1 colouring substance 2 colour produced by dyeing ▷ verb 3 to colour (hair or fabric) by applying a dye

dying *verb* present participle of **die**[1]

dyke or **dike** *noun* wall built to prevent flooding

dynamic *adjective* **1** full of energy, ambition and new ideas **2** *Physics* of energy or forces that produce motion > **dynamically** *adverb*

dynamite *noun* **1** explosive made of nitroglycerine **2** *informal* dangerous or exciting person or thing > *verb* **3** to blow (something) up with dynamite

dynamo dynamos *noun* device for converting mechanical energy into electrical energy

dynasty dynasties *noun* sequence of hereditary rulers

dysentery *noun* infection of the intestine causing severe diarrhoea

dyslexia *noun* disorder causing impaired ability to read > **dyslexic** *adjective: a dyslexic child*

e

each *adjective, pronoun* every (one) taken separately

- Wherever you use *each* other you could also use *one*
- another

eager *adjective* showing or feeling great desire, keen > **eagerly** *adverb* enthusiastically > **eagerness** *noun: an eagerness to learn*

eagle *noun* **1** large bird of prey with

keen eyesight **2** *Golf* score of two strokes under par for a hole

ear *noun* **1** organ of hearing, especially the external part of it **2** head of corn

eardrum *noun* thin piece of skin inside the ear which enables you to hear sounds

earl *noun* British nobleman ranking next below a marquess

early earlier earliest *adjective, adverb* **1** before the expected or usual time **2** in the first part of a period **3** in a period far back in time

earmark *verb* to set (something) aside for a specific purpose

earn *verb* **1** to obtain (something) by work or merit **2** (of investments etc) to gain (interest) > **earner** *noun: a wage earner*

earnest *adjective* **1** serious and sincere > *noun* **2 in earnest** seriously > **earnestly** *adverb*

earnings *plural noun* money earned

earphone *noun* receiver for a radio etc, held to or put in the ear

earring *noun* piece of jewellery worn in the ear lobe

earshot *noun* hearing range

earth *noun* **1** planet that we live on **2** land, the ground **3** soil **4** fox's hole **5** wire connecting an electrical apparatus with the earth > *verb* **6** to connect (a circuit) to earth

earthenware *noun* pottery made of baked clay

earthly *adjective* concerned with life on earth rather than heaven o life after death

earthquake noun violent vibration of the earth's surface

earthworm noun worm that burrows in the soil

earthy earthier earthiest adjective **1** coarse or crude **2** of or like earth

earwig noun small insect with a pincer-like tail

ease noun **1** freedom from difficulty, discomfort or worry **2** rest or leisure ▷ verb **3** to give bodily or mental ease to (someone or something) **4** to lessen (severity, tension, pain, etc); relieve **5** to move carefully or gradually

easel noun frame to support an artist's canvas or a blackboard

easily adverb **1** without difficulty **2** without a doubt: the song is easily one of their finest

east noun **1** (direction towards) the part of the horizon where the sun rises **2** region lying in this direction ▷ adjective **3** to or in the east **4** (of a wind) from the east ▷ adverb **5** in, to or towards the east

easter noun Christian spring festival celebrating the Resurrection of Jesus Christ

easterly adjective **1** to or towards the east **2** (of a wind) blowing from the east

eastern adjective in or from the east: a remote eastern corner of the country

eastward adjective, adverb towards the east

easy easier easiest adjective **1** not needing much work or effort **2** free from pain, care or anxiety

3 easy-going
- Although easy is an adjective,
- it can be used as an adverb
- in fixed phrases like take
- it easy

eat eats eating ate eaten verb **1** to take (food) into the mouth and swallow it **2** to have a meal > **eat away** verb (also **eat away at**) to destroy (something) slowly

eaves plural noun overhanging edges of a roof

eavesdrop eavesdrops eavesdropping eavesdropped verb to listen secretly to a private conversation

ebb verb **1** (of tide water) to flow back **2** to fall away or decline ▷ noun **3** flowing back of the tide **4** at a low ebb in a state of weakness

ebony noun **1** hard black wood ▷ adjective **2** deep black

e-book noun **1** electronic book ▷ verb **2** book (airline tickets, appointments, etc.) on the internet

ebullient adjective full of enthusiasm or excitement > **ebullience** noun

EC abbreviation European Community: a former name for the European Union

eccentric adjective **1** odd or unconventional ▷ noun **2** eccentric person > **eccentrically** adverb: eccentrically dressed > **eccentricity** noun: unusual to the point of eccentricity

ecclesiastical adjective of the Christian Church or clergy

echelon noun level of power or responsibility

echidna echidnas or ec

noun Aust Australian spiny egg-laying mammal; (also **spiny anteater**)

echo echoes echoing echoed *noun* **1** repetition of sounds by reflection of sound waves off a surface **2** close imitation ▷ *verb* **3** to be repeated as an echo **4** to imitate (what someone else has said)

eclipse *noun* **1** temporary obscuring of one star or planet by another ▷ *noun* apparent path of the sun

eco- *prefix* of ecology or the environment

ecology *noun* study of the relationships between living things and their environment > **ecological** *adjective* **1** of ecology **2** intended to protect the environment > **ecologically** *adverb*: *ecologically sound* > **ecologist** *noun* person who studies ecology

economic *adjective* **1** concerning the management of the money, industry and trade in a country **2** profitable **3** *informal* inexpensive or cheap

economical *adjective* spending money carefully and sensibly > **economically** *adverb*: *an economically depressed area*

economics *noun* **1** the study of the production and distribution of goods, services and wealth in a society and the organization of its money, industry and trade ▷ *plural* **2** financial aspects

economist *noun* specialist in economics

economy economies *noun* **1** system that a country uses to organize and manage its money, industry and trade **2** wealth that a country gets from business and industry **3** careful use of money or resources to avoid waste

ecosystem *noun* system involving interactions between a community and its environment

ecstasy ecstasies *noun* **1** state of intense delight **2** *informal* powerful drug that can produce hallucinations > **ecstatic** *adjective* very happy and excited > **ecstatically** *adverb*: *ecstatically happy*

eczema *noun* skin disease that causes the skin surface to become rough and itchy

eddy eddies eddying eddied *noun* **1** circular movement of air, water, etc ▷ *verb* **2** to move with a circular motion

edge *noun* **1** border or line where something ends or begins **2** cutting side of a blade **3 have the edge on** to have an advantage over (someone) **4 on edge** nervous or irritable ▷ *verb* **5** to provide an edge or border for (something) **6** to push (one's way) gradually

edgy edgier edgiest *adjective* nervous or irritable

edible *adjective* fit to be eaten

edifice *noun* large building

edit *verb* **1** to make changes, cuts and corrections (to a piece of writing, book, film, etc) so that it is fit for publication or broadcast **2** to be in charge of (a newspaper, magazine, etc) or a section of it

edition *noun* number of copies of a new publication printed at one time

editor *noun* **1** person who edits

2 person in charge of a newspaper or magazine or a section of it

editorial noun **1** newspaper article stating the opinion of the editor ▷ adjective **2** relating to editing or editors >**editorially** adverb

educate verb to teach (someone)

educated adjective having a high standard of learning and culture

education noun **1** gaining knowledge and understanding through learning **2** system of teaching people at school or university >**educational** adjective: educational materials; It would be very educational >**educationally** adverb

eel noun snakelike fish

eerie eerier eeriest adjective uncannily frightening or disturbing >**eerily** adverb: eerily quiet

effect noun **1** change or result caused by someone or something **2** overall impression **3 take effect** to starts to happen or start to produce results: the law will take effect next year

- Remember that effect is a noun and affect is a verb

effective adjective **1** producing a desired result **2** coming into operation or beginning officially >**effectively** adverb: to function effectively

effeminate adjective (of a man) displaying characteristics thought to be typical of a woman

efficient adjective functioning effectively and with little waste of effort >**efficiency** noun ability to function effectively and with little waste of effort >**efficiently** adverb effectively and with little

waste of effort

effigy effigies noun statue or model of a person

effluent noun liquid waste that comes out of factories or sewage works

effluvium effluvia noun unpleasant smell or gas given off by something

effort noun **1** physical or mental exertion **2** attempt

effortless adjective done easily and well >**effortlessly** adverb easily and well

e.g. abbreviation Latin for example

egalitarian adjective favouring equality for all people

egg noun **1** oval or round object laid by the females of birds and other creatures, containing a developing embryo **2** hen's egg used as food **3** (also **ovum**) cell produced in a female animal's body that can develop into a baby if it is fertilized >**egg on** verb to encourage (someone) to do something foolish or daring

eggplant noun US, Canadian, Aust, NZ dark purple pear-shaped vegetable; aubergine

ego egos noun self-esteem

egocentric adjective only thinking of oneself

egoism or **egotism** noun **1** excessive concern for one's own interests **2** excessively high opinion of oneself >**egoist** or **egotist** noun egotistical person >**egotistic** or **egotistical** or **egoistic** adjective having an excessive concern for one's own interests

Egyptian adjective **1** belonging or relating to Egypt ▷ noun

2 someone from Egypt

Eid-ul-Adha noun annual Muslim festival marking the end of pilgrimage to Mecca known as the hajj

eight adjective, noun the number 8 > **eighth** adjective, noun

eighteen adjective, noun the number 18 > **eighteenth** adjective, noun

eighty eighties adjective, noun the number 80 > **eightieth** adjective, noun

either adjective, pronoun **1** one or the other (of two) **2** each of two > conjunction **3** used preceding two or more possibilities joined by or > adverb **4** likewise: I don't eat meat and he doesn't either

ejaculate verb **1** to discharge semen **2** to utter (something) abruptly > **ejaculation** noun act of ejaculating

eject verb to force out or expel (someone or something) > **ejection** noun: the ejection of hecklers from the meeting

elaborate adjective **1** with a lot of fine detail; fancy > verb **2** to add more information or detail about (something) > **elaborately** adverb: elaborately costumed dolls > **elaboration** noun adding more detail about something

eland noun large antelope of southern Africa

elapse verb (of time) to pass by

elastic adjective **1** able to stretch easily **2** adapting easily to change > noun **3** rubber material that stretches and returns to its original shape > **elasticity** noun: to restore the skin's elasticity

elated adjective extremely happy

and excited > **elation** noun great happiness

elbow noun **1** joint between the upper arm and the forearm > verb **2** to shove or strike (someone) with the elbow

elder adjective **1** (of brother, son, daughter, etc) older > noun **2** older person **3** small tree with white flowers and black berries > **eldest** adjective (of brother, son, daughter, etc) oldest

elderly adjective (fairly) old

elect verb **1** to choose (someone) by voting **2** to decide (to do something) > adjective **3** appointed but not yet in office: president elect

election noun **1** choosing of representatives by voting **2** act of choosing > **electoral** adjective: electoral reform

electorate noun people who have the right to vote

electric adjective **1** powered or produced by electricity **2** exciting or tense

electrical adjective using or producing electricity > **electrically** adverb

electrician noun person trained to install and repair electrical equipment

electricity noun **1** form of energy associated with stationary or moving electrons or other charged particles **2** electric current or charge

electrified adjective connected to a supply of electricity

electrifying adjective very exciting

electro- prefix operated by or caused by electricity

electrocute verb to kill or

injure (someone) by electricity
> **electrocution** noun: death by
electrocution

electrode noun conductor
through which an electric current
enters or leaves a battery, vacuum
tube, etc

electron noun elementary particle
in all atoms that has a negative
electrical charge

electronic adjective having
transistors or silicon chips
which control an electric current
> **electronically** adverb

electronics noun technology
concerned with the development
of electronic devices and circuits

elegant adjective pleasing or
graceful in dress, style or design
> **elegance** noun: understated
elegance > **elegantly** adverb

elegy elegies noun mournful
poem, especially a lament for
the dead

element noun **1** component
part **2** substance that cannot be
separated into other substances
by ordinary chemical techniques
3 section of people within a
larger group: the rowdy element
4 heating wire in an electric
kettle, stove, etc **5** in your
element in a situation where
you are happiest **6** elements
a basic principles of something
b weather conditions, especially
wind, rain and cold

elemental adjective simple and
basic, but powerful

elementary adjective simple and
straightforward

elephant noun huge four-footed
thick-skinned animal with ivory
tusks and a long trunk

elevate verb **1** to raise (someone)
in rank or status **2** to lift
(something) up

elevation noun **1** raising of
someone or something to a
higher level or position **2** height
above sea level

eleven adjective, noun **1** the
number 11 ▷ noun **2** Sport team
of eleven people > **eleventh**
adjective, noun

elf elves noun (in folklore) small
mischievous fairy

elicit verb **1** to bring about (a
response or reaction) **2** to find
out (information) by careful
questioning

eligible adjective **1** meeting the
requirements or qualifications
needed **2** desirable as a spouse
> **eligibility** noun: eligibility for
benefits

eliminate verb to get rid of
(something) > **elimination** noun:
the elimination of chemical weapons

elite noun most powerful, rich
or gifted members of a group
▷ adjective

Elizabethan adjective of the
reign of Elizabeth I of England
(1558–1603)

elk noun large deer of N Europe
and Asia

ellipse noun a regular oval shape,
like a circle seen from an angle

elm noun tall tree with broad leaves

elocution noun art of speaking
clearly in public

elongated adjective long and thin

elope verb (of two people) to run
away secretly to get married

eloquent adjective able to speak
or write skilfully and with ease
> **eloquence** noun fluent powerful

use of language > **eloquently** adverb

else adjective, adverb **1** in addition or more: *what else can I do?* **2** other or different: *It was unlike anything else that had happened*

elsewhere adverb in or to another place

elude verb **1** to escape from (someone or something) by cleverness or quickness **2** to baffle (someone)

elusive adjective difficult to catch or remember

elves noun plural of **elf**

em- prefix another form of the prefix **en-**
- em- is the form used before the letters b, m and p

emaciated adjective extremely thin and weak, because of illness or lack of food

e-mail or **email** noun **1** (also **electronic mail**) sending of messages between computer terminals ▷ verb **2** to communicate with (someone) in this way

emancipation noun freeing someone from harmful or unpleasant restrictions

embargo embargoes embargoing embargoed noun **1** order by a government prohibiting trade with a country ▷ verb **2** to put an embargo on (goods)

embark verb **1** to board a ship or aircraft **2** (followed by on) to begin (a new project)

embarrass verb to cause (someone) to feel self-conscious or ashamed > **embarrassed** adjective: *an embarrassed silence*

> **embarrassing** adjective: *an embarrassing situation*

> **embarrassment** noun: *we apologize for any embarrassment this may have caused*

embassy embassies noun **1** offices or official residence of an ambassador **2** ambassador and his staff

embedded adjective **1** fixed firmly and deeply **2** (of a journalist) assigned to accompany an active military unit

ember noun glowing piece of wood or coal in a dying fire

embittered adjective feeling anger as a result of misfortune

emblazoned adjective decorated (with something)

emblem noun object or design that symbolizes a quality, type or group

embody embodies embodying embodied verb **1** to be an example or expression of (a quality or idea) **2** to comprise or include (a number of things) > **embodiment** noun: *the embodiment of vulnerability*

embossed adjective (of a design or pattern) standing out from a surface

embrace verb **1** to clasp (someone) in your arms; hug **2** to accept (an idea) eagerly ▷ noun **3** act of embracing

embroider verb to decorate (fabric) with needlework > **embroidery** noun

embroiled adjective deeply involved and entangled (in an argument or conflict)

embryo embryos noun unborn creature in the early stages of

development > **embryonic**
adjective at an early stage

emerald *noun* **1** bright green
precious stone ▷ *adjective*
2 bright green

emerge *verb* **1** to come into view
2 (followed by *from*) to come out
of (a difficult or bad experience)
3 to become known > **emergence**
noun coming into existence
> **emergent** *adjective* coming into
existence

emergency emergencies *noun*
sudden unforeseen occurrence
needing immediate action

emigrant *noun* person who goes
and settles in another country

emigrate *verb* to go and settle in
another country > **emigration**
noun process of emigrating

eminent *adjective* > well-known
and respected > **eminence** *noun*
1 position of superiority or fame
> **eminently** *adverb* very: *eminently
reasonable*

emir *noun* Muslim ruler

emission *noun* release of
something such as gas or
radiation into the atmosphere

emit emits emitting emitted *verb*
1 to give out (heat, light or a smell)
2 to utter (a sound): *She emitted a
long, low whistle*

emoticon *noun* Computers same
as **smiley**

emotion *noun* strong feeling

emotional *adjective* readily
affected by or appealing to the
emotions > **emotionally** *adverb*

emotive *adjective* tending to
arouse emotion

empathize *verb* (followed by
with) to understand the feelings
of (someone) > **empathy** *noun*
ability to understand someone
else's feelings as if they were
one's own

emperor *noun* ruler of an empire

emphasis emphases *noun*
1 special importance or
significance **2** stress on a word or
phrase in speech

emphasize *verb* to make it
known that (something) is very
important

emphatic *adjective* showing
emphasis > **emphatically** *adverb*

empire *noun* **1** group of countries
under the rule of one state or
person **2** large organization that
is directed by one person or group

employ *verb* **1** to hire (someone)
2 to provide work or occupation
for (someone) **3** to use
(something)

employee *noun* person who
works for another person or for an
organization

employer *noun* person or
organization that employs
someone

employment *noun* **1** state of
being employed **2** work done by a
person to earn money

empower *verb* to enable or
authorize (someone) to do
something

empress *noun* woman who rules
an empire, or the wife of an
emperor

**empty emptier emptiest;
empties emptying emptied**
adjective **1** containing nothing
2 unoccupied **3** without purpose
or value **4** (of words) insincere
▷ *verb* **5** to make (something)
empty > **empties** *plural noun*
empty boxes, bottles, etc

> emptiness *noun: the emptiness of the desert*

emu *noun* large Australian flightless bird with long legs

emulate *verb* to attempt to equal or surpass (someone or something) by imitating **> emulation** *noun: a role model worthy of emulation*

emulsion *noun* a water-based paint

en- *prefix* **1** to surround or cover: *enclose; encrusted* **2** to cause to be in a certain state or condition: *enamoured; endanger*

enable *verb* to provide (someone) with the means, opportunity or authority (to do something)

enact *verb* **1** to establish (a law or bill) by law **2** to perform (a story or play) **> enactment** *noun: the enactment of the Bill of Rights*

enamel enamels enamelling
enamelled *noun* **1** glasslike coating applied to metal etc to preserve the surface **▷ verb 2** to cover (an object) with enamel **> enamelled** *adjective* covered with enamel

enamoured *adjective* **be enamoured of** to like (someone or something) very much

encapsulate *verb* to contain or represent (facts or ideas) in a small space

encased *adjective* surrounded or covered with a substance: *encased in plaster*

enchanted *adjective* fascinated or charmed

enchanting *adjective* attractive, delightful or charming

encircle *verb* to form a circle around (something or someone)

enclave *noun* part of a country entirely surrounded by foreign territory

enclose *verb* **1** to surround (an object or area) completely **2** to include (something) along with something else **> enclosed** *adjective* **1** surrounded completely **2** included

enclosure *noun* area of land surrounded by a wall or fence and used for a particular purpose

encompass *verb* to include all of (a number of things)

encore *interjection* **1** again, once more **▷ noun 2** short extra performance due to enthusiastic demand

encounter *verb* **1** to meet (someone) unexpectedly **2** to be faced with (a difficulty) **▷ noun 3** unexpected meeting

encourage *verb* **1** to inspire (someone) with confidence **2** to spur (someone) on **> encouragement** *noun: my friends gave me a great deal of encouragement* **> encouraging** *adjective: the results have been encouraging*

encroach *verb* (followed by) (on) to intrude gradually on (a person's rights or land) **> encroachment** *noun* intruding gradually on something

encrusted *adjective* covered with a layer of something: *a necklace encrusted with gold*

encyclopedia or **encyclopaedia** *noun* book or set of books containing facts about many subjects, usu. in alphabetical order

encyclopedic or **encyclopaedic** *adjective* knowing or giving information about many different things

end *noun* 1 furthest point or part 2 limit 3 last part of something 4 fragment 5 death or destruction 6 purpose 7 *Sport* either of the two defended areas of a playing field 8 **make ends meet** to have just enough money for your needs ▷ *verb* 9 to come or bring (something) to a finish

endanger *verb* to put (something) in danger

endear *verb* (followed by *to*) to cause (someone) to be liked > **endearing** *adjective*: *an endearing personality* > **endearingly** *adverb*

endeavour *verb* 1 to try ▷ *noun* 2 effort

endless *adjective* having or seeming to have no end > **endlessly** *adverb*

endorse *verb* 1 to give approval to (someone or something) 2 to sign the back of (a cheque) 3 to record a conviction on (a driving licence)

endowed *adjective* **endowed with** provided with (a quality or ability)

endurance *noun* act or power of enduring

endure *verb* 1 to bear (hardship) patiently 2 to last for a long time > **enduring** *adjective*: *an enduring friendship*

enema *noun* liquid put into a person's rectum to cause their bowels to empty

enemy enemies *noun* hostile person or nation, opponent

energetic *adjective* having energy or enthusiasm; lively

> **energetically** *adverb* with great energy

energy *noun* 1 capacity for intense activity 2 capacity to do work and overcome resistance 3 source of power, such as electricity

enforce *verb* to cause (a law or rule) to be obeyed > **enforceable** *adjective*: *legally enforceable contracts* > **enforcement** *noun*: *stricter enforcement of existing laws*

engage *verb* 1 to take part or participate 2 to involve (a person or his or her attention) intensely

engaged *adjective* 1 having agreed to be married 2 in use

engagement *noun* appointment with someone

engine *noun* 1 any machine that converts energy into mechanical work 2 railway locomotive

engineer *noun* 1 person trained in any branch of engineering ▷ *verb* 2 to plan (an event or situation) in a clever manner

engineering *noun* profession of applying scientific principles to the design and construction of engines, cars, buildings or machines

English *noun* 1 official language of Britain, Ireland, Australia, New Zealand, South Africa, Canada, the US and several other countries ▷ *plural* 2 **the English** the people of England ▷ *adjective* 3 relating to England

Englishman Englishmen *noun* a man from England > **Englishwoman** *noun*

engrave *verb* to carve (a design) onto a hard surface > **engraver** *noun*

engraving *noun* print made from

a
b
c
d
e
f
g
h
i
j
k
l
m
n
o
p
q
r
s
t
u
v
w
x
y
z

an engraved plate

engrossed *adjective* having all your attention taken up: *engrossed in a video game*

engulf *verb* to cover or surround (something) completely

enhance *verb* to increase the quality, value or attractiveness of (something) > **enhancement** *noun* increase in quality, value or attractiveness

enigma *noun* puzzling thing or person

enigmatic *adjective* mysterious, puzzling or difficult to understand > **enigmatically** *adverb*

enjoy *verb* 1 to take joy in (something) 2 to experience (something)

enjoyable *adjective* giving pleasure or satisfaction

enjoyment *noun* pleasure or satisfaction from doing something enjoyable

enlarge *verb* 1 to make (something) larger 2 (followed by *on*) to speak or write about (a subject) in greater detail

enlargement *noun* 1 making something bigger 2 something, especially a photograph, that has been made bigger

enlighten *verb* to give information to (someone) > **enlightening** *adjective: an enlightening talk* > **enlightenment** *noun*

enlightened *adjective* well informed and willing to consider different opinions

enlist *verb* 1 to enter the armed forces 2 to obtain support or help from (someone)

enliven *verb* to make (something) lively or cheerful

en masse *adverb* French in a group, all together

enormity enormities *noun* 1 great wickedness 2 gross offence 3 *informal* great size

enormous *adjective* very big, vast > **enormously** *adverb* very

enough *adjective* 1 as much or as many as necessary ▷ *noun* 2 sufficient quantity ▷ *adverb* 3 sufficiently 4 fairly or quite: *that's a common enough experience*

enquire *verb* to seek information or ask (about)

enquiry enquiries *noun* 1 question 2 investigation

enrage *verb* to make (someone) very angry > **enraged** *adjective* very angry

enrich *verb* to improve the quality of (something) > **enriched** *adjective* improved in quality > **enrichment** *noun: the enrichment of society*

enrol enrols enrolling enrolled *verb* (to cause) to become a member > **enrolment** *noun* act of enrolling

en route *adverb* French on the way

ensconced *adjective* settled firmly or comfortably

ensemble *noun* 1 all the parts of something taken together 2 company of actors or musicians 3 *Music* group of musicians playing together

enshrine *verb* to cherish or treasure (something)

ensign *noun* 1 naval flag 2 US naval officer

ensue ensues ensuing ensued *verb* to come next or result > **ensuing** *adjective* following or resulting

ensure *verb* to make certain or sure (that something happens)

entangled *adjective* involved: *entangled in international politics*

enter *verb* **1** to come or go into (a place) **2** to join (an organization) **3** to become involved in or take part in (a competition or examination) **4** to record (an item) in a journal etc

enterprise *noun* **1** company or firm **2** bold or difficult undertaking >**enterprising** *adjective* full of boldness and initiative

entertain *verb* **1** to amuse (people) **2** to receive (people) as guests >**entertainer** *noun* person who amuses audiences, e.g. a comedian or singer >**entertaining** *adjective* amusing >**entertainment** *noun* anything that people watch for pleasure, e.g. shows and films

enthral *verb* **enthrals enthralling enthralled** *verb* to hold the attention of (someone) >**enthralling** *adjective* fascinating

enthuse *verb* to show enthusiasm

enthusiasm *noun* ardent interest, eagerness

enthusiastic *adjective* showing great excitement, eagerness or approval >**enthusiastically** *adverb*

entice *verb* to tempt (someone) to do something

enticing *adjective* extremely attractive and tempting

entire *adjective* including every detail, part or aspect of something >**entirely** *adverb* wholly and completely >**entirety** *noun*: *this message will now be repeated in its entirety*

entitle *verb* to give a right to (someone) >**entitlement** *noun*: *they lose their entitlement to benefit when they start work*

entity entities *noun* separate distinct thing

entourage *noun* group of people who follow or travel with a famous or important person

entrails *plural noun* **1** intestines **2** innermost parts of something

entrance[1] *noun* **1** way into a place **2** act of entering **3** right of entering

entrance[2] *verb* **1** to delight (someone) **2** to put (someone) into a trance >**entrancing** *adjective* fascinating

entrant *noun* person who enters a university, contest, etc

entrenched *adjective* (of a belief, custom or power) firmly established

entrepreneur *noun* business person who attempts to make a profit by risk and initiative >**entrepreneurial** *adjective*: *his entrepreneurial spirit*

entrust *verb* to put (something) into the care or protection of (someone)

entry entries *noun* **1** entrance, way in **2** entering **3** item entered in a journal etc

envelop *verb* to wrap (something) up, enclose (something)

envelope *noun* folded gummed paper cover for a letter

enviable *adjective* arousing envy, fortunate

envious *adjective* full of envy >**enviously** *adverb*

environment *noun* external

conditions and surroundings in which people, animals, or plants live > **environmental** adjective: environmental hazards such as wind and sun > **environmentally** adverb: environmentally friendly goods

● There is an n before the m in
● environment

environmentalist noun person concerned with the protection of the natural environment

envisage verb to conceive of (something) as a possibility

envoy noun 1 messenger 2 diplomat ranking below an ambassador

envy envies envying envied noun 1 feeling of discontent aroused by another's good fortune ▷ verb 2 to grudge (someone) his or her good fortune, success, or qualities

enzyme noun a chemical substance, usually a protein, produced by cells in the body

ephemeral adjective short-lived

epic noun 1 long poem, book or film about heroic events or actions ▷ adjective 2 very impressive or ambitious

epidemic noun 1 widespread occurrence of a disease 2 rapid spread of something

epigram noun short witty remark or poem

epigraph noun 1 quotation at the start of a book 2 inscription

epilepsy noun disorder of the nervous system causing loss of consciousness and sometimes convulsions > **epileptic** adjective 1 of or having epilepsy ▷ noun 2 person who has epilepsy

episode noun 1 incident in a series of incidents 2 section of a serialized book, television programme, etc

epistle noun letter, especially of an apostle

epitaph noun commemorative inscription on a tomb

epithet noun descriptive word or name

epitome noun typical example

● Do not use epitome to mean
● 'the peak of something'. It
● means 'the most typical
● example of something'

epoch noun long period of time

eponymous adjective after whom a book, play, etc is named: the eponymous hero of 'Erik the Viking'

equal equals equalling equalled adjective 1 identical in size, quantity, degree, etc 2 having identical rights or status 3 evenly balanced 4 (followed by to) having the necessary ability (for) ▷ noun 5 person or thing equal to another ▷ verb 6 to be equal to (something) > **equality** noun state of being equal > **equally** adverb

equate verb to make or regard (something) as equivalent to something else: you can't equate lives with money

equation noun mathematical statement that two expressions are equal

equator noun imaginary circle round the earth, lying halfway between the North and South poles > **equatorial** adjective near or at the equator

equestrian adjective relating to horses and riding

equilateral *adjective* (of a triangle) having equal sides

equilibrium *noun* steadiness or stability

equine *adjective* relating to horses

equinox *noun* time of year when day and night are of equal length

equip **equips** **equipping** **equipped** *verb* to provide (someone or something) with supplies, components, etc

equipment *noun* set of tools or devices used for a particular purpose; apparatus

equitable *adjective* fair and reasonable

equity *noun* fairness

equivalent *adjective* **1** equal in use, size, value or effect ▷ *noun* **2** something that has the same use, size, value or effect as something else > **equivalence** *noun* state of being equivalent

era *noun* period of time considered as distinctive

eradicate *verb* to destroy (something) completely > **eradication** *noun*: *the eradication of corruption*

erase *verb* to remove (something) > **eraser** *noun* object for erasing something written

erect *verb* **1** to build (something) ▷ *adjective* **2** in a straight and upright position; vertical > **erection** *noun* **1** process of erecting something **2** something that has been erected **3** stiff swollen penis in an upright position

ermine *noun* expensive white fur

erode *verb* to wear (something) away

erosion *noun* gradual wearing away and destruction of something: *soil erosion*

erotic *adjective* involving or arousing sexual desire > **erotically** *adverb*

err *verb* to make a mistake

errand *noun* short trip to do something for someone

erratic *adjective* irregular or unpredictable > **erratically** *adverb*

erroneous *adjective* incorrect, mistaken > **erroneously** *adverb*

error *noun* mistake, inaccuracy or misjudgment

erudite *adjective* having great academic knowledge

erupt *verb* **1** (of a volcano) to throw out a lot of hot lava and ash suddenly and violently **2** to burst forth suddenly and violently > **eruption** *noun*: *the volcanic eruption of Tambora*

escalate *verb* to increase in extent or intensity

escalator *noun* moving staircase

escapade *noun* mischievous adventure

escape *verb* **1** to get free of (someone or something) **2** to avoid (something unpleasant or difficult): *escape attention* **3** (of a gas, liquid, etc) to leak gradually ▷ *noun* **4** act of escaping **5** means of relaxation

escapee *noun* person who has escaped

escapism *noun* taking refuge in fantasy to avoid unpleasant reality > **escapist** *adjective*: *escapist fantasy*

eschew *verb* to avoid or keep away from (something)

escort *noun* **1** people or vehicles accompanying another person for protection or as an honour **2** person who accompanies a person of the opposite sex to a social event ▷ *verb* **3** to act as an escort to (someone)

Eskimo *Eskimos noun* offensive a name that was formerly used for the Inuit people and their language

especially *adverb* particularly

espionage *noun* spying

espouse *verb* to adopt or give support to (a cause etc)

espresso *espressos noun* strong coffee made by forcing steam or boiling water through ground coffee beans

● The second letter of *espresso* is *s* and not *x*

essay *noun* **1** short literary composition **2** short piece of writing on a subject done as an exercise by a student

essence *noun* **1** most important feature of a thing which gives it its identity **2** concentrated liquid used to flavour food

essential *adjective* **1** vitally important **2** basic or fundamental ▷ *noun* **3** something fundamental or indispensable ▷ **essentially** *adverb* fundamentally

establish *verb* **1** to set (something) up on a permanent basis **2** to make (oneself) secure or permanent in a certain place, job, etc **3** to prove (a fact) ▷ **established** *adjective: the established names of Paris fashion*

establishment *noun* **1** act of establishing **2** commercial or other institution **3 the Establishment** group of people

having authority within a society

estate *noun* **1** large area of privately owned land in the country and all the property on it **2** large area of property development, especially of new houses or factories **3** property of a deceased person

estate agent *noun* person who works for a company that sells houses and land

esteem *noun* **1** high regard ▷ *verb* **2** to think highly of (someone or something) ▷ **esteemed** *adjective* greatly admired and respected

estimate *verb* **1** to calculate (an amount or quantity) roughly **2** to form an opinion about (something) ▷ *noun* **3** approximate calculation **4** statement from a workman etc of the likely charge for a job **5** opinion

estimation *noun* considered opinion

estranged *adjective* no longer living with your husband or wife

estrogen *noun* female sex hormone that regulates the reproductive cycle

estuary *estuaries noun* mouth of a river

etc *abbreviation* et cetera

et cetera *Latin* **1** and the rest or and others **2** or the like

● As *etc* means 'and the rest', you should not write *and etc*

etch *verb* **1** to cut (a design or pattern) on a surface by using acid or a sharp tool **2** to imprint (something) vividly on someone's mind ▷ **etched** *adjective* having a design made by etching

etching *noun* picture printed

from a metal plate that has had a design cut into it

eternal *adjective* lasting forever, or seeming to last forever
> **eternally** *adverb*

eternity eternities *noun* **1** infinite time **2** timeless existence after death **3** period of time that seems to go on forever

ether *noun* colourless sweet-smelling liquid used as an anaesthetic

ethereal *adjective* extremely delicate

ethical *adjective* in agreement with accepted principles of behaviour that are thought to be right > **ethically** *adverb*

ethics *noun* **1** code of behaviour ▷ *plural* **2** study of morals

Ethiopian *adjective* **1** belonging to or relating to Ethiopia ▷ *noun* **2** someone from Ethiopia

ethnic *adjective* **1** relating to a people or group that shares a culture, religion, or language **2** belonging or relating to such a group, especially one that is a minority group in a particular place > **ethnically** *adverb*

ethos *noun* distinctive spirit and attitudes of a people, culture, etc

etiquette *noun* conventional code of conduct

etymology *noun* study of the sources and development of words

EU *abbreviation* European Union

eucalyptus or **eucalypt** eucalyptuses or eucalypts *noun* tree, mainly grown in Australia, that provides timber, gum, and medicinal oil from the leaves

Eucharist *noun* religious ceremony in which Christians remember and celebrate Christ's last meal with his disciples

eunuch *noun* castrated man, especially (formerly) a guard in a harem

euphemism *noun* inoffensive word or phrase substituted for one considered offensive or upsetting > **euphemistic** *adjective: a euphemistic way of saying that someone has been lying* > **euphemistically** *adverb*

euphoria *noun* sense of elation > **euphoric** *adjective* intensely happy and excited

euro euros *noun* unit of the single currency of the European Union

Europe *noun* second smallest continent, having Asia to the east, the Arctic to the north, the Atlantic to the west, and the Mediterranean and Africa to the south

European *noun* **1** someone from Europe ▷ *adjective* **2** of or relating to Europe

European Union *noun* economic and political association of a number of European nations

euthanasia *noun* act of killing someone painlessly, especially to relieve his or her suffering

evacuate *verb* **1** to send (someone) away from a place of danger **2** to empty (a place) > **evacuation** *noun: the evacuation of the sick and wounded* > **evacuee** *noun* person who has been sent away from a place of danger

evade *verb* **1** to get away from or avoid (a problem or question) **2** to elude (someone or something)

evaluate *verb* to find or judge

the value of (something)
> **evaluation** noun assessing the strengths and weaknesses of something

evangelical adjective of certain Protestant sects which maintain the doctrine of salvation by faith

evangelist noun travelling preacher > **evangelism** noun teaching and spreading of the Christian gospel > **evangelize** verb to preach the gospel

evaporate verb to change from a liquid or solid to a vapour
> **evaporation** noun: the evaporation of the sweat on the skin

evasion noun deliberately avoiding doing something: evasion of arrest

evasive adjective deliberately trying to avoid talking about or doing something

eve noun 1 evening or day before some special event 2 period immediately before an event

even adjective 1 flat or smooth 2 (followed by with) on the same level (as) 3 equally balanced 4 divisible by two ▷ adverb 5 equally 6 simply 7 nevertheless > **evenly** adverb

evening noun 1 end of the day or early part of the night ▷ adjective 2 of or in the evening

event noun 1 anything that takes place; happening 2 planned and organized occasion 3 contest in a sporting programme

eventful adjective full of exciting incidents

eventual adjective ultimate

eventuality eventualities noun possible event

eventually adverb at the end of a

situation or process

ever adverb 1 at any time 2 always

evergreen noun, adjective (tree or shrub) having leaves throughout the year

everlasting adjective never coming to an end

every adjective 1 each without exception 2 all possible

everybody pronoun every person

everyday adjective usual or ordinary

everyone pronoun every person

everything pronoun 1 all or the whole of something 2 the most important thing: when I was 20, friends were everything to me

everywhere adverb in all places

evict verb to legally expel (someone) from his or her home > **eviction** noun: they were facing eviction

evidence noun 1 reason for belief 2 matter produced before a law court to prove or disprove a point 3 sign, indication 4 **in evidence** conspicuous

evident adjective easily seen or understood > **evidently** adverb

evil noun 1 wickedness 2 wicked deed ▷ adjective 3 harmful 4 morally bad 5 very unpleasant

evoke verb to call or summon up (a memory, feeling, etc)

evolution noun gradual change in the characteristics of living things over successive generations, especially to a more complex form > **evolutionary** adjective: an evolutionary process

evolve verb 1 to develop gradually 2 (of an animal or plant species) to undergo evolution

ewe noun female sheep

ex- prefix former: ex-wife

exacerbate verb to make (pain, emotion or a situation) worse

exact adjective **1** correct and complete in every detail **2** precise, as opposed to approximate ▷ verb **3** to demand (something) from someone > **exactly** adverb

exaggerate verb **1** to regard or represent (something) as greater than is true **2** to make (something) greater or more noticeable > **exaggeration** noun act of exaggerating

exalted adjective very important

exam noun short for **examination**

examination noun **1** examining **2** test of a candidate's knowledge or skill

examine verb **1** to look at (something or someone) closely **2** to test the knowledge of (someone) **3** to ask questions of (someone)

examiner noun person who sets or marks an examination

example noun **1** specimen typical of its group; sample **2** person or thing worthy of imitation **3** punishment regarded as a warning to others

exasperate verb to cause great irritation to (someone) > **exasperating** adjective infuriating > **exasperation** noun: he clenched his fist in exasperation

excavate verb **1** to remove earth from the ground by digging **2** to dig up (buried objects) from a piece of land to learn about the past > **excavation** noun: the excavation of a bronze-age boat

exceed verb **1** to be greater than

(something) **2** to go beyond (a limit) > **exceedingly** adverb very

excel excels excelling excelled verb to be outstandingly good at something

Excellency Excellencies noun title used to address a high-ranking official, such as an ambassador

excellent adjective exceptionally good; superb > **excellence** noun: the top award for excellence

except preposition **1** (sometimes followed by for) other than, not including **2** except that but for the fact that **3** verb **3** not to include > **exception** noun **1** excepting **2** thing that is excluded from or does not conform to the general rule > **exceptional** adjective **1** not ordinary **2** much above the average > **exceptionally** adverb

excerpt noun passage taken from a book, speech, etc

excess noun **1** state or act of exceeding the permitted limits **2** immoderate amount **3** amount by which a thing exceeds the permitted limits

excessive adjective too great in amount or degree > **excessively** adverb too

exchange verb **1** to give or receive (something) in return for something else ▷ noun **2** act of exchanging **3** thing given or received in place of another **4** centre in which telephone lines are interconnected **5** Finance place where securities or commodities are traded **6** transfer of sums of money of equal value between different currencies

Exchequer noun Brit government department in charge of state money

excise noun 1 tax on goods produced for the home market ▷ verb 2 to cut (something) out or away

excitable adjective easily excited

excite verb 1 to arouse (someone) to strong emotion; thrill 2 to arouse or evoke (an emotion) > **excited** adjective happy and unable to relax > **excitedly** adverb > **excitement** noun state of being excited > **exciting** adjective: the race is very exciting

exclaim verb to speak suddenly, cry out

exclamation noun word or phrase spoken suddenly to express a strong feeling

exclamation mark noun punctuation mark (!) used after exclamations

exclude verb 1 to keep or leave (someone) out 2 to leave (something) out of consideration > **exclusion** noun: women's exclusion from political power

exclusive adjective 1 excluding everything else 2 not shared 3 catering for a privileged minority ▷ noun 4 story reported in only one newspaper > **exclusively** adverb

excrement noun waste matter discharged from the body

excrete verb to discharge (waste matter) from the body > **excretion** noun: the excretion of this drug from the body

excruciating adjective 1 agonizing 2 hard to bear > **excruciatingly** adverb

excursion noun short journey, especially for pleasure

excuse noun 1 explanation offered to justify a fault etc ▷ verb 2 to put forward a reason or justification for (a fault etc) 3 to forgive (a person) or overlook (a fault etc) 4 to free (someone) from a duty or responsibility 5 to allow (someone) to leave

execute verb 1 to kill (someone) as a punishment for a crime 2 to carry out or perform (a plan or action) > **execution** noun: execution by lethal injection > **executioner** noun person who executes criminals

executive noun 1 person employed by a company at a senior level 2 (in an organization) committee having authority to make decisions and ensure that they are carried out ▷ adjective 3 concerned with making important decisions and ensuring that they are carried out

executor noun person appointed to perform the instructions of a will

exemplary adjective 1 being a good example 2 serving as a warning

exemplify exemplifies exemplifying exemplified verb to be a typical example of (something)

exempt adjective 1 not subject to an obligation or rule 2 to release (someone) from an obligation or rule > **exemption** noun being excused from an obligation or rule

exercise noun 1 activity to train the body or mind 2 set of movements or tasks designed to improve or test a person's ability **3** performance of a function ▷ *verb* **4** to make use of (something): *to exercise your rights* **5** to take exercise or perform exercises

exert *verb* **1** to use (influence, authority, etc) forcefully or effectively **2 exert yourself** to make a special effort > **exertion** *noun* vigorous physical effort or exercise

exhale *verb* to breathe out

exhaust *verb* **1** to tire (someone) out **2** to use up (a supply of something) **3** to discuss (a subject) thoroughly ▷ *noun* **4** gases ejected from an engine as waste products **5** pipe through which an engine's exhaust fumes pass > **exhaustion** *noun* **1** extreme tiredness **2** exhausting

exhaustive *adjective* thorough and complete > **exhaustively** *adverb*

exhibit *verb* **1** to display (things) to the public **2** to show (a quality or feeling) ▷ *noun* **3** object exhibited to the public

exhibition *noun* **1** public display of art, skills, etc **2** exhibiting

exhibitor *noun* person whose work is being shown in an exhibition

exhilarating *adjective* exciting and thrilling

exile *noun* **1** prolonged, usually enforced, absence from your country **2** person banished or living away from his or her country ▷ *verb* **3** to expel (someone) from his or her country

exist *verb* **1** to have being or reality **2** to live

existence *noun* **1** state of being or

existing **2** way of living or being: *an idyllic existence*

exit *noun* **1** way out **2** going out **3** actor's going off stage ▷ *verb* **4** to go out **5** to go offstage: used as a stage direction

exodus *noun* departure of a large number of people

exotic *adjective* **1** having a strange allure or beauty **2** originating in a foreign country

expand *verb* **1** to become larger or make (something) larger **2** (followed by *on*) to give more details about (something) > **expansion** *noun*: *the rapid expansion of private health insurance*

expanse *noun* uninterrupted wide area

expansive *adjective* **1** wide or extensive **2** friendly and talkative

expatriate *adjective* **1** living outside your native country ▷ *noun* **2** person living outside his or her native country

expect *verb* **1** to regard (something) as probable **2** to look forward to or await (someone or something) **3** to require (something) as an obligation

expectancy *noun* feeling of anticipation

expectant *adjective* **1** expecting or hopeful **2** pregnant > **expectantly** *adverb*

expectation *noun* **1** act or state of expecting **2** something looked forward to **3** attitude of anticipation or hope

expedient *noun* **1** something that achieves a particular purpose ▷ *adjective* **2** suitable to the circumstances, appropriate > **expediency** *noun* doing what is convenient rather than what is morally right

expedition *noun* **1** organized journey, especially for exploration **2** people and equipment comprising an expedition **3** pleasure trip or excursion ▷ **expeditionary** *adjective* relating to an expedition, especially a military one

expel *verb* **expels expelling expelled** **1** to force out (a gas or liquid) from a place **2** to dismiss (someone) from a school etc permanently

expend *verb* to spend or use up (energy, time or money)

expendable *adjective* no longer useful or necessary, and therefore able to be got rid of

expenditure *noun* **1** something expended, especially money **2** amount expended

expense *noun* **1** cost **2** (cause of) spending **3** **expenses** money spent while doing something connected with work and paid back by your employer

expensive *adjective* high-priced ▷ **expensively** *adverb*

experience *noun* **1** direct personal participation **2** particular incident, feeling, etc that a person has undergone **3** accumulated knowledge ▷ *verb* **4** to participate in or undergo (something) **5** to be affected by (an emotion)

experiment *noun* **1** test to provide evidence to prove or disprove a theory **2** attempt at something new ▷ *verb* **3** to carry out an experiment ▷ **experimental** *adjective*: *an experimental air-conditioning*

system > **experimentally** *adverb* > **experimentation** *noun*: *the ethical aspects of animal experimentation*

expert *noun* **1** person with extensive skill or knowledge in a particular field; authority ▷ *adjective* **2** skilful or knowledgeable > **expertly** *adverb*

expertise *noun* special skill or knowledge

expire *verb* **1** to finish or run out **2** *literary* to die > **expiry** *noun* end, especially of a contract period

explain *verb* **1** to make (something) clear and intelligible **2** to account for (something) > **explanation** *noun*: *there was no apparent explanation for the crash* > **explanatory** *adjective*: *a series of explanatory notes*

explicit *adjective* **1** precisely and clearly expressed **2** shown in realistic detail > **explicitly** *adverb*: *she has been talking very explicitly about AIDS to these groups*

explode *verb* **1** to burst with great violence, blow up **2** to react suddenly with emotion **3** to increase rapidly

exploit *verb* **1** to take advantage of (someone) for your own purposes **2** to make the best use of (something) ▷ *noun* **3** notable feat or deed > **exploitation** *noun*: *the exploitation of the famine by local politicians*

explore *verb* **1** to think carefully about (an idea) **2** to travel into (unfamiliar regions), especially for scientific purposes > **exploration** *noun* act of exploring > **exploratory** *adjective* *exploratory surgery* > **explorer** *noun* person who explores unfamiliar regions

explosion noun sudden violent burst of energy, for example one caused by a bomb

explosive adjective 1 tending to explode ▷ noun 2 substance that causes explosions

exponent noun 1 person who advocates an idea, cause, etc 2 skilful performer, especially a musician

export noun 1 selling or shipping of goods to a foreign country 2 product shipped or sold to a foreign country ▷ verb 3 to sell or ship (goods) to a foreign country > **exporter** noun country, firm or person that sells or ships goods to a foreign country

expose verb 1 to uncover or reveal (something) 2 to make (someone) vulnerable, leave (someone) unprotected 3 to subject (a photographic film) to light

exposition noun detailed explanation of a particular subject

exposure noun 1 exposing 2 lack of shelter from the weather, especially the cold 3 appearance before the public, as on television

express verb 1 to put (an idea or feeling) into words 2 to show (an emotion) 3 to indicate (a quantity) by a symbol or formula ▷ adjective 4 of or for rapid transportation of people, mail, etc ▷ noun 5 fast train or bus stopping at only a few stations ▷ adverb 6 by express delivery

expression noun 1 expressing 2 word or phrase 3 showing or communication of emotion 4 look on the face that indicates

mood 5 Maths variable, function, or some combination of these

expressive adjective 1 showing feelings clearly 2 full of expression

expressway noun Aust road designed for fast-moving traffic

expulsion noun act of officially banning someone from a place or institution: the high number of school expulsions

exquisite adjective 1 of extreme beauty or delicacy 2 intense in feeling

extend verb 1 to continue and stretch into the distance 2 to draw (something) out, stretch (something) 3 to last for a certain time 4 to increase in size or scope 5 to offer (something): extend your sympathy > **extension** noun 1 room or rooms added to an existing building 2 additional telephone connected to the same line as another 3 extending

extensive adjective having a large extent or widespread > **extensively** adverb: to travel extensively

extent noun range over which something extends; area

exterior noun 1 part or surface on the outside 2 outward appearance ▷ adjective 3 of, on or coming from the outside

exterminate verb to destroy (animals or people) completely > **extermination** noun: the extermination of hundreds of thousands of their countrymen

external adjective of, situated on or coming from the outside > **externally** adverb: vitamins must be applied externally to the skin

extinct adjective 1 having died out 2 (of a volcano) no longer liable to erupt >**extinction** noun: to save a species from extinction

extinguish verb to put out (a fire or light)

extortionate adjective (of prices) excessive

extra adjective 1 more than is usual, expected or needed; additional ▷ noun 2 additional person or thing 3 something for which an additional charge is made 4 Films actor hired for crowd scenes ▷ adverb 5 unusually or exceptionally

extra- prefix outside or beyond an area or scope: extrasensory; extraterritorial

extract verb 1 to take or get (something) out, often by force 2 to get (information) from someone with difficulty ▷ noun 3 something extracted, such as a passage from a book etc 4 preparation containing the concentrated essence of a substance: beef extract >**extraction** noun 1 country or people that your family originally comes from: of Australian extraction 2 process of taking or getting something out of a place

extraordinary adjective unusual or surprising >**extraordinarily** adverb

extravagant adjective 1 spending money excessively 2 going beyond reasonable limits >**extravagance** noun excessive spending >**extravagantly** adverb

extravaganza noun elaborate and lavish entertainment, display, etc

extreme adjective 1 of a high or the highest degree or intensity 2 severe 3 immoderate 4 farthest or outermost ▷ noun 5 either of the two limits of a scale or range >**extremely** adverb very

extremist noun 1 person who favours immoderate methods ▷ adjective 2 holding extreme opinions >**extremism** noun: right-wing extremism

extremity extremities noun 1 farthest point 2 **extremities** hands and feet or fingers and toes

extricate verb to free (someone) from complication or difficulty

extrovert noun extrovert person

exuberant adjective high-spirited >**exuberance** noun: a burst of exuberance >**exuberantly** adverb

exude verb to make (something) apparent by mood or behaviour: exude confidence

eye eyes eyeing or eying eyed noun 1 organ of sight 2 ability to judge or appreciate: a good eye for detail 3 hole at one end of a sewing needle through which you pass thread ▷ verb 4 to look at (something) carefully or warily

eyeball noun ball-shaped part of the eye

eyebrow noun line of hair on the bony ridge above the eye

eyelash noun short hair that grows out from the eyelid

eyelid noun fold of skin that covers the eye when it is closed

eyesight noun ability to see

eyesore noun ugly object

eyewitness noun person who was present at an event and can describe what happened

eyrie noun nest of an eagle

f

fable noun 1 story with a moral; false or fictitious account 2 legend

fabled adjective made famous in legend

fabric noun 1 cloth 2 walls, roof and basic structure of a building 3 structure, laws and customs of society

fabricate verb 1 to make up (a story or lie) 2 to make or build (something) > **fabrication** noun

fabulous adjective 1 informal wonderful or very impressive 2 astounding 3 not real but told of in stories and legends

facade noun 1 front of a building 2 (false) outward appearance

face noun 1 front of the head 2 facial expression 3 distorted expression 4 outward appearance 5 front or side, especially the most important side 6 dial of a clock 7 dignity, self-respect > verb 8 to be opposite (something or someone) 9 to look or turn towards (something or someone) 10 to be confronted by (something) > **face up to** verb to accept (an unpleasant fact or reality)

faceless adjective impersonal, anonymous

face-lift noun 1 operation to tighten facial skin, to remove wrinkles 2 improvement, new look

facet noun 1 aspect 2 cut surface of a precious stone

facetious adjective witty or amusing but in a rather silly or inappropriate way

facial adjective 1 of the face > noun 2 beauty treatment for the face

facilitate verb to make (something) easier

facility facilities noun 1 talent, ability 2 facilities means or equipment for an activity

fact noun 1 event or thing known to have happened or existed 2 provable truth 3 **in fact** actually or really > **factual** adjective: factual errors > **factually** adverb: It was factually incorrect

faction noun (dissenting) minority group within a larger body

fact of life noun 1 something inescapable 2 **facts of life** details of sex and reproduction

factor noun 1 something that helps to cause a result 2 Maths one of two or more whole numbers that when multiplied together give a given number. For example, 2 and 5 are factors of 10

factory factories noun building or group of buildings where goods are manufactured

faculty faculties noun 1 physical or mental ability 2 department in a university or college

fad noun temporary fashion

fade verb 1 to lose or cause something to lose brightness, colour or strength 2 to vanish slowly

faeces plural noun solid waste matter excreted from a person's or animal's body

fag noun Brit informal cigarette

Fahrenheit noun a scale of temperature in which the freezing point of water is 32° and the boiling point is 212°

fail verb 1 to be unsuccessful 2 to stop working 3 to be or to judge someone to be below the required standard in a test 4 to disappoint or be useless to (someone) 5 to neglect to or be unable to do (something) ▷ noun 6 instance of not passing an exam or test 7 **without fail a** regularly **b** definitely

failing noun 1 weak point ▷ preposition 2 in the absence of

failure noun 1 act or instance of failing 2 unsuccessful person or thing 3 **someone's failure to do something** fact of someone not having done something

faint adjective 1 (of sound, colour or image) not easy to hear or see owing to a lack of volume, brightness or definition 2 dizzy or weak 3 slight ▷ verb 4 to lose consciousness temporarily; to black out or pass out ▷ noun 5 temporary loss of consciousness ▷ **faintly** adverb

fair adjective 1 unbiased, reasonable and just 2 quite large: *a fair amount of money* 3 quite good: *a fair attempt* 4 having light coloured hair or pale skin 5 (of weather) fine ▷ noun 6 travelling entertainment with sideshows, rides and amusements 7 exhibition of goods produced by a particular industry ▷ adverb

8 fairly ▷ **fairness** noun

fairground noun open space used for a fair

fairway noun Golf smooth area between the tee and the green

fairy fairies noun (in stories) small, supernatural creature with magic powers

fairy tale or **story** noun 1 story about fairies or magic 2 unbelievable story or explanation

faith noun 1 confidence or trust 2 religion

faithful adjective 1 loyal 2 accurate and reliable ▷ **faithfully** adverb ▷ **faithfulness** noun

fake noun 1 imitation of something meant to trick people into thinking that it is genuine; copy or sham ▷ adjective 2 imitation and not genuine; artificial ▷ verb 3 to pretend to have (an illness, emotion, etc); feign 4 to cause (something not genuine) to appear real or more valuable by fraud

falcon noun small bird of prey that can be trained to hunt other birds or small animals

fall falls falling fell fallen verb 1 (also **fall over**) to lose balance and tumble towards the ground 2 to drop from a higher to a lower place through the force of gravity 3 to land 4 to go down or decrease in number or quality 5 to pass into a specified condition; become 6 (of a soldier) to be killed 7 to occur or happen ▷ noun 8 act of falling 9 thing or amount that falls 10 decrease or reduction in value or number 11 decline in power or influence

12 US autumn **13 falls** waterfall
> **fall down** verb (of an argument or idea) to fail > **fall for** verb **1** informal to fall in love with **2** to be deceived by (a lie or trick)
> **fall out** verb to quarrel; have a disagreement > **fall through** verb (of an arrangement or plan) to fail or be abandoned

fallacy fallacies noun **1** false belief **2** unsound reasoning > **fallacious** adjective: It is a fallacious argument

fallopian tube noun one of two tubes in a woman's or female mammal's body along which the eggs pass from the ovaries to the uterus

fallout noun radioactive particles that fall to the earth after a nuclear explosion

fallow adjective (of land) ploughed but not planted so as to recover and regain fertility

false adjective **1** untrue or incorrect **2** artificial, fake **3** deceptive: false promises > **falsely** adverb > **falseness** noun: the obvious falseness of their position > **falsity** noun: efforts to establish the truth or falsity of these claims

falsehood noun **1** quality of being untrue **2** lie

falsify falsifies falsifying falsified verb to alter fraudulently > **falsification** noun: deliberate falsification of evidence

alter verb **1** to be hesitant, weak or unsure **2** to lose power momentarily **3** to talk hesitantly **4** to move unsteadily

ame noun state of being widely known or recognized

amed adjective very well-known; famous

familiar adjective **1** well-known **2** too informal and friendly **3** intimate, friendly **4** (followed by with) acquainted > **familiarity** noun > **familiarize** verb to acquaint (someone) fully with a particular subject > **familiarly** adverb

family families noun **1** group consisting of parents and their children **2** group descended from a common ancestor **3** group of related objects or beings ▷ adjective **4** suitable for parents and children together > **familial** adjective: social and familial relationships

family planning noun practice of controlling the number of children you have, usually by using contraception

famine noun severe shortage of food

famished adjective informal very hungry

famous adjective very well-known

famously adverb old-fashioned informal excellently

fan fans fanning fanned noun **1** informal enthusiastic follower of a pop star, sport or hobby **2** hand-held or mechanical device used to create a cooling draught ▷ verb **3** to blow or cool (someone or something) with a fan > **fan out** verb to spread out like a fan

fanatic noun person who is very extreme in their support for a cause or in their enthusiasm for a particular activity > **fanaticism** noun: the evils of religious fanaticism

fanatical adjective extreme and obsessive in your support or enthusiasm for something > **fanatically** adverb

fancy fancies fancying fancied;
fancier fanciest verb 1 informal to
have a wish for; want 2 informal
to be sexually attracted to 3 to
suppose 4 fancy yourself
informal to have a high opinion
of yourself ▷ noun 5 sudden
irrational liking or desire
6 uncontrolled imagination
▷ adjective 7 not plain; elaborate

fancy dress noun party costume
representing a historical figure,
animal etc

fanfare noun short loud tune
played on brass instruments

fang noun long pointed tooth

fantail noun 1 a pigeon with a
large tail that can be opened out
like a fan 2 small Australian and
New Zealand bird with a fan-
shaped tail

fantasize verb to imagine
pleasant but unlikely events or
situations; daydream

fantastic adjective 1 informal very
good 2 unrealistic or absurd
3 extremely large in degree or
amount 4 strange and difficult to
believe ▷ **fantastically** adverb

fantasy fantasies noun
1 imagined story or situation;
daydream 2 far-fetched notion
3 imagination unrestricted by
reality 4 fiction with a large
fantasy content

far farther farthest; further
furthest adverb 1 at, to or from
a great distance 2 at or to a
remote time 3 very much: far
more important 4 so far up to now
▷ adjective 5 a long way away in
space or time 6 further away or
more distant

• When you are talking about
• a physical distance you can

• use farther and farthest or
• further and furthest. If you are
• talking about extra effort or
• time, use further and furthest:
• a further delay is likely

farce noun 1 humorous play in
which ridiculous and unlikely
situations occur 2 disorganized
and ridiculous or ludicrous
situation > **farcical** adjective
ludicrous > **farcically** adverb

fare noun 1 charge for a
passenger's journey 2 passenger
3 food provided ▷ verb 4 to get
on (in a particular way): We fared
badly

Far East noun the countries of East
Asia, including China, Japan and
Malaysia > **Far Eastern** adjective

farewell interjection 1 goodbye
▷ noun, adjective 2 (of) an event
related to leaving: a farewell speech

far-fetched adjective unlikely to
be true

farm noun 1 area of land together
with the buildings on it that
forms a unit and is used for
growing crops or rearing livestock
▷ verb 2 to run a farm by rearing
livestock and/or cultivating the
land 3 to cultivate (land) 4 to rear
(livestock) > **farming** noun

farmhouse noun the main house
on a farm

farmyard noun area surrounded
by farm buildings

fascia noun -ciae or -cias 1 outer
surface of a dashboard 2 flat
surface above a shop window
3 mobile phone casing with
spaces for the buttons

fascinate verb to attract and
interest (someone) strongly;
to make motionless from fear

or awe > **fascinating** adjective: a fascinating place to visit > **fascination** noun: her fascination with politics

fascism noun extreme right-wing political ideology or system of government with a powerful dictator and state control of most activities. Nationalism is encouraged and political opposition not allowed > **fascist** adjective, noun

fashion noun **1** style of dress or way of behaving that is popular at a particular time; vogue **2** way something happens or is done > verb **3** to make or shape (something)

fashionable adjective currently popular; in vogue > **fashionably** adverb

fast adjective **1** (capable of) acting or moving quickly **2** done in or lasting a short time **3** (of a clock or watch) showing a time later than the correct time > adverb **4** quickly **5** soundly, deeply: fast asleep **6** tightly and firmly > adjective **7** (of a colour or dye) not likely to run when wet > verb **8** to go without food, especially for religious reasons > noun **9** period of fasting

fasten verb **1** to close (something), do (something) up or fix (something) in place **2** to close or do up

fast food noun hot food, such as hamburgers, that is prepared and served quickly after you have ordered it

fastidious adjective **1** very fussy about details **2** excessively concerned with cleanliness

fast-track adjective **1** taking the quickest but most competitive route to success: fast-track executives > verb **2** to speed up the progress of (a project or person)

fat fatter fattest; fats adjective **1** carrying too much weight on your body; overweight **2** (of meat) containing a lot of fat **3** thick > noun **4** extra flesh on the body **5** greasy solid or liquid substance obtained from animals or plants and often used in cooking > **fatness** noun > **fatty** adjective containing fat

fatal adjective **1** causing death **2** very damaging; disastrous > **fatally** adverb

fatality fatalities noun death caused by an accident or disaster

fate noun **1** power supposed by some to control events; destiny or providence **2** fortune that awaits a person or thing

fateful adjective having an important, often disastrous, effect

father noun **1** male parent **2** man who starts, creates or invents something: the father of Italian painting **3** **Father a** God **b** form of address for a priest in some Christian churches > verb **4** to be the father of (a child) > **fatherhood** noun: the joys of fatherhood > **fatherly** adjective: a few words of fatherly advice

father-in-law fathers-in-law noun father of your husband or wife

fathom noun **1** unit of length, used in navigation, equal to six feet (1.83 metres) > verb **2** to understand

fatigue fatigues fatiguing fatigued noun **1** extreme physical or mental tiredness **2** weakening of a material due to stress ▷ *verb* **3** to tire out

fault *noun* **1** responsibility for something wrong **2** weakness, defect or flaw **3** mistake or error **4** *Geology* large crack in rock caused by movement of the earth's crust **5** *Tennis squash, etc* incorrect and invalid serve ▷ *verb* **6** to criticize >**faultless** *adjective: an almost faultless performance* >**faulty** *adjective: faulty wiring*

favour *noun* **1** approving attitude **2** act of goodwill or generosity **3** in someone's favour of help or advantage to someone **4** in favour of a feeling approval for **b** to the benefit of ▷ *verb* **5** to prefer (someone or something) **6** to support or recommend (something)

favourable *adjective* **1** encouraging or advantageous: *a favourable review* **2** useful or beneficial: *favourable weather conditions* **3** giving consent: *They got a favourable response from the bank* >**favourably** *adverb*

favourite *adjective* **1** most liked ▷ *noun* **2** preferred person or thing **3** *Sport* competitor expected to win

favouritism *noun* practice of giving special treatment to a person or group

fawn *adjective* **1** light yellowish-brown ▷ *noun* **2** young deer ▷ *verb* **3** fawn on to seek the approval of (someone) by flattering them

fax *noun* **1** exact copy of a document sent electronically along a telephone line **2** electronic system for sending exact copies of documents by

telephone ▷ *verb* **3** to send (a document) by this system

fear *noun* **1** distress or alarm caused by approaching danger or pain **2** thought that something undesirable or unpleasant might happen ▷ *verb* **3** to be afraid of (something or someone) **4** to be afraid (that something may happen) >**fear for** *verb* to feel anxious about the safety of (someone or something)

fearful *adjective* **1** feeling fear **2** *informal* very unpleasant >**fearfully** *adverb*

fearsome *adjective* terrible or frightening

feasible *adjective* able to be done; possible >**feasibility** *noun: the feasibility of constructing a new bypass* >**feasibly** *adverb*

feast *noun* **1** large and special meal for a lot of people **2** annual religious celebration ▷ *verb* **3** to eat a feast **4** feast on to eat a large amount of (something)

feat *noun* impressive and difficult achievement

feather *noun* one of the light fluffy things covering a bird's body >**feathered** *adjective* >**feathery** *adjective*

feature *noun* **1** interesting or important part or characteristic of something **2** part of your face, such as your eyes or nose **3** special article or programme dealing with a particular subject **4** main film in a cinema programme ▷ *verb* **5** to have (someone or something) as a feature or to be a feature in (something) >**featureless** *adjective: a featureless landscape*

February *noun* second month of

the year

fed verb past of **feed**

federal adjective relating to a system of government in which a group of states is controlled by a central government, but each state has its own local powers

federation noun group of organizations or states that have joined together for a common purpose

fed up adjective informal bored or dissatisfied

fee noun charge or payment for a job, service or activity

feeble adjective 1 lacking physical or mental power 2 unconvincing

feed feeds feeding fed verb 1 to give food to (a person or animal) 2 to give (something) to (a person or animal) as food 3 to eat 4 to supply (what is needed): The information was fed into a computer database ▷ noun 5 act of feeding 6 food, especially for babies or animals

feedback noun 1 comments and information about the quality or success of something 2 condition in which some of the power, sound or information produced by electronic equipment goes back into it

feel feels feeling felt verb 1 to experience (an emotion, sensation or effect of something) 2 to believe 3 to become aware of (something or someone) by touch 4 to touch (something) 5 (of things) to give the impression of being (cold, hard, soft, etc) 6 **feel like** to wish for or want (something) ▷ noun 7 way something feels 8 act of feeling 9 impression 10 instinctive

aptitude

feeler noun organ of touch in some animals; antenna

feeling noun 1 emotion or reaction 2 physical sensation 3 ability to experience physical sensations 4 opinion 5 impression 6 sympathy or understanding 7 **feelings** emotions or beliefs

feet noun plural of **foot**

feign verb to pretend to experience (something)

feline adjective 1 belonging or relating to the cat family 2 catlike

fell verb 1 past tense of **fall** 2 to cut down (a tree)

fellow noun 1 old-fashioned man or boy 2 senior member of a learned society or a university college 3 comrade, associate or person in the same group or condition ▷ adjective 4 (of a person) in the same group or condition: his fellow editors

fellowship noun 1 feeling of friendliness and companionship experienced by those doing something together 2 group with shared aims or interests 3 paid research post in a college or university

felt verb 1 past of **feel** ▷ noun 2 matted fabric made by bonding fibres by pressure

female noun 1 person or animal that belongs to the sex that can have babies or young ▷ adjective 2 concerning or relating to females

feminine adjective 1 having qualities traditionally regarded as suitable for, or typical of, women 2 relating to women 3 belonging to a particular class of nouns, adjectives, pronouns or endings in some languages >**femininity** noun: Pink emphasizes femininity

feminism noun belief that women should have the same rights and opportunities as men >**feminist** noun, adjective

fen noun Brit low-lying, flat, marshy land

fence noun 1 wooden or wire barrier between two areas of land 2 barrier or hedge for horses to jump over in horse racing or show jumping ▷ verb 3 to surround (an area of land) with a fence 4 to fight with swords as a sport >**fencer** noun

fend verb **fend for yourself** to look after yourself >**fend off** verb to defend yourself against (a verbal or physical attack or attacker)

ferment verb (of wine, beer or fruit) to change chemically, often producing alcohol >**fermentation** noun: chemicals produced during fermentation

fern noun plant with long feathery leaves and no flowers

ferocious adjective violent and fierce >**ferociously** adverb >**ferocity** noun

ferret noun 1 small, fierce animal related to the weasel and kept for hunting rats and rabbits ▷ verb 2 to search around >**ferret out** verb to find out (information) by searching

ferry ferries ferrying ferried noun 1 boat for transporting people and vehicles ▷ verb 2 to carry (people or goods) by ferry

fertile adjective 1 capable of producing young, crops or vegetation 2 creative: a fertile

mind >**fertility** noun

fertilize verb 1 to cause (an animal or plant) to begin the process of reproduction by supplying sperm or pollen 2 to feed (soil or land) with nutrients >**fertilization** noun

fertilizer or**fertiliser** noun substance added to the soil to improve plant growth

fervent or**fervid** adjective intensely passionate, enthusiastic and sincere >**fervently** adverb

fervour noun very strong feeling for or belief in something

fester verb 1 (of a situation or problem) to grow worse and increasingly hostile 2 (of a wound) to become infected and form pus

festival noun 1 organized series of events or performances 2 day or period of celebration

festive adjective full of happiness and celebration

festivity festivities noun happy celebration

festooned adjective **festooned with** adorned with

fetch verb 1 to go to get (someone or something) 2 to be sold for (a sum of money)

fetching adjective attractive

fete noun 1 outdoor event with competitions, displays and goods for sale ▷ verb 2 to honour or entertain (someone) regally

feud noun 1 long-term and very bitter quarrel, especially between families ▷ verb 2 to carry on a feud

feudalism noun social and political system that was

common in the Middle Ages in Europe. Under this system, ordinary people were given land and protection by a lord, and in return they worked and fought for him > **feudal** adjective relating to or resembling feudalism

fever noun **1** (illness causing) high body temperature **2** nervous excitement

feverish adjective **1** suffering from fever **2** in a state of nervous excitement > **feverishly** adverb

few adjective, pronoun **1** not many **2** a few small number (of) **3** quite a few, a good few several

- You use fewer to talk about things that can be counted: fewer than five visits. When you are talking about amounts that can't be counted you should use less

fiancé noun man engaged to be married

fiancée noun woman engaged to be married

fiasco fiascos noun event or attempt that fails completely, especially in a ridiculous or disorganized way

fib fibs fibbing fibbed noun **1** small, unimportant lie > verb **2** to tell a small lie

fibre noun **1** thread that can be spun into yarn **2** part of plants that can be eaten but not digested; it helps food pass quickly through the body > **fibrous** adjective: fibrous material

fickle adjective changeable, inconstant

fiction noun **1** stories about people and events that have been invented by the author

2 invented story

fiddle verb **1** (often followed by with) to move or touch something restlessly **2** to falsify (accounts) > noun **3** informal dishonest action or scheme **4** violin > **fiddler** noun

fiddly fiddlier fiddliest adjective awkward to do or use

fidelity noun faithfulness

fidget verb **1** to move about restlessly > noun **2** someone who fidgets > **fidgety** adjective

field noun **1** enclosed piece of land where crops are grown or animals are kept **2** marked off area for sports: a hockey field **3** area rich in a specified natural resource: an oil field **4** subject or area of interest; sphere **5** Sport to catch and return (a ball) **6** to deal with (a question) successfully

fielder noun Sport player whose task is to field the ball

field marshal noun army officer of the highest rank

fieldwork noun study of something in the environment where it naturally lives or occurs, rather than in a class or laboratory

fiend noun **1** evil spirit **2** cruel or wicked person **3** informal person devoted to something: fitness fiend

fierce adjective **1** wild or aggressive **2** intense or strong > **fiercely** adverb > **fierceness** noun

fiery fierier fieriest adjective **1** consisting of or like fire **2** showing great anger, energy or passion

fifteen adjective, noun the number 15 > **fifteenth** adjective, noun

fifth adjective, noun **1** (coming as) number 5 in a series > noun **2** one

a b c d e **f** g h i j k l m n o p q r s t u v w x y z

of five equal parts

fifty fifties adjective, noun the number 70 > **fiftieth** adjective, noun

fifty-fifty adverb **1** divided equally into two portions ▷ adjective **2** just as likely not to happen as to happen: You've got a fifty-fifty chance of being right

fig noun **1** soft, sweet fruit full of tiny seeds. It grows in hot countries and is often eaten dried **2** tree bearing it

fight fights fighting fought verb **1** to take part in a battle, a war, a boxing match or some other form of physical combat **2** to battle against (someone) **3** to struggle to overcome someone or obtain something **4** to carry on (a battle or contest) **5** to make (one's way) somewhere with difficulty ▷ noun **6** situation in which people hit or try to hurt each other **7** determined attempt to prevent or achieve something: the fight for independence > **fighter** noun **1** boxer **2** determined person **3** aircraft designed to destroy other aircraft > **fight off** verb **1** to drive away (an attacker) **2** to struggle to avoid

figure noun **1** written number **2** amount expressed in numbers **3** Maths geometrical shape **4** diagram or table in a written text **5** shape of a person whom you cannot see clearly **6** shape of your body **7** person **8** representation in painting or sculpture of a human form ▷ verb **9** (usually followed by in) to be included (in) **10** informal to guess or conclude > **figure out** verb to solve (something)

or to understand (something or someone)

figurative adjective (of language) abstract, imaginative or symbolic > **figuratively** adverb

figurehead noun **1** someone who is the leader in name of a movement or organization but who has no real power **2** carved wooden model of a person or creature decorating the front of a sailing ship

figure of speech noun expression such as a simile or idiom in which words do not have their literal meaning

file noun **1** box or folder used to keep documents in order **2** documents in a file **3** information about a person or subject **4** line of people one behind the other **5** Computers organized collection of related material **6** tool with a rough surface, used for smoothing or shaping hard material ▷ verb **7** to place (a document) in a file **8** to place (a legal document) on an official record **9** to bring (a lawsuit), especially for divorce **10** to walk or march in a line **11** to smooth or shape (something) with a file

file sharing noun sharing computer data on a network, esp. the internet

fill verb **1** to make (something) full or to become full **2** to occupy (a space or gap) completely **3** to plug (a gap) **4** to satisfy (a need) **5** to hold and perform the duties of (a position) **6** to appoint someone to (a job or position) ▷ noun **7** **have your fill** to have enough for your needs or wants

> **fill in** verb **1** to complete (a form) **2** to update (someone)

fillet noun **1** boneless piece of meat or fish ▷ verb **2** to remove the bones from (meat or fish)

filling noun **1** soft food mixture inside a sandwich, cake or pie **2** small amount of metal or plastic put into a hole in a tooth by a dentist ▷ adjective **3** (of food) substantial and satisfying

filly fillies noun young female horse

film noun **1** series of moving pictures projected onto a screen and shown at the cinema or on television **2** thin flexible strip of plastic used in a camera to record images when exposed to light **3** thin sheet or layer ▷ verb **4** to record (someone or something) using a movie or video camera **5** to make a film of (a scene, story, etc) ▷ adjective **6** connected with films or the cinema

filter noun **1** device that allows some substances, lights or sounds to pass through it, but not others ▷ verb **2** to pass (a substance) through a filter **3** to pass slowly or faintly > **filtration** noun

filth noun **1** disgusting dirt **2** offensive material or language > **filthiness** noun > **filthy** adjective

fin noun **1** a thin, flat structure sticking out of a fish's body and helping it to balance and swim **2** part of the tail of an aircraft that sticks up

final adjective **1** last in a series or happening at the end of something **2** (of a decision) having no possibility of further change, action or discussion ▷ noun **3** the last game or contest in a series which decides the overall winner **4** **finals** last and most important examinations in a university or college course

finale noun last section of a piece of music or show

finalist noun competitor in a final

finalize verb to complete the remaining details of something

finally adverb **1** eventually or at last **2** lastly or in conclusion

finance verb **1** to provide or obtain funds for (a project, purchase) ▷ noun **2** management of money, loans or investments **3** funds for paying for something **4** **finances** money resources

financial adjective relating to or involving money > **financially** adverb

financier noun person or organization providing the funds for a project or for business

finch noun small songbird with a short strong beak

find finds finding found verb **1** to discover or come across (something or someone) by chance or after a search **2** to realize **3** to consider (someone or something) to have a particular quality **4** Law to pronounce (the defendant) guilty or not guilty **5** to provide (money, time) especially with difficulty ▷ noun **6** valuable or useful person or thing > **finder** noun > **find out** verb **1** to learn or discover something either by chance or after research **2** to learn about something bad, criminal or negligent done by (someone)

findings plural noun conclusions from an investigation

a
b
c
d
e
f
g
h
i
j
k
l
m
n
o
p
q
r
s
t
u
v
w
x
y
z

fine *adjective* **1** very good **2** (of weather) clear and dry **3** in good health **4** satisfactory **5** of delicate workmanship **6** very narrow or thin **7** subtle or abstruse: *a fine distinction* **8** (of a net or sieve) having very small holes **9** (of dust, powder) consisting of very small particles ▷ *adverb* **10** very well ▷ *noun* **11** payment imposed as a penalty or punishment ▷ *verb* **12** to impose a fine on (a person or organization)

finery *noun* very beautiful clothing and jewellery

finesse *noun* **1** delicate skill **2** subtlety and tact

finger *noun* **1** one of the four long jointed parts of the hand **2** part of a glove that covers a finger ▷ *verb* **3** to touch or handle (something) with your fingers

fingernail *noun* any of the hard coverings on the upper part of the ends of your fingers

fingerprint *noun* mark made showing the pattern on the skin at the tip of a person's finger

finish *verb* **1** to reach the end (of) **2** to come to an end or stop **3** to use (something) up ▷ *noun* **4** end or last part **5** texture or appearance of the surface of something

finite *adjective* having limits in space, time or size

Finn *noun* someone from Finland

Finnish *adjective* **1** belonging or relating to Finland ▷ *noun* **2** the main language spoken in Finland

fir *noun* tall pointed evergreen tree that has needle-like leaves and produces cones

fire *noun* **1** flames produced when something burns **2** pile or mass of burning material **3** piece of equipment used as a heater **4** incident involving undesirable destructive burning **5** shooting of guns **6** open fire to begin shooting ▷ *verb* **7** to operate (a weapon) so that a bullet or missile is released **8** *informal* to dismiss from employment **9** to bake (ceramics etc) in a kiln

firearm *noun* gun

fire brigade *noun* organized body of people whose job is to put out fires

fire engine *noun* vehicle carrying equipment for putting out fires

fire escape *noun* metal staircase or ladder down the outside of a building for escape in the event of fire

fire extinguisher *noun* metal cylinder containing water or foam for spraying onto a fire to put it out

firefighter *noun* member of a fire brigade

firefly *noun, plural* **fireflies** insect that glows in the dark

fireplace *noun* opening beneath a chimney where a fire can be lit

fireproof *adjective* resistant to fire

fire station *noun* building where firefighters are stationed

firework *noun* small container of gunpowder and other chemicals which explodes and produces spectacular explosions and coloured sparks when lit

firing squad *noun* group of soldiers ordered to shoot a person condemned to death

firm *adjective* **1** not soft or

yielding **2** securely in position **3** definite **4** having or showing determination and authority ▷ adverb **5** in an unyielding manner: *hold firm* ▷ noun **6** business; company ▷ **firmly** adverb ▷ **firmness** noun

first adjective **1** earliest in time or order **2** graded or ranked above all others ▷ noun **3** person or thing coming before all others **4** outset or beginning **5** first-class honours degree at university **6** lowest forward gear in a car or other vehicle ▷ adverb **7** before anything else **8** for the first time ▷ **firstly** adverb

first aid noun immediate medical assistance given to an injured person

first-class adjective **1** of the highest quality or standard **2** *Travel* (of a ticket, seat, accommodation) relating to the best and most expensive facilities **3** (of postage) quicker but more expensive

first-hand adjective **1** obtained directly from the original source ▷ adverb **2** directly from the original source

First Lady noun the wife of the president of a country

first-rate adjective excellent

fiscal adjective of government or public money, especially taxes

fish fishes fishing fished noun **1** cold-blooded creature living in water that has a spine, gills, fins and a scaly skin **2** the flesh of such a creature eaten as food ▷ verb **3** to try to catch fish **4** fish for to try to get (information) in an indirect way ▷ **fishing** noun

fishery fisheries noun area of the sea used for fishing

fishmonger noun seller of fish

fishy fishier fishiest adjective **1** smelling of fish **2** *informal* suspicious or questionable

fission noun **1** splitting **2** splitting of an atomic nucleus with the release of a large amount of energy; nuclear fission

fissure noun deep crack, especially in rock

fist noun clenched hand with the fingers curled tightly towards the palm

fit fits fitting fitted; fitter fittest verb **1** to be of the correct size or shape (for) **2** to fix or put (something) in place **3** to be appropriate or suitable for (a situation, person or thing) **4** to correspond with the facts or circumstances **5** to adjust (something) to make it the right size and shape ▷ noun **6** way in which something fits **7** sudden attack or convulsion, such as an epileptic seizure **8** sudden short burst or spell of laughter, coughing, panic **6** ▷ adjective **9** suitable or appropriate **10** in good health **11** worthy or deserving ▷ **fit in** verb **1** to make a place or time for (someone or something) **2** to conform or manage to belong ▷ **fitness** noun ▷ **fit out** verb to provide (someone or something) with the necessary equipment

fitful adjective happening at irregular intervals and not continuous: *a fitful breeze* ▷ **fitfully** adverb

fitter noun person who assembles or installs machinery

fitting adjective **1** appropriate

or suitable ▷ *noun* **2** accessory or part **3** session trying on clothes that are being adjusted to ensure a correct fit **4 fittings** furnishings and accessories in a building

five *adjective, noun* the number 5

fix *verb* **1** to mend or repair **2** to place permanently **3** to settle definitely **4** to direct (your attention) steadily **5** to arrange or organize **6** *informal* to influence the outcome of (something) unfairly ▷ *noun* **7** *informal* **a** difficult situation **b** unfair or dishonest arrangement **c** injection of a drug such as heroin >**fixed** *adjective* >**fixedly** *adverb* steadily > **fix up** *verb* **1** to arrange **2** (often followed by *with*) to provide

fixation *noun* extreme and obsessive interest in something

fixture *noun* **1** permanently fitted piece of household equipment **2** sports match or the date fixed for it

fizz *verb* **1** to make a hissing or bubbling noise **2** to give off small bubbles

fizzle *verb* to make a weak hissing or bubbling sound > **fizzle out** *verb informal* to come to nothing, fail

fizzy fizzier fizziest *adjective* (of a drink) bubbly, owing to the presence of carbon dioxide

fjord *noun* long narrow inlet of the sea between cliffs, especially in Norway

flab *noun informal* unsightly body fat

flabbergasted *adjective* completely astonished

flabby flabbier flabbiest *adjective* having flabby flesh

flag flags flagging flagged *noun* **1** rectangular or square cloth which has a particular colour and design, and is used as the symbol of a nation or as a signal **2** (also **flagstone**) flat paving-stone ▷ *verb* **3** to lose enthusiasm or vigour **4** to mark with a flag or sticker > **flag down** *verb* to signal (a vehicle) to stop by waving the arm

flagrant *adjective* openly outrageous >**flagrantly** *adverb*

flagship *noun* ship carrying the commander of the fleet

flail *verb* to wave about wildly

flair *noun* **1** natural ability **2** stylishness

flak *noun* **1** anti-aircraft fire **2** *informal* severe criticism

flake *noun* **1** small thin piece, especially chipped off something ▷ *verb* **2** to peel off in flakes >**flaked** *adjective:* flaked almonds > **flake out** *verb informal* to collapse or fall asleep from exhaustion >**flaky** *adjective:* flaky pastry

flamboyant *adjective* **1** behaving in a very noticeable, extravagant way **2** very bright and showy >**flamboyance** *noun*

flame *noun* **1** luminous burning gas coming from burning material **2 old flame** *informal* former boyfriend or girlfriend

flamenco *noun* type of rhythmical Spanish dancing or the guitar music that accompanies it

flamingo flamingos or **flamingoes** *noun* long-legged wading bird with pink or white feathers and a long neck

flammable *adjective* easily set on fire

flan *noun* open sweet or savoury tart with a pastry or cake base

flank *noun* **1** part of the side between the hips and ribs **2** side of a body of troops ▷ *verb* **3** to be at or to move along the side of

flannel *noun* **1** *Brit* small piece of cloth for washing the face **2** soft woollen fabric for clothing **3** **flannels** trousers made of flannel

flap **flaps** **flapping** **flapped** *verb* **1** to move back and forwards or up and down with a snapping sound ▷ *noun* **2** action or sound of flapping **3** piece of something such as paper, fabric or skin, attached by one edge only

flare *noun* **1** device that produces a brightly coloured flame, used especially as an emergency signal **2** **flares** flared trousers ▷ *verb* **3** to start to burn much more vigorously **4** *informal* (of temper, violence or trouble) to break out suddenly **5** (of a skirt or trousers) to become wider towards the bottom > **flared** *adjective* (of a skirt or trousers) becoming wider towards the bottom

flash *noun* **1** sudden short burst of light or flame **2** burst of (intuition or emotion) **3** very short time **4** brief unscheduled news announcement ▷ *verb* **5** to give out or to cause something to give out light suddenly or repeatedly **6** to move very fast **7** *informal* to show (something) briefly or arrogantly

flashback *noun* scene in a book, play or film, that returns to earlier events

flash drive *noun* portable computer hard drive and data storage device

flashlight *noun* US torch

flashy **flashier** **flashiest** *adjective* expensive-looking and showy, in a vulgar way

flask *noun* **1** same as **vacuum flask** **2** flat bottle for carrying alcoholic drink in the pocket

flat **flats** **flatting** **flatted**; **flatter** **flattest** *noun* **1** self-contained set of rooms, usually on one level, for living in **2** *Music* note or key a semitone lower than that described by the same letter. It is represented by the symbol (♭) **3** punctured tyre **4** mud bank exposed at low tide ▷ *verb* **5** *Aust, NZ* to live in a flat ▷ *adjective* **6** level and horizontal **7** even and smooth **8** (of a tyre, ball) deflated **9** outright **10** fixed **11** without variation or emotion **12** (of a drink) no longer fizzy **13** (of a battery) with no electrical charge **14** *Music* below the true pitch ▷ *adverb* **15** in or into a flat position **16** completely or absolutely **17** (of a rate, price) unvarying **18** *Music* too low in pitch > **flatly** *adverb* > **flatness** *noun*

flatfish *noun* sea fish, such as the sole, which has a flat body

• The plural of *flatfish* is *flatfish*

flathead *noun* common Australian edible fish

flatscreen *noun* slim lightweight TV set or computer with a flat screen

flatten *verb* to become or make (something) flat or flatter

flatter verb 1 to praise (someone) insincerely 2 to make (someone) appear more attractive 3 **flatter yourself** to believe something good about yourself that others doubt >**flattered** adjective feeling pleased and special >**flattering** adjective: a flattering colour

flattery noun flattering words or behaviour

flatting go flatting NZ to leave home and live with others in a shared house or flat

flatulence noun condition of having too much gas in your stomach or intestines

flaunt verb to display (yourself or your possessions) arrogantly

flautist noun flute player

flavour noun 1 distinctive taste 2 distinctive characteristic or quality ▷ verb 3 to add flavour to (food) >**flavouring** noun substance used to flavour food

flaw noun 1 fault or mark 2 mistake that makes a plan or argument invalid >**flawed** adjective >**flawless** adjective

flax noun plant used for making rope and cloth

flay verb 1 to strip the skin off (a dead animal) 2 to criticize (someone) severely

flea noun small wingless jumping bloodsucking insect

fleck noun small mark, streak or speck >**flecked** adjective: The wall was flecked with blood

fled verb past of **flee**

fledgling noun 1 young bird ▷ adjective 2 new or inexperienced

flee flees fleeing fled verb to run away (from)

fleece noun 1 sheep's coat of wool 2 sheepskin used as a lining for coats etc 3 warm polyester fabric 4 Brit jacket or top made of this fabric ▷ verb 5 to defraud or overcharge (someone)

fleet noun group of ships or vehicles owned by the same organization or travelling together

fleeting adjective lasting for a very short time >**fleetingly** adverb

Flemish noun language spoken in many parts of Belgium

flesh noun 1 soft part of a human or animal body 2 informal excess fat 3 meat of animals as opposed to fish or fowl 4 thick soft part of a fruit or vegetable 5 human body as opposed to the soul >**fleshy** adjective 1 plump 2 like flesh

flew verb past tense of **fly**

flex noun 1 flexible insulated electric cable ▷ verb 2 to bend (your muscles)

flexible adjective 1 easily bent 2 adaptable >**flexibility** noun

flick verb 1 to move (something) with a quick jerk of your finger 2 to move with a short sudden movement, often repeatedly ▷ noun 3 quick or sharp movement

flicker verb 1 to shine unsteadily or intermittently ▷ noun 2 unsteady brief light 3 momentary feeling

flight noun 1 journey by air 2 act or manner of flying through the air 3 ability to fly 4 aircraft flying on a scheduled journey 5 set of stairs between two landings 6 act of running away

flight attendant noun person who looks after passengers on an aircraft

flightless *adjective* (of certain birds or insects) unable to fly

flimsy flimsier flimsiest *adjective* **1** not strong or substantial **2** thin **3** not very convincing

flinch *verb* to draw back or wince, as from pain

fling flings flinging flung *verb* **1** to throw, send or move forcefully or hurriedly ▷ *noun* **2** spell of self-indulgent enjoyment **3** brief romantic or sexual relationship

flint *noun* **1** hard grey stone **2** piece of this

flip flips flipping flipped *verb* **1** to turn (something small or light) over or move (something) with a quick movement **2** to hit (something) sharply with your finger or thumb > **flip through** *verb* to look at (a book or magazine) quickly or idly

flippant *adjective* showing an inappropriate lack of seriousness > **flippancy** *noun* > **flippantly** *adverb*

flipper *noun* **1** broad, fat limb of a sea animal adapted for swimming **2** one of a pair of broad, flat pieces of rubber that you can attach to your feet to help you swim

flirt *verb* **1** to behave as if sexually attracted to someone but without serious intentions ▷ *noun* **2** person who flirts > **flirtation** *noun* > **flirtatious** *adjective* > **flirt with** *verb* to consider lightly; toy with

flit flits flitting flitted *verb* **1** *informal* to depart furtively and secretly ▷ *noun* **2** act of flitting

float *verb* **1** to be supported by a liquid **2** to move lightly and freely,

supported by the air **3** to launch (a company) as a public company, with shares available on the stock market ▷ *noun* **4** light object used to help someone or something float **5** indicator on a fishing line that moves when a fish bites **6** decorated truck in a procession **7** *Brit* small delivery vehicle **8** sum of money used for minor expenses or to provide change > **floating** *adjective* **1** moving about, changing: *floating population* **2** (of a voter) not committed to one party

flock *noun* **1** group (of birds, sheep or goats) **2** *Christianity* congregation

flog flogs flogging flogged *verb* **1** to beat (someone) with a whip or stick **2** *Brit, NZ, S Afr informal* to sell **3** *NZ informal* to steal > **flogging** *noun*

flood *noun* **1** large amount of water covering an area that is usually dry ▷ *verb* **2** to cover (something) or to become covered with water **3** to come in large numbers or quantities

floodgates *plural noun* **open the floodgates** to give a lot of people the opportunity to do something they could not do before

floodlight *noun* powerful outdoor lamp used to light up public buildings and sports grounds > **floodlit** *adjective*

floor *noun* **1** the part of a room you walk on **2** one of the levels of a building **3** flat bottom surface of something **4** (right to speak in) a legislative hall ▷ *verb* **5** *informal* (of a remark or question) to cause (someone) to be disconcerted and unable to respond adequately

floorboard noun one of the long planks of wood from which a floor is made

flop flops flopping flopped verb 1 to bend, fall or collapse loosely or carelessly 2 informal to fail ▷ noun 3 informal failure

floppy floppier floppiest adjective tending to hang loosely downwards

floppy disk or **disc** noun Computers flexible magnetic disk on which computer data is stored

floral adjective made from or decorated with flowers

florid adjective 1 highly elaborate and extravagant; ornate: florid language 2 with a red or flushed complexion

florist noun person or shop selling flowers

floss noun 1 See **dental floss** 2 fine silky fibres

flotation noun 1 launching of a business enterprise as a public company, with shares available on the stock market 2 act of floating

flotilla noun small fleet or fleet of small ships

flotsam noun wreckage or rubbish floating at sea or washed up on the shore

flounce verb 1 to walk with exaggerated movements suggesting anger or impatience about something: She flounced out of the office ▷ noun 2 ornamental frill

flounder verb 1 to move with difficulty, as in mud 2 to find it difficult to decide what to do or say ▷ noun 3 edible flatfish

● The plural of flounder in sense

● 3 can be either flounder or
● flounders

flour noun powder made by grinding grain, usually wheat, and used for baking and cooking > **floured** adjective > **floury** adjective

flourish verb 1 to be active, successful, healthy or widespread 2 to wave (something) dramatically ▷ noun 3 bold sweeping or waving motion > **flourishing** adjective: Business is flourishing

flout verb to deliberately disobey (a rule, law, etc)

flow verb 1 (of liquid) to move in a stream 2 (of blood or electricity) to circulate 3 to hang loosely ▷ noun 4 act, rate or manner of flowing 5 continuous stream of something

flow chart noun diagram showing the sequence of steps that lead to various results

flower noun 1 part of a plant containing the reproductive organs from which the fruit or seeds develop 2 plant grown for its colourful flowers ▷ verb 3 to produce flowers, bloom

flowery adjective (of language or style) elaborate

flown verb past participle of **fly**

flu noun illness similar to a very bad cold, which causes headaches, sore throat, weakness and aching muscles

fluctuate verb to change frequently and erratically: fluctuating between feeling well and not so well

flue noun passage or pipe which takes fumes and smoke away from a stove or boiler

fluent adjective **1** able to speak a foreign language correctly and without hesitation **2** able to speak or write easily and without hesitation **3** spoken or written with ease > **fluency** noun > **fluently** adverb

fluff noun **1** soft, light, woolly threads or fibres bunched together ▷ verb **2** (often followed by up) to brush or shake (something) to make it seem larger and lighter > **fluffy** adjective

fluid noun **1** liquid ▷ adjective **2** (of movement) smooth and flowing > **fluidity** noun

fluke noun accidental success or stroke of luck

flung verb past of **fling**

fluorescent adjective **1** having a very bright appearance when light is shone on it, as if it is shining itself: *fluorescent yellow dye* **2** (of a light, lamp) in the form of a tube and shining with a hard bright light

fluoride noun mixture of chemicals that is meant to prevent tooth decay

flurry flurries noun short rush of activity or movement

flush verb **1** to blush or to cause (someone) to blush **2** to send water through (a toilet or pipe) so as to clean it **3** to drive (someone or something) out of a hiding place ▷ noun **4** rosy red colour; blush **5** pleasure and excitement **6** (in card games) hand all of one suit ▷ adjective **7** level with the surrounding surface **8** informal having plenty of money > **flushed** adjective pleased and excited

flustered adjective confused, nervous and rushed

flute noun **1** wind instrument consisting of a tube with sound holes and a hole for blowing across. It is held sideways **2** tall narrow wineglass

fluted adjective having decorative grooves

flutter verb **1** to flap or wave with small, quick movements **2** to move (something) quickly and irregularly **3** (of the heart) to beat abnormally quickly ▷ noun **4** nervous agitation **5** informal small bet

flux noun state of constant change

fly flies flew flown 1 insect with two pairs of wings **2** (often plural) Brit fastening at the front of trousers **3** (also **fly sheet**) flap forming the entrance to a tent ▷ verb **4** to move through the air on wings or in an aircraft **5** to pilot (a plane) **6** to float, flutter or be displayed in the air **7** to transport (someone or something) or to be transported by air **8** to move quickly or suddenly **9** (of time) to pass rapidly **10** to flee ▷ adjective **11** informal sharp and cunning > **flying** adjective, noun

fly-fishing noun method of freshwater fishing using imitation flies as bait

flying fox noun **1** large fruit-eating bat, found in Australia and Africa **2** Aust, NZ cable car used to carry people over rivers and gorges

flying saucer noun unidentified disc-shaped flying object, supposedly from outer space

flyover noun structure carrying one road over another at a junction or intersection

foal noun **1** young horse ▷ verb **2** to give birth to a foal

foam noun **1** mass of tiny bubbles **2** light spongy material used, for example, in furniture or packaging ▷ verb **3** to produce foam

fob off verb to stop (someone) asking questions or complaining by offering excuses, telling them half truths or giving them something of inferior quality

focus focuses or focusses **focusing** or **focussing** focused or **focussed**; focuses or **foci** verb **1** to adjust (your eyes, a camera or a lens, etc) in order to see or view something clearly ▶ **focus on a** to concentrate on **b** to look at ▷ noun **3** centre of interest or activity

fodder noun food for farm animals or horses

foe noun enemy

foetus foetuses; also spelt **fetus** noun an unborn child or animal in the womb > **foetal** adjective: foetal development

fog fogs fogging fogged noun **1** thick mist of water droplets suspended in the air ▷ verb **2** (often followed by up) to cover or become covered with steam > **foggy** adjective: a foggy morning

foil verb **1** to ruin (someone's plan) ▷ noun **2** metal in a thin sheet, especially for wrapping food **3** anything or anyone that shows up the qualities of something or someone else by contrast **4** thin, light sword with a button on the tip, used in fencing

foist verb (followed by on, upon) to force or impose (something on someone)

fold verb **1** to bend (something) so that one part covers another **2** to cross (your arms) **3** Cooking to mix gently **4** informal (of business) to fail or go bankrupt ▷ noun **5** mark, crease or hollow made by folding **6** folded piece or part **7** small enclosed area for sheep **8** church or its members

folder noun piece of folded cardboard for holding loose papers

foliage noun leaves

folk noun **1** people in general **2** race of people ▷ plural **3** informal relatives ▷ adjective **4** (of music, dance or art) traditional or representative of the ordinary local people

folklore noun traditional stories and beliefs of a community

follicle noun small pouchlike structure or cavity in the body, especially one from which a hair grows

follow verb **1** to go or come after (someone or something) **2** to be a logical or natural consequence of (something) **3** to keep to the course, track or direction of (a road, river or sign) **4** to act in accordance with (instructions or advice) **5** to accept the ideas or beliefs of (someone) **6** to understand (an explanation, plot or story) **7** to have a keen interest in (something) **8** to be true or logical in consequence ▶ **follow up** verb **1** to investigate (a matter, suggestion or discovery) **2** to do a second, often similar, thing after (a first)

follower noun disciple or

supporter

folly follies noun 1 foolishness 2 foolish action or idea 3 useless extravagant building

fond adjective 1 tender or loving 2 (of a hope or belief) foolish 3 fond of having a liking for > **fondly** adverb > **fondness** noun

fondle verb to stroke tenderly

font noun 1 bowl in a church that holds water for baptisms 2 set of printing type of one style and size

food noun 1 what people and animals eat 2 substance that provides nourishment for plants

food chain noun a series of living things which are linked because each one feeds on the next one in the series. For example, a plant may be eaten by a rabbit which may be eaten by a fox

food group noun category of food based on its nutritional content

foodstuff noun substance used as food

food technology noun study of foods, what they consist of and their effect on the body

fool noun 1 person who behaves in a silly or stupid way 2 dessert of puréed fruit mixed with cream > verb 3 to deceive (someone)

foolhardy foolhardier foolhardiest adjective recklessly adventurous > **foolhardiness** noun: the foolhardiness of travelling across the world by bike

foolish adjective unwise, silly or absurd > **foolishly** adverb > **foolishness** noun: He felt ashamed of his foolishness

foolproof adjective unable to fail

foosball noun US & Canadian same as **table football**

foot feet noun 1 part of the leg below the ankle 2 lowest part of anything: the foot of the mountain 3 unit of length equal to twelve inches or about 30.5 centimetres 4 Poetry basic unit of rhythm containing two or three syllables ▷ adjective 5 (of a brake, pedal, pump) operated by your foot ▷ verb 7 **foot it** informal to walk 6 **foot the bill** to pay the entire cost

footage noun amount or length of film

football noun 1 any of various games in which the ball can be kicked, such as soccer, rugby, Australian Rules and American football 2 ball used in any of these games > **footballer** noun

foothills plural noun hills at the foot of a mountain

foothold noun 1 place where you can put your foot when climbing 2 secure position from which progress may be made

footing noun 1 secure grip by or for the feet 2 basis or foundation of a relationship or situation

footman footmen noun male servant in a large house who wears a uniform

footnote noun note printed at the foot of a page

footpath noun 1 narrow path for walkers only 2 Aust raised space alongside a road, for pedestrians

footprint noun mark left by a foot

footstep noun 1 step taken when walking 2 sound made by walking

for preposition 1 indicating the person or thing receiving or benefiting from something:

a gift for you **2** indicating the destination of something: *the train for Liverpool* **3** indicating a length of time or distance: *for three weeks; for five miles* **4** indicating the reason, cause or purpose of something: *This is my excuse for going to Italy* **5** indicating the person or thing represented by someone: *playing for his country*

forage verb to search about (for food)

foray noun **1** brief attempt to do or get something **2** brief raid or attack

forbid forbids forbidding forbade forbidden verb to prohibit or refuse to allow: *He forbade her to leave the house* > **forbidden** adjective

force verb **1** to make (someone) do something; compel **2** to break open ▷ noun **3** strength or power **4** compulsion **5** *Physics* force is a pushing or pulling influence that changes a body from a state of rest to one of motion, or changes its rate of motion **6** mental or moral strength **7** person or thing with strength or influence **8** vehemence or intensity **9** group of people organized for a particular task or duty **10 in force a** having legal validity **b** in great numbers

forceful adjective powerful and convincing > **forcefully** adverb

forceps plural noun pair of long tongs or pincers used by a doctor

forcible adjective **1** involving physical force or violence **2** strong and convincing > **forcibly** adverb

ford noun **1** shallow place where a

river may be crossed ▷ verb **2** to cross (a river) at a ford

fore adjective **1** in, at or towards the front ▷ noun **2 come to the fore** to become important or popular: *Environmental issues have come to the fore lately*

forearm noun arm from the wrist to the elbow

forebear noun ancestor

foreboding noun feeling that something bad is about to happen

forecast forecasts forecasting forecast or **forecasted** verb **1** to predict (weather, events, etc) ▷ noun **2** prediction

forecourt noun courtyard or open space in front of a building

forefather noun ancestor

forefinger noun finger next to the thumb

forefront noun leading or most active position

forego foregoes foregoing forewent foregone; also spelt **forgo** verb to do without or give up (something)

foregoing adjective formal going before; preceding

foregone conclusion noun inevitable result

foreground noun part of a view, especially in a picture, nearest the observer

forehand noun *Tennis, Squash, Badminton* stroke made with the palm of your hand facing in the direction that you hit the ball

forehead noun area of your face above your eyebrows and below your hairline

foreign adjective **1** belonging to or involving countries other than your own **2** unfamiliar or uncharacteristic **3** in an abnormal place or position: *foreign matter* > **foreigner** *noun*

foreman foremen *noun* **1** person in charge of a group of workers **2** leader of a jury

foremost *adjective, adverb* first in time, place or importance

forensic *adjective* **1** relating to or involving the scientific examination of objects involved in a crime **2** relating to or involving the legal profession

forerunner *noun* something or someone that precedes, influences or is an early sign of subsequent developments in the area

foresee foresees foreseeing foresaw foreseen *verb* to see or know beforehand; predict > **foreseeable** *adjective*: *He will continue as chairman for the foreseeable future*

foresight *noun* ability to anticipate and provide for future needs

foreskin *noun* fold of skin covering the tip of the penis

forest *noun* large area of trees growing close together

forestry *noun* **1** science of planting and caring for trees **2** management of forests

foretaste *noun* early limited experience of something to come

foretell foretells foretelling foretold *verb* to predict (something)

forever or **for ever** *adverb* permanently or continually

forewarn *verb* to warn (someone) beforehand

foreword *noun* introduction to a book

forfeit *verb* **1** to lose (something) as a penalty ▷ *noun* **2** thing lost or given up as a penalty

forge *noun* **1** place where a blacksmith works making metal goods by hand; smithy **2** furnace for melting metal ▷ *verb* **3** to make an illegal copy of (a painting, document or money, etc) **4** to shape (metal) by heating and hammering it **5** to create (a relationship etc) > **forge ahead** *verb* to progress quickly

forgery forgeries *noun* **1** illegal copy of something **2** crime of forging money, documents or paintings

forget forgets forgetting forgot forgotten *verb* **1** to fail to remember (something) **2** to neglect **3** to leave (something) behind by mistake **4** **forget yourself** to behave in an unacceptable way > **forgetful** *adjective* tending to forget > **forgetfulness** *noun*

forget-me-not *noun* plant with clusters of small blue flowers

forgive forgives forgiving forgave forgiven *verb* to cease to blame or hold resentment against (someone); pardon > **forgiveness** *noun* > **forgiving** *adjective*

forgo *verb* same as **forego**

fork *noun* **1** tool for eating food, with prongs and a handle **2** large similarly-shaped garden tool **3** point where a road, river, etc divides into two branches **4** one of the branches ▷ *verb* **5** to pick up, dig, etc (something) with a fork **6** to branch **7** to take one or other branch at a fork in the road

a
b
c
d
e
f
g
h
i
j
k
l
m
n
o
p
q
r
s
t
u
v
w
x
y
z

>**forked** *adjective* >**fork out** *verb*
informal to pay

forlorn *adjective* **1** lonely and
unhappy **2** (of a hope or
attempt) desperate and without
any expectation of success
>**forlornly** *adverb*

form *noun* **1** type or kind **2** shape
or appearance **3** mode in which
something appears **4** printed
document with spaces for details
5 physical or mental condition
6 previous record of an athlete,
racehorse, etc **7** class in school
▷ *verb* **8** to come into existence;
be made **9** to bring (something)
into existence; make **10** to make
(something) up: *events that were
to form the basis of her novel* **11** to
acquire or develop (something)

formal *adjective* **1** correct, serious
and conforming to accepted
conventions: *a very formal letter
of apology* **2** of or for formal
occasions **3** stiff in manner
4 organized **5** official and publicly
recognized: *the first formal
agreement of its kind* >**formally**
adverb

formaldehyde *noun* a poisonous,
strong-smelling gas, used for
preserving specimens in biology

formality formalities *noun*
1 requirement of custom or
etiquette **2** necessary procedure
without real importance

**format formats formatting
formatted** *noun* **1** style in which
something is arranged ▷ *verb* **2** to
arrange (something) in a format

formation *noun* **1** process
of developing and creating
something **2** structure or shape
of something **3** arrangement of
people or things acting as a unit

formative *adjective* having an
important and lasting influence
on character and development

former *adjective* **1** happening or
existing before now or in the
past ▷ *noun* **2 the former** first
mentioned of two >**formerly**
adverb

formidable *adjective* **1** frightening
because difficult to overcome or
manage **2** extremely impressive
>**formidably** *adverb*

formula formulae or **formulas**
noun **1** group of numbers, letters
or symbols expressing a scientific
or mathematical rule **2** list of
quantities of substances that
when mixed make another
substance, for example in
chemistry **3** method or rule for
doing or producing something

formulate *verb* to create and
express (a plan or thought) in a
clear and precise way

fornication *noun* formal sin
of having sex with someone
without being married to them

**forsake forsakes forsaking
forsook forsaken** *verb* to give up
or abandon (someone)

fort *noun* **1** strong building built
for defence **2 hold the fort**
informal to keep things going
during someone's absence

forte *noun* **1** something that
someone does really well;
speciality ▷ *adverb* **2** *Music* loudly

forth *adverb* forwards, out or away

forthcoming *adjective* **1** about
to appear or happen **2** available
3 (of a person) communicative

forthright *adjective* direct and
outspoken

fortification *noun* building, wall

or ditch used to protect a place

fortitude noun calm and patient courage in times of trouble or when suffering

fortnight noun two weeks >**fortnightly** adverb, adjective

fortress noun large fort or fortified town

fortuitous adjective happening by chance or good luck >**fortuitously** adverb

fortunate adjective **1** having good luck; lucky **2** occurring by good luck >**fortunately** adverb

fortune noun **1** luck, especially when favourable **2** wealth, large sum of money **3** (often plural) person's destiny

forty forties adjective, noun the number 40 >**fortieth** adjective, noun

forum forums or fora noun **1** place, meeting or medium in which people can exchange ideas and discuss public issues **2** square in Roman towns where people met to discuss business and politics

forward adverb **1** (also **forwards**) towards or at a place further ahead in space or time **2** towards the front ▷ adjective **3** directed or moving ahead **4** in, at or near the front **5** presumptuous **6** well developed or advanced **7** relating to the future ▷ noun **8** attacking player in various team games, such as soccer or hockey ▷ verb **9** to send (a letter etc) on to an ultimate destination >**forwards** adverb

fossick verb Aust, NZ to search, especially for gold or precious stones

fossil noun the remains or impression of an animal or plant from a previous age, preserved in rock >**fossilize** verb to turn into a fossil

fossil fuel noun fuel such as coal, oil or natural gas, formed by the rotting of animals and plants from millions of years ago

foster verb **1** to bring up (someone else's child) without becoming the legal parent **2** to promote the growth or development of >**foster child** noun >**foster home** noun >**foster parent** noun

fought verb past of **fight**

foul adjective **1** dirty, wicked or obscene ▷ verb **2** to make (something) dirty or polluted, especially with faeces **3** Sport to break the rules to the disadvantage of (an opponent) ▷ noun **4** Sport act of breaking the rules

found verb **1** past of **find 2** to start or set up (an organization or institution) **3** to lay the foundation of

foundation noun **1** basis or base **2** part of a building or wall below the ground **3** act of founding **4** organization set up by money left in someone's will for research or charity **5** cosmetic used as a base for make-up

founder noun **1** person responsible for setting up an institution or organization ▷ verb **2** to break down or fail **3** (of a ship) to sink

foundry foundries noun factory where metal is melted and cast

fountain noun **1** jet of water **2** structure from which such a jet spurts

fountain pen noun pen supplied with ink from a container inside it

four adjective, noun **1** the number 4 ▷ noun **2** **on all fours** on hands and knees

four-poster noun bed with four posts supporting a canopy and curtains

fourteen adjective, noun the number 14 > **fourteenth** adjective, noun

fourth adjective, noun **1** (coming as) number 4 in a series ▷ noun **2** quarter

fowl noun bird such as chicken or duck that is kept for its meat or eggs or hunted for its meat

fox foxes foxing foxed noun **1** dog-like wild animal with reddish-brown fur, a pointed face and ears, and a thick tail **2** cunning person ▷ verb **3** informal to puzzle or perplex (someone)

foxglove noun tall plant with purple or white trumpet-shaped flowers

foxhound noun breed of dog used for hunting foxes

foyer noun large area just inside the main doors of a theatre, cinema or hotel

fracas noun noisy quarrel
- The plural of *fracas* is *fracas*

fraction noun **1** part of a whole number **2** tiny amount, fragment or piece of something > **fractional** adjective > **fractionally** adverb

fractious adjective easily upset or angered

fracture noun **1** crack or break in something, especially a bone ▷ verb **2** to break

fragile adjective **1** easily broken

or damaged **2** in a weakened physical state > **fragility** noun

fragment noun **1** small piece broken off something ▷ verb **2** to break into pieces > **fragmentation** noun > **fragmented** adjective

fragmentary adjective made up of small pieces or parts that are not connected: *fragmentary notes in a journal*

fragrance noun **1** sweet or pleasant smell **2** perfume or scent

fragrant adjective smelling sweet or pleasant

frail adjective **1** physically weak **2** easily damaged > **frailty** noun physical or moral weakness

frame noun **1** structure surrounding a door, window or picture **2** structure giving shape or support **3** person's build **4** one of the many separate photographs of which a cinema film is made up **5** **frames** the part of a pair of glasses that holds the lenses ▷ verb **6** to put (a picture) into a frame **7** to put (something) into words; express **8** informal to incriminate (a person) on a false charge

framework noun **1** supporting structure **2** set of rules, beliefs or ideas which you use to decide what to do

franc noun monetary unit of Switzerland, various African countries, and formerly of France and Belgium

franchise noun **1** right to vote **2** authorization to sell a company's goods

frank adjective **1** open, honest and straightforward in what you

say ▷ *noun* **2** official mark on a letter permitting delivery ▷ *verb* **3** to put such a mark on (a letter) > **frankly** *adverb* > **frankness** *noun*

frantic *adjective* **1** made wild and uncontrolled through anxiety or fear **2** hurried and disorganized > **frantically** *adverb*

fraternal *adjective* of a brother, brotherly

fraternity fraternities *noun* **1** brotherhood **2** group of people with shared interests, aims, etc **3** US male social club at college

fraud *noun* **1** crime of getting money by deceit or trickery **2** something that deceives people in an illegal or immoral way **3** person who is not what they pretend to be

fraudulent *adjective* dishonest or deceitful

fraught *adjective* **1** tense or anxious **2 fraught with** involving, filled with

fray *verb* **1** to become or make (something) ragged at the edge **2** to become strained ▷ *noun* **3** *Brit, Aust, NZ* noisy quarrel or fight

freak *noun* **1** abnormal person or thing ▷ *adjective* **2** very unusual and unlikely to happen

freckle *noun* small brown spot on the skin > **freckled** *adjective* marked with freckles

free freer freest; frees freeing freed *adjective* **1** (of a person, group) able to act at will; not forced, restrained or imprisoned **2** (of activity, event) not controlled or limited: *the free flow of aid; free trade* **3** (of an object, event, activity) costing nothing

4 (of a person) not busy **5** (of a place, seat, machine) not in use ▷ *verb* **6** to release or liberate (someone or something) **7** to make (something or someone) available or usable

freedom *noun* **1** being free **2** right or privilege of unlimited access: *the freedom of the city*

freehold *noun* right to own a house or piece of land for life without conditions

freelance *adjective* **1** self-employed ▷ *adverb* **2** as a self-employed person ▷ *noun* **3** a self-employed person doing specific pieces of work for various employers

freely *adverb* without restriction

free-range *adjective* kept or produced in natural conditions

freestyle *noun* sports competitions, especially swimming, in which competitors can use any style or method

freeway *noun* *US, Aust* motorway

free will *noun* **of your own free will** by choice and without pressure being exerted

freeze freezes freezing froze frozen *verb* **1** (of a liquid) to become solid because of the cold **2** to preserve (food etc) by extreme cold **3** to be very cold **4** to become suddenly very still or quiet with fear, shock, etc **5** *Drama* to stop (the action in a film) at a particular frame **6** to fix (prices or wages) at a particular level ▷ *noun* **7** period of very cold weather **8** official action taken to prevent wages or prices from rising

freezer *noun* large refrigerator

which freezes and stores food for a long time

freezing *adjective informal* very cold

freight *noun* **1** cargo transported by lorries, ships, etc **2** commercial transport of goods **3** cost of this

French *noun, adjective* **1** belonging or relating to France **2** language of France, also spoken in parts of Belgium, Canada and Switzerland

French bean *noun* green pod eaten as a vegetable, which grows on a climbing plant with white or mauve flowers

French horn *noun* brass wind instrument with a coiled tube

Frenchman Frenchmen *noun* man from France >**Frenchwoman** *noun*

French window *noun* one of a pair of glass doors that lead into a garden or onto a balcony

frenetic *adjective* wild and excited >**frenetically** *adverb*

frenzy frenzies *noun* wild and uncontrolled state >**frenzied** *adjective*

frequency frequencies *noun* **1** how often something happens **2** *Physics* the rate at which a sound wave or radio wave vibrates

frequent *adjective* **1** happening often ▷ *verb* **2** to visit (a place) often >**frequently** *adverb*

fresco frescoes or **frescos** *noun* picture painted on wet plaster on a wall

fresh *adjective* **1** newly made, acquired, etc **2** original **3** further, additional **4** (of food) not preserved **5** (of water) not salty **6** (of weather) brisk or invigorating **7** not tired **8** fresh

from having recently experienced (something) >**freshly** *adverb* >**freshness** *noun*

freshwater *adjective* **1** (of a lake or pool) containing water that is not salty **2** (of a fish, animal) living in a river, lake or pool that is not salty

fret frets fretting fretted *verb* **1** to be worried ▷ *noun* **2** small bar on the fingerboard of a guitar etc

Freudian slip *noun* something that you say or do that reveals your unconscious thoughts

friar *noun* member of a male Roman Catholic religious order

friction *noun* **1** force that stops things from moving freely when they rub against each other **2** rubbing **3** clash of wills or personalities

Friday *noun* day between Friday and Sunday

fridge *noun* electrically cooled container in which you store food and drinks to keep them fresh; refrigerator

friend *noun* person you know well and like

friendly friendlier friendliest; friendlies *adjective* **1** showing or expressing liking **2** not hostile, on the same side ▷ *noun* **3** *Sport* match played for its own sake and not as part of a competition >**friendliness** *noun*

friendship *noun* **1** relationship that you have with a friend **2** state of being friends with someone

frieze *noun* decorative band on a wall

frigate *noun* medium-sized fast warship

right noun 1 sudden fear or alarm 2 sudden alarming shock

righten verb to scare or terrify (someone) > **frightened** adjective > **frightening** adjective

rightful adjective 1 horrifying 2 informal very great > **frightfully** adverb

rigid adjective 1 (of a woman) sexually unresponsive 2 cold and unfriendly

rill noun strip of cloth with many folds, attached to something as a decoration > **frilly** adjective decorated with frills or lace

ringe noun 1 hair that is cut to hang down over your forehead 2 ornamental edge of hanging threads, tassels, etc 3 outer edge 4 less important parts of an activity or group > adjective 5 (of theatre) unofficial or unconventional > **fringed** adjective

risk verb informal to search (a person) for concealed weapons etc

risky friskier friskiest adjective lively or high-spirited

ritter noun piece of food fried in batter > **fritter away** verb to waste

rivolous adjective 1 not serious or sensible 2 enjoyable but trivial > **frivolity** noun

rizzy frizzier frizziest adjective (of hair) having small, tight, wiry curls

rock noun old-fashioned dress

og noun small amphibious creature with smooth skin, prominent eyes, and long back legs which it uses for jumping

olic frolics frolicking frolicked

verb to run around and play in a lively way

from preposition 1 indicating the origin or source of something or someone: a call from a public telephone; people from a city 100 miles away 2 indicating a starting point or point of departure: She fled from the room 3 indicating the start of a range: a score from one to five 4 indicating a cause: the wreckage from the bomb blast 5 indicating a sum or amount that is reduced by another sum or amount: The money is deducted from her salary every month

frond noun long feathery leaf

front noun 1 part of something that faces forward 2 position directly before or ahead 3 place where two armies are fighting 4 Meteorology dividing line between a mass of cold air and a mass of warm air 5 outward appearance 6 informal cover for another, usually criminal, activity 7 particular field of activity: on the economic front > adjective 8 of or at the front 9 in front ahead or further forward 10 in front of a in the presence of b before > **frontal** adjective formal: the frontal region of the brain

frontage noun (of a building) wall facing onto a street, river or public place; facade

frontier noun border between two countries

frontispiece noun illustration facing the title page of a book

frost noun 1 white frozen dew or mist 2 atmospheric temperature below freezing point

frostbite noun damage to your fingers, toes or ears caused by extreme cold

frosty frostier frostiest adjective
1 below freezing **2** unfriendly
▷ **frostily** adverb

froth noun **1** mass of small bubbles
▷ verb **2** to foam ▷ **frothy** adjective

frown verb **1** to wrinkle your brows
in worry, anger or thought ▷ noun
2 cross, frowning expression

froze verb past tense of **freeze**

frozen verb **1** past participle of
freeze ▷ adjective **2** extremely
cold

fructose noun type of sugar found
in many fruits and in honey

frugal adjective **1** spending very
little money; thrifty **2** (of a meal)
small and cheap ▷ **frugality** noun
▷ **frugally** adverb

fruit noun **1** part of a plant
containing seeds, especially if
edible **2** (often plural) good result
of an action or effort

fruitful adjective useful or
productive

fruitless adjective useless or
unproductive

fruit machine noun coin-
operated gambling machine

fruit salad noun mixture of pieces
of different fruits served in a juice
as a dessert

fruity fruitier fruitiest adjective
1 of or like fruit **2** (of a voice) rich
and deep

frustrate verb **1** to make
(someone) angry or upset by
not allowing or preventing
them from doing what they
want **2** to hinder or prevent
(a plan) ▷ **frustrated** adjective:
frustrated motorists, desperate
to get moving ▷ **frustrating**
adjective: a frustrating day at work

▷ **frustration** noun: his frustration
at being left out of the team

fry fries frying fried verb to cook or
be cooked in fat or oil

fuchsia noun plant or bush with
pink, purple or white flowers that
hang downwards

fudge noun **1** soft brown sweet
made from butter, milk and sugar
▷ verb **2** to avoid making a firm
statement or decision about
(something)

fuel fuels fuelling fuelled noun
1 substance such as coal or petrol
that is burned to provide heat
or power ▷ verb **2** to provide (a
device or vehicle) with fuel

fug noun hot stale atmosphere
▷ **fuggy** adjective

fugitive noun person who flees,
especially from arrest or pursuit

-ful suffix **1** used to form adjectives
with the meaning full of: careful
2 used to form nouns which mean
the amount needed to fill: spoonful

fulcrum fulcrums or **fulcra** noun
the point at which something is
balancing or pivoting

fulfil fulfils fulfilling fulfilled
verb **1** to carry out or achieve (a
promise, duty, dream or hope)
2 (of work, an activity) to satisfy
(someone or yourself) completely
▷ **fulfilling** adjective: a happy and
fulfilling life ▷ **fulfilment** noun: It
was the fulfilment of a dream

full adjective **1** containing as
much or as many as possible
2 complete, whole **3** (of clothes)
loose and made from a lot of fabric
4 having had enough to eat **5** (of
a figure) plump **6** (of a sound or
flavour) rich and strong ▷ adverb
7 completely **8** directly ▷ noun

9 in full completely ▷ **fullness** noun > **fully** adverb

full-blooded adjective vigorous or enthusiastic

full-blown adjective fully developed

full moon noun phase of the moon when it looks round and complete

full stop noun punctuation mark (.) used at the end of a sentence and after abbreviations or initials

full-time adjective **1** involving work for the whole of each normal working week ▷ noun **2** Sport the end of a match ▷ adverb **3** (also **full time**) during the whole of each normal working week

fully-fledged adjective completely developed: I was a fully-fledged and mature human being

fulsome adjective exaggerated and elaborate, and often sounding insincere

fumble verb to handle something awkwardly

fume verb to be very angry ▷ **fumes** plural noun gases, vapours or smoke which are released from certain chemicals or burning substances and which smell unpleasant and may be toxic

fun noun **1** enjoyment or amusement **2 make fun of** to mock or tease (someone)

function noun **1** purpose something exists for **2** role or job **3** way something works **4** large or formal social event **5** Maths quantity whose value depends on the varying value of another ▷ verb **6** to operate or work **7 function as** to fill the role of

functional adjective **1** relating to the way something works

2 practical rather than decorative **3** in working order

fund noun **1** stock of money for a special purpose **2** supply or store **3 funds** money resources ▷ verb **4** to provide money for (something or someone) > **funding** noun: Where are they going to get the funding?

fundamental adjective **1** essential or primary **2** basic ▷ noun **3** basic rule or fact > **fundamentally** adverb

funeral noun ceremony or religious service for the burial or cremation of a dead person

funereal adjective gloomy or sombre

funfair noun place or event provided for outdoor entertainment, having stalls and rides on machines

fungicide noun substance that destroys fungi

fungus fungi or **funguses** noun organism such as a mushroom, toadstool or mould that does not have leaves and grows on other living things > **fungal** adjective: a fungal infection

funk verb **1** old-fashioned informal to avoid (doing something) through fear ▷ noun **2** style of music with a strong rhythm based on jazz and blues

funnel funnels funnelling funnelled noun **1** tube with a cone shape at the top for pouring liquids into a narrow opening **2** metal chimney on a ship or steam engine ▷ verb **3** to move or cause to move through or as if through a funnel

funny funnier funniest adjective

1 odd, strange or puzzling **2** causing amusement or laughter ▷ adverb **>funnily** adverb

fur noun **1** soft thick body hair of many animals **2** animal skin with the fur left on **3** coat made from this **>furry** adjective: a furry toy

furious adjective **1** very angry **2** involving great energy, effort or speed **>furiously** adverb

furlong noun unit of length equal to 220 yards (201.168 metres)

furnace noun enclosed chamber containing a very hot fire used, for example, in the steel industry for melting ore

furnish verb **1** to provide (a house or room) with furniture **2** to supply or provide (someone with something)

furnishings plural noun furniture, carpets and fittings

furniture noun large movable articles such as chairs and wardrobes: a few pieces of furniture

furore noun angry and excited reaction

furrow noun **1** long, shallow trench made by a plough **2** groove, especially a wrinkle on the forehead ▷ verb **3** furrow your brow to frown

further adjective **1** a comparative form of **far 2** additional or more **3** more distant ▷ adverb **4** in addition **5** to a greater distance or extent ▷ verb **6** to assist the progress of (something)

further education noun Brit education beyond school other than at a university

furthermore adverb formal besides

furthest adjective **1** a superlative

form of **far 2** most distant ▷ adverb **3** to the greatest distance or extent

furtive adjective sly and secretive **>furtively** adverb

fury noun violent or extreme anger

fuse noun **1** safety device for electric circuits, containing a wire that melts and breaks the connection when the circuit is overloaded **2** long cord attached to some types of simple bomb which is lit to detonate the bomb ▷ verb **3** to stop working or cause (something) to stop working as a result of a blown fuse **4** to join or combine

fuselage noun body of an aircraft

fusion noun **1** something new created by a mixture of qualities, ideas or things **2** the joining together of two or more things to form one thing **3** the melting together of two substances **4** (also **nuclear fusion**) combination of the nucleus of two atoms with the release of energy

fuss noun **1** needless activity, worry or attentiveness **2** complaint or objection ▷ verb **3** to show unnecessary concern or attention over unimportant things

fussy fussier fussiest adjective **1** inclined to fuss **2** overparticular **3** overelaborate

futile adjective having no chance of success: a futile attempt to calm the storm **>futility** noun: the futility of war

future noun **1** time to come **2** what will happen **3** prospects ▷ adjective **4** yet to come or be **5** of or relating to time to come

6 (of a verb tense) indicating that the action specified has not yet taken place

futuristic *adjective* (of a design) very modern and strange, as if belonging to a time in the future

fuzz *noun* mass of fine or curly hairs or fibres

g

g *symbol* **1** gram(s) **2** (acceleration due to) gravity

gabble *verb* **1** to speak rapidly and indistinctly ▷ *noun* **2** rapid indistinct speech

gable *noun* triangular upper part of a wall between sloping roofs

gadget *noun* small mechanical device or appliance > **gadgetry** *noun* gadgets

Gaelic *noun* any of the Celtic languages of Ireland and the Scottish Highlands

gaffe *noun* social blunder

gaffer *noun* Brit informal foreman or boss

gag gags gagging gagged *verb* **1** to choke and nearly vomit **2** to stop up the mouth of (someone) with a strip of cloth **3** to deprive (someone) of free speech ▷ *noun* **4** strip of cloth tied across the mouth **5** informal joke

gaggle *noun* **1** informal disorderly crowd **2** flock of geese

gaiety *noun* **1** cheerfulness

2 merrymaking

gaily *adverb* merrily

gain *verb* **1** to acquire or obtain (something) **2** (followed by *from*) to get an advantage from a situation **3** (of a watch or clock) to be or become too fast ▷ *noun* **4** profit or advantage **5** increase > **gain on** or **upon** *verb* to get nearer to or catch up with (someone)

gait *noun* manner of walking

gala *noun* **1** festival **2** competitive sporting event

galah *noun* Aust **1** cockatoo with a pink breast and a grey back and wings **2** informal stupid person

galaxy galaxies *noun* system of stars

gale *noun* strong wind

gall *noun* **1** informal impudence ▷ *verb* **2** to annoy (someone)

gallant *adjective* **1** brave and noble **2** (of a man) attentive to women > **gallantly** *adverb* > **gallantry** *noun* **1** showy, attentive treatment of women **2** bravery

gall bladder *noun* organ next to the liver that stores bile

galleon *noun* large three-masted sailing ship of the 15th–17th centuries

gallery galleries *noun* **1** room or building for displaying works of art **2** balcony in a church, theatre, etc

galley *noun* **1** kitchen of a ship or aircraft **2** History ship propelled by oars, usually rowed by slaves

Gallic *adjective* literary French

gallon *noun* liquid measure of eight pints, equal to 4.55 litres

gallop *noun* **1** horse's fastest pace **2** galloping ▷ *verb* **3** to go or ride at a gallop **4** to move or progress rapidly

gallows noun wooden structure used for hanging criminals

gallstone noun small painful lump formed in the gall bladder or its ducts

galore adverb in abundance: chocolates galore

galoshes plural noun Brit, Aust, NZ waterproof shoes for wearing on top of ordinary shoes

galvanized or **galvanised** adjective (of metal) coated with zinc by an electrical process to protect it from rust

gambit noun **1** opening line or move intended to secure an advantage **2** Chess opening move involving the sacrifice of a pawn

gamble verb **1** to bet money on the result of a game or race; wager **2** to risk losing (something) in the hope of gaining an advantage ▷ noun **3** risky undertaking ▷ **gambler** noun person who gambles regularly ▷ **gambling** noun activity of betting money

game noun **1** amusement or pastime **2** contest for amusement **3** single period of play in a contest **4** animals or birds hunted for sport or food **5** scheme or trick ▷ adjective **6** willing to try something unusual or difficult ▷ **gamely** adverb: he gamely defended the decision ▷ **gaming** noun gambling

gamekeeper noun Brit, Aust, S Afr person employed to look after game animals and birds on a country estate

games console noun electronic device enabling computer games

to be played on a TV screen

gammon noun cured or smoked ham

gamut noun whole range or scale (of music, emotions, etc)

gander noun male goose

gang noun group of people who join together for some purpose, e.g. to commit a crime > **gang up** on verb to join together to oppose (someone)

gangplank noun portable bridge for boarding or leaving a ship

gangrene noun decay of body tissue as a result of disease or injury > **gangrenous** adjective: gangrenous limbs

gangster noun member of a criminal gang

gannet noun large sea bird

gaol noun same as **jail**

gap noun **1** break or opening **2** great difference: the gap between fantasy and reality

gape verb **1** to stare with the mouth open in surprise **2** to be wide open > **gaping** adjective: gaping holes in the wall

garage noun **1** building where cars are kept **2** place for the refuelling, sale and repair of cars

garb noun formal clothes

garbage noun **1** rubbish, especially household rubbish **2** nonsense

garbled adjective (of a story etc) jumbled and confused

garden noun **1** piece of land for growing flowers, fruit or vegetables **2** gardens ornamental park > **gardener** noun person who looks after a garden as a job or hobby > **gardening** noun looking after a garden as a job or hobby

gargle *verb* to wash the throat with a liquid by breathing out slowly through the liquid

gargoyle *noun* waterspout carved in the form of a grotesque face, especially on a church

garish *adjective* crudely bright or colourful

garland *noun* circle of flowers worn or hung as a decoration

garlic *noun* pungent bulb of a plant of the onion family, used in cooking

garment *noun* article of clothing

garnet *noun* red semiprecious stone

garnish *verb* **1** to decorate (food) ▷ *noun* **2** decoration for food

garret *noun* attic in a house

garrison *noun* **1** troops stationed in a town or fort **2** fortified place

garrotte *verb* to strangle (someone) with a piece of wire

garter *noun* band worn round the leg to hold up a sock or stocking

gas *gases*; *gasses* *gassing* *gassed* *noun* **1** airlike substance that is not liquid or solid **2** fossil fuel in the form of a gas, used for heating **3** *Chiefly US* petrol ▷ *verb* **4** to poison (people or animals) with gas ▷ **5** *adjective* of or like gas **6** filled with gas

● The plural of the noun *gas* is *gases*. The verb forms of *gas* are spelt with a double *s*

gas chamber *noun* airtight room which is filled with poison gas to kill people or animals

gash *verb* **1** to make a long deep cut in (something) ▷ *noun* **2** long deep cut

gas mask *noun* mask with a

chemical filter to protect the wearer against poison gas

gasoline *noun US* petrol

gasp *verb* **1** to draw in breath sharply or with difficulty ▷ *noun* **2** convulsive intake of breath

gastric *adjective* of the stomach

gate *noun* **1** movable barrier, usually hinged, in a wall or fence **2** number of people attending a sporting event

gateau *gateaux* *noun* rich layered cake with cream in it

gatecrash *verb* to enter (a party) uninvited

gateway *noun* **1** entrance with a gate **2** means of access: *New York is the great gateway to America*

gather *verb* **1** to come together in a group; assemble **2** to collect (a number of things) gradually **3** to increase (something) gradually **4** to learn (something) from information given

gathering *noun* meeting of people who have come together for a particular purpose

gauche *adjective* socially awkward

gaudy *gaudier gaudiest* *adjective* vulgarly bright or colourful

gauge *verb* **1** to estimate or calculate (something) ▷ *noun* **2** measuring instrument **3** scale or standard of measurement **4** distance between the rails of a railway track

gaunt *adjective* lean and haggard

gauntlet *noun* **1** heavy glove with a long cuff **2** **run the gauntlet** to be exposed to criticism or unpleasant treatment **3** **throw down the gauntlet** to offer a challenge

gave *verb* past tense of **give**

gay adjective **1** homosexual **2** old-fashioned carefree and merry ▷ noun **3** homosexual person

- The most common meaning of *gay* now is 'homosexual'. In some older books it may have its old-fashioned meaning of 'lively and full of fun'. The noun *gaiety* is related to this older meaning of *gay*. The noun that means 'the state of being homosexual' is *gayness*.

gaze verb to look fixedly

gazelle noun small graceful antelope

gazette noun official publication containing announcements

GB abbreviation Great Britain

GCSE abbreviation (in Britain) General Certificate of Secondary Education

gear noun **1** set of toothed wheels connecting with another or with a rack to change the direction or speed of transmitted motion **2** mechanism for transmitting motion by gears **3** setting of a gear to suit engine speed: *first gear* **4** clothing or belongings **5** equipment ▷ verb **6** (followed by *to*) to prepare (someone) or organize (something) for a particular event or purpose

geek noun informal **1** boring, unattractive person **2** person highly knowledgeable in computing ▷ **geeky** adjective

geese noun plural of **goose**

gel gels gelling gelled noun **1** jelly-like substance, especially one used to set a hairstyle ▷ verb **2** to form a gel **3** informal to take on a definite form

gelatine or **gelatin** noun **1** substance made by boiling animal bones **2** edible jelly made of this

gelding noun castrated horse

gem noun **1** precious stone or jewel **2** highly valued person or thing

Gemini noun third sign of the zodiac, represented by a pair of twins

gemsbok gemsbok or gemsboks noun S Afr oryx, a type of large antelope with straight horns

gen noun informal information

gender noun **1** state of being male or female **2** Grammar classification of nouns in certain languages as masculine, feminine or neuter

gene noun part of a cell which determines inherited characteristics

general adjective **1** common or widespread **2** of or affecting all or most **3** not specific **4** including or dealing with various or miscellaneous items **5** highest in authority or rank: *general manager* ▷ noun **6** very senior army officer **7** in general mostly or usually ▷ **generally** adverb usually

general election noun election in which everyone old enough to vote can vote for the candidate they want to represent them in Parliament

generalize verb to say that something is true in most cases, ignoring minor details ▷ **generalization** noun: *That's rather a sweeping generalization*

general practitioner noun

doctor who works in the community rather than in a hospital

generate verb to produce (something) or bring (something) into being

generation noun 1 all the people born about the same time 2 average time between two generations (about 30 years)

generator noun machine for converting mechanical energy into electrical energy

generic adjective of a class, group or genus > **generically** adverb

generous adjective 1 very willing to give money or time 2 very large; ample > **generosity** noun state of being generous > **generously** adverb

genesis noun formal beginning or origin

genetic adjective relating to genes or genetics > **genetically** adverb > **genetics** noun study of heredity and variation in organisms

genial adjective cheerful and friendly > **genially** adverb in a cheerful and friendly manner

genie noun (in fairy tales) servant who appears by magic and grants wishes

genitals or **genitalia** plural noun external sexual organs

genius geniuses noun (person with) exceptional ability in a particular field

genocide noun murder of a race of people

genome noun all of the genes contained in a single cell of an organism

genre noun style of literary, musical or artistic work

genteel adjective very polite and refined

gentile adjective, noun non-Jewish (person)

gentility noun excessive politeness and refinement

gentle adjective 1 mild or kindly 2 not rough or severe 3 gradual 4 easily controlled, tame > **gentleness** noun: the gentleness with which she treated her pregnant mother > **gently** adverb

gentleman gentlemen noun 1 polite well-bred man 2 man of high social position 3 polite name for a man > **gentlemanly** adjective (of a man) having good manners

gentry plural noun people just below the nobility in social rank

genuine adjective 1 not fake, authentic 2 sincere > **genuinely** adverb > **genuineness** noun: the genuineness of their intentions

genus genera noun Biology group into which a family of animals or plants is divided

geo- prefix earth: geography; geologist

geography noun study of the earth's physical features, climate, population, etc > **geographical** or **geographic** adjective relating to geography > **geographically** adverb in a geographical sense

geology noun study of the earth's origin, structure and composition > **geological** adjective relating to geology > **geologist** noun person who studies geology

geometry noun branch of mathematics dealing with points, lines, curves, and surfaces > **geometric** or **geometrical**

adjective **1** consisting of regular lines and shapes, such as squares, triangles and circles **2** involving geometry > **geometrically** *adverb* in a geometric pattern

Georgian *adjective* of the time of any of the four kings of Britain called George, esp. 1714–1830

geranium *noun* cultivated plant with red, pink or white flowers

gerbil *noun* burrowing desert rodent of Asia and Africa

geriatrics *noun* branch of medicine dealing with old age and its diseases > **geriatric** *adjective, noun* old (person)

germ *noun* **1** very small organism that causes disease **2** *formal* beginning from which something may develop

German *noun* **1** language of Germany, Austria and part of Switzerland **2** person from Germany > *adjective* **3** of Germany or its language > **Germanic** *adjective* typical of Germany or the German people

German measles *noun* contagious disease accompanied by a cough, sore throat, and red spots

germinate *verb* **1** (of a seed) to start to grow **2** (of an idea or plan) to start to develop > **germination** *noun: the germination of a seed*

gerrymander *verb* to alter political boundaries in an area to give unfair advantage to a particular party and make it more likely that its candidate(s) will do well in elections > **gerrymandering** *noun*

gestation *noun* period of carrying of young in the womb between conception and birth

gesticulate *verb* to make expressive movements with the hands and arms > **gesticulation** *noun*

gesture *noun* **1** movement to convey meaning **2** thing said or done to show your feelings ▷ *verb* **3** to move the hands or head in order to communicate a message or feeling

get gets getting got *verb* **1** to obtain or receive (something) **2** to bring or fetch (something) **3** to become as specified: *get wet* **4** to understand (something) **5** (often followed by *to*) to come to or arrive at (a place) **6** to go on board (a plane, bus, etc) **7** to persuade (someone) to do something > **get across** *verb* to cause (something) to be understood > **get at** *verb* **1** to imply or mean (something) **2** to criticize (someone) > **get away with** *verb* not to be found out or punished for doing (something dishonest) > **get by** *verb* to manage in spite of difficulties > **get on** *verb* **1** (of two people) to like each other's company **2** to do (a task) > **get over with** *verb* to be finished with (something unpleasant) > **get through to** *verb* **1** to make (someone) understand what you are saying **2** to contact (someone) by telephone

getaway *noun* escape made by criminals

get-together *noun informal* informal meeting or party

geyser *noun* **1** spring that discharges steam and hot water **2** *Brit, S Afr* domestic gas water heater

Ghanaian adjective **1** of Ghana ▷ noun **2** person from Ghana

ghastly ghastlier ghastliest adjective extremely horrible and unpleasant

gherkin noun small pickled cucumber

ghetto ghettoes or **ghettos** noun part of a city where many poor people of a particular race live

ghost noun spirit of a dead person, believed to haunt people or places

ghoulish adjective very interested in unpleasant things such as death and murder

giant noun **1** mythical being of superhuman strength ▷ adjective **2** much larger than other similar things: giant prawns

gibberish noun speech that makes no sense at all

gibbon noun ape with very long arms

gibe noun same as **jibe**

giddy giddier giddiest adjective feeling unsteady on your feet usually because of illness > **giddily** adverb dizzily

gift noun **1** present **2** natural talent > **gifted** adjective talented

gig noun **1** rock or jazz concert **2** light two-wheeled horse-drawn carriage

gigantic adjective enormous

giggle verb **1** to laugh in a nervous or embarrassed way ▷ noun **2** short nervous laugh > **giggly** adjective laughing in a nervous or embarrassed way

gilded adjective covered with a thin layer of gold

gill¹ noun liquid measure of quarter of a pint, equal to 0.142 litres

gill² noun organs on the sides of a fish that it uses for breathing

gilt adjective **1** covered with a thin layer of gold ▷ noun **2** thin layer of gold used as decoration

gimmick noun something designed to attract attention or publicity > **gimmicky** adjective designed to attract attention or publicity

gin noun strong, colourless alcoholic drink made from grain and juniper berries

ginger noun **1** plant root with a hot, spicy flavour, used in cooking ▷ adjective **2** bright orange or red: ginger hair

gingerbread noun moist cake flavoured with ginger

gingerly adverb cautiously

gingham noun checked cotton cloth

gipsy noun same as **Gypsy**

giraffe noun a tall four-legged African mammal with a very long neck

girder noun large metal beam used in the construction of a bridge or a building

girdle noun woman's corset

girl noun female child > **girlhood** noun period of being a girl > **girlish** adjective like a young girl

girlfriend noun girl or woman with whom a person is romantically or sexually involved

giro giros noun **1** (in some countries) system of transferring money within a post office or bank directly from one account to another **2** Brit informal social security payment by giro cheque

girth noun measurement round something

gist noun substance or main point of a matter

give gives giving gave given verb 1 to present (something) to another person 2 to utter or emit (something) 3 to organize or host (a party or meal) 4 to yield or break under pressure ▷ noun 5 resilience or elasticity > **give in** verb to admit defeat > **given** adjective fixed or specified: my style can change at any given moment > **give out** verb to stop working: the electricity gave out > **give up** verb 1 to stop doing (something) 2 to admit defeat 3 to let the police know where (someone) is hiding

glacé adjective preserved in a thick sugary syrup: glacé cherries

glacier noun slow-moving mass of ice formed by accumulated snow > **glaciation** noun Geography condition of being covered with sheet ice

glad gladder gladdest adjective 1 pleased and happy 2 **glad to** very willing to (do something) > **gladly** adverb > **gladness** noun: a night of joy and gladness

glade noun open space in a forest

gladiator noun (in ancient Rome) man trained to fight in arenas to provide entertainment

gladiolus gladioli noun garden plant with sword-shaped leaves

glamour noun alluring charm or fascination > **glamorous** adjective alluring

glance verb 1 to look rapidly or briefly ▷ noun 2 brief look > **glance off** verb to strike and be deflected off (an object) at an oblique angle

gland noun organ that produces and secretes substances in the body > **glandular** adjective: glandular tissue

glare verb 1 to stare angrily ▷ noun 2 angry stare 3 unpleasant brightness

glass noun 1 hard, transparent substance that is easily broken, used to make windows and bottles 2 tumbler > **glassy** adjective 1 like glass 2 expressionless

glasses plural noun spectacles

glaze verb 1 to fit a sheet of glass into the frame of (a window) 2 to cover (pottery or food) with a smooth shiny surface ▷ noun 3 smooth shiny surface on pottery or food > **glaze over** verb (of eyes) to become dull and expressionless, as when someone is bored

glazed adjective (of a facial expression) looking bored

gleam noun 1 small beam or glow of light 2 brief or faint indication ▷ verb 3 to shine and reflect light

glean verb to gather (facts etc) bit by bit

glee noun old-fashioned triumph and delight > **gleeful** adjective happy and excited, often at someone else's bad luck > **gleefully** adverb in a gleeful manner

glen noun deep narrow valley, especially in Scotland

glide verb 1 to move easily and smoothly 2 (of an aircraft) to move without the use of engines

glider noun aircraft without an engine which floats on air currents

glimmer verb 1 to shine faintly, flicker ▷ noun 2 faint gleam 3 faint indication

glimpse noun 1 brief or incomplete view ▷ verb 2 to catch a glimpse of (someone or something)

glint verb 1 to gleam brightly ▷ noun 2 quick flash of light 3 brightness in someone's eye expressing some emotion: *a glint of mischief*

glisten verb to gleam by reflecting light

glitter verb 1 to shine with bright flashes ▷ noun 2 sparkle or brilliance 3 tiny pieces of shiny decorative material

gloat verb to cruelly show your pleasure about your own success or someone else's failure

global adjective worldwide

globalization noun trend towards the existence of a single world market dominated by multinational companies

global warming noun increase in the overall temperature worldwide believed to be caused by the greenhouse effect

lobe noun 1 sphere with a map of the earth on it 2 spherical object 3 SAfr light bulb 4 **the globe** the earth

loom noun 1 melancholy or depression 2 darkness ▷ gloomy adjective 1 melancholy or unhappy 2 dark or dim ▷ **gloomily** adverb

lorify glorifies glorifying glorified verb to make (something) seem more worthy than it is ▷ **glorification** noun: *the glorification of violence*

orious adjective 1 brilliantly

beautiful 2 delightful 3 involving great fame and success ▷ **gloriously** adverb

glory glories glorying gloried noun 1 praise or honour 2 something considered splendid or admirable ▷ verb 3 (followed by *in*) to take great delight in (something)

glory box noun Aust, NZ old-fashioned chest in which a young woman stores household goods and linen for her marriage

gloss noun 1 bright shine on a surface 2 attractive appearance that may hide less attractive qualities > **gloss over** verb to try to cover up or pass over (a fault or error)

glossary glossaries noun list of words with their explanations or translations, usually found at the back of a book

glossy glossier glossiest adjective 1 smooth and shiny 2 (of a magazine) printed on shiny paper

glove noun covering for the hand with individual sheaths for each finger and the thumb

glow verb 1 to shine with a dull steady light 2 to have a strong feeling of pleasure or happiness ▷ noun 3 dull steady light 4 strong feeling of pleasure or happiness

glower verb, noun (to) scowl

glowing adjective (of a description, report, etc) full of praise

glucose noun kind of sugar found in fruit

glue glues gluing or glueing glued noun 1 substance used for sticking things together ▷ verb 2 to stick (objects) together using glue

glum glummer glummest
adjective sullen or gloomy
> **glumly** *adverb*

glut *noun* excessive supply

gluten *noun* sticky protein found
in cereal grain

glutton *noun* **1** greedy person
2 person with a great capacity for
something > **gluttony** *noun* state
of being greedy

gnarled *adjective* rough, twisted
and knobbly

gnat *noun* small biting two-
winged fly

gnaw gnaws gnawing gnawed
verb **1** to bite or chew (something)
steadily **2** (followed by *at*) to
cause constant distress to
(someone)

gnome *noun* imaginary creature
like a little old man

gnu *noun* oxlike S African antelope

go goes going went gone *verb*
1 to move to or from a place **2** to
depart **3** to be, do or become as
specified: *She felt she was going
mad* **4** (often followed by *with*)
to blend or harmonize with
(something) **5** to fail or break
down **6** to be got rid of > *noun*
7 attempt > **go back on** *verb*
to break (a promise etc) > **go
down** *verb* to get a particular
kind of reception: *His speech
went down well* > **go for** *verb* **1** to
like (something) very much
2 to attack (someone) > **go off**
verb **1** (of a bomb) to explode
2 *informal* to stop liking (someone
or something) > **go on** *verb* **1** to
continue (doing something) **2** to
keep talking about (something)
in a rather boring way **3** to be

happening > **go through** *verb*
1 to experience (an unpleasant
event) **2** (of a law or agreement)
to be approved and become
official > **go through with** *verb* to
do (something) even though it is
unpleasant

goad *verb* to provoke (someone) to
take some kind of action, usually
in anger

go-ahead *noun* permission to do
something

goal *noun* **1** *Sport* posts through
which the ball or puck has to be
propelled to score **2** score made
in this way **3** aim or purpose

goalkeeper *noun* *Sport* player
whose task is to stop shots
entering the goal

goanna *noun* large Australian
lizard

goat *noun* animal like a sheep with
coarse hair, a beard and horns

go-away bird *noun* S Afr grey
lourie, a type of bird that lives in
open grassland

gob *noun* Brit, Aust, NZ informal
mouth

gobble *verb* **1** to eat (food) hastily
and greedily **2** to make the rapid
gurgling cry of the male turkey

gobbledygook or
gobbledegook *noun* language
or jargon that is impossible to
understand

goblet *noun* drinking cup without
handles

goblin *noun* ugly mischievous
creature in fairy stories

god *noun* **1** spirit or being
worshipped as having
supernatural power **2** object of
worship, idol **3 God** (in religions
such as Islam, Christianity and

Judaism) the Supreme Being, creator and ruler of the universe **4 the gods** top balcony in a theatre

godchild godchildren noun child for whom a person stands as godparent > **goddaughter** noun girl for whom a person stands as godparent > **godson** noun boy for whom a person stands as godparent

goddess noun female god

godparent noun person who promises at a child's baptism to bring the child up as a Christian > **godfather** noun **1** male godparent **2** head of a criminal, especially Mafia, organization > **godmother** noun female godparent

godsend noun something unexpected but welcome

goggles plural noun protective spectacles

going noun condition of the ground for walking or riding over

gold noun **1** yellow precious metal **2** coins or articles made of this ▷ adjective **3** gold-coloured

golden adjective **1** made of gold **2** gold-coloured **3** very successful or promising

golden rule noun important principle

golden wedding noun fiftieth wedding anniversary

goldfish noun orange fish kept in ponds or aquariums
- The plural of *goldfish* is *goldfish*

goldsmith noun person whose job is making jewellery out of gold

golf noun outdoor game in which a ball is struck with clubs into a series of holes > **golfer** noun person who plays golf

golf course noun area of grassy land where people play golf

gondola noun long narrow boat used in Venice

gone verb past participle of **go**

gong noun flat circular piece of metal that produces a note when struck

good better best adjective **1** pleasant, acceptable or satisfactory **2** kind, thoughtful and loving **3** skilful or successful: *good at art* **4** well-behaved **5** used to emphasize something: *a good few million pounds* **6** as **good as** virtually ▷ noun **7** benefit **8** positive moral qualities **9 for good** permanently
- *Good* is an adjective, and
- should not be used as an
- adverb. You should say that *a*
- *person did well* not *did good*

goodbye interjection, noun expression used on parting

Good Friday noun Friday before Easter, when Christians remember the crucifixion of Christ

good-natured adjective friendly, pleasant and even-tempered

goodness noun **1** quality of being kind ▷ interjection **2** exclamation of surprise

goodwill noun kindly feeling

goody goodies noun **1** informal hero in a book or film **2** enjoyable thing

goose geese noun web-footed bird like a large duck

gooseberry gooseberries noun edible yellowy-green berry

gore noun **1** blood from a wound

▷ *verb* **2** to pierce (someone) with horns

gorge *noun* **1** deep narrow valley
▷ *verb* **gorge yourself 2** to eat greedily

gorgeous *adjective* **1** strikingly beautiful or attractive **2** *informal* very pleasant

gorilla *noun* very large strong ape with very dark fur

gorse *noun* prickly yellow-flowered shrub

gory gorier goriest *adjective* **1** horrific or bloodthirsty **2** involving bloodshed

gosling *noun* young goose

gospel *noun* **1** Gospel any of the first four books of the New Testament **2** unquestionable truth **3** Black religious music originating in the churches of the Southern US

gossip gossips gossiping gossiped *noun* **1** idle talk, especially about other people **2** person who engages in gossip ▷ *verb* **3** to engage in gossip

got *verb* **1** past of **get 2** have got to possess **3** have got to to need or be required to

gouge *verb* **1** to scoop or force (something) out **2** to cut (a hole or groove) in something

goulash *noun* rich stew seasoned with paprika, originally from Hungary

gourd *noun* fleshy fruit of a climbing plant

gourmet *noun* person who enjoys good food and drink and knows a lot about it

gout *noun* disease causing inflammation of the joints, especially in the toes

govern *verb* **1** to control (a country) **2** to influence (a situation)

governess *noun* woman teacher in a private household

government *noun* **1** group of people who govern a country **2** control and organization of a country ▷ **governmental** *adjective: a governmental agency*

governor *noun* **1** person who controls and organizes a state or an institution **2** *Aust* representative of the King or Queen in a State

governor general governors general *noun* chief representative of the King or Queen in Australia, New Zealand and other Commonwealth countries

gown *noun* **1** woman's long formal dress **2** official robe worn by judges, clergymen, etc

GP *abbreviation* general practitioner

grab grabs grabbing grabbed *verb* **1** to grasp (something) suddenly, snatch (something) ▷ *noun* **2** sudden snatch

grace *noun* **1** beauty and elegance, poise **2** polite kind behaviour **3** short prayer of thanks for a meal **4** Grace title of a duke, duchess or archbishop ▷ *verb* **5** to kindly agree to be present at (an event) ▷ **graceful** *adjective: graceful ballerinas* ▷ **gracefully** *adverb*

gracious *adjective* **1** kind, polite and pleasant ▷ **interjection 2** good gracious! exclamation of surprise ▷ **graciously** *adverb*

grade *noun* **1** place on a scale of quality, rank or size **2** mark or rating ▷ *verb* **3** to arrange (things) in grades

gradient noun (degree of) slope

gradual adjective occurring, developing or moving in small stages >**gradually** adverb happening or changing slowly over a long period of time

graduate verb 1 to receive a degree or diploma 2 to progress gradually from one thing towards another ▷ 3 holder of a degree >**graduation** noun: they asked what his plans were after graduation

graffiti (plural) noun words or drawings scribbled or sprayed on walls etc

● Although *graffiti* is a plural
● in Italian, the language it
● comes from, in English it
● can be either a singular or a
● plural noun

graft noun 1 surgical transplant of skin or tissue 2 shoot of a plant set in the stalk of another 3 informal hard work ▷ verb 4 to transplant (living tissue) surgically 5 to insert (a plant shoot) in another stalk

grain noun 1 seedlike fruit of a cereal plant 2 cereal plants in general 3 small hard particle 4 very small amount 5 arrangement of fibres, as in wood 6 texture or pattern resulting from this 7 **go against the grain** to be contrary to your natural inclination

gram or **gramme** noun metric unit of mass equal to one thousandth of a kilogram

grammar noun branch of linguistics dealing with the form, function, and order of words

grammar school noun 1 Brit especially formerly, a secondary school providing an education with a strong academic bias 2 Aust private school, usually one controlled by a church

grammatical adjective according to the rules of grammar >**grammatically** adverb

gran noun Brit, Aust, NZ informal grandmother

granary granaries noun 1 storehouse for grain ▷ adjective 2 trademark (of bread) containing whole grains of wheat

grand adjective 1 large or impressive, imposing 2 dignified or haughty 3 informal excellent 4 (of a total) final ▷ noun 5 informal thousand pounds or dollars >**grandly** adverb in a manner intended to impress

grandad or **granddad** noun informal grandfather

grandchild grandchildren noun child of your son or daughter

granddaughter noun female grandchild

grandeur noun magnificence

grandfather noun male grandparent

grandfather clock noun tall standing clock with a pendulum and wooden case

grandiose adjective intended to be very impressive but seeming ridiculous

grandma noun informal grandmother

grandmother noun female grandparent

grandparent noun parent of your father or mother

grand piano noun large harp-shaped piano with the strings set horizontally

grandson noun male grandchild

grandstand noun terraced block of seats giving the best view at a sports ground

granite noun very hard rock often used in building

granny grannies noun informal grandmother

grant verb 1 to allow someone to have (something) 2 to admit the truth of (something) 3 **take for granted a** to accept (something) as true without proof **b** to take advantage of (someone) without due appreciation ▷ noun 4 sum of money provided by a government for a specific purpose, such as education

granule noun small grain

grape noun small juicy green or purple berry, eaten raw or used to produce wine, raisins, currants or sultanas

grapefruit noun large round yellow citrus fruit

grapevine noun 1 grape-bearing vine 2 informal unofficial way of spreading news

graph noun diagram in which a line shows how two sets of numbers or measurements are related

-graph suffix writer or recorder of some sort or something made by writing, drawing or recording: telegraph; autograph

graphic adjective 1 vividly descriptive 2 of or using drawing, painting, etc > **graphically** adverb in a vividly descriptive fashion > **graphics** plural noun diagrams, graphs, etc, especially as used on a television programme or computer screen

graphite noun soft black form of carbon, used in pencil leads

grapple verb (followed by with) 1 to try to cope with (something difficult) 2 to come to grips with (a person)

grasp verb 1 to grip (something) firmly 2 to understand (something) 3 noun 3 grip or clasp 4 understanding

grass noun common green plant that grows on lawns and in parks > **grassy** adjective covered in grass

grasshopper noun jumping insect with long hind legs

grate verb 1 to rub (food) into small bits against a grater 2 to scrape with a harsh rasping noise 3 (followed by on) to annoy (someone) ▷ noun 4 framework of metal bars for holding fuel in a fireplace

grateful adjective feeling or showing gratitude; thankful > **gratefully** adverb thankfully

grater noun small metal tool used for grating food

gratify gratifies gratifying gratified verb 1 to satisfy or please (someone) 2 to indulge (a desire or whim)

grating adjective 1 harsh or rasping ▷ noun 2 framework of metal bars covering an opening

gratis adverb, adjective free, for nothing

gratitude noun feeling of being thankful for a favour or gift; appreciation

gratuitous adjective unjustified: gratuitous violence > **gratuitousl** adverb unnecessarily

grave¹ graves; graver gravest
noun **1** hole for burying a corpse
▷ adjective **2** serious and solemn
> **gravely** adverb

grave² noun accent (`) over
a vowel to indicate a special
pronunciation

gravel noun mixture of small
stones and coarse sand

gravestone noun stone marking
a grave

graveyard noun area of land
where corpses are buried

gravitate verb to be drawn
towards something

gravitation noun force that
causes objects to be attracted
to each other > **gravitational**
adjective: the earth's gravitational
pull

gravity noun **1** force of attraction
of one object for another,
especially of objects to the earth
2 seriousness or importance

gravy noun **1** juices from meat in
cooking **2** sauce made from these

graze verb **1** (of animals) to feed
on grass **2** to scratch or scrape (a
body part) ▷ noun **3** slight scratch
or scrape

grease noun **1** soft melted animal
fat **2** any thick oily substance
▷ verb **3** to apply grease to
(something) > **greasy** adjective
covered with or containing
grease

great adjective **1** large in size or
number **2** important **3** informal
excellent > **greatly** adverb:
people would benefit greatly from
a pollution-free environment
> **greatness** noun: Abraham Lincoln
achieved greatness

Great Britain noun largest of

the British Isles, consisting of
England, Scotland, and Wales

Great Dane noun very large dog
with short smooth hair

great-grandfather noun father's
or mother's grandfather

great-grandmother noun
father's or mother's grandmother

greed noun excessive desire for
food, wealth, etc

greedy greedier greediest
adjective wanting more of
something than you really need
> **greedily** adverb > **greediness**
noun being greedy

Greek noun **1** language of Greece
2 person from Greece ▷ adjective
3 of Greece, the Greeks or the
Greek language

green adjective **1** of a colour
between yellow and blue
2 Green of or concerned with
environmental issues **3** informal
young and inexperienced ▷ noun
4 colour between blue and yellow
5 area of grass in the middle of a
village **6** grassy area on which
putting or bowls is played **7** area
of smooth short grass around
each hole on a golf course
8 Green person concerned with
environmental issues **9 greens**
green vegetables > **greenery** noun
vegetation

greenfly greenfly or **greenflies**
noun small green insect that
damages plants

greengrocer noun Brit shopkeeper
selling vegetables and fruit

greenhouse noun glass building
for growing plants that need to be
kept warm

greenhouse effect noun rise
in the temperature of the earth

caused by heat absorbed from the sun being unable to leave the atmosphere

green paper noun Brit, Aust, NZ report published by the government containing proposals to be discussed before decisions are made about them

greenstone noun NZ type of green jade used for Maori ornaments

greet verb 1 to meet (someone) with expressions of welcome 2 to react to (something) in a specified manner: *This decision was greeted with dismay*

greeting noun something friendly that you say to someone you meet

gregarious adjective fond of company

grenade noun small bomb thrown by hand or fired from a rifle

grevillea noun Australian evergreen tree or shrub

grew verb past tense of **grow**

grey adjective 1 of a colour between black and white 2 dull or boring ▷ noun 3 grey colour > **greying** adjective (of hair) turning grey > **greyness** noun: *winter's greyness*

greyed out adjective (of an item on a computer screen) unavailable

greyhound noun swift slender dog used in racing

grid noun 1 network of horizontal and vertical lines, bars, etc 2 national network of electricity supply cables

grief noun deep sadness; sorrow

grievance noun cause for complaint

grieve verb to feel grief or cause (someone) to feel grief

grievous adjective very serious

> **grievously** adverb: grievously injured

grill noun 1 device on a cooker that radiates heat downwards 2 a metal frame on which you cook food over a fire 3 grilled food ▷ verb 4 to cook (food) under a grill 5 to question (someone) relentlessly

grille or **grill** noun grating over an opening

grim grimmer grimmest adjective 1 (of a person) very serious or stern 2 (of a place) unattractive and depressing 3 (of a situation or piece of news) very unpleasant and worrying > **grimly** adverb in a grim manner

grimace noun 1 ugly or distorted facial expression of pain, disgust, etc ▷ verb 2 to make a grimace

grime noun ingrained dirt > **grimy** adjective: a grimy industrial city

grin verb 1 to smile broadly, showing the teeth ▷ noun 2 broad smile

grind grinds grinding ground verb 1 to crush or rub (something) to a powder; powder 2 to scrape (the teeth) together with a harsh noise

grip grips gripping gripped noun 1 firm hold or grasp 2 control over a situation 3 handle on a bat or a racket ▷ verb 4 to grasp or hold (something) tightly

grisly grislier grisliest adjective horrifying or ghastly

grit grits gritting gritted noun 1 rough particles of sand ▷ verb 2 to spread grit on (an icy road) 3 grit your teeth to decide to carry on in a difficult situation > **gritty** adjective 1 containing or covered with grit **2** brave and determined **3** (of a drama) realistic

grizzled adjective grey-haired

grizzly bear noun large greyish-brown American bear

groan noun **1** deep sound of grief or pain ▷ verb **2** to utter a groan

grocer noun shopkeeper who sells many kinds of food and other household goods

grocery groceries noun **1** business or premises of a grocer **2 groceries** goods sold by a grocer

grog noun Brit, Aust, NZ informal any alcoholic drink

groin noun place where the legs join the abdomen

groom noun **1** person who looks after horses **2** bridegroom ▷ verb **3** to brush or clean (a horse) **4** to train (someone) for a future role

groove noun long narrow channel in a surface > **grooved** adjective having deep grooves on the surface

grope verb (followed by for) **1** to search for (something you cannot see) with your hands **2** to try to think of (something such as the solution to a problem)

gross grosser grossest; grosses grossing grossed adjective **1** extremely bad: a gross betrayal **2** (of speech or behaviour) vulgar **3** informal disgusting or repulsive **4** total, without deductions **5** (of weight) including container weight ▷ noun **6** twelve dozen ▷ verb **7** to earn (an amount of money) in total > **grossly** adverb: grossly overweight

grotesque adjective **1** very strange

and ugly **2** exaggerated and absurd > **grotesquely** adverb

grotto grottoes or **grottos** noun small picturesque cave

ground noun **1** surface of the earth **2** soil **3** area used for a specific purpose: rugby ground **4** position in an argument or controversy **5 grounds a** enclosed land round a house **b** reason or motive ▷ verb **6** (followed by in) to base or establish (something) on something else **7** to ban (an aircraft) from flying **8** past of **grind**

ground floor noun floor of a building level with the ground

grounding noun basic knowledge of a subject

groundless adjective without reason

group noun **1** number of people or things regarded as a unit **2** small band of musicians or singers ▷ verb **3** to place or form (people or things) into a group

grouping noun number of things or people that are linked together in some way

grouse noun stocky game bird

● The plural of grouse is grouse

grove noun literary small group of trees

grovel grovels grovelling grovelled verb to behave humbly in order to win a superior's favour

grow grows growing grew grown verb **1** to develop physically **2** (of a plant) to exist **3** to cultivate (plants) **4** to increase in size or degree **5** to become gradually: It was growing dark > **grow on** verb informal to gradually become liked by (someone) > **grow up** verb to mature

growl verb 1 to make a low rumbling sound 2 to utter (something) with a growl ▷ noun 3 growling sound

grown-up adjective, noun adult

growth noun 1 growing 2 increase 3 process by which something develops to its full size 4 tumour

grub noun 1 legless insect larva 2 informal food

grubby grubbier grubbiest adjective dirty

grudge verb 1 to be unwilling to give or allow (someone something) ▷ noun 2 resentment

grudging adjective done or felt unwillingly: grudging admiration > **grudgingly** adverb unwillingly

gruel noun thin porridge

gruelling adjective exhausting or severe

gruesome adjective causing horror and disgust

gruff adjective rough or surly in manner or voice

grumble verb 1 to complain ▷ noun 2 complaint

grumpy grumpier grumpiest adjective bad-tempered and fed-up

grunt verb 1 to make a low short gruff sound, like a pig ▷ noun 2 pig's sound 3 gruff noise

guarantee guarantees guaranteeing guaranteed noun 1 formal assurance, especially in writing, that a product will meet certain standards 2 something that makes a specified condition or outcome certain ▷ verb 3 to make certain (that something

will happen) > **guarantor** noun person who gives or is bound by a guarantee

guard verb 1 to watch over (someone or something) to protect or to prevent escape ▷ noun 2 person or group that guards 3 official in charge of a train 4 screen for enclosing anything dangerous > **guard against** verb to take precautions against (something)

guardian noun 1 keeper or protector 2 person legally responsible for a child, mentally ill person, etc > **guardianship** noun position of being a guardian

guernsey noun 1 Aust, NZ jersey 2 Aust sleeveless top worn by an Australian Rules football player

guerrilla or **guerilla** noun member of an unofficial armed force fighting regular forces

guess verb 1 to form or express an opinion that it is the case, without having much information ▷ noun 2 estimate or conclusion reached by guessing

guest noun 1 person entertained at another's house or at another's expense 2 invited performer or speaker 3 customer at a hotel or restaurant

guffaw noun 1 crude noisy laugh ▷ verb 2 to laugh in this way

guidance noun leadership, instruction or advice

guide noun 1 person who conduct tour expeditions 2 person who shows the way 3 book of instruction or information 4 **Guide** member of an organization for girls equivalent to the Scouts ▷ **verb 5** to act as a guide for (someone) **6** to control, supervise or influence (someone)

guidebook noun book that gives information about a place

guide dog noun dog trained to lead a blind person

guideline noun set principle for doing something

guild noun organization or club

guile noun cunning or deceit > **guileless** adjective open and honest

guillotine noun machine for beheading people

guilt noun **1** fact or state of having done wrong **2** remorse for wrongdoing

guilty guiltier guiltiest adjective **1** responsible for an offence or misdeed **2** feeling or showing guilt > **guiltily** adverb

guinea noun old British unit of money, worth 21 shillings

guinea pig noun **1** small furry animal without a tail, often kept as a pet **2** person used to try something out on

guise noun misleading appearance

guitar noun stringed instrument with a flat back and a long neck, played by plucking or strumming > **guitarist** noun person who plays the guitar

gulf noun **1** large deep bay **2** large difference in opinion or understanding

gull noun long-winged sea bird

gullet noun muscular tube through which food passes from the mouth to the stomach

gullible adjective easily tricked

> **gullibility** noun being gullible

gully gullies noun channel cut by running water

gulp verb **1** to swallow (food or drink) hastily **2** to gasp ▷ noun **3** large quantity of food or drink swallowed at one time

gum noun **1** firm flesh in which the teeth are set **2** sticky substance obtained from certain trees **3** adhesive **4** chewing gum

gumboots plural noun Chiefly Brit Wellington boots

gum tree noun eucalypt tree

gun noun weapon that fires bullets or shells > **gunboat** noun small warship

gunfire noun repeated firing of guns

gunpowder noun explosive powder made from a mixture of potassium nitrate and other substances

gunshot noun shot or range of a gun

gunyah noun Aust hut or shelter in the bush

guppy guppies noun small colourful aquarium fish

gurdwara noun Sikh place of worship

gurgle verb, noun (to make) a bubbling noise

guru noun **1** Hindu or Sikh religious teacher or leader **2** leader, adviser or expert

gush verb **1** to flow out in large quantities **2** to express admiration in an exaggerated way > **gushing** adjective: he delivered a gushing speech

gust noun sudden blast of wind > **gusty** adjective

gusto noun enjoyment or zest

a b c d e f g h i j k l m n o p q r s t u v w x y z

gut guts gutting gutted *noun*
1 intestine **2 guts a** internal
organs **b** *informal* courage ▷ *verb*
3 to remove the guts from (a dead
fish) **4** (of a fire) to destroy the
inside of (a building)

gutter *noun* shallow channel for
carrying away water from a roof
or roadside ▷ **guttering** *noun*
material for gutters

guttural *adjective* (of a sound)
produced at the back of the
throat

guy *noun* **1** *informal* man or boy
2 crude model of Guy Fawkes
burnt on Nov. 5th (**Guy Fawkes
Day**) **3** rope or chain to steady or
secure something

guzzle *verb* to eat or drink
(something) greedily

gym *noun* **1** gymnasium
2 gymnastics

gymkhana *noun* horse-riding
competition

gymnasium *noun* large room
with equipment for physical
training

gymnast *noun* expert in
gymnastics ▷ **gymnastic**
adjective: *gymnastic exercises*

gymnastics *plural noun* exercises
to develop strength and agility

gynaecology *noun* branch of
medical science concerned with
the female reproductive system
▷ **gynaecological** *adjective*: *a
routine gynaecological examination*
▷ **gynaecologist** *noun* doctor who
specializes in gynaecology

Gypsy Gypsies *noun* member
of a travelling people found
throughout Europe

gyrate *verb* to move round in
a circle

h

habit *noun* **1** something that you
do often **2** something that you
keep doing and find it difficult
to stop doing **3** loose, dress-like
costume of a monk or nun

habitat *noun* natural home of an
animal or plant

hack *verb* **1** to cut or chop violently
▷ *noun* **2** (inferior) writer or
journalist

hacker *noun* *informal* someone
who uses a computer to break
into the computer system of a
company or government

hackles *plural noun* **1** hairs on
the back of an animal which rise
when it is angry **2 make your
hackles rise** to make you feel
angry or hostile

hackneyed *adjective* (of a word or
phrase) unoriginal and overused

hacksaw *noun* small saw with a
narrow blade set in a frame

haddock *noun* edible sea fish of
the North Atlantic
● The plural of *haddock* is
● *haddock*

haemoglobin *noun* substance
in red blood cells which carries
oxygen round the body

haemorrhage *noun* **1** (instance
of) heavy bleeding ▷ *verb* **2** to
bleed heavily

haemorrhoids *plural noun* painful
lumps around the anus that are
caused by swollen veins; piles

hag *noun* *offensive* ugly old woman

haggard *adjective* looking tired

and ill

haggis noun Scottish dish made from the internal organs of a sheep, boiled together with oatmeal and spices in a bag traditionally made from the sheep's stomach

haggle verb to bargain or wrangle over a price

hail noun **1** frozen rain **2** large number of insults, missiles, blows or other things ▷ verb **3** to fall as or like hail **4** to call out to (someone); greet **5** to stop (a taxi) by waving **6** to acknowledge (someone or something) publicly ▷ **hail from** verb to come originally from

hair noun **1** soft, threadlike strand that grows with others from the skin of animals and humans **2** such strands collectively, especially on the head

haircut noun the cutting of someone's hair; also the style in which it is cut

hairdo hairdos noun informal hairstyle

airdresser noun **1** person trained to cut and style hair **2** shop where people go to have their hair cut ▷ **hairdressing** noun, adjective

airline noun **1** the edge of the area at the top of the forehead where your hair starts ▷ adjective **2** (of a crack) very fine or narrow

airpin noun U-shaped wire used to hold the hair in place

air-raising adjective very frightening or exciting

airstyle noun cut and arrangement of a person's hair

airy hairier hairiest adjective **1** covered with hair **2** informal

difficult, exciting and rather frightening

hajj noun pilgrimage a Muslim makes to Mecca

haka hakas noun NZ **1** ceremonial Maori dance with chanting **2** similar dance performed by a sports team before a match

hake noun edible sea fish related to the cod

● The plural of hake is hake

hakea noun Australian tree or shrub with hard, woody fruit

halcyon adjective Literary **1** peaceful and happy **2 halcyon days** time of peace and happiness

half halves noun **1** either of two equal parts that make up a whole **2** informal half-pint of beer, cider etc **3** half-price ticket ▷ adjective **4** denoting one of two equal parts ▷ adverb **5** to the extent of half **6** partially or partly: I half expected him to explode in anger

half-baked adjective informal (of idea, theory, plan) not properly thought out

half board noun (at hotel) breakfast and dinner but not lunch

half-brother noun brother related through one parent only

half-hearted adjective unenthusiastic

half-pie adjective NZ informal incomplete

half-sister noun sister related through one parent only

half-timbered adjective (of a house) having a framework of wooden beams that are left exposed and visible in the walls

half-time noun Sport short rest period between two halves of a game

halfway adverb, adjective at or up to half the distance between two points in place or time; midway

halibut halibut or halibuts noun large edible flatfish of N Atlantic

hall noun **1** (also **hallway**) entrance passage **2** large room or building for public meetings, dances, etc **3** Brit large country house

hallmark noun **1** typical feature or quality **2** mark indicating the standard of tested gold and silver ▷ verb **3** to stamp with a hallmark

hallowed adjective respected as being holy

Halloween or **Hallowe'en** noun October 31, celebrated by children by dressing up as ghosts, witches, etc

hallucinate verb to see or experience strange things in your mind because of illness or drugs > **hallucination** noun: Drugs can cause hallucinations > **hallucinatory** adjective: a hallucinatory state

halo haloes or halos noun ring of light round the head of a holy figure

halt verb **1** to come or bring something to a stop ▷ noun **2** temporary stop

halter noun strap round a horse's head with a rope to lead it with

halve verb **1** to divide (something) in half **2** to reduce (something) or be reduced by half

ham noun **1** smoked or salted meat from a pig's thigh **2** bad actor who overacts **3** amateur radio operator

hamburger noun minced beef

shaped into a flat disc, cooked and usually served in a bread roll

hammer noun **1** tool with a heavy metal head and a wooden handle, used to drive in nails etc **2** heavy metal ball on a wire, thrown as a sport ▷ verb **3** to hit (something) repeatedly with a hammer or your fist **4** informal to punish or defeat (someone) utterly **5 hammer something into someone** to keep repeating something to someone in the hope that they will remember it

hammock noun hanging bed made of canvas or net

hamper noun **1** large wicker basket with a lid **2** selection of food and drink packed as a gift ▷ verb **3** to make it difficult for (someone or something) to move or progress

hamster noun small furry rodent with a short tail and cheek pouches that is often kept as a pet

● There is no p in hamster

hamstring noun tendon at the back of your knee

hand noun **1** part of your body at the end of your arm, consisting of a palm, four fingers and a thumb **2** style of handwriting **3** round of applause **4** pointer on a dial, especially on a clock **5** cards dealt to a player in a card game **6** manual worker **7** unit of length of four inches (10.16 centimetres) used to measure horses **8 have a hand in** to be involved in **9 give someone a hand** to help someone **10 to hand** or **at hand** or **on hand** nearby **11 on the one hand** way of introducing the first part of an argument or discussion when giving two contrasting points of view **12 on the other hand** way of introducing the second part of an argument or discussion when giving two contrasting points of view **13 out of hand** beyond control ▷ *verb* **14** to pass or give > **hand down** *verb* to pass from one generation to another

handbag *noun* woman's small bag for carrying personal articles in

handbook *noun* small reference or instruction book

handcuff *noun* one of a linked pair of metal rings designed to be locked round a prisoner's wrists by the police

handful *noun* **1** amount that can be held in the hand **2** small number **3** *informal* person or animal that is difficult to control

handicap handicaps handicapping handicapped *noun* **1** physical or mental disability **2** something that makes progress difficult **3** contest in which the competitors are given advantages or disadvantages according to their skill in an attempt to equalize their chances of winning **4** advantage or disadvantage given ▷ *verb* **5** to make it difficult for (someone) to do something

handicraft *noun* activity such as embroidery or pottery which involves making things with your hands; also the items produced

handiwork *noun* result of someone's work or activity

handkerchief *noun* small square of fabric used for blowing your nose

handle *noun* **1** part of an object that is designed for holding when you use it **2** a small lever or knob used to open and close a door or window ▷ *verb* **3** to hold, feel or move with your hands **4** to control or deal with

handlebars *plural noun* curved metal bar used to steer a cycle

handout *noun* **1** clothing, food or money given to a needy person **2** written information given out at a talk etc

hand-picked *adjective* carefully chosen

handset *noun* part (of a telephone) that you speak into and listen with

handshake *noun* the grasping and shaking of a person's hand by another person as a gesture of greeting, taking leave or agreement

handsome *adjective* **1** (especially of a man) good-looking **2** large or generous > **handsomely** *adverb*

handwriting *noun* (style of) writing by hand

handy handier handiest *adjective* **1** convenient, useful or conveniently near **2** skilful

hang hangs hanging hung *verb* **1** to attach (something) or be attached at the top with the lower part free **2** (*past*: **hanged**) to kill (someone) by suspending them by a rope around the neck **3 get the hang of** *informal* to begin to understand > **hang about** or **hang around** *verb* **1** *informal* to wait somewhere **2** hang about with to spend a lot of time with > **hang back** *verb* to hesitate or be reluctant > **hang on 1** (often followed by *to*) to hold tightly **2** *informal* to wait > **hang out with** *verb* *informal* to spend a lot of time with > **hang over** verb (of a future event or possibility) to worry or frighten (someone) > **hang up** verb to put down the receiver ending a telephone call

hangar noun large shed for storing aircraft

hanger noun curved piece of wood, wire or plastic, with a hook, for hanging up clothes; (also **coat hanger**)

hanger-on hangers-on noun unwelcome follower of an important person

hang-glider noun aircraft without an engine and consisting of a large frame covered in fabric, from which the pilot hangs in a harness > **hang-gliding** noun

hangi hangi or hangis noun NZ (in New Zealand) Maori oven consisting of a hole in the ground lined with hot stones

hangover noun headache and sickness after drinking too much alcohol

hang-up noun informal emotional problem

hanker verb (followed by after, for) to want very much > **hankering** noun: He has a hankering to go back to acting

hanky hankies; also spelt **hankie** noun informal handkerchief

Hanukkah or **Chanukah** noun eight-day Jewish festival of lights

haphazard adjective not organized or planned > **haphazardly** adverb

hapless adjective literary unlucky

happen verb 1 to take place; occur 2 to chance (to be or do something)

happiness noun feeling of great contentment or pleasure

happy happier happiest adjective 1 feeling or causing joy 2 satisfied that something is right 3 willing 4 lucky or fortunate > **happily** adverb

happy-go-lucky adjective carefree and cheerful

harangue verb 1 to talk to (someone) at length angrily, passionately and forcefully about something > noun 2 a long, angry, passionate and forceful speech

harass verb to annoy or trouble (someone) constantly > **harassed** adjective: a harassed mother trying to soothe a crying baby > **harassment** noun: Intimidation and harassment are common

harbinger noun someone or something that announces the approach of something: I hate to be the harbinger of doom

harbour noun 1 sheltered port > verb 2 to hide (someone) secretly in your house; shelter 3 to have (a feeling, hope or grudge) for a long time

hard adjective 1 firm, solid or rigid 2 difficult 3 requiring a lot of effort 4 unkind, unfeeling 5 causing pain, sorrow or hardship 6 (of water) containing calcium salts that stop soap lathering freely 7 (of a drug) strong and addictive 8 (of evidence, facts) provable and indisputable 9 (of drink, liquor) strong and alcoholic > adverb 10 with great energy or effort 11 with great intensity 12 to the extent of becoming firm, solid or rigid: The ground was baked hard > **hardness** noun

hard and fast adjective fixed and unchangeable: hard and fast rules

hardback noun a book with a stiff cover

hard core noun (in an organization) group of people most resistant to change

harden verb to become hard or get harder > **hardening** noun

hard labour noun difficult and exhausting physical work; used in some countries as a punishment for a crime

hardly adverb 1 scarcely or not at all 2 with difficulty

- You should not use hardly
- with a negative word like
- not or no: he could hardly hear
- her not he could not hardly
- hear her

hard-nosed adjective tough, practical and realistic

hard of hearing adjective unable to hear well

hardship noun 1 suffering 2 difficult circumstances

hard shoulder noun area at the edge of a motorway where you can park in the event of a breakdown

hard up adjective informal short of money

hardware noun 1 metal tools and implements 2 machinery used in a computer system 3 heavy military equipment, such as tanks and missiles

hard-wearing adjective strong, well-made and long-lasting

hardwood noun strong, hard wood from a tree such as oak or ash; also the tree itself

hardy hardier hardiest adjective able to stand difficult conditions

> **hardiness** noun

hare hares haring hared noun 1 animal like a large rabbit, with longer ears and legs > verb 2 (usually followed by off) to run (away) quickly

harem noun group of wives or mistresses of one man, especially in Muslim societies; also the place where these women live

hark verb old-fashioned to listen > **hark back** verb to return (to an earlier subject)

harlequin noun 1 stock comic character with a diamond-patterned costume and mask > adjective 2 in many colours

harm verb 1 to injure or damage > noun 2 injury or damage

harmful adjective causing injury or damage

harmless adjective 1 safe to use or be near 2 unlikely to cause problems or annoyance > **harmlessly** adverb

harmonic adjective using musical harmony

harmonica noun small musical instrument which you play by blowing and sucking while moving it across your lips; mouth organ

harmonious adjective 1 peaceful, friendly and free from disagreement 2 attractively and agreeably combined > **harmoniously** adverb

harmony harmonies noun 1 peaceful agreement and cooperation 2 pleasant combination of notes sounded at the same time 3 Music the structure and relationship of chords in a piece of music

harness noun 1 arrangement of straps for attaching a horse to a cart or plough 2 set of straps fastened round someone's body to attach something: a safety harness ▷ verb 3 to bring (something) under control in order to make use of it

harp noun large triangular stringed instrument played with the fingers > **harpist** noun

harpoon noun 1 barbed spear attached to a rope used for hunting whales ▷ verb 2 to spear (a whale or large fish) with a harpoon

harpsichord noun stringed keyboard instrument

harrowing adjective very distressing

harsh adjective 1 severe and difficult to cope with 2 unkind, unsympathetic 3 extremely hard, bright or rough > **harshly** adverb > **harshness** noun: the harshness of prison life

harvest noun 1 (season for) the gathering of crops 2 crops gathered ▷ verb 3 to gather (a ripened crop) > **harvester** noun

has-been noun informal person who is no longer popular or successful

hash noun 1 (also **hash mark**) the character (#) 2 dish of diced cooked meat and vegetables reheated 3 informal hashish 4 **make a hash of** informal to do (a job) badly

hashish noun drug made from the cannabis plant. It is usually smoked, and is illegal in many countries

hassle informal noun 1 trouble

or bother ▷ verb 2 to bother (someone) with repeated requests to do something; pester

haste noun 1 (excessive) quickness 2 **make haste** to hurry or rush

hasten verb 1 to hurry 2 to cause (something) to happen earlier than otherwise

hasty hastier hastiest adjective (too) quick > **hastily** adverb (too) quickly

hat noun 1 covering for the head, often with a brim 2 **keep something under your hat** to keep something secret

hatch verb 1 (of a bird, reptile) to come out of the egg 2 (of an egg) to break open allowing a young bird or reptile to come out 3 to devise (a plot) ▷ noun 4 covered opening in a wall, floor or ceiling

hatchback noun car with a rear door that opens upwards

hatchet noun 1 small axe 2 **bury the hatchet** to make peace

hate verb 1 to dislike (someone or something) intensely ▷ noun 2 intense dislike

hatred noun intense dislike

hat trick noun three achievements in a row, especially in sport

haughty haughtier haughtiest adjective proud, arrogant > **haughtily** adverb

haul verb 1 to pull or drag (something or someone) with effort ▷ noun 2 amount gained by effort or theft 3 **long haul** something that takes a lot of time and effort

haulage noun business or cost of transporting goods

haunches plural noun buttocks and thighs

haunt verb 1 (of a ghost) to visit (a building, place) regularly 2 (of a memory, fear) to worry or trouble (someone) continually ▷ noun 3 place visited frequently

haunted adjective 1 frequented by ghosts 2 very worried or troubled

haunting adjective memorably beautiful or sad

have has having had verb 1 to possess or hold 2 to receive, take or obtain 3 to experience or be affected by 4 (followed by to) to be obliged to; must: I had to go 5 to cause to be done 6 to give birth to (a baby, foal, kittens etc) 7 used to form past tenses (with a past participle): we have looked; she had done enough 8 **be had** to be tricked or deceived; to settle a matter by argument > **have on** verb 1 to wear (clothing) 2 informal to tease or trick (someone) > **have up** verb to bring (someone) to trial

haven noun place of safety

havoc noun disorder and confusion

hawk noun 1 bird of prey with a short hooked bill and very good eyesight 2 Politics supporter or advocate of warlike policies ▷ verb 3 to offer (goods) for sale in the street or door-to-door 4 to clear phlegm from your throat noisily

hawthorn noun thorny shrub or tree producing white blossom and red berries

hay noun grass cut and dried as animal feed

hay fever noun allergy to pollen and grass, causing sneezing and watering eyes

haystack noun large firmly built pile of hay

hazard noun 1 something that could be dangerous ▷ verb 2 to put (something) at risk 3 to make (a guess) > **hazardous** adjective: hazardous waste

haze noun mist, often caused by heat

hazel noun 1 small tree producing edible nuts ▷ adjective 2 (of eyes) greenish-brown

hazy hazier haziest adjective 1 not clear, misty 2 confused or vague

he pronoun refers to: 1 male person or animal 2 a person or animal of unknown or unspecified sex; he or she ▷ noun 3 male person or animal

head noun 1 part of your body containing your eyes, mouth, nose and brain 2 mind and mental abilities 3 upper or most forward part of anything 4 most important end of something 5 person in charge of a group, organization or school 6 pus-filled tip of a spot or boil 7 white froth on beer 8 (of a computer or tape recorder) the part that can read or write information 9 head person or animal considered as a unit 10 **off your head** informal foolish or insane 11 **can't make head nor tail of** can't understand ▷ adjective 12 chief or principal ▷ verb 13 to be at the top or front of 14 to be in charge of 15 to move (in a particular direction) 16 to hit (a ball) with your head 17 to provide (something) with a heading > **head off** verb 1 to make (someone or something) change direction 2 to prevent (something) from happening

a b c d e f g h i j k l m n o p q r s t u v w x y z

>heads adverb informal with the side of a coin which has a portrait of a head on it uppermost

headache noun **1** pain in your head **2** informal cause of worry or annoyance

header noun **1** Football hitting a ball with your head **2** headlong fall

heading noun title written or printed at the top of a page

headland noun narrow piece of land jutting out into the sea

headlight noun powerful light on the front of a vehicle

headline noun **1** title at the top of a newspaper article, especially on the front page **2 headlines** main points of a news broadcast

headmaster noun male head teacher of a school

headmistress noun female head teacher of a school

headphones plural noun pair of small speakers which you wear over your ears to listen to a radio, CD player, etc without other people hearing

headquarters plural noun centre from which the operations of an organization are directed

headroom noun amount of space below a roof, arch, bridge etc under which an object must pass or fit

headstone noun memorial stone on a grave

headstrong adjective self-willed and obstinate

head teacher noun the teacher who is in charge of a school

headway noun progress

headwind noun wind blowing against you, hindering rather than helping your progress

heady headier headiest adjective intoxicating or exciting

heal verb to become well or make (someone) well **>healer** noun

health noun **1** condition of your body and the extent to which it is free from illness **2** state of being well; fitness

health food noun food believed to be good for you, especially food that is free from additives

healthy healthier healthiest adjective **1** (of person, animal) having good health **2** (of a food, activity) good for you **3** (of an organization, system) functioning well; sound **>healthily** adverb

heap noun **1** pile of things one on top of another **2** informal (also **heaps**) large number or quantity **▷ verb 3** to gather (things) into a pile **4** (followed by on) to give a lot of (something) to (someone): He was quick to heap praise on his secretary

hear hears hearing heard verb **1** to pick up (a sound) with your ears **2** to listen to **3** to learn or be informed **4** Law to try (a case) **>hearer** noun **>hear!**

hear! exclamation of approval or agreement **>hear out** verb to listen to everything said by (someone) without interrupting

hearing noun **1** ability to hear **2** trial of a case

hearsay noun gossip, rumour

hearse noun funeral car used to carry a coffin

heart noun **1** organ that pumps blood round your body **2** centre of emotions, especially love

3 courage, spirit **4** central or most important part **5** shape representing a heart, used especially as a symbol of love **6** playing card with red heart-shaped symbols **7 by heart** from memory

heartache noun very great sadness and emotional suffering

heart attack noun serious medical condition in which the heart suddenly beats irregularly or stops completely

heartbreak noun intense grief
>**heartbreaking** adjective: the heartbreaking story of a little boy
>**heartbroken** adjective suffering intense grief

heartburn noun burning sensation in the chest caused by indigestion

heartening adjective encouraging or uplifting

heart failure noun serious condition in which someone's heart does not work as well as it should, sometimes stopping completely

heartfelt adjective felt sincerely or strongly

hearth noun floor of a fireplace

heartless adjective cruel and unkind

heart-rending adjective causing great sorrow

heart-throb noun informal very attractive man, especially a film or pop star

heart-to-heart noun discussion in which two people talk about their deepest feelings

hearty heartier heartiest adjective **1** friendly and enthusiastic **2** substantial

and nourishing **3** strongly felt
>**heartily** adverb: I'm heartily sick of it

heat noun **1** warmth or state of being hot **2** temperature **3** hot weather **4** preliminary eliminating contest or race to decide who will take part in the later stages **5 on, in heat** (of some female animals) ready for mating ▷ verb **6** to make (something) hot or become hot

heath noun Brit area of open land covered with rough grass or heather

heathen adjective, noun old-fashioned (of a) person who does not believe in one of the established religions

heather noun low-growing plant with small purple, pinkish or white flowers, that grows on heaths and moorland

heating noun equipment used to heat a building; also the process and cost of running such equipment

heatwave noun period of time when the weather is much hotter than usual

heave heaves heaving heaved verb **1** to lift, move or throw (something heavy) with effort **2** to utter (a sigh) **3** to rise and fall **4** to vomit ▷ noun **5** instance of heaving

heaven noun **1** place believed to be the home of God, where good people go when they die **2** wonderful place or state **3 the heavens** literary sky

heavenly adjective **1** of or like heaven **2** informal wonderful or beautiful

heavy **heavier** **heaviest** adjective
1 great in weight or force **2** great in degree or amount **3** solid and thick in appearance **4** using a lot of something quickly **5** informal serious and difficult to deal with or understand **6 with a heavy heart** with sadness or sorrow > **heavily** adverb > **heaviness** noun

heavy-duty adjective (of equipment, material) strong and hard-wearing

heavy-handed adjective showing a lack of care or thought and using too much authority

heavyweight noun **1** a boxer in the heaviest weight group **2** important person with a lot of influence

Hebrew noun **1** ancient language of the Hebrews **2** its modern form, used in Israel **3** Hebrew-speaking Jew living in Israel in past times > adjective **4** relating to the Hebrews and their customs

heckle verb to interrupt (a public speaker) with comments, questions or taunts > **heckler** noun

hectare noun one hundred acres or 10 000 square metres (2.471 acres)

hectic adjective rushed or busy

hedge noun **1** row of bushes forming a barrier or boundary > verb **2** to avoid answering a question or dealing with a problem **3 hedge your bets** to avoid the risk of losing completely by supporting two or more people or courses of action

hedgehog noun small brown animal with a protective covering of sharp spikes covering its back

hedonism noun belief that

pleasure is the most important thing in life > **hedonist** noun > **hedonistic** adjective: her hedonistic lifestyle

heed noun **1** careful attention > verb **2** to pay careful attention to

heel noun **1** back part of your foot **2** the part of a shoe or sock that goes under your heel **3 down at heel** shabby and untidy > verb **4** to repair the heel of (a shoe)

heeler noun Aust dog that herds cattle by biting at their heels

hefty **heftier** **heftiest** adjective of great size, force or weight

height noun **1** distance from base to top **2** distance above sea level **3** a high position or place **4** highest degree or point; peak

heighten verb to make (something) higher or more intense or to become higher or more intense

heinous adjective evil and shocking

heir noun person entitled to inherit property or title

heiress noun a woman who has inherited or is likely to inherit a large amount of money or property

heirloom noun object that has belonged to a family for generations

helicopter noun aircraft with rotating blades above it which enable it to take off vertically, hover and fly

helium noun Chemistry colourless odourless gas that is lighter than air and used to fill balloons

hell noun **1** place believed to be where wicked people go when they die **2** terrible place or state

hellbent adjective (followed by on) determined to

hellish adjective informal very unpleasant

hello interjection expression of greeting

helm noun **1** position from which a boat is steered; also the tiller or wheel for steering **2 at the helm** in a position of leadership or control

helmet noun hard hat worn to protect your head

help verb **1** to make something easier, better or quicker for (someone) **2** to improve (a situation) **3** to stop yourself from: I can't help smiling **4 help yourself** to take something, especially food or drink, without being served ▷ noun **5** assistance or support > **helper** noun

helpful adjective providing help or relief > **helpfully** adverb

helping noun single portion of food

helpless adjective weak, incapable or powerless > **helplessly** adverb > **helplessness** noun

hem hems hemming hemmed noun **1** edge (of a piece of clothing, curtain, etc) which has been turned over and sewn in place ▷ verb **2** to provide (something) with a hem > **hem in** verb to surround and prevent (someone) from moving

hemisphere noun one half of the earth, a brain or a sphere > **hemispherical** adjective

hemp noun tall plant, some varieties of which are used to make rope, and others to produce the drug cannabis

hen noun **1** female chicken **2** female of any bird

hence formal conjunction **1** for this reason ▷ adverb **2** from this time

henceforth adverb from now on

henchman henchmen noun person employed by someone powerful to carry out orders

hepatitis noun inflammation of the liver

her pronoun **1** refers to a female person or animal, or anything thought of as feminine; used as the object of a verb or preposition ▷ adjective **2** belonging to her

herald noun **1** (in the past) a messenger or announcer of important news ▷ verb **2** to be a sign of (a future event)

herb noun plant whose leaves are used in medicine or to flavour food > **herbal** adjective: herbal remedies > **herbalist** noun person who grows or specializes in the use of medicinal herbs

herbivore noun animal that eats only plants > **herbivorous** adjective: A few beetles are herbivorous

herd noun **1** large group of animals feeding and living together **2** large crowd of people ▷ verb **3** to collect (animals or people) into a herd

here adverb in, at or to this place or point

hereafter adverb **1** formal after this point or time ▷ noun **2 the hereafter** life after death

hereby adverb formal by means of this or as a result of this

hereditary adjective passed on to a child from a parent

heredity noun passing on

of characteristics from one generation to another through genes

herein adverb formal in this place or document

heresy heresies noun belief or behaviour considered wrong because it goes against accepted opinion or belief, especially religious belief

herewith adverb formal with this letter or document

heritage noun possessions or traditions that have been passed from one generation to another

hermit noun person living in solitude, especially for religious reasons

hernia noun medical condition in which part of the intestine or another organ sticks through a weak point in the surrounding tissue

hero heroes noun 1 main male character in a film, book, etc 2 person who has done something brave or good

heroic adjective 1 brave, courageous and determined 2 of or like a hero > **heroically** adverb

heroin noun highly addictive drug derived from morphine

heroine noun 1 main female character in a film, book, etc 2 woman or girl who has done something brave or good

heroism noun great courage and bravery

heron noun wading bird with very long legs and a long beak and neck

herpes noun any of several inflammatory skin diseases, including shingles and cold sores

herring herrings or **herring** noun

silvery food fish of northern seas

hers pronoun object or objects belonging to or relating to a woman, girl or female animal that has already been mentioned

herself pronoun 1 used as an object of a verb or pronoun when the woman, girl or female animal that does an action is also the woman, girl or female animal that is directly affected by it: She pulled herself out of the water 2 used to emphasize she: She herself knew nothing about it

hertz noun Physics unit of frequency equal to one cycle per second

● The plural of *hertz* is *hertz*

hesitant adjective undecided or uncertain about doing something > **hesitantly** adverb

hesitate verb 1 to pause or show uncertainty 2 to be reluctant (to do something) > **hesitation** noun: "I know," he replied, without hesitation

hessian noun thick coarse fabric used for making sacks

heterosexual adjective 1 (of a person) sexually attracted to members of the opposite sex ▷ noun 2 person who is sexually attracted to people of the opposite sex

hewn adjective carved from a substance

hexagon noun six-sided shape > **hexagonal** adjective: Choose between square and hexagonal tiles

heyday noun period of greatest success

hi interjection informal expression of greeting

hiatus hiatuses noun formal pause

or interruption

hibernate verb (of an animal) to spend the winter in a state resembling deep sleep > **hibernation** noun: The snakes have come out of hibernation

hibiscus hibiscuses noun type of tropical shrub with brightly coloured flowers

hiccup hiccups hiccupping hiccupped; also spelt **hiccough** noun 1 one of a series of short, uncontrolled intakes of breath, each accompanied by a gulping sound in your throat that you sometimes get especially if you have been eating or drinking too quickly 2 informal small problem; hitch ▷ verb 3 to make a hiccup

hide hides hiding hid hidden verb 1 to put (yourself or an object) somewhere very difficult to see or find in order to avoid discovery; conceal 2 to keep (something) secret ▷ noun 3 place of concealment, especially for a bird-watcher 4 skin of an animal > **hiding** noun 1 state of concealment: in hiding 2 informal severe beating

hideous adjective very ugly or unpleasant > **hideously** adverb

hide-out noun hiding place

hierarchy hierarchies noun system in which people or things are ranked according to how important they are > **hierarchical** adjective: a hierarchical society

hi-fi noun set of stereo equipment on which you can play compact discs and tapes

high adjective 1 of a great height; tall 2 far above ground or sea level 3 greater than usual in degree, quantity or intensity 4 of great

importance, quality or rank 5 (of a sound or note) close to the top of a range 6 informal under the influence of alcohol or drugs ▷ adverb 7 at or to a high level ▷ noun 8 a high point or level: Morale reached a new high 9 on a high informal in a very excited and optimistic mood

highbrow adjective concerned with serious, intellectual subjects

higher education noun education at colleges and universities

high jump noun athletics event involving jumping over a high bar

highlands plural noun mountainous or hilly areas

highlight verb 1 to give emphasis to ▷ noun 2 most interesting part or feature 3 lighter area of a painting, showing where light shines on things 4 lightened streak in the hair

highly adverb 1 extremely 2 very well

high-minded adjective having strong moral principles

Highness noun title used to address or refer to a royal person

high-pitched adjective (of a sound) high or rather shrill

high-rise adjective (of a building) having many storeys

high school noun secondary school

high tide noun the time when the sea is at its highest level

highway noun 1 public road 2 US, Aust, NZ main road

highwayman highwaymen noun (formerly) robber, usually on horseback, who robbed travellers at gunpoint

hijack *verb* to seize control of (an aircraft or other vehicle) during a journey > **hijacker** *noun* > **hijacking** *noun*: *an attempted hijacking*

hike *noun* 1 long walk in the country, especially for pleasure ▷ *verb* 2 to go for a long walk > **hiker** *noun*

hilarious *adjective* very funny > **hilariously** *adverb*

hilarity *noun* great amusement and laughter

hill *noun* raised part of land, higher than the land surrounding it, but less high than a mountain > **hilly** *adjective*: *a hilly area*

hillbilly hillbillies *noun US* unsophisticated country person

hilt *noun* handle of a sword or knife

him *pronoun* refers to a male person or animal; used as the object of a verb or preposition

himself *pronoun* 1 used as an object of a verb or pronoun when the man, boy or male animal that does an action is also the man, boy or male animal that is directly affected by it: *He pulled himself out of the water* 2 used to emphasize *he*: *He himself knew nothing about it*

hind *adjective* 1 situated at the back ▷ *noun* 2 female deer

hinder *verb* to get in the way of (someone or something); hamper

Hindi *noun* language spoken in northern India

hindrance *noun* 1 someone or something that causes difficulties or is an obstruction 2 act of hindering

hindsight *noun* ability to understand an event after it has taken place: *With hindsight, I*
realized how odd he is

Hindu *noun* 1 person who practises Hinduism ▷ *adjective* 2 of Hinduism > **Hinduism** *noun* dominant religion of India, which involves the worship of many gods and a belief in reincarnation

hinge *noun* 1 movable joint which attaches a door or window to its frame ▷ *verb* 2 (followed by *on*) to depend (on)

hint *noun* 1 indirect suggestion, clue or helpful piece of advice 2 small amount ▷ *verb* 3 to suggest indirectly

hinterland *noun* land lying behind a coast or near a city, especially a port

hip *noun* either side of the body between the pelvis and the thigh

hippo hippos *noun informal* hippopotamus

hippopotamus hippopotamuses or **hippopotami** *noun* large African animal with thick wrinkled skin, living near rivers

hippy hippies *noun* (esp. in the 1960s) someone rejecting conventional society and trying to live a life based on peace and love; also spelt **hippie** *noun*

hire *verb* 1 to pay to have temporary use of 2 to employ (someone) to do a job ▷ *noun* 3 temporary use in exchange for money

hirsute *adjective formal* hairy

his *adjective* 1 belonging to him ▷ *pronoun* 2 object or objects belonging to or relating to a man, boy or male animal that has already been mentioned

hiss *verb* 1 to make a long s sound,

especially to show disapproval or aggression ▷ noun **2** sound like that of a long s

histogram noun statistical graph in which the frequency of values is represented by vertical bars of varying heights and widths

historian noun person who studies and writes about history

historic adjective famous or significant in history

historical adjective **1** occurring in the past **2** based on history > **historically** adverb

history histories noun **1** study of the past **2** past events and developments **3** record or account of past events and developments **4** record of someone's past

histrionic adjective excessively dramatic > **histrionics** plural noun excessively dramatic behaviour

hit hits hitting hit verb **1** to strike (someone or something) forcefully **2** to come into violent contact with (something or someone) **3** to affect (someone) badly **4** to reach (a point or place) **5** **hit it off** informal to get on well together ▷ noun **6** instance of hitting **7** successful record, film, etc **8** Computers single visit to a website > **hit on** verb to think of (an idea)

hit and miss adjective sometimes successful and sometimes not

hit-and-run adjective (of a car accident) in which the driver responsible for the accident drives away without stopping

hitch noun **1** minor problem ▷ verb **2** informal to travel by getting lifts from passing vehicles **3** to

attach > **hitch up** verb to pull (something) up with a jerk

hitchhike verb to travel by getting lifts from passing vehicles > **hitchhiker** noun > **hitchhiking** noun

hi tech adjective using very advanced technology

hither adverb **1** old-fashioned to or towards this place **2** **hither and thither** in all directions

hitherto adverb formal until this time

HIV abbreviation human immunodeficiency virus: cause of AIDS

hive noun **1** same as **beehive** **2** **hive of activity** place where people are very busy > **hive off** verb to separate (something) from a larger group

hoard verb **1** to save or store (objects, food); stockpile ▷ noun **2** store of things that has been saved or hidden; stash > **hoarder** noun

● Do not confuse hoard with horde

hoarding noun large board for displaying advertisements by the side of the road

hoarse adjective **1** (of a voice) rough and unclear **2** having a rough and unclear voice > **hoarsely** adverb

hoax noun **1** trick or an attempt to deceive someone ▷ verb **2** to deceive or play a trick on > **hoaxer** noun

hob noun Brit a surface on top of a cooker containing rings, hotplates or gas burners for cooking things

hobble verb **1** to walk lamely **2** to

tie the legs of (a horse) together to restrict its movement

hobby hobbies noun something that you do for enjoyment in your spare time

hock noun **1** joint in the back leg of an animal such as a horse that corresponds to the human ankle **2** white German wine

hockey noun **1** team game played on a field with a ball and curved sticks **2** US ice hockey

hoe noun hoes hoeing hoed **1** long-handled tool with a small square blade, used for loosening soil or weeding ▷ verb **2** to scrape or weed with a hoe

hog hogs hogging hogged noun **1** castrated male pig **2 go the whole hog** to do something completely or thoroughly in a bold or extravagant way ▷ verb **3** informal to take more than your share of (something) or keep (something) for too long

hoist verb **1** to raise or lift (something) up ▷ noun **2** device for lifting things

hokey-pokey noun NZ brittle toffee sold in lumps

hold holds holding held verb **1** to keep or support (something) in or with your hands or arms **2** to have or possess (power, office or an opinion) **3** to arrange for (a meeting, party, election, etc) to take place **4** to consider (someone or something) to be as specified: *who are you holding responsible?* **5** to have space for (an amount or number) **6** informal to wait, especially on the telephone **7** to keep back or reserve (tickets, an order) **8** to maintain (something) in

a specified position or state ▷ noun **9** act or way of holding **10** controlling influence **11** cargo compartment on a ship or aircraft **> hold back** verb to prevent or keep control of **> hold down** verb to keep (something) or keep it under control: *How could I have children and hold down a job like this?* **> holder** noun **> hold on to** verb to continue to have (something) in spite of difficulties **> hold out** verb to stand firm and resist opposition in difficult circumstances **> hold up** verb to delay

holdall noun large strong travelling bag

hole noun **1** gap, opening or hollow **2** animal's burrow **3** informal weakness or error (in a theory or argument) **4** informal difficult situation **5** Golf small hole into which you have to hit the ball ▷ verb **6** to make holes in **7** to hit (a golf ball) into the target hole

Holi noun Hindu festival celebrated in spring

holiday noun **1** time spent away from home for rest or recreation **2** day or other period of rest from work or studies ▷ verb **3** to take a holiday (somewhere)

holidaymaker noun a person who is away from home on holiday

holiness noun **1** state of being holy **2 Your Holiness, His Holiness** title used to address or refer to the Pope

hollow adjective **1** having a hole or space inside **2** (of a sound) as if echoing in a hollow place **3** without any real value or worth ▷ noun **4** space **5** dip in the land ▷ verb **6** to form a hollow in **7** to make (something) by forming such a hollow

holly noun evergreen tree with prickly leaves and red berries

holocaust noun destruction or loss of life on a massive scale

holster noun leather case for a hand gun, hung from a belt

holy holier holiest adjective **1** relating to God or a god **2** (of a person) religious and living a very pure and good life

homage noun act of respect or honour towards someone or something

home noun **1** place where you live **2** place for the care of the elderly, orphans, etc ▷ adjective **3** connected with or involving your home or country **4** Sport played on your own ground ▷ adverb **5** to or at home

homeland noun native country

homeless adjective **1** having nowhere to live ▷ plural noun **2** people who have nowhere to live >**homelessness** noun

homely homelier homeliest adjective simple, ordinary and comfortable

homeopathy noun treatment of disease by small doses of a drug that produces symptoms of the disease in healthy people >**homeopath** noun person who practises homeopathy >**homeopathic** adjective

homeowner noun person who owns the home in which he or she lives

homesick adjective unhappy because of being away from home and missing family and friends >**homesickness** noun

homespun adjective not sophisticated or complicated: The book is simple homespun philosophy

homestead noun house and its land and other buildings, especially a farm

home truths plural noun unpleasant facts told to a person about himself or herself

homeward adjective **1** towards home ▷ adverb **2** (also **homewards**) towards home

homework noun **1** school work done at home **2** preparatory research and work

homicide noun **1** killing of a human being **2** person who kills someone >**homicidal** adjective: a homicidal maniac

homing adjective **1** (of a device) capable of guiding itself to a target **2** (of a pigeon, an instinct) with or relating to the ability to find home

homophone noun word pronounced the same as another, but with a different meaning or spelling. For example, write and right

Homo sapiens noun formal scientific name for human beings as a species

homosexual adjective **1** (of a person) sexually attracted to members of the same sex ▷ noun **2** person who is sexually attracted to people of the same sex >**homosexuality** noun

hone verb **1** to sharpen (a tool) **2** to improve and develop (a skill, ability or quality)

honest adjective **1** truthful and trustworthy **2** open and sincere >**honestly** adverb

honesty *noun* quality of being honest

honey *noun* **1** sweet edible sticky substance made by bees from nectar **2** term of endearment

honeycomb *noun* waxy structure of six-sided cells in which honey is stored by bees in a beehive

honeyeater *noun* small Australian bird that feeds on nectar from flowers

honeymoon *noun* holiday taken by a couple who have just got married

honeysuckle *noun* climbing shrub with sweet-smelling flowers

hongi *noun* NZ Maori greeting in which people touch noses

honk *noun* **1** sound made by a car horn **2** sound made by a goose ▷ *verb* **3** to make this sound **4** to cause (a horn) to make this sound

honorary *adjective* **1** (of a degree, title) held or given only as an honour **2** (of a job) unpaid

honour *noun* **1** sense of honesty and fairness **2** respect **3** award given out of respect **4** pleasure or privilege **5 honours** class of university degree of a higher standard than a pass or ordinary degree ▷ *verb* **6** to give praise and attention to **7** to give an award to (someone) out of respect **8** to pay (a cheque or bill) **9** to keep (a promise)

honourable *adjective* worthy of respect or esteem

hood *noun* **1** loose head covering, often attached to a coat or jacket **2** folding roof of a convertible car or a pram **3** US, Aust car bonnet

-hood *suffix* added at the end of words to form nouns that indicate a state or condition: *childhood*; *priesthood*

hoof **hooves** or **hoofs** *noun* horny covering of the foot of a horse, deer, etc

hook *noun* **1** curved piece of metal, plastic, etc, used to catch, hang, hold, or pull something **2** curving movement, for example of the fist in boxing, or of a golf ball **3 let someone off the hook** to cause someone to get out of a punishment or difficult situation ▷ *verb* **4** to fasten or catch (something) with or as if with a hook

hooked *adjective* **1** bent like a hook **2** (folowed by *on*) *informal* addicted (to) or obsessed (with)

hooligan *noun* destructive and violent young person > **hooliganism** *noun*

hoop *noun* large ring, often used as a toy

hooray *interjection* same as **hurray**

hoot *noun* **1** sound of a car horn **2** cry of an owl **3** similar sound to that of an owl ▷ *verb* **4** to sound (a car horn) **5** to make a long *oo* sound like an owl

Hoover® *noun* **1** vacuum cleaner ▷ *verb* **2 hoover** to clean with a vacuum cleaner

hooves *noun* a plural of **hoof**

hop **hops** **hopping** **hopped** *verb* **1** to jump on one foot **2** to move in short jumps **3** *informal* to move quickly ▷ *noun* **4** instance of hopping **5** (often plural) climbing plant, the dried flowers of which are used to make beer

hope *verb* **1** to want (something to happen or be true) ▷ *noun* **2** wish or feeling of desire and expectation

hopeless adjective **1** having no hope **2** certain to fail or be unsuccessful **3** unable to do something well; useless: *I'm hopeless at remembering birthdays* > **hopelessly** adverb > **hopelessness** noun

hopper noun large, funnel-shaped container for storing substances such as grain or sand

horde noun large crowd

horizon noun **1** apparent line that divides the earth and the sky **2** horizons limits of what you want to do or are interested in: *Travel broadens your horizons*

horizontal adjective flat and parallel to the horizon > **horizontally** adverb

hormone noun **1** substance secreted by certain glands which stimulates certain organs of the body **2** synthetic substance with the same effect > **hormonal** adjective: *hormonal changes*.

horn noun **1** one of a pair of bony growths sticking out of the heads of cattle, sheep, etc **2** substance of which horns are made **3** musical instrument with a tube or pipe of brass fitted with a mouthpiece **4** device on a vehicle sounded as a warning

hornet noun type of large wasp with a severe sting

horoscope noun prediction about a person's future based on the positions of the planets, sun and moon at his or her birth

horrendous adjective very unpleasant and shocking

horrible adjective **1** disagreeable and unpleasant **2** causing shock,

fear or disgust > **horribly** adverb

horrid adjective disagreeable and unpleasant

horrific adjective causing horror: *a horrific attack*

horrifies horrifying **horrified** verb to cause (someone) to feel horror or shock > **horrified** adjective: *He had been horrified at the discovery* > **horrifying** adjective: *a horrifying experience*

horror noun terror or hatred

horse noun **1** large animal with hooves, a mane and a tail, used for riding and pulling carts etc **2** piece of gymnastic equipment used for vaulting over

horseback noun **1** on horseback riding a horse > adjective **2** on a horse or on horses

horsepower noun unit of power (equivalent to 745.7 watts), used to measure the power of an engine

horseradish noun strong-tasting root of a plant, often made into a sauce

horseshoe noun protective U-shaped piece of iron nailed to a horse's hoof, regarded as a symbol of good luck

horsey or **horsy** adjective very keen on horses

horticulture noun art or science of growing flowers, fruit and vegetables > **horticultural** adjective

hose hoses hosing hosed noun **1** flexible pipe along which liquid or gas can be passed ▷ verb **2** to wash or water (something) with a hose

hosiery noun stockings, socks and tights collectively

hospice noun nursing home for people who are dying

hospitable adjective welcoming to strangers or guests

hospital noun place where people who are sick or injured are looked after and treated

host noun **1** person who entertains guests **2** place or country providing the facilities for an event **3** compere of a show **4** animal or plant on which a parasite lives **5** large number ▷ verb **6** to be the host of (an event, party)

hostage noun person who is illegally held prisoner and threatened with injury or death unless certain demands are met by other people

hostel noun building providing accommodation at a low cost for a specific group of people such as students, travellers, homeless people, etc

hostess noun woman who entertains guests

hostile adjective **1** unfriendly **2** (followed by to) opposed (to) **3** relating to or involving the enemies of a country

hostility hostilities noun **1** unfriendly and aggressive feelings or behaviour **2** hostilities acts of warfare

hot hotter hottest adjective **1** having a high temperature **2** strong, spicy **3** (of news) very recent **4** (of a temper) quick to rouse **5** liked very much: a hot favourite **6** dangerous or difficult to deal with **7** informal stolen ▷ **hotly** adverb

hotbed noun any place encouraging a particular activity: hotbeds of unrest

hot dog noun long roll split lengthways with a hot sausage inside

hotel noun building where people stay, paying for their room and meals

hothouse noun **1** greenhouse **2** place or situation of intense intellectual or emotional activity: a hothouse of radical socialist ideas

hot seat noun **in the hot seat** informal having to make difficult decisions for which you will be held responsible

hound noun **1** hunting dog ▷ verb **2** to pursue (someone) relentlessly

hour noun **1** unit of time equal to sixty minutes and a twenty-fourth part of a day **2** time **3** hours period regularly appointed for work or business

house houses housing housed noun **1** building used as a home **2** building used for some specific purpose: the opera house **3** business firm **4** law-making body or the hall where it meets **5** family or dynasty **6** theatre or cinema audience ▷ verb **7** to give accommodation to **8** to contain or cover

houseboat noun boat tied up at a particular place on a river or canal and used as a home

household noun **1** all the people living in a house ▷ adjective **2** household name very well-known person

housekeeper noun person employed to run someone's household

House of Commons noun the more powerful of the two parts of the British Parliament. Its members are elected by the public

House of Lords noun the less powerful of the two parts of the British Parliament. Its members are unelected

House of Representatives noun 1 (in Australia) the larger of the two parts of the Federal Parliament 2 (n New Zealand) the Parliament

housewife housewives noun married woman who runs her own household and does not have a paid job

housing noun 1 houses and flats or apartments 2 the providing of houses

hovel noun small house or hut that is dirty or badly in need of repair

hover verb 1 (of a bird etc) to hang in the air 2 to stand around in a state of indecision

hovercraft or **hovercrafts** noun vehicle which can travel over both land and sea on a cushion of air

how adverb 1 in what way, by what means 2 to what degree: I know how hard it is; How much is it for the weekend? 3 used to emphasize: How odd!

however adverb 1 nevertheless 2 by whatever means 3 no matter how: however much it hurt, he could do it

howl verb 1 (of wolf, dog, person) to make a long, loud wailing noise ▷ noun 2 loud wailing cry 3 loud burst of laughter

HQ an abbreviation for **headquarters**

hub noun 1 centre of a wheel,

through which the axle passes 2 the most important or active part of a place or organization

hubbub noun great noise or confusion

huddle verb 1 to keep your arms and legs close to your body often in response to cold or fear 2 (of people, animals) to crowd closely together ▷ noun 3 small group

hue noun colour, shade

huff noun **in a huff** in an angry and resentful mood > **huffy** adjective > **huffily** adverb: "There's no need to be sarcastic," he replied huffily

hug hugs hugging hugged verb 1 to clasp (someone) tightly in your arms as a gesture of affection 2 to keep close to (the ground, kerb, etc) ▷ noun 3 tight or fond embrace

huge adjective very big > **hugely** adverb: a hugely successful career

hui hui or **huis** noun NZ 1 meeting of Maori people 2 informal party

hulk noun 1 large heavy person or thing 2 body of an abandoned ship > **hulking** adjective bulky, unwieldy

hull noun main body of a boat that sits in the water

hum hums humming hummed verb 1 to make a low continuous low noise 2 to sing with the lips closed 3 informal (of a place) be very busy ▷ noun 4 humming sound

human adjective 1 of or typical of people ▷ noun 2 person; human being > **humanly** adverb by human powers or means

human being noun man, woman or child

humane adjective kind or merciful

> **humanely** adverb

humanism noun belief in mankind's ability to achieve happiness and fulfilment without the need for religion > **humanist** noun

humanitarian noun 1 person who works for the welfare of mankind or who has the interests of humankind at heart ▷ adjective 2 concerned with the welfare of mankind > **humanitarianism** noun

humanity humanities noun 1 human race 2 the quality of being human 3 kindness or mercy 4 **humanities** study of literature, philosophy and the arts

human rights plural noun rights of individuals to freedom and justice

humble adjective 1 conscious of your failings 2 modest, unpretentious 3 unimportant ▷ verb 4 to cause (someone) to feel humble; humiliate 1 **humbly** adverb

humbug noun 1 Brit hard striped peppermint sweet 2 speech or writing that is obviously dishonest or untrue

humdrum adjective ordinary, dull

humid adjective damp and hot

humidity noun amount of moisture in the air, or the state of being humid

humiliate verb to make (someone) feel ashamed or appear stupid in front of other people > **humiliating** adjective: a degrading and humiliating experience > **humiliation** noun

humility noun quality of being humble

hummingbird noun very small American bird whose powerful wings make a humming noise as they beat

humour noun 1 quality of being funny 2 ability to say amusing things or find things amusing 3 state of mind; mood ▷ verb 4 to be kind and indulgent to

hump noun 1 raised piece of ground 2 large lump on the back of an animal or person ▷ verb 3 informal to carry or heave 4 **get, take the hump** informal to be annoyed, sulk

hunch noun 1 feeling or suspicion not based on facts ▷ verb 2 to draw (one's shoulders) up or together

hunchback noun old-fashioned person with an abnormal curvature of the spine

hundred adjective, noun 1 the number 100 ▷ noun 2 **hundreds** large but unspecified number; lots > **hundredth** adjective, noun

Hungarian adjective 1 belonging or relating to Hungary ▷ noun 2 person from Hungary 3 main language spoken in Hungary

hunger noun 1 need or desire to eat 2 desire or craving > **hunger for** verb to want very much

hunger strike noun refusal to eat, as a means of protest

hungry hungrier hungriest adjective needing or wanting to eat > **hungrily** adverb

hunk noun 1 large piece 2 informal sexually attractive man

hunt verb 1 to seek out and kill (wild animals) for food or sport 2 (followed by for) to search (for) ▷ noun 3 instance of hunting

> **hunter** noun person or animal that hunts wild animals for food or sport > **hunting** adjective, noun

huntaway noun Aust, NZ sheepdog trained to drive sheep by barking

hurdle noun 1 Sport light barrier for jumping over in some races 2 problem or difficulty 3 **hurdles** race involving hurdles > **hurdler** noun

hurl verb 1 to throw (something) forcefully 2 to utter (insults) forcefully

hurray or **hurrah** interjection exclamation of joy or applause

hurricane noun very violent wind or storm

hurry hurries hurrying hurried verb 1 to move or do something as quickly as possible 2 to cause (something or someone) to move or do something more quickly than otherwise > noun 3 haste or rush > **hurried** adjective > **hurriedly** adverb

hurt hurts hurting hurt verb 1 to injure or cause physical pain to 2 to be painful 3 to make (someone) unhappy by being unkind or thoughtless towards them > noun 4 physical or mental pain > **hurtful** adjective unkind: a hurtful remark

hurtle verb to move quickly or violently

husband noun 1 woman's partner in marriage > verb 2 to use (resources) economically

husbandry noun 1 farming 2 management of resources

hush verb 1 to be silent or make (someone) silent > noun 2 stillness or silence > **hushed** adjective > **hush up** verb to

suppress information about

husk noun dry outer covering of certain seeds and fruits > verb

husky huskier huskiest; huskies adjective 1 (of a voice) slightly hoarse > noun 2 Arctic sledge dog with thick hair and a curled tail > **huskily** adverb

hustle verb 1 to push (someone) about; jostle > noun 2 lively activity or bustle

hut noun small house, shelter or shed

hutch noun wooden box with wire mesh at one side, for keeping pet rabbits etc

hyacinth noun sweet-smelling spring flower that grows from a bulb

hybrid noun 1 plant or animal that has been bred from two different types of plant or animal 2 anything that is a mixture of two other things > adjective 3 of mixed origin

hydra hydras or **hydrae** noun microscopic freshwater creature that has a slender tubular body and tentacles round the mouth

hydrangea noun ornamental shrub with clusters of pink, blue or white flowers

hydraulic adjective operated by pressure forced through a pipe by a liquid such as water or oil > **hydraulically** adverb > **hydraulics** noun study of the mechanical properties of fluids as they apply to practical engineering

hydro- prefix 1 water: hydroelectric 2 containing hydrogen: hydrochloric acid

hydrogen noun Chemistry light

flammable colourless gas that combines with oxygen to form water

hyena *noun* wild doglike animal of Africa and Asia that hunts in packs

hygiene *noun* practice of keeping yourself and your surroundings clean, especially to stop the spread of disease >**hygienic** *adjective* >**hygienically** *adverb*

hymn *noun* Christian song in praise of God

hyper- *prefix* very much, over or excessively: *hyperactive*

hyperactive *adjective* (of person) unable to relax and always in a state of restless activity

hyperbole *noun* deliberate exaggeration for effect

hypertension *noun formal* high blood pressure

hyphen *noun* punctuation mark (-) indicating that two words or syllables are connected >**hyphenate** *verb* to separate (words or syllables) with a hyphen >**hyphenated** *adjective* (of two words or syllables) having a hyphen between them >**hyphenation** *noun*

hypnosis *noun* artificially induced state of relaxation in which the mind is more than usually receptive to suggestion

hypnotize *verb* to put (someone) into a state in which they seem to be asleep but can respond to questions and suggestions

hypochondria *noun* undue preoccupation with your health >**hypochondriac** *noun* person who continually worries about their health

hypocrisy hypocrisies *noun* pretence that you have beliefs or qualities that you do not really have, so that you seem a better person than you are >**hypocrite** *noun* person who pretends to be what he or she is not >**hypocritical** *adjective* >**hypocritically** *adverb*

hypodermic *noun* syringe or needle used to inject a drug beneath the skin

hypothermia *noun* condition in which a person's body temperature is dangerously low as a result of prolonged exposure to severe cold

hypothesis hypotheses *noun* explanation or theory which has not yet been proved to be correct

hypothetical *adjective* based on assumption rather than on fact or reality >**hypothetically** *adverb*

hysterectomy hysterectomies *noun* surgical removal of the womb

hysteria *noun* state of uncontrolled excitement or panic

hysterical *adjective* in a state of uncontrolled excitement or panic >**hysterically** *adverb*

I *pronoun* used by a speaker or writer to refer to himself or herself as the subject of a verb

ibis ibises *noun* large wading bird

with long legs

-ible *suffix* another form of the suffix **-able**

-ic or **-ical** *suffix* used to form adjectives: *ironic; ironical*

ice *noun* **1** frozen water **2** *Chiefly Brit* ice cream **3 break the ice** to create a relaxed atmosphere, especially between people meeting for the first time ▷ *verb* **4** (followed by *up, over*) to become covered with ice **5** to cover (a cake) with icing

Ice Age *noun* period lasting thousands of years when much of the earth's surface was covered in ice

iceberg *noun* large floating mass of ice

icecap *noun* mass of ice permanently covering an area

ice cream *noun* sweet creamy frozen food

ice cube *noun* small square block of ice added to a drink to cool it

ice hockey *noun* type of hockey played on ice

Icelandic *noun* main language spoken in Iceland

ice-skate *verb* to move about on ice wearing ice-skates >**ice-skater** *noun*

icicle *noun* piece of ice shaped like a pointed stick hanging down where water has dripped

icing *noun* mixture of powdered sugar and water or egg whites, used to decorate cakes

icon *noun* **1** picture on a computer screen representing a program that can be activated by clicking on it **2** picture of Christ or another religious figure, regarded as holy

ICT *abbreviation* information and communications technology

icy *adjective* **icier iciest 1** very cold **2** covered with ice **3** unfriendly and cold >**icily** *adverb*

id *noun Psychology* basic instincts and unconscious thoughts

idea *noun* **1** plan or thought formed in the mind **2** belief or opinion **3** knowledge

ideal *adjective* **1** most suitable **2** perfect ▷ *noun* **3** principle or idea that you try to achieve because it seems perfect to you **4** perfect example (of a person or thing)

idealism *noun* tendency to seek perfection in everything >**idealist** *noun* >**idealistic** *adjective*

idealize *verb* to regard or portray (someone or something) as perfect or nearly perfect >**idealization** *noun*

ideally *adverb* **1** if everything were perfect; in a perfect world: *Ideally, they'd have their own home* **2** perfectly

identical *adjective* exactly the same >**identically** *adverb*

identification *noun* **1** act of identifying **2** document such as a driver's licence or passport, which proves who you are

identify **identifies identifying identified** *verb* to recognize (someone or something) as being or prove (someone or something) to be a particular person or thing >**identifiable** *adjective: a clearly identifiable cause of stress* >**identify with** *verb* to understand and sympathize with the feelings and ideas of (a person or group)

identity identities noun characteristics that make you who you are

ideology ideologies noun body of ideas and beliefs of a group, nation, etc > **ideological** adjective > **ideologically** adverb

idiom noun group of words whose meaning together is different from all the words taken individually. For example, 'It is raining cats and dogs' is an idiom

idiosyncrasy idiosyncrasies noun personal peculiarity of mind, habit or behaviour > **idiosyncratic** adjective

idiot noun foolish or stupid person

idiotic adjective extremely foolish or silly > **idiotically** adverb

idle adjective **1** not doing anything **2** not willing to work; lazy **3** not being used **4** useless or meaningless: *an idle threat* ▷ verb **5** (of an engine) to run slowly out of gear > **idleness** noun > **idly** adverb

idol noun **1** famous person who is loved and admired by fans **2** picture or statue which is worshipped as if it were a god

idyll noun scene or time of great peace and happiness > **idyllic** adjective: *an idyllic place to stay*

i.e. abbreviation Latin that is to say

if conjunction **1** on the condition that **2** whether **3** even though

igloo igloos noun dome-shaped Inuit house made of snow and ice

igneous adjective technical (of rock) formed as molten rock cools and hardens

ignite verb to set fire to (something) or catch fire

ignition noun system that ignites the fuel-and-air mixture to start an engine

ignominious adjective shameful or considered wrong > **ignominiously** adverb

ignoramus ignoramuses noun ignorant person

ignorant adjective **1** lacking knowledge **2** informal rude through lack of knowledge of good manners > **ignorance** noun > **ignorantly** adverb

ignore verb to refuse to notice (someone or something); disregard

iguana noun large tropical American lizard

il- prefix not or the opposite of: the form of in- that is used before the letter l: *illegible*

ill adjective **1** not in good health **2** harmful or unpleasant: *ill effect* ▷ noun **3** ills difficulties or problems ▷ adverb **4** badly **5** hardly, with difficulty: *I can ill afford to lose him*

ill at ease adjective uncomfortable or unable to relax

illegal adjective against the law > **illegality** noun > **illegally** adverb

illegible adjective (of writing) unclear and difficult or impossible to read

illegitimate adjective **1** born of parents not married to each other **2** not lawful > **illegitimacy** noun

ill-fated adjective doomed to end unhappy

illicit adjective **1** illegal **2** forbidden or disapproved of by society

illiterate adjective **1** unable to read or write ▷ noun **2** someone who is unable to read or write

> **illiteracy** noun

illness noun 1 experience of being ill 2 particular disease

illogical adjective 1 not reasonable or sensible 2 not logical
> **illogically** adverb

ill-treat verb to treat (someone or something) badly, causing hurt, harm or damage > **ill-treatment** noun

illuminate verb 1 to light (something) up 2 to make (something) clear; explain 3 History to decorate (a manuscript) with brightly coloured pictures > **illuminating** adjective

illumination noun 1 lighting 2 **illuminations** coloured lights put up to decorate a town

illusion noun 1 false belief 2 deceptive impression of reality which deceives the eye

illusory adjective seeming to be true, but actually false

illustrate verb 1 to explain (something) by use of examples 2 to provide (a book or text) with pictures 3 to be an example of
> **illustrative** adjective: illustrative examples > **illustrator** noun

illustration noun 1 picture or diagram 2 example

illustrious adjective famous and distinguished

ill will noun feeling of hostility

im- prefix not or the opposite of: the form of in- used before the letters b, m and p: imbalance; immature

IM abbreviation instant messaging

image noun 1 mental picture of someone or something 2 impression people have of a person, organization, etc

3 representation of a person or thing in a work of art

imagery noun descriptive language used in a poem or book

imaginary adjective existing only in the imagination

imagination noun 1 the ability to form new and exciting ideas 2 ability to make mental images of things that you may not have seen

imaginative adjective having or showing a lot of creative mental ability > **imaginatively** adverb

imagine verb 1 to form a mental image of 2 to think, believe or guess > **imaginable** adjective: hats of every imaginable shape and size

imam noun 1 leader of prayers in a mosque 2 title of some Islamic leaders

imbalance noun lack of balance or proportion

imbecile noun stupid person

imitate verb to copy > **imitative** adjective > **imitator** noun

imitation noun 1 copy of an original 2 instance of imitating

immaculate adjective 1 completely clean or tidy 2 without any mistakes at all
> **immaculately** adverb

immaterial adjective not important or not relevant

immature adjective 1 not fully developed 2 lacking the wisdom and good sense expected of a person of this age > **immaturity** noun

immediate adjective 1 occurring at once 2 next or nearest in time, space or relationship
> **immediacy** noun

immediately adverb 1 straight

away **2** just: *immediately behind the house*

immemorial *adjective* since, from **time immemorial** longer than anyone can remember

immense *adjective* extremely large >**immensely** *adverb* to a very great degree >**immensity** *noun*

immerse *verb* **1** to involve (someone) deeply; engross **2** to plunge (something or someone) into liquid >**immersion** *noun: damage due to immersion in water*

immigrant *noun* someone who has come to live permanently in a new country >**immigrate** *verb* to come to live >**immigration** *noun* coming to live in a foreign country in order to live there

imminent *adjective* about to happen >**imminence** *noun* >**imminently** *adverb*

immobile *adjective* **1** not moving **2** unable to move >**immobility** *noun: Weeks of immobility had left every muscle stiff*

immoral *adjective* morally wrong; corrupt >**immorality** *noun*

- Do not confuse *immoral* and *amoral*. You use *immoral* to talk about people who are aware of moral standards, but go against them. *Amoral* applies to people with no moral standards

immortal *adjective* **1** living forever **2** famous for all time >**immortalize** *verb*

immortality *noun* state of living forever and never dying

immovable or **immoveable** *adjective* fixed and unable to be moved >**immovably** *adverb*

immune *adjective* **1** protected

against a specific disease **2** (followed by *to*) secure (against)

immune system *noun* body's system of defence against disease

imp *noun* (in folklore) mischievous small creature with magical powers >**impish** *adjective*

impact *noun* **1** strong effect **2** (force of) a collision

impair *verb* to weaken or damage (something) >**impairment** *noun*

impale *verb* to pierce with a sharp object

impart *verb formal* to pass on (information)

impartial *adjective* not favouring one side or the other; fair and objective >**impartially** *adverb* >**impartiality** *noun*

impasse *noun* situation in which progress is impossible

impassioned *adjective* full of emotion

impassive *adjective* showing no emotion, calm >**impassively** *adverb*

impasto *noun Art* technique of painting with thick paint so that brush strokes or palette knife marks can be seen

impatient *adjective* **1** irritable at any delay or difficulty **2** restless (to have or do something) >**impatiently** *adverb* >**impatience** *noun*

impeccable *adjective* excellent and without any faults >**impeccably** *adverb*

impede *verb* to hinder (someone) in action or progress

impediment *noun* something that makes action, speech or progress difficult

impelled *adjective* driven (to do

something)

impending adjective (esp. of something bad) about to happen

impenetrable adjective
1 impossible to get through
2 impossible to understand

imperative adjective 1 extremely urgent or important; vital ▷ noun
2 Grammar form of a verb that is used for giving orders

imperfect adjective 1 having faults or mistakes 2 Grammar indicating a tense of verbs describing continuous, incomplete or repeated past actions ▷ noun 3 Grammar (also **imperfect tense**) tense of verbs describing continuous, incomplete or repeated past actions > **imperfectly** adverb

imperial adjective 1 relating to an empire, emperor or empress
2 denoting a system of weights and measures that uses inches, feet, and yards, ounces and pounds, pints and gallons
> **imperialism** noun system of rule in which a rich and powerful nation controls other nations
> **imperialist** adjective, noun

imperious adjective proud and domineering > **imperiously** adverb

impersonal adjective 1 lacking human warmth or sympathy
2 not relating to any particular person; objective 3 Grammar (of a verb) without a personal subject: It is snowing > **impersonally** adverb

impersonate verb to pretend to be (another person)
> **impersonation** noun
> **impersonator** noun

impertinent adjective disrespectful or rude
> **impertinently** adverb
> **impertinence** noun

impetuous adjective hasty and lacking in forethought; rash > **impetuosity** noun
> **impetuously** adverb

impetus impetuses noun
1 incentive, impulse 2 Physics force that starts a body moving

impinge verb **impinge on, upon** to affect or restrict

implacable adjective not prepared to be appeased; unyielding > **implacability** noun
> **implacably** adverb

implant verb 1 to put (something) into someone's body, usually by surgical operation 2 to fix (something) firmly in someone's mind ▷ noun 3 Medicine something put into someone's body, usually by surgical operation

implausible adjective very unlikely
> **implausibly** adverb

implement verb 1 to carry out (a plan, instructions, etc) ▷ noun 2 tool or instrument
> **implementation** noun: We need to discuss the implementation of the new plan

implicate verb to show (someone) to be involved in something, especially a crime

implication noun something suggested indirectly or implied

implicit adjective 1 expressed indirectly 2 absolute and unquestioning: implicit support
> **implicitly** adverb

implore verb to beg (someone) earnestly

imply implies implying implied
verb to suggest or hint (that
something is the case)

import verb 1 to bring in
(goods) from another country
▷ noun 2 something imported
> **importation** noun > **importer**
noun

important adjective 1 very
valuable, necessary or significant
2 having influence or power
> **importance** noun value,
necessity or significance: the
importance of having a balanced diet
> **importantly** adverb

impose verb 1 to force the
acceptance of (something)
2 (often followed by on) to
take unfair advantage (of)
> **imposition** noun unreasonable
demand

imposing adjective grand and
impressive

impossible adjective not
able to be done or to happen
> **impossibility** noun > **impossibly**
adverb

imposter or **impostor** noun
person who pretends to be
someone else in order to get
things they want

impotent adjective 1 powerless
2 (of a man) incapable of having or
maintaining an erection during
sexual intercourse > **impotence**
noun > **impotently** adverb

impound verb to take legal
possession of; confiscate

impoverished adjective poor

impractical adjective not
practical, sensible or realistic

impregnable adjective impossible
to break into

impregnated adjective saturated
or soaked

impresario impresarios noun
person who runs theatre
performances, concerts, etc

impress verb 1 to cause (someone)
to feel admiration or respect
2 **impress something on**
someone to make someone
understand the importance
of something 3 to stress or
emphasize

impression noun 1 effect,
especially a strong or
favourable one 2 vague
idea 3 impersonation for
entertainment 4 mark made by
pressing

impressionable adjective easily
impressed or influenced

impressionism noun style of
painting which is concerned with
the impressions created by light
and shapes, rather than with
exact details > **impressionist**
noun

impressive adjective making a
strong impression, especially
through size, importance, or
quality

imprint noun 1 lasting effect
(on the mind) 2 mark left by
something causing pressure
▷ verb 3 to fix (something in
someone's memory) 4 to produce
(a mark) by printing or stamping

imprison verb to put (someone) in
prison > **imprisonment** noun

improbable adjective not
likely to be true or to happen
> **improbability** noun
> **improbably** adverb

impromptu adjective without
planning or preparation

improper adjective 1 indecent

or shocking **2** illegal or dishonest **3** not suitable or correct **> improperly** adverb **> impropriety** noun formal unsuitable or slightly improper behaviour

improve verb to become better or to make (something) better **> improvement** noun: There's no sign of any improvement yet

improvise verb **1** to make use of whatever materials are available **2** to make up (a piece of music, speech, etc) as you go along **> improvisation** noun **> improvised** adjective: They're making do with improvised shelters

impudent adjective cheeky and disrespectful **> impudence** noun **> impudently** adverb

impulse noun **1** sudden urge to do something **2** Physics short electrical signal passing along a wire or nerve or through the air **3 on impulse** suddenly and without planning **> impulsive** adjective **1** (of a person) tending to do things on the spur of the moment without thinking about them carefully **2** (of an action, decision, etc) carried out or taken on the spur of the moment without too much thinking **> impulsively** adverb

impure adjective **1** having dirty or unwanted substances mixed in **2** immoral, obscene

impurity **impurities** noun **1** quality of being impure **2** trace of dirt or another substance that should not be present

in preposition **1** indicating position inside (something): in the box **2** indicating state or situation, etc: in a mess **3** indicating time

or manner: in the afternoon; in a husky voice ▷ adverb **4** indicating position inside, entry into, etc: she stayed in; come in ▷ adjective **5** fashionable

in- prefix **1** added to the beginning of some words to form a word with the opposite meaning: insincere **2** in, into or in the course of: infiltrate

inability noun lack of means or skill to do something

inaccessible adjective impossible or very difficult to reach

inaccurate adjective not correct

inadequate adjective **1** not enough **2** not good enough **> inadequacy** noun **> inadequately** adverb

inadvertent adjective unintentional **> inadvertently** adverb

inane adjective silly or stupid **> inanely** adverb **> inanity** noun

inanimate adjective not living

inappropriate adjective not suitable **> inappropriately** adverb

inarticulate adjective unable to express yourself clearly or well

inasmuch as conjunction because or in so far as

inaudible adjective not loud enough to be heard **> inaudibly** adverb

inaugurate verb **1** to open (a building) especially with ceremony **2** to begin to use (a new system) **3** to formally establish (a new leader) in office **> inaugural** adjective **> inauguration** noun

inborn adjective existing from birth; natural

incandescent adjective glowing

with heat >**incandescence** noun

incapable adjective **1** (followed by of) unable (to do something) **2** incompetent

incarcerate verb to imprison >**incarceration** noun

incarnate adjective in human form >**incarnation** noun

incendiary adjective (of a bomb, attack, etc) designed to cause fires

incense noun substance that gives off a sweet perfume when burned

incensed adjective extremely angry

incentive noun something that encourages effort or action

inception noun formal beginning

incessant adjective never stopping >**incessantly** adverb

incest noun sexual intercourse between two people too closely related to marry >**incestuous** adjective: an incestuous relationship

inch noun **1** unit of length equal to about 2.54 centimetres ▷ verb **2** to move slowly and gradually

incident noun event

incidental adjective occurring as a minor part of something >**incidentally** adverb

incinerate verb to burn >**incineration** noun

incinerator noun special container for burning rubbish

incipient adjective just starting to appear or happen

incision noun a sharp cut, made especially by a surgeon operating on a patient

incisive adjective direct and forceful

incite verb **1** to stir up (trouble, violence, criminal behaviour,

etc) **2** to provoke (someone) into doing something >**incitement** noun

inclination noun **1** liking, tendency or preference **2** slope

incline verb **1** to make (someone) likely (to do something) **2** **be inclined** to tend (to do something) ▷ noun **3** slope

include verb to have (something or someone) as part of something or make them part of it >**including** preposition: everybody, including me

inclusion noun act of making (something or someone) part of something

inclusive adjective including everything (specified) >**inclusively** adverb

incognito adjective, adverb in disguise or with a false identity

incoherent adjective unclear and impossible to understand >**incoherence** noun >**incoherently** adverb

income noun amount of money earned from work, investments, etc

income tax noun tax on annual income

incoming adjective **1** coming in **2** about to come into office

incomparable adjective beyond comparison; unequalled >**incomparably** adverb

incompatible adjective unable to live or exist together because of differences >**incompatibility** noun

incompetent adjective not having the necessary ability or skill to do something >**incompetence** noun >**incompetently** adverb

incomplete adjective not complete

or finished > **incompletely** adverb

incomprehensible adjective not able to be understood

inconceivable adjective impossible to believe

inconclusive adjective not leading to a decision or a definite result

incongruous adjective inappropriate or out of place > **incongruously** adverb

inconsequential adjective unimportant or insignificant

inconsistent adjective not always behaving in the same way; unpredictable > **inconsistency** noun > **inconsistently** adverb

inconspicuous adjective not easily seen or obvious > **inconspicuously** adverb

incontinent adjective unable to control your bladder or bowels > **incontinence** noun

inconvenience noun 1 trouble or difficulty ▷ verb 2 to cause (someone) trouble or difficulty > **inconvenient** adjective > **inconveniently** adverb

incorporate verb to include (something or someone) as part of a larger unit > **incorporation** noun

incorrect adjective wrong or untrue > **incorrectly** adverb

increase verb 1 to become or make (something) greater in size, number, etc ▷ noun 2 rise in number, size, etc 3 amount by which something increases > **increasingly** adverb

incredible adjective 1 hard to believe or imagine 2 informal marvellous; amazing > **incredibly** adverb

incredulous adjective not able to

believe something > **incredulity** noun > **incredulously** adverb

increment noun increase in money or value, especially a regular salary increase > **incremental** adjective

incriminate verb to make (someone) seem guilty of a crime > **incriminating** adjective: incriminating evidence

incubate verb (of eggs) to be kept warm until ready to hatch > **incubation** noun > **incubator** noun piece of hospital equipment in which sick or weak newborn babies are kept warm

incumbent adjective 1 **it is incumbent on** it is the duty of (someone to do something) ▷ noun 2 person holding a particular office or position

incur incurs incurring incurred verb to cause (something unpleasant) to happen

incurable adjective not able to be cured > **incurably** adverb

indebted adjective grateful (to someone for help or favours) > **indebtedness** noun

indecent adjective 1 morally or sexually offensive or unseemly: indecent haste > **indecency** noun > **indecently** adverb

indeed adverb really or certainly

indefatigable adjective never getting tired

indefinite adjective 1 without exact limits: for an indefinite period 2 vague, unclear > **indefinitely** adverb

indefinite article noun grammatical term for a or an

indelible adjective impossible to

erase or remove >**indelibly** adverb

indemnity indemnities noun formal insurance against loss or damage

indentation noun dent or groove in a surface or edge

independence noun 1 not relying on anyone else 2 self-rule

independent adjective 1 free from the control or influence of others 2 separate 3 financially self-reliant 4 capable of acting for yourself or on your own ▷ noun 5 politician who does not represent any political party >**independently** adverb

indeterminate adjective not certain and not fixed

index noun **indexes** or **indices** 1 alphabetical list of names or subjects dealt with in a book 2 alphabetical list of all the books in a library, arranged by title, author or subject

index finger noun finger next to your thumb

Indian adjective 1 belonging or relating to India ▷ noun 2 someone from India 3 Native American

indicate verb 1 to be a sign or symptom of 2 to point (something) out 3 to state (something) briefly 4 (of a measuring instrument) to show a reading of 5 (of a driver) to give a signal showing which way you are going to turn

indication noun a sign of what someone feels or what is likely to happen

indicative adjective 1 **indicative of** suggesting ▷ noun 2 Grammar indicative mood

indicator noun 1 something acting as a sign or indication 2 flashing light on a vehicle showing the driver's intention to turn 3 Chemistry substance that shows if another substance is an acid or alkali by changing colour when it comes into contact with it

indict verb to charge (someone) officially with a crime >**indictable** adjective: an indictable offence >**indictment** noun

indifferent adjective 1 (often followed by to) showing no interest or concern (in) 2 of poor quality >**indifference** noun >**indifferently** adverb

indigenous adjective born in or native to a country

indigestion noun discomfort or pain caused by difficulty in digesting food >**indigestible** adjective difficult to digest

indignant adjective angry at something unfair or wrong >**indignantly** adverb

indignation noun anger at something unfair or wrong

indignity indignities noun something causing embarrassment or humiliation

indigo noun or adjective deep violet-blue

indirect adjective not direct >**indirectly** adverb

indiscriminate adjective showing lack of careful thought or choice >**indiscriminately** adverb

indispensable adjective absolutely essential

indistinct adjective not clear >**indistinctly** adverb

individual adjective 1 relating to

one particular person or thing
2 separate; distinct **3** distinctive
or unusual ▷ noun **4** single person
or thing > **individually** adverb

individualist noun someone who
likes to do things in their own
way > **individualistic** adjective: a
very individualistic society

individuality noun quality of
being different from all other
things, and therefore interesting
and noticeable

indomitable adjective formal
too strong to be defeated or
discouraged

Indonesian adjective **1** belonging
or relating to Indonesia ▷ noun
2 someone from Indonesia
3 official language of Indonesia

indoor adjective inside a building

indoors adverb inside a building

induce verb **1** to cause (a state
or condition) **2** to persuade
or influence (someone to do
something) **3** Medicine to cause (a
woman) to go into labour or bring
on (labour) by the use of drugs etc

inducement noun something
used to persuade someone to do
something

indulge verb **1** to allow yourself to
do something that you enjoy **2** to
allow (someone) to have or do
what they want

indulgence noun **1** something
allowed because it gives pleasure
2 act of indulging yourself or
someone else

indulgent adjective showing
kindness, generosity and
understanding towards
someone, often to an excessive
degree > **indulgently** adverb

industrial adjective relating to
industry

industrial action noun any
action, such as striking or
working to rule, that is used by
workers as a way of protesting
about their pay and conditions
with the aim of bringing about
change

industrialist noun person who
owns or controls a lot of factories

Industrial Revolution noun the
transformation of Britain and
other countries in the eighteenth
and nineteenth century into
industrial nations, through
greater use of machinery

industrious adjective hard-
working

industry industries noun **1** work
and processes involved in
manufacturing things in factories
2 all the people and processes
involved in manufacturing a
particular thing

inedible adjective not fit to be
eaten

inefficient adjective badly
organized, wasteful and
slow > **inefficiency** noun
> **inefficiently** adverb

inept adjective clumsy or lacking
skill > **ineptitude** noun

inequality inequalities noun
difference in size, status, wealth
or position, between different
things, groups or people

inert adjective **1** without the
power of motion or resistance
2 chemically unreactive
> **inertness** noun

inertia noun feeling of
unwillingness to do anything

inevitable adjective unavoidable,
sure to happen > **inevitability**

noun >**inevitably** adverb

inexhaustible adjective incapable of running out or being used up

inexorable adjective unable to be prevented from continuing or progressing >**inexorably** adverb

inexpensive adjective not costing much

inexperienced adjective lacking experience of a situation or activity >**inexperience** noun

inexplicable adjective impossible to explain >**inexplicably** adverb

inextricably adverb without possibility of separation

infallible adjective never wrong >**infallibility** noun

infamous adjective well-known for something bad

infant noun very young child

infantry noun soldiers who fight on foot

infatuated adjective feeling such intense love or passion for someone that you cannot think sensibly about them >**infatuation** noun intense unreasoning passion

infect verb to give (someone or something) a disease

infection noun 1 disease caused by germs 2 being infected

infectious adjective 1 (of a disease) spreading without actual contact 2 spreading from person to person: *infectious enthusiasm*

infer infers inferring inferred verb to work (something) out from evidence >**inference** noun conclusion

● Do not use *infer* to mean the
● same as *imply*

inferior adjective 1 lower in quality, position or status ▷ noun

2 person of lower position or status >**inferiority** noun

infernal adjective 1 old-fashioned informal very irritating 2 relating to hell

inferno infernos noun intense raging fire

infertile adjective 1 (of soil) poor in quality and not good for growing plants 2 unable to produce children or young >**infertility** noun

infested adjective inhabited or overrun by a large number of animals or insects >**infestation** noun

infidelity infidelities noun being unfaithful to your husband, wife or partner

infighting noun quarrelling within a group

infiltrate verb to become part of (an organization) gradually and secretly with the aim of finding out information about its activities >**infiltration** noun >**infiltrator** noun

infinite adjective without any limit or end >**infinitely** adverb

infinitive noun Grammar form of a verb not showing tense, person or number, e.g. *to sleep*

infinity noun endless space, time or number

infirmary infirmaries noun hospital

inflamed adjective (of part of the body) red, swollen and painful because of infection

inflammable adjective easily set on fire

inflammation noun painful redness or swelling of part of the body

inflammatory adjective likely to

provoke anger

inflate verb to fill (something) with air or gas > **inflatable** adjective able to be inflated

inflation noun increase in prices and fall in the value of money > **inflationary** adjective

inflection or **inflexion** noun Grammar change in the form of a word according to function, tense, number, etc

inflexible adjective **1** unwilling to be persuaded, obstinate **2** (of a policy etc) firmly fixed, unalterable

inflict verb to impose (something unpleasant) on

influence noun **1** power of a person to have an effect over others **2** effect of a person or thing on another ▷ verb **3** to have an effect on

influential adjective having a lot of influence

influenza noun formal flu

influx noun arrival or entry of many people or things

inform verb **1** to tell (someone) of something **2** to give information to the police revealing the involvement of a particular person in a crime > **informant** noun person who gives information

informal adjective **1** relaxed and friendly **2** appropriate for everyday life or use > **informality** noun > **informally** adverb

information noun knowledge or facts

informative adjective giving useful information

informer noun person who gives information to the police revealing the involvement of a

particular person in a crime

infrastructure noun basic facilities, services and equipment needed for a country or organization to function properly

infringe verb **1** to break (a law or agreement) **2** to interfere with (people's rights), preventing them from using them > **infringement** noun

infuriate verb to make (someone) very angry > **infuriating** adjective

infuse verb **1** to fill (someone with an emotion or quality) **2** to leave (something) to soak in hot water so that the water absorbs its flavours, etc > **infusion** noun

ingenious adjective showing cleverness and originality > **ingeniously** adverb

ingenuity noun cleverness and originality at inventing things or working out plans

ingot noun oblong block of metal, especially gold

ingrained adjective firmly fixed

ingredient noun one of the things from which a dish or mixture is made

inhabit verb to live in

inhabitant noun person who lives in a place

inhale verb to breathe in (air, smoke, etc) > **inhalation** noun

inherent adjective forming an inseparable part of something > **inherently** adverb

inherit verb **1** to receive (money etc) from someone who has died **2** to receive (a characteristic) from an earlier generation > **inheritance** noun > **inheritor** noun

inhibit verb **1** to prevent

(someone) from doing something **2** to hinder or prevent (something) from happening

inhibited *adjective* finding it difficult to relax and show emotions

inhibition *noun* feeling of fear or embarrassment that stops you from behaving naturally

inhospitable *adjective* **1** difficult to live in; harsh **2** not welcoming or friendly

inhuman *adjective* **1** cruel or brutal **2** not human

inhumane *adjective* cruel or brutal > **inhumanity** *noun*

inimitable *adjective* impossible to imitate; unique

initial *adjective* **1** first or at the beginning ▷ *noun* **2** first letter, especially of a person's name > **initially** *adverb*

initiate *verb* **1** to begin or set (something) up **2** to admit (someone) into a closed group, especially by means of a special ceremony > **initiation** *noun* > **initiator** *noun*

initiative *noun* **1** attempt to get something done **2** first step, commencing move **3** ability to act independently

inject *verb* **1** to put (a substance) into someone's body with a syringe **2** to introduce (a new element) > **injection** *noun*: *I was given an injection*

injunction *noun* court order not to do something

injure *verb* to hurt (a person or animal)

injury injuries *noun* hurt or damage

injustice *noun* **1** lack of justice and fairness **2** unfair action **3** do

someone an injustice to criticize someone unfairly

ink *noun* coloured liquid used for writing or printing

inkling *noun* slight idea or suspicion

inlaid *adjective* decorated with small pieces of wood, metal or stone

inland *adjective* or *adverb* in or towards the interior of a country, away from the sea

in-laws *plural noun* the family of your husband or wife

inlet *noun* **1** narrow strip of water extending from the sea into the land **2** valve etc through which liquid or gas enters

inmate *noun* person living in an institution such as a prison

inn *noun* pub or small hotel, especially in the country

innards *plural noun informal* internal parts

innate *adjective* being part of someone's nature; inborn > **innately** *adverb*

inner *adjective* happening or located inside

innermost *adjective* deepest and most secret

innings *noun Sport* player's or side's turn of batting

innocent *adjective* **1** not guilty of a crime **2** without experience of evil **3** without malicious intent > **innocence** *noun* > **innocently** *adverb*

innocuous *adjective* not harmful

innovation *noun* **1** new idea or method **2** introduction of new ideas or methods > **innovative** *adjective* fresh and new

innuendo innuendos *or*

innuendoes noun indirect reference to something rude or unpleasant

innumerable adjective too many to be counted

input noun 1 resources put into a project etc 2 data fed into a computer

inquest noun official inquiry into a sudden death

inquire verb to seek information or ask (about) > **inquiring** adjective

inquisition noun thorough official investigation, often using harsh methods of questioning

inquisitive adjective curious and keen to find out about things > **inquisitively** adverb

inroads plural noun **make inroads into** to start affecting or reducing (something)

insane adjective 1 mentally ill 2 stupidly irresponsible > **insanely** adverb > **insanity** noun

insatiable adjective unable to be satisfied > **insatiably** adverb

inscribe verb 1 to write or carve (words) on something 2 to write on or carve (something) with words

inscription noun words written or carved on something

inscrutable adjective revealing nothing or giving nothing away

insect noun small animal with six legs and usually wings

insecticide noun substance for killing insects

insecure adjective 1 anxious, not confident 2 not safe or well-protected > **insecurity** noun

insensitive adjective unaware of or ignoring other people's feelings > **insensitivity** noun

insert verb to put (something)

inside or include (something) > **insertion** noun

inshore adjective 1 close to the shore ▷ adjective or adverb 2 towards the shore

inside preposition 1 in or into the interior of ▷ adjective 2 on or relating to the inside 3 by or from someone within an organization: *inside information* ▷ adverb 4 on, in or into the inside; indoors ▷ noun 5 inner side, surface or part 6 **inside out** with the inside facing outwards 7 **know something inside out** to know something thoroughly 8 *informal* **insides** stomach and bowels

- Do not use *of* after *inside*. You
- should write *she was waiting*
- *inside the school* and not *inside*
- *of the school*

insider noun member of a group who has privileged knowledge about it

insidious adjective dangerous and developing slowly without being noticed > **insidiously** adverb

insight noun deep understanding

insignia noun badge or emblem of a particular organization

insignificant adjective small and unimportant > **insignificance** noun

insincere adjective pretending to have certain feelings; not genuine > **insincerely** adverb > **insincerity** noun

insinuate verb 1 to suggest (something unpleasant) indirectly; hint at 2 to work (yourself) into a position gradually and cleverly > **insinuation** noun

insipid adjective lacking interest,

spirit or flavour

insist *verb* to demand or state firmly

insolent *adjective* rude and disrespectful >**insolence** *noun* >**insolently** *adverb*

insoluble *adjective* **1** impossible to solve **2** impossible to dissolve

insolvent *adjective* unable to pay your debts >**insolvency** *noun*

insomnia *noun* difficulty in sleeping >**insomniac** *noun* person who has difficulty in sleeping

inspect *verb* to check (someone or something) closely or officially >**inspection** *noun*

inspector *noun* **1** person who inspects **2** high-ranking police officer

inspire *verb* **1** to fill (someone) with enthusiasm; stimulate **2** to arouse (an emotion) >**inspiration** *noun* **1** creative influence or stimulus **2** brilliant idea >**inspired** *adjective* >**inspiring** *adjective*

instability *noun* lack of stability

install *verb* **1** to put in and prepare (equipment) for use **2** to place (a person) formally in a position or rank **3** to settle (yourself) in a place >**installation** *noun* **1** installing **2** equipment installed **3** place containing equipment for a particular purpose: *oil installations*

instalment *noun* one of a series of successive parts

instance *noun* **1** particular example **2 for instance** as an example

instant *noun* **1** very brief time **2** particular moment ▷ *adjective* **3** happening at once; immediate **4** (of foods) requiring little preparation >**instantly** *adverb*

instantaneous *adjective* happening at once >**instantaneously** *adverb*

instead *adverb* in place of something

instigate *verb* to cause (something) to happen >**instigation** *noun: The search was carried out at the instigation of the president* >**instigator** *noun*

instil instils instilling instilled *verb* to introduce (an idea etc) gradually into someone's mind

instinct *noun* natural tendency to behave in a certain way >**instinctive** *adjective* >**instinctively** *adverb*

institute *noun* **1** organization set up for a specific purpose, especially for research or teaching ▷ *verb* **2** *formal* to start or establish (a rule or system)

institution *noun* **1** long-established custom **2** large important organization such as a university or bank >**institutional** *adjective*

instruct *verb* **1** to tell (someone) to do something **2** to teach (someone) how to do something >**instruction** *noun* >**instructive** *adjective* informative or helpful >**instructor** *noun: a driving instructor*

instrument *noun* **1** tool or device used for a particular job **2** object, such as a piano or flute, played to make music **3** measuring device to show height, speed, etc

instrumental *adjective* **1** (followed by *in*) having an important role (in doing something) **2** (of music) played by or composed for musical instruments

insufficient *adjective* not enough

> **insufficiently** adverb

insular adjective not open to new ideas; narrow-minded > **insularity** noun

insulate verb 1 to cover (something) with a layer to keep it warm or to stop electricity passing through it 2 to protect (someone) from harmful things > **insulation** noun > **insulator** noun

insulin noun hormone produced in the pancreas that controls the amount of sugar in the blood

insult verb 1 to behave rudely to (someone); offend ▷ noun 2 rude remark or action which offends you > **insulting** adjective

insure verb 1 to protect (something or yourself) by paying for insurance 2 **insure against** to take action to prevent (something) from happening or to provide protection if it does happen

insurrection noun rebellion

intact adjective not changed or damaged in any way

intake noun amount or number of something taken in

integral adjective being an essential part of a whole

integrate verb 1 (of person) to become part of a group or community 2 to combine (things) so that they become part of a whole > **integration** noun

integrity noun 1 quality of being honest and following your principles 2 quality of being united

intellect noun ability to think and reason

intellectual adjective 1 involving thought, ideas and understanding 2 clever,

intelligent ▷ noun 3 person who enjoys thinking about complicated ideas > **intellectually** adverb

intelligence noun 1 quality of being able to understand and to learn things quickly and well 2 information about the aims and activities, especially military or terrorist ones, of an organization, government, etc 3 people or department collecting such information

intelligent adjective 1 able to understand, learn and think things out quickly 2 (of a computerized device) able to react to events > **intelligently** adverb

intelligentsia noun intellectual or cultured people in a society

intelligible adjective able to be understood > **intelligibility** noun

intend verb 1 to propose or plan (to do something) 2 **be intended to do something** to have something as your purpose or task

intense adjective 1 very great in strength or amount 2 deeply emotional > **intensely** adverb > **intensity** noun

intensify intensifies intensifying intensified verb to become or make (something) greater or stronger > **intensification** noun

intensive adjective using or needing a lot of energy or effort over a short time

intent noun 1 formal intention ▷ adjective 2 **intent on doing something** determined to do something > **intently** adverb

intention noun plan

intentional adjective done on purpose; deliberate

>**intentionally** adverb

inter- prefix between or among: international

interact verb to act, work or communicate together
>**interaction** noun

interactive adjective (of television, computer, game, etc) reacting to decisions taken by the viewer, user or player

intercept verb to seize or stop (someone or something) on their way somewhere

interchange noun act or process of exchanging things or ideas
>**interchangeable** adjective

intercom noun internal communication system resembling a telephone

intercourse noun (also **sexual intercourse**) act of having sex

interest noun 1 desire to know or hear more about something 2 something in which you are interested 3 (often plural) advantage or benefit 4 reason for wanting something to happen 5 sum paid for the use of borrowed money 6 (often plural) right or share ▷ verb 7 to attract the attention of (someone) because they want to know or hear more

interesting adjective of interest
>**interestingly** adverb

interface noun 1 area where two things interact or link 2 user interface presentation on screen of a computer program and how easy it is to operate

interfere verb 1 to try to influence other people's affairs when it is not really your business to do so 2 (followed by with) to clash

(with) or get in the way (of)
>**interference** noun >**interfering** adjective

interim adjective temporary or provisional

interior noun 1 inside 2 inland region ▷ adjective 3 inside or inner

interjection noun word or phrase spoken suddenly to express surprise, pain or anger

interlude noun short rest or break in an activity or event

intermediary intermediaries noun someone who tries to get two groups of people to come to an agreement

intermediate adjective occurring in the middle, between two other stages

interminable adjective seemingly endless because boring
>**interminably** adverb

intermission noun interval between parts of a play, film, etc

intermittent adjective occurring at intervals >**intermittently** adverb

internal adjective happening inside a person, place or object
>**internally** adverb

international adjective 1 of or involving two or more countries ▷ noun 2 game or match between teams of different countries
>**internationally** adverb

Internet or **internet** noun worldwide computer communication network

interplay noun the way two things react with one another

interpret verb 1 to explain the meaning of 2 to translate orally what someone says in one language into another language

for the benefit of others **3** to convey the meaning of (a poem, song, etc) in performance
> **interpretation** noun
> **interpreter** noun

interrogate verb to question (someone) closely
> **interrogation** noun
> **interrogator** noun

interrupt verb **1** to start talking while someone else is talking **2** to break into (a conversation etc) **3** to stop (a process or activity) temporarily (> **interruption** noun

intersect verb (of roads) to meet and cross > **intersection** noun

interspersed adjective scattered (among, between or on)

interval noun **1** time between two particular moments or events **2** break between parts of a play, concert, etc **3** difference in pitch between musical notes **4 at intervals a** repeatedly **b** with spaces left between

intervene verb to step in to a situation, especially to prevent conflict > **intervention** noun

intervening adjective (of time) in between

interview noun **1** formal discussion, especially between an employer and someone trying to get a job **2** questioning of a well-known person about his or her career, views, etc, by a reporter > verb **3** to conduct an interview with > **interviewee** noun someone interviewed > **interviewer** noun someone conducting an interview

intestine noun (often plural) tube that carries food from your stomach to your bowels, and in which the food is digested

intimate adjective **1** having a close personal relationship **2** personal or private **3** (of knowledge) extensive and detailed **4** having a quiet and friendly atmosphere > verb **5** to hint or suggest
> **intimacy** noun: the intimacy of the relationship between the players > **intimately** adverb > **intimation** noun: The first intimation that something could be amiss

intimidate verb to frighten (someone) deliberately with the aim of influencing their behaviour > **intimidated** adjective frightened > **intimidating** adjective frightening: I found it quite intimidating > **intimidation** noun

into preposition **1** indicating motion towards the inside of something: into the valley **2** indicating the result of change or division turned into a madman; cut into pieces **3** indicating destination: Their car crashed into a tree **4** informal interested in: Nowadays I'm really into healthy food

intolerable adjective more than can be endured > **intolerably** adverb

intonation noun the way that your voice rises and falls as you speak

intoxicated adjective **1** drunk **2** overexcited

intra- prefix within or inside: intra-European conflicts

intractable adjective formal stubborn and difficult to deal with

intransitive adjective (of a verb) not taking a direct object

intravenous adjective given into a vein > **intravenously** adverb

intrepid adjective fearless or bold

>**intrepidity** *noun* >**intrepidly** *adverb*

intricate *adjective* **1** involved or complicated **2** full of fine detail >**intricacy** *noun*: *the intricacy of the design* >**intricately** *adverb*

intrigue intrigues intriguing intrigued *verb* **1** to make (someone) interested or curious **2** to plot secretly ▷ *noun* **3** secret planning or plotting >**intriguing** *adjective*

intrinsic *adjective* essential to the basic nature of something >**intrinsically** *adverb*

introduce *verb* **1** to present (someone) by name (to another person) **2** to say a few explanatory words at the beginning of (a radio or television programme) **3** to make (someone) aware of or get them interested in something for the first time **4** to insert (something) >**introductory** *adjective*

introduction *noun* **1** act of presenting a person or thing for the first time **2** piece of writing at the beginning of a book, usually telling you what the book is about

introvert *noun* person concerned more with his or her thoughts and feelings than with the outside world >**introversion** *noun* >**introverted** *adjective*

intrude *verb* to come in or join in without being invited: *I don't want to intrude on your parents* >**intrusion** *noun* >**intrusive** *adjective*

intuition *noun* feeling you have about something that you cannot explain >**intuitive** *adjective* >**intuitively** *adverb*

Inuit *noun* **1** member of a group of people who live in Northern

Canada, Greenland, Alaska and Eastern Siberia, formerly known as Eskimos **2** language spoken by the Inuit people

inundated *adjective* **1** overwhelmed (with letters, requests, etc) **2** flooded

invade *verb* **1** to enter (a country) by force **2** to disturb (someone's privacy) >**invader** *noun*

invalid[1] *noun* disabled or chronically ill person >**invalidity** *noun*

invalid[2] *adjective* **1** (of an argument etc) not valid because based on a mistake **2** not acceptable legally >**invalidate** *verb* to make (something) invalid >**invalidity** *noun*

invaluable *adjective* extremely useful

invariably *adverb* almost always

invasion *noun* **1** entry by force; invading **2** intrusion: *an invasion of privacy*

invective *noun formal* abusive language used by someone who is angry

invent *verb* **1** to think up or create (something new) **2** to make up (a story, excuse, etc) >**invention** *noun* **1** something invented **2** ability to invent >**inventive** *adjective* creative and resourceful >**inventiveness** *noun* >**inventor** *noun*

inventory inventories *noun* detailed list of all the objects in a place

inverse *adjective* **1** reversed in effect, sequence, direction, etc ▷ *noun* **2** exact opposite >**inversely** *adverb*

invertebrate *noun technical* animal with no backbone

inverted *adjective* upside down or back to front

inverted commas *plural noun* the punctuation marks `" "` or `''`, used to show where speech begins and ends; quotation marks

invest *verb* 1 to pay (money) into a bank or buy shares with it in the expectation of receiving a profit 2 to spend (money, time, etc) on something in the hope of making it a success > **invest in** *verb* to buy > **investment** *noun* > **investor** *noun*

investigate *verb* to try to find out all the facts about (something) > **investigation** *noun* > **investigative** *adjective* > **investigator** *noun*

inveterate *adjective* firmly established in a habit or condition and unlikely to stop

invincible *adjective* impossible to defeat > **invincibility** *noun*

invisible *adjective* not able to be seen > **invisibility** *noun* > **invisibly** *adverb*

invite *verb* 1 to ask (someone) to an event 2 to ask (someone to do something) > **invitation** *noun* > **inviting** *adjective* tempting or attractive

invoice *noun* 1 bill for goods or services supplied ▷ *verb* 2 to present (someone) with a bill for goods or services supplied

invoke *verb* to use (a law) to justify something

involuntary *adjective* sudden and uncontrollable; unintentional > **involuntarily** *adverb*

involve *verb* 1 to include (someone or something) as a necessary part 2 to affect or

concern > **involvement** *noun*

inward *adjective* 1 directed towards the inside or middle 2 situated within 3 spiritual or mental ▷ *adverb* 4 (also **inwards**) towards the inside or middle > **inwardly** *adverb*

iodine *noun* Chemistry bluish-black substance used in medicine and photography

ion *noun* electrically charged atom

iota *noun* very small amount

IQ *abbreviation* intelligence quotient: level of intelligence shown by the results of a special test

ir- *prefix* not or the opposite of; the form of *in-* used before the letter r: *irrational*

Iranian *adjective* 1 belonging or relating to Iran ▷ *noun* 2 someone from Iran 3 main language spoken in Iran; Farsi

Iraqi *adjective* 1 belonging or relating to Iraq ▷ *noun* 2 someone from Iraq

irate *adjective* very angry

iris *irises* *noun* 1 round, coloured part of your eye 2 tall plant with purple, yellow or white flowers

Irish *adjective* 1 belonging or relating to the Irish Republic, or to the whole of Ireland ▷ *noun* 2 (also **Irish Gaelic**) language spoken in some parts of Ireland

Irishman Irishmen *noun* man from Ireland

irk *verb* to irritate or annoy > **irksome** *adjective* irritating or annoying

iron *noun* 1 hard dark metal used to make steel, and things like gates and fences. Small amounts of iron are found in blood 2 device that heats up in order to press clothes

3 metal-headed golf club **4 irons** chains or restraints ▷ adjective **5** made of iron **6** strong, inflexible: iron will ▷ verb **7** to smooth (clothes or fabric) with an iron > **ironing** noun clothes to be ironed > **iron out** verb to solve (difficulties)

Iron Age noun era about three thousand years ago when people first started to make tools out of iron

ironbark noun Australian eucalypt with a hard, rough bark

irony ironies noun **1** mildly sarcastic use of words to imply the opposite of what is said **2** aspect of a situation that is odd or amusing because it is the opposite of what you would expect

irrational adjective not based on or not using logical reasoning > **irrationality** noun > **irrationally** adverb

irregular adjective **1** not regular or even **2** not conforming to accepted practice **3** (of a word) not following the typical pattern of formation in a language > **irregularity** noun > **irregularly** adverb

irrelevant adjective not directly connected with the matter in hand > **irrelevance** noun > **irrelevantly** adverb

irrepressible adjective unfailingly lively and cheerful

irresistible adjective too attractive or strong to resist > **irresistibly** adverb

irrespective of preposition without taking account of

irresponsible adjective not giving enough thought or

taking enough care about the consequences of your actions or attitudes > **irresponsibility** noun > **irresponsibly** adverb

irrigate verb to supply (land) with water by artificial channels or pipes > **irrigation** noun

irritate verb **1** to annoy **2** to cause (a body part) to itch or become inflamed > **irritable** adjective easily annoyed > **irritably** adverb > **irritant** noun, adjective (person or thing) causing irritation > **irritation** noun

is verb third person singular present tense of **be**

-ish suffix used to form adjectives that mean 'fairly' or 'rather': smallish

Islam noun Muslim religion teaching that there is one God and that Mohammed is his prophet. The holy book of Islam is the Koran > **Islamic** adjective

island noun piece of land surrounded by water > **islander** noun person who lives on an island

isle noun literary island

-ism suffix **1** used to form nouns that refer to an action or condition: criticism; heroism **2** used to form nouns that refer to a political or economic system or a system of beliefs: Marxism; Sikhism **3** used to form nouns that refer to a type of prejudice: racism; sexism

isolate verb to set (someone) apart > **isolated** adjective > **isolation** noun

isosceles triangle noun triangle with two sides of equal length

ISP abbreviation Internet service provider

Israeli Israelis *adjective*
1 belonging or relating to Israel
▷ *noun* 2 someone from Israel

issue issues issuing issued
noun 1 important subject
that people are talking about
2 particular edition of a magazine
or newspaper 3 reason for
quarrelling ▷ *verb* 4 to make
(a statement etc) publicly 5 to
supply (someone) officially (with)
6 to produce and make available

-ist *suffix* 1 used to form nouns
and adjectives which refer to
someone who is involved in a
certain activity or who believes
in a certain system or religion:
chemist; *motorist*; *Buddhist* 2 used
to form nouns and adjectives
which refer to someone who has a
certain prejudice: *racist*

isthmus isthmuses *noun* narrow
strip of land with water on either
side connecting two areas of land

it *pronoun* 1 refers to any inanimate
object 2 refers to a baby or
animal whose sex is unknown
or unimportant 3 refers to
a thing mentioned or being
discussed 4 used as the subject of
impersonal verbs: *It's windy* > **it's**
1 it is 2 it has

Italian *adjective* 1 belonging
or relating to Italy ▷ *noun*
2 someone from Italy 3 main
language spoken in Italy

italic *adjective* (of printing type)
sloping to the right > **italics** *plural
noun* this type, used for emphasis

itch *verb* 1 to have an itch 2 **be
itching to do something** to
be impatient to do something
▷ *noun* 3 skin irritation causing a
desire to scratch > **itchy** *adjective*

item *noun* 1 single thing in a list

or collection 2 newspaper or
magazine article

itinerary itineraries *noun*
detailed plan of a journey

-itis *suffix* added to names of parts
of the body to refer to a condition
involving inflammation of that
part: *appendicitis*; *tonsillitis*

its *adjective, pronoun* belonging to it

itself *pronoun* 1 used as an object
of a verb or pronoun when the
thing that does an action is also
the thing directly affected by
it: *It switches itself off* 2 used for
emphasis: *The site itself forms a
large rectangle*

-ity *suffix* used to form nouns that
refer to a state or condition:
continuity; *technicality*

-ive *suffix* used to form adjectives
and some nouns: *massive*; *detective*

ivory *noun* 1 hard white bony
substance forming the tusks of
elephants ▷ *adjective* 2 yellowish-
white

ivy ivies *noun* evergreen climbing
plant

iwi *noun* NZ Maori tribe

-ize or **-ise** *suffix* used to form
verbs. Most verbs can be spelt
with either ending, though there
are some that can only be spelt
with '-ise', for example *advertise*,
improvise and *revise*

j

jab jabs jabbing jabbed *verb* 1 to
poke (something) sharply ▷ *noun*

2 quick punch or poke **3** *informal* injection

jabiru *noun* white and green Australian stork with red legs

jack *noun* **1** device for raising a motor vehicle or other heavy object **2** playing card with a picture of a pageboy, whose value is between a ten and a queen **3** *Bowls* small white bowl aimed at by the players **4** socket in electrical equipment into which a plug fits >**jack up** *verb* **1** to raise (a motor vehicle) with a jack **2** to increase (prices or salaries) **3** *NZ informal* to organize by dishonest means

jackal *noun* doglike wild animal of Africa and Asia

jackaroo jackaroos *noun Aust* trainee on a sheep or cattle station

jackdaw *noun* bird like a small crow with black and grey feathers

jacket *noun* **1** short coat **2** skin of a baked potato **3** outer paper cover on a hardback book

jackpot *noun* **1** largest prize that may be won in a gambling game **2** **hit the jackpot** *informal* to be very successful through luck

jade *noun* **1** hard green stone used for making jewellery and ornaments ▷ *adjective* **2** bluish-green

jagged *adjective* having an uneven edge with sharp points

jaguar *noun* large member of the cat family, with spots on its back

jail or **gaol** *noun* **1** prison ▷ *verb* **2** to send to prison >**jailer** *noun* person who is in charge of the prisoners in a jail

jam jams jamming jammed *verb* **1** to pack tightly into a place **2** to

crowd or congest **3** to make or become stuck **4** *Radio* to block (a radio signal) and prevent it from being heard properly **5** **jam on the brakes** to apply the brakes fiercely ▷ *noun* **6** hold-up of traffic **7** *informal* awkward situation **8** food made from fruit boiled with sugar

Jamaican *adjective* **1** belonging or relating to Jamaica ▷ *noun* **2** someone from Jamaica

jamboree *noun* large gathering of people enjoying themselves

Jandal® *noun NZ* sandal with a strap between the big toe and other toes and over the foot

jangle *verb* **1** to (cause to) make a harsh ringing noise **2** (of nerves) to be upset or irritated

janitor *noun* caretaker of a school or other building

January *noun* first month of the year

Japanese *adjective* **1** belonging or relating to Japan ▷ *noun* **2** someone from Japan **3** main language spoken in Japan

jar jars jarring jarred *noun* **1** wide-mouthed container, usually round and made of glass ▷ *verb* **2** to have a disturbing or unpleasant effect **3** to jolt or bump ▷ *noun* **4** to jolt or shock

jargon *noun* words that are used in special or technical ways by particular groups of people, often making the language difficult to understand

jarrah *noun* Australian eucalypt tree that produces valuable timber

jasmine *noun* climbing plant with sweet-smelling yellow or white flowers

jaundice *noun* disease affecting

the liver, causing yellowness of the skin

jaundiced *adjective* (of an attitude or opinion) bitter or cynical

jaunt *noun* short journey for pleasure

jaunty jauntier jauntiest *adjective* expressing cheerfulness and self-confidence: *a jaunty tune* > **jauntily** *adverb*

javelin *noun* light spear thrown in sports competitions

jaw *noun* **1** one of the bones in which the teeth are set **2 jaws a** mouth **b** gripping part of a tool

jay *noun* bird with a pinkish body and blue-and-black wings

jazz *noun* kind of music with an exciting rhythm, usually involving improvisation > **jazz up** *verb informal* to make (something) more lively or colourful

jazzy jazzier jazziest *adjective informal* flashy or showy

jealous *adjective* **1** fearful of losing a partner or possession to a rival **2** envious **3** suspiciously watchful > **jealously** *adverb* > **jealousy** *noun* feeling of anger or bitterness caused by desire for another's possessions or abilities

jeans *plural noun* casual denim trousers

jeep® *noun* four-wheel-drive motor vehicle

jeer *verb* **1** (followed by *at*) to insult (someone) in a loud, unpleasant way ▷ *noun* **2** rude or insulting remark > **jeering** *adjective*

Jehovah *noun* name of God in the Old Testament

jelly jellies *noun* **1** soft food made of liquid set with gelatine **2** jam made from fruit juice and sugar

jellyfish *noun* small jelly-like sea animal with tentacles which may sting

● The plural of *jellyfish* is *jellyfish*

jeopardize *verb* to place (something) in danger

jeopardy *noun* danger: *Setbacks have put the whole project in jeopardy*

jerk *verb* **1** to move suddenly and sharply ▷ *noun* **2** sudden sharp movement **3** *informal* stupid or ignorant person

jerkin *noun* short sleeveless jacket

jersey *noun* **1** knitted jumper **2** machine-knitted fabric **3 Jersey** breed of dairy cow that produces very rich milk

jest *verb* **1** to speak jokingly ▷ *noun* **2** joke

jester *noun History* professional clown at a royal court

jet jets jetting jetted *verb* **1** to fly by jet aircraft ▷ *noun* **2** aircraft driven by jet propulsion **3** stream of liquid or gas, especially one forced from a small hole **4** nozzle from which gas or liquid is forced **5** hard black mineral

jet boat *noun* motorboat propelled by a jet of water

jet lag *noun* tiredness and confusion felt by people after a long flight across different time zones

jettison *verb* **1** to abandon (something) **2** to throw (something) overboard

jetty jetties *noun* wooden platform at the edge of the sea or a river, where boats can be moored

Jew *noun* **1** person whose religion is Judaism **2** descendant of the ancient Hebrews > **Jewish** *adjective*

jewel *noun* **1** precious stone

2 special person or thing
>**jewelled** adjective

jeweller noun person who makes
jewellery or who sells and repairs
jewellery and watches

jewellery noun ornaments that
people wear, made of valuable
metals and sometimes decorated
with precious stones

jib jibs jibbing jibbed noun
1 triangular sail set in front of a
mast **2** projecting arm of a crane
or derrick ▷ **jib at** verb to object to
(a proposal etc)

jibe noun **1** an insulting remark
▷ verb **2** to make insulting or
taunting remarks

jig jigs jigging jigged noun **1** type
of lively folk dance; also the music
that accompanies it ▷ verb **2** to
dance or jump around in a lively
bouncy manner

jiggle verb to move up and down
with short jerky movements

jigsaw noun **1** (also **jigsaw puzzle**)
picture cut into interlocking
pieces, which the user tries to fit
together again **2** mechanical saw
for cutting along curved lines

jihad verb Islamic holy war
against those who reject the
teachings of Islam

jilt verb to leave or reject (one's
lover) >**jilted** adjective

jingle noun **1** catchy verse or song
used in a radio or television
advert **2** gentle ringing sound
▷ verb **3** to make a gentle ringing
sound

jinks plural noun **high jinks** noisy
and mischievous behaviour

jinx noun person or thing that is
thought to bring bad luck

jinxed adjective considered to be

unlucky

jitters plural noun informal **the
jitters** worried nervousness: I had
the jitters during my speech >**jittery**
adjective nervous

job noun **1** occupation or paid
employment **2** task to be done
3 informal difficult task **4** Brit,
Aust, NZ informal crime, especially
robbery **5 just the job** exactly
right or exactly what is required

job centre noun government
office where people can find out
about job vacancies

jobless adjective without any work

jockey noun **1** (professional) rider
of racehorses ▷ verb **2 jockey for
position** to manoeuvre in order to
obtain an advantage

jocular adjective intended to make
people laugh: a jocular remark
>**jocularly** adverb

jodhpurs plural noun riding
trousers, loose-fitting above the
knee but tight below

joey noun Aust young kangaroo

jog jogs jogging jogged verb **1** to
run at a gentle pace, often as
a form of exercise **2** to nudge
(something) slightly **3 jog
someone's memory** to remind
someone of something ▷ noun
4 slow run >**jogger** noun person
who jogs for exercise >**jogging**
noun activity of running at a
gentle pace for exercise

join verb **1** to become a member
(of) **2** to come into someone's
company **3** to take part (in) **4** to
come or bring together ▷ noun
5 place where two things are
joined >**join up** verb to enlist in
the armed services

joiner noun person who makes

wooden furniture, doors and window frames

joinery noun work done by a joiner

joint adjective **1** shared by two or more ▷ noun **2** place where bones meet but can move **3** junction of two or more parts or objects **4** piece of meat for roasting **5** informal house or place, especially a disreputable bar or nightclub **6** informal marijuana cigarette **7** out of joint a disorganized **b** (of a bone) knocked out of its normal position ▷ verb **8** to divide meat into joints ▷ jointed adjective **1** having joints that move **2** (of a large piece of meat) cut into pieces and ready to cook ▷ jointly adverb

joist noun horizontal beam that helps support a floor or ceiling

joke noun **1** thing said or done to cause laughter **2** ridiculous person or thing that is not worthy of respect: The decision was a joke ▷ verb **3** to make jokes ▷ jokingly adverb

joker noun **1** person who jokes **2** extra card in a pack of cards, counted as any other in some games

jolly jollier jolliest; jollies jollying jollied adjective **1** (of a person) happy and cheerful **2** (of an occasion) merry and festive ▷ verb **3** jolly along to try to keep (someone) cheerful by flattery or coaxing ▷ adverb **4** informal very: I'm going to have a jolly good try

jolt noun **1** unpleasant surprise or shock **2** sudden jerk or bump ▷ verb **3** to surprise or shock **4** to bump against (someone or something) with a sudden violent movement

jostle verb to knock or push against roughly

jot jots jotting jotted verb **1** (followed by down) to write a brief note of ▷ noun **2** very small amount ▷ jottings plural noun notes jotted down

jotter noun notebook

joule noun Physics unit of work or energy

journal noun **1** magazine that deals with a particular subject, trade or profession **2** diary which someone keeps regularly

journalism noun work of collecting, writing and publishing news in newspapers, magazines and on television and radio ▷ **journalist** noun person whose job is writing for newspapers and magazines ▷ **journalistic** adjective

journey noun **1** act or process of travelling from one place to another ▷ verb **2** to travel: He intended to journey up the Amazon

joust History noun **1** competition in medieval times between knights fighting on horseback, using lances ▷ verb **2** to fight on horseback using lances

jovial adjective happy and cheerful ▷ **joviality** noun cheerful friendliness ▷ **jovially** adverb

joy noun **1** feeling of great delight or pleasure **2** something or someone that causes happiness **3** informal success or luck: Any joy with your insurance claim?

joyful adjective **1** causing pleasure and happiness **2** extremely happy ▷ **joyfully** adverb

joyous adjective formal extremely happy and enthusiastic ▷ **joyously** adverb

joyride noun drive in a stolen car for pleasure >**joyrider** noun >**joyriding** noun

joystick noun control device for an aircraft or computer

jube noun Aust, NZ informal a fruit-flavoured jelly sweet

jubilant adjective feeling or expressing great joy or triumph >**jubilantly** adverb

jubilation noun feeling of great happiness or triumph

jubilee noun special anniversary, especially 25th (**silver jubilee**) or 50th (**golden jubilee**)

Judaism noun religion of the Jews, based on the Old Testament and the Talmud >**Judaic** adjective

judder verb 1 to shake and vibrate noisily and violently ▷ noun 2 violent vibration

judder bar noun NZ raised strip across a road designed to slow down vehicles

judge noun 1 public official who tries cases and passes sentence in a court of law 2 person who decides the outcome of a contest ▷ verb 3 to act as a judge 4 to form an opinion about (someone or something) 5 to decide the result of (a competition)

judgment or **judgement** noun 1 opinion reached after careful thought 2 verdict of a judge 3 ability to make sensible decisions or achieve a balanced viewpoint

judicial adjective relating to the legal system: an independent judicial inquiry >**judicially** adverb

judiciary noun judiciaries branch of government concerned with justice and the legal system

judicious adjective well-judged and sensible >**judiciously** adverb

judo noun sport, originating from Japan, in which two opponents try to force each other to the ground using special throwing techniques

jug noun container for liquids, with a handle and small spout

juggernaut noun Brit large heavy truck

juggle verb 1 to throw and catch (several objects) so that most are in the air at the same time 2 to keep (several activities) in progress at the same time >**juggler** noun person who juggles in order to entertain people

jugular or **jugular vein** noun one of three large veins of the neck that return blood from the head to the heart

juice noun 1 liquid part of vegetables, fruit or meat 2 **juices** fluids in the body: gastric juices

juicy juicier juiciest adjective 1 full of juice 2 interesting, exciting or scandalous: juicy gossip >**juiciness** noun

jukebox noun coin-operated machine found in cafés and pubs, on which CDs or videos can be played

July noun seventh month of the year

jumble noun 1 untidy muddle of things 2 articles for a jumble sale ▷ verb 3 (followed by up) to mix (things) untidily

jumble sale noun event at which cheap second-hand items are sold to raise money, often for a charity

jumbo jumbos adjective 1 informal very large: jumbo packs of elastic bands ▷ noun 2 (also **jumbo jet**) large jet airliner

jumbuck noun Aust old-fashioned sheep

jump verb 1 to leap or spring into the air using the leg muscles 2 to move quickly and suddenly 3 to make a sudden sharp movement of surprise 4 to increase suddenly: The number of crimes jumped by 10% last year 5 **jump the gun** to do something before the proper or right time 6 **jump the queue** not to wait your turn ▷ noun 7 act of jumping 8 sudden rise 9 break in continuity > **jump at** verb to accept (a chance etc) gladly > **jump on** verb to criticize (someone) suddenly and forcefully

jumper noun sweater or pullover

jumpy jumpier jumpiest adjective nervous and worried

junction noun place where routes, railway lines or roads meet

June noun sixth month of the year

jungle noun 1 tropical forest of dense tangled vegetation 2 confusion or mess: a jungle of complex rules

junior adjective 1 holding a low-ranking position in an organization 2 younger 3 relating to childhood: a junior school ▷ noun 4 person who holds an unimportant position in an organization

juniper noun evergreen shrub with purple berries used in cooking and medicine

junk noun 1 discarded or useless objects 2 rubbish 3 flat-bottomed Chinese sailing boat

junk food noun food of low nutritional value

junkie noun informal drug addict

Jupiter noun largest planet in the solar system and fifth from the sun

jurisdiction noun formal 1 right or power to apply laws and make legal judgments: The Court did not have the jurisdiction to examine the case 2 power or authority: The airport was under French jurisdiction

juror noun member of a jury

jury juries noun group of people in a court of law who have been chosen to listen to the facts of a case on trial, and to decide whether the accused person is guilty or not

just adverb 1 very recently 2 at this instant 3 merely, only 4 exactly 5 barely: They only just won 6 really 7 **just now** S Afr in a little while ▷ adjective 8 fair or impartial in action or judgment 9 proper or right > **justly** adverb > **justness** noun

justice noun 1 fairness and reasonableness: There is no justice in this world! 2 administration of law in a country 3 judge or magistrate

justify justifies justifying justified verb 1 to prove (a decision, action or idea) to be reasonable or necessary: This decision was fully justified by economic conditions 2 to adjust (text) so that the margins are straight > **justifiable** adjective acceptable or reasonable > **justifiably** adverb > **justification** noun acceptable or reasonable explanation for something

jut juts jutting jutted verb to stick out beyond or above a surface or edge

jute noun strong fibre made from the bark of an Asian plant, used to make rope and sacking

juvenile adjective 1 young 2 of

or suitable for young people **3** immature and rather silly ▷ *noun* **4** young person or child

juxtapose *verb* to put (things or ideas) close together in order to emphasize the differences > **juxtaposition** *noun*

k

kaleidoscope *noun* tube-shaped toy containing loose coloured pieces reflected by mirrors so that changing patterns form when the tube is twisted > **kaleidoscopic** *adjective* colourful and constantly changing

kamikaze *noun* **1** (in World War II) Japanese pilot who performed a suicide mission ▷ *adjective* **2** (of an action) undertaken in the knowledge that it will kill or injure the person performing it

kangaroo kangaroos *noun* Australian animal which moves by jumping with its powerful hind legs

karate *noun* Japanese system of unarmed combat using blows with the feet, hands, elbows and legs

karma *noun* Buddhism, Hinduism person's actions affecting his or her fate in future lives

Karoo Karoos; also spelt **Karroo** *noun* S Afr area of very dry land

karri karris *noun* **1** Australian eucalypt **2** its wood, used for building

kauri kauri or **kauris** *noun* NZ large New Zealand tree that produces

wood used for building and making furniture

kayak *noun* **1** Inuit canoe made of sealskins stretched over a frame **2** fibreglass or canvas-covered canoe of this design

kea keas *noun* NZ **1** large greenish New Zealand parrot **2 the Keas** youngest members of the Scouts

kebab *noun* **1** dish of small pieces of meat grilled on skewers **2** (also **doner kebab**) grilled minced lamb served in a split slice of unleavened bread

keel *noun* main lengthways timber or steel support along the base of a ship > **keel over** *verb* **1** to turn upside down **2** *informal* to collapse suddenly

keen *adjective* **1** eager or enthusiastic **2** intense or strong **3** intellectually acute **4** (of the senses) capable of recognizing small distinctions **5** sharp > **keenly** *adverb* > **keenness** *noun*: *keenness to please*

keep keeps keeping kept *verb* **1** to have or retain possession of (something or someone) **2** to store (something) **3** to stay or cause (something or someone) to stay in, on or at a place or position **4** to continue or persist **5** to detain (someone) **6** to look after or provide for (something or someone) ▷ *noun* **7** cost of food and everyday expenses > **keep up** *verb* to maintain (something) at the current level > **keep up with** *verb* to move at a pace set by (someone)

keeper *noun* **1** person who looks after animals in a zoo **2** person in charge of a museum or collection **3** short for **goalkeeper**

keeping noun 1 care or charge 2 in, out of keeping with appropriate or inappropriate for

keepsake noun gift treasured for the sake of the giver

keg noun small metal beer barrel

kelpie noun Australian sheepdog with a smooth coat and upright ears

kennel noun 1 hutlike shelter for a dog 2 kennels place for breeding, boarding or training dogs

Kenyan adjective 1 belonging or relating to Kenya ▷ noun 2 someone from Kenya

kerb noun edging to a pavement

kernel noun 1 seed of a nut, cereal or fruit; stone 2 central and essential part of something

kerosene noun US, Canadian, Aust, NZ liquid mixture distilled from petroleum and used as a fuel or solvent

kestrel noun type of small falcon

ketchup noun thick cold sauce, usually made of tomatoes

kettle noun container with a spout and handle used for boiling water

key noun 1 device for locking and unlocking a lock by moving a bolt 2 device turned to wind a clock, operate a machine, etc 3 any of a set of levers or buttons pressed to use a typewriter, computer or musical keyboard instrument 4 Music set of related notes 5 something crucial in providing an explanation or interpretation 6 means of achieving a desired end 7 list of explanations of codes, symbols, etc ▷ adjective 8 of great importance ▷ verb 9 (also key in) to type in (text) using a keyboard

keyboard noun 1 set of keys on a piano, computer, etc 2 musical instrument played using a keyboard

Key Stage noun in England and Wales, one of the four age-group divisions to which each level of the National Curriculum applies (5–7; 7–11; 11–14; 14v16)

kg symbol kilogram(s)

khaki adjective 1 dull yellowish-brown ▷ noun 2 hard-wearing fabric of this colour used for military uniforms

khanda noun sword used by Sikhs in the Amrit ceremony

kia ora interjection NZ Maori greeting

kibbutz kibbutzim noun farm or factory in Israel where the workers live together and share everything

kick verb 1 to drive, push or strike (something or someone) with the foot 2 (of a gun) to recoil when fired 3 (followed by against) informal to object (to something) or resist (something) 4 informal to free yourself of (an addiction) 5 Rugby to score (a goal) with a kick ▷ noun 6 thrust or blow with the foot 7 recoil of a gun when fired 8 informal excitement or thrill ▷ kick off verb 1 to start a game of soccer 2 informal to begin ▷ kick up verb informal to create (a fuss)

kid kids kidding kidded noun 1 informal child 2 young goat 3 leather made from the skin of a young goat ▷ verb 4 informal to tease or deceive (someone)

kidnap kidnaps kidnapping kidnapped verb to take (someone) away by force and hold (him or her) to ransom

> **kidnapper** noun person who kidnaps someone > **kidnapping** noun

kidney noun **1** either of the pair of organs that remove waste products from the blood **2** animal kidney used as food

kill verb **1** to cause the death of (a person or an animal) **2** informal to cause (someone) pain or discomfort **3** to put an end to (a conversation or an activity) **4** to pass (time) > noun **5** act of killing **6** animals or birds killed in a hunt > **killer** noun person who kills someone > **killing** informal adjective **1** very tiring **2** very funny > noun **3** sudden financial success

kiln noun oven for baking or drying pottery, bricks, etc

kilo kilos noun short for **kilogram**

kilogram or **kilogramme** noun one thousand grams

kilohertz noun one thousand hertz

● The plural of kilohertz is kilohertz

kilometre noun one thousand metres

kilowatt noun Electricity one thousand watts

kilt noun knee-length pleated tartan skirt worn originally by Scottish Highlanders

kimono kimonos noun loose wide-sleeved Japanese robe, fastened with a sash

kin or **kinsfolk** plural noun person's relatives collectively

kind adjective **1** considerate, friendly and helpful > noun **2** class or group with common characteristics **3** essential nature or character **4** in kind a (of payment) in goods rather than money **b** with something similar **5** kind of to a certain extent > **kindness** noun: we have been treated with such kindness

kindergarten noun class or school for children under six years old

kindle verb **1** to set (a fire) alight **2** (of a fire) to start to burn **3** to arouse (a feeling) or (of a feeling) to be aroused

kindling noun dry wood or straw for starting fires

kindred adjective **1** having similar qualities **2** related by blood or marriage > noun **3** same as **kin**

kinetic energy noun energy produced when something moves

king noun **1** male ruler of a monarchy **2** ruler or chief **3** best or most important of its kind **4** piece in chess that must be defended **5** playing card with a picture of a king on it

kingdom noun **1** country ruled by a king or queen **2** division of the natural world

kingfisher noun small bird, often with a bright-coloured plumage, that dives for fish

king-size or **king-sized** adjective larger than standard size

kink noun **1** twist or bend in rope, wire, hair, etc **2** informal quirk in someone's personality

kinky kinkier kinkiest adjective **1** informal having peculiar sexual tastes **2** full of kinks

kinship noun family relationship to other people

kiosk noun **1** small booth selling drinks, cigarettes, newspapers, etc **2** public telephone box

kip kips kipping kipped informal verb **1** to sleep > noun **2** sleep

kipper noun cleaned, salted and smoked herring

kirk noun Scot church

kiss verb 1 to touch (someone) with the lips in affection or greeting 2 to join lips with (someone) in love or desire ▷ noun 3 touch with the lips

kiss of life noun method of reviving someone by blowing air into his or her lungs

kit kits kitting kitted noun 1 outfit or equipment for a specific purpose 2 set of pieces of equipment sold ready to be put together 3 NZ flax basket > **kit out** verb to provide (someone) with clothes or equipment needed for a particular activity

kitchen noun room used for cooking

kite noun 1 light frame covered with a thin material flown on a string in the wind 2 large hawk with a forked tail

kitset noun NZ set of parts for putting together to make a house or a piece of furniture

kitten noun young cat

kitty kitties noun 1 fund of money given by a group of people to pay for things together 2 total amount bet in certain gambling games

kiwi kiwi or kiwis noun 1 New Zealand bird with a long beak and no tail, which cannot fly 2 informal New Zealander

kiwi fruit noun edible fruit with a fuzzy brownish skin and green flesh

km symbol kilometre(s)

knack noun 1 skilful way of doing something 2 innate ability

knead verb 1 to work (dough) into a smooth mixture with the hands 2 to squeeze or press (something) with the hands

knee noun 1 joint between thigh and lower leg 2 lap 3 part of a garment covering the knee ▷ verb 4 to strike or push (someone) with the knee

kneecap kneecaps kneecapping kneecapped noun 1 bone in front of the knee ▷ verb 2 to shoot (someone) in the kneecap

kneel kneels kneeling knelt verb to fall or rest on one's knees

knell noun 1 sound of a bell, especially at a funeral or death 2 sign of something bad about to happen

knickers plural noun woman's or girl's undergarment covering the lower trunk and having holes for the legs; pants

knick-knack noun small ornament

knife knives; knifes knifing knifed noun 1 cutting tool or weapon consisting of a sharp-edged blade with a handle ▷ verb 2 to cut (something) or stab (someone) with a knife

knight noun 1 man who has been given a knighthood 2 History man who served a monarch or lord as a mounted soldier 3 chess piece shaped like a horse's head ▷ verb 4 to award a knighthood to (a man) > **knighthood** noun honorary title given to a man by the British sovereign

knit knits knitting knitted verb 1 to make (a garment) by working lengths of wool together using needles or a machine 2 to join closely together 3 to draw (one's eyebrows) together > **knitting** noun 1 garment being knitted

2 the activity of knitting

knob noun **1** rounded switch on a machine such as a radio **2** rounded handle on a door or drawer **3** small amount (of butter)

knock verb **1** to give a blow or push to (someone or something) **2** to tap on (something) with the knuckles **3** to make or drive (someone or something) into a certain position by striking **4** informal to criticize (someone) **5** (of an engine) to make a regular banging noise as a result of a fault ▷ noun **6** blow or rap **7** knocking sound >**knock about** or **around** verb **1** to wander or spend time aimlessly **2** to hit or kick (someone) brutally >**knock back** verb informal **1** to drink (a drink) quickly **2** to cost (someone) a certain amount **3** to reject or refuse (someone) >**knock down** verb **1** to demolish (a building) **2** to reduce (a price) >**knock off** verb **1** informal to cease work **2** informal to make or do (something) hurriedly or easily **3** to take (a specified amount) off a price **4** Brit, Aust, NZ informal to steal (something) >**knock out** verb **1** to hit (someone) so hard that he or she becomes unconscious **2** informal to overwhelm or amaze (someone) **3** to defeat (a competitor) in a knockout competition >**knock up** verb **1** informal to put (something) together quickly **2** informal to waken (someone)

knocker noun metal fitting for knocking on a door

knockout noun **1** blow so hard that it makes an opponent unconscious **2** competition

in which competitors are eliminated in each round until only the winner is left **3** informal extremely attractive person or thing

knoll noun small rounded hill

knot knots knotting knotted noun **1** fastening made by looping and pulling tight strands of string, cord or rope **2** tangle (of hair) **3** small cluster or huddled group (of people) **4** round lump or spot in timber **5** feeling of tightness in the stomach, caused by tension or nervousness **6** unit of speed used by ships, equal to one nautical mile (1.85 kilometres) per hour ▷ verb **7** to tie (something) with or into a knot

know knows knowing knew known verb **1** to be or feel certain of the truth of (information etc) **2** to be acquainted with (a person or place) **3** to have a grasp of or understand (a skill or language) **4** to be aware of (a fact) ▷ noun **5** in the know informal informed or aware of something few people know about

know-how noun informal ability to do something difficult or technical

knowing adjective suggesting secret knowledge >**knowingly** adverb **1** deliberately **2** in a way that suggests secret knowledge

knowledge noun **1** facts or experiences known by a person **2** state of knowing **3** specific information on a subject

knowledgeable or **knowledgable** adjective intelligent or well-informed

knuckle noun **1** bone at the finger joint **2** knee joint of a calf or pig **3** near the knuckle informal rather rude or offensive > **knuckle under** verb to yield or give in

koala noun Australian animal with grey fur that lives in trees

kohanga reo or **kohanga** noun NZ infant class where children are taught in Maori
- The plural of kohanga reo is
- kohanga reo

kookaburra noun large Australian kingfisher with a cackling cry

kopje or **koppie** noun SAfr small hill

Koran noun sacred book of Islam

Korean adjective **1** relating or belonging to Korea ▷ noun **2** someone from Korea **3** main language spoken in Korea

kosher adjective **1** (of food) prepared according to Jewish law **2** informal correct or genuine ▷ noun **3** kosher food

kowhai kowhais noun small New Zealand tree with clusters of yellow flowers

kraal noun S African village surrounded by a strong fence

kudu noun SAfr large African antelope with curled horns

kung fu noun Chinese martial art combining hand, foot and weapon techniques

kura kaupapa Maori noun NZ primary school where the teaching is done in Maori

Kurd noun member of a group of people who live mainly in eastern Turkey, northern Iraq and western Iran

Kurdish adjective **1** belonging or relating to the Kurds ▷ noun **2** language spoken by the Kurds

l symbol litre

lab noun informal short for laboratory

label labels labelling labelled noun **1** piece of paper or plastic attached to something as an identification ▷ verb **2** to put a label on (something)

laboratory laboratories noun building or room designed for scientific research or for the teaching of practical science

laborious adjective involving great prolonged effort > **laboriously** adverb

Labor Party noun Aust main left-wing political party in Australia

labour or **labor** (US & Aust) noun **1** physical work or exertion **2** workers in industry **3** final stage of pregnancy, leading to childbirth ▷ verb **4** old-fashioned to work hard > **labourer** noun person who labours, especially someone doing manual work for wages

labrador noun large retriever dog with a usually gold or black coat

labyrinth noun complicated network of passages

lace noun **1** delicate decorative fabric made from threads woven into an open weblike pattern **2** cord drawn through eyelets and tied ▷ verb **3** to fasten (shoes) with laces **4** to add a small amount of alcohol, a drug, etc to (food or drink) > **lacy** adjective fine, like lace

lack noun 1 shortage or absence of something needed or wanted ▷ verb 2 not to be present when or where needed 3 to need or be short of (something)

lacklustre adjective lacking brilliance or vitality

laconic adjective using only a few words

lacquer noun hard varnish for wood or metal

lacrosse noun sport in which teams catch and throw a ball using long sticks with a net at the end, in an attempt to score goals

lad noun boy or young man

ladder noun 1 frame of two poles connected by horizontal steps used for climbing 2 line of stitches that have come undone in tights or stockings ▷ verb 3 to have such a line of undone stitches in (one's tights or stockings)

laden adjective (often followed by with) carrying a lot (of something): I came home laden with cardboard boxes

ladle noun 1 spoon with a long handle and a large bowl, used for serving soup etc ▷ verb 2 to serve out (soup etc)

lady ladies noun 1 woman regarded as having characteristics of good breeding or high rank 2 polite term of address for a woman 3 Lady title of some female members of the British nobility

ladybird noun small red flying beetle with black spots

lady-in-waiting ladies-in-waiting noun female servant of a queen or princess

ladylike adjective polite and dignified

Ladyship noun Your Ladyship term of address for a woman with the title Lady

lag lags lagging lagged verb to wrap (a boiler, pipes, etc) with insulating material > **lag behind** verb to make slower progress than other people

lager noun light-coloured beer

lagoon noun area of water cut off from the open sea by coral reefs or sand bars

laid verb past of **lay**

lain verb past participle of **lie²**

lair noun resting place of a wild animal

laird noun landowner in Scotland

lake noun area of fresh water surrounded by land

lama noun Buddhist priest or monk

lamb noun 1 young sheep 2 its meat

lame adjective 1 having an injured or disabled leg or foot 2 (of an excuse) unconvincing; feeble > **lamely** adverb in an unconvincing manner > **lameness** noun state of being lame

lament verb 1 to feel or express sorrow for (something) ▷ noun 2 passionate expression of grief 3 song or poem expressing grief at someone's death

lamentable adjective very disappointing

laminated adjective consisting of several thin sheets or layers stuck together: laminated glass

lamp noun device that produces light from electricity, oil or gas

lamppost noun post supporting a lamp in the street

lampshade noun decorative

covering over an electric light bulb that prevents the bulb giving out too harsh a light

lance noun **1** long spear used by a mounted soldier ▷ verb **2** to pierce (a boil or abscess) with a sharp instrument

land noun **1** solid part of the earth's surface **2** ground, especially with reference to its type or use **3** country or region ▷ verb **4** to come to earth after a flight, jump or fall **5** informal to succeed in getting (something) **6** to catch (a fish) **7** (followed by with) to cause (someone) to have to deal with something unpleasant

landing noun **1** floor area at the top of a flight of stairs **2** bringing or coming to land

landlady landladies noun woman who owns a house or small hotel and who lets rooms to people

landlord noun man who owns a house or small hotel and who lets rooms to people

landmark noun **1** prominent feature of a landscape **2** event, decision, etc considered as an important development

landowner noun person who owns land, especially a large area of the countryside

landscape noun **1** extensive piece of inland scenery seen from one place **2** picture of it

landslide noun **1** (also **landslip**) falling of soil, rock, etc down the side of a mountain **2** overwhelming electoral victory

lane noun **1** narrow road, especially in the country **2** one of the strips on a road marked with lines to guide drivers

language noun **1** system of sounds, symbols, etc for communicating thought **2** particular system used by a nation or people **3** style in which a person expresses himself or herself: *his language is often obscure*

languid adjective lacking energy or enthusiasm >**languidly** adverb

languish verb to suffer neglect or hardship

lanky lankier lankiest adjective ungracefully tall and thin

lantana noun Aust shrub with orange or yellow flowers, considered a weed in Australia

lantern noun light in a transparent protective case

lap laps lapping lapped noun **1** part between the waist and knees of a person when sitting **2** single circuit of a racecourse or track ▷ verb **3** to overtake (an opponent) in a race so as to be one or more circuits ahead **4** (of waves) to beat softly against a shore etc >**lap up** verb (of an animal) to drink (liquid) by scooping up with the tongue

lapel noun part of the front of a coat or jacket folded back towards the shoulders

lapse noun **1** slight mistake **2** instance of bad behaviour by someone usually well-behaved **3** period of time between two events ▷ verb **4 lapse into** to give way to (a regrettable kind of behaviour); fall into: *the offenders lapsed into a sullen silence* **5** to end or become invalid, especially through disuse

lard noun fat from a pig, used in cooking

larder noun storeroom for food

large adjective 1 great in size, number or extent ▷ noun 2 **at large** (of a prisoner) escaped from prison ▷ **largely** adverb to a great extent: the public are largely unaware of this

lark noun 1 small brown songbird, skylark 2 informal harmless piece of mischief or fun

larrikin noun Aust, NZ informal mischievous or unruly person

larva larvae noun insect in an immature stage, often resembling a worm

laryngitis noun inflammation of the larynx, causing loss of voice

larynx larynxes or **larynges** noun part of the throat containing the vocal cords

lasagne noun dish made from layers of pasta in wide flat sheets, meat and cheese

laser noun device that produces a very narrow intense beam of light, used for cutting very hard materials and in surgery etc

lash noun 1 eyelash 2 strip of leather at the end of a whip 3 sharp blow with a whip ▷ **lash out** verb (followed by at) to make a sudden physical or verbal attack on (someone)

lass noun Scot, N English girl

lasso lassoes or **lassos lassoing lassoed** noun 1 rope with a noose for catching cattle and horses ▷ verb 2 to catch (an animal) with a lasso

last adjective, adverb 1 coming at the end or after all others 2 most recent(ly) ▷ adjective 3 only remaining ▷ verb 4 to continue to exist or happen 5 to remain fresh,

uninjured or unaltered ▷ **lastly** adverb: Lastly, I would like to ask about your future plans

last-ditch adjective done as a final resort

latch noun 1 fastening for a door with a bar and lever 2 lock that can only be opened from the outside with a key ▷ **latch onto** verb to become attached to (a person or idea)

late adjective 1 after the normal or expected time 2 towards the end of a period 3 recently dead ▷ adverb 4 after the normal or expected time ▷ **lately** adverb in recent times

latent adjective hidden and not yet developed

lateral adjective of or relating to the side or sides

lathe noun machine for turning wood or metal while it is being shaped

lather noun froth of soap and water

Latin noun 1 language of the ancient Romans 2 member of a people who speak languages closely related to Latin, such as French, Italian, Spanish and Portuguese

Latin America noun parts of South and Central America whose official language is Spanish or Portuguese ▷ **Latin American** noun, adjective

latitude noun distance north or south of the equator measured in degrees

latrine noun hole or trench in the ground used as a toilet at a camp

latter adjective, noun 1 second of two ▷ adjective 2 being the second or end part of something:

the latter part of his career ▷ **latterly** adverb formal recently

- You use **latter** to talk about the second of two items. To talk about the last of three or more items you should use **last-named**

lattice noun structure made of strips crossed over each other diagonally with holes in between

laudable adjective praiseworthy ▷ **laudably** adverb in a praiseworthy manner

laugh verb **1** to make a noise with the voice that expresses amusement or happiness ▷ noun **2** act or instance of laughing ▷ **laughable** adjective ridiculously inadequate ▷ **laughter** noun sound or action of laughing

laughing stock noun person who has been made to seem ridiculous

launch verb **1** to put (a ship or boat) into the water, especially for the first time **2** to put (a new product) on the market **3** to send (a missile or spacecraft) into space or the air ▷ noun **4** launching **5** open motorboat

launch pad or **launching pad** noun place from which space rockets take off

launder verb old-fashioned to wash and iron (clothes and linen)

laundry laundries noun **1** clothes etc for washing or that have recently been washed **2** business that washes and irons clothes and sheets

laurel noun evergreen tree with shiny leaves

lava noun molten rock thrown out by volcanoes, which hardens as it cools

lavatory lavatories noun toilet

lavender noun **1** shrub with fragrant flowers ▷ adjective **2** bluish-purple

lavish adjective **1** giving or spending generously ▷ verb **2** (followed by on) to give (money, affection, etc) generously: he lavished praise on our contribution ▷ **lavishly** adverb

law noun **1** system of rules developed by a government, which regulate what people may and may not do and deals with people who break these rules **2** one of these rules **3** profession of people such as lawyers, whose job involves the application of the laws of a country **4** scientific fact that explains how things work in the physical world ▷ **lawful** adjective allowed by law ▷ **lawfully** adverb as allowed by the law ▷ **lawless** adjective having no regard for the law

law-abiding adjective obeying the laws

lawn noun area of cultivated grass; fine linen or cotton fabric

lawnmower noun machine for cutting grass

lawsuit noun court case brought by one person or group against another

lawyer noun person who is qualified in law, and who advises people about the law and represents them in court

lax adjective not strict

laxative noun medicine taken to stop constipation

lay lays laying laid verb **1** to put (something) down so that it lies somewhere **2** (of a bird or

a b c d e f g h i j k l m n o p q r s t u v w x y z

reptile) to produce (an egg) out of its body **3** to arrange (a table) for a meal **4** to set (a trap) for someone **5** to put (emphasis) on something to indicate that it is very important **6** past tense of **lie 7 lay odds on** to bet that (something) will happen ▷ *adjective* **8** of people who are involved with a Christian church but are not members of the clergy ▷ **lay off** *verb* **1** to dismiss (staff) during a slack period **2** *informal* to stop doing something annoying ▷ **lay on** *verb* to provide (a meal or entertainment)

● People often get confused about *lay* and *lie*. The verb *to lay* (past tense *laid*) takes an object: *lay the table please; the Queen laid a wreath.* The verb *to lie* (past tense *lay*) does not take an object: *the book was lying on the table; I lay on the bed*

lay-by *noun* **1** stopping place for traffic beside a road **2** *Aust, NZ* system whereby a customer pays a deposit on an item in a shop so that it will be kept for him or her until the rest of the price is paid

layer *noun* single thickness of something, such as a cover or coating on a surface

layman laymen *noun* **1** person who is not a member of the clergy **2** person without specialist knowledge

layout *noun* arrangement, especially of matter for printing or of a building

laze *verb* to be idle or lazy

lazy lazier laziest *adjective* idle and not inclined to work or make much effort ▷ **lazily** *adverb*

▷ **laziness** *noun* the state of being idle

lb *abbreviation* pound (weight)

lbw *abbreviation* Cricket leg before wicket

leach *verb* to remove (minerals) from rocks by a liquid passing through the rock

lead¹ leads leading led *verb* **1** to guide or conduct (someone) somewhere **2** to cause (someone) to feel, think or behave in a certain way **3** to control or direct (a group of people) **4** **lead to** to result in (something happening) ▷ *noun* **5** clue that might help the police to solve a crime **6** length of leather or chain attached to a dog's collar to control it ▷ **leading** *adjective* **1** principal **2** in the first position

lead² *noun* soft heavy grey metal

leaden *adjective* **1** heavy and slow-moving **2** dull grey

leader *noun* **1** person who leads **2** article in a newspaper expressing editorial views ▷ **leadership** *noun* **1** group of people in charge of an organization **2** ability to be a good leader

leaf leaves; leafs leafing leafed *noun* flat usually green blade attached to the stem of a plant ▷ **leaf through** *verb* to turn the pages of (a book, magazine or newspaper) without reading them ▷ **leafy** *adjective*: *tall leafy trees*

leaflet *noun* sheet of printed matter for distribution

league *noun* **1** association promoting the interests of its members **2** association of sports clubs organizing competitions between its members **3** obsolete measure of distance, about three miles

leak noun **1** hole or defect that allows the escape or entrance of liquid, gas, radiation, etc **2** disclosure of secrets ▷ verb **3** to let liquid etc in or out **4** (of liquid etc) to find its way through a leak **5** to disclose (secret information) > **leakage** noun escape of liquid etc from a pipe or container > **leaky** adjective: the leaky roof

lean leans leaning leant or leaned; leaner leanest verb **1** to bend or slope from an upright position: He leaned forward ▷ adjective **2** thin but healthy-looking **3** (of meat) lacking fat **4** (of a period) during which food or money is in short supply > **lean on** or **upon** verb **1** to rest against (something) **2** to depend on (someone) > **lean towards** verb to have an inclination or tendency to follow (particular ideas): parents who lean towards strictness

leap leaps leaping leapt or leaped verb **1** to make a sudden powerful jump ▷ noun **2** sudden powerful jump

leap year noun year with February 29th as an extra day

learn learns learning learnt or learned verb **1** to gain skill or knowledge by study, practice or teaching **2** to memorize (something) **3** to find out about or discover (something) > **learned** adjective having a lot of knowledge gained from years of study > **learner** noun person who is learning about something > **learning** noun knowledge got

by study

lease noun **1** contract by which property is rented for a stated time by the owner to a tenant ▷ verb **2** to let or rent (property) by lease

leash noun lead for a dog

least adjective **1** superlative of **little 2** smallest ▷ noun **3** smallest possible amount **4 at least** no fewer or less than (a specified number or amount) ▷ adverb **5** in the smallest degree

leather noun material made from specially treated animal skins > **leathery** adjective like leather; tough

leave leaves leaving left verb **1** to go away from (a place) **2** to allow (someone) to remain somewhere, accidentally or deliberately **3** to stop being part of (a job or organization) **4** to arrange for (money or possessions) to be given to someone after one's death **5** to cause (a number) to remain after subtracting one number from another ▷ noun **6** period of holiday or absence from work or duty

Lebanese adjective **1** of Lebanon ▷ noun **2** person from Lebanon

lecherous adjective constantly thinking about sex

lectern noun sloping reading desk, especially in a church

lecture noun **1** informative talk to an audience on a subject **2** lengthy scolding ▷ verb **3** to teach in a college or university

lecturer noun teacher in a college or university

led past of **lead**[1]

ledge noun **1** narrow shelf sticking

out from a wall **2** shelflike projection from a cliff etc

ledger *noun* book of debit and credit accounts of a firm

lee *noun* **1** sheltered part or side ▷ *adjective* **2** denoting the side of a ship away from the wind

leech *noun* small worm that lives in water and feeds by sucking the blood from other animals

leek *noun* vegetable of the onion family with a long bulb and thick stem

leer *verb* **1** to look or grin at someone in a sneering or suggestive manner ▷ *noun* **2** sneering or suggestive look or grin

leeway *noun* room for free movement within limits

left *adjective* **1** of the side that faces west when the front faces north ▷ *adverb* **2** on or towards the left ▷ *noun* **3** left side or part **4** *Politics* people and political groups supporting socialism or communism rather than capitalism ▷ *verb* **5** past of **leave** >**leftist** *noun, adjective* (person) of the political left

left-handed *adjective* more adept with the left hand than with the right

leftovers *plural noun* unused bits of food or material

left-wing *adjective* supporting socialism or communism rather than capitalism >**left-winger** *noun*

leg *noun* **1** one of the limbs on which a person or animal walks, runs or stands **2** part of a garment covering the leg **3** one of the parts of an object such as a table

that rest on the floor and support its weight **4** stage of a journey **5** *Sport* one of two matches played between two sports teams

legacy legacies *noun* **1** thing left in a will **2** something that exists as a result of a previous event or time: *the legacy of a Catholic upbringing*

legal *adjective* **1** allowed by the law **2** relating to law or lawyers >**legally** *adverb*

legal aid *noun* system providing the services of a lawyer free, or very cheaply, to people who cannot afford the full fees

legality *noun* (of an action) fact of being allowed by the law: *they challenged the legality of the scheme*

legalize *verb* to make (something) legal >**legalization** *noun: the legalization of drugs*

legend *noun* **1** traditional story or myth **2** famous person or event >**legendary** *adjective* **1** famous **2** of or in legend

leggings *plural noun* **1** closefitting trousers for women or children **2** protective or waterproof covering worn over trousers

legible *adjective* easily read

legion *noun* **1** large military force **2** famous number **3** infantry unit in the Roman army

legislate *verb formal* to make laws

legislation *noun* law or set of laws created by a government

legislative *adjective* of the making of new laws

legislator *noun formal* maker of laws

legislature *noun formal* parliament in a country, which is responsible for making new laws

legitimate adjective reasonable or acceptable according to existing laws or standards > **legitimacy** noun state of being reasonable or acceptable > **legitimately** adverb: the government has been legitimately elected by the people

leisure noun 1 time for relaxation or hobbies 2 at (one's) leisure when one has time > **leisurely** adjective 1 deliberate, unhurried ▷ adverb 2 slowly

lekker adjective S Afr informal 1 attractive or nice 2 tasty

lemming noun small rodent of cold northern regions, reputed to run into the sea and drown during mass migrations

lemon noun 1 sour-tasting yellow oval fruit that grows on trees ▷ adjective 2 pale-yellow

lemonade noun lemon-flavoured soft drink, often fizzy

lend lends lending lent verb 1 to give someone the temporary use of (something) 2 (of a bank etc) to provide (money) temporarily, often for interest > **lender** noun: mortgage lenders

length noun 1 extent or measurement from end to end 2 period of time for which something happens 3 quality of being long 4 piece of something narrow and long 5 at length for a long time

lengthen verb to make (something) longer

lengthways or **lengthwise** adverb horizontally from one end to the other

lengthy lengthier lengthiest adjective lasting for a long time

lenient adjective tolerant, not strict or severe > **leniency** noun: the judge rejected pleas for leniency > **leniently** adverb

lens noun 1 piece of glass or similar material with one or both sides curved, used to bring together or spread light rays in cameras, spectacles, telescopes, etc 2 transparent structure in the eye that focuses light

lent verb past of **lend**

lentil noun small dried red or brown seed, cooked and eaten in soups and curries

Leo noun fifth sign of the zodiac, represented by a lion

leopard noun wild Asian or African big cat, with yellow fur and black or brown spots

leotard noun tight-fitting costume covering the body and sometimes the legs, worn for dancing or exercise

leper noun person suffering from leprosy

leprosy noun disease attacking the nerves and skin, resulting in loss of feeling in the affected parts

lesbian noun homosexual woman > **lesbianism** noun female homosexuality

lesion noun injury or wound

less adjective 1 smaller in extent, degree or duration 2 not so much 3 comparative of **little** ▷ adverb 4 to a smaller extent or degree ▷ preposition 5 after deducting, minus

-less suffix without: hopeless

lessen verb to be reduced in amount, size or quality; decrease

lesser adjective not as great in

quantity, size or worth

● You use *less* to talk about things that can't be counted: *less time*. When you are talking about amounts that can be counted you should use *fewer*

lesson *noun* **1** single period of instruction in a subject **2** experience that makes one understand something important

lest *conjunction* so as to prevent any possibility that

let lets letting let *verb* **1** to allow (someone) to do something **2** used as an auxiliary to express a proposal, command, threat, or assumption: *let's go* **3** to grant the use of (a house or flat) for rent **4 let oneself in for** to agree to do (something one does not really want to do) >**let down** *verb* **1** to fail (someone); disappoint **2** to deflate >**let off** *verb* **1** to excuse (someone) from a punishment **2** to light (a firework) or detonate (an explosive)

lethal *adjective* deadly: *a lethal weapon*

lethargy *noun* lack of energy and enthusiasm >**lethargic** *adjective* having no energy or enthusiasm

letter *noun* **1** written message, usually sent by post **2** alphabetical symbol

letter box *noun* **1** slot in a door through which letters are delivered **2** box in a street or post office where letters are posted

lettering *noun* writing, especially the type of letters used: *bold lettering*

lettuce *noun* plant with large green leaves used in salads

leukaemia or **leukemia** *noun* disease caused by uncontrolled overproduction of white blood cells

level levels levelling levelled *adjective* **1** (of a surface) smooth, flat and parallel to the ground ▷ *verb* **2** to make (a piece of land) flat **3** to direct (a criticism, accusation, etc) at someone ▷ *adverb* **4 draw level with** to get closer to (someone) so that one is moving next to him or her ▷ *noun* **5** point on a scale measuring the amount, importance or difficulty of something **6** height that a liquid comes up to in a container >**level off** or **level out** *verb* to stop increasing or decreasing

level crossing *noun* point where a railway line and road cross

level-headed *adjective* not apt to be carried away by emotion

lever *noun* **1** handle used to operate machinery **2** bar used to move a heavy object or to open something

leverage *noun* **1** action or power of a lever **2** influence that can be used to make someone do something

leveret *noun* young hare

levy levies levying levied *verb* **1** to impose and collect (a tax) ▷ *noun* **2** formal amount of money that one pays in tax

lewd *adjective* lustful or indecent

lexicography *noun* the profession of writing dictionaries >**lexicographer** *noun* writer of dictionaries

liability liabilities *noun* **1** responsibility for wrongdoing

2 *informal* person who causes a lot of problems or embarrassment **3 liabilities** business debts

liable *adjective* **1** (followed by *to*) likely (to happen) **2** (followed by *for*) legally responsible (for something)

liaise *verb* to establish and maintain communication with (a person or organization)

liaison *noun* communication and contact between groups

liar *noun* person who tells lies

libel libels libelling libelled *noun* **1** published statement falsely damaging a person's reputation ▷ *verb* **2** to falsely damage the reputation of (someone) ▷ **libellous** *adjective: he claimed the articles were libellous*

liberal *adjective* **1** tolerant of a wide range of behaviour, standards or opinions **2** generous (with something) **3** (of a quantity) large ▷ *noun* **4** person who has liberal ideas or opinions > **liberalism** *noun* belief in democratic reforms and individual freedom > **liberally** *adverb* in large quantities

Liberal Democrat or **Lib Dem** *noun* member of the Liberal Democrats, a British political party favouring a mixed economy and individual freedom

liberate *verb* to free (people) from prison or from an unpleasant situation > **liberation** *noun: the women's liberation movement* > **liberator** *noun* person who sets people free

liberty liberties *noun* freedom to choose how one wants to live, without government restrictions

libido libidos *noun* sexual drive

Libra *noun* seventh sign of the zodiac, represented by a pair of scales

librarian *noun* person in charge of a library

library libraries *noun* **1** building where books are kept for people to come and read or borrow **2** collection of books, records, etc for consultation or borrowing

Libyan *adjective* **1** of Libya ▷ *noun* **2** person from Libya

lice *noun* plural of **louse**

licence *noun* **1** official document giving official permission to do something **2** freedom to do what one wants, especially when considered irresponsible

● The noun **licence** ends in *ce*

license *verb* to give official permission for (an activity) to be carried out

● The verb **license** ends in *se*

lichen *noun* green moss-like growth on rocks or tree trunks

lick *verb* **1** to pass the tongue over (something) ▷ *noun* **2** licking

lid *noun* movable cover for a container

lie¹ lies lying lied *verb* **1** to say something that is not true ▷ *noun* **2** something said that is not true

lie² lies lying lay lain *verb* **1** to be in a horizontal position **2** to be situated

● The past tense of this verb *lie* is *lay*. Do not confuse it with the verb *to lay* (past tense *laid*) meaning 'put'

lieu *noun* **in lieu of** instead of

lieutenant *noun* junior officer in the army or navy

life lives noun **1** quality of being able to grow and develop, which is present in people, plants and animals **2** period between birth and death or between birth and the present time **3** amount of time something is active or functions **4** liveliness or high spirits **5** imprisonment for the rest of your life or until granted parole

life assurance noun insurance that provides a sum of money in the event of the policy holder's death

lifeblood noun most essential part of something

lifeboat noun **1** boat kept on shore, used for rescuing people at sea **2** small boat kept on a ship, used if the ship starts to sink

life expectancy noun number of years a person can expect to live

lifeguard noun person whose job is to rescue people in difficulty at sea or in a swimming pool

life jacket noun sleeveless inflatable jacket that keeps a person afloat in water

lifeless adjective **1** dead **2** not lively or exciting

lifelike adjective (of a picture or sculpture) looking very real or alive

lifeline noun **1** means of contact or support **2** rope used in rescuing a person in danger

lifelong adjective lasting all of a person's life

lifesaver noun Aust, NZ person whose job is to rescue people who are in difficulty at sea

life span noun **1** length of time during which a person is alive

2 length of time a product or organization exists or is useful

lifetime noun length of time a person is alive

lift verb **1** to move (something) upwards in position, status, volume, etc **2** to remove or cancel (a ban) **3** informal to steal (something) ▷ noun **4** cage raised and lowered in a vertical shaft to transport people or goods **5** ride in a car etc as a passenger

ligament noun band of tissue joining bones

light lights lighting lighted or lit; lighter lightest noun **1** brightness from the sun, fire or lamps, by which things are visible **2** lamp or other device that gives out brightness **3** match or lighter to light a cigarette: have you got a light? ▷ adjective **4** (of a place) bright **5** (of a colour) pale **6** (of an object) not weighing much **7** (of a task) fairly easy **8** (of books or music) not serious or profound ▷ verb **9** to cause (a fire) to start burning **10** to cause (a place) to be filled with light ▷ **lightly** adverb: cook the onions until lightly browned ▷ **lightness** noun: the lightness of the large bedroom

▷ **light on** or **upon** verb literary (of eyes, gaze, person) to find (something) by chance

lighten verb **1** to become less dark **2** to make (something) less heavy

lighter noun device for lighting cigarettes etc

light-headed adjective feeling faint, dizzy

light-hearted adjective cheerful and carefree

lighthouse noun tower by the sea with a powerful light to guide ships

lighting noun 1 way that a room or building is lit 2 apparatus for and use of artificial light in theatres, films, etc

lightning noun bright flashes of light in the sky, produced by natural electricity during a thunderstorm

lightweight noun, adjective 1 not weighing much ▷ noun 2 boxer weighing up to 135lb (professional) or 60kg (amateur)

light year noun Astronomy distance light travels in one year, about six million million miles

likable or **likeable** adjective pleasant and friendly

like preposition, adjective 1 indicating similarity, comparison, etc 2 feel like to want to do or to have (something): I feel like a walk ▷ verb 3 to find (something or someone) pleasant

-like suffix resembling or similar to: a balloonlike object

likelihood noun probability

likely adjective probable

liken verb to compare (one thing) to another

likeness noun resemblance

likewise adverb similarly

liking noun fondness for (someone or something)

lilac noun 1 shrub with pale mauve or white flowers ▷ adjective 2 light-purple

lilt noun pleasing musical quality in speaking ▷ **lilting** adjective: a lilting northern accent

lily lilies noun plant that grows from a bulb and has large, often white, flowers

limb noun 1 arm, leg or wing 2 main branch of a tree **go out on a limb** 3 to say or do something risky

limber up verb to stretch your muscles in preparation for doing sport

limbo limbos noun 1 West Indian dance in which dancers lean backwards to pass under a bar 2 **in limbo** not knowing the result or next stage of something and powerless to influence it

lime noun 1 calcium compound used as a fertilizer or in making cement 2 small green citrus fruit 3 deciduous tree with heart-shaped leaves and fragrant flowers

limelight noun glare of publicity

limerick noun humorous verse of five lines

limestone noun white rock used in building

limit noun 1 boundary or extreme beyond which something cannot go: the speed limit ▷ verb 2 to prevent (something) from becoming bigger, spreading or making progress ▷ **limited** adjective rather small in amount or extent

limitation noun 1 reducing or controlling of something 2 **limitations** limits of the abilities of someone or something

limousine noun large luxurious car, usually driven by a chauffeur

limp verb 1 to walk with an uneven step because of an injured leg or foot ▷ noun 2 limping walk ▷ adjective 3 without firmness or stiffness

limpet noun shellfish that sticks tightly to rocks

line noun 1 long narrow mark 2 telephone connection 3 railway track 4 course or direction of movement 5 attitude towards something 6 kind of work someone does 7 row or queue of people 8 type of product 9 row of words 10 lines words of a theatrical part ▷ verb 11 to cover the inside of (something) > **line up** verb 1 to stand in a line 2 to arrange (something) for a special occasion

lineage noun all the people from whom someone is directly descended

linear adjective arranged in a line or in a strict sequence, or happening at a constant rate

line dancing noun form of dancing performed by rows of people to country and western music

linen noun 1 cloth or thread made from flax 2 sheets, tablecloths, etc

liner noun large passenger ship or aircraft

linesman linesmen noun (in some sports) an official who helps the referee or umpire

-ling suffix small: duckling

linger verb to remain for a long time

lingerie noun women's underwear or nightwear

lingo lingoes noun informal foreign or unfamiliar language

linguist noun person who studies foreign languages or the way language works

lining noun any material used to line the inside of something

link noun 1 relationship or connection between two things: the link between sunbathing and skin cancer 2 person or thing forming a connection 3 any of the rings forming a chain ▷ verb 4 to join (people, places or things) together > **linkage** noun: there is no formal linkage between the two agreements

lino noun short for linoleum

linoleum noun floor covering with a shiny surface

lint noun soft material for dressing a wound

lion noun large animal of the cat family, the male of which has a shaggy mane

lip noun 1 either of the fleshy edges of the mouth 2 rim of a jug etc

lip-read lip-reads lip-reading lip-read verb to understand speech by following lip movements; a skill often used by deaf people > **lip-reading** noun

lipstick noun cosmetic in stick form, for colouring the lips

liqueur noun flavoured and sweetened alcoholic spirit, usually drunk after a meal

liquid noun 1 substance in a physical state which can change shape but not size ▷ adjective 2 of or being a liquid 3 (of assets) in the form of money or easily converted into money

liquidate verb 1 to dissolve (a company) and share its assets among creditors 2 informal to wipe out or kill (someone) > **liquidation** noun: the company went into liquidation > **liquidator** noun official appointed to liquidate a business

liquor noun any strong alcoholic

drink

liquorice noun **1** root used to flavour sweets **2** sweets flavoured with liquorice

lira *lire* noun unit of currency of Turkey and formerly of Italy

lisp noun **1** speech defect in which s and z are pronounced th ▷ verb **2** to speak with a lisp

list noun **1** item-by-item record of names or things, usually written one below another ▷ verb **2** to make a list of (a number of things) **3** (of a ship) to lean to one side

listen verb to heed or pay attention (to something) > **listener** noun: *I'm a regular listener to her show*

listless adjective lacking interest or energy > **listlessly** adverb without interest or energy

lit verb past of **light**

litany *litanies* noun **1** prayer with responses from the congregation **2** any tedious recital

literacy noun ability to read and write

literal adjective **1** according to the explicit meaning of a word or text, not figurative **2** (of a translation) word for word > **literally** adverb: *the views are literally breath-taking*

- Be careful where you use
- *literally*. It can emphasize
- something without
- changing the meaning: *the*
- *house was literally only five*
- *minutes walk away*. However,
- it can make nonsense of
- some things: *he literally swept*
- *me off my feet*. This sentence
- is ridiculous unless he
- actually took a broom
- and swept the speaker
- over

literary adjective of or knowledgeable about literature

literature noun **1** written works such as novels, plays and poetry **2** books and writings of a country, period or subject

lithe adjective flexible or supple

litmus noun Chemistry blue dye turned red by acids and restored to blue by alkalis

litmus test noun something regarded as a simple and accurate test of a particular thing

litre noun unit of liquid measure equal to 1000 cubic centimetres or 1.76 pints

litter noun **1** untidy rubbish dropped in public places **2** group of young animals produced at one birth **3** dry material to absorb a cat's excrement ▷ verb **4** to scatter things about untidily in (a place)

little adjective **1** small or smaller than average ▷ adverb **2** not a lot or not often ▷ noun **3** small amount, extent or duration

live¹ verb **1** to be alive **2** to reside > **live down** verb to wait till people forget (a past mistake or misdeed) > **live up to** verb to meet (one's expectations)

live² adjective **1** living; alive **2** (of a broadcast) transmitted during the actual performance **3** (of a wire, circuit, etc) carrying an electric current **4** causing interest or controversy **5** capable of exploding

livelihood noun occupation or employment

lively *livelier liveliest* adjective full of life or vigour; energetic > **liveliness** noun vigour and enthusiasm

liven up verb to make (things) more lively

liver noun **1** large organ in the body that cleans the blood and aids digestion **2** animal liver as food

livestock noun farm animals

livid adjective **1** informal angry or furious **2** bluish-grey

living adjective **1** alive ▷ noun **2 for a living** in order to earn money to live: What does he do for a living?

living room noun room in a house used for relaxation and entertainment

lizard noun four-footed reptile with a long body and tail

llama noun woolly animal of the camel family found in S America

load noun **1** something being carried **2** loads informal lots ▷ verb **3** to put a load onto (an animal) or into (a vehicle)

loaf loaves; loafs loafing loafed noun **1** shaped mass of baked bread ▷ verb **2** to be lazy and not do any work

loan noun **1** sum of money borrowed **2** lending ▷ verb **3** to lend (something) to someone

loath or **loth** adjective unwilling or reluctant (to do something)

loathe verb to hate or be disgusted by (someone or something) >**loathing** noun: She looked at him with loathing >**loathsome** adjective: a loathsome spectacle

lob lobs lobbing lobbed Sport noun **1** ball struck or thrown high in the air ▷ verb **2** to strike or throw (a ball) high in the air

lobby lobbies lobbying lobbied noun **1** corridor into which rooms open **2** group which tries

to influence an organization ▷ verb **3** to try to influence (an MP or organization) in the formulation of policy >**lobbyist** noun person who lobbies an MP or organization

lobe noun **1** any rounded part of something **2** soft hanging part of the ear

lobster noun shellfish with a long tail and claws, which turns red when boiled

local adjective **1** of the area close to your home **2** (of an anaesthetic) producing loss of feeling in one part of the body ▷ noun **3** person belonging to a particular district **4** informal pub close to your home >**locally** adverb: cards designed by someone locally

locality localities noun neighbourhood or area

localized or **localised** adjective existing or happening in only one place: localized pain

locate verb **1** to discover the whereabouts of (someone or something) **2** to situate (something) in a place

location noun **1** site or position **2** site of a film production away from the studio **3** S Afr Black African or coloured township

loch noun Scot lake

lock noun **1** appliance for fastening a door, case, etc **2** section of a canal shut off by gates between which the water level can be altered to aid boats moving from one level to another **3** small bunch of hair ▷ verb **4** to close and fasten (something) with a key **5** to move into place and become firmly fixed there

locker noun small cupboard with a lock

locket noun small hinged pendant for a portrait etc, worn on a chain round the neck

locksmith noun person who makes and mends locks

locomotive noun railway engine

locust noun destructive African insect that flies in swarms and eats crops

lodge noun 1 small house in the grounds of a large country house 2 small house used for holidays ▷ verb 3 to live in another's house at a fixed charge 4 to stick or become stuck (in a place) 5 to make (a complaint) formally

lodger noun person who lives in someone's house and pays rent

lodgings plural noun rented room or rooms in another person's house

loft noun space between the top storey and roof of a building

lofty loftier loftiest adjective 1 of great height 2 very noble or important 3 proud and superior

log logs logging logged noun 1 portion of a felled tree stripped of branches 2 detailed record of a journey of a ship, aircraft, etc ▷ verb 3 to make a record of (something) in a ship's log > **log in** verb to gain access (to a computer system) by keying in a special command > **log out** verb to leave (a computer system) by keying in a special command

logic noun 1 way of reasoning involving a series of statements, each of which must be true if the statement before it is true 2 any sensible thinking or reasonable

decision

logical adjective 1 (of an argument) using logic 2 (of a course of action or a decision) sensible or reasonable in the circumstances > **logically** adverb: to look at things logically

logistics noun detailed planning and organization of a large, especially military, operation

logo logos noun emblem used by a company or other organization

-logy suffix study of something: biology; geology

loin noun 1 piece of meat from the back or sides of an animal 2 **loins** old-fashioned front part of the body between the waist and the thighs, especially the sexual parts

loiter verb to stand or wait aimlessly or idly

loll verb 1 to lounge lazily 2 (of a head or tongue) to hang loosely

lollipop noun hard sweet on a small wooden stick

lolly lollies noun 1 lollipop or ice lolly 2 Aust, NZ sweet

lolly scramble noun NZ sweets scattered on the ground for children to collect

lone adjective solitary or single

lonely lonelier loneliest adjective 1 sad because alone 2 (of a place) isolated and unfrequented > **loneliness** noun: a fear of loneliness

loner noun informal person who prefers to be alone

lonesome adjective lonely and sad

long adjective 1 having length, especially great length, in space or time ▷ adverb 2 for an extensive period 3 **as long as** only if 4 **before long** soon 5 **no**

longer not any more ▷ *verb* **6** (followed by *for*) to have a strong desire for (something) >**longing** *noun* yearning

longevity *noun* long life

longhand *noun* ordinary writing, not shorthand or typing

longitude *noun* distance east or west from a line passing through Greenwich, measured in degrees

long jump *noun* athletics event involving jumping as far as possible after taking a long run

long-range *adjective* **1** extending into the future **2** (of vehicles, weapons, etc) designed to cover great distances

long-sighted *adjective* able to see distant objects in focus but not nearby ones

long-standing *adjective* existing for a long time

long-suffering *adjective* enduring trouble or unhappiness without complaint

long-term *adjective* lasting or effective for a long time

long-winded *adjective* speaking or writing at tedious length

loo loos *noun informal* toilet

look *verb* **1** (followed by *at*) to direct the eyes or attention towards (something or someone) **2** to have the appearance of being (as specified) **3** to search for (something or someone) ▷ *noun* **4** instance of looking; glance **5** facial expression **6 looks** attractiveness >**look after** *verb* to take care of (someone or something) >**look down on** *verb* to treat (someone) as inferior or unimportant >**look forward to** *verb* to anticipate (something)

with pleasure >**look out** *verb* to be careful >**look up** *verb* **1** to discover or confirm (information) by checking in a book **2** (of a situation) to improve **3** to visit (someone) after a long gap >**look up to** *verb* to respect (someone)

lookalike *noun* person who is the double of another

lookout *noun* **1** person who is watching for danger; guard **2** place for watching **3 on the lookout** watching or waiting expectantly (for something)

loom *noun* **1** machine for weaving cloth ▷ *verb* **2** to appear suddenly and unclearly or threateningly **3** to seem ominously close

loony loonies *informal adjective* **1** foolish or insane ▷ *noun* **2** foolish or insane person

loop *noun* **1** rounded shape made by a curved line or rope crossing itself ▷ *verb* **2** to fasten (something) with a loop

loophole *noun* means of evading a rule without breaking it

loose *adjective* **1** not tight, fastened, fixed or tense **2** at a **loose end** bored, with nothing to do ▷ *adverb* **3** free from captivity >**loosely** *adverb*

- The adjective and adverb
- *loose* is spelt with two os.
- Do not confuse it with the
- verb *lose*

loosen *verb* to make (something) looser

loot *verb* **1** to steal goods from (shops and houses) during a battle or riot ▷ *noun* **2** stolen money and goods

lop lops lopping lopped *verb* to chop (something) off with one quick stroke

lopsided adjective greater in height, weight or size on one side

lord noun 1 male member of the British nobility 2 **Lord a** God or Jesus **b** (in Britain) title given to certain male officials and peers ▷ verb 3 **lord it over** to act in a superior manner towards (someone)

Lordship noun (in Britain) title of some male officials and peers

lore noun all the traditional knowledge and stories about a subject

lorikeet noun small brightly coloured Australian parrot

lorry lorries noun Brit, S Afr large vehicle for transporting goods by road

lory lories noun small, brightly coloured parrot found in Australia

lose loses losing lost verb 1 to come to be without (something), especially by accident or carelessness 2 to be deprived of (something) 3 to be deprived of (a relative or friend) through his or her death 4 to be defeated in (a competition etc) 5 (of a business) to spend more (money) than it earns 6 to be or become engrossed: lost in thought ▷ **loser** noun 1 person or thing that loses 2 informal person who seems destined to fail

- The verb **lose** is spelt with
- one o. Do not confuse it with
- the adjective and adverb
- **loose**

loss noun 1 losing 2 **at a loss** confused or bewildered

lost verb 1 past of **lose** ▷ adjective 2 unable to find your way

3 unable to be found

lot noun 1 item at auction 2 **a lot a** a great number or quantity: a lot of noise **b** very much or very often: He's out a lot 3 **the lot** or **the whole lot** the whole amount or number: He bet all his wages and lost the lot 4 **lots** great numbers or quantities: We took lots of photos

lotion noun medical or cosmetic liquid for use on the skin

lottery lotteries noun method of raising money by selling tickets that win prizes by chance

lotus noun large water lily of Africa and Asia

loud adjective 1 having a high volume of sound 2 (of clothing) too bright ▷ **loudly** adverb ▷ **loudness** noun: she was startled at their loudness

loudspeaker noun piece of equipment that makes your voice louder when you speak into a microphone connected to it

lounge noun 1 living room in a private house 2 more expensive bar in a pub ▷ verb 3 to sit, lie or stand in a relaxed manner

lourie noun S Afr one of two types of bird found in South Africa: the grey lourie, which lives in open grassland, and the more brightly coloured species, which lives in forests

louse lice noun small insect that lives on people's bodies

lousy lousier lousiest adjective informal 1 mean or unpleasant 2 bad, inferior 3 unwell

lout noun young man who behaves in an aggressive and rude way

lovable or **loveable** adjective having very attractive qualities and therefore easy to love

love verb **1** to have a great affection for (someone) **2** to enjoy (something) very much **3** would love to to want very much to (do something): I would love to live there ▷ noun **4** great affection **5** Tennis squash, etc score of nothing **6** in love feeling a strong emotional and sexual attraction (for someone) **7** make love (often followed by to) to have sexual intercourse with (someone) > **loving** adjective affectionate, tender > **lovingly** adverb

love affair noun romantic or sexual relationship between two people who are not married to each other

love life noun person's romantic or sexual relationships

lovely lovelier loveliest adjective very beautiful, attractive and pleasant > **loveliness** noun: a vision of loveliness

lover noun **1** person having a sexual relationship outside marriage **2** person who loves a specified person or thing

low adjective **1** not tall or high **2** of little or less than the usual amount, degree, quality or cost **3** coarse or vulgar **4** not loud **5** deep in pitch ▷ adverb **6** in or to a low position, level or degree ▷ noun **7** low position, level or degree

lowboy noun Aust, NZ small wardrobe or chest of drawers

lower verb **1** to move (something) downwards **2** to lessen (something)

lowlands plural noun area of flat low land > **lowland** adjective:

lowland areas

lowly lowlier lowliest adjective low in importance, rank or status

low tide noun time, usually twice a day, when the sea is at its lowest level

loyal adjective faithful to your friends, country or government > **loyally** adverb > **loyalty** noun: an oath of loyalty to the monarchy

loyalist noun person who remains firm in support for a government or ruler

lozenge noun **1** medicated tablet held in the mouth until it dissolves **2** diamond-shaped figure

LP noun long-playing record

LSD noun lysergic acid diethylamide, a very powerful drug that causes hallucinations

Ltd abbreviation Brit Limited (Liability)

lubra noun Aust Australian Aboriginal woman

lubricate verb to oil or grease (something) to lessen friction > **lubricant** noun lubricating substance, such as oil > **lubrication** noun: use linseed oil for lubrication

lucid adjective **1** (of writing or speech) clear and easily understood **2** (of a person) able to think clearly

luck noun fortune, good or bad

luckless adjective having bad luck

lucky luckier luckiest adjective having or bringing good luck > **luckily** adverb fortunately

lucrative adjective very profitable

ludicrous adjective absurd or ridiculous

lug lugs lugging lugged verb to

carry or drag (something) with great effort

luggage noun traveller's cases, bags, etc

lukewarm adjective 1 moderately warm, tepid 2 indifferent or half-hearted

lull verb 1 to calm the fears or suspicions of (someone) by deception ▷ noun 2 a brief time of quiet in a storm etc

lullaby lullabies noun quiet song to send a child to sleep

lumber noun 1 Brit unwanted or disused household articles 2 Chiefly US sawn timber ▷ verb 3 to move heavily and awkwardly 4 informal to burden (someone) with something unpleasant

luminaries noun literary famous person

luminous adjective glowing in the dark, usually because treated with a special substance > **luminosity** noun 1 brightness 2 (of a person's skin) healthy glow

lump noun 1 shapeless piece or mass 2 swelling 3 informal awkward or stupid person ▷ verb 4 to consider (people or things) as a single group 5 **lump it** informal to tolerate or put up with something > **lumpy** adjective containing or covered with lumps

lump sum noun large sum of money paid at one time

lunacy noun 1 extremely foolish or eccentric behaviour 2 old-fashioned severe mental illness

lunar adjective relating to the moon

lunatic adjective 1 foolish and irresponsible ▷ noun 2 foolish or annoying person 3 old-fashioned

insane person

lunch noun 1 meal taken in the middle of the day ▷ verb 2 to eat lunch

luncheon noun formal lunch

lung noun organ that allows an animal or bird to breathe air: humans have two lungs in the chest

lunge noun 1 sudden forward motion 2 thrust with a sword ▷ verb 3 to move with a lunge

lurch verb 1 to make a sudden jerky movement ▷ noun 2 lurching movement 3 **leave someone in the lurch** to abandon someone in difficulties

lure verb 1 to tempt or attract (someone) by the promise of reward ▷ noun 2 person or thing that lures

lurid adjective 1 vivid in shocking detail, sensational 2 glaring in colour

lurk verb to lie hidden or move stealthily, especially for sinister purposes

luscious adjective extremely pleasurable to taste or smell

lush adjective (of grass etc) growing thickly and healthily

lust noun 1 strong sexual desire 2 any strong desire ▷ verb 3 (followed by after or for) to have a strong desire for (someone or something)

lustre noun gloss, sheen

lute noun ancient guitar-like musical instrument with a body shaped like a half pear

luxuriant adjective (of plants or gardens) large, healthy and growing strongly

luxurious adjective very expensive

and full of luxury; splendid
> **luxuriously** adverb: luxuriously furnished

luxury luxuries noun **1** enjoyment of rich, very comfortable living **2** enjoyable but not essential thing

-ly suffix **1** forming adjectives that describe a quality: friendly **2** forming adjectives that refer to how often something happens: yearly **3** forming adverbs that refer to how something is done: quickly; nicely

lying noun telling lies ▷ verb **2** present participle of **lie¹**

lynch verb (of a crowd) to put (someone) to death without a trial

lynx lynxes noun wildcat with tufted ears and a short tail

lyre noun ancient musical instrument like a U-shaped harp

lyric adjective (of poetry) expressing personal emotion in songlike style > **lyrical** adjective poetic and romantic

m

m symbol **1** metre(s) **2** mile(s)

macabre adjective strange and horrible, gruesome

macadamia noun Australian tree with edible nuts

macaroni noun pasta in short tube shapes

macaroon noun small biscuit or cake made with ground almonds

mace noun ornamental pole carried by an official during ceremonies as a symbol of authority

machete noun broad heavy knife used for cutting or as a weapon

machine noun **1** apparatus, usually powered by electricity, designed to perform a particular task ▷ verb **2** to make or produce (something) with a machine

machine gun noun automatic gun that fires rapidly and continuously

machinery noun machines or machine parts collectively

machismo noun exaggerated or strong masculinity

macho adjective strongly or exaggeratedly masculine

mackerel noun edible sea fish with blue and silver stripes

mackintosh noun raincoat made from specially treated waterproof cloth

mad madder maddest adjective **1** mentally deranged; insane **2** very foolish **3** informal angry **4** (followed by about) very enthusiastic (about someone or something) > **madly** adverb in a fast excited way > **madness** noun driven to the brink of madness

madam noun polite form of address to a woman

maddening adjective irritating or frustrating

madrigal noun song sung by several people without instruments

Mafia noun international secret criminal organization founded in Sicily

magazine noun 1 weekly or monthly publication with articles and photographs 2 compartment in a gun for cartridges

magenta noun, adjective deep purplish-red

maggot noun larva of an insect

magic noun 1 in fairy stories, a special power that can make impossible things happen 2 art of performing tricks to entertain people > **magical** adjective 1 of, using or like magic 2 informal wonderful, marvellous > **magically** adverb by or as if by magic

magician noun 1 person who performs tricks as entertainment 2 in fairy stories, a man with magical powers

magistrate noun official who acts as a judge in a law court that deals with less serious crimes

magnanimous adjective noble and generous

magnate noun influential or wealthy person, especially in industry

magnet noun piece of iron or steel capable of attracting iron and pointing north when suspended

magnificent adjective extremely beautiful or impressive > **magnificence** noun: the magnificence of the Swiss mountains > **magnificently** adverb

magnify magnifies magnifying magnified verb (of a microscope or lens) to make (something) appear bigger than it actually is > **magnification** noun 1 act of magnifying 2 degree to which something is magnified

magnifying glass noun lens which makes things appear bigger than they really are

magnitude noun relative importance or size

magnolia noun shrub or tree with showy white or pink flowers

magpie noun black-and-white bird

mahogany noun hard reddish-brown wood of several tropical trees

maid or **maidservant** noun female servant

maiden noun 1 literary young unmarried woman > adjective 2 first: maiden voyage

maiden name noun woman's surname before marriage

mail noun 1 letters and packages delivered by the post office > verb 2 to send (a letter) by mail

mail order noun system of buying goods by post

maim verb to injure (someone) very badly for life

main adjective 1 chief or principal > noun 2 principal pipe or line carrying water, gas or electricity 3 **mains** main distribution network for water, gas or electricity > **mainly** adverb for the most part, chiefly

mainframe noun Computers high-speed general-purpose computer

mainland noun stretch of land which forms the main part of a country

mainstay noun most important part of something

mainstream noun most ordinary and conventional group of people or ideas in a society

maintain verb 1 to keep (something) going or keep (something) at a particular rate or level **2** to support (someone) financially **3** to assert that (something) is true

maintenance noun **1** process of keeping something in good condition **2** money that a person sends regularly to someone to provide for the things he or she needs

maize noun type of corn with spikes of yellow grains

majesty noun **1** great dignity and impressiveness **2** **His Majesty, Her Majesty** way of referring to a king or queen

major adjective **1** greater in number, quality or extent **2** significant or serious **3** denoting the key in which most European music is written ▷ noun **4** middle-ranking army officer

majority **majorities** noun **1** greater number **2** number by which the votes on one side exceed those on the other

- You should use *majority* only to talk about things that can be counted: *the majority of car owners.* To talk about an amount that cannot be counted you should use *most: most of the harvest was saved*

make **makes** **making** **made** verb **1** to create, construct or establish (something) **2** to force (someone) to do something **3** to bring about or produce (something) **4** to perform (an action) **5** **make do** to manage with an inferior alternative ▷ noun **6** brand, type or style >**maker** noun manufacturer >**make up** verb **1** to form or constitute (something) **2** to invent (a story) **3** (followed by

for) to compensate for (something that you have done wrong) **4** to apply cosmetics to (oneself or someone else) **5** **make it up** to settle a quarrel >**making** noun **1** creation or production **2** **in the making** gradually becoming (something): *a captain in the making*

make-up noun **1** cosmetics **2** character or personality

maladjusted adjective Psychology unable to meet the demands of society

malaise noun vague feeling of unease, illness or depression

malaria noun infectious disease caused by the bite of some mosquitoes

Malaysian adjective **1** of Malaysia ▷ noun **2** person from Malaysia

male adjective **1** of the sex which can fertilize female reproductive cells ▷ noun **2** male person or animal

male chauvinist noun man who thinks that men are better than women

malevolent adjective wishing evil to others; spiteful >**malevolence** noun: *a streak of malevolence*

malfunction verb **1** to function imperfectly or fail to function ▷ noun **2** defective functioning or failure to function

malice noun desire to cause harm to others

malicious adjective intended to harm: *malicious gossip*

malign verb to say unpleasant and untrue things about (someone)

malignant adjective (of a tumour) harmful and uncontrollable

mallard noun wild duck, the male of which has a green head

mallee noun Aust low-growing eucalypt in dry regions

mallet noun wooden hammer with a square head

malnutrition noun inadequate nutrition

malodorous adjective bad-smelling

malpractice noun immoral, illegal or unethical professional conduct

malt noun grain, such as barley, prepared for use in making beer or whisky

mammal noun animal of the type that suckles its young

mammoth noun **1** extinct elephant-like mammal ▷ adjective **2** colossal

man men; **man's** manning

manned noun **1** adult male **2** humankind: one of the hardest substances known to man **3** men people: all men are equal ▷ verb **4** to be in charge of or operate (something)

mana noun NZ authority or influence

manacles plural noun metal rings or clamps attached to a prisoner's wrists or ankles

manage verb **1** to succeed in doing something **2** to be in charge of or administer (an organization or business)

manageable adjective able to be dealt with

management noun **1** managers collectively **2** administration or organization

manager noun person responsible for running a business or

organization
- In business, the word *manager* can apply to either
- a man or a woman

manageress noun woman responsible for running a business or organization

managing director noun company director responsible for the way the company is managed

mandarin noun kind of small orange

mandate noun authorization or instruction from an electorate to its representative or government

mandatory adjective compulsory

mandir noun Hindu temple

mandolin noun musical instrument with four pairs of strings

mane noun long hair on the neck of a horse, lion, etc

manger noun eating trough in a stable or barn

mangle verb **1** to destroy (something) by crushing and twisting ▷ noun **2** machine with rollers for squeezing water from washed clothes

mango mangoes or mangos noun tropical fruit with sweet juicy yellow flesh

manhole noun hole with a cover, through which a person can enter a drain or sewer

manhood noun state of being a man rather than a boy

mania noun **1** extreme enthusiasm: my wife's mania for plant collecting **2** mental illness

maniac noun mad person who is violent and dangerous

manic adjective **1** energetic and excited **2** affected by mania

manicure noun cosmetic care of the fingernails and hands
>**manicurist** noun person whose job is the cosmetic care of fingernails and hands

manifest adjective **1** easily noticed, obvious ▷ verb **2** to show or reveal (something): Fear can manifest itself in many ways

manifestation noun sign that something is happening or exists: a manifestation of stress

manifesto manifestoes or **manifestos** noun declaration of policy as issued by a political party

manipulate verb **1** to control or influence (people or events) to produce a particular result **2** to control (a piece of equipment) in a skilful way >**manipulation** noun: political manipulation >**manipulative** adjective influencing people to produce a desired result >**manipulator** noun person who manipulates people

mankind noun human beings collectively

manly manlier manliest adjective possessing qualities that are typically masculine

manna noun **appear like manna from heaven** to appear suddenly as if by a miracle to help someone in a difficult situation

manner noun **1** way a thing happens or is done **2** person's bearing or behaviour **3** manners (polite) social behaviour

mannerism noun person's distinctive habit or trait

manoeuvre noun **1** skilful movement **2** contrived,

complicated and possibly deceptive plan or action ▷ verb **3** to skilfully move (something) into a place

manor noun Brit large country house and its lands

manpower noun available number of workers

mansion noun large house

manslaughter noun Law unlawful but unintentional killing of a person

mantelpiece noun shelf above a fireplace

mantle noun literary responsibilities and duties which go with a particular job or position

mantra noun word or short piece of sacred text or prayer continually repeated to help concentration

manual adjective **1** of or done with the hands **2** by human labour rather than automatic means ▷ noun **3** instruction book explaining how to use a machine >**manually** adverb

manufacture verb **1** to process or make (goods) on a large scale using machinery **2** to invent or concoct (an excuse etc)

manure noun animal excrement used as a fertilizer

manuscript noun handwritten or typed document, especially a version of a book before it is printed

Manx adjective of the Isle of Man

many adjective **1** numerous ▷ pronoun **2** large number

Maori noun **1** person descended from the people who lived in New Zealand before Europeans arrive

2 language of the Maoris

map maps mapping mapped
noun representation of the earth's surface or some part of it, showing geographical features > **map out** verb to work out (a plan)

maple noun tree with broad leaves, a variety of which (**sugar maple**) yields sugar

mar mars marring marred verb to spoil (something)

marae noun NZ **1** enclosed space in front of a Maori meeting house **2** Maori meeting house and its buildings

marathon noun **1** long-distance race of 26 miles 385 yards (42.195 kilometres) > adjective **2** (of a task) large and taking a long time

marble noun **1** kind of limestone with a mottled appearance, which can be highly polished **2** small glass ball used in a children's game **3 marbles** game of rolling these at one another

march verb **1** to walk with a military step **2** to walk quickly in a determined way > noun **3** organized protest in which a large group of people walk somewhere together

mare noun female horse

margarine noun butter substitute made from animal or vegetable fats

margin noun **1** blank space at each side of a printed or written page **2** additional amount or one greater than necessary **3 win by a large margin** to win (a contest) by a large or small amount

marginal adjective **1** insignificant, unimportant **2** Politics (of a

constituency) won by only a small margin > **marginally** adverb to only a small extent

marigold noun plant with yellow or orange flowers

marijuana noun dried flowers and leaves of the cannabis plant, used as a drug, especially in cigarettes

marina noun harbour for yachts and other pleasure boats

marinate verb to soak (fish or meat) in a seasoned liquid before cooking

marine adjective **1** of the sea or shipping > noun **2** (especially in Britain and the US) soldier trained for land and sea combat

marital adjective relating to marriage

maritime adjective relating to shipping

marjoram noun herb used for seasoning food and in salads

mark noun **1** line, dot, scar, etc visible on a surface **2** written or printed symbol **3** letter or number used to grade academic work **4** unit of currency formerly used in Germany > verb **5** to make a mark on (a surface) **6** to be a sign of (something) **7** to grade (academic work) **8** to stay close to (a sporting opponent) to hamper his or her play

marked adjective noticeable > **markedly** adverb

market noun **1** place where goods or animals are bought and sold **2** place with many small stalls selling different goods **3** demand for goods > verb **4** to sell (a product) in an organized way

marketing noun part of a business that controls the way that goods or services are sold

market research noun research into consumers' needs and purchases

marksman marksmen noun person skilled at shooting

marlin noun Aust large fish found in tropical seas that has a very long upper jaw

marmalade noun jam made from citrus fruits

maroon adjective reddish-purple

marooned adjective **1** abandoned ashore, especially on an island **2** isolated without resources

marquee noun large tent used for a party or exhibition

marriage noun **1** state of being married; matrimony **2** wedding

marrow noun long thick striped green vegetable with whitish flesh

marry marries marrying married verb **1** to take (someone) as a husband or wife **2** to join (a couple) in marriage > **married** adjective: a married man

Mars noun fourth planet from the sun in the solar system

marsh noun low-lying wet land

marshal marshals marshalling marshalled noun **1** official who organizes ceremonies or events > verb **2** to gather (things or people) together and organize them

marshmallow noun spongy pink or white sweet

marsupial noun animal that carries its young in a pouch, such as a kangaroo

martial art noun any of various philosophies and techniques of self-defence, originating in the

Far East, such as karate

Martian noun supposed inhabitant of Mars

martyr noun **1** person who dies or suffers for his or her beliefs > verb **2** to make a martyr of (someone) > **martyrdom** noun: They see martyrdom as the ultimate glory

marvel marvels marvelling marvelled verb **1** to be filled with wonder > noun **2** wonderful thing

marvellous adjective wonderful or excellent > **marvellously** adverb

Marxism noun political philosophy of Karl Marx, which states that society will develop towards communism through the struggle between different social classes > **Marxist** noun **1** person who believes in Marxism > adjective **2** believing in Marxism

marzipan noun paste of ground almonds, sugar and egg whites, put on top of cakes or used to make small sweets

mascara noun cosmetic for darkening and lengthening the eyelashes

mascot noun person, animal or thing supposed to bring good luck

masculine adjective **1** typical of men rather than women **2** Grammar of the gender of nouns that includes some male animate things > **masculinity** noun: the link between masculinity and violence

mash verb to crush (cooked vegetables) into a soft mass

mask noun **1** covering for the face, as a disguise or protection > verb **2** to hide or disguise (something)

masochism noun condition in which pleasure is obtained from feeling pain or from being humiliated >**masochist** noun someone who gets pleasure from his or her own suffering

mason noun person who works with stone

masonry noun pieces of stone forming part of a wall or building

masquerade verb (followed by as) to pretend to be (someone or something else)

mass noun 1 large quantity 2 Physics amount of matter in an object **the masses** ordinary people ▷ adjective 4 involving many people ▷ verb 5 to gather together in a large group

massacre noun 1 indiscriminate killing of large numbers of people ▷ verb 2 to kill (people) in large numbers

massage noun 1 rubbing and kneading of parts of the body to reduce pain or stiffness ▷ verb 2 to give a massage to (someone)

massive adjective large and heavy >**massively** adverb extremely

mass-produce verb to manufacture (standardized goods) in large quantities

mast noun tall pole for supporting something, especially a ship's sails

master noun 1 person in control, such as an employer or an owner of slaves or animals 2 male teacher ▷ adjective 3 overall or controlling 4 main or principal ▷ verb 5 to acquire knowledge of or skill in (something) 6 to succeed in controlling (a difficult situation)

masterful adjective showing control and authority

masterly adjective showing

great skill

mastermind verb 1 to plan and direct (a complex task) ▷ noun 2 person who plans and directs a complex task

masterpiece noun outstanding work of art

masturbate verb to stroke or rub one's genitals for sexual pleasure >**masturbation** noun masturbating

mat noun piece of fabric used as a floor covering or to protect a surface

matador noun man who kills the bull in bullfights

match noun 1 contest in a game or sport 2 small stick with a tip that produces a flame when scraped on a rough surface ▷ verb 3 to be exactly like, equal to or in harmony with (something)

mate noun 1 informal friend 2 sexual partner of an animal 3 officer in a merchant ship ▷ verb 4 (of animals) to be paired for reproduction

material noun 1 substance of which a thing is made 2 cloth 3 information on which a piece of work may be based 4 materials equipment needed for an activity ▷ adjective 5 involving possessions or money >**materially** adverb considerably

materialism noun excessive interest in or desire for money and possessions >**materialistic** adjective: a materialistic society

materialize verb to happen in fact or appear

maternal adjective 1 of a mother 2 related through one's mother

maternity adjective of or for

pregnant women

mathematics noun study of numbers, quantities and shapes > **mathematical** adjective: mathematical calculations > **mathematically** adverb: mathematically minded > **mathematician** noun person trained in the study of numbers, quantities and shapes

maths noun informal mathematics

Matilda noun **1** Aust old-fashioned swagman's bundle of belongings **2** waltz Matilda Aust to travel about carrying your bundle of belongings

matinée noun afternoon performance in a theatre or cinema

matrimony noun formal marriage > **matrimonial** adjective: the matrimonial home

matrix matrices noun **1** substance or situation in which something originates, takes form or is enclosed **2** Maths rectangular array of numbers or elements

matron noun **1** Brit **a** (in a nursing home or, formerly, in a hospital) senior nurse in charge of the nursing staff **b** (in a boarding school) woman responsible for looking after the health of the children **2** staid or dignified married woman

matt adjective dull, not shiny

matted adjective (of hair) tangled, with strands sticking together

matter noun **1** substance of which something is made **2** physical substance **3** event, situation or subject **4** written material in general **5** what's the matter? what is wrong? > verb **6** to be of

importance

matter-of-fact adjective showing no emotion

matting noun thick woven material such as rope or straw, used as a floor covering

mattress noun large stuffed flat case, often with springs, used on or as a bed

mature adjective **1** fully developed or grown-up > verb **2** to become mature **3** (of a bill or bond) to become due for payment > **maturely** adverb in a mature fashion > **maturity** noun state of being mature

maudlin adjective foolishly or tearfully sentimental

maul verb (of an animal) to attack (someone) savagely

mausoleum noun stately tomb

mauve adjective pale purple

maxim noun general truth or principle

maximize verb to increase (something) to a maximum

maximum adjective, noun greatest possible (amount or number)

may verb used as an auxiliary to express possibility, permission, opportunity, etc

maybe adverb perhaps, possibly

mayhem noun violent destruction or confusion

mayonnaise noun thick salad dressing made with egg yolks, oil and vinegar

mayor noun person elected to lead and represent the people of a town

maze noun complex network of paths or lines designed to puzzle

MBE abbreviation (in Britain) Member of the Order of the

British Empire

MD *abbreviation* **1** Doctor of Medicine **2** managing director

me *pronoun* objective form of **I**

meadow *noun* piece of grassland

meagre *adjective* scanty or insufficient

meal *noun* **1** occasion when food is served and eaten **2** the food itself

mealie *noun* S Afr maize

mean means meaning meant *verb* **1** to intend to convey or express (something) **2** to signify or denote (something) **3** to intend (to do something) **4** to have importance as specified: *It would mean a lot to them to win* ▷ *adjective* **5** miserly, ungenerous or petty **6** unkind or cruel ▷ *noun* **7** Maths average of a set of numbers > **meanly** *adverb* > **meanness** *noun*: *his meanness over money*

meander *verb* to follow a winding course

meaning *noun* **1** sense, significance **2** worth, purpose: *a challenge that gives meaning to life* > **meaningful** *adjective*: *a meaningful event* > **meaningfully** *adverb*: *He glanced meaningfully at the other policeman* > **meaningless** *adjective*: *a meaningless existence*

means test *noun* inquiry into a person's means to decide on eligibility for financial aid

meantime *noun* intervening period

meanwhile *adverb* **1** during the intervening period ▷ *noun* **2** intervening period

measles *noun* infectious disease producing red spots

measly measlier measliest
adjective informal meagre

measure *noun* **1** unit of size or quantity **2** certain amount (of something): *a measure of agreement* **3** **measures** actions taken ▷ *verb* **4** to determine the size or quantity of (something) **5** to be (a specified amount) in size or quantity

measured *adjective* **1** slow and steady **2** carefully considered

measurement *noun* **1** measuring **2** size

meat *noun* animal flesh as food > **meaty** *adjective* (tasting) of or like meat

Mecca *noun* **1** holy city of Islam **2** place that attracts visitors
- Most Muslims dislike this form and use the Arabic
- Makkah

mechanic *noun* person skilled in repairing or operating machinery

mechanical *adjective* **1** of or done by machines **2** (of an action) without thought or feeling > **mechanically** *adverb*

mechanism *noun* **1** piece of machinery **2** process or technique

medal *noun* piece of metal with an inscription etc, given as a reward or memento

medallion *noun* disc-shaped ornament worn on a chain round the neck

medallist *noun* winner of a medal

meddle *verb* to interfere annoyingly

media *plural noun* television, radio and newspapers collectively
- Although *media* is a plural noun, it is becoming more common for it to be used

● as a singular: *the media is obsessed with violence*

mediaeval *adjective* same as **medieval**

median *adjective, noun* Geometry middle (point or line)

mediate *verb* to intervene in a dispute to bring about agreement >**mediation** *noun: United Nations mediation between the two sides* >**mediator** *noun: acting as mediator between the rebels and the authorities*

medical *adjective* **1** of or relating to the science of medicine ▷ *noun* **2** *informal* medical examination >**medically** *adverb: medically qualified*

medication *noun* medicinal substance

medicinal *adjective* relating to the treatment of illness

medicine *noun* **1** substance used to treat disease **2** science of preventing, diagnosing or curing disease

medieval *adjective* of the Middle Ages

mediocre *adjective* of rather poor quality >**mediocrity** *noun: the mediocrity of most contemporary literature*

meditate *verb* **1** to reflect deeply, especially on spiritual matters **2** (followed by *on*) to think about or plan (something) >**meditation** *noun* act of meditating ▷ *adjective*

Mediterranean *noun* **1** large sea between southern Europe and northern Africa ▷ *adjective* **2** of the Mediterranean or the European countries adjoining it

medium **mediums** or **media**

adjective **1** midway between extremes, average ▷ *noun* **2** means of communicating news or information to the public, such as radio or newspapers **3** person who can supposedly communicate with the dead

medley *noun* **1** miscellaneous mixture **2** musical sequence of different tunes

meek *adjective* submissive or humble >**meekly** *adverb* >**meekness** *noun* submissiveness or humility

meet **meets meeting met** *verb* **1** to come together with (someone) **2** to come into contact with (someone) **3** to be at the place of arrival of (someone) **4** to satisfy (a need etc) **5** to experience (a situation, attitude or problem) **6** **meet with** or **be met with** to get (a particular reaction): *I was met with silence*

meeting *noun* **1** event in which people discuss proposals and make decisions together **2** act of meeting someone

megabyte *noun* Computers 2²⁰ or 1 048 576 bytes

melaleuca *noun* Australian shrub or tree with a white trunk and black branches

melancholy *noun* **1** sadness or gloom ▷ *adjective* **2** sad or gloomy

mêlée *noun* noisy confused fight or crowd

mellow *adjective* **1** (of light) soft, not harsh **2** (of a sound) smooth and pleasant to listen to ▷ *verb* **3** to become more pleasant or relaxed

melodic *adjective* relating to melody

melodious adjective pleasing to the ear

melodrama noun play full of extravagant action and emotion

melodramatic adjective behaving in an exaggerated, emotional way; theatrical

melody melodies noun series of musical notes which make a tune

melon noun large round juicy fruit with a hard rind

melt verb to become liquid or cause (a solid) to become liquid by heat

member noun 1 one of the people or things belonging to a group 2 individual making up a body or society ▷ adjective 3 (of a country or state) belonging to an international organization

Member of Parliament noun person elected to parliament

membership noun 1 state of being a member of an organization 2 people belonging to an organization

membrane noun thin flexible tissue in a plant or animal body

memento mementos noun thing serving to remind, souvenir

memo memos noun short for **memorandum**

memoirs plural noun biography or historical account based on personal knowledge

memorable adjective worth remembering, noteworthy > **memorably** adverb

memorandum memorandums or **memoranda** noun 1 written record or communication within a business 2 note of things to be remembered

memorial noun 1 something

serving to commemorate a person or thing ▷ adjective 2 serving as a memorial

memory memories noun 1 ability to remember 2 particular recollection 3 part of a computer that stores information

men noun plural of **man**

menace noun 1 someone or something likely to cause serious harm 2 quality of being threatening > verb 3 to threaten or endanger (someone) > **menacingly** adverb threateningly

menagerie noun collection of wild animals for exhibition

mend verb to repair or patch (something)

menial adjective involving boring work of low status

meningitis noun inflammation of the membranes of the brain

menopause noun time when a woman's menstrual cycle ceases

menorah noun candelabra that usually has seven parts and is used in Jewish temples

menstruate verb (of a woman) to have an approximately monthly discharge of blood from the womb > **menstrual** adjective: the menstrual cycle > **menstruation** noun approximately monthly discharge of blood and cellular debris from the womb of a woman who is not pregnant

-ment suffix state or feeling: contentment; resentment

mental adjective 1 of, in or done by the mind 2 of or for mental illness > **mentally** adverb

mentality mentalities noun way of thinking

mention *verb* **1** to refer to (something) briefly ▷ *noun* **2** brief reference to a person or thing

mentor *noun* adviser or guide

menu *noun* **1** list of dishes to be served, or from which to order **2** *Computers* list of options displayed on a screen

mercenary mercenaries *adjective* **1** mainly interested in getting money ▷ *noun* **2** soldier paid to fight for a foreign country

merchandise *noun* goods that are sold

merchant *noun* person engaged in trade, wholesale trader

merchant navy *noun* ships or crew engaged in a nation's commercial shipping

merciful *adjective*
1 compassionate, kind
2 considered to be fortunate as a relief from suffering: *Death came as a merciful release* >**mercifully** *adverb*

merciless *adjective* showing no kindness or forgiveness; heartless >**mercilessly** *adverb*

mercury *noun* silvery liquid metal

mercy mercies *noun* compassionate treatment of an offender or enemy who is in one's power

mere merest *adjective* nothing more than: *mere chance* >**merely** *adverb*

merge *verb* to combine or blend

meringue *noun* baked mixture of egg whites and sugar

merino merinos *noun* breed of sheep, common in Australia and New Zealand, with fine soft wool

merit *noun* **1** excellence or worth **2** merits admirable qualities

▷ *verb* **3** to deserve (something)

mermaid *noun* imaginary sea creature with the upper part of a woman and the lower part of a fish

merry merrier merriest *adjective* **1** cheerful or jolly **2** *informal* slightly drunk >**merrily** *adverb*: *He laughed merrily*

merry-go-round *noun* roundabout

mesh *noun* network or net

mess *noun* **1** untidy or dirty confusion **2** trouble or difficulty **3** place where members of the armed forces eat ▷ *verb* **4** (followed by *about*) to potter about >**mess up** *verb* to spoil (something) or do (something) wrong

message *noun* **1** communication sent **2** meaning or moral

message board *noun* internet discussion forum

messaging *noun* sending messages between mobile phones, using letters and numbers to produce shortened forms of words

messenger *noun* someone who takes a message to someone for someone else

Messiah *noun* **1** Jews' promised deliverer **2** Christ

Messrs *noun* plural of **Mr**

met *verb* past of **meet**

metabolism *noun* chemical processes of a living body >**metabolic** *adjective*: *people with low metabolic rate*

metal *noun* chemical element, such as iron or copper, that is malleable and capable of conducting heat and electricity

> **metallic** adjective made of or resembling metal

metamorphic adjective (of rocks) changed in texture or structure by heat and pressure

metamorphosis
metamorphoses noun change of form or character

metaphor noun figure of speech in which a word is used to refer to something it does not mean literally in order to suggest a resemblance: He is a lion in battle > **metaphorical** adjective: talking in metaphorical terms
> **metaphorically** adverb: speaking metaphorically

meteor noun piece of rock or metal that burns very brightly when it enters the earth's atmosphere from space

meteoric adjective (of someone's rise to power or success) happening very quickly

meteorite noun meteor that has fallen to earth

meteorology noun study of the earth's atmosphere, especially for weather forecasting
> **meteorological** adjective relating to the weather or weather forecasting

meter noun instrument for measuring and recording something, such as the consumption of gas or electricity

methane noun colourless inflammable gas

method noun **1** way or manner **2** technique

methodical adjective orderly
> **methodically** adverb

Methodist noun **1** member of any of the Protestant churches originated by John Wesley and his followers ▷ adjective **2** of Methodists or their Church

meticulous adjective very careful about details > **meticulously** adverb

metre noun **1** basic unit of length equal to about 1.094 yards (100 centimetres) **2** rhythm of poetry

metric adjective relating to the decimal system of weights and measures based on the metre

metropolis metropolises noun chief city of a country or region

metropolitan adjective of a metropolis

mettle noun **on your mettle** ready to do something as well as you can in a test or challenge

mew noun **1** cry of a cat ▷ verb **2** to utter this cry

Mexican adjective **1** of Mexico ▷ noun **2** person from Mexico

mg symbol milligram(s)

miasma miasmas or miasmata noun unwholesome or foreboding atmosphere

mice noun plural of **mouse**

micro- prefix very small

microchip noun small wafer of silicon containing electronic circuits

microphone noun instrument for amplifying or transmitting sounds

microprocessor noun integrated circuit acting as the central processing unit in a small computer

microscope noun instrument with lens(es) that produces a magnified image of a very small object

microscopic adjective very small

microwave *noun* **1** electromagnetic wave with a wavelength of a few centimetres, used in radar and cooking **2** microwave oven ▷ *verb* **3** to cook (food) in a microwave oven

mid- *prefix* middle: *mid-Atlantic; the mid-70s*

midday *noun* noon

middle *adjective* **1** equally distant from two extremes **2** medium, intermediate ▷ *noun* **3** middle point or part

middle age *noun* period of life between about 40 and 60 years old ▷ **middle-aged** *adjective* aged between about 40 and 60 years old

Middle Ages *plural noun* period from about 1000 AD to the 15th century

middle class *noun* social class of business and professional people ▷ **middle-class** *adjective* belonging to the middle class

Middle East *noun* area around the eastern Mediterranean up to and including Iran

Middle English *noun* the form of the English language that existed from about 1100 AD until about 1450 AD

middle-of-the-road *adjective* (of opinions) moderate

middle school *noun* in England and Wales, a school for children aged between about 8 and 12

middling *adjective* of average quality or ability

midge *noun* small mosquito-like insect

midget *noun* very small person or thing

midnight *noun* twelve o'clock at night

midriff *noun* middle part of the body

midst *noun* **in the midst of** in the middle of

midsummer *adjective* of or relating to the period in the middle of summer

midway *adverb* halfway

midwife **midwives** *noun* trained nurse who assists at childbirth ▷ **midwifery** *noun* work of a midwife

might *verb* **1** past tense of **may**: *I might stay a while; You might like to go and see it* ▷ *noun* **2** literary power or strength

mightily *adverb* old-fashioned to a great degree or extent

mighty **mightier** **mightiest** *adjective* literary powerful or strong

migraine *noun* severe headache, often with nausea and visual disturbances

migrate *verb* **1** to move from one place to settle in another **2** (of animals) to move at a particular season to a different place ▷ **migration** *noun: the migration of Soviet Jews to Israel* ▷ **migratory** *adjective* (of an animal) migrating every year

mike *noun informal* microphone

mild *adjective* **1** not strongly flavoured **2** gentle **3** calm or temperate ▷ **mildly** *adverb: to put it mildly*

mildew *noun* destructive fungus on plants or things exposed to damp

mile *noun* unit of length equal to 1760 yards or 1.609 kilometres

mileage *noun* **1** distance travelled in miles **2** miles travelled by a motor vehicle per gallon of petrol **3** *informal* usefulness of something

militant *adjective* **1** aggressive or vigorous in support of a cause ▷ *noun* **2** person who tries to bring about extreme political or social change > **militancy** *noun: the rise of trade-union militancy*

military *adjective* **1** of or for soldiers, armies or war ▷ *noun* **2** armed services > **militarily** *adverb*

militia *noun* military force of trained citizens for use in emergency only

milk *noun* **1** white fluid produced by female mammals to feed their young **2** milk of cows, goats, etc, used by humans as food ▷ *verb* **3** to draw milk from the udders of (a cow or goat) **4** to exploit (a person or situation)

milk teeth *noun* first set of teeth in young children

milky milkier milkiest *adjective* **1** pale creamy white **2** containing a lot of milk

Milky Way *noun* luminous band of stars stretching across the night sky

mill *noun* **1** building where grain is crushed to make flour **2** factory for making materials such as steel, wool or cotton **3** small device for grinding coffee or spices into powder

millennium millennia or **millenniums** *noun* period of a thousand years

miller *noun* person who works in a mill

milligram *noun* thousandth of a gram

millilitre *noun* thousandth of

a litre

millimetre *noun* thousandth part of a metre

million *adjective, noun* **1** one thousand thousands; 1,000,000 **2 millions** large but unspecified number; lots > **millionth** *adjective, noun* the millionth truck; a millionth of a second

millionaire *noun* person who owns at least a million pounds, dollars, etc

millstone *noun* **millstone round your neck** unpleasant problem or responsibility that you cannot escape from

mime *noun* **1** acting without the use of words ▷ *verb* **2** to describe or express (something) in mime

mimic mimics mimicking mimicked *verb* **1** to imitate (a person or manner), especially in an amusing way ▷ *noun* **2** person who is good at mimicking > **mimicry** *noun* action of mimicking someone

minaret *noun* tall slender tower of a mosque

mince *verb* **1** to cut or grind (meat) into very small pieces **2** to walk in an affected manner ▷ *noun* **3** minced meat

mind *noun* **1** ability to think **2** memory or attention **3 change your mind** to change a decision that you have made ▷ *verb* **4** to take offence at (something) **5** to take care of (a child or an object)

mindful *adjective* (followed by *of*) heedful of (something)

mindless *adjective* stupid and destructive

mine *pronoun* **1** belonging to me ▷ *noun* **2** deep hole for digging out coal, ores, etc **3** bomb placed under the ground or in water ▷ *verb* **4** to dig (minerals) from a mine ▷ **miner** *noun* person who works in a mine ▷ **mining** *noun*: *traditional industries such as coal mining*

minefield *noun* area of land or water containing mines

mineral *noun* naturally occurring inorganic substance, such as metal

mineral water *noun* water that comes from a natural spring

minestrone *noun* soup containing vegetables and pasta

minesweeper *noun* ship for clearing away mines

mingle *verb* to mix or blend

mini- *prefix* smaller or less important: *a TV mini-series*

miniature *noun* **1** small portrait, model or copy ▷ *adjective* **2** small-scale

minibus *noun* small bus

minim *noun* *Music* note half the length of a semibreve

minimal *adjective* minimum ▷ **minimally** *adverb* to the minimum degree

minimize *verb* to reduce (something) to a minimum

minimum *adjective, noun* least possible (amount or number)

minister *noun* **1** head of a government department **2** (in a Protestant church) member of the clergy

ministerial *adjective* of a government minister

ministry ministries *noun* **1** ministers collectively **2** government department

mink *noun* **1** stoatlike animal **2** its

highly valued fur

minnow *noun* very small freshwater fish

minor *adjective* **1** lesser **2** *Music* (of a scale) having a semitone between the second and third notes ▷ *noun* **3** person regarded legally as a child

minority minorities *noun* **1** lesser number **2** group in a minority in any state

minstrel *noun* medieval singer or musician

mint *noun* **1** herb used for flavouring in cooking **2** peppermint-flavoured sweet **3** place where money is coined ▷ *verb* **4** to make (coins) ▷ *adjective* **5** in mint condition in very good condition, like new

minus *preposition* **1** indicating subtraction ▷ *adjective* **2** less than zero ▷ *noun* **3** sign (-) denoting subtraction or a number less than zero

minuscule *adjective* very small indeed

minute¹ *noun* **1** 60th part of an hour or degree **2** moment **3** minutes record of the proceedings of a meeting ▷ *verb* **4** to write the official notes of (a meeting)

minute² *adjective* extremely small ▷ **minutely** *adverb* in great detail

minutiae *plural noun* trifling or precise details

miracle *noun* **1** wonderful and surprising event, believed to have been caused by God **2** any very surprising and fortunate event ▷ **miraculous** *adjective: He made a miraculous recovery* ▷ **miraculously** *adverb*

mirage noun optical illusion, especially one caused by hot air

mire noun literary swampy ground or mud

mirror noun 1 coated glass surface for reflecting images ▷ verb 2 to reflect (something) in or as if in a mirror

mirth noun literary laughter, merriment or gaiety

mis- prefix wrong(ly), bad(ly)

misbehave verb to be naughty or behave badly > **misbehaviour** noun naughty or bad behaviour

miscarriage noun 1 spontaneous premature expulsion of a fetus from the womb 2 failure: a miscarriage of justice

miscellaneous adjective mixed or assorted

mischief noun eagerness to have fun by teasing people or playing tricks > **mischievous** adjective full of mischief

misconception noun wrong idea or belief

misconduct noun bad or unacceptable behaviour by a professional person

misdemeanour noun minor wrongdoing

miser noun person who hoards money and hates spending it > **miserly** adjective reluctant to spend money; mean

miserable adjective 1 very unhappy and sad; dejected 2 causing misery > **miserably** adverb

misery miseries noun great unhappiness

misfire verb (of a plan) to fail to turn out as intended

misfit noun person not suited to his or her social environment

misfortune noun piece of bad luck

misgiving noun feeling of fear or doubt

misguided adjective mistaken or unwise

misinform verb to give incorrect information to (someone) > **misinformation** noun incorrect information

misinterpret verb to make an incorrect interpretation of

misjudge verb to judge (someone or something) wrongly or unfairly

mislay mislays mislaying mislaid verb to lose (something) temporarily

mislead misleads misleading misled verb to give false or confusing information to (someone)

misplaced adjective (of a feeling) inappropriate or directed at the wrong thing or person: misplaced loyalty

misprint noun printing error

misrepresent verb to represent (someone) wrongly or inaccurately > **misrepresentation** noun: misrepresentation of the facts

miss verb 1 to fail to notice, hear, hit, reach, find or catch (something) 2 not to be in time for (a bus, train or plane) 3 to notice or regret the absence of (someone or something) 4 to fail to take advantage of (a chance or opportunity) ▷ noun 5 fact or instance of missing

missile noun object or weapon thrown, shot or launched at a target

mission noun 1 specific task or

duty **2** group of people sent on a mission **3** journey made by a military aeroplane or space rocket to carry out a task **4** building in which missionaries work

missionary missionaries noun person sent abroad to do religious and social work

missive noun old-fashioned letter

mist noun **1** thin fog ▷ verb **2** (of eyes) to become blurred with tears **3** (followed by *up* or *over*) (of a glass) to become opaque because covered with condensation

mistake mistakes mistaking mistook mistaken noun **1** error or blunder ▷ verb **2** to confuse (a person or thing) with another

mistaken adjective **1** (of a person) wrong: *I was mistaken about you* **2** (of a belief or opinion) incorrect >**mistakenly** adverb incorrectly

Mister noun polite form of address to a man

mistletoe noun evergreen plant with white berries growing as a parasite on trees, used as a Christmas decoration

mistook verb past of **mistake**

mistreat verb to treat (a person or animal) badly

mistress noun **1** woman who has a continuing sexual relationship with a married man **2** female employer of a servant **3** female teacher

mistrust verb **1** to have doubts or suspicions about (someone) ▷ noun **2** lack of trust

misty mistier mistiest adjective full of or covered with mist

misunderstand misunderstands

misunderstanding

misunderstood verb to fail to understand (someone) properly >**misunderstanding** noun slight quarrel or disagreement

misuse noun **1** incorrect, improper or careless use ▷ verb **2** to use (something) wrongly

mite noun very tiny creature that lives in the fur of animals

mitigating adjective formal (of circumstances) making a crime easier to understand or justify

mitten noun glove with one section for the thumb and one for the four fingers together

mix verb to combine or blend (things) into one mass >**mix up** verb to confuse (two things or people)

mixed adjective **1** consisting of several things of the same general kind **2** involving people from two or more different races: *mixed marriages* **3** (of education or accommodation) for both males and females

mixed up adjective **1** confused **2** (followed by *in*) involved in (a crime or a scandal)

mixer noun machine used for mixing things together

mixture noun **1** several different things mixed together **2** substance consisting of other substances that have been stirred or shaken together

mix-up noun mistake in something that was planned

ml symbol millilitre(s)

mm symbol millimetre(s)

moa noun large extinct flightless New Zealand bird

moan noun **1** low cry of pain

2 *informal* grumble ▷ *verb* **3** to make a low cry of pain **4** *informal* to grumble

moat *noun* deep wide ditch, especially round a castle

mob mobs mobbing mobbed *noun* **1** disorderly crowd ▷ *verb* **2** to surround (someone) in a disorderly crowd

mobile *adjective* **1** able to move or be moved freely and easily: *a mobile library* **2** able to travel or move about from one place to another ▷ *noun* **3** same as **mobile phone 4** hanging structure designed to move in air currents > **mobility** *noun* condition of being mobile

mobile phone *noun* cordless phone powered by batteries

moccasin *noun* soft leather shoe

mock *verb* **1** to make fun of, mimic or ridicule (someone) ▷ *adjective* **2** sham or imitation **3** (of an examination) done as a practice before the real examination

mockery **mockeries** *noun* expression of scorn or ridicule

mode *noun* **1** method or manner **2** *Maths* biggest in a set of groups

model **models** **modelling** **modelled** *noun* **1** (miniature) representation **2** pattern **3** person or thing worthy of imitation **4** person who poses for an artist or photographer **5** person who wears clothes to display them to prospective buyers ▷ *adjective* **6** denoting a (miniature) representation of something **7** excellent: *a model pupil* ▷ *verb* **8** to display (clothes) by wearing them **9** to make (shapes or figures) out of clay or wood **10** **model yourself on** to

copy the behaviour of (someone that you admire)

modem *noun* device for connecting two computers by a telephone line

moderate *adjective* **1** not extreme **2** average ▷ *noun* **3** person of moderate views ▷ *verb* **4** to become less violent or extreme or make (something) less violent or extreme > **moderately** *adverb* > **moderation** *noun*: *a man of fairness and moderation*

modern *adjective* **1** of present or recent times **2** up-to-date > **modernity** *noun*: *the clash between tradition and modernity*

modernize *verb* to bring (something) up to date

modest *adjective* **1** not vain or boastful **2** quite small in size or amount **3** shy and easily embarrassed > **modestly** *adverb* in a modest manner > **modesty** *noun* quality of being modest

modify **modifies** **modifying** **modified** *verb* to change (something) slightly in order to improve it > **modification** *noun* small change made to improve something

module *noun* **1** one of the parts that when put together form a whole unit or object **2** part of a machine or system that does a particular task **3** part of a spacecraft that can do certain things away from the main body > **modular** *adjective*: *the course is modular in structure*

mohair *noun* very soft, fluffy wool obtained from angora goats

moist *adjective* slightly wet

moisten *verb* to make (something)

moist

moisture *noun* tiny drops of water in the air or on the ground

molar *noun* large back tooth used for grinding

mole *noun* **1** small dark raised spot on the skin **2** small burrowing animal with black fur **3** *informal* member of an organization who is working as a spy for a rival organization

molecule *noun* the smallest amount of a substance that can exist >**molecular** *adjective*: *the molecular structure of fuel*

molest *verb* to touch (a child) in a sexual way >**molester** *noun*: *a child molester*

mollify mollifies mollifying mollified *verb* to make (someone) less upset or angry

mollusc *noun* soft-bodied, usually hard-shelled, animal, such as a snail or oyster

molten *adjective* liquefied or melted

moment *noun* **1** very short space of time; second **2** point in time **3** **at the moment** now

momentary *adjective* lasting only a moment >**momentarily** *adverb*

● Some Americans say
● *momentarily* when they mean
● 'very soon', rather than 'for a
● moment'

momentous *adjective* of great significance

momentum momenta or **momentums** *noun* **1** ability to keep developing: *the campaign is gaining momentum* **2** impetus of a moving body

monarch *noun* sovereign ruler of a state

monarchy monarchies *noun* government by or a state ruled by a sovereign

monastery monasteries *noun* residence of a community of monks >**monastic** *adjective* of monks, nuns or monasteries

Monday *noun* day between Sunday and Tuesday

money *noun* medium of exchange, coins or banknotes

mongrel *noun* dog of mixed breed

monitor *noun* **1** person or device that checks, controls, warns or keeps a record of something **2** visual display unit of a computer **3** *Brit, Aust, NZ* pupil assisting a teacher with duties ▷ *verb* **4** to watch and check on (something)

monk *noun* member of an all-male religious community bound by vows

monkey *noun* animal that has a long tail and climbs trees

mono- *prefix* single: *monosyllable*

monocle *noun* eyeglass for one eye only

monogamy *noun* custom of being married to one person at a time >**monogamous** *adjective* being married to one person at a time

monologue *noun* long speech by one person during a play or a conversation

monopoly monopolies *noun* exclusive possession of or right to do something

monotone *noun* unvaried pitch in speech or sound

monotonous *adjective* tedious due to lack of variety >**monotony** *noun*: *to break the monotony*

monotreme *noun* Australian mammal with a single opening in its body for the passage of eggs, sperm, faeces and urine

monounsaturated *adjective* (of an oil) made mainly from vegetable fat > **monounsaturate** *noun*

monsoon *noun* season of very heavy rain in South-east Asia

monster *noun* **1** large imaginary frightening beast **2** very wicked person > *adjective* **3** huge

monstrosity monstrosities *noun* large ugly thing

monstrous *adjective* extremely shocking or unfair > **monstrously** *adverb*

montage *noun* picture or film consisting of a combination of several different items arranged to produce an unusual effect

month *noun* one of the twelve divisions of the calendar year

monthly *adjective* happening or payable once a month

monument *noun* something, especially a building or statue, that commemorates something

monumental *adjective* **1** (of a monumental building or sculpture) very large and important **2** very large or extreme

moo *verb* to make the long deep cry of a cow

mood *noun* temporary (gloomy) state of mind

moody moodier moodiest *adjective* **1** sullen or gloomy **2** changeable in mood

moon *noun* natural satellite of the earth

moonlight moonlights moonlighting moonlighted *noun* **1** light from the moon > *verb* **2** informal to work at a secondary

job, especially illegally

moor *noun* **1** high area of open land > *verb* **2** to secure (a ship) with ropes etc

mooring *noun* place for mooring a ship

moose *noun* large N American deer

● The plural of *moose* is *moose*

moot *verb* to bring (something) up for discussion

mop mops mopping mopped *noun* **1** long stick with twists of cotton or a sponge on the end, used for washing floors **2** thick mass of hair > *verb* **3** to clean (a surface) with or as if with a mop

mope *verb* to feel miserable and not interested in anything

moped *noun* type of small motorcycle

mopoke *noun* small spotted owl found in Australia and New Zealand

moral *adjective* **1** concerned with right and wrong conduct > *noun* **2** lesson to be obtained from a story or event **3** morals values based on beliefs about the correct and acceptable way to behave > **morality** *noun* **1** good moral conduct **2** moral goodness or badness > **morally** *adverb*

morale *noun* degree of confidence or hope of a person or group

morbid *adjective* unduly interested in death or unpleasant events

more *adjective* **1** greater in amount or degree **2** comparative of **much** or **many** **3** additional or further > *adverb* **4** to a greater extent **5** in addition > *pronoun* **6** greater or additional amount or number

moreover *adverb* in addition to what has already been said

morepork noun NZ same as **mopoke**

morgue noun building where dead bodies are kept before being buried or cremated

moribund adjective without force or vitality

morning noun 1 part of the day before noon 2 part of the day between midnight and noon

Moroccan adjective 1 of Morocco ▷ noun 2 person from Morocco

moron noun informal foolish or stupid person > **moronic** adjective: moronic vandalism

morose adjective sullen or moody

morphine noun drug extracted from opium, used as an anaesthetic and sedative

Morse or **Morse code** noun code used for sending messages in which each letter is represented by a series of dots and dashes

morsel noun small piece of food

mortal adjective 1 unable to live forever 2 (of a wound) causing death ▷ noun 3 human being

mortality mortalities noun 1 state of being mortal 2 great loss of life 3 death rate

mortar noun 1 small cannon with a short range 2 mixture of lime, sand and water for holding bricks and stones together

mortgage noun 1 loan from a bank or a building society to buy a house ▷ verb 2 to use (one's house) as a guarantee to a company in order to borrow money from them

mortifying adjective embarrassing or humiliating

mortuary mortuaries noun building where corpses are kept

before burial or cremation

mosaic noun design or decoration using small pieces of coloured stone or glass

Moslem noun, adjective same as **Muslim**

mosque noun Muslim temple

mosquito mosquitoes or mosquitos noun blood-sucking flying insect

moss noun small flowerless plant growing in masses on moist surfaces > **mossy** adjective: a mossy wall

most noun 1 greatest number or degree ▷ adjective 2 greatest in number or degree 3 superlative of **much** or **many** ▷ adverb 4 in the greatest degree

mostly adverb for the most part, generally

MOT noun (in Britain) compulsory annual test of the roadworthiness of vehicles over a certain age

motel noun roadside hotel for motorists

moth noun insect like a butterfly which usually flies at night

mother noun 1 female parent ▷ verb 2 to look after (someone) as a mother

motherhood noun state of being a mother

mother-in-law mothers-in-law noun mother of your husband or wife

motif noun (recurring) theme or design

motion noun 1 process, action or way of moving 2 action or gesture 3 proposal in a meeting ▷ verb 4 to direct (someone) by gesture

motionless adjective not moving

motivate verb 1 to inspire (someone) to behave in a particular way 2 to make (someone) feel determined to do something > **motivated** adjective: highly motivated employees > **motivation** noun: his lack of motivation at work

motive noun reason for a course of action

motley adjective miscellaneous

motor noun 1 engine, especially of a vehicle 2 machine that converts electrical energy into mechanical energy ▷ verb 3 to travel by car

motorboat noun boat with an engine

motorcycle noun two-wheeled vehicle with an engine that is ridden like a bicycle > **motorcyclist** noun person who rides a motorcycle

motoring adjective relating to cars and driving: a motoring correspondent

motorist noun person who drives a car

motorway noun main road for fast-moving traffic

mottled adjective marked with blotches

motto **mottoes** or **mottos** noun saying expressing an ideal or rule of conduct

mould noun 1 hollow container in which metal etc is cast 2 fungal growth caused by dampness ▷ verb 3 to shape (a substance) 4 to influence or direct (someone or something) > **mouldy** adjective covered with mould

moult verb to shed feathers, hair or skin to make way for new growth

mound noun 1 heap, especially of earth or stones 2 small hill

mount verb 1 to climb or ascend (something) 2 to get up on (a horse etc) 3 to increase or accumulate 4 to fix (an object) in a particular place to display it 5 to organize (a campaign or event) ▷ noun 6 mountain

mountain noun 1 hill of great size 2 large heap

mountaineer noun person who climbs mountains

mountainous adjective full of mountains

mourn verb to feel or express sorrow for (a dead person or lost thing)

mourner noun person attending a funeral

mournful adjective sad or dismal

mourning noun conventional symbols of grief for death, such as the wearing of black

mouse **mice** noun 1 small long-tailed rodent 2 Computers hand-held device for moving the cursor without keying

mousse noun dish of flavoured cream whipped and set

moustache noun hair on a man's upper lip

mouth noun 1 opening in the head for eating and issuing sounds 2 entrance to a cave or a hole 3 point where a river enters the sea ▷ verb 4 to form (words) with the lips without speaking

mouthpiece noun 1 part of a telephone into which a person speaks 2 part of a wind instrument into which the player blows 3 spokesperson

movable or **moveable** adjective able to be moved from one place to another

move verb 1 to change in place or position 2 to change the place or position of (something) 3 to change (one's house etc) 4 to stir the emotions of (someone) 5 to suggest (a proposal) formally ▷ noun 6 moving 7 act of putting a piece or counter in a game in a different position: It's your move next

movement noun 1 action or process of moving 2 group with a common aim: the peace movement 3 division of a piece of classical music 4 **movements** everything that you do during a period of time

moving adjective causing you to feel deep sadness or emotion ▷ **movingly** adverb

mow mows mowing mowed mown verb to cut (grass or crops) > **mow down** to kill (people) in large numbers > **mower** noun machine for cutting grass

MP abbreviation Member of Parliament

MP3 player noun device that plays audio or video files, often used for listening to music downloaded from the Internet

mpg abbreviation miles per gallon

mph abbreviation miles per hour

Mr title used before a man's name

Mrs title used before a married woman's name

Ms title used instead of Miss or Mrs

MSP abbreviation (in Britain) Member of the Scottish Parliament

much adjective 1 large amount or degree of ▷ noun 2 large amount or degree ▷ adverb 3 to a great degree 4 often: He didn't talk much about the war

muck noun 1 informal dirt, filth 2 manure > **muck about** informal to behave stupidly and waste time > **mucky** adjective informal very dirty

mucus noun liquid produced in parts of the body, e.g. the nose

mud noun wet soft earth

muddle verb 1 to confuse (someone) 2 to mix (things) up ▷ noun 3 state of confusion

muddy muddier muddiest adjective 1 covered in mud 2 (of a colour) dull and not clear

muesli noun mixture of grain, nuts and dried fruit, eaten with milk

muffin noun a small round cake eaten hot

muffled adjective (of a sound) quiet or difficult to hear: a muffled explosion

mug mugs mugging mugged noun 1 large drinking cup 2 informal gullible person ▷ verb 3 informal to attack and rob (someone) > **mugger** noun person who attacks and robs someone > **mugging** noun act of attacking and robbing someone

muggy muggier muggiest adjective (of weather) unpleasantly warm and damp

mule noun offspring of a horse and a donkey

mulga noun 1 Australian acacia shrub growing in desert regions 2 Aust informal the outback

● The plural of mulga is mulga

mull verb **mull over** to think (something) over or ponder (something)

mullet noun common edible fish found in Australian and New Zealand waters

mulloway noun large edible fish found in Australian waters

multi- prefix many: multicultural; multistorey

multimedia noun 1 Computing sound, pictures, film and ordinary text used to convey information 2 TV, computers and books used as teaching aids

multinational noun very large company with branches in many countries

multiple adjective 1 having many parts ▷ noun 2 quantity which contains another an exact number of times

multiple sclerosis noun serious disease that attacks the nervous system, affecting the ability to move

multiplication noun 1 process of multiplying one number by another 2 large increase in number

multiplicity noun large number or great variety

multiply multiplies multiplying multiplied verb 1 to increase in number, quantity or degree 2 to add (a number or quantity) to itself a given number of times

multitude noun formal very large number of people or things

mum noun informal mother

mumble verb to speak indistinctly, mutter

mummy mummies noun 1 child's word for **mother** 2 body embalmed and wrapped for burial in ancient Egypt

mumps noun infectious disease with swelling in the glands of the neck

munch verb to chew (food) noisily and steadily

mundane adjective very ordinary and not interesting or unusual

municipal adjective relating to a city or town

munitions plural noun military stores

mural noun picture painted on a wall

murder noun 1 unlawful intentional killing of a human being ▷ verb 2 to kill (someone) in this way > **murderer** noun person who has murdered someone > **murderous** adjective 1 likely to murder someone 2 (of an attack or other action) resulting in the death of many people

murky murkier murkiest adjective dark or gloomy

murmur verb 1 to speak in a quiet indistinct way ▷ noun 2 something that someone says that can hardly be heard

muscle noun tissue in the body which produces movement by contracting > **muscle in on** verb informal to force your way into (a situation in which one is not welcome)

muscular adjective 1 with well-developed muscles 2 of muscles

muse verb literary to think about something for a long time

museum noun building where natural, artistic, historical or scientific objects are exhibited and preserved

mush noun soft pulpy mass

mushroom noun 1 edible fungus with a stem and cap ▷ verb 2 to grow rapidly

mushy mushier mushiest adjective 1 (of a fruit or vegetable) too soft 2 informal (of a story) too sentimental

music noun 1 art form using a melodious and harmonious combination of notes 2 written or printed form of this

musical adjective 1 of or like music 2 talented in or fond of music ▷ noun 3 play or film with songs and dancing >**musically** adverb

musician noun person who plays a musical instrument

musk noun scent obtained from a gland of the musk deer or produced synthetically >**musky** adjective (of a smell) strong, warm and sweet

musket noun History long-barrelled gun

Muslim or **Moslem** noun 1 follower of the religion of Islam ▷ adjective 2 of or relating to Islam

muslin noun fine cotton fabric

mussel noun edible shellfish with a dark hinged shell

must verb 1 used as an auxiliary to express obligation, certainty or resolution ▷ noun 2 essential or necessary thing

mustard noun paste made from the powdered seeds of a plant, used as a condiment

muster verb to gather together (energy, support, etc)

musty mustier mustiest adjective smelling mouldy and stale

mutate verb to change and develop in a new way, especially genetically >**mutant** noun, adjective: New species are merely mutants of earlier ones; mutant genes

mute adjective formal not giving out sound or speech

muted adjective 1 (of sound or colour) softened 2 (of a reaction) subdued

muti noun S Afr informal medicine, especially herbal medicine

mutilate verb 1 to deprive (something) of a limb or other part 2 to damage (a book or text) >**mutilation** noun: cases of torture and mutilation

mutiny mutinies mutinying mutinied noun 1 rebellion against authority, especially by soldiers or sailors ▷ verb 2 to commit mutiny

mutter verb 1 to speak indistinctly 2 to grumble

mutton noun flesh of a sheep, used as food

mutton bird noun 1 Aust sea bird with dark plumage 2 NZ any of a number of migratory sea birds, the young of which are a Maori delicacy

mutual adjective 1 felt or expressed by each of two people about the other 2 common to both or all >**mutually** adverb: a mutually supportive relationship

● It used to be that mutual
● could only be used of
● something that was shared
● between two people or
● groups. Nowadays you
● can use it to mean 'shared
● between two or more people
● or groups'

muzzle noun 1 animal's mouth and nose 2 cover for a dog's muzzle to prevent biting 3 open end of a gun 4 verb to put a muzzle on (a dog)

my adjective belonging to me

mynah bird noun tropical bird that can mimic human speech

myriad adjective 1 very many ▷ noun 2 large indefinite number

myrrh noun fragrant substance used in perfume and incense

myself pronoun emphatic or reflexive form of I or **me**

mysterious adjective **1** strange and not well understood **2** secretive >**mysteriously** adverb

mystery mysteries noun something that is not understood or known about

mystic noun **1** person who seeks spiritual knowledge ⊳ adjective **2** mystical >**mystical** adjective having a spiritual or religious significance beyond human understanding >**mysticism** noun religious practice in which people search for truth and closeness to God through meditation and prayer

mystify verb **mystifies mystifying mystified** to bewilder or puzzle (someone)

mystique noun atmosphere of mystery or power

myth noun **1** tale with supernatural characters, usually of how the world and humankind began **2** untrue idea or explanation

mythical adjective imaginary, untrue or existing only in myths

mythology noun myths collectively >**mythological** adjective: a mythological beast

n

naartjie noun S Afr tangerine
nag nags nagging nagged verb

1 to scold or find fault constantly **2** to be a constant source of discomfort or worry to ⊳ noun **3** person who nags >**nagging** adjective, noun

nail noun **1** pointed piece of metal with a head, hit with a hammer to join two objects together **2** hard covering of the upper tips of the fingers and toes **3 hit the nail on the head** to say something exactly correct ⊳ verb **4** to attach (something) with nails **5** informal to catch or arrest

naive or **naïve** adjective **1** innocent and easily fooled **2** simple and unsophisticated >**naively** adverb >**naivety** or **naïveté** noun

naked adjective **1** without clothes **2** without any covering **3 the naked eye** the eye unassisted by binoculars, telescope, etc >**nakedness** noun

name noun **1** word by which a person or thing is known **2** reputation, especially a good one **3 call someone names** or **a name** to use insulting words to describe him or her ⊳ verb **4** to give a name to **5** to refer to (someone or something) by name **6** to fix or specify

nameless adjective **1** without a name **2** unspecified **3** too horrible to be mentioned

namely adverb that is to say

namesake noun person with the same name as another

nanny nannies noun woman whose job is looking after young children

nap naps napping napped noun **1** short sleep ⊳ verb **2** to have a short sleep

nape noun back of the neck

napkin noun piece of cloth or paper for wiping the mouth or protecting the clothes while eating

nappy nappies noun piece of absorbent material fastened round a baby's bottom to absorb urine and faeces

narcotic noun, adjective (of) a drug, such as morphine or opium, designed to produce numbness and drowsiness

narrate verb 1 to tell (a story) 2 to speak words that accompany and explain what is happening in a film or TV programme > **narration** noun

narrative noun account, story

narrator noun 1 a person who tells a story 2 a person who speaks the words accompanying and explaining a film or TV programme

narrow adjective 1 small in breadth in comparison to length 2 limited in range, extent or outlook 3 with little margin: *a narrow escape* ▷ verb 4 to make or become narrow 5 (often followed by *down*) to limit or restrict > **narrowly** adverb > **narrowness** noun > **narrows** plural noun narrow part of a strait, river or current

narrow-minded adjective intolerant or bigoted

nasal adjective 1 of the nose 2 (of a sound) pronounced with air passing through the nose > **nasally** adverb

nasty nastier nastiest adjective 1 unpleasant 2 (of an injury) dangerous or painful 3 spiteful or unkind > **nastily** adverb > **nastiness** noun

nation noun people of one or more cultures or races organized as a single state

national adjective 1 typical of a particular nation ▷ noun 2 citizen of a nation > **nationally** adverb

national anthem noun official song of a country

nationalism noun 1 policy of national independence 2 patriotism, sometimes to an excessive degree > **nationalist** noun, adjective > **nationalistic** adjective

nationality nationalities noun 1 fact of being a citizen of a particular nation 2 group of people of the same race

nationalize verb to put (an industry or a company) under state control > **nationalization** noun

National Party noun major political party in Australia and New Zealand

national service noun compulsory military service

nationwide adjective, adverb happening all over a country

native adjective 1 relating to a place where a person was born 2 born in a specified place 3 (followed by *to*) originating (in) 4 inborn ▷ noun 5 person born in a specified place 6 indigenous animal or plant 7 member of the original race of a country

Nativity noun Christianity birth of Jesus Christ

natter informal verb 1 to talk idly or chatter ▷ noun 2 long idle chat

natural adjective 1 normal or

to be expected **2** genuine or spontaneous **3** of, according to, existing in or produced by nature **4** not created by human beings **5** not synthetic ▷ noun **6** person with an inborn talent or skill > **naturally** adverb **1** of course **2** in a natural or normal way **3** instinctively

nature noun **1** whole system of the existence, forces and events of the physical world that are not controlled by human beings **2** fundamental or essential qualities **3** kind or sort

naughty naughtier naughtiest adjective **1** disobedient or mischievous **2** mildly indecent > **naughtily** adverb > **naughtiness** noun

nausea noun feeling of being about to vomit > **nauseous** adjective **1** as if about to vomit **2** sickening

nautical adjective of the sea or ships

naval adjective of or relating to a navy or ships

navel noun hollow in the middle of the abdomen where the umbilical cord was attached

navigate verb **1** to direct or plot the path or position of a ship, aircraft or car **2** to travel over or through > **navigation** noun > **navigator** noun

navy navies noun **1** branch of a country's armed services that fights at sea **2** warships of a nation ▷ adjective **3** very dark blue; (also **navy-blue**)

Nazi Nazis noun **1** member of the fascist National Socialist Party, which held power in Germany under Adolf Hitler ▷ adjective **2** of

or relating to the Nazis > **Nazism** noun

NB abbreviation note well

near preposition, adverb, adjective **1** indicating a place or time not far away ▷ adjective **2** almost being the thing specified: a near disaster ▷ verb **3** to draw close (to) > **nearness** noun

nearby adjective not far away

nearly adverb almost

neat adjective **1** tidy and clean **2** smoothly or competently done **3** undiluted > **neatly** adverb > **neatness** noun

necessarily adverb inevitably or certainly

necessary adjective **1** needed to achieve the desired result: the necessary skills **2** certain or unavoidable: the necessary consequences

necessity necessities noun **1** circumstances that inevitably require a certain result **2** something needed

neck noun **1** part of the body joining the head to the shoulders **2** part of a garment round the neck **3** long narrow part of a bottle or violin ▷ verb **4** informal to kiss and cuddle

necklace noun **1** decorative piece of jewellery worn around the neck

nectar noun **1** sweet liquid collected from flowers by bees **2** drink of the gods

nectarine noun smooth-skinned peach

née preposition indicating the surname that a woman had before marrying

need verb **1** to require or be in want of **2** to be obliged

(to do something) ▷ noun
3 condition of lacking something
4 requirement or necessity
5 poverty

needle noun **1** thin pointed piece of metal with an eye through which thread is passed for sewing **2** long pointed rod used in knitting **3** pointed part of a hypodermic syringe **4** small pointed part in a record player that touches the record and picks up the sound signals, stylus **5** pointer on a measuring instrument or compass **6** long narrow stiff leaf ▷ verb **7** informal to goad or provoke

needless adjective unnecessary
> **needlessly** adverb

needy needier neediest adjective poor and in need of financial support

negative adjective **1** expressing a denial or refusal **2** lacking positive qualities **3** (of an electrical charge) having the same electrical charge as an electron ▷ noun **4** negative word or statement **5** Photography image with a reversal of tones or colours from which positive prints are made > **negatively** adverb

neglect verb **1** to take no care of **2** to fail (to do something) through carelessness **3** to disregard ▷ noun **4** neglecting or being neglected > **neglectful** adjective

negligent adjective neglectful or careless > **negligence** noun > **negligently** adverb

negligible adjective very small or unimportant

negotiable adjective able to be negotiated

negotiate verb **1** to discuss in order to reach (an agreement) **2** to succeed in passing round or over (a place or problem) > **negotiation** noun > **negotiator** noun

Negro Negroes noun old-fashioned member of any of the Black peoples originating in Africa

neigh noun **1** loud high-pitched sound made by a horse ▷ verb **2** to make this sound

neighbour noun person who lives or is situated near another

neighbourhood noun **1** district **2** surroundings **3** people of a district

neighbouring adjective situated nearby

neither adjective, pronoun **1** not one nor the other ▷ conjunction **2** not

neo- prefix new, recent or a modern form of: neoclassicism

nephew noun son of your brother or sister

Neptune noun eighth planet from the sun in the solar system

nerve noun **1** cordlike bundle of fibres that conducts impulses between the brain and other parts of the body **2** bravery and determination **3** impudence **4** nerves **a** anxiety or tension **b** ability or inability to remain calm in a difficult situation

nerve-racking adjective very distressing or harrowing

nervous adjective **1** apprehensive or worried **2** of or relating to the nerves > **nervously** adverb > **nervousness** noun

nervous breakdown noun mental illness in which someone

suffers from severe depression and needs psychiatric treatment

nervous system *noun* nerves, brain and spinal cord

nest *noun* **1** place or structure in which birds or certain animals lay eggs or give birth to young **2** secluded place **3** set of things of graduated sizes designed to fit together ▷ *verb* **4** to make or inhabit a nest

nestle *verb* **1** to snuggle **2** to be in a sheltered position

nestling *noun* bird too young to leave the nest

net nets netting netted *noun* **1** fabric of meshes of string, thread or wire with many openings **2** piece of net used to protect or hold things or to trap animals **3** Internet ▷ *verb* **4** to catch (a fish or animal) in a net

netball *noun* team game in which a ball has to be thrown through a net hanging from a ring at the top of a pole

netting *noun* material made of net

nettle *noun* plant with stinging hairs on the leaves

network *noun* **1** system of intersecting lines, roads, etc **2** interconnecting group or system **3** group of broadcasting stations that all transmit the same programmes at the same time

neuron or **neurone** *noun* cell carrying nerve impulses in the nervous system

neurosis neuroses *noun* mental disorder producing hysteria, anxiety, depression or obsessive behaviour

neurotic *adjective* **1** emotionally

unstable **2** suffering from neurosis ▷ *noun* **3** neurotic person

neuter *adjective* **1** (of grammatical inflections in some languages) neither masculine nor feminine ▷ *verb* **2** to remove the reproductive organs of (an animal)

neutral *adjective* **1** taking neither side in a war or dispute **2** of or belonging to a neutral party or country **3** (of a colour) not definite or striking ▷ *noun* **4** neutral person or nation **5** neutral gear ▷ **neutrality** *noun*

neutron *noun* electrically neutral elementary particle of about the same mass as a proton

never *adverb* at no time

nevertheless *adverb* in spite of that

new *adjective* **1** not existing before **2** recently acquired **3** having lately come into some state **4** additional **5** (followed by to) unfamiliar ▷ **newness** *noun*

newborn *adjective* recently or just born

newcomer *noun* recent arrival or participant

newly *adverb* recently: *the newly arrived visitors*

new moon *noun* moon when it appears as a narrow crescent at the beginning of its cycle

news *noun* **1** important or interesting new happenings **2** information about such events reported in the media

newsagent *noun* Brit shopkeeper who sells newspapers and magazines

newspaper *noun* weekly or daily

publication containing news

newt noun small amphibious creature with a long slender body and tail

New Testament noun second main division of the Bible

New Year noun beginning of a calendar year

New Zealander noun person from New Zealand

next adjective, adverb **1** immediately following **2** nearest

next door adjective, adverb in or to the adjacent house

NHS abbreviation (in Britain) National Health Service

nib noun writing point of a pen

nibble verb **1** to take little bites (of) ▷ noun **2** little bite

nice adjective **1** pleasant **2** kind **3** good or satisfactory **4** subtle: a nice distinction > **nicely** adverb > **niceness** noun

nicety niceties noun **1** subtle point **2** refinement or delicacy

niche noun **1** hollow area in a wall **2** suitable position for a particular person

nick verb **1** to make a small cut in **2** Chiefly Brit informal to steal **3** Chiefly Brit informal to arrest ▷ noun **4** small cut **5** informal prison or police station

nickel noun **1** Chemistry silvery-white metal often used in alloys **2** US coin worth five cents

nickname noun **1** familiar name given to a person or place ▷ verb **2** to call (someone or something) by a nickname

nicotine noun addictive substance found in tobacco

niece noun daughter of your

brother or sister

nifty niftier niftiest adjective informal neat or smart

Nigerian adjective **1** of Nigeria ▷ noun **2** person from Nigeria

niggle verb **1** to worry slightly **2** to continually find fault (with) ▷ noun **3** small worry or doubt

night noun time of darkness between sunset and sunrise

nightclub noun place for dancing, music, etc, open late at night

nightdress noun woman's loose dress worn in bed

nightfall noun time when it starts to get dark

nightie noun informal nightdress

nightingale noun small bird with a musical song usually heard at night

nightly adjective **1** happening every night ▷ adverb **2** every night

nightmare noun **1** very bad dream **2** very unpleasant experience > **nightmarish** adjective

nil noun nothing, zero

nimble adjective **1** agile and quick **2** mentally alert or acute > **nimbly** adverb

nine adjective, noun the number 9 > **ninth** adjective, noun

nineteen adjective, noun the number 19 > **nineteenth** adjective, noun

ninety adjective, noun the number 90 > **ninetieth** adjective, noun

nip nips nipping nipped verb **1** informal to hurry **2** to pinch or squeeze **3** to bite lightly ▷ noun **4** pinch or light bite **5** sharp coldness

nipple noun projection in the centre of a breast

nirvana noun Buddhism, Hinduism absolute spiritual enlightenment and bliss

nit noun 1 egg or larva of a louse 2 informal stupid person

nitrogen noun Chemistry colourless odourless gas that forms four fifths of the air

no noes or nos interjection 1 expresses denial, disagreement or refusal ▷ adjective 2 not any, not a ▷ adverb 3 not at all ▷ noun 4 negative answer or vote against something

no. abbreviation number

nobility nobilities noun 1 quality of being noble 2 class of people holding titles and high social rank

noble adjective 1 showing or having high moral qualities 2 of the nobility 3 impressive and magnificent ▷ noun 4 member of the nobility > **nobly** adverb

nobleman noblemen noun member of the nobility > **noblewoman** noun

nobody nobodies pronoun 1 no person ▷ noun 2 person of no importance

nocturnal adjective 1 of the night 2 active at night

nod nods nodding nodded verb 1 to lower and raise (one's head) briefly in agreement or greeting ▷ noun 2 act of nodding > **nod off** verb informal to fall asleep

noise noun sound, usually a loud or disturbing one

noisy noisier noisiest adjective 1 making a lot of noise 2 full of noise > **noisily** adverb > **noisiness** noun

nomad noun member of a tribe with no fixed dwelling place,

wanderer > **nomadic** adjective

nominal adjective 1 in name only 2 very small in comparison with real worth > **nominally** adverb

nominate verb 1 to suggest as a candidate 2 to appoint to an office or position > **nomination** noun

non- prefix indicating: 1 negation: nonexistent 2 refusal or failure: noncooperation 3 exclusion from a specified class: nonfiction 4 lack or absence: nonevent

nonchalant adjective casually unconcerned or indifferent > **nonchalance** noun > **nonchalantly** adverb

noncommissioned officer noun (in the armed forces) a subordinate officer, risen from the ranks

nondescript adjective lacking outstanding features

none pronoun 1 not any 2 no-one

nonfiction noun writing that is factual rather than about imaginary events

nonplussed adjective perplexed

nonsense noun 1 something that has or makes no sense 2 absurd language 3 foolish behaviour > **nonsensical** adjective

nonstop adjective, adverb without a stop

noodles plural noun long thin strips of pasta

nook noun sheltered place

noon noun twelve o'clock midday

no-one or **no one** pronoun nobody

noose noun loop in the end of a rope, tied with a slipknot

nor conjunction and not

norm noun standard that is regarded as normal

normal *adjective* **1** usual, regular or typical **2** meeting standards or conventions > **normality** *noun*

normally *adverb* **1** usually **2** in a normal way

north *noun* **1** direction towards the North Pole, opposite south **2** area lying in or towards the north ▷ *adjective* **3** to or in the north **4** (of a wind) from the north ▷ *adverb* **5** in, to or towards the north

North America *noun* continent consisting of Canada, the United States and Mexico > **North American** *adjective*

northeast *noun* **1** direction midway between north and east **2** area lying in or towards the northeast ▷ *adjective* **3** to or in the northeast **4** (of a wind) from the northeast ▷ *adverb* **5** in, to or towards the northeast

northeasterly northeasterlies *adjective, adverb* **1** in, towards or from the northeast ▷ *noun* **2** wind blowing from the northeast

northeastern *adjective* in or from the northeast

northerly northerlies *adjective, adverb* **1** in, towards or from the north ▷ *noun* **2** wind blowing from the north

northern *adjective* in or from the north

North Pole *noun* northernmost point on the earth's axis

northward *adjective, adverb* in or towards the north

northwest northwesterlies *noun* **1** direction midway between north and west **2** area lying in or towards the northwest ▷ *adjective* **3** to or in the northwest **4** (of

a wind) from the northwest ▷ *adverb* **5** in, to or towards the northwest

northwesterly *adjective, adverb* **1** in, towards or from the northwest ▷ *adverb* **2** wind blowing from the northwest

northwestern *adjective* in or from the northwest

Norwegian *adjective* **1** of Norway ▷ *noun* **2** person from Norway **3** language of Norway

nose *noun* **1** organ of smell, used also in breathing **2** front part of a vehicle ▷ *verb* **3** to move forward slowly and carefully **4** to pry or snoop

nostalgia *noun* sentimental longing for the past > **nostalgic** *adjective*

nostril *noun* either of the two openings at the end of the nose

nosy nosier nosiest; also spelt **nosey** *adjective informal* prying or inquisitive

not *adverb* expressing negation, refusal or denial

notable *adjective* **1** worthy of being noted, remarkable ▷ *noun* **2** person of distinction > **notably** *adverb*

notch *noun* **1** V-shaped cut **2** *informal* step or level ▷ *verb* **3** to make a notch in

note *noun* **1** short letter **2** brief comment or record **3** banknote **4** (symbol for) a musical sound **5** hint or mood ▷ *verb* **6** to notice or pay attention to **7** to record (something) in writing **8** to remark upon (something) > **note down** *verb* to write (something) down to have as a record

notebook *noun* book for writing in

noted *adjective* well-known

nothing *pronoun* 1 not anything 2 matter of no importance 3 figure o ▷ *adverb* 4 not at all

notice *noun* 1 observation or attention 2 sign giving warning or an announcement 3 advance warning of intention to end a contract of employment ▷ *verb* 4 to observe or become aware of 5 to point out or remark upon

noticeable *adjective* easily seen or detected, appreciable >**noticeably** *adverb*

noticeboard *noun* board where notices are displayed

notify notifies notifying notified *verb* to inform >**notification** *noun*

notion *noun* 1 idea or opinion 2 whim

notorious *adjective* well known for something bad >**notoriety** *noun* >**notoriously** *adverb*

notwithstanding *preposition* in spite of

nougat *noun* chewy sweet containing nuts and fruit

nought *noun* 1 figure o 2 nothing

noun *noun* word that refers to a person, place or thing

nourish *verb* 1 to feed 2 to encourage or foster (an idea or feeling)

nourishing *adjective* providing the food necessary for life and growth

nourishment *noun* food necessary for life and growth

novel *noun* 1 long fictitious story in book form ▷ *adjective* 2 fresh, new or original

novelist *noun* person who writes novels

novelty novelties *noun* 1 newness 2 something new or

unusual

November *noun* eleventh month of the year

novice *noun* 1 beginner 2 person who has entered a religious order but has not yet taken vows

now *adverb* 1 at or for the present time 2 immediately ▷ *conjunction* 3 seeing that, since

nowadays *adverb* in these times

nowhere *adverb* not anywhere

noxious *adjective* 1 poisonous or harmful 2 extremely unpleasant

nozzle *noun* projecting spout through which fluid is discharged

nuance *noun* subtle difference in colour, meaning or tone

nubile *adjective* (of a young woman) 1 sexually attractive 2 old enough to get married

nuclear *adjective* 1 of nuclear weapons or energy 2 of a nucleus, especially the nucleus of an atom

nuclear reactor *noun* device in which a nuclear reaction is maintained and controlled to produce nuclear energy

nucleus nuclei *noun* 1 central part of an atom or cell 2 basic central part of something

nude *adjective* 1 naked ▷ *noun* 2 naked figure in painting, sculpture or photography >**nudity** *noun*

nudge *verb* 1 to push gently, especially with the elbow ▷ *noun* 2 gentle push or touch

nudist *noun* person who believes in not wearing clothes >**nudism** *noun*

nugget *noun* 1 small lump of gold in its natural state 2 something small but valuable ▷ *verb* 3 NZ, S Afr to polish footwear

nuisance noun something or someone that causes annoyance or bother

null adjective **null and void** not legally valid

nulla-nulla noun wooden club used by Australian Aborigines

numb adjective **1** without feeling, as through cold, shock or fear ▷ verb **2** to make numb

numbat noun small Australian marsupial with a long snout and tongue

number noun **1** sum or quantity **2** word or symbol used to express a sum or quantity, numeral **3** numeral or string of numerals used to identify a person or thing **4** one of a series, such as a copy of a magazine **5** song or piece of music **6** group of people **7** Grammar classification of words depending on how many persons or things are referred to ▷ verb **8** to count **9** to give a number to **10** to amount to **11** to include in a group

numeral noun word or symbol used to express a sum or quantity

numerical adjective measured or expressed in numbers > **numerically** adverb

numerous adjective existing or happening in large numbers

nun noun female member of a religious order

nurse noun **1** person whose job is looking after sick people, usually in a hospital **2** woman whose job is looking after children ▷ verb **3** to look after (a sick person) **4** to breast-feed (a baby) **5** to try to cure (an ailment) **6** to harbour or foster (a feeling)

nursery nurseries noun **1** room where children sleep or play **2** place where children are taken care of while their parents are at work **3** place where plants are grown for sale

nursery school noun school for children from 3 to 5 years old

nursing home noun private hospital or home for old people

nurture noun **1** act or process of promoting the development of a child or young plant ▷ verb **2** to promote or encourage the development of

nut noun **1** fruit consisting of a hard shell and a kernel **2** small piece of metal that screws onto a bolt **3** informal insane or eccentric person **4** informal head

nutmeg noun spice made from the seed of a tropical tree

nutrient noun substance that provides nourishment

nutrition noun **1** process of taking in and absorbing nutrients **2** process of being nourished > **nutritional** adjective > **nutritionist** noun professional advising on diet

nutritious or **nutritive** adjective nourishing

nutty nuttier nuttiest adjective **1** containing or resembling nuts **2** informal insane or eccentric

nylon noun **1** synthetic material used for clothing etc **2** nylons old-fashioned stockings made of nylon

GUIDE TO PARTS OF SPEECH

ADJECTIVE: a *describing word* that tells you more about a noun or pronoun:

a **good** man • They're **French** • two **fluffy white** clouds • a **southern** accent • I'm **better** now • the **worst** holiday we've had

➤ **comparative adjectives are adjectives ending in** *-er* **(or preceded by** *more* **or** *less***) that show that the thing described has more or less of a particular quality then the thing with which it is being compared:**

He's **taller** than me • the **more ambitious** twin • the **less studious** brother

➤ **superlative adjectives are adjectives ending in** *-est* **(or preceded by** *most* **or** *least***) that show that the thing described has more or less of a particular quality than** *all* **of the other things with which it is being compared:**

the **fastest** runner • the **most successful** businesswoman • the **least effective** method

....

ADVERB: a word that is usually used with verbs, adjectives or other adverbs and gives more information about *how, where, when* or *in what circumstances* something happens or *to what degree* something is true. Many adverbs are formed by adding *-ly* to a related adjective:

Mark laughed **loudly** • She fell **awkwardly**

- The children behaved **badly** • a **horribly** violent film
- Work **hard**. • He ran **faster** than me • Try getting here **earlier** • He played **well** • The river runs **south**
- Children travel **free** • Do it **now**. • It should arrive **soon** • She's very **pretty** • I **almost** slipped.

....

ARTICLE: *a*, *an* (indefinite articles) or *the* (definite article)

➤ **Use *a* rather than *an* before nouns that begin with, or sound as if they begin with, a consonant:**

a man • a country • a union • a European

➤ **Remember to use an before a noun that begins with, or sounds as if it begins with, a vowel:**

an elephant • an honour

....

CONJUNCTION: a *joining* word or expression that joins two words or two parts of a sentence together:

salt **and** pepper • tea **or** coffee • strange **but** true
- It's faded **because** it's been washed so often.

➤ **Sometimes conjunctions are made up of more than one word or are used in pairs:**

She covered her face **so that** I wouldn't see her tears
- He smiled **even though** he felt like hitting her •
She speaks **both** French **and** Spanish. • Use **either** butter **or** margarine. • That's **neither** here **nor** there.

....

INTERJECTION or **EXCLAMATION**: a word or short phrase that expresses a feeling or emotion:

Ouch! • Good gracious! • Whew! • Mmm! • Hooray! • Tut, tut! • Hi! • See you! • Congratulations! • Thanks!

➤ **Interjections often stand alone, but if an interjection is used within a sentence, it is usually separated by commas or dashes:**

I turned the key, and, **hey presto**, the engine started.

....

NOUN: a *naming word* that refers to a person, thing or idea

➤ **common nouns, which start with small letters, are the words used to talk about any of the members of a particular category:**

mountain • horse • book • tree • man • girl

➤ **proper nouns, which start with capital letters, give the name of a particular person, place or object:**

Harry Potter • New Zealand • Great Expectations

➤ **concrete nouns are common nouns that name things you can touch:**

a chair • water • her hand

➤ **abstract nouns are common nouns that name things you cannot touch:**

hatred • beauty • ambition • popularity

➤ **collective nouns are words used to indicate groups or collections of things:**

flock • team • family

....

PREPOSITION: a word that is used before a noun, pronoun or a word ending in -*ing* to relate it to other words. Prepositions may tell you the place of something in relation to another thing, or indicate movement or time:

a bird **in** a tree • The marble rolled **under** the bed • Put the cart **before** the horse • He burst **through** the doors. • They're only here **for** the day. • We'll arrive **on** Monday. • It's used **for** cleaning brass.

....

PRONOUN: a word used in place of a noun or instead of naming a person or thing:

The cat likes fish. **It** likes cream too. • **She** rings every week.

➤ **personal pronouns** (*I, me, we, us, you, he, him, she, her, they, them, it*) **replace the subject or object of a sentence:**

He phoned *me*

> **Tip:** If you're not sure whether to use *and me* or *and I* in a sentence, try using me or I on their own in the same position. If it sounds correct, you've made the right choice:
>
> *(My brother and) I love football* not *(My brother and) me love football* • *Pat is always arguing with (Mum and) me* not *Pat is always arguing with (Mum and) I*

> **Note:** you may have to change *are* to *am* when doing this test:
>
> My cousin and I *are* going shopping
> • I *am* going shopping

➤ **reflexive pronouns** (*myself, yourself, himself, herself, ourselves, yourselves, themselves*) replace the object of a sentence when the object is the same person or thing as the subject:

Kathy burnt herself.

➤ **possessive pronouns** are the words *mine, ours, yours, his, hers* and *theirs*.

➤ **indefinite pronouns** replace a subject or object and are used to refer to a broad or vague range of people or things:

Somebody must know the answer • Can you see anything?

➤ **demonstrative pronouns** (*this, that, these, those*) replace the subject or object of a sentence:

That is a novel • Those are dictionaries • Have you seen this?

➤ **interrogative pronouns** are the words *what, which, who, whose* and *whom* used to ask questions:

What is this? • Who did it?

➤ **relative pronouns** (*which, who, whom, that*) are used to link two different parts of a sentence and always refer back to a word in the earlier part of the sentence:

We ate at the local café, **which** serves very good snacks. • They have friends **who** live in the country. • He is a man in **whom** you can put your trust • a girl **that** I know

••

VERB: a *doing word* that expresses an action or state of being:

He **hates** beans • We **saw** Jack at the concert

➤ **auxiliary verbs are verbs used in combination with other verbs to form tenses or express requests, suggestions, intentions, politeness, likelihood, or obligation:**

He **is** living abroad • They **were** laughing • She **has** decided to stay. • We **had** already left. • I **didn't** want to disturb you. • **Do** you know where I can find him? • **Shall** I open a window? • I **won't** hurt you.
• **Can** you dance? • **Could** you pass me the salt?
• I **might** go shopping later. • It **may** be possible to go another day. • He **would** like an ice cream.
• She **must** finish her essay by Monday.

GUIDE TO PUNCTUATION

Punctuation marks are essential parts of written language. They help the reader understand what the writer wants to convey, and how something should be read.

APOSTROPHE (')1: used to show possession

's is added to the end of singular words:

a child's cry • Hannah's book

's is added to the end of plural words not ending in s:

children's games • women's clothes

' An apostrophe alone is added to plural words ending in s:

workers' rights • ladies' fashion

's is added to the end of names and singular words ending in s:

James's car • the octopus's tentacles

But if the word is a classical Greek name, an apostrophe alone is preferred:

Socrates' Athens

> **Tip:** To test whether an apostrophe is in the right place, think about who the owner is, since the apostrophe always follows the noun or name referring to the owner:
>
> the **boy's** books [= the books belonging to the **boy**]
> the **boys'** books [= the books belonging to the **boys**]

Note: An apostrophe is not used to form possessive pronouns, possessive adjectives, or plurals:

Is it yours? • *Its cover is torn.* • *2 kilos of potatoes*

APOSTROPHE (') 2: used in shortened forms of words where letters have been missed out:

It's [= It is] a lovely day. • *He'll* [= He will] be pleased.

BRACKETS ( ): used to enclose a word or words which can be left out and still leave a meaningful sentence:

The area planted with conifers (see map below) is approximately 4000 hectares.

COLON (:): used to introduce a list, a quotation, or an explanation:

I used three colours: green, blue, and pink. • He received a telegram which read: "Return home immediately." • They didn't like the room: it was small and dingy.

COMMA (,): marks a short pause between different elements in a sentence:

➤ **separating subsidiary parts of the sentence from the main part:**

If we get another goal before full-time, we'll have won the league. • He'll be there, come what may. When you're ready, give me a call.

➤ **before and after words like** *however*, *therefore*, **and** *moreover*:

The forecasters got it wrong. There was no warning,

viii

therefore, of the heavy rain and flooding that hit the south.

➤ **separating off extra, non-essential information starting with *who*, *which*, or *that* from the main part of the sentence:**

A new model, which will be made in Spain, is to be introduced in the spring.

> **Tip:** Don't include a comma if the part starting with *who*, *which*, or *that* is essential in order to understand who or what is being talked about:
>
> *The boy who's just come in is my brother.*

➤ **separating the name of the person or people being addressed from the rest of the sentence:**

And now, ladies and gentlemen, please raise your glasses in a toast.

➤ **separating items in a list or series:**

bread, butter, and jam • Winners of a Highly-Commended Prize: Alice Howard, Ayesha Singh, Thomas McAdam.

➤ **separating words in quotation marks from the rest of the sentence, when there is no question mark or exclamation mark at the end of the quotation:**

"I don't understand this question," said Peter.

> **Tip:** Note that the comma comes before the closing quotation mark in such cases.

➤ after reporting verbs such as *say*, *ask*, and *exclaim*, when they are followed by a quotation:

Tom said, "Dream on!"

DASH (–) marks an abrupt change in the flow of a sentence, either showing a sudden change of subject, or marking off extra information:

Now children – Kenneth, stop that immediately! – open your books at page 20. • Boots and shoes – all shapes, sizes, and colours – tumbled out of the cupboard.

EXCLAMATION MARK (!): used after exclamations and emphatic expressions:

I can't believe it! • Oh, no! Look at this mess!

> **Tip:** The exclamation mark can lose its effect if overused. Use a full stop instead after a sentence expressing only mild excitement or humour:
>
> *It was such a beautiful day.*

FULL STOP (.): used to mark the end of any sentence that is not a question or an exclamation:

Harry loves football.

➤ Full stops are also sometimes used after initials or abbreviations, especially if the last letter of the abbreviation isn't the last letter of the word it's standing in for:

C. Bell • etc. • Rev. Adams • misc.

➤ A full stop is used after an indirect question or instructions phrased as polite requests:

He asked if the London train had arrived. • May I see the menu.

HYPHEN (-): separates different parts of words. It is used when there would otherwise be an awkward combination of letters, or confusion with another word:

re-elect • re-covering furniture • a no-nonsense approach

INVERTED COMMAS or QUOTATION MARKS (" " or ' '): mark the beginning and end of *direct speech* (a speaker's words written down exactly as they were said):

"I didn't understand," said Peter. • Mr Evans declared abruptly, "We're leaving."

➤ Inverted commas are not used for *indirect* or *reported speech* (an account of what someone has said rather than their exact words):

Peter said that he didn't understand the question. • Mr Evans declared abruptly that they were leaving.

➤ Inverted commas are used to indicate the title of a book, poem, piece of music, film, or work of art:

Have you read "The Lord of the Rings"? • music from "Swan Lake"

➤ Inverted commas are also used to show that a word is being used in an unusual way, or that the word itself is being discussed:

Braille allows a blind person to "see" with the fingers.
• What is the French for "egg"?

QUESTION MARK (?) marks the end of a question:

When will we get there? • Do you like hockey?

➤ A full stop, rather than a question mark, is used after an indirect question or a polite request:

George asked when we would get there. • Will you please return the completed forms to me.

SEMICOLON (;): marks a stronger break than a comma, but a weaker one than a full stop. It is used to mark a break between two main clauses when there is a balance or contrast between the clauses, and to separate clauses or items in a long list:

I'm not that interested in jazz; I prefer classical music. • The holiday was a disaster: the flight was four hours late; the hotel was overbooked; and it rained for the whole fortnight.

SLASH (/): separates letters, words or numbers. It is used to indicate alternatives and ratios and ranges:

he/she/it • you and/or your partner • 200 km/hr
• the 2009/10 accounting year

COMMONLY CONFUSED WORDS

We all have blindspots when it comes to certain words, especially words that have similar pronunciations. Use this quick guide if you're unsure of what spelling to use.

accept *verb*: Please accept this gift
except *preposition*: every day except Friday

advice *noun*: He always gives good advice
advise *verb*: I wouldn't advise doing that

affect *verb*: Tiredness affects concentration
effect *noun*: the beneficial effects of eating fruit

a lot *noun*: A lot of people were at the concert
allot *verb*: Space was allotted for visitors' cars

bought *verb*: He bought a newspaper at the kiosk
brought *verb*: She brought the book with her yesterday

braking *verb*: The train has an automatic braking system
breaking *verb*: breaking the world record

choose *verb*: Please choose your favourite
chose *verb*: She chose a silver MP3 player

compliment *noun, verb*: My compliments to the chef
• He complimented her on her taste
complement *noun, verb*: our full complement of staff
• wine to complement your meal

conscience *noun*: He seems to have a guilty conscience
conscious *adjective*: She's conscious of the fact

dependent *adjective*: We're dependent on food aid
dependant *noun*: Have you any children or other dependants?

xiii

desert *noun*, *verb*: the Gobi desert • He had deserted his post

dessert *noun*: What's for dessert?

draft *noun*, *verb*: my first draft • He's drafting his reply

draught *noun*: a cold draught

its *adjective*: Her cat had hurt its paw

it's *short form*: It's a lovely day• It's been fun

licence *noun*: a driving licence

license *verb*: licensed to drive heavy goods vehicles

miner *noun*: a coal miner

minor *adjective*, *noun*: a minor problem • a 14-year-old minor

practice *noun*: a common practice

practise *verb*: You should practise more

precede *verb*: as summer preceded autumn

proceed *verb*: Let's proceed with the meeting

principal *noun*, *adjective*: the school principal
• the principal reason

principle *noun*: It's against my principles

quiet *adjective*: Please be quiet!

quite *adjective*: He said their new album was quite good

threw *verb*: He threw the ball as hard as he could

through *preposition*, *adjective*: They managed to crawl through the tunnel • I'm through with this

to *preposition*: She gave a bunch of flowers to her Mum

too *adverb*: The food was too spicy for him

two *adjective*, *noun*: Could I have two coffees, please?
• Two is a prime number

WORDS THAT ARE OFTEN SPELLED INCORRECTLY

To make them easier to remember, the following words have been grouped alongside words that share certain letter clusters:

-sion and -tion

aggression	concentration	pronunciation
conclusion	participation	proportion
extension	creation	proposition
obsession	evaluation	reaction
occasion	explanation	recommendation
possession	preparation	

-ance and -ence

performance	consequence	sequence
extravagance	evidence	existence
relevance	reference	occurrence
audience		

-ate and -ite

definite	accommodate	desperate
chocolate	commemorate	resuscitate
unfortunately	commiserate	separate

-our and -ous

glamour	continuous	nervous
humour	jealous	glamorous
resources	miscellaneous	humorous

cc, dd, ee

accelerator	occur	committee
broccoli	success	foresee
moccasin	address	

ff, gg, ll

graffiti	actually	galloping
paraffin	parallel	millionaire
aggravating	appalling	usually

mm, nn, pp

commit	mayonnaise	opportunity
commitment	questionnaire	disappear
recommend	unnecessary	disappointment
beginning	appal	happened
cinnamon	apparent	supplement

rr, ss, tt

curriculum	marriage	harassment
diarrhoea	tomorrow	necessary
embarrass	assessment	obsess
embarrassed	business	pattern
haemorrhage	issue	boycott
interrupt	process	omelette

O

oaf noun stupid or clumsy person

oak noun 1 deciduous forest tree 2 its wood, used for furniture

OAP abbreviation (in Britain) old-age pensioner

oar noun pole with a broad blade, used for rowing a boat

oasis oases noun fertile area in a desert

oat noun 1 hard cereal grown as food 2 oats grain of this cereal

oath noun solemn promise, especially to be truthful in court

oatmeal noun rough flour made from oats

OBE abbreviation (in Britain) Officer of the Order of the British Empire

obedient adjective obeying or willing to obey > **obedience** noun: unquestioning obedience > **obediently** adverb

obelisk noun four-sided stone column tapering to a pyramid at the top, built in honour of a person or event

obese adjective very fat > **obesity** noun: Obesity rates among children are increasing

obey verb to carry out instructions or orders

obituary obituaries noun announcement of someone's death, especially in a newspaper

object noun 1 physical thing 2 focus of thoughts or action 3 aim or purpose 4 Grammar word that a verb or preposition affects 5 to express disapproval

objection noun 1 expression or feeling of opposition or disapproval 2 reason for opposing something

objectionable adjective unpleasant and offensive

objective noun 1 aim or purpose ▷ adjective 2 not biased 3 existing in the real world outside the human mind > **objectively** adverb > **objectivity** noun: The press strives for balance and objectivity

obligation noun duty

obligatory adjective required by a rule or law

oblige verb 1 to compel (someone) morally or by law to do something 2 to do a favour for (someone)

oblique adjective 1 slanting 2 indirect > **obliquely** adverb

obliterate verb to destroy every trace of > **obliteration** noun: the obliteration of three rainforests

oblivion noun 1 state of being forgotten 2 state of being unaware or unconscious

oblong adjective 1 having two long sides, two short sides and four right angles ▷ noun 2 oblong figure

obnoxious adjective offensive

oboe noun double-reeded woodwind instrument > **oboist** noun

obscene adjective 1 portraying sex offensively 2 disgusting > **obscenely** adverb

obscure adjective 1 not well known 2 hard to understand 3 indistinct ▷ verb 4 to make (something) obscure > **obscurity** noun: She was plucked from obscurity

observance noun observing of

a custom

observant *adjective* quick to notice things

observation *noun* 1 action or habit of observing 2 remark

observatory observatories *noun* building equipped for studying the weather and the stars

observe *verb* 1 to see or notice 2 to watch (someone or something) carefully 3 to remark 4 to act according to (a law or custom) > **observable** *adjective*: *This had no observable effect on their behaviour*

obsession *noun* something that preoccupies a person to the exclusion of other things > **obsessional** *adjective*: *She became almost obsessional about the way she looked*

obsolete *adjective* no longer in use

obstacle *noun* something that makes progress difficult

obstetrics *noun* branch of medicine concerned with pregnancy and childbirth > **obstetric** *adjective*: *obstetric care* > **obstetrician** *noun*: *an appointment to see the obstetrician*

obstinate *adjective* 1 stubborn 2 difficult to remove or change > **obstinacy** *noun*: *the streak of obstinacy in me that would not let me stop* > **obstinately** *adverb*

obstruct *verb* to block with an obstacle > **obstruction** *noun*: *vehicles causing an obstruction* > **obstructive** *adjective*: *She was obstructive and refused to follow procedure*

obtain *verb* to acquire intentionally > **obtainable** *adjective*: *It's obtainable from most health shops*

obtrusive *adjective* unpleasantly noticeable

obtuse *adjective* 1 mentally slow 2 *Maths* (of an angle) between 90° and 180° 3 not pointed

obvious *adjective* easy to see or understand, evident > **obviously** *adverb*

occasion *noun* 1 time at which a particular thing happens 2 reason: *no occasion for complaint* 3 special event ▷ *verb formal* 4 to cause

occasional *adjective* happening sometimes > **occasionally** *adverb*

occult *adjective* 1 relating to the supernatural ▷ *noun* 2 **the occult** knowledge or study of the supernatural

occupancy occupancies *noun* (length of) a person's stay in a specified place

occupant *noun* person occupying a specified place

occupation *noun* 1 profession 2 activity that occupies your time 3 control of a country by a foreign military power 4 being occupied > **occupational** *adjective*: *occupational health and safety issues*

occupy occupies occupying occupied *verb* 1 to live or work in (a building) 2 to take up the attention of (someone) 3 to take up (space or time) 4 to take possession of (a place) by force > **occupier** *noun*: *the occupier of the flat*

occur occurs occurring occurred *verb* 1 to happen 2 to exist 3 *occur to* to come to the mind of

occurrence *noun* 1 something that occurs 2 fact of occurring

ocean noun **1** vast area of sea between continents **2** *literary* sea > **oceanic** adjective: *oceanic islands*

o'clock adverb used after a number to specify an hour

octagon noun geometric figure with eight sides > **octagonal** adjective: *an octagonal box*

octave noun *Music* (interval between the first and) eighth note of a scale

October noun tenth month of the year

octopus octopuses noun sea creature with a soft body and eight tentacles

odd adjective **1** unusual **2** occasional **3** not divisible by two **4** not part of a set **5** odds (ratio showing) the probability of something happening > **oddly** adverb > **oddness** noun: *the oddness of his opinions*

oddity oddities noun odd person or thing

oddments plural noun things left over

odds and ends plural noun small miscellaneous items

ode noun lyric poem, usually addressed to a particular subject

odious adjective offensive

odour noun particular smell > **odorous** adjective: *odorous air emissions*

odyssey noun long eventful journey

oesophagus oesophagi noun passage between the mouth and stomach

oestrogen noun female hormone that controls the reproductive cycle

of preposition **1** belonging to **2** consisting of **3** connected with **4** characteristic of

off preposition **1** away from ▷ adverb **2** away ▷ adjective **3** not operating **4** cancelled **5** (of food) gone bad

offline adjective not connected to the Internet

offal noun edible organs of an animal, such as liver or kidneys

offence noun **1** (cause of) hurt feelings or annoyance **2** illegal act **3** give offence to cause to feel upset or angry **4** take offence to feel hurt or offended

offend verb **1** to hurt the feelings of (a person) **2** *formal* to commit a crime

offensive adjective **1** disagreeable **2** insulting **3** aggressive ▷ noun **4** position or action of attack > **offensively** adverb

offer verb **1** to present (something) for acceptance or rejection **2** to provide **3** to be willing (to do something) **4** to propose as payment ▷ noun **5** instance of offering something

offering noun thing offered

offhand adjective **1** casual, curt ▷ adverb **2** without preparation

office noun **1** room or building where people work at desks **2** department of a commercial organization **3** formal position of responsibility **4** place where tickets or information can be obtained

officer noun **1** person in authority in the armed services **2** member of the police force **3** person with special responsibility in an organization

official adjective **1** of a position of authority **2** approved or arranged by someone in authority ▷ *noun* **3** person who holds a position of authority ▷ **officially** *adverb*

officialdom *noun* officials collectively

officiate *verb* to act in an official role

offing *noun* **in the offing** likely to happen soon

off-licence *noun* Brit shop licensed to sell alcohol for drinking elsewhere

offline *adjective* (of a computer) not connected to the Internet

offset **offsets** **offsetting** **offset** *verb* to cancel out or compensate for

offshoot *noun* something developed from something else

offshore *adjective, adverb* in or from the part of the sea near the shore

offside *adjective, adverb* **1** Sport (positioned) illegally ahead of the ball ▷ *noun* **2** side of a vehicle that is furthest from the pavement

offspring *noun* immediate descendant or descendants of a person or animal

often *adverb* frequently, much of the time

ogle *verb* to stare at (someone) lustfully

ogre *noun* **1** giant that eats human flesh **2** monstrous or cruel person

ohm *noun* unit of electrical resistance

oil *noun* **1** viscous liquid, insoluble in water and usually flammable **2** same as **petroleum** **3** petroleum derivative, used as a fuel or lubricant **4** **oils** oil-based paints used in art ▷ *verb* **5** to lubricate (a machine) with oil

oil painting *noun* picture painted using oil-based paints

oilskin *noun* (garment made from) waterproof material

oily **oilier** **oiliest** *adjective* **1** covered with or containing oil **2** like oil

ointment *noun* greasy substance used for healing skin or as a cosmetic

OK or **okay** *informal interjection* **1** expression of approval ▷ *noun* **2** approval

old *adjective* **1** having lived or existed for a long time **2** of a specified age: *two years old* **3** former

olden *adjective* old: *in the olden days*

Old English *noun* form of the English language that existed from the fifth century AD until about 1100; also known as **Anglo-Saxon**

old-fashioned *adjective* **1** no longer commonly used or valued **2** favouring or denoting the styles or ideas of a former time

Old Norse *noun* language spoken in Norway and Iceland from about 700 AD to about 1350 AD and from which many English words are derived

Old Testament *noun* part of the Bible recording Hebrew history

oleander *noun* Mediterranean flowering evergreen shrub

olive *noun* **1** small green or black fruit used as food or pressed for its oil **2** tree on which this fruit grows ▷ *adjective* **3** greyish-green

-ology *suffix* used to form words that refer to the study of something: *biology*; *geology*

Olympic Games *plural noun*

four-yearly international sports competition

ombudsman **ombudsmen** noun official who investigates complaints against government organizations

omelette noun dish of eggs beaten and fried

omen noun happening or object thought to foretell success or misfortune

ominous adjective worrying, seeming to foretell misfortune > **ominously** adverb

omission noun 1 something that has not been included or done 2 act of missing out or failing to do something

omit **omits** **omitting** **omitted** verb 1 to leave out 2 to neglect (to do something)

omnibus **omnibuses** noun 1 several books or TV or radio programmes made into one 2 old-fashioned bus

omnipotent adjective having unlimited power > **omnipotence** noun: the omnipotence of God

omnivore noun animal that eats all kinds of food, including meat and plants > **omnivorous** adjective: Brown bears are omnivorous

lights were on 10 taking place: What's on at the cinema?

once adverb 1 on one occasion 2 formerly ▷ conjunction 3 as soon as ▷ noun 4 one occasion or case 5 **at once a** immediately **b** simultaneously

one adjective, noun 1 the number 1 ▷ adjective 2 single, lone 3 used emphatically to mean a or an: They got one almighty shock ▷ noun 4 single unit ▷ pronoun 5 any person 6 referring back to something or someone already mentioned or known about: the pretty one; His business was a successful one

one-off noun something that happens or is made only once

onerous adjective (of a task) difficult to carry out

oneself pronoun reflexive form of **one**

one-sided adjective 1 considering only one point of view 2 having all the advantage on one side

one-way adjective moving or allowing travel in one direction only

ongoing adjective in progress, continuing

onion noun strongly flavoured edible bulb

online adjective relating to the Internet: online shopping

onlooker noun person who watches without taking part

on preposition 1 touching or attached to: lying on the ground; a puppet on a string; on the coast 2 inside: on a train 3 indicating when: on Mondays 4 using: on the phone 5 about: a talk on dictionary skills ▷ adverb 6 in operation: He left the lights on 7 continuing: He stayed on after his family left 8 forwards: from that day on ▷ adjective 9 operating: All the

only adjective 1 alone of its kind ▷ adverb 2 exclusively 3 merely 4 no more than 5 **only too** extremely ▷ conjunction 6 but

onomatopoeia noun use of a word which imitates the sound it represents, such as hiss

> **onomatopoeic** adjective: Buzz is
an onomatopoeic word

onset noun beginning

onslaught noun violent attack

onto preposition **1** to a position on
2 aware of: She's onto us

onus onuses noun formal
responsibility or burden

onward adjective **1** directed or
moving forward ▷ adverb **2** (also
onwards) ahead, forward

onyx noun type of quartz with
coloured layers

ooze verb **1** to flow slowly ▷ noun
2 soft mud at the bottom of a lake
or river

opal noun iridescent precious
stone

opaque adjective **1** not able to be
seen through, not transparent
2 difficult to understand

open adjective **1** not closed **2** not
covered **3** unfolded **4** ready for
business **5** free from obstruction,
accessible **6** frank ▷ verb **7** to
(cause to) become open **8** to
begin ▷ noun **9** in the open
a outdoors **b** not secret

opening noun **1** opportunity
2 hole **3** first part ▷ adjective
4 first

open-minded adjective receptive
to new ideas

open-plan adjective (of a house or
office) having few interior walls

opera noun drama in which the
text is sung to an orchestral
accompaniment > **operatic**
adjective: an amateur operatic society

operate verb **1** to work **2** to
control the working of (a
machine) **3** to perform a surgical
operation (on a person or animal)

operation noun **1** method or

procedure of working **2** medical
procedure in which the body is
worked on to repair a damaged
part **3** in operation working or
being used

operational adjective **1** in working
order **2** occurring while a plan is
being carried out

operative adjective **1** working
▷ noun **2** worker with a special
skill

operator noun **1** someone who
works at a telephone exchange
or on a switchboard **2** someone
who operates a machine
3 someone who runs a business: a
tour operator

opinion noun personal belief or
judgment

opinionated adjective having
strong opinions

opium noun addictive narcotic
drug made from poppy seeds

opponent noun person you are
competing, fighting or arguing
against in a contest, battle or
argument

opportune adjective formal
happening at a suitable time

opportunism noun doing
whatever is advantageous
without regard for principles
> **opportunist** noun: Car thieves are
opportunists

opportunity opportunities noun
1 favourable time or condition
2 good chance

oppose verb **1** to work against
2 be opposed to to disagree with
or disapprove of

opposed adjective **1** opposed to
against (something or someone)
in speech or action **2** opposite or
very different **3** as opposed to in

opposite *adjective* **1** situated on the other side **2** facing **3** completely different ▷ *noun* **4** person or thing that is opposite ▷ *preposition* **5** facing ▷ *adverb* **6** on the other side

opposition *noun* **1** obstruction or hostility **2** group opposing another **3 the Opposition** political parties not in power

oppressed *adjective* treated cruelly or unfairly >**oppression** *noun*: *political oppression* >**oppress** *verb* >**oppressor** *noun*: *They tried to resist their oppressors by non-violent means*

oppressive *adjective* **1** tyrannical **2** uncomfortable or depressing **3** (of weather) hot and humid >**oppressively** *adverb*

opt *verb* **1** to show preference (for) or choose (to do something) **2 opt out** to choose not to be part (of)

optical *adjective* **1** concerned with vision, light or images **2** relating to the appearance of things: *an optical illusion*

optician *noun* **1** (also **ophthalmic optician**) person qualified to prescribe glasses **2** (also **dispensing optician**) person who supplies and fits glasses

optimism *noun* tendency to take the most hopeful view >**optimist** *noun*: *Optimists predict the economy will grow steadily* >**optimistic** *adjective*: *She was in a jovial and optimistic mood* >**optimistically** *adverb*

optimum optima or **optimums** *noun* **1** best possible conditions ▷ *adjective* **2** most favourable

option *noun* **1** choice **2** thing chosen **3** right to buy or sell something at a specified price within a given time

opulent *adjective* having or indicating wealth >**opulence** *noun*: *the elegant opulence of the German embassy*

opus opuses or **opera** *noun* artistic creation, especially a musical work

or *conjunction* **1** used to join alternatives: *tea or coffee* **2** used to introduce a warning: *Do as I say or else I'll shoot*

-or *suffix* used to form nouns from verbs: *actor; conductor*

oracle *noun* **1** shrine of an ancient god **2** prophecy, often obscure, revealed at a shrine **3** person believed to make infallible predictions

oral *adjective* **1** spoken **2** (of a drug) to be taken by mouth ▷ *noun* **3** spoken examination >**orally** *adverb*

orange *noun* **1** reddish-yellow citrus fruit ▷ *adjective* **2** reddish-yellow

orang-utan or **orang-utang** *noun* large reddish-brown ape with long arms

orator *noun* skilful public speaker

oratory oratories *noun* **1** art of making speeches **2** small private chapel

orbit *noun* **1** curved path of a planet, satellite or spacecraft around another body **2** sphere of influence ▷ *verb* **3** to move in an orbit around **4** to put (a satellite or spacecraft) into orbit

orchard *noun* area where fruit trees are grown

orchestra noun 1 large group of musicians, especially playing a variety of instruments 2 (also **orchestra pit**) area of a theatre in front of the stage, reserved for the musicians > **orchestral** adjective: an orchestral concert

orchestrate verb 1 to arrange (music) for orchestra 2 to organize (something) to produce a particular result > **orchestration** noun: Mahler's imaginative orchestration

orchid noun plant with flowers that have unusual lip-shaped petals

ordain verb to make (someone) a member of the clergy

ordeal noun painful or difficult experience

order noun 1 instruction to be carried out 2 methodical arrangement or sequence 3 established social system 4 condition of a law-abiding society 5 request for goods to be supplied 6 kind, sort 7 religious society of monks or nuns 8 **in order that** so that it is possible ▷ verb 9 to command or instruct (to do something) 10 to request (something) to be supplied in return for payment

orderly orderlies adjective 1 well-organized 2 well-behaved ▷ noun 3 male hospital attendant

ordinarily adverb usually

ordinary adjective 1 usual or normal 2 dull or commonplace

ordination noun act of making someone a member of the clergy

ordnance noun weapons and military supplies

ore noun (rock containing) a mineral which yields metal

oregano noun sweet-smelling herb used in cooking

organ noun 1 part of an animal or plant that has a particular function, such as the heart or lungs 2 musical keyboard instrument in which notes are produced by forcing air through pipes

organic adjective 1 of or produced from animals or plants 2 grown without artificial fertilizers or pesticides 3 Chemistry relating to compounds of carbon > **organically** adverb

organism noun any living animal or plant

organist noun organ player

organization noun 1 group of people working together 2 act of organizing > **organizational** adjective: organizational skills

organize verb 1 to plan and arrange (something) 2 to arrange systematically > **organized** adjective: organized resistance > **organizer** noun: She is a good organizer

orgasm noun most intense point of sexual pleasure

orgy orgies noun 1 party involving promiscuous sexual activity 2 unrestrained indulgence: an orgy of destruction

orient verb 1 to position (yourself) according to your surroundings 2 to position (a map) in relation to the points of the compass

Oriental adjective relating to eastern or south-eastern Asia: Oriental carpets

orientation noun 1 activities and aims that a person or

organization is interested in **2** position of an object with relation to the points of the compass or other specific directions

oriented or **orientated** adjective interested (in) or directed (toward something): Medical care needs to be oriented towards prevention > **-oriented** or **-orientated** suffix: career-oriented women

orienteering noun sport in which competitors hike over a course using a compass and map

origin noun **1** point from which something develops **2** ancestry

original adjective **1** first or earliest **2** new, not copied or based on something else **3** able to think up new ideas > **original** noun **1** first version, from which others are copied > **originality** noun: ideas of startling originality > **originally** adverb

originate verb to come or bring into existence > **originator** noun: the originator of the theory of relativity

ornament noun **1** decorative object ▷ verb **2** to decorate

ornamental adjective designed to be attractive rather than useful

ornamentation noun decoration on a building, a piece of furniture or a work of art

ornate adjective highly decorated, elaborate

ornithology noun study of birds > **ornithological** adjective: an ornithological society > **ornithologist** noun: a keen amateur ornithologist

orphan noun **1** child whose parents are dead ▷ verb **2** to cause (someone) to become an orphan

orphanage noun children's home for orphans

orthodox adjective conforming to established views > **orthodoxy** noun: He rebelled against religious orthodoxy

osmosis osmoses noun **1** movement of a liquid through a membrane from a lower to a higher concentration **2** process of subtle influence

osprey noun large fish-eating bird of prey

ostensible adjective apparent, seeming > **ostensibly** adverb

ostentatious adjective **1** intended to impress people, for example by looking expensive **2** flaunting your wealth or making a show of your importance > **ostentation** noun: a notable lack of ostentation > **ostentatiously** adverb

ostinato ostinatos noun Music musical phrase that is continuously repeated throughout a piece

ostrich ostriches noun large African bird that runs fast but cannot fly

other adjective **1** different from the ones specified or understood **2** additional **3** the other day a few days ago ▷ noun **4** other person or thing

otherwise conjunction **1** or else, if not ▷ adverb **2** differently, in another way

otter noun small brown freshwater mammal that eats fish

ouch interjection exclamation of sudden pain

ought verb used to express: **1** obligation: You ought to pay **2** advisability: You ought to diet

3 probability: *You ought to know by then*

ounce *noun* unit of weight equal to one sixteenth of a pound (28.4 grams)

our *adjective* belonging to us

ours *pronoun* thing(s) belonging to us

ourselves *pronoun* emphatic and reflexive form of **we** or **us**

oust *verb* to force (someone) out of a position

out *adverb* **1** towards the outside of a place: *Two dogs rushed out of the house* **2** not at home **3** in the open air: *They are playing out in bright sunshine* **4** no longer shining or burning: *The lights went out* ▷ *adjective* **5** on strike: *1000 construction workers are out in sympathy* **6** unacceptable or unfashionable: *Miniskirts are out* **7** incorrect: *Logan's timing was out in the first two rounds*

out- *prefix* **1** surpassing: *outlive; outdistance* **2** on the outside or away from the centre: *outpost*

out-and-out *adjective* entire or complete: *an out-and-out lie*

outback *noun* remote bush country of Australia

outboard motor *noun* engine externally attached to the stern of a boat

outbreak *noun* sudden occurrence (of something unpleasant)

outburst *noun* sudden expression of emotion

outcast *noun* person rejected by a particular group

outclassed *adjective* surpassed in quality

outcome *noun* result

outcrop *noun* part of a rock

formation that sticks out of the earth

outcry outcries *noun* vehement or widespread protest

outdated *adjective* no longer in fashion

outdo outdoes outdoing outdid outdone *verb* to be more successful or better than (someone or something) in performance

outdoor *adjective* happening or used outside

outdoors *adverb* **1** in(to) the open air ▷ *noun* **2** the open air

outer *adjective* on the outside

outer space *noun* space beyond the earth's atmosphere

outfit *noun* **1** matching set of clothes **2** *informal* group of people working together

outgoing *adjective* **1** leaving **2** sociable **3** outgoings expenses

outgrow outgrows outgrowing outgrew outgrown *verb* to become too large or too old for

outhouse *noun* building near a main building

outing *noun* leisure trip

outlandish *adjective* extremely unconventional

outlaw *verb* **1** to make (something) illegal ▷ *noun* **2** *History* criminal deprived of legal protection

outlay outlays *noun* expenditure

outlet *noun* **1** means of expressing emotion **2** market for a product **3** place where a product is sold **4** opening or way out

outline *noun* **1** short general explanation **2** line defining the shape of something ▷ *verb* **3** to give the main features or general idea of (something) **4** to show the general shape of an object but not its details

outlive *verb* to live longer than someone

outlook *noun* **1** attitude **2** probable outcome

outlying *adjective* distant from the main area

outmoded *adjective* no longer fashionable or accepted

outnumber *verb* to exceed in number

out of *preposition* **1** because of: *She went along out of curiosity* **2** from (a material or source): *old instruments made out of wood* **3** no longer in a specified state or condition: *out of work* **4** at or to a point outside: *The train pulled out of the station* **5** away from, not in: *out of focus*

out-of-date *adjective* old-fashioned

out of doors *adverb* outside

outpatient *noun* patient who does not stay in hospital overnight

outpost *noun* outlying settlement

output ouputs outputting outputted or **output** *noun* **1** amount produced **2** power, voltage or current delivered by an electrical circuit **3** Computers data produced ▷ *verb* **4** Computers to produce (data) at the end of a process

outrage *noun* **1** great moral indignation **2** gross violation of morality ▷ *verb* **3** to cause deep indignation, anger or resentment in (someone)

outright *adjective, adverb* **1** absolute(ly) **2** open(ly) and

direct(ly)

outset *noun* beginning

outshine outshines outshining outshone *verb* to surpass (someone) in excellence

outside *preposition, adjective, adverb* **1** indicating movement to or position on the exterior ▷ *adjective* **2** unlikely: *an outside chance* **3** coming from outside ▷ *noun* **4** external area or surface

outsider *noun* **1** person outside a specific group **2** contestant thought unlikely to win

outsize or **outsized** *adjective* larger than normal

outskirts *plural noun* outer areas, especially of a town

outspoken *adjective* **1** tending to say what you think, regardless of how others may react **2** said openly

outstanding *adjective* **1** excellent **2** still to be dealt with or paid

outstretched *adjective* extended or stretched out as far as possible

outstrip outstrips outstripping outstripped *verb* **1** to surpass (someone) in a particular activity **2** to go faster than (someone)

outward *adjective* **1** apparent ▷ *adverb* **2** (also **outwards**) away from somewhere ▷ **outwardly** *adverb*

outwards *adverb* away from a place or towards the outside: *The door opened outwards*

outweigh *verb* to be more important, significant or influential than

outwit outwits outwitting outwitted *verb* to get the better of (someone) by cunning

oval *adjective* egg-shaped ▷ *noun*

a b c d e f g h i j k l m n o p q r s t u v w x y z

2 anything that is oval in shape

ovary *ovaries noun* female egg-producing organ

ovation *noun* enthusiastic round of applause

oven *noun* heated compartment or container for cooking or for drying or firing ceramics

over *preposition, adverb* **1** indicating position on the top of, movement to the other side of, amount greater than, etc: *a room over the garage; climbing over the fence; over fifty pounds* ▷ *adjective* **2** finished ▷ *noun* **3** Cricket series of six balls bowled from one end

over- *prefix* **1** too much: *overeat* **2** above: *overlord* **3** on top: *overshoe*

overall *adjective, adverb* **1** in total ▷ *noun* **2** overalls protective garment consisting of trousers with a jacket or bib and braces attached

overawe *verb* to fill (someone) with respect or fear ▷ **overawed** *adjective: He had been overawed to meet the Prime Minister*

overbearing *adjective* unpleasantly forceful

overboard *adverb* **1** from a boat into the water **2** go overboard to go to extremes, especially in enthusiasm

overcast *adjective* (of the sky) covered by clouds

overcoat *noun* heavy coat

overcome *overcomes overcoming overcame* **overcome** *verb* **1** to gain control over an effort **2** (of an emotion) to affect strongly

overcrowded *adjective* containing more people or things than is desirable

overdo *overdoes overdoing overdid overdone verb* **1** to do to excess **2** to exaggerate (something)

overdose *noun* **1** excessive dose of a drug ▷ *verb* **2** to take more of a drug than is safe, either accidentally or deliberately

overdraft *noun* **1** overdrawing **2** amount overdrawn

overdrawn *adjective* **1** having taken out more money than you had in your bank account **2** (of an account) in debit

overdrive *noun* extra, higher gear in a vehicle, which is used at high speeds to reduce engine wear and save petrol

overdue *adjective* still due after the time allowed

overestimate *verb* to believe something or someone to be bigger, more important, or better than is the case

overflow *overflows overflowing overflowed* or **overflown** *verb* **1** to flow over (a brim) **2** to be filled beyond capacity so as to spill over ▷ *noun* **2** outlet that enables surplus liquid to be drained off

overgrown *adjective* thickly covered with plants and weeds

overhang *overhangs overhanging overhung* *verb* **1** to project or hang over beyond (something) ▷ *noun* **2** overhanging part or object

overhaul *verb* **1** to examine (a system or an idea) carefully for faults **2** to make repairs or adjustments to (a vehicle or machine)

overhead *adverb, adjective* above your head

overhear overhears
overhearing overheard verb
to hear (a speaker or remark)
unintentionally or without the
speaker's knowledge

overjoyed adjective extremely
pleased

overlaid adjective overlaid with
covered with

overland adjective, adverb by land

overlander noun Aust history man
who drove cattle or sheep long
distances through the outback

overlap overlaps overlapping
overlapped verb 1 to share part of
the same space or period of time
(as) ▷ noun 2 area overlapping

overleaf adverb on the back of the
current page

overload verb to put too large a
load on or in (something)

overlook verb 1 to fail to notice
2 to ignore (misbehaviour or
a fault)

overly adverb excessively

overnight adjective, adverb
1 (taking place) during one night
2 (happening) very quickly

overpower verb 1 to subdue
or overcome (someone) 2 to
have such a strong effect on as
to make helpless or ineffective
▷ **overpowering** adjective:
overpowering anger

overrate verb to have too high an
opinion of ▷ **overrated** adjective:
The food here is overrated

overreact verb to react more
strongly or forcefully than is
necessary

overriding adjective more
important than anything else

overrule verb to reverse the
decision of (a person with less
power)

overrun overruns overrunning
overran overrun verb 1 to
conquer (territory) rapidly by
force of numbers 2 to spread
over (a place) rapidly 3 to extend
beyond a set limit

overseas adverb, adjective to, of or
from a distant country

oversee oversees overseeing
oversaw overseen verb to watch
over from a position of authority
▷ **overseer** noun: I was promoted
to overseer

overshadow verb to reduce the
significance of (a person or thing)
by comparison

oversight noun mistake caused by
not noticing something

overspill noun Brit rehousing of
people from crowded cities in
smaller towns

overstate verb to state
(something) too strongly

overstep oversteps
overstepping overstepped verb
overstep the mark to go too far
and behave in an unacceptable
way

overt adjective open, not hidden
▷ **overtly** adverb

overtake overtakes overtaking
overtook overtaken verb to
move past (a vehicle or person)
travelling in the same direction

overthrow overthrows
overthrowing overthrew
overthrown verb to defeat and
replace (a ruler or government)
by force

overtime noun, adverb (paid work
done) in addition to your normal
working hours

overtones plural noun additional

meaning: *the political overtones of the trial*

overture *noun* **1** *Music* orchestral introduction **2 overtures** opening moves in a new relationship

overturn *verb* **1** to turn upside down **2** to overrule (a legal decision)

overview *noun* general understanding or description of a situation

overweight *adjective* weighing more than is healthy

overwhelm *verb* **1** to overpower the thoughts, emotions or senses of (someone) **2** to overcome (people) with irresistible force > **overwhelming** *adjective: an overwhelming majority* > **overwhelmingly** *adverb*

overwork *verb* to work too hard or too long

overwrought *adjective* nervous and agitated

ovulate *verb* to produce or release an egg cell from an ovary

ovum ova *noun* unfertilized egg cell

owe *verb* **1** to be obliged to pay (a sum of money) to (a person) **2** to feel an obligation to do or give

owl *noun* night bird of prey

own *adjective* **1** used to emphasize possession: *my own idea* ▷ *pronoun* **2** the one or ones belonging to a particular person: *I had one of my own* **3 on your own a** alone **b** without help ▷ *verb* **4** to have (something) as your possession

owner *noun* person to whom something belongs

ownership *noun* state or fact of being an owner

ox oxen *noun* castrated bull

oxide *noun* compound of oxygen and one other element

oxidize *verb* to combine chemically with oxygen, as in burning or rusting > **oxidation** *noun: the oxidation of metals*

oxygen *noun* *Chemistry* gaseous element essential to life and combustion

oxymoron *noun* figure of speech that combines two apparently contradictory ideas: *cruel kindness*

oyster *noun* edible shellfish

oz. *abbreviation* ounce

ozone *noun* strong-smelling form of oxygen

ozone layer *noun* layer of ozone in the upper atmosphere that filters out ultraviolet radiation

p

p *abbreviation* **1** *Brit, Aust, NZ* penny **2** *Brit* pence

pa or **pah** *noun* NZ (formerly) a fortified Maori settlement

pace *noun* **1** single step in walking **2** length of a step **3** rate of progress ▷ *verb* **4** to walk up and down, especially in anxiety **5 pace out** to cross or measure with steps

pacemaker *noun* electronic device surgically implanted in a person with heart disease to regulate the heartbeat

Pacific *noun* ocean separating

North and South America from
Asia and Australia

pacifist noun person who refuses
on principle to take part in war
▷ **pacifism** noun

pacify pacifies pacifying pacified
verb to soothe or calm

pack verb 1 to put (clothes etc)
together in a suitcase or bag 2 to
put (goods) into containers or
parcels 3 to fill with people or
things ▷ noun 4 bag carried on a
person's or animal's back *Chiefly
US* same as **packet** 6 set of
playing cards 7 group of dogs or
wolves that hunt together > **pack
in** verb informal to stop doing
(something) > **pack up** verb 1 to
put (your things) in a bag because
you are leaving 2 (of machine) to
stop working

package noun 1 small parcel
2 (also **package deal**) deal
in which separate items are
presented together as a unit
▷ verb 3 to put (something) into
a package

packaging noun container or
wrapping in which an item is
sold or sent

packed adjective very full

packet noun 1 small container
(and contents) 2 small parcel
3 informal large sum of money

pact noun formal agreement

pad pads padding padded noun
1 piece of soft material used for
protection, support, absorption
of liquid, etc 2 number of sheets
of paper fastened at the edge
3 fleshy underpart of an animal's
paw 4 place for launching
rockets 5 informal home ▷ verb
6 to protect or fill (something)
with soft material 7 to walk with

soft steps

paddle noun 1 short oar with a
broad blade at one or each end
▷ verb 2 to move (a canoe etc)
with a paddle 3 to walk barefoot
in shallow water

paddock noun small field or
enclosure for horses

paddy paddies noun Brit informal
fit of temper

padlock noun 1 detachable lock
with a hinged hoop fastened over
a ring on the object to be secured
▷ verb 2 to fasten (something)
with a padlock

padre noun chaplain to the armed
forces

paediatrician noun doctor who
specializes in treating children

paediatrics noun branch of
medicine concerned with
diseases of children > **paediatric**
adjective: paediatric medicine

pagan adjective 1 not belonging to
one of the world's main religions
▷ noun 2 someone who believes
in a pagan religion > **paganism**
noun

page pages paging paged noun
1 (one side of) a sheet of paper
forming a book etc 2 screenful
of information from a website or
teletext service 3 (also **pageboy**)
small boy who attends a bride
at her wedding 4 History boy in
training for knighthood ▷ verb
5 to summon (someone) by
bleeper or loudspeaker, in order to
pass on a message

pageant noun parade or display
of people in costume, usually
illustrating a scene from history

pagoda noun pyramid-shaped
Asian temple or tower

pail noun (contents of) a bucket

pain noun **1** physical or mental suffering **2 pains** trouble or effort **3 on pain of** subject to the penalty of

painful adjective causing emotional or physical pain
> **painfully** adverb

painkiller noun drug that relieves pain

painstaking adjective extremely thorough and careful

paint noun **1** coloured substance, spread on a surface with a brush or roller ▷ verb **2** to colour or coat with paint **3** to use paint to make a picture of

pair noun **1** set of two things matched for use together ▷ verb **2** to group or be grouped in twos

Pakeha Pakehas noun NZ New Zealander who is not of Maori descent

Pakistani adjective **1** belonging or relating to Pakistan ▷ noun **2** someone from Pakistan

pal noun informal old-fashioned in NZ friend

palace noun **1** residence of a king, bishop, etc **2** large grand building

Palagi Palagi or **Palagis** noun NZ Samoan name for a Pakeha

palatable adjective pleasant to taste

palate noun **1** roof of the mouth **2** sense of taste

pale adjective **1** light, whitish **2** whitish in the face, especially through illness or shock ▷ noun **3** wooden or metal post used in fences **4 beyond the pale** outside the limits of social convention ▷ verb **5** to become pale or paler

Palestinian adjective belonging or relating to the region formerly called Palestine or its people ▷ noun Arab from this region

palette noun artist's flat board for mixing colours on

pall noun **1** cloth spread over a coffin **2** dark cloud (of smoke) **3** depressing oppressive atmosphere ▷ verb **4** to become boring

palm noun **1** inner surface of the hand **2** tropical tree with long pointed leaves growing out of the top of a straight trunk ▷ verb **3 palm off** to get rid of (an unwanted thing or person), especially by deceit

Palm Sunday noun Sunday before Easter

palpable adjective **1** obvious: *a palpable hit* **2** so intense as to seem capable of being touched: *the tension is almost palpable*
> **palpably** adverb

paltry paltrier paltriest adjective (of an amount) very small

pamper verb to treat (someone) with great indulgence, spoil

pamphlet noun thin paper-covered booklet

pan pans panning panned noun **1** wide long-handled metal container used in cooking **2** bowl of a toilet ▷ verb **3** to sift gravel from (a river) in a pan to search for gold **4** informal to criticize harshly **5** (of a film camera) to be moved slowly so as to cover a whole scene or follow a moving object
> **pan out** verb to work out

panacea noun remedy for all diseases or problems

panache noun confident elegant

style

pancake noun thin flat circle of fried batter

pancreas noun large gland behind the stomach that produces insulin and helps digestion

panda noun large black-and-white bearlike mammal from China

panda car noun Brit police patrol car

pandemonium noun wild confusion, uproar

pander verb **pander to** to indulge (a person in his or her desires)

pane noun sheet of glass in a window or door

panel panels panelling panelled **1** flat distinct section of a larger surface, for example in a door **2** group of people as a team in a quiz etc **3** list of jurors, doctors, etc **4** board or surface containing switches and controls to operate equipment ▷ verb **5** to cover or decorate with panels > **panelled** adjective

panelling noun panels collectively, especially on a wall

pang noun sudden sharp feeling of pain or sadness

panic panics panicking panicked noun **1** sudden overwhelming fear, often affecting a whole group of people ▷ verb **2** to feel or cause to feel panic

panorama noun wide unbroken view of a scene ▷ adjective: panoramic views

pansy pansies noun small garden flower with velvety purple, yellow or white petals

pant verb to breathe quickly and noisily during or after exertion

panther noun leopard, especially a black one

pantomime noun play based on a fairy tale, performed at Christmas time

pantry pantries noun small room or cupboard for storing food

pants plural noun **1** undergarment for the lower part of the body **2** US, Canadian, Aust, NZ trousers

papaya or **pawpaw** noun large sweet West Indian fruit

paper noun **1** material made in sheets from wood pulp or other fibres **2** printed sheet of this **3** newspaper **4** set of examination questions **5** article or essay **6 papers** personal documents ▷ verb **7** to cover (walls) with wallpaper

paperback noun book with covers made of flexible card

paperwork noun clerical work, such as writing reports and letters

papier-mâché noun material made from paper mixed with paste and moulded when moist

paprika noun mild powdered seasoning made from red peppers

par noun **1** usual or average condition: feeling under par **2** Golf expected standard score **3** face value of stocks and shares **4 on a par with** equal to

parable noun story that illustrates a religious teaching

parachute noun **1** large fabric canopy that slows the descent of a person or object from an aircraft ▷ verb **2** to land or drop by parachute > **parachutist** noun

parade noun **1** procession or march **2** street or promenade ▷ verb **3** to display or flaunt **4** to march in procession

paradise noun 1 heaven 2 place or situation that is near-perfect

paradox noun statement that seems self-contradictory but may be true > **paradoxical** adjective: a paradoxical effect

paraffin noun Brit, S Afr liquid mixture distilled from petroleum and used as a fuel or solvent

paragon noun model of perfection

paragraph noun section of a piece of writing starting on a new line

parallel parallels paralleling or **parallelling parelleled** or **paralleled** adjective 1 separated by an equal distance at every point 2 exactly corresponding ▷ noun 3 line separated from another by an equal distance at every point 4 thing with similar features to another 5 line of latitude ▷ verb 6 to correspond to

parallelogram noun Maths four-sided geometric figure with opposite sides parallel

paralyse verb 1 to affect with paralysis 2 to make temporarily unable to move or take action

paralysis paralyses noun inability to move or feel, because of damage to the nervous system

paramedic noun person working in support of the medical profession

parameter noun limiting factor or boundary

paramilitary adjective organized on military lines

paramount adjective of the greatest importance

paranoia noun 1 mental illness causing delusions of grandeur or persecution 2 informal intense fear or suspicion

paranoid adjective having undue suspicion or fear of persecution

parapet noun low wall or railing along the edge of a balcony or roof

paraphernalia noun personal belongings or bits of equipment

paraphrase verb to put (a statement or text) into other words

parasite noun 1 animal or plant living in or on another 2 person who lives at the expense of others > **parasitic** adjective: parasitic diseases

parasol noun umbrella-like sunshade

paratroops or **paratroopers** plural noun soldiers trained to be dropped by parachute into a battle area

parcel parcels parcelling parcelled noun 1 something wrapped up, package ▷ verb 2 parcel up to wrap up 3 parcel out to divide into parts

parched adjective 1 very hot and dry 2 informal thirsty

parchment noun thick smooth writing material made from animal skin

pardon verb 1 to forgive or excuse ▷ noun 2 forgiveness 3 official release from punishment for a crime

pare verb 1 to cut off the skin or top layer of 2 pare down to reduce in size or amount

parent noun father or mother > **parental** adjective: parental duties

parentage noun ancestry or family

parish noun area that has its own church and a priest or pastor

parishioner noun inhabitant of a parish

parity noun formal equality or equivalence

park noun 1 area of open land for recreational use by the public 2 area containing a number of related enterprises: a business park 3 Brit area of private land around a large country house ▷ verb 4 to stop and leave (a vehicle) temporarily > parked adjective: parked cars > parking noun: free parking

parliament noun law-making assembly of a country > parliamentary adjective: parliamentary debates

parlour noun old-fashioned living room for receiving visitors

parochial adjective 1 narrow in outlook 2 of a parish

parody parodies parodying parodied noun 1 exaggerated and amusing imitation of someone else's style ▷ verb 2 to make a parody of

parole noun 1 early freeing of a prisoner on condition that he or she behaves well 2 on parole (of a prisoner) released on condition that he or she behaves well ▷ verb 3 to place (a person) on parole

parrot noun 1 tropical bird with a short hooked beak and an ability to imitate human speech ▷ verb 2 to repeat (someone else's words) without thinking

parry parries parrying parried verb 1 to ward off (an attack) 2 to avoid (an awkward question) in a clever way

parsley noun herb used for seasoning and decorating food

parsnip noun long tapering cream-coloured root vegetable

parson noun 1 Anglican parish priest 2 any member of the clergy

part noun 1 one of the pieces that make up a whole 2 one of several equal divisions 3 actor's role 4 component of a vehicle or machine 5 parts region or area 6 take someone's part to support someone in an argument etc 7 take (something) in good part to respond to (teasing or criticism) with good humour ▷ verb 8 to divide or separate from one another 9 (of people) to leave each other > part with verb to give away or hand over

partake partakes partaking partook partaken verb 1 (followed by of) to take (food or drink) 2 (followed by in) to take part in

partial adjective 1 not complete 2 prejudiced 3 partial to having a liking for > partially adverb

participate verb to become actively involved in > participant noun: participants in the course > participation noun: participation in religious activities

participle noun form of a verb used in compound tenses, e.g. written; writing

particle noun 1 extremely small piece or amount 2 Physics minute piece of matter, such as a proton or electron

particular adjective 1 relating to one person or thing, not general 2 exceptional or special 3 very exact 4 difficult to please, fastidious ▷ noun 5 particulars items of information, details > particularly adverb

parting noun 1 occasion when one person leaves another 2 line of scalp between sections of hair combed in opposite directions 3 dividing or separating

partisan noun 1 strong supporter of a party or group 2 member of a resistance movement ▷ adjective 3 prejudiced or one-sided

partition noun 1 screen or thin wall that divides a room 2 division of a country into independent parts ▷ verb 3 to divide (something) into separate parts

partly adverb not completely

partner noun 1 either member of a couple in a relationship or activity 2 member of a business partnership ▷ verb 3 to be the partner of

part of speech noun particular grammatical class of words, such as noun or verb

partook the past tense of **partake**

partridge noun game bird of the grouse family

part-time adjective occupying or working less than the full working week

party parties noun 1 social gathering for pleasure 2 group of people travelling or working together 3 group of people with a common political aim 4 formal person or people forming one side in a lawsuit or dispute

pass verb 1 to go by, past or through 2 to be successful in (a test or examination) 3 to spend (time) or (of time) to go by 4 to give or hand 5 to be inherited by 6 Sport to hit, kick or throw (the ball) to another player 7 (of a law-making body) to agree to (a law) 8 to exceed 9 to announce (a judicial decision) ▷ noun 9 successful result in a test or examination 10 permit or licence 11 **make a pass at** informal to make sexual advances to ▷ **pass away** verb to die ▷ **pass out** verb informal to faint ▷ **pass up** verb informal to fail to take advantage of (something)

passable adjective 1 (just) acceptable 2 (of a road) capable of being travelled along

passage noun 1 channel or opening providing a way through 2 hall or corridor 3 section of a book etc 4 journey by sea 5 right or freedom to pass

passé adjective out-of-date

passenger noun 1 person travelling in a vehicle driven by someone else 2 member of a team who does not pull his or her weight

passer-by passers-by noun person who is walking past something or someone

passing adjective 1 brief or transitory 2 cursory or casual

passion noun 1 intense sexual love 2 any strong emotion 3 great enthusiasm 4 **Passion** Christianity the suffering of Christ

passionate adjective expressing very strong feelings about something ▷ **passionately** adverb

passive adjective 1 not playing an active part 2 submissive and receptive to outside forces 3 Grammar (of a verb) in a form indicating that the subject receives the action, e.g. was jeered in he was jeered by the crowd ▷ **passively** adverb ▷ **passivity** noun: the passivity of the public under military occupation

Passover noun Jewish festival commemorating the sparing of the Jews in Egypt

passport noun official document of nationality granting permission to travel abroad

password noun 1 secret word or phrase that ensures admission 2 a sequence of characters that must be keyed in order to get access to some computers or computer files

past adjective 1 of the time before the present 2 ended, gone by 3 Grammar (of a verb tense) indicating that the action specified took place earlier ▷ noun 4 period of time before the present 5 person's earlier life, especially a disreputable period 6 Grammar past tense ▷ adverb 7 by, along ▷ preposition 8 beyond 9 **past it** informal unable to do the things you could do when younger

pasta noun type of food, such as spaghetti, that is made in different shapes from flour and water

paste noun 1 moist soft mixture, such as toothpaste 2 adhesive, especially for paper 3 Brit pastry dough 4 shiny glass used to make imitation jewellery ▷ verb 5 to fasten with paste

pastel noun 1 coloured chalk crayon for drawing 2 picture drawn in pastels 3 pale delicate colour ▷ adjective 4 pale and delicate in colour

pasteurized adjective (of food or drinks) treated with a special heating process to kill bacteria

pastime noun activity that makes time pass pleasantly

pastor noun member of the clergy in charge of a congregation

pastoral adjective 1 of or depicting country life 2 of a clergyman or his duties

past participle noun Grammar the form of a verb, usually ending in ed or en, that is used to make some past tenses and the passive. For example killed in she has killed the goldfish and broken in a window had been broken are past participles

pastry pastries noun 1 baking dough made of flour, fat and water 2 cake or pie

past tense noun Grammar tense of a verb that is used mainly to refer to things that happened or existed before the time of writing or speaking

pasture noun grassy land for farm animals to graze on

pasty¹ **pastier pastiest** adjective (of a complexion) pale and unhealthy

pasty² **pasties** noun round of pastry folded over a savoury filling

pat pats patting patted verb 1 to tap lightly ▷ noun 2 gentle tap or stroke 3 small shaped mass of butter etc ▷ adjective 4 quick, ready or glib 5 **off pat** learned thoroughly

patch noun 1 piece of material sewn on a garment 2 small contrasting section 3 plot of ground 4 protective pad for the eye ▷ verb 5 to mend with a patch ▷ **patch up** verb 1 to repair clumsily 2 to make up (a quarrel)

patchwork noun needlework made of pieces of different materials sewn together

patchy patchier patchiest

adjective of uneven quality or intensity

pâté *noun* spread of finely minced liver etc

patent *noun* **1** document giving the exclusive right to make or sell an invention ▷ *adjective* **2** obvious: *It's patent nonsense* ▷ *verb* **3** to obtain a patent for (an invention) >**patently** *adverb*

paternal *adjective* **1** fatherly **2** related through your father

paternity *noun* fact or state of being a father

path *noun* **1** surfaced walk or track **2** course of action

pathetic *adjective* **1** causing feelings of pity or sadness **2** distressingly inadequate >**pathetically** *adverb*

pathological *adjective* **1** of pathology **2** *informal* extreme and uncontrollable >**pathologically** *adverb*

pathology *noun* scientific study of diseases >**pathologist** *noun: an experienced pathologist*

pathos *noun* power of arousing pity or sadness

pathway *noun* path

patience *noun* **1** quality of being patient **2** card game for one

patient *adjective* **1** enduring difficulties or delays calmly ▷ *noun* **2** person receiving medical treatment >**patiently** *adverb*

patio *patios noun* paved area adjoining a house

patriarch *noun* **1** male head of a family or tribe **2** highest-ranking bishop in Orthodox Churches

patrician *formal noun* **1** member of the nobility ▷ *adjective* **2** of noble birth

patriot *noun* person who loves his or her country and supports its interests >**patriotic** *adjective: patriotic songs* >**patriotism** *noun: He joined the army out of a sense of patriotism*

patrol *patrols patrolling patrolled noun* **1** regular circuit by a guard **2** person or small group patrolling **3** unit of Scouts or Guides ▷ *verb* **4** to engage in a patrol of (a place)

patron *noun* **1** person who gives financial support to charities, artists, etc **2** regular customer of a shop, pub, etc

patronize *verb* **1** to treat in a condescending way **2** to be a patron of >**patronizing** *adjective: The tone of the interview was patronizing*

patron saint *noun* saint regarded as the guardian of a country or group

patter *verb* **1** to make repeated soft tapping sounds ▷ *noun* **2** quick succession of taps **3** glib rapid speech

pattern *noun* **1** arrangement of repeated parts or decorative designs **2** regular way that something is done **3** diagram or shape used as a guide to make something

paunch *noun* protruding belly

pauper *noun* old-fashioned very poor person

pause *verb* **1** to stop for a time ▷ *noun* **2** stop or rest in speech or action

pave *verb* to form (a surface) with stone or brick

pavement *noun* paved path for

pedestrians

pavilion *noun* 1 building on a playing field etc 2 building for housing an exhibition etc

paw *noun* 1 animal's foot with claws and pads ▷ *verb* 2 to scrape with the paw or hoof 3 *informal* to touch in a rough or overfamiliar way

pawn *verb* 1 to deposit (an article) as security for money borrowed ▷ *noun* 2 chessman of the lowest value 3 person manipulated by someone else

pawnbroker *noun* lender of money on goods deposited

pawpaw *noun* same as **papaya**

pay pays paying paid *verb* 1 to give money etc in return for goods or services 2 to settle a debt or obligation 3 to compensate (for) 4 to give 5 to be profitable to ▷ *noun* 6 wages or salary

payable *adjective* due to be paid

payment *noun* 1 act of paying 2 money paid

payroll *noun* list of paid employees of an organization

PC *abbreviation* 1 personal computer 2 (in Britain) Police Constable 3 politically correct

PE *abbreviation* physical education

pea *noun* 1 climbing plant with seeds growing in pods 2 its seed, eaten as a vegetable

peace *noun* 1 calm, quietness 2 absence of anxiety 3 freedom from war 4 harmony between people

peaceful *adjective* quiet and calm ▷ **peacefully** *adverb*

peach *noun* 1 soft juicy fruit with a stone and a downy skin 2 *informal* very pleasing person or thing

▷ *adjective* 3 pinkish-orange

peacock *noun* large male bird with a brilliantly coloured fanlike tail

peak *noun* 1 pointed top, especially of a mountain 2 point of greatest development etc 3 projecting piece on the front of a cap ▷ *verb* 4 to form or reach a peak ▷ *adjective* 5 of or at the point of greatest demand

peal *noun* 1 long loud echoing sound, especially of bells or thunder ▷ *verb* 2 to sound with a peal or peals

peanut *noun* 1 pea-shaped nut that ripens underground 2 **peanuts** *informal* trifling amount of money

pear *noun* sweet juicy fruit with a narrow top and rounded base

pearl *noun* hard round shiny object found inside some oyster shells and used as a jewel

peasant *noun* person working on the land, especially in poorer countries or in the past

peat *noun* decayed vegetable material found in bogs, used as fertilizer or fuel

pebble *noun* small roundish stone

peck *verb* 1 to strike or pick up with the beak 2 *informal* to kiss quickly 3 **peck at** to nibble or eat reluctantly ▷ *noun* 4 pecking movement

peculiar *adjective* 1 strange 2 distinct, special 3 belonging exclusively to > **peculiarly** *adverb*

pedal pedals pedalling pedalled *noun* 1 foot-operated lever used to control a vehicle or machine, or to modify the tone of a musical instrument ▷ *verb* 2 to propel (a bicycle) by using its pedals

pedantic adjective excessively concerned with details and rules, especially in academic work

peddle verb to sell (goods) from door to door

pedestal noun base supporting a column, statue, etc

pedestrian noun 1 person who walks ▷ adjective 2 dull, uninspiring

pedestrian crossing noun place marked where pedestrians may cross a road

pediatrician another spelling of **paediatrician**

pediatrics another spelling of **paediatrics**

pedigree noun register of ancestors, especially of a purebred animal

peek verb 1 to glance quickly or secretly ▷ noun 2 a quick look at something

peel verb 1 to remove the skin or rind of (a vegetable or fruit) 2 (of skin or a surface) to come off in flakes ▷ noun 3 rind or skin

peep verb 1 to look slyly or quickly 2 to make a small shrill noise ▷ noun 3 peeping look 4 small shrill noise

peer verb 1 to look closely and intently ▷ noun 2 (feminine **peeress**) (in Britain) member of the nobility 3 person of the same status, age, etc

peerage noun plural Brit 1 whole body of peers 2 rank of a peer

peer group noun group of people of similar age, status, etc

peerless adjective so magnificent or perfect that nothing can equal it

peewee noun black-and-white Australian bird

peg pegs pegging pegged noun 1 pin or clip for joining, fastening, marking, etc 2 hook or knob for hanging things on 3 off the peg (of clothes) ready-to-wear, not tailor-made ▷ verb 4 to fasten with pegs 5 to stabilize (prices)

peggy square noun NZ small hand-knitted square

pejorative adjective (of words etc) with an insulting or critical meaning

Pekinese noun small dog with a short wrinkled muzzle

● The plural of Pekinese is Pekinese

pelican noun large water bird with a pouch beneath its bill for storing fish

pellet noun small ball of something

pelt verb 1 to throw (missiles) at 2 **pelt along** to run fast, rush 3 to rain heavily ▷ noun 4 skin of a fur-bearing animal 5 **at full pelt** at top speed

pelvis pelvises noun framework of bones at the base of the spine, to which the hips are attached ▷ **pelvic** adjective: the pelvic bone

pen pens penning penned noun 1 instrument for writing in ink 2 small enclosure for domestic animals ▷ verb 3 to write or compose 4 to enclose (animals) in a pen 5 **penned in** being or feeling trapped or confined

penal adjective of or used in punishment

penalize verb 1 to impose a penalty on 2 to handicap or hinder

penalty penalties noun 1 punishment for a crime or

offence **2** *Sport* handicap or disadvantage imposed for breaking a rule, such as a free shot at goal by the opposition

penance *noun* voluntary self-punishment to make amends for wrongdoing

pence *noun Brit* a plural of **penny**

penchant *noun formal* inclination or liking

pencil pencils pencilling pencilled *noun* **1** thin cylindrical instrument containing graphite, for writing or drawing ▷ *verb* **2** to draw, write or mark with a pencil

pendant *noun* ornament worn on a chain round the neck

pending *formal preposition* **1** while waiting for ▷ *adjective* **2** not yet decided or settled

pendulum *noun* suspended weight swinging to and fro, especially as a regulator for a clock

penetrate *verb* **1** to find or force a way into or through **2** to arrive at the meaning of

penetrating *adjective* **1** (of a sound) loud and unpleasant **2** quick to understand

pen friend *noun* friend with whom a person corresponds without meeting

penguin *noun* flightless black-and-white sea bird of the southern hemisphere

penicillin *noun* antibiotic drug effective against a wide range of diseases and infections

peninsula *noun* strip of land nearly surrounded by water

penis penises *noun* organ of copulation and urination in male mammals

penitent *adjective* **1** feeling sorry for having done wrong ▷ *noun* **2** someone who is penitent
> **penitence** *noun: a gesture of penitence*

penknife penknives *noun* small knife with blade(s) folding into the handle

pennant *noun* triangular flag, especially one used by ships as a signal

penniless *adjective* very poor

penny pence or **pennies** *noun* **1** British bronze coin worth one hundredth of a pound **2** former British and Australian coin worth one twelfth of a shilling

pension *noun* regular payment to people above a certain age, retired employees, widows, etc

pensioner *noun* person receiving a pension

pensive *adjective* deeply thoughtful, often with a tinge of sadness

pentagon *noun* geometric figure with five sides

pentathlon *noun* sports contest in which athletes compete in five different events

penthouse *noun* flat built on the roof or top floor of a building

pent-up *adjective* (of an emotion) not released, repressed

penultimate *adjective* second last

peony peonies *noun* garden plant with showy red, pink or white flowers

people peoples peopling peopled *plural noun* **1** persons generally **2** the community **3** your family ▷ *noun* **4** race or nation ▷ *verb* **5** to provide with inhabitants

pepper noun 1 sharp hot condiment made from the fruit of an East Indian climbing plant 2 colourful tropical fruit used as a vegetable, capsicum ▷ verb 3 to season with pepper 4 to sprinkle or dot

peppermint noun 1 plant that yields an oil with a strong sharp flavour 2 sweet flavoured with this

per preposition 1 for each 2 as per in accordance with

perceive verb 1 to become aware of (something) through the senses 2 to understand

per cent adverb in each hundred

percentage noun proportion or rate per hundred

perceptible adjective able to be perceived, recognizable

perception noun 1 act of perceiving 2 intuitive judgment

perceptive adjective able to realize or notice things that are not obvious > **perceptively** adverb

perch noun 1 resting place for a bird 2 any of various edible fishes ▷ verb 3 to alight, rest or place on or as if on a perch

percolator noun coffeepot in which boiling water is forced through a tube and filters down through coffee

percussion noun 1 striking of one thing against another 2 percussion instruments collectively

perennial adjective 1 lasting through many years ▷ noun 2 plant lasting more than two years

perfect adjective 1 having all the essential elements 2 faultless

3 correct or precise 4 utter or absolute 5 excellent ▷ noun 6 Grammar perfect tense ▷ verb 7 to improve 8 to make fully correct > **perfectly** adverb

perfectionist noun person who demands the highest standards of excellence

perforated adjective pierced with holes > **perforation** noun: perforation of the eardrum

perform verb 1 to carry out (an action) 2 to act, sing or present a play before an audience 3 to fulfil (a promise etc) > **performer** noun: a world-class performer

performance noun 1 act of performing 2 artistic or dramatic production 3 manner of quality of functioning: the poor performance of our economy

perfume noun 1 liquid cosmetic worn for its pleasant smell 2 fragrance ▷ verb 3 to give a pleasant smell to > **perfumed** adjective: a perfumed envelope

perfunctory adjective done only as a matter of routine, superficial

perhaps adverb possibly, maybe

peril noun great danger > **perilous** adjective: a perilous journey > **perilously** adverb

perimeter noun (length of) the outer edge of an area

period noun 1 particular portion of time 2 single occurrence of menstruation 3 division of time at school etc when a particular subject is taught 4 US full stop ▷ adjective 5 (of furniture, dress, a play, etc) dating from or in the style of an earlier time

periodical noun 1 magazine issued at regular intervals

▷ *adjective* **2** periodic

peripheral *adjective*
1 unimportant, not central **2** on or relating to the edge of an area

periphery peripheries *noun*
1 boundary or edge **2** fringes of a field of activity

perish *verb* **1** to be destroyed or die **2** to decay or rot

perjury perjuries *noun Law* act or crime of lying while under oath in a court

perk *noun informal* incidental benefit gained from a job, such as a company car ▷ **perk up** *verb* to cheer up

perm *noun* **1** long-lasting curly hairstyle produced by treating the hair with chemicals ▷ *verb* **2** to give (hair) a perm

permanent *adjective* lasting forever ▷ **permanence** *noun*: *belief in the permanence of nature* ▷ **permanently** *adverb*

permeable *adjective formal* able to be permeated, especially by liquid

permeate *verb* to penetrate or spread throughout (something)

permissible *adjective* allowed by the rules

permission *noun* authorization to do something

permissive *adjective* tolerant or lenient, especially in sexual matters ▷ **permissiveness** *noun*: *An atmosphere of permissiveness prevails*

permit permits permitting permitted *verb* **1** to give permission, allow ▷ *noun* **2** document giving permission to do something

permutation *noun* any of the ways a number of things can be arranged or combined

pernicious *adjective formal*
1 wicked **2** extremely harmful, deadly

peroxide *noun* **1** hydrogen peroxide used as a hair bleach **2** oxide containing a high proportion of oxygen

perpendicular *adjective* **1** at right angles to a line or surface **2** upright or vertical ▷ *noun* **3** line or plane at right angles to another

perpetrate *verb* to commit or be responsible for (a wrongdoing) ▷ **perpetrator** *noun*: *the perpetrator of this crime*

perpetual *adjective* **1** lasting forever **2** continually repeated ▷ **perpetually** *adverb*

perpetuate *verb* to cause to continue or be remembered

perplexed *adjective* puzzled or bewildered

persecute *verb* **1** to treat cruelly because of race, religion, etc **2** to subject to persistent harassment ▷ **persecution** *noun*: *political persecution* ▷ **persecutor** *noun*: *They rose up against their persecutors*

persevere *verb* to keep making an effort despite difficulties ▷ **perseverance** *noun*: *This will require enormous patience and perseverance*

Persian *adjective, noun* old word for Iranian, used especially when referring to the older forms of the language

persimmon *noun* sweet red tropical fruit

persist *verb* **1** to continue to be or happen **2** to continue in spite of obstacles or objections ▷ **persistence** *noun*: *Skill only*

a b c d e f g h i j k l m n o p q r s t u v w x y z

comes with practice and persistence
> **persistent** *adjective:* *persistent*
rain

person **people** or **persons** *noun*
1 human being **2** body of a
human being **3** *Grammar* form of
pronouns and verbs that shows if
a person is speaking, spoken to,
or spoken of **4 in person** actually
present

- The usual plural of *person* is
- *people*. *Persons* is much less
- common, and is used only in
- formal or official English

personal *adjective* **1** individual
or private **2** of the body: *personal*
hygiene **3** (of a remark etc)
offensive

personality **personalities**
noun **1** person's distinctive
characteristics **2** celebrity

personification *noun* **1** form of
imagery in which something
inanimate is described as if it
has human qualities **2** living
example of a particular quality:
the personification of evil

personify **personifies**
personifying **personified** *verb*
1 to give human characteristics to
2 to be an example of, typify

personnel *noun* **1** people
employed in an organization
2 department in an organization
that appoints or keeps records of
employees

perspective *noun* **1** view of the
relative importance of situations
or facts **2** method of drawing that
gives the effect of solidity and
relative distances and sizes

perspiration *noun* sweat

perspire *verb* to sweat

persuade *verb* **1** to make

(someone) do something by
argument, charm, etc **2** to
convince

pertaining *adjective formal*
pertaining to about or
concerning

pertinent *adjective* relevant

perturbed *adjective* greatly
worried

Peruvian *adjective* **1** belonging
or relating to Peru ▷ *noun*
2 someone from Peru

pervade *verb* to spread right
through (something) > **pervasive**
adjective: *the pervasive influence of*
the army in national life

perverse *adjective* deliberately
doing something different from
what is thought normal or proper
> **perversely** *adverb* > **perversity**
noun: *What sort of perversity causes*
people to resist so obvious a good?

pervert *verb* **1** to use or alter for
a wrong purpose **2** to lead into
abnormal (sexual) behaviour
▷ *noun* **3** person who practises
sexual perversion

perverted *adjective* **1** having
disgusting or unacceptable
behaviour or ideas, especially
sexual behaviour or ideas
2 completely wrong: *a perverted*
sense of value

peseta *noun* former monetary unit
of Spain

peso **pesos** *noun* main unit
of currency in several South
American countries

pessimism *noun* tendency to
expect the worst in all things
> **pessimist** *noun:* *I'm a natural*
pessimist; I usually expect the
worst > **pessimistic** *adjective:* *a*
pessimistic view of life

pest *noun* **1** annoying person **2** insect or animal that damages crops

pester *verb* to annoy or nag continually

pesticide *noun* chemical for killing insect pests

pet *pets petting petted noun* **1** animal kept for pleasure and companionship **2** person favoured or indulged ▷ *adjective* **3** particularly cherished ▷ *verb* **4** to treat as a pet **5** to pat or stroke affectionately **6** *old-fashioned* to kiss and caress erotically

petal *noun* one of the brightly coloured outer parts of a flower

peter out *verb* to come gradually to an end

petite *adjective* (of a woman) small and slim

petition *noun* **1** formal request, especially one signed by many people and presented to a government or other authority ▷ *verb* **2** to present a petition to (a government or someone in authority)

petrified *adjective* very frightened

petrol *noun* flammable liquid obtained from petroleum, used as fuel in internal-combustion engines

petroleum *noun* thick dark oil found underground

petticoat *noun* woman's skirt-shaped undergarment

petty *pettier pettiest adjective* **1** unimportant or trivial **2** small-minded **3** on a small scale: *petty crime*

petulant *adjective* childishly irritable or peevish ▷ **petulance**

noun: His petulance made her impatient > **petulantly** *adverb*

petunia *noun* garden plant with funnel-shaped flowers

pew *noun* fixed benchlike seat in a church

pewter *noun* greyish metal made of tin and lead

pH *noun Chemistry* measure of the acidity of a solution

phalanger *noun* long-tailed Australian tree-dwelling marsupial

phallus *phalluses* or **phalli** *noun* penis, especially as a symbol of reproductive power in primitive rites > **phallic** *adjective: a phallic symbol*

phantom *noun* **1** ghost **2** unreal vision

pharaoh *noun* king (of ancient Egypt)

pharmaceutical *adjective* connected with the industrial production of medicines

pharmacist *noun* person who is qualified to prepare and sell medicines

pharmacy *pharmacies noun* **1** preparation and dispensing of drugs and medicines **2** pharmacist's shop

phase *noun* **1** any distinct or characteristic stage in a development or chain of events ▷ *verb* **2** to arrange or carry out in stages or to coincide with something else > **phase in** *verb* to introduce gradually > **phase out** *verb* to discontinue gradually

PhD *abbreviation* Doctor of Philosophy: degree awarded to someone who has done advanced research in a subject

pheasant *noun* game bird with bright plumage

phenomenal *adjective* extraordinarily great or good >**phenomenally** *adverb*

phenomenon phenomena *noun* 1 anything appearing or observed 2 remarkable person or thing

philanthropist *noun* someone who freely gives help or money to people in need >**philanthropic** *adjective: philanthropic organizations* >**philanthropy** *noun: a retired banker well known for his philanthropy*

philistine *adjective, noun* person who is hostile towards culture and the arts

philosophical or**philosophic** *adjective* 1 of philosophy 2 calm in the face of difficulties or disappointments

philosophy philosophies *noun* 1 study of the meaning of life, knowledge, thought, etc 2 theory or set of ideas held by a particular philosopher 3 person's outlook on life >**philosopher** *noun*

phishing *noun* practice of tricking computer users into revealing their financial data in order to defraud them

phlegm *noun* thick yellowish substance formed in the nose and throat during a cold

phobia *noun* intense and unreasoning fear or dislike >**phobic** *adjective: He is phobic about getting in lifts*

-phobia *suffix* fear of: *claustrophobia*

phoenix *noun* legendary bird said to set fire to itself and rise anew from its ashes

phone *informal noun* 1 telephone ▷ *verb* 2 to call or talk to (a person) by telephone

-phone *suffix* giving off sound: *telephone*

phoney phonier phoniest; phoneys phonies *informal adjective* 1 not genuine 2 insincere ▷ *noun* 3 phoney person or thing

photo photos *noun* short for photograph

photo- *prefix* of light or using light: *photography*

photocopy photocopies photocopying photocopied *noun* 1 photographic reproduction ▷ *verb* 2 to make a photocopy of >**photocopier** *noun*

photogenic *adjective* always looking attractive in photographs

photograph *noun* 1 picture made by the chemical action of light on sensitive film ▷ *verb* 2 to take a photograph of

photographic *adjective* 1 connected with photography 2 (of a person's memory) able to retain facts or appearances in precise detail

photosynthesis *noun* process by which a green plant uses sunlight to build up carbohydrate reserves

phrasal verb *noun* phrase consisting of a verb and an adverb or preposition, with a meaning different from the parts, such as *take in* meaning *deceive*

phrase *noun* 1 group of words forming a unit of meaning, especially within a sentence 2 short effective expression ▷ *verb* 3 to express in words

physical *adjective* 1 of the body, as

contrasted with the mind or spirit **2** of material things or nature **3** of physics > **physically** adverb

physical education noun training and practice in sports and gymnastics

physician noun doctor of medicine

physics noun science of the properties of matter and energy > **physicist** noun: a nuclear physicist

physio- prefix to do with the body or natural functions: physiotherapy

physiology noun science of the normal function of living things

physiotherapy noun treatment of disease or injury by physical means such as massage, rather than by drugs > **physiotherapist** noun: She sees a physiotherapist once a week

physique noun person's bodily build and muscular development

pi noun Maths a number, approximately 3.142 and symbolized by the Greek letter π. It is the ratio of the circumference of a circle to its diameter

piano pianos noun **1** musical instrument with strings which are struck by hammers worked by a keyboard; (also **pianoforte**) > adverb **2** Music quietly > **pianist** noun

piccolo piccolos noun small flute

pick verb **1** to choose **2** to remove (flowers or fruit) from a plant **3** to take hold of and move with the fingers **4** to provoke (a fight etc) **5** to open (a lock) deliberately by means other than a key > noun **6** choice **7** best part **8** tool with a curved iron crossbar and wooden shaft, for breaking up

hard ground or rocks > **pick on** verb to continually treat someone unfairly > **pick out** verb **1** to select for use or special consideration **2** to recognize (a person or thing) > **pick up** verb **1** to raise or lift **2** to collect **3** to improve

pickaxe noun large pick

picket noun **1** person or group standing outside a workplace to deter would-be workers during a strike > verb **2** to form a picket outside (a workplace)

pickings plural noun money easily acquired

pickle noun **1** food preserved in vinegar or salt water **2** informal awkward situation > verb **3** to preserve in vinegar or salt water

pickpocket noun thief who steals from someone's pocket

picnic picnics picnicking picnicked noun **1** informal meal out of doors > verb **2** to have a picnic

pictorial adjective of or in painting or pictures

picture noun **1** drawing or painting **2** photograph **3** mental image **4** beautiful or picturesque object **5** image on a TV screen **6 the pictures** cinema > verb **7** to visualize or imagine **8** to represent in a picture

picturesque adjective **1** (of a place or view) pleasant to look at **2** (of language) forceful or vivid

pie noun dish of meat, fruit, etc baked in pastry

piece noun **1** separate bit or part **2** instance: a piece of luck **3** example or specimen **4** literary or musical composition **5** coin **6** small object used in draughts, chess, etc ▷ *verb* **7 piece together** to make or assemble bit by bit

piecemeal *adverb* bit by bit

pier *noun* **1** platform on stilts sticking out into the sea **2** pillar, especially one supporting a bridge

pierce *verb* **1** to make a hole in or through with a sharp instrument **2** to make a way through

piercing *adjective* **1** (of a sound) shrill and high-pitched **2** (of eyes or a stare) intense and penetrating

piety pieties *noun* deep devotion to God and religion

pig *noun* **1** animal kept and killed for pork, ham and bacon **2** *informal* greedy, dirty or rude person

pigeon *noun* bird with a heavy body and short legs, sometimes trained to carry messages

pigeonhole *noun* **1** compartment for papers in a desk etc ▷ *verb* **2** to classify

piggyback *noun* **1** ride on someone's shoulders ▷ *adverb* **2** carried on someone's shoulders

piglet *noun* young pig

pigment *noun* colouring matter, paint or dye > **pigmentation** *noun: the pigmentation of the skin*

pigsty pigsties *noun* hut with a small enclosed area where pigs are kept

pigtail *noun* plait of hair hanging from the back or either side of the head

pike *noun* **1** large freshwater fish with strong teeth **2** *History* pointed metal blade attached to a long pole, used as a weapon

pilchard *noun* small edible sea fish of the herring family

pile *noun* **1** number of things lying on top of each other **2** *informal* large amount **3** fibres of a carpet or a fabric, especially velvet, that stand up from the weave ▷ *verb* **4** to collect into a pile

pile-up *noun informal* traffic accident involving several vehicles

pilfer *verb* to steal (minor items) in small quantities

pilgrim *noun* person who journeys to a holy place > **pilgrimage** *noun: the pilgrimage to Mecca*

pill *noun* **1** small ball of medicine swallowed whole **2 the pill** pill taken by a woman to prevent pregnancy

pillage *verb* **1** to steal property by violence in war ▷ *noun* **2** violent seizure of goods, especially in war

pillar *noun* **1** upright post, usually supporting a roof **2** strong supporter

pillar box *noun* (in Britain) red pillar-shaped letter box in the street

pillory pillories pillorying pilloried *verb* to ridicule publicly

pillow *noun* stuffed cloth bag for supporting the head in bed

pillowcase or **pillowslip** *noun* removable cover for a pillow

pilot *noun* **1** person qualified to fly an aircraft or spacecraft **2** person employed to steer a ship entering or leaving a harbour ▷ *adjective* **3** experimental and preliminary ▷ *verb* **4** to act as the pilot of **5** to guide or lead (a project or people)

pimp *noun* man who gets customers for a prostitute in

return for a share of his or her
earnings

pimple noun small pus-filled spot
on the skin ▷ **pimply** adjective:
pimply teenagers

pin pins pinning pinned noun
1 short thin piece of stiff wire with
a point and head, for fastening
things **2** wooden or metal peg
or stake ▷ verb **3** to fasten with a
pin **4** to seize and hold fast ▷ **pin
down** verb **1** to force (someone) to
make a decision, take action, etc
2 to define clearly

PIN abbreviation personal
identification number: a number
used by the holder of a cash card
or credit card

pinafore noun **1** apron **2** dress
with a bib top

pincers plural noun **1** tool
consisting of two hinged arms,
for gripping **2** claws of a lobster
etc

pinch verb **1** to squeeze
(something) between finger and
thumb **2** to cause pain by being
too tight **3** informal to steal ▷ noun
4 act of pinching **5** as much as
can be taken up between the
finger and thumb **6 at a pinch** if
absolutely necessary

pinched adjective (of someone's
face) thin and pale

pine verb **1 pine for** to feel great
longing (for) ▷ noun **2** evergreen
coniferous tree with very thin
leaves **3** its wood

pineapple noun large tropical
fruit with juicy yellow flesh and
a hard skin

Ping-Pong® noun table tennis

pink noun **1** pale reddish colour
2 fragrant garden plant **3 in the**
pink in good health ▷ adjective
4 of the colour pink

pinnacle noun **1** highest point of
fame or success **2** mountain peak

pinpoint verb **1** to locate or
identify exactly ▷ adjective
2 exact: pinpoint accuracy

pinstripe noun **1** very narrow
stripe in fabric **2** the fabric itself

pint noun liquid measure, 1/8
gallon (.568 litre)

pioneer noun **1** explorer or
early settler of a new country
2 originator or developer of
something new ▷ verb **3** to be the
pioneer or leader of

pious adjective deeply religious

pip noun **1** small seed in a fruit
2 high-pitched sound used as a
time signal on radio

pipe noun **1** tube for conveying
liquid or gas **2** tube with a small
bowl at the end for smoking
tobacco **3** tubular musical
instrument **4 the pipes**
bagpipes ▷ verb **5** to convey (a
liquid such as oil) by pipe

pipeline noun **1** long pipe for
transporting oil, water, etc
2 means of communication

piper noun player on a pipe or
bagpipes

piping noun **1** system of pipes
2 fancy edging on clothes etc

piranha noun small fierce
freshwater fish of tropical
America

pirate noun sea robber

pirouette noun spinning turn
balanced on the toes of one foot

Pisces noun twelfth sign of the
zodiac, represented by two fish

pistil noun seed-bearing part of
a flower

pistol noun short-barrelled handgun

piston noun cylindrical part in an engine that slides to and fro in a cylinder

pit pits pitting pitted noun 1 deep hole in the ground 2 coal mine 3 dent or depression 4 pits servicing and refuelling area on a motor-racing track 5 same as **orchestra pit** ▷ verb 6 to mark with small dents or scars

pitch verb 1 to throw or hurl 2 to set up (a tent) 3 to fall headlong 4 (of a ship or plane) to move with the front and back going up and down alternately 5 to set the level or tone of ▷ noun 6 area marked out for playing sport 7 degree or angle of slope 8 degree of highness or lowness of a (musical) sound 9 dark sticky substance obtained from tar

pitcher noun large jug with a narrow neck

pitfall noun hidden difficulty or danger

pith noun soft white lining of the rind of oranges etc

pitiful adjective 1 arousing pity 2 woeful, contemptible

pittance noun very small amount of money

pitted adjective covered in small hollows

pity pities pitying pitied noun 1 sympathy or sorrow for others' suffering 2 regrettable fact ▷ verb 3 to feel pity for

pivot noun 1 central shaft on which something turns ▷ verb 2 to provide with or turn on a pivot

pixie pixies noun (in folklore) fairy

pizza noun flat disc of dough covered with a wide variety of savoury toppings and baked

placard noun notice that is carried or displayed in public

placate verb to make (someone) stop feeling angry or upset

place noun 1 particular part of an area or space 2 particular town, building, etc 3 position or point reached 4 seat or space 5 usual position 6 **take place** to happen ▷ verb 7 to put in a particular place 8 to identify, put in context 9 to make (an order, bet, etc)

placebo placebos or placeboes noun substance given to a patient in place of a drug and from which, though it has no active ingredients, the patient may imagine they get some benefit

placenta placentas or placentae noun organ formed in the womb during pregnancy, providing nutrients for the fetus

placid adjective not easily excited or upset, calm > **placidly** adverb

plagiarism noun copying ideas or passages from someone else's work and pretending it is your own > **plagiarist** noun

plague plagues plaguing plagued noun 1 fast-spreading fatal disease 2 History bubonic plague 3 overwhelming number of things that afflict or harass ▷ verb 4 to trouble or annoy continually

plaice noun edible European flatfish

plaid noun tartan cloth or pattern

plain adjective 1 easy to see or understand 2 expressed honestly and clearly 3 without decoration

or pattern **4** not beautiful
5 simple or ordinary ▷ *noun*
6 large stretch of level country
▷ *adverb* **7** clearly or simply: *plain
stupid* > **plainly** *adverb*

plaintiff *noun* person who sues in
a court of law

plait *noun* **1** intertwined length
of hair ▷ *verb* **2** to intertwine
separate strands in a pattern

plan plans planning planned
noun **1** way thought out to do or
achieve something **2** diagram
showing the layout or design of
something ▷ *verb* **3** to arrange
beforehand **4** to make a diagram
of

plane *noun* **1** aeroplane **2** Maths
flat surface **3** level of attainment
etc **4** tool for smoothing wood
▷ *adjective* **5** perfectly flat or level
▷ *verb* **6** to smooth (wood) with
a plane

planet *noun* large body in space
that revolves round the sun
or another star > **planetary**
adjective: planetary systems

plank *noun* long flat piece of sawn
timber

plankton *noun* minute animals
and plants floating in the surface
water of a sea or lake

plant *noun* **1** living organism that
grows in the ground and has no
power to move **2** equipment
or machinery used in industrial
processes **3** factory or other
industrial premises ▷ *verb* **4** to
set (seeds or crops) into the
ground to grow **5** to place firmly
in position

plantation *noun* **1** estate for the
cultivation of tea, tobacco, etc
2 wood of cultivated trees

plaque *noun* **1** flat piece of metal
which is fixed to a wall and has
an inscription in memory of a
famous person or event **2** filmy
deposit on teeth that causes
decay

plasma *noun* clear liquid part
of blood

plaster *noun* **1** mixture of lime,
sand, etc for coating walls
2 adhesive strip of material for
dressing cuts etc ▷ *verb* **3** to coat
(a wall or ceiling) with plaster
4 to coat thickly > **plasterer** *noun*

plastered *adjective* **1** plastered
to stuck to **2** plastered **with**
covered with

plastic *noun* **1** synthetic material
that can be moulded when soft
but sets in a hard long-lasting
shape **2** credit cards etc as
opposed to cash ▷ *adjective*
3 made of plastic **4** easily
moulded, pliant

plastic surgery *noun* repair or
reconstruction of missing or
malformed parts of the body

plate *noun* **1** shallow dish for
holding food **2** flat thin sheet of
metal, glass, etc **3** thin coating
of metal on another metal ▷ *verb*
4 to coat (a metal surface) with a
thin coating of another metal

plateau plateaus or plateaux
noun **1** area of level high land
2 stage when there is no change
or development

platform *noun* **1** raised floor
2 raised area in a station from
which passengers board trains
3 structure in the sea which holds
machinery, stores, etc for drilling
an oil well **4** programme of a
political party

platinum *noun* Chemistry valuable

silvery-white metal

platitude *noun* remark that is true but not interesting or original

platonic *adjective* (of a relationship) friendly or affectionate but not sexual

platoon *noun* smaller unit within a company of soldiers

platter *noun* large dish

platypus *platypuses noun* Australian egg-laying amphibious mammal, with dense fur, webbed feet and a ducklike bill; (also **duck-billed platypus**)

plaudits *plural noun* expressions of approval

plausible *adjective* **1** apparently true or reasonable **2** persuasive but insincere > **plausibility** *noun: the plausibility of the theory* > **plausibly** *adverb*

play *verb* **1** to occupy yourself in (a game or recreation) **2** to compete against (someone) in a game or sport **3** to act (a part) on the stage **4** to perform on (a musical instrument) **5** to cause (a radio, CD player, etc) to give out sound ▷ *noun* **6** story performed on stage or broadcast **7** activities children take part in for amusement **8** playing of a game **9** conduct: *fair play* **10** (scope for) freedom of movement

playboy *noun* rich man who lives only for pleasure

playful *adjective* **1** friendly and light-hearted **2** lively > **playfully** *adverb*

playground *noun* outdoor area for children to play in

playgroup *noun* regular meeting of very young children for supervised play

playing card *noun* one of a set of 52 cards used in card games

playing field *noun* extensive piece of ground for sport

playwright *noun* author of plays

plaza *noun* **1** open space or square **2** modern shopping complex

plea *noun* **1** serious or urgent request, entreaty **2** statement of a prisoner or defendant **3** excuse

plead *verb* **1** to ask urgently or with deep feeling **2** to give as an excuse **3** *Law* to declare yourself to be guilty or innocent of a charge made against you

pleasant *adjective* pleasing or enjoyable > **pleasantly** *adverb*

please *verb* **1** to give pleasure or satisfaction to (someone) ▷ *adverb* **2** polite word of request > **pleased** *adjective: I'm pleased to be going home*

pleasing *adjective* attractive, satisfying or enjoyable

pleasure *noun* **1** feeling of happiness and satisfaction **2** something that causes this

pleat *noun* **1** fold made by doubling material back on itself ▷ *verb* **2** to arrange (material) in pleats

plebiscite *noun* decision by direct voting of the people of a country

pledge *noun* **1** solemn promise **2** something valuable given as a guarantee that a promise will be kept or a debt paid ▷ *verb* **3** to promise solemnly **4** to bind by or as if by a pledge

plentiful *adjective* existing in large amounts or numbers > **plentifully** *adverb*

plenty *noun* **1** large amount or number **2** quite enough

plethora noun excess

pleurisy noun inflammation of the membrane covering the lungs

pliable adjective 1 easily bent 2 easily influenced

pliers plural noun tool with hinged arms and jaws for gripping

plight noun difficult or dangerous situation ▷ verb

plinth noun slab forming the base of a statue, column, etc

plod plods plodding plodded verb 1 to walk with slow heavy steps 2 to work slowly but determinedly

plonk verb to put (something) down heavily and carelessly

plop plops plopping plopped noun 1 sound of an object falling into water without a splash ▷ verb 2 to make this sound

plot plots plotting plotted noun 1 secret plan to do something illegal or wrong 2 story of a film, novel, etc 3 small piece of land ▷ verb 4 to plan secretly, conspire 5 to mark the position or course of (a ship or aircraft) on a map 6 to mark and join up (points on a graph)

plough noun 1 agricultural tool for turning over soil ▷ verb 2 to turn over (earth) with a plough 3 **plough through** to move or work through slowly and laboriously

ploy noun manoeuvre designed to gain an advantage

pluck verb 1 to pull or pick off 2 to pull out the feathers of (a bird for cooking) 3 to sound the strings of (a guitar etc) with the fingers ▷ noun 4 bravery or courage

plug plugs plugging plugged noun 1 thing fitting into and filling a hole 2 device connecting an appliance to an electricity supply ▷ verb 3 to block or seal (a hole or gap) with a plug 4 informal to advertise (a product etc) by constant repetition

plum noun 1 oval usually dark red fruit with a stone in the middle ▷ adjective 2 dark purplish-red

plumage noun bird's feathers

plumber noun person who fits and repairs pipes and fixtures for water and drainage systems

plumbing noun pipes and fixtures used in water and drainage systems

plume noun feather, especially one worn as an ornament

plummet plummets plummeting plummeted verb to plunge downward

plump adjective moderately fat

plunder verb 1 to seize (valuables) from (a place) by force, especially in wartime ▷ noun 2 things plundered, spoils

plunge verb 1 to put or throw forcibly or suddenly (into) 2 to descend steeply 3 **plunge into** to become deeply involved in ▷ noun 4 plunging, dive

Plunket Society noun organization for the care of mothers and babies, now called the Royal New Zealand Society for the Health of Women and Children

plural adjective 1 of or consisting of more than one 2 noun word indicating more than one

plural noun noun name given to a noun normally used only in the plural, for example 'scissors' or 'police'

pluralism noun existence and toleration of a variety of peoples, opinions, etc in a society ▷ **pluralist** adjective: a pluralist democracy

plus preposition, adjective **1** indicating addition ▷ adjective **2** more than zero **3** positive **4** advantageous ▷ noun **5** sign (+) denoting addition **6** advantage

plush noun **1** fabric with long velvety pile ▷ adjective **2** (also **plushy**) luxurious

Pluto noun smallest planet in the solar system and farthest from the sun

ply plies plying plied verb **1** to work at (a job or trade) **2** to use (a tool) **3** ply with to supply with or subject to persistently ▷ noun **4** thickness of wool, fabric, etc

plywood noun board made of thin layers of wood glued together

p.m. abbreviation after noon

pneumatic adjective worked by or inflated with wind or air

pneumonia noun inflammation of the lungs

poach verb **1** to catch (animals) illegally on someone else's land **2** to simmer (food) gently in liquid

pocket noun **1** small bag sewn into clothing for carrying things **2** pouchlike container, especially for catching balls at the edge of a snooker table **3** isolated or distinct group or area ▷ verb **4** to put (something) into your pocket **5** to take (something) secretly or dishonestly

pocket money noun small regular allowance given to children by parents

pod noun long narrow seed case of peas, beans, etc

poddy poddies noun Aust calf or lamb that is being fed by hand

podcast noun **1** audio file similar to a radio broadcast which can be downloaded to a computer, MP3 player, etc. ▷ verb **2** to create such files and make them available for downloading

podium podiums or **podia** noun small raised platform for a conductor or speaker

poem noun imaginative piece of writing in rhythmic lines

poet noun writer of poems

poetic adjective of or like poetry ▷ **poetically** adverb

poetry noun **1** poems **2** art of writing poems

poignant adjective sharply painful to the feelings ▷ **poignancy** noun: the film contains moments of almost unbearable poignancy

point noun **1** main idea in a discussion, argument, etc **2** aim or purpose **3** detail or item **4** characteristic **5** particular position, stage or time **6** dot indicating decimals **7** sharp end **8** unit for recording a value or score **9** one of the direction marks of a compass **10** electrical socket **11** on the point of very shortly going to ▷ verb **12** to show the direction or draw attention to it by extending a finger or other pointed object towards it **13** to direct or face towards

point-blank adjective **1** fired at a very close target **2** (of a remark or question) direct, blunt ▷ adverb **3** directly or bluntly

pointed adjective **1** having a sharp

end **2** (of a remark) obviously directed at a particular person > **pointedly** adverb

pointer noun helpful hint

pointless adjective meaningless or irrelevant > **pointlessly** adverb

point of view points of view noun way of considering something

poise noun calm dignified manner

poised adjective **1** absolutely ready **2** behaving with or showing poise

poison noun **1** substance that kills or injures when swallowed or absorbed ▷ verb **2** to give poison to someone **3** to have a harmful or evil effect on

poisonous adjective **1** containing a harmful substance that could kill you or make you ill **2** (of an animal) producing a venom that can cause death or illness in anyone bitten or stung by it

poke verb **1** to jab or prod with your finger, a stick, etc **2** to thrust forward or out ▷ noun **3** poking

poker noun **1** metal rod for stirring a fire **2** card game in which players bet on the hands dealt

polar adjective of or near either of the earth's poles

polar bear noun white bear that lives in the regions around the North Pole

pole noun **1** long rounded piece of wood etc **2** point furthest north or south on the earth's axis of rotation **3** either of the opposite ends of a magnet or electric cell

Pole noun someone from Poland

pole vault noun athletics event in which contestants jump over a high bar using a long flexible pole to lift themselves into the air

police noun **1** organized force in a state which keeps law and order ▷ verb **2** to control or watch over with police or a similar body

policeman policemen noun member of a police force > **policewoman** noun

policy policies noun **1** plan of action adopted by a person, group or state **2** document containing an insurance contract

polio noun disease affecting the spinal cord, which often causes paralysis; (also **poliomyelitis**)

polish verb **1** to make smooth and shiny by rubbing **2** to make more nearly perfect ▷ noun **3** substance used for polishing **4** pleasing elegant style

Polish adjective **1** belonging or relating to Poland ▷ noun **2** main language spoken in Poland

polite adjective **1** showing consideration for others in your manners, speech, etc **2** socially correct or refined > **politely** adverb > **politeness** noun: She listened out of politeness

political adjective of the state, government or public administration > **politically** adverb

politically correct adjective (of language) intended to avoid any implied prejudice

politician noun person actively engaged in politics, especially a member of parliament

politics noun **1** winning and using of power to govern society **2** (study of) the art of government **3** person's beliefs about how a country should be governed

polka noun **1** lively 19th-century

dance **2** music for this

poll noun **1** (also **opinion poll**) questioning of a random sample of people to find out general opinion **2** voting **3** number of votes recorded **4** **the polls** political election ▷ verb **5** to receive (votes) **6** to question (a person) in an opinion poll

pollen noun fine dust produced by flowers to fertilize other flowers

pollinate verb to fertilize by the transfer of pollen ▷ **pollination** noun: without sufficient pollination, the growth of the corn is stunted

pollutant noun something that pollutes

pollute verb to contaminate with something poisonous or harmful ▷ **polluted** adjective: polluted rivers

pollution noun harmful or poisonous substances introduced into an environment

polo noun game like hockey played by teams of players on horseback

polo-neck noun sweater with high turned-over collar

polyester noun man-made material used to make plastics and clothes

polygamy noun practice of having more than one husband or wife at the same time ▷ **polygamous** adjective: polygamous societies

polygon noun geometrical figure with three or more angles and sides

polystyrene noun synthetic material used especially as white rigid foam for packing and insulation

polythene noun light plastic used for bags etc

polyunsaturated adjective

of a group of fats that do not form cholesterol in the blood ▷ **polyunsaturate** noun: spreads containing polyunsaturates

pomegranate noun round tropical fruit with a thick rind containing many seeds in a red pulp

pomp noun stately display or ceremony

pompous adjective foolishly serious and grand, self-important ▷ **pomposity** noun: the pomposity of some politicians ▷ **pompously** adverb

pond noun small area of still water

ponder verb to think thoroughly or deeply (about)

ponderous adjective **1** serious and dull **2** heavy and unwieldy **3** (of movement) slow and clumsy ▷ **ponderously** adverb

pong noun informal strong unpleasant smell

pontiff noun formal the Pope

pony ponies noun small horse

ponytail noun long hair tied in one bunch at the back of the head

pony trekking noun leisure activity in which people ride across country on ponies

poodle noun dog with curly hair often clipped fancifully

pool noun **1** small body of still water **2** swimming pool **3** shared fund or group of workers or resources **4** game in which players try to hit coloured balls into pockets around the table using long sticks called cues ▷ verb **5** to put in a common fund

poor adjective **1** having little money and few possessions **2** less, smaller or weaker than is

needed or expected **3** inferior
4 unlucky, pitiable

poorly adverb **1** in a poor manner
▷ adjective **2** not in good health

pop pops popping popped verb
1 to make or cause to make a
small explosive sound **2** informal
to go, put or come unexpectedly
or suddenly ▷ noun **3** music of
general appeal, especially to
young people **4** small explosive
sound **5** Brit nonalcoholic fizzy
drink

popcorn noun grains of maize
heated until they puff up and
burst

Pope noun head of the Roman
Catholic Church

poplar noun tall slender tree

poppy poppies noun plant with a
large red flower

populace noun formal the ordinary
people

popular adjective **1** widely liked
and admired **2** of or for the public
in general ▷ **popularity** noun: the
growing popularity of Chilean wines
▷ **popularly** adverb

populate verb **1** to live in, inhabit
2 to fill with inhabitants

population noun **1** all the people
who live in a particular place
2 the number of people living in a
particular place

pop-up noun Computers image that
appears above the open window
on a computer screen

porcelain noun **1** fine china
2 objects made of it

porch noun covered approach to
the entrance of a building

porcupine noun animal covered
with long pointed quills

pore noun **1** tiny opening in the
skin or in the surface of a plant
2 pore over to examine or study
intently

pork noun pig meat

pornography noun writing,
films or pictures designed to be
sexually exciting ▷ **pornographic**
adjective: pornographic magazines

porpoise noun fishlike sea
mammal

porridge noun breakfast food
made of oatmeal cooked in water
or milk

port noun **1** (town with) a harbour
2 left side of a ship or aircraft
when facing the front of it
3 strong sweet wine, usually red

-port suffix carrying: transport

portable adjective easily carried

porter noun **1** man who carries
luggage **2** hospital worker who
transfers patients between rooms
3 doorman or gatekeeper of a
building

portfolio portfolios noun **1** (flat
case for carrying) examples
of an artist's work **2** area of
responsibility of a government
minister **3** list of investments
held by an investor

porthole noun small round
window in a ship or aircraft

portion noun **1** part or share
2 helping of food for one person
3 destiny or fate

portrait noun **1** picture of a person
2 lifelike description

portray verb to describe or
represent by artistic means, as in
writing or film ▷ **portrayal** noun:
his portrayal of Hamlet

Portuguese adjective **1** of
Portugal, its people or their
language ▷ noun **2** person from

Portugal **3** language of Portugal and Brazil

pose *verb* **1** to place in or take up a particular position to be photographed or drawn **2** to raise (a problem) **3** to ask (a question) **4 pose as** to pretend to be ▷ *noun* **5** position while posing **6** behaviour adopted for effect

poser *noun* **1** puzzling question **2** poseur

posh *adjective informal* **1** smart, luxurious **2** upper-class

position *noun* **1** place **2** usual or expected place **3** way in which something is placed or arranged **4** attitude, point of view **5** job ▷ *verb* **6** to place

positive *adjective* **1** feeling no doubts, certain **2** confident, hopeful **3** helpful, providing encouragement **4** absolute, downright **5** *Maths* greater than zero **6** (of an electrical charge) having a deficiency of electrons ▷ **positively** *adverb*

possess *verb* **1** to have or own (something) **2** (of a feeling, belief, etc) to have complete control of, dominate ▷ **possessor** *noun: the proud possessor of a new car*

possession *noun* **1** state of possessing; ownership **2 possessions** things a person possesses

possessive *adjective* **1** wanting all the attention or love of another person **2** (of a word) indicating the person or thing that something belongs to

possibility possibilities *noun* something that might be true or might happen

possible *adjective* **1** able to exist, happen or be done **2** worthy of consideration ▷ *noun* **3** person or thing that might be suitable or chosen

possum *noun* **1** same as **opossum** **2** *Aust, NZ* phalanger, a marsupial with thick fur and a long tail

post *noun* **1** official system of delivering letters and parcels **2** (single collection or delivery of) letters and parcels sent by this system **3** length of wood, concrete, etc fixed upright to support or mark something **4** job ▷ *verb* **5** to send by post **6** to put up (a notice) in a public place **7** to send (a person) to a new place to work; to supply someone regularly with the latest information

post- *prefix* after, later than: *postwar*

postage *noun* charge for sending a letter or parcel by post

postal order *noun Brit* written money order sent by post and cashed at a post office by the person who receives it

postbox *noun* metal box with a hole in it which you put letters into for collection by the postman

postcard *noun* card for sending a message by post without an envelope

postcode *noun* system of letters and numbers used to aid the sorting of mail

poster *noun* large picture or notice stuck on a wall

posterior *noun* **1** buttocks ▷ *adjective* **2** behind, at the back of

posterity *noun formal* future generations, descendants

posthumous *adjective* occurring

after a person's death: *a posthumous award for bravery*
> **posthumously** *adverb*

postman postmen *noun* person who collects and delivers post

postmortem *noun* medical examination of a body to establish the cause of death

post office *noun* 1 place where postal business is conducted 2 **Post Office** *Brit* government department responsible for postal services

postpone *verb* to put off to a later time > **postponement** *noun*: *the postponement was due to the weather*

posture *noun* 1 position or way in which someone stands, walks, etc > *verb* 2 to behave in an exaggerated way to get attention

posy posies *noun* small bunch of flowers

pot pots potting potted *noun* 1 round deep container 2 teapot > *verb* 3 to put (a plant) in soil in a flowerpot

potassium nitrate *noun* white chemical compound used to make gunpowder, fireworks and fertilizers; (also **saltpetre**)

potato potatoes *noun* roundish starchy vegetable that grows underground

potent *adjective* 1 effective or powerful 2 (of a male) capable of having sexual intercourse > **potency** *noun*: *the potency of the wine*

potential *adjective* 1 possible but not yet actual > *noun* 2 ability or talent not yet fully used > **potentially** *adverb*

potential energy *noun* energy stored in something

pothole *noun* 1 hole in the surface of a road 2 deep hole in a limestone area

potion *noun* dose of medicine or poison

potted *adjective* 1 grown in a pot 2 (of meat or fish) cooked or preserved in a pot

potter *noun* 1 person who makes pottery ▷ *verb* 2 **potter about, around** or **away** to be busy in a pleasant but aimless way

pottery potteries *noun* 1 articles made from baked clay 2 craft of making pottery

potty potties; pottier pottiest *noun* 1 bowl used by a small child as a toilet ▷ *adjective* 2 *informal* crazy or silly

pouch *noun* 1 small bag 2 baglike pocket of skin on an animal

poultry *noun* domestic fowls

pounce *verb* 1 **pounce on** to spring upon suddenly to attack or capture ▷ *noun* 2 pouncing

pound *noun* 1 monetary unit of Britain and some other countries 2 unit of weight equal to 0.454 kg 3 enclosure for stray animals or officially removed vehicles ▷ *verb* 4 to hit heavily and repeatedly 5 to crush to pieces or powder 6 (of the heart) to throb heavily 7 to run heavily

pour *verb* 1 to flow or cause to flow out in a stream 2 to rain heavily 3 to come or go in large numbers

pout *verb* 1 to thrust out (the lips) sullenly or provocatively ▷ *noun* 2 pouting look

poverty *noun* 1 state of being without enough food or money 2 lack of, scarcity

powder noun 1 substance in the form of tiny loose particles 2 medicine or cosmetic in this form ▷ verb 3 to cover or sprinkle with powder ▷ **powdery** adjective

power noun 1 ability to do or act 2 strength 3 position of authority or control 4 Maths product from continuous multiplication of a number by itself 5 Physics rate at which work is done 6 electricity supply 7 particular form of energy: nuclear power ▷ verb 8 to supply with power

powerful adjective strong, influential or effective: a powerful car ▷ **powerfully** adverb

powerless adjective unable to control or influence events

power station noun installation for generating and distributing electric power

practicable adjective 1 capable of being done successfully 2 usable

practical adjective 1 involving experience or actual use rather than theory 2 sensible, useful and effective 3 good at making or doing things 4 in effect though not in name ▷ noun 5 examination in which something has to be done or made ▷ **practicality** noun: the practicalities of everyday life

practically adverb 1 almost but not completely or exactly 2 in a practical way

practice noun 1 something done regularly or habitually 2 repetition of something so as to gain skill 3 doctor's or lawyer's place of work

practise verb 1 to do repeatedly so as to gain skill 2 to take part in, follow (a religion etc) 3 to work

at: to practise medicine 4 to do habitually

practised adjective expert or skilled as a result of long experience

practitioner noun person who practises a profession

pragmatic adjective concerned with practical consequences rather than theory ▷ **pragmatically** adverb ▷ **pragmatism** noun: a reputation for clear thinking and pragmatism

prairie noun large treeless area of grassland, especially in N America and Canada

praise verb 1 to express approval or admiration of (someone or something) 2 to express honour and thanks to (one's God) ▷ noun 3 something said or written to show approval or admiration

pram noun four-wheeled carriage for a baby, pushed by hand

prance verb to walk with exaggerated bouncing steps

prank noun mischievous trick

prattle verb 1 to chatter in a childish or foolish way ▷ noun 2 childish or foolish talk

prawn noun edible shellfish like a large shrimp

pray verb 1 to say prayers (to God) 2 to ask earnestly

prayer noun 1 thanks or appeal addressed to God 2 set form of words used in praying 3 earnest request

pre- prefix before, beforehand: prenatal; prerecorded; preshrunk

preach verb 1 to give a talk on a religious theme as part of a church service 2 to speak in support of (an idea, principle, etc)

precarious *adjective* (of a position or situation) dangerous or insecure > **precariously** *adverb*

precaution *noun* action taken in advance to prevent something bad happening > **precautionary** *adjective: the curfew is a precautionary measure*

precede *verb* to go or be before (someone or something) in time, place or rank > **preceding** *adjective* coming before: *the preceding day*

precedence *noun* formal order of rank or position

precedent *noun* previous case or occurrence regarded as an example to be followed

precinct *noun* **1** Brit, Aust, S Afr area in a town closed to traffic **2** Brit, Aust, S Afr enclosed area round a building **3** US administrative area of a city **4** surrounding region

precious *adjective* **1** of great value and importance **2** loved and treasured

precipice *noun* very steep face of cliff or rockface

precipitate *verb* formal to cause to happen suddenly

precipitation *formal noun* rain, snow, sleet or hail

precise *adjective* **1** exact, accurate in every detail **2** strict in observing rules or standards > **precisely** *adverb* > **precision** *noun: The work requires great precision*

preclude *verb* formal to make impossible to happen

precocious *adjective* having developed or matured early or too soon

preconceived *adjective* (of

an idea) formed without real experience or reliable information > **preconception** *noun: preconceptions about the sort of people who study computing*

precondition *noun* something that must happen or exist before something else can

precursor *noun* something that precedes and is a signal of something else, forerunner

predator *noun* animal that kills and eats other animals > **predatory** *adjective: predatory birds*

predecessor *noun* **1** person who precedes another in an office or position **2** ancestor

predetermined *adjective* decided in advance

predicament *noun* embarrassing or difficult situation

predict *verb* to tell about in advance: prophesy > **predictable** *adjective*: a predictable outcome > **prediction** *noun* forecast or prophesy: *He was unwilling to make a prediction*

predominant *adjective* more important or more noticeable than anything else in a particular set of people or things > **predominantly** *adverb*

predominate *verb* to be the main or controlling element > **predominance** *noun*: *the predominance of English on the Internet*

pre-eminent *adjective* excelling all others, outstanding > **preeminence** *noun*: *London's pre-eminence among European financial centres*

pre-empt *verb* formal to prevent an

action by doing something which makes it pointless or impossible

preen verb (of a bird) to clean or trim (feathers) with the beak

preface noun **1** introduction to a book ▷ verb **2** to serve as an introduction to (a book, speech, etc)

prefect noun senior pupil in a school, with limited power over others

prefer prefers preferring preferred verb to like better

preference noun **1** liking for one thing above another or above the rest **2** person or thing preferred

preferential adjective showing preference

prefix noun letter or group of letters put at the beginning of a word to make a new word, such as un- in unhappy

pregnant adjective carrying a fetus in the womb >**pregnancy** noun: Cut out all alcohol during pregnancy

prehistoric adjective of the period before written history begins

prejudice noun **1** unreasonable or unfair dislike or preference ▷ verb **2** to cause (someone) to have a prejudice >**prejudiced** adjective: racially prejudiced >**prejudicial** adjective: rumours considered prejudicial to security

preliminary preliminaries adjective **1** happening before and in preparation, introductory ▷ noun **2** preliminary remark, contest, etc

prelude noun event preceding and introducing something else

premature adjective **1** happening or done before the normal or expected time **2** (of a baby)

born before the end of the normal period of pregnancy >**prematurely** adverb

premeditated adjective planned in advance

première noun first performance of a play, film, etc

premise noun statement assumed to be true and used as the basis of reasoning

premium noun **1** additional sum of money, as on a wage or charge **2** (regular) sum paid for insurance

premonition noun feeling that something unpleasant is going to happen

preoccupation noun something that holds the attention completely

preoccupied adjective absorbed in something, especially your own thoughts

preparatory adjective preparing for

prepare verb to make or get ready

prepared adjective **1** willing **2** ready

preposition noun word used before a noun or pronoun to show its relationship with other words, such as by in go by bus

preposterous adjective utterly absurd

prerequisite noun formal something required before something else is possible

prerogative noun formal special power or privilege

prescribe verb to recommend the use of (a medicine)

prescription noun written instructions from a doctor for the making up and use of a medicine

presence noun **1** fact of being in

a specified place **2** impressive dignified appearance

present *adjective* **1** being in a specified place **2** existing or happening now **3** *Grammar* (of a verb tense) indicating that the action specified is taking place now ▷ *noun* **4** present time or tense **5** something given to bring pleasure to another person ▷ *verb* **6** to introduce formally or publicly **7** to introduce and compere (a TV or radio show) **8** to cause: *present a difficulty* **9** to give or offer formally

presentable *adjective* attractive, neat, fit for people to see

presentation *noun* **1** act of presenting or a way of presenting something **2** manner of presenting **3** formal ceremony in which an award is made **4** talk or demonstration

present-day *adjective* existing or happening now: *present-day farming practices*

presently *adverb* **1** soon **2** *US, Scot* at the moment

present participle *noun Grammar* the form of a verb that ends in *-ing*, used to form some tenses and to form adjectives and nouns from a verb

present tense *noun Grammar* tense of a verb that is used mainly to talk about things that happen or exist at the time of writing or speaking

preservative *noun* chemical that prevents decay

preserve *verb* **1** to keep from being damaged, changed or ended **2** to treat (food) to prevent it decaying ▷ *noun* **3** area of interest restricted to a particular person or group **4** fruit preserved by cooking in sugar ▷ **preservation** *noun*: *the preservation of natural resources*

preside *verb* to be in charge, especially of a meeting

president *noun* **1** head of state in many countries **2** head of a society, institution, etc ▷ **presidential** *adjective*: *presidential elections*

press *verb* **1** to apply force or weight to **2** to squeeze **3** to smooth by applying pressure or heat **4** to urge (someone) insistently **5** to crowd or push ▷ *noun* **6 the press a** news media collectively, especially newspapers **b** journalists collectively **7** printing machine

press conference *noun* interview for reporters given by a celebrity

pressing *adjective* urgent

pressure *noun* **1** force produced by pressing **2** urgent claims or demands **3** *Physics* force applied to a surface per unit of area ▷ *verb* **4** to persuade forcefully

pressurize *verb* to put pressure on (someone) in an attempt to persuade them to do something

prestige *noun* high status or respect resulting from success or achievements ▷ **prestigious** *adjective*: *one of the country's most prestigious schools*

presumably *adverb* one supposes (that)

presume *verb* **1** to take (something) for granted **2** to dare (to)

presumptuous *adjective* doing things you have no right to do

pretence *noun* behaviour

intended to deceive

pretend verb to claim or give the appearance of (something untrue) to deceive or in play

pretender noun person who makes a false or disputed claim to a position of power

pretension noun false claim to merit or importance

pretentious adjective making (unjustified) claims to special merit or importance

pretext noun false reason given to hide the real one

pretty prettier prettiest adjective 1 pleasing to look at ▷ adverb 2 fairly, moderately: I'm pretty certain >**prettily** adverb >**prettiness** noun: the prettiness of the village

prevail verb 1 to gain mastery 2 to be generally established

prevalent adjective widespread, common >**prevalence** noun: the prevalence of asthma in Britain

prevent verb to keep from happening or doing >**preventable** adjective: preventable illnesses >**prevention** noun: crime prevention

preventive adjective intended to help prevent things such as disease or crime

preview noun 1 advance showing of a film or exhibition before it is shown to the public 2 part of a computer program which allows the user to look at what has been keyed or added to a document or spreadsheet as it will appear when it is printed

previous adjective coming or happening before >**previously** adverb

prey noun 1 animal hunted and killed for food by another animal 2 victim ▷ verb 3 **prey on a** to hunt and kill for food **b** to worry or obsess

price noun 1 amount of money for which a thing is bought or sold 2 unpleasant thing that must be endured to get something desirable ▷ verb 3 to fix or ask the price of

priceless adjective 1 very valuable 2 informal very funny

pricey pricier priciest adjective informal expensive

prick verb 1 to pierce lightly with a sharp point 2 to cause to feel mental pain ▷ noun 3 sudden sharp pain caused by pricking 4 mark made by pricking

prickle noun 1 thorn or spike on a plant ▷ verb 2 to feel a tingling or pricking sensation

pride noun 1 feeling of pleasure and satisfaction when you have done well 2 too high an opinion of yourself 3 sense of dignity and self-respect 4 something that causes you to feel pride 5 group of lions ▷ verb 6 **pride yourself on** to feel pride about

priest noun 1 (in the Christian church) a person who can administer the sacraments and preach 2 (in some other religions) an official who performs religious ceremonies >**priestly** adjective: his priestly duties

priestess noun a female priest in a non-Christian religion

priesthood noun position of being a priest

prim primmer primmest adjective formal, proper and rather prudish

primaeval adjective same as **primeval**

primarily adverb chiefly or mainly

primary adjective **1** chief, most important **2** being the first stage, elementary

primary colours plural noun (in physics) red, green and blue or (in art) red, yellow and blue, from which all other colours can be produced by mixing

primary school noun school for children from five to eleven years or (in New Zealand) between five to thirteen years

primate noun **1** member of an order of mammals including monkeys and humans **2** archbishop

prime adjective **1** main, most important **2** of the highest quality ▷ noun **3** time when someone is at his or her best or most vigorous ▷ verb **4** to give (someone) information in advance to prepare them for something **5** to prepare (a gun, pump, etc) for use

Prime Minister noun leader of a government

primeval adjective of the earliest age of the world

primitive adjective **1** of an early simple stage of development **2** basic, crude

primrose noun pale yellow spring flower

prince noun **1** male member of a royal family, especially the son of the king or queen **2** male ruler of a small country

princess noun female member of a royal family, especially the daughter of the king or queen

principal adjective **1** main, most important ▷ noun **2** head of a school or college **3** person taking a leading part in something **4** sum of money lent on which interest is paid ▷ **principally** adverb

● Do not confuse principal with principle

principality principalities noun territory ruled by a prince

principle noun **1** moral rule guiding behaviour **2** general or basic truth **3** scientific law concerning the working of something

● Do not confuse principle with principal

print verb **1** to reproduce (a newspaper, book, etc) in large quantities by mechanical or electronic means **2** to reproduce (text or pictures) by pressing ink onto paper etc **3** to write in letters that are not joined up **4** to stamp (fabric) with a design **5** Photography to produce (pictures) from negatives ▷ noun **6** printed words etc **7** printed copy of a painting **8** printed lettering **9** photograph **10** printed fabric **11** mark left on a surface by something that has pressed against it

printing noun **1** process of producing printed matter **2** printed text **3** all the copies of a book printed at one time **4** form of writing in which the letters are not joined together

print-out noun printed information from a computer

prior adjective **1** earlier **2** prior to before ▷ noun **3** head monk in a priory

a
b
c
d
e
f
g
h
i
j
k
l
m
n
o
p
q
r
s
t
u
v
w
x
y
z

prioritize verb to arrange (items to be attended to) in order of their relative importance

priority priorities noun 1 most important thing that must be dealt with first 2 right to be or go before others

priory priories noun place where certain orders of monks or nuns live

prise or **prize** verb to force open by levering

prism noun transparent block usually with triangular ends and rectangular sides, used to disperse light into a spectrum or refract it in optical instruments

prison noun building where criminals and accused people are held

prisoner noun person held captive

pristine adjective clean, new and unused

private adjective 1 for the use of one person or group only 2 secret 3 personal or unconnected with your work 4 owned or paid for by individuals rather than by the government 5 quiet, not likely to be disturbed ▷ noun 6 soldier of the lowest rank ▶ **privacy** noun: an invasion of privacy ▶ **privately** adverb

private school noun school that does not receive money from the government, and parents pay for their children to attend

privatize verb to sell (a publicly owned company) to individuals or a private company ▶ **privatization** noun: the privatization of public transport

privilege noun advantage or favour that only some people have

privy adjective sharing knowledge of something secret

prize noun 1 reward given for success in a competition etc ▷ adjective 2 winning or likely to win a prize ▷ verb 3 to value highly 4 same as **prise**

pro pros adverb, preposition 1 in favour of 2 **pros and cons** arguments for and against ▷ noun 3 informal professional

pro- prefix 1 in favour of: pro-Russian 2 instead of: pronoun

probability probabilities noun 1 condition of being probable 2 event or other thing that is likely to happen or be true 3 Maths measure of the likelihood of an event happening

probable adjective likely to happen or be true

probably adverb in all likelihood

probation noun 1 system of dealing with law-breakers, especially juvenile ones, by placing them under supervision 2 period when someone is assessed for suitability for a job etc ▶ **probationary** adjective: a probationary period of two years

probe verb 1 to search into or examine closely ▷ noun 2 surgical instrument used to examine a wound, cavity, etc

problem noun 1 something difficult to deal with or solve 2 question or puzzle set for solution ▶ **problematic** adjective: Getting there will be problematic

procedure noun way of doing something, especially the correct or usual one ▶ **procedural** adjective: The judge rejected the case on procedural grounds

proceed verb 1 to start or continue doing 2 formal to walk or go

proceedings plural noun 1 organized or related series of events 2 minutes of a meeting 3 legal action

process noun 1 series of actions or changes 2 method of doing or producing something ▷ verb 3 to handle or prepare by a special method of manufacture

procession noun line of people or vehicles moving forward together in order

processor noun central chip in a computer which controls its operations

proclaim verb to declare publicly ▷ **proclamation** noun: a proclamation of independence

procure verb to get or provide

prod prods prodding prodded verb 1 to poke with something pointed ▷ noun 2 prodding

prodigy prodigies noun person with some marvellous talent

produce verb 1 to bring (something) into existence 2 to present to view 3 to make or manufacture ▷ noun 4 food grown for sale

producer noun 1 person with control over the making of a film, record, etc 2 person or company that produces something

product noun 1 something produced 2 number resulting from multiplication

production noun 1 process of manufacturing or growing something in large quantities 2 amount of goods manufactured or food grown by a country or company 3 presentation of a play,

opera, etc

productive adjective 1 producing large quantities 2 useful, profitable

productivity noun rate at which things are produced or dealt with

profane adjective showing disrespect for religion or holy things

profess verb formal 1 to claim (something to be true), sometimes falsely 2 to declare or express (something)

profession noun 1 type of work, such as being a doctor, that needs special training 2 all the people employed in a profession: the legal profession

professional adjective 1 working in a profession 2 taking part in an activity, such as sport or music, for money 3 very competent ▷ noun 4 person who works in a profession 5 person paid to take part in sport, music, etc ▷ **professionally** adverb

professor noun teacher of the highest rank in a university ▷ **professorial** adjective: professorial posts

proficient adjective skilled, expert ▷ **proficiency** noun: proficiency in English

profile noun 1 outline, especially of the face, as seen from the side 2 brief biographical sketch

profit noun 1 money gained 2 benefit obtained ▷ verb 3 to gain or benefit

profound adjective 1 showing or needing great knowledge 2 strongly felt, intense ▷ **profoundly** adverb ▷ **profundity** noun: His work lacks depth and *profundity*

profuse *adjective* plentiful
> **profusely** *adverb* > **profusion**
noun: *a profusion of wild flowers*

**program programs
programming programmed**
noun **1** sequence of coded
instructions for a computer ▷ *verb*
2 to arrange (data) so that it can
be processed by a computer **3** to
feed a program into (a computer)
> **programmer** *noun*

programme *noun* **1** planned
series of events **2** broadcast
on radio or television **3** list
of items or performers in an
entertainment

progress *noun* **1** improvement,
development **2** movement
forward **3 in progress** taking
place ▷ *verb* **4** to become more
advanced or skilful **5** to move
forward > **progression** *noun*:
*Both drugs slow the progression of
the disease*

progressive *adjective* **1** favouring
political or social reform
2 happening gradually

prohibit *verb* to forbid or prevent
from happening

prohibitive *adjective* (of prices)
too high to be affordable
> **prohibitively** *adverb*

project *noun* **1** planned scheme to
do or examine something over a
period ▷ *verb* **2** to make a forecast
based on known data **3** to make
(a film or slide) appear on a
screen **4** to communicate (an
impression) **5** to stick out beyond
a surface or edge > **projection**
noun: *sales projections*

projector *noun* apparatus for
projecting photographic images,
films or slides on a screen

proletariat *noun formal* working
class > **proletarian** *adjective*:
proletarian revolution

proliferate *verb* to increase rapidly
in numbers > **proliferation** *noun*:
the proliferation of nuclear weapons

prolific *adjective* very productive
> **prolifically** *adverb*

prologue *noun* introduction to a
play or book

prolong *verb* to make (something)
last longer > **prolonged** *adjective*:
prolonged negotiations

prom *noun informal* concert at
which some of the audience
stand; (also **promenade concert**)

promenade *noun Chiefly Brit* paved
walkway along the seafront at a
holiday resort

prominent *adjective* **1** very
noticeable **2** famous, widely
known > **prominence** *noun*: *He
came to prominence during the war*
> **prominently** *adverb*

promiscuous *adjective* having
many casual sexual relationships
> **promiscuity** *noun*: *male
promiscuity*

promise *verb* **1** to say that you will
definitely do or not do something
2 to show signs of, seem likely
▷ *noun* **3** undertaking to do or not
to do something **4** indication of
future success

promontory promontories *noun*
point of high land jutting out
into the sea

promote *verb* **1** to help to make
(something) happen or increase
2 to raise to a higher rank or
position **3** to encourage the sale
of (a product) by advertising
> **promotion** *noun*: *promotion
through the ranks* > **promotional**

adjective: promotional material

prompt *verb* **1** to cause (an action) **2** to remind (an actor or speaker) of words that he or she has forgotten ▷ *adjective* **3** done without delay ▷ *adverb* **4** exactly: *six o'clock prompt* ▷ **promptly** or **prompt** *adverb*

prone *adjective* **1** prone to likely to do or be affected by (something) **2** lying face downwards

prong *noun* one spike of a fork or similar instrument

pronoun *noun* word, such as *she* or *it*, used to replace a noun

pronounce *verb* **1** to form the sounds of (words or letters), especially clearly or in a particular way **2** to declare formally or officially

pronounced *adjective* very noticeable

pronouncement *noun* formal announcement

pronunciation *noun* way in which a word or language is pronounced

proof *noun* **1** evidence that shows that something is true or has happened **2** copy of something printed, such as the pages of a book, for checking before final production ▷ *adjective* **3** able to withstand: *proof against criticism* **4** denoting the strength of an alcoholic drink: *seventy proof*

prop **props propping propped** *verb* **1** to support (something) so that it stays upright or in place ▷ *noun* **2** pole, beam, etc used as a support **3** movable object used on the set of a film or play

propaganda *noun* (organized promotion of) information to assist or damage the cause of a government or movement

propagate *verb* **1** to spread (information and ideas) **2** to reproduce, breed or grow ▷ **propagation** *noun*: *the propagation of true Buddhism*

propel **propels propelling propelled** *verb* to cause to move forward

propeller *noun* revolving shaft with blades for driving a ship or aircraft

propensity **propensities** *noun formal* natural tendency

proper *adjective* **1** real or genuine **2** suited to a particular purpose **3** correct in behaviour **4** *Brit, Aust, NZ informal* complete ▷ **properly** *adverb*

proper noun *noun* name of a person, place or institution

property **properties** *noun* **1** something owned **2** possessions collectively **3** land or buildings owned by somebody **4** quality or attribute

prophecy **prophecies** *noun* **1** prediction **2** message revealing God's will

prophesy **prophesies prophesying prophesied** *verb* to foretell

prophet *noun* **1** person supposedly chosen by God to spread His word **2** person who predicts the future

prophetic *adjective* correctly predicting what will happen ▷ **prophetically** *adverb*

proportion *noun* **1** relative size or extent **2** correct relation between connected parts **3** part considered with respect to the whole **4** **proportions**

dimensions or size **5 in
proportion a** comparable in size,
rate of increase, etc **b** without
exaggerating ▷ *verb* **6** to adjust
in relative amount or size

proportional or **proportionate**
adjective being in proportion
>**proportionally** or
proportionately *adverb*

proportional representation
noun system of voting in
elections in which the number
of representatives of each party
is in proportion to the number of
people who voted for it

proposal *noun* **1** plan that has
been suggested **2** offer of
marriage

propose *verb* **1** to put forward
(a plan) for consideration **2** to
nominate (someone) for a
position **3** to intend or plan
(to do) **4** to make an offer of
marriage

proposition *noun* **1** offer
2 statement or assertion
3 *informal* thing to be dealt with

proprietor *noun* owner of a
business establishment

propriety *noun formal* correct
conduct

propulsion *noun* **1** method by
which something is propelled
2 act of propelling or state of
being propelled

prose *noun* ordinary speech or
writing in contrast to poetry

prosecute *verb* **1** to bring
a criminal charge against
(someone) **2** to continue to do
(something) >**prosecutor** *noun*:
the public prosecutor

prosecution *noun* **1** bringing
of criminal charges against

someone **2** lawyers who try to
prove that a person on trial is
guilty

prospect prospectuses *noun*
1 something anticipated
2 prospects probability of
future success ▷ *verb* **3** to
explore, especially for gold or
oil >**prospector** *noun*: *a gold
prospector*

prospective *adjective* **1** future
2 expected

prospectus *noun* booklet giving
details of a university, company,
etc

prosper *verb* to be successful
>**prosperous** *adjective*: *a
prosperous family*

prostitute *noun* person who offers
sexual intercourse in return for
payment >**prostitution** *noun*

prostrate *adjective* **1** lying face
downwards **2** physically or
emotionally exhausted

protagonist *noun formal*
1 supporter of a cause **2** leading
character in a play or a story

protea *noun* African shrub with
showy flowers

protect *verb* to defend
from trouble, harm or loss
>**protection** *noun*: *protection for
our children*

protégé *noun* person who is
protected and helped by another
>**protégée** woman or girl who is
protected and helped by another
person

protein *noun* any of a group of
complex organic compounds that
are essential for life

protest *noun* **1** declaration or
demonstration of objection
▷ *verb* **2** to object or disagree **3** to

assert formally

Protestant noun **1** follower of any of the Christian churches that split from the Roman Catholic Church in the sixteenth century ▷ adjective **2** of or relating to such a church

protestation noun strong declaration

protocol noun rules of behaviour for formal occasions

proton noun positively charged particle in the nucleus of an atom

prototype noun original or model to be copied or developed

protracted adjective lengthened or extended

protractor noun instrument for measuring angles

protrude verb to stick out or project >**protrusion** noun: a protrusion of rock

proud adjective **1** feeling pleasure and satisfaction **2** feeling honoured **3** thinking yourself superior to other people **4** dignified >**proudly** adverb

prove proves proving proved proved or proven verb **1** to establish the validity of **2** to demonstrate or test **3** to be found to be

proverb noun short saying that expresses a truth or gives a warning >**proverbial** adjective: the proverbial man in the street

provide verb **1** to make available **2** provide for **a** to take precautions (against) **b** to support financially >**provider** noun: providers of sports facilities

providence noun God or nature seen as a protective force that arranges people's lives

province noun **1** area governed as a unit of a country or empire **2** area of learning, activity, etc **3** provinces parts of a country outside the capital

provincial adjective **1** of a province or the provinces **2** unsophisticated and narrow-minded

provision noun **1** act of supplying something **2** something supplied **3** Law condition incorporated in a document **4** provisions food

provisional adjective temporary or conditional >**provisionally** adverb

proviso provisos or provisoes noun condition in an agreement

provocation noun act done deliberately to annoy someone

provocative adjective **1** intended to annoy people or make them react: a provocative speech **2** intended to make someone feel sexual desire: provocative poses

provoke verb **1** to deliberately anger **2** to cause (an adverse reaction)

prow noun bow of a vessel

prowess noun superior skill or ability

prowl verb to move stealthily around a place as if in search of prey or plunder

proximity noun formal **1** nearness in space or time **2** nearness or closeness in a series

proxy proxies noun **1** person authorized to act on behalf of someone else **2** authority to act on behalf of someone else

prude noun person who is excessively modest, prim or proper >**prudish** adjective: I'm

a
b
c
d
e
f
g
h
i
j
k
l
m
n
o
p
q
r
s
t
u
v
w
x
y
z

not prudish but I was offended by those photos

prudent *adjective* cautious, discreet and sensible > **prudence** *noun: A lack of prudence may lead to financial problems* > **prudently** *adverb*

prune *noun* **1** dried plum **2** to cut off dead parts or excessive branches from (a tree or plant) **3** to shorten or reduce

pry pries prying pried *verb* to make an impertinent or uninvited inquiry (about a private matter)

PS *abbreviation* postscript

PSHE *abbreviation* Personal Social and Health Education: a lesson in which students are taught about social and personal issues

psalm *noun* sacred song

pseudo- *prefix* false, pretending or unauthentic: *pseudoclassical*

pseudonym *noun* fictitious name adopted especially by an author

psyche *noun* human mind or soul

psychiatry *noun* branch of medicine concerned with mental disorders > **psychiatric** *adjective: chronic psychiatric illnesses* > **psychiatrist** *noun: a psychiatrist of many years experience*

psychic *adjective* **1** having mental powers which cannot be explained by natural laws **2** relating to the mind ▷ *noun* **3** person with psychic powers

psychoanalysis *noun* method of treating mental and emotional disorders by discussion and analysis of the person's thoughts and feelings > **psychoanalyst** *noun: I saw a psychoanalyst for several years*

psychology psychologies *noun*

1 study of human and animal behaviour **2** *informal* person's mental make-up > **psychologist** *noun: She trained as a psychologist*

psychopath *noun* person afflicted with a personality disorder causing him or her to commit antisocial or violent acts > **psychopathic** *adjective: a psychopathic killer*

psychosis psychoses *noun* severe mental disorder in which the sufferer's contact with reality becomes distorted > **psychotic** *adjective: psychotic disorders*

pterodactyl *noun* extinct flying reptile with batlike wings

PTO *abbreviation* please turn over

pub *noun* building with a bar licensed to sell alcoholic drinks

puberty *noun* beginning of sexual maturity

pubic *adjective* of the lower abdomen: *pubic hair*

public *adjective* **1** of or concerning the people as a whole **2** for use by everyone **3** well-known **4** performed or made openly ▷ *noun* **5** the community, people in general > **publicly** *adverb*

publican *noun Brit, Aust, NZ* person who owns or runs a pub

publication *noun* **1** publishing of a printed work **2** printed work: *medical publications*

publicity *noun* **1** process or information used to arouse public attention **2** public interest so aroused

publicize *verb* to bring to public attention

public school *noun* private fee-paying school in Britain

public servant *noun Aust, NZ*

someone who works in the public service

public service noun Aust, NZ government departments responsible for the administration of the country

publish verb **1** to produce and issue (printed matter) for sale **2** to announce formally or in public > **publishing** noun

publisher noun company or person that publishes books, periodicals, music, etc

pudding noun **1** dessert, especially a cooked one served hot **2** savoury dish with pastry or batter: steak-and-kidney pudding **3** sausage-like mass of meat: black pudding

puddle noun small pool of water, especially of rain

puerile adjective silly and childish

puff noun **1** (sound of) a short blast of breath, wind, etc **2** act of inhaling cigarette smoke **3 out of puff** out of breath ▷ verb **4** to blow or breathe in short quick draughts **5** to take draws at (a cigarette) **6 puff up** or **out** to swell > **puffy** adjective: dark-ringed puffy eyes

puffin noun black-and-white sea bird with a brightly-coloured beak

pug noun small snub-nosed dog

puja noun variety of practices which make up Hindu worship

puke informal verb **1** to vomit ▷ noun **2** vomited matter

pull verb **1** to exert force on (an object) to move it towards the source of the force **2** to strain or stretch **3** to remove or extract **4** to attract ▷ noun **5** act of pulling **6** force used in pulling

7 informal power, influence > **pull down** verb to destroy or demolish > **pull out** verb **1** (of a vehicle or driver) to move away from the side of the road or move out to overtake **2** (of a train) to depart **3** to withdraw **4** to remove by pulling > **pull through** verb to recover from a serious illness

pulley noun wheel with a grooved rim in which a belt, chain or piece of rope runs in order to lift weights by a downward pull

pullover noun sweater that is pulled on over the head

pulmonary adjective formal of the lungs

pulp noun **1** soft wet substance made from crushed or beaten matter **2** flesh of a fruit

pulpit noun raised platform for a preacher

pulse noun **1** regular beating of blood through the arteries at each heartbeat **2** any regular beat or vibration **3** edible seed of a pod-bearing plant such as a bean or pea ▷ verb **4** to beat, throb or vibrate

puma noun large American wild cat with a greyish-brown coat

pumice noun light porous stone used for scouring

pummel pummels pummelling pummelled verb to strike repeatedly with or as if with the fists

pump noun **1** machine used to force a liquid or gas to move in a particular direction **2** light flat-soled shoe ▷ verb **3** to raise or drive (air, liquid, etc) with a pump **4 pump into** to supply in large amounts: pumping money into the economy

pumpkin *noun* large round fruit with an orange rind, soft flesh and many seeds

pun *noun* use of words to exploit double meanings for humorous effect

punch *verb* 1 to strike at with a clenched fist ▷ *noun* 2 blow with a clenched fist 3 tool or machine for shaping, piercing or engraving 4 drink made from a mixture of wine, spirits, fruit, sugar and spices

punctual *adjective* arriving or taking place at the correct time >**punctuality** *noun*: train punctuality >**punctually** *adverb*

punctuate *verb* 1 to put punctuation marks into (a written text) 2 to interrupt at frequent intervals

punctuation (use of) marks such as commas, colons, etc in writing, to assist in making the sense clear

puncture *noun* 1 small hole made by a sharp object, especially in a tyre ▷ *verb* 2 to pierce a hole in (something) with a sharp object

pungent *adjective* having a strong sharp bitter flavour >**pungency** *noun*: the spices that give Jamaican food its pungency

punish *verb* to cause (someone) to suffer or undergo a penalty for some wrongdoing

punishment *noun* something unpleasant done to someone because they have done something wrong

punitive *adjective* relating to punishment

Punjabi *adjective* 1 belonging or

relating to the Punjab, a state in north-western India ▷ *noun* 2 someone from the Punjab 3 language spoken in the Punjab

punk *noun* 1 aggressive style of rock music 2 follower of this music

punt *noun* open flat-bottomed boat propelled by a pole

puny *punier puniest adjective* small and feeble

pup *noun* young of certain animals, such as dogs and seals

pupil *noun* 1 person who is taught by a teacher 2 round dark opening in the centre of the eye

puppet *noun* small doll or figure moved by strings or by the operator's hand

puppy puppies *noun* young dog

purchase *verb* 1 to obtain (goods) by payment 2 thing that is bought 3 act of buying >**purchaser** *noun*: We need to find a purchaser

pure *adjective* 1 unmixed or untainted 2 innocent 3 complete: pure delight 4 concerned with theory only: pure mathematics

purée *noun* food which has been mashed or blended to a thick, smooth consistency

purely *adverb* involving only one feature and not including anything else

Purgatory *noun* (in Roman Catholic belief) place where spirits of the dead are sent to suffer for their sins before going to Heaven

purge *verb* 1 to rid (something) of

undesirable qualities **2** to rid (an organization, etc) of undesirable people

purify **purifies purifying purified** verb to free (something) of harmful or inferior matter > **purification** noun: *a water purification plant*

purist noun person concerned with strict obedience to the traditions of a subject

puritan noun someone who believes in strict moral principles and avoids physical pleasures > **puritanical** adjective: *puritanical attitudes towards sex*

purple noun **1** colour between red and blue ▷ adjective **2** of this colour

purport verb to claim (to be or do something)

purpose noun **1** reason for which something is done or exists **2** determination **3** practical advantage or use: *use the time to good purpose*

purr verb **1** (of cats) to make a low vibrant sound, usually when pleased ▷ noun **2** this sound

purse noun **1** small bag for money **2** US, NZ handbag ▷ verb **3** to draw (one's lips) together into a small round shape

purser noun ship's officer who keeps the accounts

pursue **pursues pursuing pursued** verb **1** to follow (a person, vehicle or animal) in order to capture or overtake **2** to follow (a goal) **3** to engage in > **pursuer** noun: *They had to shake off their pursuers*

purveyor noun formal person who sells or provides goods or services

pus noun yellowish matter produced by infected tissue

push verb **1** to move or try to move by steady force **2** to drive or spur (oneself or another person) to do something **3** informal to sell (drugs) illegally ▷ noun **4** act of pushing **5** special effort **6 the push** informal dismissal from a job or relationship > **push off** verb informal to go away

pushchair noun small folding chair on wheels in which a baby or toddler can be wheeled around

pusher noun informal person who sells illegal drugs

pushing preposition almost or nearly (a certain age, speed, etc): *pushing sixty*

pushover noun informal **1** something that is easy **2** someone who is easily persuaded or defeated

pushy **pushier pushiest** adjective informal too assertive or ambitious

pussy **pussies** noun informal cat

put **puts putting put** verb **1** to cause to be (in a position or place) **2** to cause to be (in a state or condition) **3** to lay (blame, emphasis, etc) on a person or thing **4** to express **5** to estimate or judge ▷ noun **6** throw in putting the shot > **put down** verb **1** informal to belittle or humiliate **2** to put (a sick animal) to death > **put off** verb **1** to postpone **2** to cause to lose interest in > **put out** verb **1** to extinguish (a fire, light, etc) **2** to annoy or anger **3** to dislocate: *He put his back out gardening* > **put up** verb **1** to build or erect **2** to accommodate **3** put

up with *informal* to endure or tolerate

putt *Golf noun* **1** stroke on the putting green to roll the ball into or near the hole ▷ *verb* **2** to strike (the ball) in this way

putting *noun* golf played with a putter on a course of very short holes

putty *noun* adhesive used to fix glass into frames and fill cracks in woodwork

puzzle *verb* **1** to perplex and confuse or be perplexed or confused ▷ *noun* **2** problem that cannot be easily solved **3** toy, game or question that requires skill or ingenuity to solve > **puzzled** *adjective: There was a puzzled expression on her face* > **puzzlement** *noun: He frowned in puzzlement* > **puzzling** *adjective: a number of puzzling questions*

PVC *abbreviation* polyvinyl chloride: plastic material used in clothes etc

Pygmy Pygmies *noun* **1** member of one of the very short peoples of Equatorial Africa ▷ *adjective* **2** pygmy very small

pyjamas *plural noun* loose-fitting trousers and top worn in bed

pylon *noun* steel tower-like structure supporting electrical cables

pyramid *noun* **1** solid figure with a flat base and triangular sides sloping upwards to a point **2** building of this shape, especially an ancient Egyptian one

pyre *noun* pile of wood for burning a corpse on

python *noun* large nonpoisonous snake that crushes its prey

q

quack *verb* **1** (of a duck) to make a loud harsh sound ▷ *noun* **2** sound made by a duck **3** unqualified person who claims medical knowledge

quad *noun* **1** see **quadrangle** **2** short for **quadruplet**

quad bike or **quad** *noun* vehicle like a small motorcycle with four large wheels, designed for agricultural and sporting uses

quadrangle *noun* (also **quad**) rectangular courtyard with buildings on all four sides > **quadrangular** *adjective*

quadri- *prefix* four: *quadrilateral*

quadriceps *noun* large muscle in four parts at the front of your thigh

quadrilateral *Maths adjective* **1** having four sides ▷ *noun* **2** polygon with four sides

quadruped *noun* any animal with four legs

quadruple *verb* **1** (of an amount or number) to become four times as large as previously **2** to make (an amount or number) four times as large as previously; multiply by four ▷ *adjective* **3** four times as much or as many

quadruplet *noun* one of four children born at the same time to the same mother

quagmire *noun* soft wet area of land

quail *noun* **1** small game bird of the partridge family ▷ *verb* **2** to feel or look afraid

quaint adjective attractively unusual, especially in an old-fashioned style ▷ **quaintly** adverb

quake verb to shake and tremble with or as if with fear

Quaker noun member of a Christian sect, the Society of Friends

qualification noun 1 official record of achievement in a course or examination 2 quality or skill needed for a particular activity 3 something you add to a statement to make it less strong

qualify qualifies qualifying qualified verb 1 to pass the necessary examinations or tests to do a particular job or to take part in a sporting event 2 to make (someone) suitable for something 3 to moderate or restrict (a statement) by adding a detail or explanation to make it less strong ▷ **qualified** adjective

quality qualities noun 1 how good something is 2 characteristic 3 basic character or nature of something

qualm noun 1 pang of conscience 2 sudden sensation of misgiving

quandary quandaries noun difficult situation or dilemma

quango quangos noun body responsible for a particular area of public administration, which is financed by the government but is outside direct government control. Quango is short for quasi-autonomous non-governmental organization

quantity quantities noun 1 amount you can measure or count 2 amount of something

that there is: emphasis on quantity rather than quality

quarantine noun period or state of isolation to prevent the spread of disease between people or animals

quarrel quarrels quarrelling quarrelled noun 1 angry argument ▷ verb 2 to have an angry argument ▷ **quarrelsome** adjective prone to get into arguments

quarry quarries quarrying quarried noun 1 place where stone is dug from the surface of the earth 2 person or animal that is being hunted ▷ verb 3 to extract (stone) from a quarry

quart noun unit of liquid measure equal to two pints (1.136 litres)

quarter noun 1 one of four equal parts of something 2 US 25-cent piece 3 region or district of a town or city 4 fourth part of a year 5 informal unit of weight equal to 4 ounces 6 **quarters** lodgings ▷ verb 7 to divide (something) into four equal parts

quarterly quarterlies adjective 1 occurring, due or issued every three months ▷ noun 2 magazine or journal issued every three months ▷ adverb 3 once every three months

quartet noun 1 group of four performers 2 music for such a group

quartz noun kind of hard, shiny crystal used in making very accurate watches and clocks

quash verb to throw out (a decision or judgment)

quasi- prefix almost but not really: quasi-religious; a quasi-scholar

a
b
c
d
e
f
g
h
i
j
k
l
m
n
o
p
q
r
s
t
u
v
w
x
y
z

quaver verb 1 (of a voice) to quiver or tremble ▷ noun 2 Music note (♪) half the length of a crotchet and an eighth the length of a semibreve. In the United States and Canada, a quaver is known as an eighth note

quay noun place where boats are tied up and loaded or unloaded

queasy queasier queasiest adjective feeling slightly sick > **queasiness** noun

queen noun 1 female monarch or a woman married to a king 2 the only female bee, wasp or ant in a colony that can lay eggs 3 the most powerful piece in chess

queen mother noun the widow of a king and the mother of the reigning monarch

queer adjective very strange

quell verb 1 to put an end to or suppress (a rebellion or riot) 2 to overcome (a feeling)

quench verb to satisfy (one's thirst)

query queries querying queried noun 1 question 2 question mark ▷ verb 3 to express uncertainty, doubt or an objection concerning (something); question

quest noun long and difficult search ▷ verb

question noun 1 a sentence which asks for information 2 problem that needs to be discussed; matter 3 difficulty or uncertainty 4 **in question** under discussion 5 **out of the question** impossible ▷ verb 6 to put a question or questions to (a person) 7 to express uncertainty about; query

questionable adjective of disputable value or authority > **questionably** adverb

question mark noun punctuation mark (?) written at the end of questions

questionnaire noun set of questions on a form, used to collect information from people

queue queues queuing or queueing queued noun 1 line of people or vehicles waiting for something ▷ verb 2 (often followed by up) to form or remain in a line while waiting

quibble verb 1 to make trivial objections ▷ noun 2 trivial objection

quiche noun savoury tart with an egg custard filling to which vegetables etc are added

quick adjective 1 speedy, fast 2 lasting or taking a short time 3 happening without any delay 4 intelligent and able to understand things easily ▷ noun 5 area of sensitive flesh under a nail ▷ adverb 6 informal in a rapid manner > **quickly** adverb

quicksand noun area of deep wet sand that you sink into if you walk on it

quid noun Brit informal pound (sterling)

quiet adjective 1 making little or no noise 2 calm or peaceful 3 involving very little fuss or publicity ▷ noun 4 quietness > **quietly** adverb > **quietness** noun

● Do not confuse the spellings of **quiet** and the adverb **quite**.

quieten verb (often followed by down) to become or make (someone) quiet

quill noun 1 pen made from the feather of a bird's wing or tail 2 stiff hollow spine of a hedgehog or porcupine

quilt noun padded covering for a bed

quilted adjective consisting of two layers of fabric with a layer of soft material between them

quin noun short for **quintuplet**

quince noun acid-tasting fruit used for making jam and marmalade

quintessence noun formal most perfect representation of a quality or state >**quintessential** adjective: It was the quintessential Hollywood party

quintet noun 1 group of five performers 2 music for such a group

quintuplet noun one of five children born at the same time to the same mother

quip quips quipping quipped noun 1 witty remark ▷ verb 2 to make a witty remark

quirk noun 1 odd habit or characteristic 2 unexpected event or development: a quirk of fate >**quirky** adjective

quit quits quitting quit verb 1 to stop (doing something) 2 to give up (a job) 3 to depart from (a place)

quite adverb 1 fairly but not very: She's quite pretty 2 absolutely or completely: You're quite right 3 emphasizing how large or impressive something is: It was quite a party ▷ interjection 4 expression of agreement

● Do not confuse the spellings
● of quite and the adjective
● quiet

quiver verb 1 to shake with a tremulous movement ▷ noun

2 shaking or trembling 3 case for arrows

quiz quizzes quizzing quizzed noun 1 game in which the competitors are asked questions to test their knowledge ▷ verb 2 to question (someone) closely about something

quizzical adjective amused and questioning: a quizzical look >**quizzically** adverb

quota noun number or quantity of something which is officially allowed

quotation noun 1 extract from a book or speech which is quoted 2 statement of how much a piece of work will cost

quotation marks plural noun raised commas used in writing to mark the beginning or end of a quotation or passage of speech

quote verb 1 to repeat (words) exactly from (an earlier work, speech or conversation) 2 to state (a price) for goods or a job of work ▷ noun 3 quotation 4 quotes informal the same as **quotation marks**

Qur'an another spelling of **Koran**

r

RAAF abbreviation Royal Australian Air Force

rabbi rabbis noun Jewish spiritual leader

rabbit noun small burrowing

a
b
c
d
e
f
g
h
i
j
k
l
m
n
o
p
q
r
s
t
u
v
w
x
y
z

mammal with long ears

rabble noun disorderly crowd of noisy people

rabid adjective **1** fanatical **2** having rabies

rabies noun usually fatal viral disease transmitted by dogs and certain other animals

raccoon noun small N American mammal with a long striped tail

race noun **1** contest of speed **2** group of people of common ancestry with distinguishing physical features, such as skin colour **3 the races** series of contests of speed between horses or greyhounds over a fixed course ▷ verb **4** to take part in a contest of speed with someone **5** to run swiftly > **racer** noun: a champion powerboat racer

racecourse noun grass track, sometimes with jumps, along which horses race

racehorse noun horse trained to run in races

racial adjective relating to the different races that people belong to > **racially** adverb

racism or **racialism** noun hostile attitude or behaviour to members of other races, based on a belief in the innate superiority of one's own race > **racist** or **racialist** adjective, noun: a racist attack; He's a racist

rack noun **1** framework for holding particular articles, such as coats or luggage **2 go to rack and ruin** to be destroyed ▷ verb **3** to cause great suffering to **4 rack your brains** informal to try very hard to remember

racket noun **1** noisy disturbance

2 occupation by which money is made illegally **3** another spelling of **racquet**

racquet or **racket** noun bat with strings across it used in tennis and similar games

radar noun device for tracking distant objects by bouncing high-frequency radio pulses off them

radiant adjective **1** looking happy **2** shining **3** emitting radiation > **radiance** noun

radiate verb **1** to spread out from a centre **2** to show (an emotion or quality) to a great degree

radiation noun **1** transmission of energy from one body to another **2** particles or waves emitted in nuclear decay **3** process of radiating

radiator noun **1** Brit arrangement of pipes containing hot water or steam to heat a room **2** tubes containing water as a cooling apparatus for a car engine **3** Aust, NZ electric fire

radical adjective **1** fundamental **2** thorough **3** advocating fundamental change ▷ noun **4** person advocating fundamental (political) change > **radicalism** noun: a long tradition of radicalism > **radically** adverb

radii noun a plural of **radius**

radio radios radioing radioed noun **1** system of sending sound over a distance by transmitting electrical signals **2** piece of equipment for listening to radio programmes **3** communications device for sending and receiving messages using radio waves **4** broadcasting of programmes to the public by radio ▷ verb **5** to transmit (a message) by radio

radioactive adjective emitting radiation as a result of nuclear decay ▷ **radioactivity** noun: high levels of radioactivity

radiotherapy noun treatment of disease, especially cancer, by radiation ▷ **radiotherapist** noun

radish noun small hot-flavoured root vegetable eaten raw in salads

radium noun Chemistry radioactive metallic element

radius radii or **radiuses** noun (length of) a straight line from the centre to the circumference of a circle

RAF abbreviation (in Britain) Royal Air Force

raffia noun prepared palm fibre for weaving mats etc

raffle noun 1 lottery with goods as prizes ▷ verb 2 to offer as a prize in a raffle

raft noun floating platform of logs, planks, etc

rafter noun one of the main beams of a roof

rag noun 1 fragment of cloth 2 informal newspaper 3 **rags** tattered clothing

rage noun 1 violent anger or passion ▷ verb 2 to feel or show intense anger 3 to proceed violently and without restraint

ragged adjective 1 (of clothes) old and torn 2 untidy

raid noun 1 sudden surprise attack or search ▷ verb 2 to make a raid on 3 to sneak into (a place) in order to steal ▷ **raider** noun

rail noun 1 horizontal bar, especially as part of a fence or track 2 railway considered as a means of transport ▷ verb 3 **rail at** or **against** to complain bitterly

or loudly about

railing noun fence made of rails supported by posts

railway noun 1 track of iron rails on which trains run 2 company operating a railway

rain noun 1 water falling in drops from the clouds ▷ verb 2 to fall or pour down as rain 3 to fall rapidly and in large quantities

rainbird noun S African bird whose call is believed to be a sign that it will rain

rainbow noun arch of colours in the sky

raincoat noun water-resistant overcoat

rainfall noun amount of rain

rainforest noun dense forest in tropical and temperate areas

rainwater noun rain that has been stored

raise verb 1 to lift up 2 to set upright 3 to increase in amount or intensity 4 to collect or levy 5 to bring up (a family) 6 to put forward for consideration

raisin noun dried grape

rake noun 1 tool with a long handle and a crosspiece with teeth, used for smoothing earth or gathering leaves, hay, etc ▷ verb 2 to gather or smooth with a rake 3 to search (through) ▷ **rake up** verb to revive memories of (a forgotten unpleasant event)

rally rallies rallying rallied noun 1 large gathering of people for a meeting 2 marked recovery of strength 3 Tennis etc lively exchange of strokes 4 car-driving competition on public roads ▷ verb 5 to bring or come together after dispersal or for a common cause **6** to regain health or strength

ram *rams ramming rammed* noun **1** adult male sheep ▷ *verb* **2** to strike against with force **3** to force or drive

RAM *abbreviation Computers* random access memory: storage space which can be filled with data but which loses its contents when the machine is switched off

Ramadan *noun* **1** 9th Muslim month **2** strict fasting from dawn to dusk observed during this time

ramble *verb* **1** to walk without a definite route **2** to talk in a confused manner ▷ *noun* **3** long walk in the countryside

ramifications *plural noun* consequences resulting from an action

ramp *noun* slope joining two level surfaces

rampage *verb* **1** to rush about violently **2 go on the rampage** to behave violently or destructively

rampant *adjective* growing or spreading uncontrollably

rampart *noun* mound or wall for defence

ramshackle *adjective* tumbledown, rickety or makeshift

ranch *noun* large cattle farm in the American West

rancid *adjective* (of butter, bacon, etc) stale and having an offensive smell

rancour *noun* deep bitter hate ▷ **rancorous** *adjective: a series of rancorous disputes*

rand *noun* monetary unit of S Africa

random *adjective* **1** made or done by chance or without plan **2 at random** haphazard(ly) ▷ **randomly** *adverb*

range *noun* **1** limits of effectiveness or variation **2** distance that a missile or plane can travel **3** distance of a mark shot at **4** whole set of related things **5** chain of mountains **6** place for shooting practice or rocket testing ▷ *verb* **7** to vary between one point and another **8** to cover or extend over **9** to roam (over)

ranger *noun* official in charge of a nature reserve etc

rank *noun* **1** relative place or position **2** status **3** social class **4** row or line **5 rank and file** ordinary people or members **6 the ranks** common soldiers ▷ *verb* **7** to have a specific rank or position **8** to arrange in rows or lines ▷ *adjective* **9** complete or absolute: *rank favouritism* **10** smelling offensively strong

ransack *verb* **1** to search through every part of (a place or thing) **2** to pillage or plunder

ransom *noun* money demanded in return for the release of someone who has been kidnapped

rant *verb* to talk in a loud and excited way

rap *raps rapping rapped verb* **1** to hit with a sharp quick blow **2** to utter (a command) abruptly **3** to perform a rhythmic monologue with musical backing ▷ *noun* **4** quick sharp blow **5** rhythmic monologue performed to music ▷ **rapper** *noun: rappers such as Jay-Z and 50 Cent*

rape *verb* **1** to force (someone)

to submit to sexual intercourse ▷ *noun* 2 act of raping 3 plant with oil-yielding seeds, also used as fodder > **rapist** *noun: a convicted rapist*

rapid *adjective* 1 quick, swift ▷ *noun* 2 **rapids** part of a river with a fast turbulent current > **rapidity** *noun: Water rushed through with great rapidity* > **rapidly** *adverb*

rapier *noun* fine-bladed sword

rapport *noun* harmony or agreement

rapt *adjective* engrossed or spellbound

rapture *noun* feeling of extreme delight > **rapturous** *adjective: a rapturous welcome* > **rapturously** *adverb*

rare *adjective* 1 uncommon 2 infrequent 3 of uncommonly high quality 4 (of meat) lightly cooked > **rarely** *adverb* seldom

rarefied *adjective* 1 highly specialized, exalted 2 (of air) thin

raring *adjective* **raring to** enthusiastic, willing or ready to

rarity rarities *noun* 1 something that is valuable because it is unusual 2 state of being rare

rascal *noun* 1 rogue 2 naughty (young) person

rash *adjective* 1 hasty, reckless or incautious ▷ *noun* 2 eruption of spots or patches on the skin 3 outbreak of (unpleasant) occurrences > **rashly** *adverb*

rasher *noun* thin slice of bacon

rasp *noun* 1 harsh grating noise 2 coarse file ▷ *verb* 3 to make a harsh grating noise

raspberry raspberries *noun* red juicy edible berry

rat *noun* 1 small rodent 2 *informal* contemptible person, especially a deserter or informer

rate *noun* 1 degree of speed or progress 2 proportion between two things 3 charge 4 **at any rate** in any case ▷ *verb* 5 to consider or value 6 to estimate the value of

rather *adverb* 1 to some extent 2 more truly or appropriately 3 more willingly

ratify ratifies ratifying ratified *verb* to give formal approval to > **ratification** *noun: the ratification of the treaty*

rating *noun* 1 valuation or assessment 2 classification 3 **ratings** size of the audience for a TV programme

ratio ratios *noun* relationship between two numbers or amounts expressed as a proportion

ration *noun* 1 fixed allowance of food etc 2 **rations** fixed daily allowance of food, such as that given to a soldier ▷ *verb* 3 to restrict the distribution of (something)

rational *adjective* 1 reasonable, sensible 2 capable of reasoning > **rationality** *noun: We live in an era of rationality* > **rationally** *adverb*

rationale *noun* reason for an action or decision

rattle *verb* 1 to give out a succession of short sharp sounds 2 to shake briskly causing sharp sounds 3 *informal* to confuse or fluster ▷ *noun* 4 short sharp sound 5 baby's toy that rattles when shaken

rattlesnake *noun* poisonous

snake with loose horny segments on the tail that make a rattling sound

raucous adjective hoarse or harsh

ravage formal verb **1** to cause extensive damage to ▷ noun **2** ravages damaging effects

rave verb **1** to talk in a wild or incoherent manner **2** informal to write or speak (about) with great enthusiasm ▷ noun **3** informal large-scale party with electronic dance music **4** rave review informal enthusiastic praise

raven noun **1** black bird like a large crow ▷ adjective **2** (of hair) shiny black

ravenous adjective very hungry

ravine noun narrow steep-sided valley worn by a stream

raving adjective **1** delirious **2** informal exceptional: a raving beauty ▷ noun **3** ravings frenzied or wildly extravagant talk

ravioli plural noun small squares of pasta with a savoury filling

ravishing adjective lovely or entrancing

raw adjective **1** uncooked **2** not manufactured or refined **3** inexperienced **4** chilly **5** raw deal unfair or dishonest treatment

raw material noun natural substance used to make something

ray noun **1** single line or narrow beam of light **2** small amount that makes an unpleasant situation seem slightly better: a ray of hope **3** large sea fish with a flat body and a whiplike tail

raze verb to destroy (buildings or a town) completely

razor noun sharp instrument for shaving

razor blade noun small, sharp, flat piece of metal fitted into a razor for shaving

re- prefix again: re-enter; retrial

reach verb **1** to arrive at or get to (a place) **2** to make a movement (towards), as if to grasp or touch **3** to succeed in touching **4** to make contact or communication with **5** to extend as far as (a point or place) ▷ noun **6** distance that you can reach **7** range of influence > **reachable** adjective: a reachable target

react verb **1** to act in response (to) **2** react against to act in an opposing or contrary manner

reaction noun **1** physical or emotional response to a stimulus **2** any action resisting another **3** opposition to change **4** chemical or nuclear change, combination or decomposition

reactionary reactionaries adjective **1** opposed to change, especially in politics ▷ noun **2** person opposed to change

reactor noun apparatus in which a nuclear reaction is maintained and controlled to produce nuclear energy

read reads reading read verb **1** to look at and understand or take in (written or printed matter) **2** to look at and say aloud **3** to interpret in a specified way **4** (of an instrument) to register **5** to undertake a course of study in (a subject) ▷ noun **6** matter suitable for reading: a good read

reader noun **1** person who reads **2** textbook **3** Chiefly Brit senior university lecturer

readership noun readers of a publication collectively

readily adverb **1** willingly and eagerly **2** easily done or quickly obtainable > **readiness** noun: readiness to help out

reading noun **1** activity of reading books **2** figure or measurement shown on a meter or gauge

readjust verb to adapt to a new situation

ready readier readiest adjective **1** prepared for use or action **2** willing, prompt **3** easily produced or obtained: ready cash

ready-made adjective for immediate use by any customer

reaffirm verb to state again

real adjective **1** existing in fact **2** actual **3** genuine

real estate noun property consisting of land and houses

realism noun recognition of the true nature of a situation > **realist** noun

realistic adjective seeing and accepting things as they really are > **realistically** adverb

reality realities noun state of things as they are

realize verb **1** to become aware or grasp the significance of **2** formal to achieve (a plan, hopes, etc) **3** to convert (property or goods) into money > **realization** noun: the realization that things cannot go on like this

really adverb **1** very **2** truly ▷ interjection **3** exclamation of dismay, doubt or surprise

realm noun formal **1** kingdom **2** sphere of interest

reap verb **1** to cut and gather (a harvest) **2** to receive as the result of a previous activity

reappear verb to appear again > **reappearance** noun

reappraisal noun formal the assessment again of the value or quality of a person or thing

rear noun **1** back part **2** part of an army, procession, etc behind the others ▷ verb **3** to care for and educate (children) **4** to breed (animals) **5** (of a horse) to rise on its hind feet

rear admiral noun high-ranking naval officer

rearrange verb to organize differently

reason noun **1** cause or motive **2** faculty of rational thought **3** sanity ▷ verb **4** to think logically in forming conclusions **5 reason with** to persuade by logical argument into doing something

reasonable adjective **1** sensible **2** not excessive **3** logical > **reasonably** adverb

reasoning noun process by which you draw conclusions from facts or evidence

reassess verb to reconsider the value or importance of > **reassessment** noun: a reassessment of the company's worth

reassure verb to relieve (someone) of anxieties > **reassurance** noun: She needed some reassurance

rebate noun discount or refund

rebel rebels rebelling rebelled verb **1** to revolt against the ruling power **2** to reject accepted conventions ▷ noun **3** person who rebels

rebellion noun organized open resistance to authority

rebellious adjective unwilling to

obey and likely to rebel against authority

rebuff *verb* **1** to reject or snub ▷ *noun* **2** blunt refusal, snub

rebuild rebuilds rebuilding rebuilt *verb* to build (a building or town again), after severe damage

rebuke *verb* **1** to scold sternly ▷ *noun* **2** stern scolding

recall *verb* **1** to recollect or remember **2** to order to return **3** to annul or cancel

recap recaps recapping recapped *informal verb* to recapitulate

recapture *verb* **1** to relive (a former experience or sensation) **2** to capture again

recede *verb* **1** to move to a more distant place **2** (of the hair) to stop growing at the front

receipt *noun* **1** written acknowledgment of money or goods received **2** receiving or being received **3** receipts money taken in over a particular period by a shop or business

receive *verb* **1** to get (something offered or sent to you) **2** to experience **3** to greet (guests) **4** to react to: *The news was well received*

receiver *noun* **1** part of a telephone that is held to the ear **2** equipment in a telephone, radio or television that converts electrical signals into sound **3** person appointed by a court to manage the property of a bankrupt

recent *adjective* **1** having happened lately **2** new ▷ **recently** *adverb*

reception *noun* **1** area for

receiving guests, clients, etc **2** formal party **3** manner of receiving **4** welcome **5** (in broadcasting) quality of signals received

receptionist *noun* person who receives guests, clients, etc

receptive *adjective* willing to accept new ideas, suggestions, etc

recess *noun* **1** niche or alcove **2** holiday between sessions of work

recession *noun* period of economic difficulty when little is being bought or sold

recharge *verb* to charge (a battery) with electricity again after it has been used

recipe *noun* **1** directions for cooking a dish **2** method for achieving something

recipient *noun* person who receives something

reciprocal *adjective* **1** mutual **2** given or done in return ▷ **reciprocally** *adverb*

reciprocate *verb* **1** to give or feel in return **2** (of a machine part) to move backwards and forwards

recital *noun* **1** musical performance by a soloist or soloists **2** act of reciting

recite *verb* to repeat (a poem etc) aloud to an audience

reckless *adjective* heedless of danger ▷ **recklessly** *adverb* ▷ **recklessness** *noun*: *a surge of recklessness*

reckon *verb* **1** to be of the opinion **2** to consider **3** to calculate **4** to expect **5** reckon with or without to take into account or fail to take into account

reckoning noun 1 counting or calculating 2 retribution for your actions

reclaim verb 1 to regain possession of 2 to convert (unsuitable or submerged land) into land suitable for farming or building on >**reclamation** noun: the reclamation of land from the marshes

recline verb to rest in a leaning position

recluse noun person who avoids other people >**reclusive** adjective: a reclusive billionaire

recognize verb 1 to identify as (a person or thing) already known 2 to accept or be aware of (a fact or problem) 3 to acknowledge formally the status or legality of (someone or something) 4 to show appreciation of (something) >**recognition** noun: Her work has received popular recognition >**recognizable** adjective: His features were easily recognizable >**recognizably** adverb

recommend verb 1 to advise or counsel 2 to praise or commend 3 to make acceptable >**recommendation** noun: the committee's recommendations

reconcile verb 1 to harmonize (conflicting beliefs etc) 2 to re-establish friendly relations with (a person or people) or between (people) 3 to accept or cause to accept (an unpleasant situation) >**reconciliation** noun: hopes for a reconciliation between the two countries

reconnaissance noun survey for military or engineering purposes

reconsider verb to think about again >**reconsideration** noun: reconsideration of the decision

reconstruct verb 1 to rebuild 2 to form a picture of (a past event, especially a crime) >**reconstruction** noun: post-war reconstruction

record noun 1 document or other thing that preserves information 2 disc with indentations which a record player transforms into sound 3 best recorded achievement 4 known facts about a person's past ▷ verb 5 to put in writing 6 to preserve (sound, TV programmes, etc) on plastic disc, magnetic tape, etc, for reproduction on a playback device 7 to show or register

recorder noun 1 person or machine that records, especially a video, cassette or tape recorder 2 type of flute, held vertically

recording noun 1 something that has been recorded 2 process of storing sounds or visual signals for later use

recount verb to tell in detail

recoup verb to regain or make good (a loss)

recourse noun formal 1 source of help 2 **have recourse to** to turn to a source of help or course of action

recover verb 1 (of a person) to regain health, spirits or composure 2 to regain a former condition 3 to find again or obtain the return of (something lost) 4 to get back (a loss or expense)

recovery recoveries noun 1 act of recovering from sickness, a shock or a setback 2 restoration to a former and better condition 3 regaining of something lost

recreate verb to make happen or exist again

recreation noun agreeable or refreshing occupation, relaxation or amusement ▷ **recreational** adjective: recreational activities

recrimination noun mutual blame

recruit verb 1 to enlist (new soldiers, members, etc) ▷ noun 2 newly enlisted soldier, member or supporter ▷ **recruitment** noun: the recruitment of civil servants

rectangle noun oblong four-sided figure with four right angles ▷ **rectangular** adjective: a rectangular box

rectify rectifies rectifying rectified verb to put right, correct

rector noun 1 clergyman in charge of a parish 2 head of certain academic institutions

rectory rectories noun rector's house

rectum rectums or **recta** noun final section of the large intestine ▷ **rectal** adjective: rectal cancer

recuperate verb to recover from illness ▷ **recuperation** noun: powers of recuperation

recur recurs recurring recurred verb to happen again

recurring adjective 1 happening or occurring many times 2 (of a digit) repeated over and over again after the decimal point in a decimal fraction

recycle verb to reprocess (used materials) for further use ▷ **recyclable** adjective: recyclable glass

red redder reddest; reds adjective 1 of a colour varying from crimson to orange and seen in blood, fire, etc 2 flushed in the face from anger, shame, etc ▷ noun 3 red colour 4 **in the red** informal in debt

redback noun small Australian spider with a poisonous bite

redcurrant noun small round edible red berry

redeem verb 1 to make up for 2 to reinstate (oneself) in someone's good opinion 3 Christianity to free from sin

redemption noun state of being redeemed

red-handed adjective informal (caught) in the act of doing something wrong or illegal

red-hot adjective 1 glowing red 2 extremely hot

redress formal verb 1 to make amends for ▷ noun 2 compensation or amends

red tape noun excessive adherence to official rules

reduce verb 1 to bring down or lower 2 to lessen or weaken

reduction noun 1 act of reducing 2 amount by which something is reduced

redundancy redundancies noun 1 state of being redundant 2 person or job made redundant

redundant adjective 1 (of a worker) no longer needed 2 superfluous

reed noun 1 tall grass that grows in swamps and shallow water 2 tall straight stem of this plant 3 Music vibrating cane or metal strip in certain wind instruments

reef noun 1 ridge of rock or coral near the surface of the sea 2 part of a sail which can be rolled up to reduce its area

reek verb **1** to smell strongly **2 reek of** to give a strong suggestion of ▷ noun **3** strong unpleasant smell

reel noun **1** cylindrical object on which film, tape, thread or wire is wound **2** winding apparatus, as of a fishing rod **3** lively Scottish dance ▷ verb **4** to move unsteadily or spin around **5** to be in a state of confusion or stress > **reel off** verb to recite or write fluently or quickly

re-elect verb to vote for (someone) to retain his or her position, for example as a Member of Parliament

refer refers referring referred verb **refer to 1** to allude (to) **2** to be relevant (to) **3** to send (to) for information **4** to submit (to) for a decision

referee noun **1** umpire in sports, especially soccer or boxing **2** person willing to testify to someone's character etc

reference noun **1** act of referring **2** citation or direction in a book **3** written testimonial regarding character or qualifications **4 with reference to** concerning

referendum referendums or referenda noun direct vote of the electorate on an important question

refine verb **1** to purify **2** to improve

refined adjective **1** cultured or polite **2** purified

refinement noun **1** improvement or elaboration **2** fineness of taste or manners

refinery refineries noun place where sugar, oil, etc is refined

reflect verb **1** (of a surface or object) to throw back light, heat or sound **2** (of a mirror) to form an image of (something) by reflection **3** to show **4** to consider carefully

reflection noun **1** act of reflecting **2** return of rays of heat, light, etc from a surface **3** image of an object given back by a mirror etc **4** conscious thought or meditation **5** Maths transformation of a shape in which right or left, or top and bottom, are reversed

reflex noun **1** involuntary response to a stimulus or situation ▷ adjective **2** (of a muscular action) involuntary **3** reflected **4** (of an angle) more than 180°

reflexive adjective Grammar denoting a verb whose subject is the same as its object, e.g. He's cut himself

reform noun **1** improvement ▷ verb **2** to improve (a law or institution) by correcting abuses **3** to give up or cause to give up a bad habit or way of life > **reformer** noun: reformers of the legal system

reformation noun **1** act or instance of something being reformed **2 Reformation** religious movement in 16th-century Europe that resulted in the establishment of the Protestant Churches

refract verb to change the course of (light etc) passing from one medium to another > **refraction** noun: the refraction of light on the waves

refrain verb **1 refrain from** to keep yourself from doing ▷ noun

2 frequently repeated part of a song

refresh verb **1** to revive or reinvigorate, as through food, drink or rest **2** to stimulate (the memory)

refreshing adjective **1** having a reviving effect **2** pleasantly different or new

refreshment noun something that refreshes, especially food or drink

refrigerator noun full name for **fridge**

refuel refuels refuelling refuelled verb to supply or be supplied with fresh fuel

refuge noun **1** (source of) shelter or protection **2** place, person or thing that offers protection or help

refugee noun person who seeks refuge, especially in a foreign country

refund verb **1** to give back (money) ▷ noun **2** return of money **3** amount returned

refurbish verb formal to renovate and brighten up >**refurbishment** noun: The office is in need of complete refurbishment

refusal noun denial of anything demanded or offered

refuse[1] verb **1** to be determined not to do something) **2** to decline to give or allow (something) to (someone)

refuse[2] noun rubbish or useless matter

refute verb to prove (a statement or theory) to be false

regain verb **1** to get back or recover **2** to reach again

regal adjective of or like a king or queen >**regally** adverb

regard verb **1** to look upon or think of in a specified way **2** to look closely at (something or someone) **3** to take notice of **4** as regards on the subject of ▷ noun **5** respect or esteem **6** attention **7** regards expression of goodwill

regardless adjective **1** regardless of taking no notice of ▷ adverb **2** in spite of everything

regatta noun meeting for yacht or boat races

regency regencies noun period when a country is ruled by a regent

regenerate verb **1** to (cause to) undergo spiritual, economic or physical renewal **2** to come or bring into existence once again >**regeneration** noun: economic regeneration ▷ adjective

regent noun ruler of a kingdom during the absence, childhood or illness of its monarch ▷ adjective **2** ruling as a regent: prince regent

reggae noun style of Jamaican popular music with a strong beat

regime noun **1** system of government **2** particular administration

regiment noun organized body of troops as a unit of the army >**regimental** adjective: a regimental reunion

regimented adjective very strictly controlled >**regimentation** noun: bureaucratic regimentation

region noun **1** administrative division of a country **2** area considered as a unit but with no definite boundaries **3** part of the body **4** in the region

of approximately > **regional**
adjective: regional government
> **regionally** *adverb*

register *noun* **1** (book containing)
an official list or record of things
2 range of a voice or instrument
3 style of speaking or writing,
such as slang, used in particular
circumstances > *verb* **4** to
enter (an event, person's name,
ownership, etc) in a register
5 to show on a scale or other
measuring instrument **6** to show
on a person's face > **registration**
noun: compulsory registration of dogs

registrar *noun* **1** keeper of official
records **2** senior hospital doctor,
junior to a consultant **3** senior
administrative official at a
university

registration number *noun*
numbers and letters displayed on
a vehicle to identify it

registry registries *noun* place
where official records are kept

registry office *noun* place where
births, marriages and deaths
are recorded, and where people
can marry without a religious
ceremony

**regret regrets regretting
regretted** *verb* **1** to feel sorry
about **2** to express apology
or distress > *noun* **3** feeling of
repentance, guilt or sorrow
> **regretful** *adjective: a regretful
smile* > **regretfully** *adverb*

regrettable *adjective* unfortunate
and undesirable > **regrettably**
adverb

regular *adjective* **1** normal,
customary or usual
2 symmetrical or even **3** done
or occurring according to a
rule **4** periodical **5** employed

continuously in the armed forces
> *noun* **6** regular soldier **7** *informal*
frequent customer > **regularity**
noun: monotonous regularity
> **regularly** *adverb*

regulate *verb* **1** to control by
means of rules **2** to adjust slightly

regulation *noun* **1** rule
2 regulating

regurgitate *verb* **1** to vomit **2** (of
some birds and animals) to bring
back (partly digested) food into
the mouth **3** to reproduce (ideas,
facts, etc) without understanding
them

rehabilitate *verb* **1** to help (a
person) to readjust to society
after illness, imprisonment,
etc > **rehabilitation** *noun: the
rehabilitation of young offenders*

rehearsal *noun* practice of a
performance in preparation for
the actual event

rehearse *verb* **1** to practise (a play,
concert, etc) **2** to repeat aloud

reign *noun* **1** period of a sovereign's
rule > *verb* **2** to rule (a country)
3 to be supreme

rein *noun* **1 reins a** narrow straps
attached to a bit to guide a horse
b means of control **2 keep a
tight rein on** to control carefully

reincarnation *noun* **1** rebirth of a
soul in successive bodies **2** one of
a series of such transmigrations

reindeer reindeer or **reindeers**
noun deer of arctic regions with
large branched antlers

reinforce *verb* **1** to give added
emphasis to (an idea or feeling)
2 to make physically stronger
or harder

reinforcement *noun* **1** reinforcing
of something **2** reinforcements

additional soldiers sent to join an army in battle

reinstate verb 1 to restore to a former position 2 to cause to exist or be important again > **reinstatement** noun: parents campaigned for her reinstatement

reiterate verb formal to repeat again and again > **reiteration** noun: a reiteration of the same old ideas

reject verb 1 to refuse to accept or believe 2 to deny to (a person) the feelings hoped for 3 to discard as useless ▷ noun 4 person or thing rejected as not up to standard > **rejection** noun: feelings of rejection; be prepared for lots of rejections

rejoice verb to feel or express great happiness

rejoin verb to come together with (someone or something) again

rejuvenate verb to restore youth or vitality to > **rejuvenation** noun: the whole system needs rejuvenation

relapse verb 1 to fall back into bad habits, illness, etc ▷ noun 2 return of bad habits, illness, etc

relate verb 1 to establish a relation between 2 to have reference or relation to 3 to have an understanding (of people or ideas) 4 to tell (a story) or describe (an event)

relation noun 1 connection between things 2 relative 3 connection by blood or marriage 4 act of relating (a story) 5 **relations a** social or political dealings **b** family

relationship noun 1 dealings and feelings between people or countries 2 emotional or sexual affair 3 connection between two things

relative adjective 1 dependent on relation to something else, not absolute 2 having reference or relation (to) 3 Grammar referring to a word or clause earlier in the sentence ▷ noun 4 person connected by blood or marriage

relative pronoun noun pronoun that replaces a noun that links two parts of a sentence

relax verb 1 to make or become looser, less tense or less rigid 2 to ease up from effort or attention 3 to make (rules or discipline) less strict 4 to become more friendly > **relaxation** noun: rest and relaxation

relay noun 1 race between teams in which each runner races part of the distance ▷ verb 2 to pass on (a message) 3 to broadcast (a performance or event) as it happens

release verb 1 to free (a person or animal) from captivity or imprisonment 2 to free (something) from (one's grip) 3 to issue (a record, film, etc) for sale or public showing 4 to give out heat, energy, etc ▷ noun 5 setting free 6 statement to the press 7 act of issuing for sale or publication 8 newly issued film, record, etc

relegate verb 1 to put in a less important position 2 to demote (a sports team) to a lower league > **relegation** noun

relent verb 1 to change your mind about some decision 2 to become milder or less severe

relentless adjective 1 never stopping and never becoming

less intense **2** merciless
> **relentlessly** adverb

relevant adjective to do with the matter in hand > **relevance** noun: *a fact of little relevance*

reliable adjective able to be trusted, dependable > **reliability** noun: *her car's reliability* > **reliably** adverb

reliant adjective dependant > **reliance** noun: *reliance on public transport*

relic noun **1** something that has survived from the past **2** body or possession of a saint, regarded as holy **3** relics remains or traces

relief noun **1** gladness at the end or removal of pain, distress, etc **2** release from monotony or duty **3** money or food given to victims of disaster, poverty, etc

relief map noun map showing the shape and height of land by shading

relieve verb **1** to lessen (pain, distress, boredom, etc) **2** to bring assistance to (someone in need) **3** to free (someone) from an obligation **4** to take over the duties of (someone) **5** relieve **yourself** to urinate or defecate

religion noun system of belief in and worship of a supernatural power or god

religious adjective **1** of religion **2** pious or devout **3** scrupulous or conscientious

religiously adverb regularly as a duty: *he stuck religiously to the rules*

relinquish verb **1** to give up **2** to renounce (a claim or right)

relish verb **1** to savour or enjoy (an experience) to the full ▷ noun **2** liking or enjoyment **3** appetizing savoury food, such

as pickle

relive verb to remember (a past experience) very vividly, imagining it happening again

relocate verb to move to a new place to live or work > **relocation** noun: *relocation to London*

reluctant adjective unwilling or disinclined > **reluctance** noun: *he has shown reluctance to explain his position* > **reluctantly** adverb

rely relies relying relied verb **rely on** or **upon a** to be dependent on **b** to have trust in

remain verb **1** to continue to be **2** to stay behind or in the same place **3** to be left after use or the passage of time **4** to be left to be done, said, etc

remainder noun **1** part which is left **2** amount left over after subtraction or division

remand verb **1** to send (a prisoner or accused person) back into custody or put on bail before trial ▷ noun **2 on remand** in custody or on bail before trial

remark verb **1** to make a casual comment (on) **2** to say **3** to observe or notice ▷ noun **4** observation or comment

remarkable adjective **1** worthy of note or attention **2** striking or unusual > **remarkably** adverb

remarry remarries remarrying remarried verb to marry again

remedial adjective **1** intended to correct a specific disability, handicap, etc **2** designed to improve someone's ability in something

remedy remedies remedying remedied noun **1** means of curing pain or a disease **2** means of solving a problem ▷ verb **3** to put right or improve

remember verb **1** to become aware of (something forgotten) again **2** to keep (an idea, intention, etc) in your mind

remembrance noun **1** memory **2** honouring of the memory of a person or event

remind verb **1** to cause to remember **2** to put in mind (of)

reminder noun **1** something that recalls the past **2** note to remind a person of something not done

reminiscent adjective reminding or suggestive (of)

remission noun **1** reduction in the length of a prison term **2** easing of intensity, as of an illness

remit noun area of competence or authority

remittance noun formal money sent as payment

remnant noun **1** small piece, especially of fabric, left over **2** surviving trace

remorse formal noun feeling of sorrow and regret for something you did ▷ **remorseful** adjective: he was genuinely remorseful

remote adjective **1** far away, distant **2** aloof **3** slight or faint ▷ **remoteness** noun: the remoteness of the farmhouse

remote control noun control of an apparatus from a distance by an electrical device

remotely adverb used to emphasize a negative statement

removal noun removing, especially changing residence

remove verb **1** to take away **2** to take (clothing) off **3** to get rid of **4** to dismiss (someone) from

office > **removable** adjective: a tin with a removable base

renaissance noun **1** revival or rebirth **2** **Renaissance** revival of learning in the 14th–16th centuries

renal adjective of the kidneys

rename verb to give (something) a new name

render verb **1** to cause to become **2** to give or provide (aid, a service, etc) **3** to represent in painting, music or acting

rendezvous noun **1** appointment **2** meeting place

● The plural of rendezvous is rendezvous

rendition noun formal **1** performance **2** translation

renew verb **1** to begin again **2** to make valid again **3** to grow again **4** to restore to a former state ▷ **renewal** noun: the renewal of my TV licence

renewable adjective **1** able to be renewed **2** **renewables** sources of alternative energy, such as wind and wave power

renounce verb formal **1** to give up (a belief, habit, etc) voluntarily **2** to give up (a title or claim) formally ▷ **renunciation** noun: progress requires a renunciation of terrorism

renovate verb to restore to good condition ▷ **renovation** noun: property which will need extensive renovation

renowned adjective well-known for something good ▷ **renown** noun: a singer of some renown

rent verb to give or have use of (land, a building, a machine, etc) in return for regular payments

▷ *noun* **2** regular payment for use of land, a building, machine, etc

rental *noun* **1** concerned with the renting out of goods and services **2** sum payable as rent

reorganize *verb* to organize in a new and more efficient way
>**reorganization** *noun*: *the reorganization of the legal system*

rep *noun* short for **representative**: *a sales rep*

repair *verb* **1** to restore (something damaged or broken) to good condition **2** to make up for (a mistake or injury) **3** to go to (a place) ▷ *noun* **4** act of repairing **5** repaired part

repay repays repaying repaid *verb* **1** to pay back or refund **2** to make a return for (something): *repay hospitality* >**repayment** *noun*: *monthly repayments*

repeal *verb* **1** to cancel (a law) officially ▷ *noun* **2** act of repealing

repeat *verb* **1** to say, write or do again **2** to tell to another person (the secrets told to you by someone else) **3** to happen again ▷ *noun* **4** act or instance of repeating **5** programme broadcast again >**repeated** *adjective*: *repeated reminders* >**repeatedly** *adverb*

repel repels repelling repelled *verb* **1** to cause (someone) to feel disgusted **2** to force or drive back (someone or something) **3** to reject or spurn

repellent *adjective* **1** distasteful **2** resisting water etc ▷ *noun* **3** something that repels, especially a chemical to repel insects

repent *verb formal* to feel regret for (a deed or omission)
>**repentance** *noun*: *they showed no repentance during the trial*
>**repentant** *adjective*: *a repentant arms dealer*

repercussions *plural noun* indirect effects, often unpleasant

repertoire *noun* stock of plays, songs, etc that a player or company can give

repertory repertories *noun* repertoire

repetition *noun* **1** act of repeating **2** thing repeated

repetitive or **repetitious** *adjective* full of repetition

replace *verb* **1** to take the place of **2** to substitute a person or thing for (another) **3** to put (something) back in its rightful place

replacement *noun* **1** act or process of replacement **2** person or thing that replaces another

replay *noun* **1** (also **action replay**) immediate reshowing on TV of an incident in sport, especially in slow motion **2** second sports match, especially one following an earlier draw ▷ *verb* **3** to play (a match, recording, etc) again

replenish *verb formal* to make full or complete again by supplying what has been used up

replica *noun* exact copy

reply replies replying replied *verb* **1** to make answer (to) in words or writing or by an action **2** to say (something) in answer ▷ *noun* **3** answer or response

report *verb* **1** to give an account of **2** to make a report (on) **3** to make a formal complaint about **4** to present yourself (to) **5** to be

responsible (to) ▷ *noun* **6** account or statement **7** rumour **8** written statement of a child's progress at school

reported speech *noun* report of what someone said that gives the content of the speech without repeating the exact words

reporter *noun* person who gathers news for a newspaper, TV, etc

repossess *verb* (of a lender) to take back (property) from a customer who is behind with payments

represent *verb* **1** to act as a delegate or substitute for (a person, country, etc) **2** to stand as an equivalent of **3** to be a means of expressing **4** to display the characteristics of **5** to portray, as in art

representation *noun* **1** state of being represented by someone **2** anything that represents, such as a pictorial portrait **3 representations** formal requests or complaints made to an official body

representative *noun* **1** person chosen to stand for a group **2** (travelling) salesperson ▷ *adjective* **3** typical

repress *verb* **1** to keep (feelings) in check **2** to restrict the freedom of > **repression** *noun*: *political repression*

repressive *adjective* restricting freedom by the use of force

reprieve *verb* **1** to postpone the execution of (a condemned person) **2** to give temporary relief to ▷ *noun* **3** (document granting) postponement or cancellation of a punishment **4** temporary relief

reprimand *verb* **1** to blame

(someone) officially for a fault ▷ *noun* **2** official blame

reprisal *noun* retaliation

reproach *verb* **1** to express disapproval (of someone's actions) ▷ *noun* **2** blame **3 beyond reproach** beyond criticism > **reproachful** *adjective*: *a reproachful look* > **reproachfully** *adverb*

reproduce *verb* **1** to produce a copy of **2** to produce offspring **3** to re-create

reproduction *noun* **1** process of reproducing **2** facsimile, as of a painting or picture **3** quality of sound from an audio system

reproductive *adjective* relating to the reproduction of living things

reptile *noun* cold-blooded egg-laying vertebrate with horny scales or plates, such as a snake or tortoise > **reptilian** *adjective*: *reptilian creatures*

republic *noun* **1** form of government in which the people or their elected representatives possess the supreme power **2** country in which a president is the head of state > **republican** *noun*, *adjective*: *republican beliefs; a staunch republican* > **republicanism** *noun*: *the growth of republicanism in Australia*

repulse *verb* **1** to be disgusting to **2** to drive (an army) back **3** to reject with coldness or discourtesy

repulsion *noun* **1** distaste or aversion **2** *Physics* force separating two objects

repulsive *adjective* horrible and disgusting

reputable *adjective* of good

reputation, respectable

reputation noun estimation in which a person is held

reputed adjective supposed > **reputedly** adverb: he reputedly earns £30,000 per week

request verb 1 to ask for > noun 2 asking 3 thing asked for

Requiem noun 1 Mass for the dead 2 music for this

require verb 1 to want or need 2 to be a necessary condition

requirement noun 1 essential condition 2 specific need or want

requisite formal adjective 1 necessary, essential > noun 2 essential thing

rescue rescues rescuing rescued verb 1 to bring (someone or something) out of danger or trouble > noun 2 rescuing > **rescuer** noun: It took rescuers hours to reach the trapped men

research noun 1 systematic investigation to discover facts or collect information > verb 2 to carry out investigations into (a subject) > **researcher** noun: a government researcher

resemblance noun similarity

resemble verb to be or look like

resent verb to feel bitter about > **resentment** noun: resentment against his supervisor

resentful adjective bitter and angry > **resentfully** adverb

reservation noun 1 doubt 2 exception or limitation 3 seat, room, etc that has been reserved 4 area of land reserved for use by a particular group 5 Brit strip of ground separating the two carriageways of a dual carriageway or motorway

reserve verb 1 to set aside, keep for future use 2 to obtain by arranging beforehand, book 3 to keep (something) for yourself > noun 4 something, especially money or troops, kept for emergencies 5 area of land reserved for a particular purpose 6 Sport substitute 7 concealment of feelings or friendliness

reservoir noun natural or artificial lake storing water for community supplies

reshuffle noun reorganization

reside verb formal to live permanently (in a place)

residence noun formal home or house

resident noun 1 person who lives in a place > adjective 2 living in a place

residential adjective 1 (of part of a town) consisting mainly of houses 2 providing living accommodation

residue noun what is left, remainder > **residual** adjective: residual radiation

resign verb 1 to give up office, a job, etc 2 to reconcile (oneself) to

resignation noun 1 resigning 2 passive endurance of difficulties

resilient adjective 1 (of a person) recovering quickly from a shock etc 2 able to return to normal shape after stretching etc > **resilience** noun: Londoners' resilience during the Blitz

resin noun 1 sticky substance from plants, especially pines 2 similar synthetic substance

resist verb 1 to withstand or oppose 2 to refrain from despite temptation 3 to be proof against

>**resistible** *adjective*

resistance *noun* **1** act of resisting **2** capacity to withstand something **3** *Electricity* opposition offered by a circuit to the passage of a current through it

resistant *adjective* **1** opposed to something and wanting to prevent it **2** not harmed or affected by

resolute *adjective* firm in purpose >**resolutely** *adverb*

resolution *noun* **1** firmness of conduct or character **2** thing resolved upon **3** decision of a court or vote of an assembly **4** act of resolving

resolve *verb* **1** to decide with an effort of will **2** to form (a resolution) by a vote ▷ *noun* **3** absolute determination

resonance *noun* **1** echoing, especially with a deep sound **2** sound produced in one object by sound waves coming from another object

resonate *verb* to vibrate and produce a deep, strong sound

resort *verb* **1** to have recourse (to) for help etc ▷ *noun* **2** place for holidays **3** the use of something as a means or aid

resounding *adjective* **1** echoing **2** clear and emphatic

resource *noun* **1** thing resorted to for support **2** ingenuity **3** means of achieving something **4 resources a** sources of economic wealth **b** stock that can be drawn on, funds

resourceful *adjective* capable and full of initiative >**resourcefulness** *noun: a person of great experience and*

resourcefulness

respect *noun* **1** consideration **2** deference or esteem **3** point or aspect **4** reference or relation: *with respect to* **5 in respect of** or **with respect to** in reference or relation to ▷ *verb* **6** to treat with esteem **7** to show consideration for

respectable *adjective* **1** worthy of respect **2** fairly good >**respectability** *noun: she has lost all respectability* >**respectably** *adverb*

respectful *adjective* showing respect for someone >**respectfully** *adverb*

respective *adjective* relating separately to each of those in question >**respectively** *adverb*

respiration *noun* breathing

respiratory *adjective* of breathing

respire *verb* to breathe

respite *noun* formal **1** pause or interval of rest **2** delay

respond *verb* **1** to state or utter (something) in reply **2** to act in answer to any stimulus **3** to react favourably

respondent *noun* **1** person who answers a questionnaire or a request for information **2** *Law* defendant

response *noun* **1** answer **2** reaction to a stimulus

responsibility responsibilities *noun* **1** state of being responsible **2** person or thing for which you are responsible

responsible *adjective* **1** having control and authority **2** reporting or accountable (to) **3** sensible and dependable **4** involving responsibility >**responsibly**

adverb

responsive *adjective* readily reacting to some influence

rest *noun* **1** freedom from exertion etc **2** repose **3** pause, especially in music **4** object used for support **5** what is left **6** others ▷ *verb* **7** to take a rest **8** to give a rest (to) **9** to be supported **10** to place for support or steadying

restaurant *noun* commercial establishment serving meals

restaurateur *noun* person who owns or runs a restaurant

restful *adjective* relaxing or soothing

restless *adjective* finding it hard to remain still or relaxed because of boredom or impatience ▷ **restlessly** *adverb* ▷ **restlessness** *noun: restlessness in the audience*

restore *verb* **1** to return (a building, painting, etc) to its original condition **2** to cause to recover health or spirits **3** to return (something lost or stolen) to its owner **4** to reinforce or re-establish ▷ **restoration** *noun: the restoration of old houses*

restrain *verb* **1** to hold (someone) back from action **2** to control or restrict

restrained *adjective* not displaying emotion

restraint *noun* **1** control, , especially self-control **2** something that restrains

restrict *verb* to confine to certain limits ▷ **restrictive** *adjective*

restriction *noun* rule or situation that limits what you can do

result *noun* **1** outcome or consequence **2** score **3** number obtained from a calculation **4** exam mark or grade ▷ *verb* **5 result from** to be the outcome or consequence (of) **6 result in** to end (in) ▷ **resultant** *adjective: civil war and the resultant famine*

resume *verb* **1** to begin again or go on with (something interrupted) **2** to occupy or take again ▷ **resumption** *noun: a resumption of negotiations*

resurgence *noun* rising again to vigour ▷ **resurgent** *adjective: resurgent extremism*

resurrect *verb* **1** to restore to life **2** to use once more (something discarded etc)

resurrection *noun* **1** rising again (especially from the dead) **2** revival **3 the Resurrection** *Christianity* the coming back to life of Jesus Christ three days after he had been killed

resuscitate *verb* to restore to consciousness ▷ **resuscitation** *noun: mouth-to-mouth resuscitation*

retail *noun* **1** selling of goods individually or in small amounts to the public ▷ *adverb* **2** by retail ▷ *verb* **3** to sell or be sold retail

retain *verb* to keep in your possession

retaliate *verb* to repay an injury or wrong in kind ▷ **retaliation** *noun: retaliation for the recent bombings*

retarded *adjective* underdeveloped, especially mentally

rethink **rethinks** **rethinking** **rethought** *verb* to consider again, especially with a view to changing your tactics

reticent *adjective* not willing to say or tell much ▷ **reticence** *noun: a lack of reticence*

retina retinas or retinae noun light-sensitive membrane at the back of the eye

retinue noun band of attendants

retire verb 1 to (cause to) give up office or work, especially through age 2 formal to go away or withdraw 3 to go to bed

retort verb 1 to reply quickly, wittily or angrily ▷ noun 2 quick, witty or angry reply

retract verb 1 to withdraw (a statement etc) 2 to draw in (a part or appendage) > **retraction** noun: a retraction of his comments

retreat verb 1 to move back from a position, withdraw ▷ noun 2 act of or military signal for retiring or withdrawal 3 place to which anyone retires, refuge

retribution noun punishment or vengeance for evil deeds

retrieve verb 1 to fetch back again 2 to restore to a better state 3 to recover (information) from a computer > **retrieval** noun: the retrieval of confiscated items

retriever noun large dog often used by hunters to bring back birds and animals which have been shot

retro- prefix back or backwards: retrospective

retrospect noun **in retrospect** when looking back on the past

retrospective adjective 1 looking back in time 2 applying from a date in the past > **retrospectively** adverb

return verb 1 to go or come back 2 to give, put or send back 3 to hit, throw or play (a ball) back 4 (of a jury) to deliver (a verdict) ▷ noun 5 returning 6 (thing)

being returned 7 profit 8 official report, as of taxable income 9 return ticket 10 **in return** in exchange

reunion noun meeting of people who have been apart

reunite verb to bring or come together after a separation

rev revs revving revved informal noun 1 revolution (of an engine) ▷ verb 2 **rev up** to increase the speed of revolution of (an engine)

revamp verb to renovate or restore

reveal verb 1 to disclose or divulge (a secret) 2 to expose to view (something concealed)

revel revels revelling revelled verb 1 to take pleasure (in something) 2 to make merry

revelation noun 1 surprising or interesting fact made known to people 2 person or experience that proves to be different from expectations

revenge noun 1 retaliation for wrong done ▷ verb 2 to avenge (oneself or another)

revenue noun income, especially of a state

revered adjective respected and admired

reverence noun awe mingled with respect and esteem

Reverend adjective title of respect for a clergyman

reverse verb 1 to turn upside down or the other way round 2 to change completely 3 to move (a vehicle) backwards ▷ noun 4 opposite 5 back side 6 change for the worse 7 reverse gear ▷ adjective 8 opposite or contrary > **reversal** noun: a complete reversal of previous policy

reversible *adjective* **1** capable of being reversed **2** (of clothing) made so that either side may be used as the outer side

revert *verb formal* **1** to return to a former state **2** to come back to a subject

review *noun* **1** critical assessment of a book, concert, etc **2** publication with critical articles **3** general survey ▷ *verb* **4** to hold or write a review of **5** to examine, reconsider or look back on

revise *verb* **1** to change or alter **2** to restudy (work) in preparation for an examination > **revision** *noun: another revision of the report*

revive *verb* to bring or come back to life, vigour, use, etc

revolt *noun* **1** uprising against authority ▷ *verb* **2** to rise up in rebellion **3** to cause to feel disgust

revolting *adjective* disgusting and horrible

revolution *noun* **1** overthrow of a government by the governed **2** great change **3** complete rotation

revolutionary *revolutionaries adjective* **1** advocating or engaged in revolution **2** radically new or different ▷ *noun* **3** person advocating or engaged in revolution

revolve *verb* **1** to move or cause to move around a centre **2** **revolve around** to be centred on

revolver *noun* small gun held in the hand

revulsion *noun* strong disgust

reward *noun* **1** something given in return for a service **2** sum of money offered for finding a criminal or missing property ▷ *verb* **3** to pay or give something to (someone) for a service, information, etc

rewarding *adjective* giving personal satisfaction, worthwhile

rewind *rewinds rewinding rewound* *verb* to run (a tape or film) back to an earlier point in order to replay it

rhapsody *rhapsodies noun* freely structured emotional piece of music

rhetoric *noun* **1** art of effective speaking or writing **2** artificial or exaggerated language

rhetorical *adjective* **1** (of a question) not requiring an answer **2** (of language) intended to be grand and impressive

rheumatism *noun* painful inflammation of joints or muscles

rhino *noun* short for **rhinoceros**

rhinoceros *rhinoceroses* or **rhinoceros** *noun* large thick-skinned animal with one or two horns on its nose

rhododendron *noun* evergreen flowering shrub

rhombus *rhombuses* or *rhombi noun* parallelogram with sides of equal length but no right angles, diamond-shaped figure

rhubarb *noun* garden plant of which the fleshy stalks are cooked as fruit

rhyme *noun* **1** sameness of the final sounds at the ends of lines of verse, or in words **2** word identical in sound to another in its final sounds **3** verse marked by rhyme ▷ *verb* **4** (of a rhyme) to form a rhyme with another word

a b c d e f g h i j k l m n o p q r s t u v w x y z

rhythm noun **1** any regular movement or beat **2** arrangement of the durations of and stress on the notes of a piece of music, usually grouped into a regular pattern **3** (in poetry) arrangement of words to form a regular pattern of stresses ▷ **rhythmic** or **rhythmical** adjective: rhythmic breathing ▷ **rhythmically** adverb

rib noun **1** one of the curved bones forming the framework of the upper part of the body **2** cut of meat including the rib(s) **3** curved supporting part, as in the hull of a boat ▷ **ribbed** adjective: ribbed sweaters

ribbon noun narrow band of fabric used for trimming, tying, etc

ribcage noun bony structure of ribs enclosing the lungs

rice noun **1** cereal plant grown on wet ground in warm countries **2** its seeds as food

rich adjective **1** owning a lot of money or property, wealthy **2** abounding **3** fertile **4** (of food) containing much fat or sugar **5** (of colours, smells and sounds) strong and pleasant ▷ **richness** noun: the richness of Tibet's mineral deposits

richly adverb **1** elaborately **2** fully

rick noun **1** stack of hay etc ▷ verb **2** to sprain or wrench (a joint)

rickets noun disease of children marked by softening of the bones, bow legs, etc, caused by vitamin D deficiency

rickety adjective shaky or unstable

rickshaw noun light two-wheeled man-drawn Asian vehicle

ricochet ricochets ricocheting or ricochetting ricocheted or ricochetted verb **1** (of a bullet) to rebound from a solid surface ▷ noun **2** such a rebound

rid rids ridding rid verb **1** formal to relieve (oneself) or make a place free of (something undesirable) **2** get rid of to free yourself of (something undesirable)

riddle noun **1** puzzling question designed to test people's ingenuity **2** puzzling person or thing ▷ verb **3** to pierce with many holes **4** riddled with full of (something undesirable)

ride rides riding rode ridden verb **1** to sit on and control or propel (a horse, bicycle, etc) **2** to go on horseback or in a vehicle **3** to travel over ▷ noun **4** journey on a horse etc or in a vehicle

rider noun **1** person who rides **2** supplementary clause added to a document

ridge noun **1** long narrow hill **2** long narrow raised part on a surface **3** line where two sloping surfaces meet **4** Meteorology elongated area of high pressure

ridicule noun **1** treatment of a person or thing as ridiculous ▷ verb **2** to laugh at, make fun of

ridiculous adjective deserving to be laughed at, absurd ▷ **ridiculously** adverb

rife adjective **1** widespread or common **2** rife with full of

rifle noun **1** firearm with a long barrel ▷ verb **2** to search (a house or safe) and steal from it

rift noun **1** break in friendly relations **2** crack, split or cleft

rig rigs rigging rigged verb **1** to arrange in a dishonest way for profit or advantage ▷ noun **2** apparatus for drilling for oil and gas ▷ **rig up** verb to set up or build temporarily

right adjective **1** just **2** true or correct **3** proper **4** in a satisfactory condition **5** of the side that faces east when the front is turned to the north **6** of the outer side of a fabric ▷ adverb **7** properly **8** straight or directly **9** on or to the right side ▷ noun **10** claim, title, etc allowed or due **11** what is just or due **12 in the right** morally or legally correct **13 Right** conservative political party or group ▷ verb **14** to bring or come back to a normal or correct state

right angle noun angle of 90°

righteous adjective **1** upright, godly or virtuous **2** morally justified

rightful adjective **1** in accordance with what is right **2** having a legally or morally just claim ▷**rightfully** adverb

right-handed adjective using or for the right hand

right-wing adjective believing more strongly in capitalism or conservatism, or less strongly in socialism, than other members of the same party or group ▷**right-winger** noun: a veteran right-winger

rigid adjective **1** inflexible or strict **2** unyielding or stiff ▷**rigidity** noun: the rigidity of government policy ▷**rigidly** adverb

rigorous adjective harsh, severe or stern ▷**rigorously** adverb

rigour noun **1** harshness, severity or strictness **2** hardship

rim noun **1** edge or border **2** outer

ring of a wheel ▷**rimmed** adjective: rimmed with gold

rimu rimus noun NZ New Zealand tree whose wood is used for building and furniture

rind noun tough outer coating of fruits, cheese or bacon

ring rings ringing rang rung verb **1** to give out a clear resonant sound, as a bell **2** to cause (a bell) to sound **3** to call (a person) by telephone **4** (of a building or place) to be filled with sound **5** to put a ring round **6** ringing **7** telephone call **8** circle of gold etc, especially for a finger **9** any circular band, coil or rim **10** circle of people **11** enclosed area, especially a circle for a circus or a roped-in square for boxing **12** group operating (illegal) control of a market ▷**ring off** verb **1** to end a telephone call ▷**ring up** verb **1** to make a telephone call to **2** to record on a cash register

ringbark verb Aust to kill (a tree) by cutting away a strip of bark from around its trunk

ringer noun **1** informal person or thing apparently identical to another **2** Aust person who works on a sheep farm **3** Aust, NZ fastest shearer in a woolshed

ring-in noun informal **1** Aust person or thing that is not normally a member of a particular group **2** Aust, NZ someone who is brought in at the last minute as a replacement for someone else

ringleader noun instigator of a mutiny, riot, etc

rink noun **1** sheet of ice for skating or curling **2** floor for roller-skating

rinse verb **1** to remove soap from

(washed clothes, hair, etc) by applying clean water **2** to wash lightly ▷ *noun* **3** rinsing **4** liquid to tint hair

riot *noun* **1** disorderly unruly disturbance **2 run riot** to behave without restraint ▷ *verb* **3** to take part in a riot

rip rip ripping ripped *verb* **1** to tear or be torn violently **2** to remove hastily or roughly **3** *informal* to move violently or hurriedly ▷ *noun* **4** split or tear > **rip off** *verb* *informal* to cheat (someone) by overcharging

RIP *abbreviation* rest in peace

ripe *adjective* **1** ready to be reaped, eaten, etc **2** matured **3** ready or suitable **4 ripe old age** an elderly but healthy age > **ripeness** *noun*

ripen *verb* **1** to make or become ripe **2** to mature

ripper *noun* *Aust, NZ informal* excellent person or thing

ripple *noun* **1** slight wave or ruffling of a surface **2** sound like ripples of water: *a ripple of applause* ▷ *verb* **3** to flow or form into little waves (on)

rise rising rose risen *verb* **1** to get up from a lying, sitting or kneeling position **2** to get out of bed, especially to begin the day **3** to move upwards **4** (of the sun or moon) to appear above the horizon **5** to reach a higher level **6** (of an amount or price) to increase **7** to rebel **8** (of a court) to adjourn ▷ *noun* **9** rising **10** upward slope **11** increase, especially of wages

riser *noun* person who rises, especially from bed

risk *noun* **1** chance of disaster or

loss **2** person or thing considered as a potential hazard ▷ *verb* **3** to act in spite of the possibility of (injury or loss) **4** to expose to danger or loss

rite *noun* formal practice or custom, especially religious

ritual *noun* **1** prescribed order of rites **2** regular repeated action or behaviour ▷ *adjective* **3** concerning rites

rival rivals rivalling rivalled *noun* **1** person or thing that competes with or equals another for favour, success, etc ▷ *adjective* **2** in the position of a rival ▷ *verb* **3** to (try to) equal

rivalry rivalries *noun* keen competition

river *noun* **1** large natural stream of water **2** plentiful flow

rivet *noun* **1** bolt for fastening metal plates, the end being put through holes and then beaten flat ▷ *verb* **2** to fasten with rivets **3** to cause a person's attention to be fixed, as in fascination

riveting *adjective* very interesting and exciting

road *noun* **1** way prepared for passengers, vehicles, etc **2** route in a town or city with houses along it **3** way or course: *the road to fame*

road rage *noun* aggressive behaviour by a driver as a reaction to the behaviour of another driver

road train *noun* *Aust* line of linked trailers pulled by a truck, used for transporting cattle or sheep

roadworks *plural noun* repairs to a road, especially blocking part of the road

roam *verb* to walk about with no

fixed purpose or direction

roar *verb* **1** to make a very loud noise **2** (of lions, etc) to make loud growling cries **3** to shout (something) as in anger **4** to laugh loudly ▷ *noun* **5** such a sound

roast *verb* **1** to cook (food) by dry heat, as in an oven **2** to make or be very hot ▷ *noun* **3** roasted joint of meat ▷ *adjective* **4** roasted

rob robs robbing robbed *verb* **1** to take something from (a person or place) illegally **2** to deprive, especially of something deserved

robber *noun* criminal who steals money or property using force or threats > **robbery** *noun*: a bank robbery

robe *noun* long loose outer garment

robin *noun* small brown bird with a red breast

robot *noun* **1** automated machine, especially one performing functions in a human manner **2** person of machine-like efficiency **3** S Afr set of coloured lights at a junction to control the traffic flow > **robotic** *adjective*

robust *adjective* very strong and healthy > **robustly** *adverb*

rock *noun* **1** hard mineral substance that makes up part of the earth's crust, stone **2** large rugged mass of stone **3** hard sweet in sticks **4** (also **rock music**) style of pop music with a heavy beat **5** **on the rocks a** (of a marriage) about to end **b** (of an alcoholic drink) served with ice ▷ *verb* **6** to (cause to) sway to and fro

rock and roll or **rock'n'roll**

noun style of pop music blending rhythm and blues and country music

rocket *noun* **1** self-propelling device powered by the burning of explosive contents (used as a firework, weapon, etc) **2** vehicle propelled by a rocket engine, as a weapon or carrying a spacecraft **3** firework that explodes when it is high in the air ▷ *verb* **4** to increase rapidly

rocking chair *noun* chair allowing the sitter to rock backwards and forwards

rock melon *noun* US, Aust, NZ kind of melon with sweet orange flesh

rocky rockier rockiest *adjective* **1** shaky or unstable **2** having many rocks

rod *noun* **1** slender straight bar, stick **2** cane

rodent *noun* animal with teeth specialized for gnawing, such as a rat, mouse or squirrel

rodeo rodeos *noun* display of skill by cowboys, such as bareback riding

roe *noun* **1** mass of eggs in a fish, sometimes eaten as food **2** small species of deer

rogue *noun* **1** dishonest or unprincipled person **2** mischief-loving person ▷ *adjective* **3** (of a wild beast) having a savage temper and living apart from the herd

role or **rôle** *noun* **1** task or function **2** actor's part

roll *verb* **1** to move along by turning over and over **2** to move along on wheels or rollers **3** to curl or make by curling into a ball or tube **4** to move along in an undulating movement **5** to smooth out with a roller **6** to rotate wholly or partially: *He rolled his eyes* **7** (of a ship or aircraft) to turn from side to side about a line from nose to tail ▷ *noun* **8** act of rolling over or from side to side **9** piece of paper etc rolled up **10** small round individually baked piece of bread **11** list or register **12** continuous sound, as of drums, thunder, etc **13** swaying unsteady movement or gait ▷**roll up** *verb* **1** to form into a cylindrical shape **2** *informal* to appear or arrive

roll call *noun* calling out of a list of names to check who is present

roller *noun* **1** rotating cylinder used for smoothing or supporting a thing to be moved, spreading paint, etc **2** small tube around which hair may be wound in order to make it curly

Rollerblade® *noun* roller skate with the wheels set in one straight line

roller coaster *noun* (at a funfair) narrow railway with steep slopes

roller-skate *noun* **1** shoe with four small wheels that enable the wearer to glide swiftly over a flat surface ▷ *verb* **2** to move on roller-skates

rolling pin *noun* cylindrical roller for flattening pastry

ROM *abbreviation Computers* read only memory: storage device that holds data permanently and cannot be altered by the programmer

Roman Catholic *adjective* **1** of that section of the Christian Church that acknowledges the supremacy of the Pope ▷ *noun* **2** person who belongs to the Roman Catholic church ▷**Roman Catholicism** *noun: the spread of Roman Catholicism*

romance *noun* **1** love affair **2** mysterious or exciting quality **3** novel or film dealing with love, especially sentimentally

Romanian or **Rumanian** *adjective* **1** belonging or relating to Romania ▷ *noun* **2** someone from Romania **3** main language spoken in Romania

romantic *adjective* **1** of or dealing with love **2** idealistic but impractical **3** (of literature, music, etc) displaying passion and imagination rather than order and form ▷ *noun* **4** romantic person or artist ▷**romantically** *adverb* ▷**romanticism** *noun*

rondavel *noun SAfr* small circular building with a conical roof

roo *noun Aust informal* kangaroo

roof *noun* outside upper covering of a building, car, etc

roofing *noun* material used for covering roofs

rooftop *noun* outside part of the roof of a building

rook *noun* **1** Eurasian bird of the crow family **2** chess piece shaped like a castle

room *noun* **1** enclosed area in a building **2** unoccupied space **3** scope or opportunity **4** rooms lodgings

roost *noun* **1** place where birds rest or sleep ▷ *verb* **2** to rest or sleep on a roost

root *noun* **1** part of a plant that grows down into the earth obtaining nourishment **2** plant with an edible root, such as a carrot **3** part of a tooth, hair, etc below the skin **4** source or origin **5** form of a word from which other words and forms are derived **6** roots person's sense of belonging ▷ *verb* **7** to establish a root and start to grow **8** to dig or burrow > **root out** *verb* to get rid of completely

rooted *adjective* developed from or strongly influenced by something

rope *noun* **1** thick cord ▷ *verb* **2** to tie with a rope

rosary *rosaries noun* **1** series of prayers **2** string of beads for counting these prayers

rose *noun* **1** shrub or climbing plant with prickly stems and fragrant flowers **2** flower of this plant **3** pink colour ▷ *adjective* **4** pink ▷ *verb* **5** past tense of *rise*

rosella *noun* type of Australian parrot

rosemary *noun* **1** fragrant flowering shrub **2** its leaves as a herb

rosette *noun* large badge of coloured ribbons gathered into a circle, which is worn as a prize in a competition or to support a political party

Rosh Hashanah or **Rosh Hashana** *noun* festival celebrating the Jewish New Year

roster *noun* list of people and their turns of duty

rostrum *rostrums* or *rostra noun* platform or stage

rosy *rosier rosiest adjective* **1** pink-coloured **2** hopeful or promising

rot *rots rotting rotted verb* **1** to decay or cause to decay **2** to deteriorate slowly, physically or mentally ▷ *noun* **3** decay

rota *noun* list of people who take it in turn to do a particular task

rotate *verb* **1** to (cause to) move round a centre or on a pivot **2** to (cause to) follow a set sequence > **rotation** *noun: the daily rotation of the earth*

rotor *noun* **1** revolving portion of a dynamo, motor or turbine **2** rotating device with long blades that provides thrust to lift a helicopter

rotten *adjective* **1** decaying **2** *informal* very bad **3** corrupt

rouble *noun* monetary unit of Russia and Tajikistan

rough *adjective* **1** uneven or irregular **2** not careful or gentle **3** difficult or unpleasant **4** approximate **5** violent, stormy or boisterous **6** in preliminary form **7** lacking refinement ▷ *verb* **8** to make rough ▷ *noun* **9** rough state or area **10** *Golf* part of the course where the grass is uncut > **roughly** *adverb* > **roughness** *noun: the roughness of the surface*

roulette *noun* gambling game in which a ball is dropped onto a revolving wheel with numbered holes in it

round *adjective* **1** spherical, cylindrical, circular or curved ▷ *adverb, preposition* **2** indicating an encircling movement, presence on all sides, etc: *tied round the waist; books scattered round the room* ▷ *verb* **3** to move round ▷ *noun* **4** customary course, as of a milkman **5** game (of golf) **6** stage in a competition **7** one of several periods in a boxing match etc **8** number of drinks bought at one time **9** bullet or shell for a gun > **round up** *verb* to gather (people or animals) together

roundabout noun **1** road junction at which traffic passes round a central island **2** revolving circular platform on which people ride for amusement ▷ adjective **3** not straightforward

rounded adjective curved in shape, without any points or sharp edges

rounders noun bat-and-ball team game

round-the-clock adjective throughout the day and night

rouse verb **1** to wake up **2** to provoke or excite

rouseabout noun Aust, NZ labourer in a shearing shed

rout noun **1** overwhelming defeat **2** disorderly retreat ▷ verb **3** to defeat and put to flight

route noun **1** roads taken to reach a destination **2** chosen way

routine noun **1** usual or regular method of procedure **2** set sequence ▷ adjective **3** ordinary or regular ▷ **routinely** adverb

roving adjective **1** wandering or roaming **2** not restricted to any particular location or area

row¹ noun **1** straight line of people or things ▷ verb **2** to propel (a boat) by oars

row² informal noun **1** dispute **2** disturbance **3** reprimand ▷ verb **4** to quarrel noisily

rowdy rowdier rowdiest adjective disorderly, noisy and rough

royal adjective **1** of, befitting or supported by a king or queen **2** splendid ▷ noun **3** informal member of a royal family

royalist noun supporter of monarchy

royalty royalties noun **1** royal

people **2** rank or power of a monarch **3** payment to an author, musician, inventor, etc

RSS abbreviation Really Simple Syndication: a way of allowing web users to receive updates on their browsers from selected websites

rub rubs rubbing rubbed verb **1** to apply pressure and friction to (something) with a circular or backwards-and-forwards movement **2** to clean, polish or dry by rubbing **3** to chafe or fray through rubbing **4 rub it in** to emphasize an unpleasant fact ▷ **rub out** verb to remove or be removed with a rubber

rubber noun **1** strong waterproof elastic material, originally made from the dried sap of a tropical tree, now usually synthetic **2** piece of rubber used for erasing writing **3** series of matches ▷ adjective **4** made of or producing rubber

rubbish noun **1** waste matter **2** anything worthless **3** nonsense

rubble noun fragments of broken stone, brick, etc

rubric noun formal set of instructions at the beginning of an official document

ruby rubies noun **1** red precious gemstone ▷ adjective **2** deep red

rucksack noun large pack carried on the back

rudder noun vertical hinged piece at the stern of a boat or at the rear of an aircraft, for steering

rude adjective **1** impolite or insulting **2** coarse, vulgar or obscene **3** unexpected and unpleasant **4** roughly

made **5** robust > **rudely** adverb
> **rudeness** noun: I was angry at
her rudeness

rudimentary adjective formal
basic, elementary

rudiments plural noun simplest
and most basic stages of a subject

ruff noun **1** starched and frilled
collar **2** natural collar of feathers,
fur, etc on certain birds and
animals

ruffle verb **1** to disturb the calm
of **2** to annoy or irritate > noun
3 frill or pleat

rug noun **1** small carpet **2** thick
woollen blanket

rugby noun form of football played
with an oval ball which may be
handled by the players. Rugby
League is played with 13 players in
each side, Rugby Union is played
with 15 players in each side

rugged adjective **1** rocky or steep
2 uneven and jagged **3** strong-
featured **4** tough and sturdy

rugger noun Chiefly Brit informal
rugby

ruin verb **1** to destroy or
spoil completely **2** to cause
(someone) to lose money > noun
3 destruction or decay **4** loss of
wealth, position, etc **5** broken-
down unused building

rule noun **1** statement of what
is allowed, for example in a
game or procedure **2** what is
usual **3** government, authority
or control **4** measuring device
with a straight edge **5 as a rule**
usually > verb **6** to govern (people
or a political unit) **7** to be pre-
eminent or superior **8** to give a
formal decision > **rule out** verb to
dismiss from consideration

ruler noun **1** person who governs
2 measuring device with a
straight edge

rum noun strong alcoholic drink
distilled from sugar cane

Rumanian another spelling of
Romanian

rumble verb **1** to make a low
continuous noise **2** Brit informal
to discover the (disreputable)
truth about > noun **3** deep
resonant sound

rummage verb **1** to search
untidily and at length > noun
2 untidy search through a
collection of things

rumour noun **1** unproved
statement **2** gossip or common
talk

rump noun **1** buttocks **2** rear of
an animal

run runs running ran run verb
1 to move with a more rapid gait
than walking **2** to take part in
(a race) **3** to travel according
to schedule **4** to function **5** to
manage **6** to stand as a candidate
for political or other office **7** to
continue in a particular direction
or for a specified period **8** to
expose yourself to (a risk) **9** to
flow **10** to spread > noun **11** act
or spell of running **12** ride in a car
13 continuous period **14** series
of unravelled stitches, ladder
15 Cricket score of one made by a
batsman > **run away** verb to make
your escape; flee > **run down** verb
1 to be rude about **2** to reduce in
number or size **3** to stop working
> **run out** verb to use up or (of a
supply) to be used up > **run over**
verb to knock down (a person)
with a moving vehicle

runaway noun person or animal

a b c d e f g h i j k l m n o p r s t u v w x y z

that has run away

run-down adjective **1** exhausted **2** shabby or dilapidated ▷ noun **rundown 3** reduction in number or size **4** brief overview or summary

rung noun **1** crossbar on a ladder ▷ verb **2** past participle of **ring**

runner noun **1** competitor in a race **2** messenger **3** part underneath an ice skate etc, on which it slides **4** slender horizontal stem of a plant, such as a strawberry, running along the ground and forming new roots at intervals **5** long strip of carpet or decorative cloth

runner bean noun long green pod eaten as a vegetable

runner-up runners-up noun person who comes second in a competition

running adjective **1** continuous **2** consecutive **3** (of water) flowing ▷ noun **4** act of moving or flowing quickly **5** management of a business etc

runny runnier runniest adjective **1** tending to flow **2** exuding moisture

runt noun smallest animal in a litter

runway noun hard level roadway where aircraft take off and land

rupee noun monetary unit of India and Pakistan

rupture noun **1** breaking, breach **2** hernia ▷ verb **3** to break, burst or sever

rural adjective in or of the countryside

ruse noun formal trick

rush verb **1** to move or do very quickly **2** to force (someone) to act hastily **3** to make a sudden attack upon (a person or place) ▷ noun **4** sudden quick or violent movement **5** marsh plant with a slender pithy stem **6** rushes first unedited prints of a scene for a film ▷ adjective **7** done with speed, hasty

rush hour noun period at the beginning and end of the working day, when many people are travelling to or from work

rusk noun hard brown crisp biscuit, used especially for feeding babies

Russian adjective **1** belonging or relating to Russia ▷ noun **2** someone from Russia **3** main language spoken in Russia

rust noun **1** reddish-brown coating formed on iron etc that has been exposed to moisture ▷ adjective **2** reddish-brown ▷ verb **3** to become coated with rust

rustic adjective simple in a way considered to be typical of the countryside

rustle verb to make a low whispering sound > **rustling** adjective: a rustling sound

rusty rustier rustiest adjective **1** coated with rust **2** of a rust colour **3** out of practice

rut noun **1** furrow made by wheels **2** dull settled habits or way of living

ruthless adjective pitiless, merciless > **ruthlessly** adverb > **ruthlessness** noun: she has a reputation for ruthlessness

rye noun kind of grain used for fodder and bread

S

Sabbath noun day for worship and rest in some religions: Saturday for Jews, Sunday for Christians

sable noun dark fur from a small weasel-like Arctic animal

sabotage noun 1 damage done to machinery, systems, etc in order to cause disruption ▷ verb 2 to damage in order to disrupt

sabre noun 1 heavy curved sword 2 Fencing light sword

saccharin noun artificial sweetener

sachet noun small envelope or bag containing a single portion of something

sack noun 1 large bag without handles 2 plundering (of a captured town) 3 the sack informal dismissal ▷ verb 4 informal to dismiss 5 to plunder (a captured town)

sacrament noun a ceremony of the Christian Church, especially Communion

sacred adjective holy or connected with religion

sacrifice noun 1 giving up (of something valuable or important) to help someone or something else 2 thing given up 3 killing (of an animal) as an offering to a god 4 thing offered ▷ verb 5 to give up (something valuable or important) for the good of someone or something else 6 to kill (an animal) as an offering to a god > **sacrificial** adjective: sacrificial offerings

sacrilege noun behaviour that shows great disrespect for something holy or worthy of respect > **sacrilegious** adjective: It would be sacrilegious to waste this

sacrosanct adjective regarded as too important to be criticized or changed

sad sadder saddest adjective 1 unhappy, filled with sorrow 2 causing unhappiness or sorrow: a sad story 3 very bad: a sad day for democracy 4 Brit informal pathetic and inadequate: What a sad person! > **sadly** adverb > **sadness** noun: His joy was tinged with sadness

sadden verb to make (someone) sad

saddle noun 1 rider's seat on a horse or bicycle 2 joint (of meat) ▷ verb 3 to put a saddle on (a horse) 4 to burden (with a responsibility)

sadism noun gaining of pleasure from making someone suffer > **sadist** noun person who gains pleasure from causing suffering > **sadistic** adjective: a sadistic bully > **sadistically** adverb

safari noun expedition for hunting or observing wild animals, especially in Africa

safari park noun park where wild animals such as lions and elephants roam freely

safe adjective 1 not in danger 2 not harmful or dangerous ▷ noun 3 strong lockable container > **safely** adverb > **safety** noun: a threat to public safety

safeguard verb 1 to protect ▷ noun 2 protection

safekeeping noun keeping or being held in a place of safety;

protection

sag sags sagging sagged verb to sink in the middle or hang loosely >**sagging** adjective

saga noun 1 legend of Norse heroes 2 any long story or series of events

sage noun 1 herb used in cooking 2 literary very wise person

Sagittarius noun ninth sign of the zodiac, represented by a half-horse half-man creature with a bow and arrow

sail noun 1 sheet of fabric that when raised on the mast of a sailing vessel catches the wind and causes it to be blown along 2 one of the arms of a windmill that move round in the wind ▷ verb 3 to travel by water 4 to begin a voyage 5 to move smoothly

sailor noun member of the crew of a ship or boat

saint noun 1 Christianity dead person honoured by the Church for their holy life 2 very good person

saintly saintlier saintliest adjective behaving in a very good or holy way

sake noun 1 benefit 2 purpose

salad noun mixture of raw vegetables

salami noun kind of sausage that is eaten cold

salary salaries noun regular monthly payment to an employee >**salaried** adjective with a salary

sale noun 1 exchange of goods for money 2 event at which goods are sold for unusually low prices 3 auction >**saleable** adjective fit to be sold

salesman salesmen noun man who sells products for a company >**saleswoman** noun

salient adjective formal prominent, noticeable

saliva noun liquid that forms in the mouth and helps you chew food

sallow adjective (of skin) pale and unhealthy

salmon noun large silver-coloured fish with orange-pink flesh

  ● The plural of salmon is salmon

salmonella noun kind of bacterium that causes severe food poisoning

salon noun place where hairdressers or beauticians work

saloon noun 1 car with a fixed roof and a separate boot 2 in America, a place where alcoholic drinks are sold and drunk

salt noun 1 white substance used to flavour and preserve food 2 chemical compound formed from an acid base ▷ verb 3 to season or preserve with salt

salty saltier saltiest adjective containing salt or tasting of salt

salute noun 1 formal sign of respect that often involves raising your right hand to your forehead 2 firing of guns as a military greeting of honour ▷ verb 3 to greet with a salute 4 to make a salute

salvage verb 1 to save from destruction or waste 2 ships or cargoes that are saved or reclaimed from the sea 3 goods that are saved from destruction

salvation noun fact or state of being saved from harm or the consequences of sin

salvo salvos or salvoes noun

1 firing of several guns or missiles at the same time **2** burst (of applause or questions)

same *adjective, pronoun* **1** identical, not different, unchanged **2** just mentioned

Samoan *adjective* **1** belonging or relating to Samoa ▷ *noun* **2** person from Samoa

sample *noun* **1** small amount of something for trying or testing **2** *Music* short extract from an existing recording mixed into a backing track to produce a new recording ▷ *verb* **3** to try a sample of **4** *Music* to take a short extract from (one recording) and mix it into a backing track **5** to record (a sound) and feed it into a computerized synthesizer so that it can be reproduced at any pitch

samurai *noun* member of an ancient Japanese warrior class

● The plural of *samurai* is
● *samurai*

sanctimonious *adjective* pretending to be religious and virtuous

sanction *noun* **1** official approval **2** punishment or penalty intended to make a person, group or country obey a particular rule or law ▷ *verb* **3** to authorize or permit

sanctity *noun* quality of being important and deserving respect

sanctuary sanctuaries *noun* **1** place where you are safe from harm or danger **2** place where wildlife is protected

sand *noun* **1** substance consisting of small grains of rock. Beaches are made of sand ▷ *verb* **2** to smooth with sandpaper

sandal *noun* open shoe with straps

sandpaper *noun* strong paper coated with sand and used for smoothing surfaces

sandshoe *noun Brit, Aust, NZ* light canvas shoe with a rubber sole

sandstone *noun* type of rock formed from sand

sandwich *noun* **1** two slices of bread with a layer of food between ▷ *verb* **2** to insert between two other things: *a shop sandwiched between two pubs*

sandy sandier sandiest *adjective* **1** covered with sand **2** (of hair) reddish-fair

sane *adjective* **1** of sound mind **2** sensible, rational

sanguine *adjective formal* cheerful and confident

sanitary *adjective* concerned with cleanliness and hygiene

sanitary towel *noun* absorbent pad worn by women during their periods

sanitation *noun* sanitary measures, especially drainage or sewerage

sanity *noun* ability to think and act in a mentally stable way

sap saps sapping sapped *noun* **1** watery liquid found in plants ▷ *verb* **2** to undermine, weaken or destroy

sapling *noun* young tree

sapphire *noun* blue gemstone

sarcastic *adjective* relating to or involving the mocking or insulting use of irony ▷ **sarcastically** *adverb*: *"Thanks, Mum," I said sarcastically*

sarcophagus sarcophagi or **sarcophaguses** *noun* stone coffin

sardine sardines *noun* small sea

fish of the herring family

sardonic *adjective* mocking or scornful >**sardonically** *adverb*

sari saris *noun* long piece of cloth draped around the body and over one shoulder, worn by Hindu women

sarmie *noun* S Afr informal sandwich

sartorial *adjective* formal relating to men's clothes

sash *noun* decorative strip of cloth worn round the waist or over one shoulder

Satan 1 the Devil **2 Great Satan** radical Islamic term for the United States

satanic *adjective* caused by or influenced by Satan

satchel *noun* bag with a shoulder strap, for carrying books

satellite *noun* **1** man-made device orbiting the earth and collecting and relaying information **2** natural object in space that moves round a planet or star **3** country that is dependent on a more powerful one

satin *noun* silky fabric with a glossy surface on one side

satire *noun* **1** use of mocking or ironical humour, especially in literature, to show how foolish or bad someone or something is **2** play, novel or poem that does this >**satirical** *adjective: a satirical magazine*

satisfaction *noun* feeling of pleasure you have when you do or get something you wanted or that was necessary

satisfactory *adjective* acceptable or adequate >**satisfactorily** *adverb*

satisfy satisfies satisfying satisfied *verb* **1** to make (someone) content or pleased by doing something well enough or by giving them enough of something **2** to provide enough for **3** to convince or persuade >**satisfied** *adjective: He is satisfied with my work*

satisfying *adjective* pleasing or fulfilling

satsuma *noun* fruit like a small orange

saturated *adjective* **1** very wet **2** completely full

Saturday *noun* day between Friday and Sunday

Saturn *noun* sixth planet from the sun in the solar system

sauce *noun* one of many kinds of thin or thick, sweet or savoury liquids served with food

saucepan *noun* deep metal cooking pot with a handle

saucer *noun* small round dish put under a cup

saucy saucier sauciest *adjective* cheeky in an amusing way

Saudi *adjective* **1** belonging or relating to Saudi Arabia ▷ *noun* **2** person from Saudi Arabia

sauna *noun* **1** activity of alternately sitting in a steamy room sweating then having a cold bath or shower **2** place where you do this

saunter *verb* **1** to walk in a leisurely manner, stroll ▷ *noun* **2** leisurely walk

sausage *noun* minced meat in an edible tube-shaped skin

sauté sautés sautéing or sautéeing sautéed *verb* to fry quickly in a little fat

savage adjective **1** wild, untamed
2 cruel and violent ▷ noun
3 violent and uncivilized person
▷ verb **4** to attack ferociously
>**savagely** adverb

savagery savageries noun cruel
and violent behaviour

save verb **1** to rescue or preserve
from harm, protect **2** to keep for
the future, set aside **3** to spare or
prevent (someone having to do
something) **4** Sport to prevent
the scoring of (a goal) ▷ noun
5 Sport act of preventing a goal
▷ preposition **6** formal (often
followed by for) except: I was alone
save for the cat >**saver** noun person
who saves money

saving noun **1** reduction in the
amount of time or money used
2 savings money you have saved

saviour noun person who rescues
you

savour verb to enjoy fully; relish
▷ noun

savoury savouries adjective
1 salty or spicy **2** pleasant or
respectable ▷ noun **3** (usually
plural) savoury dish served before
or after a meal

saw¹ **saws sawing sawed sawn**
noun **1** tool, with a blade with
sharp teeth along one edge, for
cutting wood ▷ verb **2** to cut
with a saw

saw² verb past tense of **see**

sawdust noun fine, powdery wood
fragments produced when you
saw wood

saxophone noun brass wind
instrument with keys and a
curved body often played in jazz
bands

say says saying said verb **1** to

express in words, utter **2** to give
as your opinion **3** to suppose
▷ noun **4** right or chance to speak
or influence a decision

saying noun well-known phrase or
proverb that tells you something
about human life

scab noun **1** crust that forms over a
wound **2** offensive someone who
works with their colleagues are
on strike; a blackleg >**scabby**
adjective

scaffolding noun framework
of poles and boards used by
workmen to stand on when
working on the outside of a
building

scald verb **1** to burn with hot liquid
or steam ▷ noun **2** burn caused
by scalding

scale noun **1** size or extent (of
something): the sheer scale of the
disaster **2** set of levels or numbers
used for measuring things:
The earthquake measured 3.5 on
the Richter scale **3** relationship
between the size of something
on a map, plan, or in a model and
its size in the real world: a scale of
1:10,000 **4** upward or downward
sequence of eight musical notes
5 one of the small pieces of hard
skin that form the skin of fishes
and reptiles **6** coating that forms
in kettles etc due to hard water
▷ verb **7** to climb

scalene adjective (of a triangle)
with sides that are all of different
lengths

scallop noun edible shellfish with
two flat fan-shaped shells

scalp noun **1** skin under the hair
on your head **2** piece of skin and
hair removed when someone is
scalped ▷ verb **3** to cut off the skin

and hair from someone's head in one piece

scalpel noun small surgical knife

scaly scalier scaliest adjective covered with scales

scamper verb to run about quickly and lightly, perhaps in play

scampi plural noun large prawns, often eaten fried in breadcrumbs

scan scans scanning scanned verb **1** to look (at something) carefully **2** to glance over (something) quickly **3** to examine or search (something) by x-raying it or by passing a radar or sonar beam over it **4** (of verse) to conform to metrical rules ▷ noun **5** examination or search by a scanner

scandal noun situation or event considered shocking and immoral ▷ **scandalous** adjective: This is a scandalous waste of money

Scandinavia noun name given to a group of countries in Northern Europe, including Norway, Sweden, Denmark and sometimes Finland and Iceland ▷ **Scandinavian** noun, adjective

scanner noun **1** machine used to examine, identify or record things by means of a beam of light or X-rays **2** machine that converts text or images into a form that can be stored on a computer

scant adjective barely enough, meagre

scapegoat noun someone made to bear the blame for something that may not be their fault

scar scars scarring scarred noun **1** mark left after a wound has healed **2** permanent emotional damage left by a bad experience ▷ verb **3** to leave a permanent mark on **4** to have a permanent effect on

scarce adjective **1** not enough to meet demand **2** not common, rarely found **3 make yourself scarce** informal to leave quickly ▷ **scarcity** noun: the scarcity of housing

scarcely adverb hardly

- As scarcely already has a
- negative sense, it is followed
- by ever or any, and not by
- never or no

scare verb **1** to frighten or be frightened ▷ noun **2** fright **3** panic ▷ **scared** adjective: I was really scared

scarecrow noun figure dressed in old clothes, set up to scare birds away from crops

scarf scarfs or scarves noun piece of material worn round the neck, head or shoulders

scarlet adjective, noun bright red

scary scarier scariest adjective informal frightening

scathing adjective harshly critical: They were scathing about his idea

scatter verb **1** to throw or drop all over an area **2** to move away in different directions

scattering noun small number (of things) spread over a large area

scavenge verb to search for (anything usable) among discarded material

scenario scenarios noun **1** summary of the plot of a play or film **2** way a situation might develop in the future

scene noun **1** place where a real or imaginary event happens **2** part of a play or film in which a series of events happen in one place **3** picture or view: *a village scene* **4** display of emotion: *Don't make a scene* **5** informal area of activity: *the fashion scene* **6 behind the scenes** **a** backstage **b** in secret

scenery *sceneries noun* **1** natural features of a landscape **2** painted backcloths or screens used on stage to represent the scene of action

scenic *adjective* with nice views, picturesque

scent *noun* **1** smell, especially a pleasant one **2** series of clues **3** perfume ▷ *verb* **4** to detect by smell **5** to fill with fragrance

sceptic *noun* person who doubts things that are widely believed > **sceptical** *adjective*: *She was deeply sceptical about the idea* > **scepticism** *noun*: *his scepticism about some of their claims*

sceptre *noun* ornamental rod symbolizing royal power

schedule *noun* **1** plan listing events or tasks together with the times they are to happen; timetable **2** list ▷ *verb* **3** to plan and arrange (something) for a particular time

schema *schemata noun* **1** *technical* outline of a plan or theory **2** mental model used by the mind to understand new experiences or view the world

scheme *noun* **1** plan or arrangement **2** secret plot ▷ *verb* **3** to plan in an underhand manner

schism *noun* split or division in a group or organization

schizophrenia *noun* serious mental illness in which the sufferer has thoughts and feelings that do not relate to reality

scholar *noun* **1** a learned person **2** a student receiving a scholarship **3** *SAfr* pupil

scholarly *adjective* having or showing a lot of knowledge; learned

scholarship *noun* **1** award given to a student in recognition of their academic ability in order to finance their studies **2** academic knowledge and learning

school *noun* **1** place where children are educated or instruction is given in a subject **2** group of artists, thinkers, etc with shared beliefs or methods **3** shoal (of fish, whales, dolphins, etc) ▷ *verb* **4** to educate or train

schoolchild *schoolchildren noun* child who goes to school > **schoolboy** *noun* > **schoolgirl** *noun*

schooling *noun* the education you receive at school

schooner *noun* sailing ship

science *noun* **1** study of and knowledge about natural and physical phenomena **2** a branch of science, for example physics or biology

science fiction *noun* stories about events happening in the future or in other parts of the universe

scientific *adjective* **1** relating to science or to a particular science: *scientific knowledge* **2** systematic: *this scientific method* > **scientifically** *adverb*

scientist *noun* person who studies or practises a science

scintillating *adjective* lively and witty

scissors *plural noun* cutting tool with two crossed blades

scoff *verb* **1** to speak scornfully **2** *informal* to eat (food) quickly and greedily

scold *verb* to rebuke, reprimand or tell (someone) off

scone *noun* small plain cake made from flour and fat and usually eaten with butter

scoop *verb* (often followed by *up*) **1** to pick up or remove using a spoon, shovel or the palm of your hand ▷ *noun* **2** tool like a large spoon or shovel used for picking up ice cream, mashed potato and other substances **3** important news story reported in one newspaper before it appears elsewhere

scooter *noun* **1** light motorcycle **2** a simple vehicle consisting of a platform on wheels and a handlebar; to make it work you stand on the platform on one leg and use your other leg to push on the ground

scope *noun* **1** opportunity for doing something **2** range of activity

-scope *suffix* used to form nouns which refer to an instrument used for observing or detecting: *microscope; telescope*

scorching *adjective* extremely hot

score *verb* **1** to gain (a point, goal, run) in a game **2** to record the score obtained by the players **3** to cut a line in **4** to achieve (a success, victory) **5 score out** to cross out ▷ *noun* **6** number of points, goals, runs gained by each competitor or competing team in a game or competition **7** written version of a piece of music showing parts for each musician **8** grievance: *settle old scores* **9** old-fashioned twenty or about twenty **10 scores** lots: *Ros entertained scores of celebrities* **>scorer** *noun* person who scores

scorn *noun* **1** open contempt ▷ *verb* **2** to despise **3** *formal* to reject with contempt

scornful *adjective* showing contempt; contemptuous **>scornfully** *adverb*

Scorpio *noun* eighth sign of the zodiac, represented by a scorpion

scorpion *noun* small lobster-shaped animal with a poisonous sting at the end of a jointed tail

Scot *noun* person from Scotland **>Scots** *adjective* Scottish

scotch *noun* whisky made in Scotland

Scotsman *Scotsmen noun* man from Scotland **>Scotswoman** *noun*

Scottish *adjective* belonging or relating to Scotland

scoundrel *noun* old-fashioned cheat or deceiver

scour *verb* **1** to clean or polish by rubbing with something rough **2** to carry out a thorough search of (a place)

scourge *noun* **1** person or thing causing severe suffering **2** whip ▷ *verb* **3** to cause severe suffering to **4** to whip

scout *noun* **1** person sent out to see what an area is like and to find out the position of things **2** member of the Scout Association, an organization for boys which aims to develop character and promotes outdoor activities ▷ *verb* **3** to act as a scout **4** (especially followed by *around*) to look around (for something)

scowl verb **1** to frown in an angry or sullen way ▷ noun **2** an angry or sullen expression

scrabble verb to scrape at with the hands, feet or claws

scramble verb **1** to climb or crawl hastily or awkwardly using your hands to help you **2** to cook (eggs beaten up with milk) ▷ noun **3** motorcycle race over rough ground **4** rough climb

scrap scraps scrapping scrapped noun **1** small piece **2** (also **scrap metal**) waste metal collected for reprocessing **3** *informal* fight or quarrel **4** scraps leftover food ▷ verb **5** to get rid of

scrapbook noun book with blank pages in which you stick things such as pictures or newspaper articles

scrape verb **1** to clean (something off) using something rough or sharp: *scraping the fallen snow off the track* **2** to rub (against something) with a harsh noise: *The chair scraped across the floorboards.* ▷ noun **3** act or sound of scraping **4** mark or wound caused by scraping

scratch verb **1** to mark or cut with claws, nails or anything rough or sharp **2** to rub at (skin) with nails or fingertips to relieve itching ▷ noun **3** a small cut or mark **4** from scratch from the very beginning **5** up to scratch up to standard

scratchcard noun ticket with a surface that you scratch off to show whether or not you have won a prize in a competition

scrawl verb **1** to write (words, etc) carelessly or hastily ▷ noun **2** careless or untidy writing

scrawny scrawnier scrawniest adjective thin and bony

scream verb **1** to shout or cry in a loud, high-pitched voice, especially when afraid or in pain ▷ noun **2** shrill piercing cry **3** *informal* very funny person or thing

screech verb **1** to give a shrill cry or a high-pitched sound ▷ noun **2** shrill cry

screen noun **1** vertical surface on which pictures or films are shown or projected **2** a movable vertical panel used to separate different parts of a room or to protect something ▷ verb **3** to show (a film or television programme) **4** to shelter or conceal (someone or something) with or as if with a screen **5** to investigate (a person or group) to check their suitability for a task

screenplay noun script (of a film)

screenshot noun *Computers* copied image of a computer screen at a particular moment

screw noun **1** metal pin with a spiral ridge round its shaft and a slot for a screwdriver on its head, used for fastening things together ▷ verb **2** to fasten with screws **3** to twist (something) round and round in order to fasten it onto something else: *He screwed the top on the bottle* > **screw up** verb **1** to twist or squeeze (something) into a distorted shape **2** *informal* to bungle or spoil

screwdriver noun tool for turning screws

scribble verb **1** to write

(something) hastily or illegibly **2** to make meaningless or illegible marks ▷ noun **3** something written or drawn quickly or roughly

scrimp verb to live cheaply, spending as little money as possible

script noun **1** text of a film, play or TV programme **2** system of writing: Arabic script

scripture noun sacred writings, especially the Bible ▷ **scriptural** adjective: scriptural references

scroll noun **1** roll of parchment or paper **2** ornamental carving shaped like a scroll ▷ verb **3** to move (text) up or down on a VDU screen in order to find something

scrounge verb informal to get (something) by cadging or begging ▷ **scrounger** noun someone who makes a habit of scrounging

scrub scrubs scrubbing scrubbed verb **1** to clean by rubbing, often with a hard brush and water ▷ noun **2** scrubbing: You'll have to give them a scrub **3** low trees and bushes **4** area of land covered with scrub

scruff noun back (of your neck or collar); informal untidy person

scruffy scruffier scruffiest adjective dirty and untidy or shabby

scrum noun Rugby restarting of play in which groups of opposing forwards push against each other to gain possession of the ball

scrunchie noun a loop of elastic loosely covered with material which is used to hold hair in a ponytail

scruple noun moral principles that make you unwilling to do something that seems wrong

scrupulous adjective **1** very conscientious or honest about what one does **2** very careful or precise ▷ **scrupulously** adverb

scrutinize verb to examine very carefully

scrutiny noun close examination

scuba diving noun sport of swimming underwater using tanks of compressed air and breathing apparatus

scuff verb **1** to drag (your feet) while walking **2** to scrape (your shoes) by doing so

scuffle noun **1** short, disorderly fight ▷ verb **2** to fight in a disorderly manner

scullery sculleries noun small room next to a kitchen where washing and cleaning are done

sculpt verb to carve or shape (figures and objects) using materials such as stone, wood or clay

sculptor noun someone who makes sculptures

sculpture noun **1** a work of art produced by carving or shaping materials such as stone, wood or clay **2** art of making figures or designs in wood, stone, clay, etc ▷ **sculptural** adjective: sculptural pieces

scum noun **1** a layer of a dirty substance on the surface of a liquid **2** informal worthless people

scungy scungier scungiest adjective Aust, NZ informal sordid or dirty

scurrilous adjective offensive and damaging to someone's good name

scurry scurries scurrying scurried verb to run quickly with short steps

scurvy noun disease caused by lack of vitamin C

scuttle verb 1 to run with short quick steps 2 to make a hole in (a ship) to sink it ▷ noun 3 fireside container for coal

scythe noun 1 long-handled tool with a curved blade for cutting grass ▷ verb 2 to cut with a scythe

sea noun 1 the salty water that covers three quarters of the earth's surface 2 particular area of this 3 a large mass (of people or things) 4 **at sea a** in a ship on the ocean **b** confused or bewildered

seagull noun common bird with white, grey and black plumage that lives near the sea; gull

seahorse noun small fish that swims upright, with a head that looks like a horse's head

seal noun 1 amphibious mammal with flippers as limbs 2 official mark or stamped piece of wax on a document which shows that it is genuine 3 embossed piece of wax or lead fixed over the opening part of a container or envelope to show that it has not been tampered with 4 device used to close an opening tightly ▷ verb 5 to stick down (an envelope) 6 to close with or as if with a seal 7 to make (something) airtight or watertight ▷ **seal off** verb to enclose or isolate (a place) completely

sea lion noun a type of large seal

seam noun 1 line of stitches joining two pieces of cloth 2 thin layer of coal or ore

seaman seamen noun sailor

seance noun meeting at which people attempt to communicate with the dead

search verb 1 to examine (someone or something) closely in order to find something 2 to look (for someone or something); seek ▷ noun 3 an attempt to find something

search engine noun Computers Internet service enabling users to search for items of interest

searching adjective keen or thorough: searching questions

searchlight noun powerful light with a beam that can be shone in any direction

searing adjective (of pain) very sharp

seashore noun the land along the edge of the sea

seasick adjective feeling sick because of the movement of a boat > **seasickness** noun: The crew were all suffering from seasickness

seaside noun area next to the sea

season noun 1 any of the four periods of the year (spring, summer, autumn or winter), each having their own typical weather conditions 2 period of the year when something usually happens: the football season 3 fitting or proper time (for something) ▷ verb 4 to add salt, pepper or spices to (a dish)

seasonal adjective depending on or varying with the seasons: seasonal work

seasoned adjective very experienced: a seasoned

professional

seasoning *noun* salt, herbs and other flavourings and condiments that are added to food to enhance flavour

season ticket *noun* ticket for something that you can use as many times as you like within a certain period

seat *noun* 1 something you can sit on 2 the part (of a piece of clothing) that covers your bottom 3 buttocks 4 membership of a legislative or administrative body: *his chances of winning a seat in parliament* ▷ *verb* 5 to cause (someone) to take a seat 6 to provide seating for: *The theatre seats 570 people*

seat belt *noun* strap fixed to an aeroplane or car seat that you fasten round yourself to hold you in

seating *noun* the number of seats or the way seats are arranged in a place

seaweed *noun* plant growing in the sea

secateurs *plural noun* small pruning shears

secluded *adjective* private, sheltered

second¹ *adjective* 1 following the first 2 alternate, additional ▷ *noun* 3 one of the sixty parts that a minute is divided into 4 moment 5 person or thing coming second 6 someone who attends to the needs of one of the participants in a duel or boxing match 7 (*usually in plural*) slightly defective goods sold cheaply ▷ *verb* 8 to express formal support for (a proposal) >**secondly** *adverb*

second² *verb* to transfer (a person) temporarily to another job >**secondment** *noun* temporary transfer to another job: *She was on secondment from the local authority*

secondary *adjective* 1 of less importance 2 coming after or derived from what is primary or first 3 relating to the education of pupils between the ages of 11 and 18 or, in New Zealand, between 13 and 18

secondary school *noun* a school for pupils between the ages of eleven and eighteen

second-class *adjective* 1 inferior 2 cheaper, slower or less comfortable than first-class ▷ *adverb* 3 by second-class mail, transport, etc

second cousin *noun* Your second cousins are the children of your parents' first cousins

second-hand *adjective* 1 not bought or acquired when new but after someone else's use: *a second-hand car* ▷ *adverb* 2 following on by someone else: *We bought it second-hand* 3 indirectly: *I heard it second-hand*

second-rate *adjective* of poor quality

secret *adjective* 1 kept from the knowledge of others ▷ *noun* 2 something kept secret 3 underlying explanation: *the secret of my success* 4 **in secret** without other people knowing >**secrecy** *noun*: *The whole event was shrouded in secrecy* >**secretly** *adverb*

secret agent *noun* spy

secretary secretaries *noun* 1 person employed by an organization to keep records,

write letters and do office work
2 Secretary head of a state
department: *the Health Secretary*
>secretarial *adjective: secretarial
work*

secrete *verb* **1** (of an organ, gland,
etc) to produce and release (a
substance) **2** *formal* to hide or
conceal

secretive *adjective* inclined to
keep things secret

secret service *noun* government
department in charge of
espionage

sect *noun* religious or political
group which has broken away
from a larger group

sectarian *adjective* strongly
supporting a particular sect:
sectarian violence

section *noun* **1** part or subdivision
of something **2** cross-section
▷ *verb* **3** to cut or divide into
sections

sector *noun* **1** part or subdivision
(of something) **2** part of a circle
enclosed by two radii and the arc
which they cut off

secular *adjective* not connected
with religion or the church

secure *adjective* **1** locked or well
protected **2** free from danger
3 free from anxiety **4** firmly
fixed ▷ *verb* **5** *formal* to obtain:
They secured the rights to her story
6 to fasten (something) firmly
>securely *adverb*

security securities *noun* **1** state
of being secure **2** precautions
against theft, espionage or
other danger **3** something
given or pledged to guarantee
payment of a loan **4** securities
stocks, shares, bonds or other

investments ▷ *adjective* **5** relating
to precautions against theft,
espionage or other danger:
Security forces arrested one member

sedate *adjective* **1** calm and
dignified **2** slow or unhurried
▷ *verb* **3** to give (someone) a drug
to calm them down or make
them sleep **>sedately** *adverb*
>sedation *noun: under sedation*

sedative *adjective* **1** having a
soothing or calming effect ▷ *noun*
2 sedative drug

sedentary *adjective* done sitting
down, involving little exercise

sediment *noun* **1** solid material
that settles at the bottom of a
liquid **2** material deposited by
water, ice or wind

sedimentary *adjective* (of rocks
such as sandstone and limestone)
formed from fragments of
compressed shells or rocks

seduce *verb* **1** to persuade into
sexual intercourse **2** to tempt
into wrongdoing **>seduction**
*noun: a classic tale of lust, seduction
and revenge* **>seductive** *adjective: a
seductive offer* **>seductively** *adverb*

see sees seeing saw seen *verb* **1** to
observe: *He saw us on TV* **2** to meet
or visit: *I went to see my dentist* **3** to
understand: *I see what you mean*
4 to watch: *She wanted to see a
horror movie* **5** to find out: *I'll see
what's happening* **6** to make sure
(of something): *I'll see that she gets
it* **7** to make an effort, try: *I'll see if
I can find it* **8** to have experience
of; witness: *The next couple of years
saw two momentous developments*
9 to accompany (someone to a
place): *he offered to see her home*
10 see to to deal with: *I'll see to
your breakfast* ▷ *noun* **11** diocese

of a bishop > **see through** verb to understand the real nature of

seed noun **1** the grain of a plant from which a new plant can grow **2** origin or beginning: *the seeds of mistrust* **3** *Sport* tennis player ranked according to his or her ability

seedling noun young plant grown from a seed

seedy seedier seediest adjective shabby: *a seedy hotel*

seek seeks seeking sought verb **1** to try to find or obtain (someone or something) **2** to try (to do something): *He sought to reunite the country*

seem verb to appear to be: *He seemed such a quiet chap*

seeming adjective appearing to be real or genuine; apparent > **seemingly** adverb

seep verb to trickle through slowly; ooze

seesaw noun **1** plank balanced in the middle so that two people seated on either end ride up and down alternately > verb **2** to move up and down

seething adjective **1** very agitated and angry **2** crowded and full of restless activity

segment noun **1** one of several sections into which something may be divided **2** one of the two parts of a circle formed when you draw a straight line across it

segregate verb to set apart > **segregated** adjective: *Rival fans had broken out of their segregated area.* > **segregation** noun: *segregation, based on race, colour or creed*

seize verb **1** to take hold of forcibly

or quickly **2** to take immediate advantage of > **seize on** verb to show great and sudden interest in (something): *MPs have seized on a new report* > **seize up** verb **1** (of body parts) to become stiff and painful **2** (of mechanical parts) to become jammed through overheating

seizure noun **1** sudden violent attack of an illness, especially a heart attack **2** act of seizing or being seized: *the largest seizure of drugs in US history*

seldom adverb not often; rarely: *They seldom speak to each other*

select verb **1** to pick out or choose > adjective **2** chosen in preference to others: *an invitation to a select few* **3** restricted to a particular group, exclusive: *one of the select band of players to have won both trophies* > **selector** noun someone that selects people or things

selection noun **1** selecting: *the selection of parliamentary candidates* **2** things or people that have been selected **3** range from which something may be selected

selective adjective choosing carefully; choosy: *I am selective about what I eat* > **selectively** adverb

self selves noun **1** distinct individuality or identity of a person or thing **2** your basic nature **3** your own welfare or interests

self- prefix used with many main words to mean: **1** done to yourself or by yourself: *self-help; self-control* **2** automatic(ally): *a self-loading rifle*

self-assured adjective confident

self-centred adjective thinking

only about yourself and not about other people

self-confessed adjective by your own admission

self-confident adjective confident of your own abilities or worth > **self-confidence** noun: her lack of self-confidence

self-conscious adjective nervous, easily embarrassed and worried about what other people think of you > **self-consciously** adverb

self-control noun ability to restrain yourself and not show your feelings

self-defence noun knowledge of and ability to use means to protect yourself if attacked

self-employed adjective working for yourself, with responsibility for your own tax payments, rather than working for an employer

self-esteem noun your good opinion of yourself

self-evident adjective obvious without proof

self-indulgent adjective having a habit of allowing yourself treats or letting yourself do things you enjoy

self-interest noun personal advantage

selfish adjective caring too much about yourself and not enough about other people > **selfishly** adverb > **selfishness** noun: I can't bear greed and selfishness

selfless adjective putting other people's interests before your own; unselfish

self-made adjective rich and successful through your own efforts

self-raising adjective (of flour) containing baking powder to make baking rise

self-respect noun confidence and pride in your own abilities and worth

self-righteous adjective thinking yourself more virtuous than others > **self-righteousness** noun the arrogance and self-righteousness of politicians

self-service adjective (of shops, cafés or garages) requiring you to serve yourself and then pay a cashier

self-sufficient adjective able to provide for yourself without help

sell sells selling sold verb **1** to exchange (something) for money **2** to stock or deal in **3** (of goods) to be sold **4** **sell for** to be priced at **5** informal to persuade (someone) to accept (something) **6** **sell yourself** to present yourself well, so that people have confidence in your ability: You've got to sell yourself at the interview > **seller** noun: a newspaper seller > **sell out** verb to sell your entire stock of (something)

Sellotape® noun **1** type of adhesive tape ▷ verb **2** to stick (something) with Sellotape

semblance noun outward or superficial appearance: an effort to restore a semblance of normality

semen noun sperm-carrying fluid produced by men and male animals

semi- prefix used with many main words to mean: **1** half: semicircle **2** partly or almost: semiskilled workers

semibreve noun musical note (o) four beats long

semicircle noun half of a circle, or something with this shape >**semicircular** adjective: a semicircular alcove

semicolon noun the punctuation mark (;)

semidetached adjective (of a house) joined to another on one side

semifinal noun match or round before the final >**semifinalist** noun competitor or competing team that has reached the match or round before the final

seminar noun meeting of a group of students for discussion

semipermeable adjective (of materials) allowing certain substances with small enough molecules to go through while providing a barrier for substances with larger molecules

semiprecious adjective (of gemstones) having less value than precious stones

semitone noun smallest interval between two notes in Western music

Senate noun the smaller, more important of the two councils in the government of some countries, for example Australia, Canada and the USA

senator noun member of a Senate

send sends sending sent verb 1 to cause (a person or thing) to go to or be taken or transmitted to a place 2 to bring into a specified state or condition: The blow sent him tumbling to the ground >**send for** verb to ask (someone) to come and see you >**send up** verb informal to make fun of (someone or something) by imitating

senile adjective mentally or physically weak because of old age >**senility** noun: the onset of senility

senior adjective 1 superior in rank or standing 2 older 3 of or for older pupils ▷ noun 4 senior person >**seniority** noun: Promotion appeared to be based on seniority

senior citizen noun an elderly person, especially one receiving an old-age pension

sensation noun 1 physical feeling 2 general feeling or awareness 3 ability to feel things physically 4 exciting person or thing

sensational adjective 1 causing intense shock, anger or excitement 2 informal very good >**sensationally** adverb

sense noun 1 any of the faculties of perception or feeling (sight, hearing, touch, taste or smell) 2 feeling: a sense of guilt 3 ability to think and behave sensibly 4 meaning 5 **make sense** to be understandable or seem sensible ▷ verb 6 to become aware of; perceive

senseless adjective 1 (of an act) without meaning or purpose 2 (of a person) unconscious

sensibilities sensibilities noun ability to experience deep feelings

sensible adjective 1 having or showing good sense 2 practical >**sensibly** adverb

sensitive adjective 1 responsive and able to react with understanding 2 easily hurt or offended 3 (of a subject) liable to arouse controversy or strong feelings if not dealt with carefully 4 capable of being affected or harmed **5** (of an instrument) responsive to slight changes > **sensitively** adverb > **sensitivity** noun: *a matter that needs to be handled with sensitivity*

sensor noun device that detects or measures the presence of something, such as radiation, light or heat

sensual adjective **1** having a strong liking for physical pleasures **2** giving pleasure to the body and senses rather than the mind > **sensuality** noun > **sensually** adverb

sensuous adjective pleasing to the senses > **sensuously** adverb

sentence noun **1** sequence of words capable of standing alone as a statement, question or command **2** punishment passed on a criminal ▷ verb **3** to pass sentence on (a convicted person)

sentiment noun **1** feeling, attitude or attitude **2** feelings such as tenderness or sadness: *There's no room for sentiment in business*

sentimental adjective **1** excessively romantic or nostalgic **2** relating to a person's emotions > **sentimentalism** noun > **sentimentality** noun

sentinel noun sentry

sentry sentries noun soldier on guard duty

separate adjective **1** not the same, different **2** set apart **3** not shared, individual ▷ verb **4** (of a couple) to stop living together **5** to act as a barrier between **6** to distinguish between **7** to divide up into parts > **separately** adverb > **separation** noun **1** separating or being separated **2** *Law* living

apart of a married couple without divorce

sepia adjective, noun reddish-brown (pigment)

September noun ninth month of the year

septic adjective (of a wound) infected

sepulchre noun *literary* tomb or burial vault

sequel noun **1** novel, play or film that continues the story of an earlier one **2** consequence, result

sequence noun **1** string (of events) **2** arrangement of two or more things in successive order: *Do things in the right sequence*

sequin noun small, shiny metal disc sewn on clothes to decorate them

Serbian adjective **1** of Serbia ▷ noun **2** person from Serbia **3** form of Serbo-Croat spoken in Serbia

Serbo-Croat adjective, noun (of) the main language spoken in Serbia and Croatia

serenade noun **1** music played or sung outside a woman's window by a lover ▷ verb **2** to sing or play a serenade to (someone)

serene adjective calm, peaceful > **serenely** adverb > **serenity** noun: *It is a place of peace and serenity*

serf noun medieval farm labourer who could not leave the land he worked on

sergeant noun **1** noncommissioned officer in the army or air force **2** police officer ranking between constable and inspector

sergeant major noun noncommissioned army officer of

the highest rank

serial *noun* story or play produced in successive instalments: *a television serial*

serial number *noun* a number given on a product that identifies it and distinguishes it from other products of the same kind

series *noun* **1** group or succession of related things, usually arranged in order **2** set of radio or TV programmes about the same subject or characters

● The plural of *series* is *series*

serious *adjective* **1** giving cause for concern: **2** concerned with important matters **3** not cheerful, grave **4** sincere, not joking >**seriously** *adverb* >**seriousness** *noun*: *He has accepted the seriousness of the situation*

sermon *noun* **1** talk on a religious or moral subject given as part of a church service **2** long moralizing speech

serpent *noun* literary snake

serrated *adjective* having an edge like a saw with toothlike points

servant *noun* person employed to do household work for another

serve *verb* **1** to do useful work for (a person, community, country or cause) **2** to attend to (customers) **3** to dish out food or pour out drinks for (someone) **4** to provide with a service **5** to be a member of the armed forces **6** to spend (time) in prison **7** to act or be used: *the room that served as their office* **8** *Tennis etc* to put (the ball) into play **9** **serve right** to be the just and deserved reward for (someone) ▷ *noun* **10** *Tennis*,

Badminton act of serving the ball

server *noun* Computers computer or computer program that supplies data to other machines on a network

service *noun* **1** system that provides something needed by the public: *the bus service* **2** governmental organization: *the diplomatic service* **3** help and efforts: *services to the community* **4** overhaul of a machine or vehicle **5** formal religious ceremony **6** *Tennis etc* act, manner or right of serving the ball **7** set of matching plates or cups and saucers etc **8 services a** armed forces **b** (on a motorway etc) garage, eating and toilet facilities **9 be of service** to help **10 in service** available for use or in use ▷ *verb* **11** to examine and repair (a machine or vehicle)

serviceman, servicemen *noun* member of the armed forces >**servicewoman** *noun*

service station *noun* garage selling fuel for motor vehicles

servile *adjective* too eager to obey people, fawning; subservient; obsequious >**servility** *noun*

serving *noun* **1** helping (of food) ▷ *adjective* **2** (of a spoon, dish) used for serving food **3** (of an officer, soldier) on active service

session *noun* **1** period spent in an activity **2** meeting of a court, parliament, council or other official group **3** a period during which meetings are held regularly: *the end of the parliamentary session* **4** period during which an activity takes place: *a drinking session*

set sets setting set *noun* **1** number of things or people that belong together or form a group **2** *Maths* group of numbers or objects that satisfy a given condition or share a property **3** television or radio **4** *Tennis* a group of six or more games played as part of a match **5** scenery used in a play or film ▷ *verb* **6** to put in a specified position or state **7** to make ready **8** to make or become firm, solid or hard **9** to establish, arrange **10** to prescribe, assign **11** (of the sun) to go down ▷ *adjective* **12** fixed or established beforehand **13** rigid or inflexible **14 set on** determined to (do something): *He is set on becoming a wrestler* > **set about** *verb* to start > **set back** *verb* **1** to delay **2** *informal* to cost (someone): *A short taxi ride will set you back £12.50* > **set off** *verb* **1** to start a journey **2** to cause (something) to start > **set out** *verb* **1** to start a journey **2** to give yourself the task of (doing something): *I didn't set out to be controversial* > **set up** *verb* to make all the preparations for (something): *He has set up a website*

setback *noun* anything that delays progress

settee *noun* padded seat with arms at either end for two or three people to sit on; sofa

setter *noun* long-haired gun dog

setting *noun* **1** background or surroundings **2** time and place where a film, book, etc is supposed to have taken place **3** plates and cutlery for a single place at table **4** position or level to which the controls of a machine can be adjusted

settle *verb* **1** to arrange or put in order **2** to come to rest **3** to set up home **4** to make quiet, calm or stable **5** to pay (a bill) **6 settle for** or **on** to opt for or agree to: *We settled for orange juice and coffee* > **settle down** *verb* **1** to start living quietly in one place, especially on getting married **2** to become quiet or calm

settlement *noun* **1** an official agreement between people who have been involved in a conflict **2** a place where people have settled and built homes **3** subsidence (of a building)

settler *noun* someone who settles in a new country

seven *adjective, noun* the number 7 > **seventh** *adjective* **1** (coming as) number 7 in a series ▷ *noun* **2** one of seven equal parts

seventeen *adjective, noun* the number 17 > **seventeenth** *adjective, noun* **seventy** *adjective, noun* the number 70 > **seventieth** *adjective, noun*

sever *verb* **1** to cut through or off **2** to break off (a relationship)

several *adjective* **1** some, a few **2** various, separate

severe *adjective* **1** extremely bad or unpleasant **2** stern, strict or harsh **3** plain, sober and forbidding > **severely** *adverb* > **severity** *noun*

sew sews sewing sewed sewn *verb* to join, make or embroider items using a needle and thread or a sewing machine > **sewing** *noun*

sewage *noun* waste matter or excrement carried away in sewers

sewer *noun* drain to remove waste water and sewage

sewerage noun system of sewers

sex noun 1 male or female group: *the two sexes* 2 state of being male or female; gender: *We didn't want to know the sex of the baby* 3 sexual intercourse 4 sexual feelings or behaviour

sexism noun discrimination on the basis of a person's sex

sextet noun 1 group of six performers 2 music for such a group

sextuplet noun one of six children born to the same mother from the same pregnancy

sexual adjective 1 connected with the act of sex or with people's desire for sex: *sexual attraction* 2 relating to the difference between males and females: *sexual equality* 3 relating to the biological process by which people and animals produce young: *sexual reproduction* >**sexually** adverb

sexual intercourse noun physical act of sex between two people

sexuality noun 1 the ability to experience sexual feelings 2 the state of being heterosexual, homosexual or bisexual

sexy sexier sexiest adjective 1 sexually exciting or attractive 2 informal exciting or trendy

shabby shabbier shabbiest adjective 1 old and worn in appearance 2 mean or unfair >**shabbily** adverb

shack noun rough hut

shackle noun 1 one of a pair of metal rings joined by a chain, for fastening around a person's wrists or ankles ▷ verb 2 to fasten with shackles 3 literary to restrict or hamper

shade noun 1 an area of darkness and coolness sheltered from direct sunlight 2 cover used to provide protection from a direct source of light 3 particular hue, tone or variety of a colour 4 **shades** informal sunglasses ▷ verb 5 to screen (something or someone) from light

shadow noun 1 dark shape cast on a surface when something stands between the surface and a source of light 2 patch of shade 3 **be a shadow of your former self** to be much weaker or less impressive than you used to be ▷ verb 4 to cast a shadow over 5 to follow secretly

shadow cabinet noun those members of the main opposition party in Parliament who would be ministers if their party were in power

shadowy adjective 1 (of a place) dark and full of shadows 2 (of a figure or shape) difficult to make out

shady shadier shadiest adjective 1 situated in or giving shade 2 of doubtful honesty or legality

shaft noun 1 long straight and narrow part (of a tool or weapon) 2 ray of light 3 revolving rod that transmits power in a machine: *the drive shaft* 4 vertical passageway: *a lift shaft* 5 one of the bars between which a horse, donkey, etc is harnessed to a cart

shaggy shaggier shaggiest adjective 1 covered with rough hair or wool 2 (of hair, fur) long and untidy

shake shakes shaking shook shaken verb 1 to move quickly up and down or back and forth **2** to move (your head) from side to side in order to say 'no' **3** to make unsteady **4** to tremble **5** to grasp (someone's hand) in greeting or agreement **6** to shock or upset ▷ *noun* **7** shaking **8** vibration

shaky shakier shakiest *adjective* weak and unsteady >**shakily** *adverb*

shall *verb* **1** used as an auxiliary verb to form the future tense or to indicate intention or inevitability **2** used as an auxiliary verb when making suggestions or asking what to do: *Shall I check?*; *Shall we eat out tonight?*

shallow *adjective* **1** not deep **2** not given to deep thought or understanding; superficial

sham shams shamming shammed *noun* **1** thing or person that is not genuine ▷ *adjective* **2** not genuine ▷ *verb* **3** to fake, feign

shambles *noun* confused and disorganized situation or event

shame *noun* **1** guilt and embarrassment that comes from realizing that you have done something bad or foolish **2** capacity to feel such guilt and embarrassment **3** cause of shame: *There is no shame in that* **4** cause for regret: *It's a shame you can't come* ▷ *verb* **5** to cause to feel shame **6** to compel by shame: *They shamed their parents into giving up cigarettes* ▷ *interjection* **7** S Afr informal exclamation of sympathy

shameful *adjective* causing or deserving shame >**shamefully** *adverb*

shameless *adjective* with no sense of shame >**shamelessly** *adverb*

shampoo shampoos shampooing shampooed *noun* **1** soapy liquid used for washing hair, carpets or upholstery **2** wash with shampoo ▷ *verb* **3** to wash (something) with shampoo

shamrock *noun* plant with three round leaves on each stem used as the national emblem of Ireland

shanghai shanghais shanghaiing shanghaied *verb* **1** to force or trick (someone) into doing something ▷ *noun* **2** Aust, NZ catapult

shanty shanties *noun* **1** shack or crude dwelling **2** sailor's traditional song

shape *noun* **1** outward form of an object **2** pattern or mould **3** way in which something is organized **4 in good shape** in good condition or in a good state of health ▷ *verb* **5** to form or mould **6** to influence the development of

shapeless *adjective* without a definite shape

shapely shapelier shapeliest *adjective* (of woman) having an attractive figure

shard *noun* broken piece of pottery or glass

share *verb* **1** to hold (something) jointly or to join with others in doing, using or having (something): *We shared a bottle of champagne* **2** to divide (something) up equally: *We could share the cost between us* ▷ *noun* **3** part of something that belongs to or is contributed by a person **4** one of the equal parts into which the capital stock of a public company is divided >**share out** *verb* to divide (something) equally among a group of people

shareholder noun a person who owns shares in a company

share-milker noun NZ person who works on a dairy farm and shares the profit from the sale of its produce

shark noun 1 large, powerful fish with sharp teeth 2 person who cheats others

sharp adjective 1 (of a knife, needle) having a fine edge or point that is good for cutting or piercing things 2 not gradual 3 clearly defined 4 quick-witted 5 shrill 6 bitter or sour in taste 7 Music above the true pitch ▷ adverb 8 promptly 9 Music too high in pitch ▷ noun 10 Music note, or the symbol for it (♯), that is one semitone above the natural pitch > **sharply** adverb > **sharpness** noun

sharpen verb to make or become sharp or sharper

shatter verb 1 to break into pieces 2 to destroy completely

shattered adjective informal 1 completely exhausted 2 badly upset

shattering adjective causing shock or exhaustion

shave shaves shaving shaved verb 1 to remove (hair) from (the face, head or body) with a razor or shaver 2 to pare away ▷ noun 3 shaving 4 **close shave** informal narrow escape

shaven adjective shaved

shaver noun electric razor

shavings plural noun small, very thin pieces of wood cut off a larger piece; parings

shawl noun piece of cloth worn over a woman's head or shoulders or wrapped around a baby

she pronoun refers to: 1 female person or animal previously mentioned 2 something regarded as female, such as a car, ship or nation

sheaf sheaves noun 1 bundle (of papers) 2 tied bundle (of reaped corn)

shear shears shearing sheared or **shorn** verb 1 to clip hair or wool from (a sheep) 2 to cut through

shearer noun someone whose job is to shear sheep

sheath noun 1 close-fitting cover, especially for a knife or sword 2 Brit, Aust, NZ condom

shed sheds shedding shed noun 1 building used for storage or shelter or as a workshop ▷ verb 2 to cast off (skin, hair or leaves) 3 to weep (tears) 4 formal to get rid of: The firm is to shed 700 jobs 5 to drop (a load): A lorry had shed a load 6 **shed light (on)** to make clearer

sheen noun soft shine on the surface of something

sheep noun farm animal bred for wool and meat

● The plural of sheep is sheep

sheep-dip noun liquid disinfectant used to keep sheep clean and free of pests

sheepdog noun breed of dog often used for herding sheep

sheepish adjective embarrassed because of feeling foolish > **sheepishly** adverb

sheepskin noun skin of a sheep with the fleece still on, used for making rugs and coats

sheer adjective 1 absolute, complete: sheer folly

2 perpendicular, steep: *a sheer cliff* **3** (of material) so fine as to be transparent

sheet *noun* **1** large piece of fine cloth used under blankets or duvets as bedding **2** fine rectangular piece of any material

sheikh or **sheik** *noun* Arab chief

shelf shelves *noun* flat piece of wood, metal or glass fixed horizontally and used for putting things on

shell *noun* **1** hard outer covering of an egg, nut or certain animals **2** external frame of something: *The room was just an empty shell* **3** explosive device fired from a large gun ▷ *verb* **4** to remove the shell or outer covering from (peas, nuts) **5** to fire at (a place) with artillery shells

shellfish shellfish or **shellfishes** *noun* a small, usually edible, sea creature with a shell

shelter *noun* **1** building or structure providing protection from danger or the weather **2** protection ▷ *verb* **3** to give shelter to **4** to take shelter

sheltered *adjective* **1** (of a place) protected from wind and rain **2** (of a life) away from unpleasant or upsetting things **3** (of accommodation for the elderly or handicapped) offering specially equipped and monitored facilities

shelve *verb* to put aside or postpone

shepherd *noun* **1** person who tends sheep ▷ *verb* **2** to guide or watch over (people)

sheriff *noun* **1** (in the US) chief law enforcement officer of a county **2** (in England and Wales) person

appointed by the king or queen to carry out ceremonial duties **3** (in Scotland) chief judge of a district **4** (in Australia) officer of the Supreme Court

sherry sherries *noun* pale or dark brown fortified wine

shield *noun* **1** piece of armour carried on the arm to protect the body from blows or missiles **2** anything that protects ▷ *verb* **3** to protect

shift *verb* **1** to move **2** to transfer (blame or responsibility) **3** to remove or be removed **4** (of an opinion, situation) to change ▷ *noun* **5** set period during which different groups of people work in a factory or the people assigned to a particular period: *the night shift*

shilling *noun* former British, Australian and New Zealand coin worth one-twentieth of a pound; in Britain replaced by the 5p piece

shimmer *verb* **1** to shine with a faint flickering light ▷ *noun* **2** a faint, flickering light

shin shins shinning shinned *noun* **1** front of the lower leg ▷ *verb* **2** to climb (a pole or tree) quickly, gripping with your arms and legs

shine *verb* **shines shining shone** **1** to give out or reflect light **2** to aim (a light or torch) **3** to be very good (at something) ▷ *noun* **4** brightness or lustre

shingle *noun* **1** small pebble found on beaches **2** small wooden roof tile

shining *adjective* **1** bright, gleaming **2** **shining example** very good or typical example

shiny shinier shiniest *adjective* bright, polished-looking

ship ships shipping shipped
noun 1 a large boat which carries passengers or cargo; vessel ▷ verb 2 to send or transport (something or someone) somewhere, sometimes by ship

-ship suffix used to form nouns that refer to a condition or position: fellowship

shipment noun 1 a quantity of goods transported somewhere: a shipment of olive oil 2 transporting (of cargo)

shipping noun 1 business of transporting cargo on ships 2 ships collectively

shipwreck noun 1 destruction of a ship through storm or collision 2 wrecked ship ▷ verb 3 to leave (someone) a survivor of a shipwreck

shipyard noun place where ships are built

shiralee noun Aust old-fashioned bundle of possessions carried by a swagman

shire noun 1 Brit old-fashioned county 2 Aust rural area with an elected council

shirk verb to avoid (duty or work)

shirt noun lightweight, blouse-like piece of clothing worn especially by men and boys, typically having a collar, sleeves and buttons down the front

shiver verb 1 to tremble, as from cold or fear ▷ noun 2 slight tremble, as from cold or fear

shoal noun large number of fish swimming together

shock noun 1 sudden upsetting experience 2 sudden violent blow or impact 3 something causing this 4 serious medical condition in which the blood cannot circulate properly, brought about by physical or mental shock 5 pain and muscular spasm caused by an electric current passing through the body 6 bushy mass (of hair) ▷ verb 7 to horrify or astonish 8 to offend or scandalize >shocked adjective >shocker noun >shocking adjective 1 informal very bad 2 rude or immoral

shock absorber noun one of the devices fitted near a vehicle's wheels to help prevent it bouncing up and down

shoddy shoddier shoddiest adjective made or done badly

shoe shoes shoeing shod noun 1 type of protective footwear that covers the foot, ends below the ankle and has a hard sole 2 horseshoe ▷ verb 3 to fit (a horse) with a horseshoe or horseshoes

shoestring noun on a shoestring using a very small amount of money

shoot shoots shooting shot verb 1 to hit, wound or kill (a person or animal) by firing a gun at them 2 to fire (an arrow or a bolt) from a bow or crossbow 3 to hunt 4 to send out or move rapidly: They shot back into Green Street 5 (of a plant) to sprout 6 to photograph or film: The whole film was shot in California 7 Sport to take a shot at goal ▷ noun 8 new branch or sprout of a plant 9 hunting expedition

shooting noun an incident in which someone is shot

shooting star noun meteor

shop shops shopping shopped

noun 1 place where things are sold 2 workshop: *a bicycle repair shop* 3 **talk shop** to discuss work, especially on a social occasion ▷ **verb** 4 to go to the shops to buy things 5 *Brit, Aust, NZ informal* to inform against ▷ **shopper** *noun*: *Christmas shoppers*

shopkeeper *noun* someone who owns or manages a small shop

shoplifting *noun* practice of stealing goods from shops

shopping *noun* 1 goods bought from shops 2 activity of buying things

shop steward *noun* (in some countries) trade-union official elected to represent his or her fellow workers

shore *noun* 1 edge of a sea or lake ▷ **verb** 2 **shore up** to reinforce, strengthen or prop (something) up

shoreline *noun* the edge of a sea, lake or wide river

shorn *verb* 1 a past participle of **shear** ▷ **adjective** 2 (of grass, hair) cut very short

short *adjective* 1 not long: *a short distance* 2 not tall: *He's short and plump.* 3 not lasting long, brief: *a short time* 4 deficient: *short of cash* 5 abrupt, rude: *She was a bit short with me.* 6 (of a drink) consisting chiefly of a spirit 7 (of pastry) crumbly ▷ **adverb** 8 abruptly ▷ **noun** 9 drink of spirits 10 short film 11 *informal* short circuit

shortage *noun* deficiency

shortbread or **shortcake** *noun* crumbly biscuit made with butter

short circuit *noun* electrical fault that occurs when two points accidentally become connected

and the electricity travels directly between them rather than through the complete circuit

shortcoming *noun* failing or defect

shortcut *noun* quicker route or method

shorten *verb* to make or become shorter

shortfall *noun* smaller amount than needed

shorthand *noun* system of rapid writing using symbols to represent words

short-list *verb* to put on a short list

shortly *adverb* 1 soon 2 rudely

short-sighted *adjective* 1 unable to see distant things clearly 2 not taking account of possible future events

short-term *adjective* happening or having an effect within a short time or for a short time

shot *verb* 1 past of **shoot** ▷ *noun* 2 shooting 3 small lead pellets used in a shotgun 4 person with specified skill in shooting: *a good shot* 5 *informal* attempt: *someone who would have a shot at explaining it* 6 *Sport* act or instance of hitting, kicking or throwing the ball 7 photograph 8 uninterrupted film sequence 9 *informal* injection 10 **like a shot** *informal* quickly and eagerly

shotgun *noun* gun for firing a lot of small pellets at once

shot put *noun* athletic event in which contestants throw a heavy metal ball as far as possible ▷ **shot-putter** *noun* person who takes part in shot putting events

should *verb* 1 ought to: *He should*

have done better. **2** to be likely to: *He should have heard by now.* **3** *formal* would: *I should like to express my thanks.* **4** sometimes used in subordinate clauses after *that: It is inevitable that you should go* **5** was to or were to: *if he should die prematurely*

shoulder *noun* **1** part of the body to which an arm, foreleg or wing is attached **2** part of a piece of clothing that covers your shoulders **3** cut of meat including the upper foreleg **4** side of a road ▷ *verb* **5** to bear (a burden or responsibility) **6** to put on your shoulder

shoulder blade *noun* either of the two large flat triangular bones in the upper part of your back, below your shoulders

shout *noun* **1** loud cry ▷ *verb* **2** to cry out loudly > **shout down** *verb* to silence (someone) or to prevent (someone) from being heard by shouting

shove *verb* **1** to push roughly **2** *informal* to put ▷ *noun* **3** rough push > **shove off** *verb informal* to go away

shovel shovels shovelling shovelled *noun* **1** tool for lifting or moving loose material ▷ *verb* **2** to lift or move (something) as with a shovel

show shows showing showed shown *verb* **1** to make, be or become noticeable or visible **2** to exhibit or display: *Show me your passport* **3** to indicate or prove **4** to demonstrate: *Show me how it works.* **5** to guide or lead: *I'll show you to your room.* **6** to reveal or display (an emotion) ▷ *noun* **7** public exhibition

8 entertainment on television or at the theatre etc **9** mere display or pretence > **show off** *verb* **1** *informal* to try to impress people by behaving in a flamboyant manner **2** to allow others to see (something) to invite admiration > **show up** *verb* **1** *informal* to arrive **2** to reveal or be revealed clearly **3** to expose the faults or defects of **4** *informal* to embarrass

show business *noun* the entertainment industry

showdown *noun informal* confrontation that settles a dispute

shower *noun* **1** device for washing that sprays you with water **2** wash under such a device **3** short period of rain, hail or snow **4** sudden fall of a lot of objects ▷ *verb* **5** to wash in a shower **6** to give (a lot of things) or present (someone) with a lot of things

showing *noun* public presentation or viewing (of a film or television programme)

showjumping *noun* competitive sport of riding horses to demonstrate skill in jumping

show-off *noun informal* person who tries to impress people with their knowledge or skills

showroom *noun* room in which goods for sale are on display

showy showier showiest *adjective* large or bright and intended to impress; ostentatious > **showily** *adverb*

shrapnel *noun* **1** artillery shell filled with pellets which scatter on explosion **2** fragments from this

shred shreds shredding

shredded noun **1** long narrow strip torn from something **2** small amount ▷ verb **3** to tear to shreds

shrew noun **1** small mouselike animal **2** offensive bad-tempered nagging woman

shrewd adjective clever and perceptive > **shrewdly** adverb > **shrewdness** noun: the shrewdness of that decision

shriek noun **1** shrill cry ▷ verb **2** to utter (with) a shriek

shrill adjective (of a sound) sharp and high-pitched > **shrillness** noun > **shrilly** adverb

shrimp noun small edible shellfish

shrine noun place of worship associated with a sacred person or object

shrink shrinks shrinking shrank shrunk verb **1** to become or make smaller **2** to recoil or withdraw ▷ noun **3** informal psychiatrist > **shrinkage** noun decrease in size, value or weight

shrivel shrivels shrivelling shrivelled verb to shrink and wither

shroud noun **1** piece of cloth used to wrap a dead body **2** anything which conceals ▷ verb **3** to conceal: achievements that have remained shrouded in mystery

shrub noun a low, bushy plant

shrug shrugs shrugging shrugged verb **1** to raise and then drop (the shoulders) as a sign of indifference, ignorance or doubt ▷ noun **2** act of shrugging your shoulders

shrunken adjective formal reduced in size: a shrunken old man

shudder verb **1** to shake or tremble violently, especially with horror ▷ noun **2** shiver of fear or horror

shuffle verb **1** to walk without lifting your feet properly **2** shuffle about to move about and fidget **3** to mix (cards) up thoroughly ▷ noun **4** act of shuffling

shun shuns shunning shunned verb to avoid

shunt verb to move (objects or people) to a different position

shut shuts shutting shut verb to close > **shut down** verb to close permanently > **shut up** verb informal to stop talking

shutter noun **1** hinged doorlike cover for closing off a window **2** device in a camera that opens to allow light through the lens when a photograph is taken

shuttle noun **1** plane or other vehicle that goes to and fro between two places **2** instrument that passes the weft thread between the warp threads in weaving ▷ adjective **3** (of services) involving a plane, bus or train service that travels to and fro between two places

shuttlecock noun feathered object used as a ball in the game of badminton

shy shyer shyest; shies shying shied adjective **1** nervous and uncomfortable in company; timid **2** shy of cautious or wary of ▷ verb **3** (of a horse) to move away suddenly because startled or afraid **4** to shy away from to avoid (doing something) through fear or lack of confidence > **shyly** adverb > **shyness** noun

sibling noun formal brother or sister

sick *adjective* **1** ill **2 feel sick** to feel nauseous and likely to vomit **3 be sick** to vomit **4** *informal* (of a person, story, joke) showing an unpleasant and frivolous disrespect for something sad **5 sick of** *informal* disgusted by or weary of >**sickness** *noun*

sicken *verb* to make (someone) nauseated or disgusted >**sickening** *adjective: a string of sickening attacks*

sickle *noun* tool with a short handle and a curved blade for cutting grass or grain

sickly sicklier sickliest *adjective* **1** unhealthy or weak **2** causing revulsion or nausea

side *noun* **1** either of two halves into which something can be divided **2** either surface of a flat object **3** surface or edge of something, especially when neither the front nor the back **4** area immediately next to a person or thing **5** aspect or part **6** one of two opposing groups or teams **7** slope (of a hill) **8** television channel **9 on the side a** as an extra **b** unofficially ▷ *adjective* **10** at or on the side: *the side door* **11** of lesser importance: *a side road* > **side with** *verb* to support (one side in a dispute)

sideboard *noun* a long, low cupboard for plates and glasses in a dining room

sideburns *plural noun* areas of hair growing on a man's cheeks in front of his ears

side effect *noun* (of a drug) additional undesirable effect

sidekick *noun informal* close friend or associate

sideline *noun* **1** extra interest or source of income **2** *Sport* line marking the boundary of a playing area

sideshow *noun* stall at a fairground

sidestep sidesteps sidestepping sidestepped *verb* to dodge (an issue)

sidewalk *noun* US paved path for pedestrians, at the side of a road; pavement

sideways *adverb* **1** to or from the side **2** obliquely

siding *noun* short stretch of railway track beside the main tracks where engines and carriages are left when not in use

sidle *verb* to walk in a furtive manner

siege *noun* military operation in which an army surrounds a place and prevents food or help from reaching the people inside

sieve *noun* **1** utensil with mesh through which a substance is sifted or strained ▷ *verb* **2** to sift or strain through a sieve

sift *verb* **1** to pass (a substance) through a sieve to remove lumps **2** to examine (information or evidence) to select what is important

sigh *noun* **1** long audible breath expressing sadness, tiredness, relief or longing ▷ *verb* **2** to let out a sigh

sight *noun* **1** ability to see **2** range of vision **3** something seen: *It was a ghastly sight* **4** thing worth seeing: *Tim was eager to see the sights.* **5** device for guiding the eye while using a gun or optical instrument **6** *informal* a lot ▷ *verb*

7 to catch sight of
- Do not confuse the spellings of *sight* and *site*

sighted *adjective* able to see

sighting *noun* instance of something rare or unexpected being seen

sightseeing *noun* visiting places that tourists usually visit >**sightseer** *noun*: *For centuries, sightseers have flocked to this site*

sign *noun* **1** indication of something not immediately or outwardly observable **2** gesture, mark or symbol conveying a meaning **3** notice displayed to advertise, inform or warn **4** omen ▷ *verb* **5** to write (your name) on (a document or letter) to show its authenticity or your agreement **6** to communicate using sign language **7** to make a sign or gesture >**sign on** *verb* to register as unemployed >**sign up** *verb* to sign a document committing yourself to a job, course, etc

signal signals signalling signalled *noun* **1** sign or gesture to convey information **2** piece of equipment beside a railway track which tells train drivers whether to stop or not **3** sequence of electrical impulses or radio waves transmitted or received ▷ *verb* **4** to convey (information) by signal

signature *noun* **1** person's name written by himself or herself in his or her usual style when signing **2** sign at the start of a piece of music to show the key or tempo

significant *adjective* **1** important **2** having or expressing a meaning **3** (of amount) large >**significance** *noun*: *We didn't appreciate the significance of this till later* >**significantly** *adverb*

signify signifies signifying signified *verb* **1** to indicate or suggest **2** to be a symbol or sign for

sign language or **signing** *noun* system of communication by gestures, as used by deaf people

signpost *noun* road sign with information on it, such as the name of a town and how far away it is

Sikh *noun* person who believes in Sikhism, an Indian religion which separated from Hinduism in the sixteenth century and which teaches that there is only one God >**Sikhism** *noun*

silence *noun* **1** absence of noise or speech ▷ *verb* **2** to make (someone or something) silent

silent *adjective* **1** not saying a word; uncommunicative **2** not making a sound; quiet >**silently** *adverb*

silhouette *noun* outline of a dark shape seen against a light background >**silhouetted** *adjective*: *chimney-stacks silhouetted against the sky*

silicon *noun* brittle nonmetallic element widely used in chemistry and industry

silk *noun* **1** fibre made by the silkworm **2** thread or fabric made from this

silkworm *noun* larva of a particular kind of moth

silky or **silken** *adjective* of or like silk; smooth and soft

sill *noun* ledge at the bottom of a window or door

silly sillier silliest *adjective* foolish

silt noun **1** mud deposited by moving water ▷ verb **2** **silt up** (of a river, lake) to fill or be choked with silt

silver noun **1** valuable greyish-white metallic element used for making jewellery and ornaments **2** coins or articles made of silver or silver-coloured metal ▷ adjective, noun **3** greyish-white

silverbeet noun Aust, NZ leafy green vegetable with white stalks

silver fern noun NZ tall fern found in New Zealand. It is the symbol of New Zealand national sports teams

silverfish silverfishes or **silverfish** noun small silver-coloured insect with no wings

silver jubilee noun 25th anniversary of an important event

silver medal noun a medal made from silver, or something resembling this, awarded to the competitor who comes second in a competition

silver wedding noun 25th wedding anniversary

silvery adjective having the appearance or colour of silver

similar adjective **1** alike but not identical **2** Geometry (of triangles) having the same angles ▷ **similarly** adverb

similarity similarities noun similar quality; resemblance

simile noun figure of speech comparing one thing to another, using as or like: He's as white as a sheet; She runs like a deer

simmer verb **1** to cook gently at just below boiling point **2** to be in a state of suppressed rage

simple adjective **1** easy to understand or do **2** plain or unpretentious **3** not combined or complex **4** having some degree of mental retardation **5** no more than; mere > **simplicity** noun quality of being simple

simple-minded adjective not very intelligent or sophisticated

simplify simplifies simplifying simplified verb to make less complicated > **simplification** noun

simplistic adjective too simple or naive

simply adverb **1** merely or just **2** in a way that is easy to understand **3** plainly or unpretentiously

simulate verb **1** to make a pretence of **2** to reproduce the characteristics of **3** to have the appearance of > **simulation** noun > **simulator** noun device designed to reproduce actual conditions, for example in order to train pilots or astronauts

simultaneous adjective occurring at the same time > **simultaneously** adverb

sin sinning sinned noun **1** wicked and immoral behaviour **2** offence against a principle or standard, especially a religious one **3** **live in sin** old-fashioned (of an unmarried couple) to live together as if married ▷ verb **4** to do something wicked and immoral

since preposition **1** during the period of time from: I've been waiting here since half past three ▷ conjunction **2** from the time when: We've known each other since we were kids **3** for the reason that: I'm forever on a diet, since I put on weight easily ▷ adverb **4** from that time: *They split up and he has since remarried*

sincere *adjective* without pretence or deceit > **sincerity** *noun*: *There is no doubting their sincerity*

sincerely *adverb* **1** genuinely **2 Yours sincerely** ending for formal letters addressed and written to a named person

sinew *noun* **1** tough fibrous tissue joining muscle to bone **2** muscles or strength

sinful *adjective* wicked and immoral

sing sings singing sang sung *verb* **1** to make musical sounds with the voice **2** to perform (a song) **3** (of a bird, insect) to make a humming or whistling sound > **singer** *noun* person who sings, especially professionally

singe singes singeing singed *verb* **1** to burn the surface of ▷ *noun* **2** a slight burn

single *adjective* **1** one only **2** unmarried **3** designed for one user: *a single bed* **4** (of a ticket) valid for an outward journey only **5 in single file** (of people or things) arranged in one line ▷ *noun* **6** thing intended for one person **7** single ticket **8** recording of one or two short pieces of music on a record, CD or cassette **9 singles** game between two players > **single out** *verb* to pick out from others > **singly** *adverb* on your own or one by one

single-handed *adjective* without assistance

single-minded *adjective* having one aim only

singular *adjective* **1** (of a word or form) denoting one person or thing **2** remarkable, unusual ▷ *noun* **3** singular form of a word > **singularity** *noun* > **singularly** *adverb*

sinister *adjective* seeming evil or harmful

sink sinks sinking sank sunk or **sunken** *noun* **1 a** a basin with taps supplying water, usually in a kitchen ▷ *verb* **2** to move or cause to move downwards, especially through water: *An Indian cargo ship sank in icy seas* **3** to descend or cause to descend: *He sank into black despair* **4** to decline in value or amount **5** to become weaker **6** to dig or drill (a hole or shaft) **7** to make (a knife, your teeth) go deeply into something **8** to invest (money) > **sink in** *verb* (of a fact) to penetrate the mind

sinner *noun* person who has committed a sin

sinus **sinuses** *noun* air passage in the skull

sip sips sipping sipped *verb* **1** to drink in small mouthfuls ▷ *noun* **2** amount sipped

siphon or **syphon** *verb* to draw (a liquid) out of something through a tube and transfer it to another place

sir *noun* **1** polite term of address for a man **2 Sir** title of a knight or baronet

siren *noun* **1** device making a loud wailing noise as a warning **2** *literary* dangerously alluring woman

sirloin *noun* prime cut of loin of beef

sis or **sies** *interjection* S Afr informal

exclamation of disgust

sister noun **1** girl or woman with the same parents as another person **2** female fellow-member of a group **3** senior nurse **4** nun ▷ adjective **5** closely related; similar

sisterhood noun strong feeling of companionship between women

sister-in-law sisters-in-law noun **1** your husband's or wife's sister **2** your brother's wife

sit sits sitting sat verb **1** to have your body bent at the hips so that your weight is on your buttocks rather than your feet **2** (also **sit down**) to lower yourself to a sitting position **3** to perch **4** (of an official body) to hold a session **5** to take (an examination)

sitcom noun informal a television comedy series which shows characters in amusing situations; situation comedy

site noun **1** piece of ground where a particular thing happens or is situated **2** same as **website** ▷ verb **3** to provide with a site

● Do not confuse the spellings of site and sight.

sitting noun **1** one of the times when a meal is served **2** one of the occasions when a parliament or law court meets and carries out its work

sitting room noun room in a house where people sit and relax; living room

situated adjective located

situation noun **1** state of affairs **2** old-fashioned location and surroundings **3** position of employment

Siva proper noun Hindu god and one of the Trimurti

six adjective, noun the number 6

sixteen adjective, noun the number 16 ▷ **sixteenth** adjective, noun

sixth adjective, noun **1** (coming as) number 6 in a series ▷ noun **2** one of six equal parts

sixth sense noun instinctive awareness

sixty sixties adjective, noun the number 60 ▷ **sixtieth** adjective, noun

sizable or **sizeable** adjective quite large

size noun **1** dimensions, bigness **2** one of a series of standard measurements of goods ▷ **size up** verb informal to assess

sizzle verb to make a hissing sound like frying fat

sjambok noun S Afr long whip made from animal hide

skate skates skating skated noun **1** boot with a steel blade attached to the sole for gliding over ice; ice skate **2** item of footwear with a set of wheels attached for gliding over a hard surface; roller skate **3** large edible sea fish ▷ verb **4** to glide on or as if on skates ▷ **skate over** or **round** verb to avoid discussing or dealing with (a matter) fully

skateboard noun narrow board on small wheels for riding on while standing up

skeleton noun **1** framework of bones inside a person's or animal's body ▷ adjective **2** (of staff, a workforce) reduced to a minimum

sketch noun **1** quick, rough drawing **2** brief description **3** short humorous play ▷ verb **4** to make a sketch (of something or someone) **5** to give a brief description of

sketchy sketchier sketchiest *adjective* incomplete or inadequate

skew or **skewed** *adjective* slanting or crooked

skewer *noun* **1** pin to hold meat together during cooking ▷ *verb* **2** to push a skewer through

ski skis skiing skied *noun* **1** one of a pair of long runners fastened to boots for gliding over snow or water ▷ *verb* **2** to travel on skis > **skier** *noun* person who skis

skid skids skidding skidded *verb* **1** (of a moving vehicle) to slide sideways uncontrollably ▷ *noun* **2** instance of skidding

skilful *adjective* having or showing skill; able > **skilfully** *adverb*

skill *noun* **1** special ability or expertise **2** something requiring special training or expertise

skilled *adjective* **1** having the knowledge and ability to do something well **2** (of work) requiring special training

skim skims skimming skimmed *verb* **1** to remove floating matter from the surface of (a liquid) **2** to glide smoothly over (a surface) **3** to read (a book) quickly

skimmed milk *noun* milk from which the cream has been removed

skin skins skinning skinned *noun* **1** outer covering of the body **2** complexion **3** outer layer or covering **4** film on a liquid **5** animal skin used as a material or container ▷ *verb* **6** to remove the skin of (an animal)

skinny skinnier skinniest *adjective* very thin

skip skips skipping skipped *verb* **1** to leap lightly from one foot to the other **2** to jump over a rope as it is swung under one **3** *informal* to pass over or omit ▷ *noun* **4** little jump from one foot to the other **5** large metal container for holding rubbish and rubble

skipper *noun* *informal* captain (of a ship)

skirmish *noun* brief or minor fight or argument ▷ *verb*

skirt *noun* **1** piece of woman's clothing that hangs down over the legs from the waist ▷ *verb* **2** to border **3** to go round **4** to avoid dealing with (an issue)

skirting board *noun* narrow board round the bottom of an interior wall

skite *Aust, NZ informal verb* **1** to boast ▷ *noun* **2** boast

skittle *noun* bottle-shaped object used as a target in some games

skull *noun* bony part of the head surrounding the brain

skunk *noun* small black-and-white North American mammal which lets out a foul-smelling fluid when attacked

sky skies *noun* the space around the earth which you can see when you look upwards

skylight *noun* window in a roof or ceiling

skyline *noun* **1** line where the earth and the sky appear to meet **2** outline of buildings, trees, etc against the sky

skyscraper *noun* very tall building

slab *noun* thick, flat piece of something

slack adjective **1** not tight **2** not busy **3** not thorough; negligent ▷ noun **4** part (of a rope) that is not taut ▷ verb **5** to neglect your work or duty >**slackness** noun

slacken verb to make or become slack

slag slags slagging slagged noun **1** waste material left after ore has been melted down to remove the metal ▷ verb **2 slag off** informal to criticize

slalom noun skiing competition in which competitors have to twist and turn quickly to avoid obstacles

slam slams slamming slammed verb **1** to shut, put down or hit (something) violently and noisily ▷ noun **2** act or sound of slamming

slander noun **1** false and potentially damaging claim about a person **2** crime of making such a statement ▷ verb **3** to make false and potentially damaging claims about a person >**slanderous** adjective: false or slanderous statements that damage a person's reputation

slang noun very informal language

slant verb **1** to lean at an angle; slope **2** to present (information) in a biased way ▷ noun **3** slope **4** point of view, especially a biased one

slap slaps slapping slapped noun **1** blow with the open hand or a flat object ▷ verb **2** to strike with the open hand or a flat object **3** informal to put (someone or something somewhere) forcefully or carelessly

slash verb **1** to cut with a long, sweeping stroke **2** to reduce drastically ▷ noun **3** a diagonal line used for separating letters, words or numbers (/); stroke

slat noun narrow strip of wood or metal >**slatted** adjective: slatted wooden blinds

slate noun **1** rock which splits easily into thin layers **2** piece of this for covering a roof or, formerly, for writing on ▷ verb **3** informal to criticize (something or someone) harshly

slaughter verb **1** to kill (animals) for food **2** to kill (people) savagely or indiscriminately ▷ noun **3** mass killing; massacre

slave noun **1** person owned by another person and forced to work for them **2** person who is dominated by another person or by a habit ▷ verb **3** to work like a slave >**slavery** noun **1** state or condition of being a slave **2** practice of owning slaves

slay slays slaying slew slain verb literary to kill

sleazy sleazier sleaziest adjective run-down or sordid

sled noun sledge

sledge noun vehicle on runners for sliding on snow

sledgehammer noun large, heavy hammer

sleek adjective **1** glossy, smooth and shiny **2** (of a person) rich and elegant in appearance

sleep sleeps sleeping slept noun **1** natural state of rest in which your eyes are closed and you are unconscious **2** period spent sleeping; nap **3 put to sleep** to kill (a sick or injured animal) painlessly ▷ verb **4** to be asleep **5** (of a house, flat, etc) to have beds for (a specified number of people) > **sleep together** verb to have sexual intercourse > **sleep with** verb to have sexual intercourse with

sleeper noun 1 person who sleeps in a specified way: *I'm a very heavy sleeper* 2 bed on a train 3 railway car fitted for sleeping in 4 beam supporting the rails of a railway 5 ring worn in a pierced ear to stop the hole from closing up

sleeping bag noun padded bag for sleeping in

sleeping pill noun pill which you take to help you sleep

sleepout noun 1 *Aust* area of veranda or porch closed off for use as a bedroom 2 *NZ* small building for sleeping in

sleepover noun *informal* overnight stay at someone else's house

sleepwalk verb to walk around while asleep

sleepy sleepier sleepiest adjective 1 tired and ready to go to sleep 2 (of a town or village) very quiet > **sleepily** adverb > **sleepiness** noun

sleet noun mixed rain and snow or hail

sleeve noun 1 part of a piece of clothing that covers your arms or upper arms 2 tubelike cover 3 (of a record) cover > **sleeveless** adjective: *a sleeveless pullover*

sleigh noun sledge

slender adjective 1 attractively slim 2 small in amount

sleuth noun detective

slew verb 1 past tense of **slay** 2 (of a vehicle) to skid or swing round

slice noun 1 thin flat piece cut from something 2 share 3 kitchen

utensil with a broad flat blade 4 *Sport* instance of hitting a ball so that it goes to one side rather than straight ahead ▷ verb 5 to cut into slices 6 *Sport* to hit (a ball) with a slice 7 **slice through** to cut or move through (something) quickly, like a knife

slick adjective 1 (of an action) skilfully and quickly done 2 (of a person) persuasive but insincere 3 (of a book, film) well-made and attractive, but superficial ▷ noun 4 patch of oil on water

slide slides sliding slid verb 1 to slip smoothly along (a surface) ▷ noun 2 small piece of photographic film which can be projected onto a screen so that you can see the picture 3 small piece of glass on which you put something for viewing under a microscope 4 structure with a steep, slippery slope for children to slide down 5 ornamental hair clip

slight adjective 1 small in quantity or extent 2 not important 3 slim and delicate ▷ verb 4 to snub ▷ noun 5 snub > **slightly** adverb

slim slimmer slimmest; slims slimming slimmed adjective 1 not heavy or stout, thin 2 slight ▷ verb 3 to make or become slim by diet and exercise > **slimmer** noun

slime noun unpleasant, thick, slippery substance

slimy slimier slimiest adjective 1 like slime or covered with slime 2 showing excessive and insincere helpfulness and friendliness; ingratiating

sling slings slinging slung noun 1 bandage hung from the neck to support an injured hand or arm **2** rope or strap for lifting something **3** strap with a string at each end for throwing a stone ▷ *verb* **4** to throw or put as if with a sling

slip slips slipping slipped *verb* **1** to slide accidentally, losing your balance **2** to go smoothly, easily or quietly: *She slipped out of the house* **3** to put something (somewhere) easily or quickly **4** to pass out of (your mind): *It slipped my mind* ▷ *noun* **5** act of slipping **6** mistake **7** piece of clothing worn under a dress or skirt; petticoat **8** small piece of paper) **9** give someone the slip to escape from someone >**slip up** *verb* to make a mistake

slipped disc *noun* painful condition in which one of the discs connecting the bones of your spine moves out of its position

slipper *noun* loose, soft shoe for indoor wear

slippery *adjective* **1** smooth, wet or greasy and therefore difficult to hold or walk on **2** (of a person) untrustworthy

slippery dip *noun Aust informal* children's slide at a playground or funfair

slip rail *noun Aust, NZ* fence that can be slipped out of place to make an opening

slipstream *noun* the flow of air behind a fast-moving object, such as a car or plane

slit slits slitting slit *noun* **1** long narrow cut or opening ▷ *verb* **2** to make a long, straight cut in

slither *verb* to slide in an uneven manner

sliver *noun* small thin piece

slob *noun informal* lazy and untidy person

slog slogs slogging slogged *verb* to work hard and steadily

slogan *noun* a short, easily-remembered phrase used in politics or advertising; catch-phrase

slop slops slopping slopped *verb* **1** to splash or spill ▷ *noun* **2** slops dirty water or liquid waste

slope *noun* **1** surface that is higher at one end than at the other; incline **2** the angle at which something slopes; gradient **3** slopes hills ▷ *verb* **4** (of a surface) to be higher at one end than at the other **5** to lean to one side: *sloping handwriting*

sloppy sloppier sloppiest *adjective* **1** careless or untidy **2** foolishly sentimental >**sloppily** *adverb* >**sloppiness** *noun*

slot slots slotting slotted *noun* **1** narrow opening for putting something in **2** *informal* place in a schedule, scheme or organization ▷ *verb* **3** to fit into a slot

sloth *noun* **1** laziness **2** a South and Central American animal that moves very slowly and hangs upside down from the branches of trees

slouch *verb* to sit, stand or move with a drooping posture

slouch hat *noun Aust* hat with a wide, flexible brim, especially an Australian army hat with the left side of the brim turned up

Slovak *adjective* **1** belonging to or relating to Slovakia ▷ *noun* **2** someone from Slovakia **3** language spoken in Slovakia

slow *adjective* **1** taking a longer time than is usual or expected **2** not fast **3** (of a clock or watch) showing a time earlier than the correct one **4** not clever ▷ *verb* **5** (often followed by *down, up*) to become less fast **6** to reduce the speed (of) >**slowly** *adverb* >**slowness** *noun*

slow motion *noun* movement that is much slower than normal, especially in a film

sludge *noun* **1** thick mud **2** sewage

slug *noun* **1** small, slow-moving creature with a slimy body, like a snail without a shell **2** *informal* mouthful (of an alcoholic drink) **3** bullet

sluggish *adjective* slow-moving, lacking energy >**sluggishly** *adverb* >**sluggishness** *noun*: *the sluggishness of the economy*

sluice *noun* **1** channel carrying off water **2** sliding gate used to control the flow of water in this; sluicegate ▷ *verb* **3** to pour water over or through

slum slums slumming slummed *noun* **1** squalid overcrowded house or area ▷ *verb* **2** to be temporarily experiencing poorer places or conditions than usual

slumber *literary noun* **1** sleep ▷ *verb* **2** to sleep

slump *verb* **1** (of prices or demand) to fall suddenly and dramatically **2** (of a person) to sink or fall heavily ▷ *noun* **3** a sudden, severe drop in prices or demand **4** time of unemployment and economic decline

slur slurs slurring slurred *verb* **1** to pronounce or say (words) indistinctly **2** *Music* to sing or play (notes) smoothly without a break ▷ *noun* **3** slurring of words **4** remark intended to discredit someone **5** *Music* **a** slurring of notes **b** curved line indicating notes to be slurred

slurp *informal verb* **1** to eat or drink noisily ▷ *noun* **2** slurping sound

slush *noun* **1** wet, melting snow **2** *informal* sloppy sentimental talk or writing >**slushy** *adjective*: *a slushy romance*

slut *noun offensive* **1** dirty, untidy woman **2** immoral woman

sly slyer or **slier slyest** or **sliest** *adjective* **1** crafty **2** secretive and cunning **3** roguish **4 on the sly** secretly >**slyly** *adverb*

smack *verb* **1** to slap (someone) sharply **2 smack of** to suggest or be reminiscent of: *His tale smacks of fantasy* **3 smack your lips** to open and close (your lips) loudly in enjoyment or anticipation ▷ *noun* **4** sharp slap **5** slapping sound **6** small fishing boat **7** *informal* heroin ▷ *adverb* **8** *informal* squarely or directly: *smack in the middle*

small *adjective* **1** not large in size, number or amount **2** unimportant ▷ *noun* **3** narrow part of the lower back >**smallness** *noun*: *the smallness of the cell*

smallpox *noun* serious contagious disease with blisters that leave scars

small talk *noun* light social conversation

smart *adjective* **1** neat and tidy **2** clever **3** fashionable **4** brisk ▷ *verb* **5** to feel or cause stinging pain >**smartly** *adverb* >**smartness** *noun*

smarten *verb* to make or become smart

smash *verb* 1 to break violently and noisily 2 to strike (against something) violently 3 to destroy ▷ *noun* 4 act or sound of smashing 5 violent collision of vehicles 6 *informal* (also **smash hit**) popular success 7 *Sport* powerful overhead shot

smashing *adjective informal* excellent

smattering *noun* slight knowledge

smear *noun* 1 dirty, greasy mark or smudge 2 untrue and malicious rumour 3 *Medicine* bodily sample smeared on to a slide for examination under a microscope ▷ *verb* 4 to spread with a greasy or sticky substance 5 to rub so as to produce a dirty mark or smudge 6 to slander

smell smells smelling smelled or **smelt** *noun* 1 odour or scent 2 ability to perceive odours by the nose ▷ *verb* 3 to have or give off a smell: *He smelled of tobacco and garlic* 4 to have an unpleasant smell 5 to sniff (something) 6 to perceive (a scent or odour) by means of the nose 7 to detect by instinct

smelly smellier smelliest *adjective* having a nasty smell

smelt smelts smelting smelted *verb* 1 a past of **smell** 2 to extract (a metal) from (an ore) by heating

smile *verb* 1 to turn up the corners of your mouth slightly because you are pleased or amused or want to convey friendliness ▷ *noun* 2 turning up of the corners of the mouth to show pleasure, amusement or friendliness

smirk *noun* 1 smug smile ▷ *verb* 2 to give a smirk

smith *noun* worker in metal

smitten *adjective* in love (with someone) or very enthusiastic (about them)

smock *noun* 1 loose top resembling a long blouse ▷ *verb* 2 to gather (material) by sewing in a honeycomb pattern

smog *noun* mixture of smoke and fog

smoke *noun* 1 cloudy mixture of gas and small particles sent into the air when something burns 2 act of smoking tobacco ▷ *verb* 3 to give off smoke 4 to suck in and blow out smoke from (a cigarette, cigar or pipe) 5 to use cigarettes, cigars or a pipe habitually 6 to cure (meat, fish or cheese) by treating with smoke > **smoker** *noun*: *a heavy smoker* > **smoking** *noun*

smoky smokier smokiest *adjective* full of smoke

smooth *adjective* 1 even and without roughness, holes or lumps 2 without obstructions or difficulties 3 charming and polite but possibly insincere 4 free from jolts 5 not harsh in taste ▷ *verb* 6 to make smooth > **smoothly** *adverb* > **smoothness** *noun*

smoothie *noun* thick drink made from milk, blended fruit and ice

smother *verb* 1 to kill (someone) by covering their mouth and nose so that they cannot breathe 2 to provide (someone) with love and protection to an excessive degree 3 to suppress or stifle (an emotion) 4 to cover (a dish) thickly with something

smothered *adjective* completely covered (in or with something)

smoulder *verb* **1** to burn slowly with smoke but no flame **2** (of feelings) to exist in a suppressed state

smudge *verb* **1** to make or become dirty or messy through contact with something ▷ *noun* **2** dirty or blurred mark

smug smugger smuggest *adjective* self-satisfied > **smugly** *adverb* > **smugness** *noun*

smuggle *verb* **1** to import or export (goods) secretly and illegally **2** to take (something or someone) somewhere secretly

smuggler *noun* someone who smuggles goods illegally into a country

snack *noun* light quick meal

snag snags snagging snagged *noun* **1** small problem or disadvantage **2** hole in fabric caused by a sharp object **3** *Aust, NZ informal* sausage ▷ *verb* **4** to catch or tear (clothing on a point)

snail *noun* **1** small, slow-moving creature with a long, shiny body and a shell on its back **2 at a snail's pace** at a very slow speed

snail mail *noun informal* conventional post, as opposed to e-mail

snake *noun* **1** long, thin, scaly reptile without limbs ▷ *verb* **2** to move in a winding course like a snake

snap snaps snapping snapped *verb* **1** to break suddenly **2** to (cause) to make a sharp cracking sound **3** to bite (at) suddenly **4** to speak sharply and angrily **5** to take a snapshot of ▷ *noun* **6** act

or sound of snapping **7** *informal* snapshot; photo **8** sudden brief spell of cold weather **9** card game in which the word snap is called when two similar cards are put down ▷ *adjective* **10** (of a decision) made on the spur of the moment > **snap up** *verb* to take eagerly and quickly

snapper *noun* type of edible fish, found in waters around Australia and New Zealand

snapshot *noun* photograph taken quickly and casually

snare *noun* **1** trap for catching birds or small animals involving a noose ▷ *verb* **2** to catch (an animal or bird) in or as if in a snare

snarl *verb* **1** (of an animal) to growl with bared teeth **2** to speak or utter fiercely **3** to make tangled ▷ *noun* **4** act or sound of snarling **5** tangled mess

snatch *verb* **1** to seize or try to seize suddenly **2** to take (food, rest, etc) hurriedly ▷ *noun* **3** act of snatching **4** fragment (of conversation or song)

sneak *verb* **1** to move furtively **2** to bring, take or put furtively **3** *informal* to tell tales ▷ *noun* **4** someone who reports other people's bad behaviour or naughtiness to those in authority

sneakers *plural noun* casual shoes with rubber soles

sneaking *adjective* (of a feeling) slight but persistent and a little worrying

sneaky sneakier sneakiest *adjective informal* underhand

sneer *noun* **1** scornful and contemptuous expression or remark, intended to show your low opinion of someone or something ▷ *verb* **2** to show contempt for someone or something by giving a sneer

sneeze *verb* **1** to react to a tickle in the nose by involuntarily letting out air and droplets of water from the nose and mouth suddenly and noisily ▷ *noun* **2** act or sound of sneezing

snide *adjective* (of a comment, remark) critical in an unfair and nasty way

sniff *verb* **1** to breathe in through the nose in short breaths that can be heard **2** to smell (something) by sniffing ▷ *noun* **3** act or sound of sniffing >**sniff at** *verb* to express contempt for

snigger *noun* **1** sly, disrespectful laugh, especially one partly stifled ▷ *verb* **2** to let out a snigger

snip *snips snipping snipped verb* **1** to cut in small quick strokes with scissors or shears ▷ *noun* **2** *informal* bargain **3** act or sound of snipping

snippet *noun* small piece (of information, news)

snob *noun* **1** someone who admires upper-class people and looks down on lower-class people **2** someone who believes that they are better than other people >**snobbery** *noun*: *intellectual snobbery* >**snobbish** *adjective*: *snobbish attitudes*

snooker *noun* game played on a large table covered with smooth green cloth. Players score points by hitting different coloured balls into side pockets using a long stick called a cue

snoop *informal verb* **1** to pry ▷ *noun* **2** act of snooping >**snooper** *noun*:

the ease with which snoopers can obtain personal data about you

snooze *informal verb* **1** to sleep lightly for a short time, especially during the day ▷ *noun* **2** short light sleep

snore *verb* **1** to make snorting sounds while sleeping ▷ *noun* **2** sound of snoring

snorkel *snorkels snorkelling snorkelled noun* **1** tube allowing a swimmer to breathe while face down in the water ▷ *verb* **2** to swim using a snorkel >**snorkelling** *noun*: *We went snorkelling there*

snort *verb* **1** to breathe out noisily through the nostrils **2** to express contempt or anger by snorting ▷ *noun* **3** act or sound of snorting

snout *noun* nose and jaws (of an animal)

snow *noun* **1** flakes of ice crystals which fall from the sky in cold weather ▷ *verb* **2** to fall as or like snow

snowball *noun* **1** snow shaped into a ball for throwing ▷ *verb* **2** to increase rapidly

snowdrift *noun* deep pile of snow formed by the wind

snowdrop *noun* small white bell-shaped spring flower

snowman *snowmen noun* figure shaped out of snow

snub *snubs snubbing snubbed verb* **1** to insult (someone) deliberately, especially by making an insulting remark or by ignoring them ▷ *noun* **2** deliberate insult ▷ *adjective* **3** (of a nose) short and turned-up

snuff *noun* **1** powdered tobacco for sniffing up the nostrils ▷ *verb* **2** to put out (a candle)

snug snugger snuggest adjective
1 warm and comfortable
2 comfortably close-fitting
▷ noun **3** (in Britain and Ireland) small room in a pub >**snugly** adverb

snuggle verb to nestle into a person or thing for warmth or from affection

so adverb **1** to such an extent: Why are you so cruel? **2** very: I'm so tired **3** also; too: He laughed, and so did Jarvis **4** in such a manner: She's a good student and we'd like her to remain so **5** that is the case: Have you locked the keys? If so, where were the keys? **6** so much or so many limited: There are only so many questions we can ask **7** so long **a** for a limited time **b** goodbye ▷ conjunction **8** therefore **9** (often followed by that) **a** in order that: He left for work late so that he could talk to the children **b** with the result that: We were late leaving so that it was dark when we arrived **10** so as to ▷ interjection **11** exclamation of surprise, triumph or realization: So! You finally made it

soak verb **1** to make (something) thoroughly wet **2** to put (something) in liquid or to lie in liquid so as to become thoroughly wet **3** (of liquid) to go into, permeate or saturate ▷ noun **4** soaking >**soak up** to absorb

soaked adjective extremely wet

soaking adjective If something is soaking, it is very wet

soap noun **1** substance made of natural oils and fats and used for washing **2** informal soap opera

▷ verb **3** to apply soap to (a person, thing) >**soapy** adjective

soap opera noun radio or television serial dealing with people's daily lives

soar verb **1** (of a value, price, amount) to increase suddenly **2** to rise or fly upwards >**soaring** adjective: soaring temperatures

sob sobs sobbing sobbed verb **1** to cry noisily, with gasps and short breaths **2** to say while sobbing ▷ noun **3** act or sound of sobbing

sober adjective **1** not drunk **2** serious and thoughtful **3** (of colours) plain and dull **4** to make (someone) sober or to become sober >**soberly** adverb >**sober up** verb to become sober after being drunk

sobering adjective causing you to become serious and thoughtful: the sobering lesson of the last year

so-called adjective misleadingly called

soccer noun football played by two teams of eleven players kicking a ball in an attempt to score goals

sociable adjective **1** friendly or companionable **2** (of an occasion) providing companionship >**sociability** noun: man's natural sociability

social adjective **1** relating to society or how it is organized **2** living in a community **3** sociable **4** relating to activities that involve meeting others >**socially** adverb

socialism noun political system or ideas promoting public ownership of industries, resources and transport >**socialist** noun, adjective

socialize verb to meet others socially

social security noun **1** payments made to the unemployed, elderly or sick by the state **2** system responsible for making such payments

social work noun work which involves helping or advising people with serious financial or family problems > **social worker** noun

society societies noun **1** human beings considered as a group within a particular country or region **2** organization for people who have the same interest or aim: *the school debating society* **3** rich, upper-class or fashionable people collectively **4** companionship

sociology noun study of human societies > **sociological** adjective: *the sociological study of social relations* > **sociologist** noun

sock noun piece of clothing that covers your foot and ankle

socket noun **1** place on a wall or on a piece of electrical equipment into which you can put a plug or bulb **2** hollow part or opening into which another part fits: *eye sockets*

sod noun literary surface of the ground, together with the grass and roots growing in it; turf

soda noun **1** soda water **2** sodium in the form of crystals or powder, used for baking or cleaning

soda water noun fizzy drink made from water charged with carbon dioxide

sodden adjective soaked

sodium noun silvery-white chemical element which combines with other chemicals. Salt is a sodium compound

sofa noun padded seat with arms at either end for two or three people to sit on; settee

soft adjective **1** not hard, stiff, firm or rough **2** (of a voice, sound) not loud or harsh; quiet **3** (of colour, light) not bright **4** (of a breeze or climate) mild **5** (of a person) (too) lenient **6** (of a person) weak and easily influenced **7** (of drugs) not liable to cause addiction > **softly** adverb

soft drink noun any cold, nonalcoholic drink

soften verb **1** to make (something) soft or softer or to become soft or softer **2** (of a person) to become more sympathetic and less critical

software noun computer programs

soggy soggier soggiest adjective unpleasantly wet or full of water

soil noun **1** top layer of earth in which plants grow ▷ verb **2** to make (something) dirty > **soiled** adjective

solace noun literary comfort when sad or distressed

solar adjective **1** relating or belonging to the sun **2** using the energy of the sun

solar system noun the sun and the planets, comets and asteroids that go round it

solder verb **1** to join (two pieces of metal) using molten metal ▷ noun **2** soft metal alloy used to join two metal surfaces

soldier noun **1** member of an army ▷ verb **2** to serve in an army > **soldier on** verb to persist doggedly

sole soles soling soled adjective 1 one and only 2 not shared, exclusive ▷ noun 3 underside of your foot or shoe 4 small edible flatfish ▷ verb 5 to put a sole on (a shoe)

solely adverb only, alone

solemn adjective 1 serious, deeply sincere 2 formal > **solemnity** noun: the solemnity of the occasion > **solemnly** adverb

solicitor noun Brit, Aust, NZ lawyer who gives legal advice to clients and prepares documents and cases

solid adjective 1 (of a substance, object) hard or firm 2 not liquid or gas 3 not hollow 4 of the same substance throughout 5 strong or substantial 6 (of a person, firm) sound or reliable 7 whole or without interruption: I cried for two solid days ▷ noun 8 solid substance or object > **solidity** noun: The extensive use of wood gives a feeling of solidity > **solidly** adverb

solidarity noun unity and mutual support

soliloquy soliloquies noun speech made by a person while alone, especially in a play

solitary adjective 1 (of an activity) done alone 2 (of a person, animal) used to being alone 3 single, lonely

solitary confinement noun the state of being kept alone, without company, in a prison cell; isolation

solitude noun state of being alone

solo solos noun 1 music for one performer 2 act performed by one

person alone ▷ adjective 3 done alone: my first solo flight ▷ adverb 4 by oneself, alone

soloist noun musician or dancer who performs a solo

solstice noun either the shortest winter day or the longest summer day

soluble adjective 1 (of a substance) able to be dissolved 2 (of a problem) able to be solved > **solubility** noun

solution noun 1 answer to a problem 2 act of solving a problem 3 liquid in which a solid substance has been dissolved

solve verb to find the answer to (a problem)

solvent adjective 1 having enough money to pay your debts ▷ noun 2 liquid capable of dissolving other substances > **solvency** noun state of having enough money to pay your debts

Somali Somalis adjective 1 belonging to or relating to Somalia ▷ noun 2 person from Somalia 3 language spoken by Somalis

sombre adjective 1 (of a colour, place) dark, gloomy 2 (of a person, atmosphere) serious, sad or gloomy

some adjective 1 a number or quantity of 2 unknown or unspecified 3 a considerable number or amount of 4 informal remarkable ▷ pronoun 5 a number or quantity ▷ adverb 6 about or approximately

somebody pronoun some person; someone

some day adverb at an unknown date in the future

somehow adverb in some

unspecified way

someone pronoun some person; somebody

somersault noun 1 forwards or backwards roll in which the head is placed on the ground and the body is brought over it ▷ verb 2 to perform a somersault

something pronoun 1 unknown or unspecified thing 2 impressive or important thing

sometime adverb 1 at some unspecified time ▷ adjective 2 former

sometimes adverb from time to time, now and then; occasionally

somewhat adverb to some extent, rather

somewhere adverb 1 in, to or at some unspecified or unknown place 2 some time, some number or some quantity: somewhere between the winter of 1999 and the summer of 2004

son noun male child

sonar noun device for calculating the depth of the sea or the position of an underwater object using sound waves

sonata noun piece of music, usually in three or four movements, for the piano or another instrument with or without piano

song noun 1 music with words that are sung to the tune 2 tuneful sound made by certain birds 3 **for a song** very cheaply

songbird noun any bird with a musical call

son-in-law sons-in-law noun daughter's husband

sonnet noun poem consisting of 14 lines with a fixed rhyme scheme

soon adverb in a short time

soot noun black powder that rises in the smoke from a fire >**sooty** adjective: a black sooty substance

soothe verb 1 to make (someone) calm 2 to relieve (pain etc) >**soothing** adjective: soothing music

sophisticated adjective 1 (of a person) having refined or cultured tastes or habits 2 (of a machine, device) made using advanced and complicated methods; complex >**sophistication** noun: the sophistication of communications technology

soppy soppier soppiest adjective informal too sentimental

soprano sopranos noun 1 (singer with) the highest female or boy's voice 2 highest pitched of a family of instruments

sorcerer noun magician

sorceress noun female sorcerer

sorcery noun witchcraft or black magic

sordid adjective 1 dishonest or immoral 2 dirty or squalid

sore adjective 1 painful 2 resentful 3 (of a need) urgent ▷ noun 4 painful place where your skin has become infected >**sorely** adverb greatly She will be sorely missed >**soreness** noun: Bleeding and soreness can follow

sorghum noun kind of grass cultivated for grain

sorrow noun 1 grief or sadness 2 cause of sorrow

sorry sorrier sorriest adjective 1 feeling sadness, sympathy or regret 2 pitiful or wretched

sort noun 1 group sharing certain qualities or characteristics; kind;

type **2 out of sorts** slightly unwell or bad-tempered ▷ *verb* **3** to arrange into different groups according to kind **4** (also **sort out**) to mend, fix or solve

- When you use *sort* in its singular form, the adjective before it should also be singular: *that sort of car.*
- When you use the plural form *sorts*, the adjective before it should be plural: *those sorts of shops*

SOS *noun* signal that you are in danger and need help

so-so *adjective informal* neither good nor bad; mediocre

soufflé or **souffle** *noun* light fluffy dish made with beaten egg whites and other ingredients and baked in the oven

sought *verb* past of **seek**

soul *noun* **1** spiritual part of a human being, believed by many to be immortal **2** essential part or fundamental nature **3** deep and sincere feelings **4** person regarded as typifying some quality: *Sonia was the soul of patience* **5** person: *There was not a soul there* **6** type of music combining blues, pop and gospel

sound *noun* **1** something heard; noise **2** everything heard **3** impression formed from hearing about someone or something: *I like the sound of your aunt* **4** channel or strait ▷ *verb* **5** to make a sound or cause (something) to make a sound **6** to seem to be as specified **7** to pronounce **8** to find the depth of (water etc) **9** to examine (the body, heart etc) by tapping or

listening with a stethoscope **10** to find out the views of ▷ *adjective* **11** in good condition **12** firm, substantial **13** financially reliable **14** showing good judgment **15** ethically correct **16** (of sleep) deep **17** thorough ▷ **soundly** *adverb*: *to sleep soundly*

sound bite *noun* short, memorable sentence or phrase extracted from a longer speech, especially by a politician, for use on television or radio

sound effect *noun* sound created artificially to make a play more realistic, especially a radio play

soundproof *adjective* **1** (of a room) not penetrable by sound ▷ *verb* **2** to make (something) soundproof

soundtrack *noun* the part of a film that you hear

soup *noun* liquid food made from meat, vegetables, etc and water

sour *adjective* **1** sharp-tasting; acid **2** (of milk) gone bad **3** (of a person's temperament) bad-tempered and unfriendly ▷ *verb* **4** to make (something) sour or become sour

source *noun* **1** origin or starting point **2** person, book, etc providing information **3** spring where a river or stream begins

- Do not confuse the spellings of *source* and *sauce*

sour grapes *plural noun* scornful remark or action that is born of envy

south *noun* **1** direction towards the South Pole, opposite north **2** area lying in or towards the south ▷ *adjective* **3** to or in the south **4** (of a wind) from the

south ▷ *adverb* **5** in, to or towards the south

South America *noun* fourth largest continent, having the Pacific Ocean on its west side, the Atlantic on its east side and the Antarctic to the south. South America is joined to North America by the Isthmus of Panama > **South American** *adjective*

south-east *noun, adverb, adjective* halfway between south and east

south-easterly *adjective* **1** to or towards the south-east **2** (of a wind) from the south-east

south-eastern *adjective* in or from the south-east

southerly *adjective* **1** to or towards the south **2** (of a wind) from the south

southern *adjective* in or from the south > **southerner** *noun* person from the south of a country or area

Southern Cross *noun* group of stars which can be seen from the southern part of the earth, and which is represented by the national flags of Australia and New Zealand

South Pole *noun* southernmost point of the earth

southward *adjective* **1** towards the south ▷ *adverb* **2** towards the south

south-west *noun, adverb, adjective* halfway between south and west

south-westerly *adjective* **1** to or towards the south-west **2** (of a wind) from the south-west

south-western *adjective* in or from the south-west

souvenir *noun* keepsake, memento

sovereign *noun* **1** king, queen or other royal ruler of a country **2** former British gold coin worth one pound ▷ *adjective* **3** (of a state) independent

sovereignty *noun* political power that a country has to govern itself

Soviet *adjective* belonging or relating to the country that used to be the Soviet Union

sow¹ **sows sowing sowed sown** *verb* **1** to scatter or plant (seed) **2** to plant seed in (the ground) **3** to implant or introduce (undesirable feelings or attitudes)

sow² *noun* female adult pig

soya *noun* plant whose edible bean (**soya bean**) is used for food and as a source of oil

soya bean *noun* type of edible Asian bean

spa *noun* resort with a mineral-water spring

space *noun* **1** unlimited expanse in which all objects exist and move **2** interval **3** blank portion **4** unoccupied area **5** the universe beyond the earth's atmosphere ▷ *verb* **6** to place (a series of things) at intervals

spacecraft *noun* vehicle for travel beyond the earth's atmosphere

spaceman spacemen *noun* someone who travels in space

spaceship *noun* a spacecraft that carries people through space

space shuttle *noun* vehicle for repeated space flights

spacious *adjective* having or providing a lot of space; roomy

spade *noun* **1** tool for digging **2** playing card of the suit marked with black leaf-shaped symbols

spaghetti *noun* long, thin pieces of pasta

spam *verb* **spams spamming spammed** **1** to send unsolicited e-mail or text messages to multiple recipients ▷ *noun* **2** unsolicited e-mail or text messages sent in this way

span **spans spanning spanned** *noun* **1** the period of time between two dates or events during which something exists or functions **2** distance between two extreme points (of something) **3** distance from thumb to little finger of the expanded hand ▷ *verb* **4** to last throughout (a period of time) **5** (of a bridge) to stretch across (a river, valley)

spangle *noun* **1** small, sparkling piece of metal or plastic used to decorate clothing or hair ▷ *verb* **2** to decorate with spangles

Spaniard *noun* someone from Spain

spaniel *noun* type of dog with long ears and silky hair

Spanish *adjective* **1** belonging or relating to Spain ▷ *noun* **2** main language spoken in Spain, also spoken by many people in Central and South America ▷ *plural noun* **3** the Spanish the people of Spain

spank *verb* to slap with the open hand, on the buttocks or legs

spanner *noun* tool for gripping and turning a nut or bolt

spar **spars sparring sparred** *verb* **1** to box or fight using light blows for practice **2** to argue (with someone) ▷ *noun* **3** pole that a sail is attached to on a ship or yacht

spare *adjective* **1** extra **2** in reserve **3** (of time) free ▷ *noun* **4** duplicate kept in case of damage or loss ▷ *verb* **5** to refrain from punishing or harming (someone) **6** to save (someone) from (something unpleasant) **7** to afford to give

sparing *adjective* economical > **sparingly** *adverb*

spark *noun* **1** tiny, bright piece of burning material thrown out from a fire **2** fiery particle caused by friction **3** flash of light caused by electricity **4** trace or hint (of a particular quality) ▷ *verb* **5** to give off sparks > **spark off** *verb* to set off or give rise to

sparkle *verb* **1** to glitter with lots of small, bright points of light **2** to be lively, intelligent and witty ▷ *noun* **3** sparkling point of light **4** vivacity or wit > **sparkling** *adjective* **1** (of wine or mineral water) slightly fizzy **2** glittering

sparrow *noun* common, small bird with brown and grey feathers

sparse *adjective* thinly scattered or spread > **sparsely** *adverb*: sparsely populated areas

spartan *adjective* simple and without luxuries; austere

spasm *noun* **1** involuntary muscular contraction **2** sudden burst of activity or feeling

spasmodic *adjective* occurring for short periods of time or at irregular intervals > **spasmodically** *adverb*

spastic *noun* **1** person with cerebral palsy ▷ *adjective* **2** suffering from cerebral palsy

spate *noun* large number of things happening within a short period of time

spatial *adjective* of or in space

spatter verb **1** to scatter or be scattered in drops over (something) ▷ noun **2** something spattered in drops

spawn noun **1** jelly-like mass containing the eggs of fish or amphibians such as frogs ▷ verb **2** (of fish, frogs) to lay eggs **3** to give rise to

speak speaks speaking spoke spoken verb **1** to say words; talk **2** to give a speech or lecture **3** to know how to talk in (a specified language) **4** to communicate or express in words > **speak out** verb to publicly state an opinion

speaker noun **1** person who speaks, especially at a formal occasion **2** loudspeaker **3** Speaker (in Parliament) the official chairperson whose role is to control proceedings

speakerphone noun telephone with a microphone and loudspeaker allowing more than one person to participate in a call

spear noun **1** weapon consisting of a long shaft with a sharp point **2** slender shoot ▷ verb **3** to pierce with a spear or other pointed object

spearhead verb to lead (an attack or campaign)

spec noun on spec informal as a risk or gamble

special adjective **1** distinguished from others of its kind **2** for a specific purpose **3** exceptional **4** particular

specialist noun **1** expert in a particular activity or subject ▷ adjective **2** having a skill or knowing a lot about a particular subject > **specialism** noun

speciality specialities noun **1** special interest or skill **2** product specialized in

specialize verb to be a specialist > **specialization** noun: Farmers began to abandon mixed farms in favour of greater specialization

specialized or **specialised** adjective developed for a particular purpose or trained in a particular area of knowledge

specially adverb particularly

species noun group of plants or animals that are related closely enough to interbreed naturally

● The plural of species is species

specific adjective particular > **specifically** adverb

specification noun detailed description of something to be made or done

specify specifies specifying specified verb to refer to or state specifically

specimen noun **1** example or small sample (of something) that gives an idea of what the whole is like **2** sample of urine, blood, etc taken for analysis

speck noun small spot or particle

speckled adjective covered in small marks or spots

spectacle noun **1** strange, interesting or ridiculous sight **2** impressive public show

spectacular adjective impressive > **spectacularly** adverb

spectator noun person watching something; onlooker

spectra a plural of **spectrum**

spectre noun **1** ghost **2** frightening idea or image

spectrum spectra or **spectrums** noun **1** range of colours found in a rainbow and produced when light passes through a prism or a drop of water **2** range (of opinions, emotions) **3** entire range of anything

speculate verb **1** to weigh up and make guesses about something **2** to buy property, shares, etc in the hope of selling them at a profit >**speculation** noun

speculative adjective **1** based on guesses and opinions rather than known facts **2** (of an expression) suggesting that the person concerned is weighing up and making guesses about something

speech noun **1** ability to speak **2** act or manner of speaking **3** talk given to an audience **4** group of lines spoken by one of the characters in a play **5** language or dialect

speechless adjective unable to speak because of great emotion

speed speeds speeding sped or **speeded** verb **1** fast movement or travel; swiftness; rapidity **2** rate at which something moves or happens; velocity ▷ verb **3** to go quickly **4** to drive faster than the legal limit >**speed up** verb to accelerate

speedboat noun light fast motorboat

speed limit noun maximum speed at which vehicles are legally allowed to drive on a particular road

speedway noun **1** track for motorcycle racing **2** US, Canadian, NZ track for motor racing

speedy speedier speediest adjective rapid >**speedily** adverb

spell spells spelling spelt or

spelled verb **1** to provide the letters that form (a word) in the correct order **2** (of letters) to make up (a word) **3** to indicate or suggest: This method could spell disaster ▷ noun **4** a word or sequence of words used to perform magic **5** effect of a spell **6** period of time of weather or activity >**spell out** verb to explain in detail

spellbound adjective so fascinated by something that you cannot think about anything else

spelling noun **1** way a word is spelt **2** person's ability to spell

spend spends spending spent verb **1** to pay out (money) **2** to use or pass (time) **3** to use (energy)

spent adjective used: spent matches

sperm sperms or **sperm** noun cell produced in the sex organ of a male animal which can enter a female animal's egg and fertilize it

spew verb to come out or to send (something) out in a stream >**spew up** verb informal to vomit

sphere noun **1** perfectly round solid object **2** field of activity or interest >**spherical** adjective round

sphinx sphinxes noun monster with a lion's body and a human head

spice noun **1** powder or seeds from a plant added to food to give it flavour **2** something which makes life more exciting ▷ verb **3** to flavour with spices >**spice up** verb to make (something) more exciting

spicy spicier spiciest adjective strongly flavoured with spices

spider noun small eight-legged creature which spins a web to catch insects for food

spike noun 1 sharp point 2 sharp pointed metal object 3 **spikes** sports shoes with spikes for greater grip ▷ verb 4 to pierce or fasten with a spike 5 to add alcohol to (a drink)

spiky spikier spikiest adjective having sharp points

spill spills spilling spilled or **spilt** 1 to allow (something) accidentally to pour out of something 2 to pour from or as if from a container

spillage noun the spilling of something, or something that has been spilt

spin spins spinning spun verb 1 to turn quickly or to cause (something) to turn quickly round a central point 2 to make thread or yarn by twisting together fibres using a spinning machine or spinning wheel 3 (of a spider) to make (a web) 4 informal to present information in a way that creates a favourable impression ▷ noun 5 a rapid turning motion around a central point 6 continuous spiral descent of an aircraft 7 informal short drive for pleasure 8 informal presentation of information in a way that creates a favourable impression > **spin out** verb to make (something) last an unusually long time; to prolong

spinach noun dark green leafy vegetable

spinal adjective relating to your spine

spine noun 1 backbone 2 edge of a book on which the title is printed

3 sharp point on an animal or plant

spinifex noun coarse spiny Australian grass

spinning wheel noun a wooden machine for spinning flax or wool

spin-off noun unexpected benefit

spinster noun woman who has never married

spiny spinier spiniest adjective covered with spines

spiral spirals spiralling spiralled noun 1 something that forms a continuous curve winding round and round a central point so that a circle of increasingly bigger loops winds out from the middle, or else a tubular shape is formed consisting of loops above loops 2 steadily accelerating increase or decrease ▷ adjective 3 in the shape of a spiral ▷ verb 4 to move in a spiral 5 to increase or decrease with steady acceleration

spire noun pointed part at the top of some church towers

spirit noun 1 nonphysical part of a person connected with their deepest thoughts and feelings 2 nonphysical part of a person believed to live on after death 3 supernatural being; ghost 4 courage and liveliness 5 essential meaning as opposed to literal interpretation 6 liquid obtained by distillation 7 **spirits** emotional state ▷ verb 8 (usually followed by away, off) to carry (something or someone) away mysteriously

spirited adjective lively and courageous

spirit level noun glass tube containing a bubble in liquid, used to check whether a surface is level

spiritual adjective **1** relating to the spirit **2** relating to sacred things ▷ noun **3** type of religious folk song originating among Black slaves in America > **spirituality** noun: People still want spirituality in their lives > **spiritually** adverb

spit spits spitting spat verb **1** to eject (saliva or food) from the mouth **2** to rain slightly ▷ noun **3** saliva **4** sharp rod on which meat is skewered for roasting

spite noun **1** deliberate nastiness; malice **2 in spite of** in defiance of or regardless of ▷ verb **3** to spite to annoy or hurt (someone) from spite

spiteful adjective deliberately nasty; malicious

spitting image noun informal person who looks very like another

splash verb **1** to scatter liquid on (something) **2** to scatter (a liquid) in drops **3** (of a liquid) to be scattered in drops **4** to print (a story or photograph) prominently in a newspaper ▷ noun **5** splashing sound **6** small amount (of a liquid) **7** contrastive patch (of a colour or light) **8** extravagant display **9** small amount of liquid added to a drink > **splash out** informal to spend extravagantly

splatter verb **1** to splash ▷ noun **2** splash

spleen noun organ near your stomach that filters bacteria from the blood

splendid adjective **1** excellent **2** beautiful and impressive > **splendidly** adverb

splendour noun quality of being beautiful and impressive

splint noun long piece of wood or metal used as support for a broken bone

splinter noun **1** thin sharp piece broken off, especially from wood ▷ verb **2** to break into fragments

split splits splitting split verb **1** to break into separate pieces **2** to separate **3** to tear or crack **4** to share (something) ▷ noun **5** crack, tear or division caused by splitting **6** splits act of sitting with the legs outstretched in opposite directions > **split up** verb to end a relationship or marriage

split second noun extremely short period of time

splitting adjective (of a headache) very painful

splutter verb **1** to speak in a confused way because of embarrassment **2** to make hissing or spitting sounds

spoil spoils spoiling spoiled or spoilt verb **1** to damage **2** to harm the character of (a child) by giving or pampering them too much **3** to treat (someone) **4** to rot, go bad

spoilsport noun person who spoils people's fun

spoke verb **1** past tense of **speak** ▷ noun **2** bar joining the hub of a wheel to the rim

spokesperson noun person chosen to speak on behalf of a group > **spokesman** noun > **spokeswoman** noun

sponge noun **1** sea animal with a porous absorbent skeleton **2** part of the very light skeleton of a sponge, or something resembling it, used for washing and cleaning **3** type of light cake ▷ verb **4** to wipe (something) with a sponge **5** (followed by *off, on*) to live at the expense of (others)

sponsor *verb* **1** to provide financial support for (an event or training) **2** to agree to pay a sum to (a charity fund-raiser) if they successfully complete an activity **3** to put forward and support (a proposal or suggestion) ▷ *noun* **4** person or organization sponsoring something or someone >**sponsorship** *noun: He also received corporate sponsorship from big businesses*

spontaneous *adjective* **1** not planned or arranged **2** occurring through natural processes without outside influence >**spontaneity** *noun* ability to act without planning or prior arrangement >**spontaneously** *adverb*

spoof *noun* mildly satirical parody

spooky spookier spookiest *adjective* eerie and frightening

spool *noun* cylindrical object onto which thread, tape or film can be wound

spoon *noun* **1** object shaped like a small shallow bowl with a long handle, used for eating, stirring and serving food ▷ *verb* **2** to lift (something) with a spoon

spoonful spoonfuls or **spoonsful** *noun* the amount held by a spoon

sporadic *adjective* happening at irregular intervals >**sporadically** *adverb*

spore *noun technical* minute reproductive body of some plants and bacteria

sporran *noun* pouch worn in front of a kilt

sport *noun* **1** any activity for pleasure, competition or exercise requiring physical effort and skill **2** such activities collectively **3** enjoyment **4** person who reacts cheerfully ▷ *verb* **5** to wear proudly

sporting *adjective* **1** relating to sport **2** behaving in a fair and decent way **3 a sporting chance** reasonable chance of success

sports car *noun* fast low-built car, usually open-topped

sportsman sportsmen *noun* person who plays sports

sportswoman sportswomen *noun* woman who plays sports

sporty sportier sportiest *adjective* **1** (of a car) fast and flashy **2** (of a person) good at sports

spot spots spotting spotted *noun* **1** small, round, coloured area on a surface **2** small lump on your skin, caused by infection or allergy; pimple **3** place or location **4** *informal* small quantity **5** (on a television show) part regularly reserved for a particular performer or type of entertainment **6 on the spot a** at the place in question **b** immediately **c** in an awkward predicament ▷ *verb* **7** to notice

spot check *noun* random examination

spotless *adjective* absolutely clean >**spotlessly** *adverb*

spotlight spotlights spotlighting spotlit or **spotlighted** *noun* **1** powerful light which can be directed to light up a small area ▷ *verb* **2** to draws the public's attention to (a situation or problem)

spot-on *adjective informal* absolutely accurate

spotted *adjective* having a pattern of spots

spotter *noun* person whose hobby is watching for things of a particular kind: *a train spotter*

spotty spottier spottiest *adjective* with spots

spouse *noun* husband or wife

spout *verb* 1 to pour out in a stream or jet 2 *informal* to utter (a stream of words) lengthily ▷ *noun* 3 tube with a lip-like end for pouring liquid 4 stream or jet of liquid

sprain *verb* 1 to injure (a joint) by a sudden twist ▷ *noun* 2 such an injury

sprawl *verb* 1 to lie or sit with your legs and arms spread out 2 (of a place) to spread out in a straggling manner ▷ *noun* 3 something that has spread untidily over a large area >**sprawling** *adjective*: *a sprawling city*

spray *noun* 1 fine drops of liquid splashed or forced into the air 2 liquid kept under pressure in a can or other container 3 piece of equipment for spraying liquid 4 branch with buds, leaves, flowers or berries on it ▷ *verb* 5 to scatter in fine drops 6 to cover with a spray

spread spreads spreading **spread** *verb* 1 to open (something) out or to arrange (something) so that all or most of it can be seen easily 2 to stretch out 3 to put a thin layer of (a

substance or coating) on a surface 4 to reach or affect a wider and wider area 5 to distribute (something) evenly ▷ *noun* 6 extent reached or distribution (of something) 7 wide variety 8 *informal* large meal 9 soft food which can be put on bread, biscuits, etc

spread-eagled *adjective* with arms and legs outstretched

spreadsheet *noun* computer program for entering and arranging figures and sums

spree *noun* period of time spent doing something enjoyable to excess: *a shopping spree*

sprig *noun* 1 twig or shoot 2 *Aust, NZ* stud on the sole of a soccer or rugby boot

sprightly sprightlier sprightliest *adjective* lively and active

spring springs springing sprang sprung *noun* 1 season between winter and summer 2 coil of wire which returns to its natural shape after being pressed or pulled 3 place where water comes up through the ground 4 jump 5 elasticity; bounce ▷ *verb* 6 to move suddenly upwards or forwards in a single motion; jump 7 to move suddenly and quickly 8 to result or originate (from) 9 (followed by *on*) to give (a surprising piece of news, task) to (someone)

springboard *noun* 1 flexible board on which a diver or gymnast jumps to gain height 2 something that provides a helpful starting point (for an activity or enterprise)

springbok *noun* 1 S African antelope 2 person who has

represented South Africa in a sports team

spring-clean *verb* to clean (a house) thoroughly

spring onion *noun* small onion with long green shoots, often eaten raw in salads

sprinkle *verb* to scatter (a liquid or powder) in tiny drops or particles over (something)

sprinkling *noun* small quantity or number

sprint *noun* **1** short fast race **2** fast run ▷ *verb* **3** to run a short distance at top speed

sprinter *noun* athlete who runs fast over short distances

sprite *noun* type of fairy; elf

sprout *verb* **1** to produce shoots **2** to begin to grow or develop **3** (followed by *up*) to appear rapidly ▷ *noun* **4** short for **Brussels sprout**

spruce *noun* **1** kind of fir tree ▷ *adjective* **2** neat and smart ▷ *verb* **3** **spruce up** to make neat and smart

spunk *noun informal* **1** *old-fashioned* courage, spirit **2** *Aust, NZ* good-looking person

spur *spurs spurring spurred verb* **1** to urge on, incite (someone) ▷ *noun* **2** encouragement or incentive; stimulus **3** spiked wheel on the heel of a rider's boot used to urge on a horse **4** ridge sticking out from a mountain or hillside **5** **on the spur of the moment** on impulse

spurious *adjective* not genuine or real

spurn *verb* to refuse to accept; reject

spurt *verb* **1** to gush out in a jet ▷ *noun* **2** sudden gush **3** short sudden burst of activity or speed

spy *spies spying spied noun* **1** person employed to obtain secret information **2** person who secretly watches others ▷ *verb* **3** to act as a spy **4** to catch sight of

squabble *verb* **1** to quarrel about something trivial ▷ *noun* **2** a quarrel

squad *noun* small group of people working or training together

squadron *noun* section of one of the armed forces, especially the air force

squalid *adjective* **1** dirty and unpleasant **2** unpleasant, unwholesome and perhaps dishonest; sordid

squall *noun* **1** sudden strong wind ▷ *verb* **2** to cry noisily, yell

squalor *noun* bad or dirty conditions or surroundings

squander *verb* to waste (money or resources)

square *noun* **1** shape with four equal sides and four right angles **2** flat open area in a town, bordered by buildings or streets **3** product of a number multiplied by itself ▷ *adjective* **4** square in shape **5** in area: 10 *million square feet of office space* **6** in length on each side: *a towel measuring a foot square* **7** straight or level **8** with all accounts or debts settled ▷ *verb* **9** to multiply (a number) by itself **10** to make (something) square ▷ *adverb* **11** squarely, directly

squarely *adverb* **1** in a direct way **2** in an honest and frank manner

square root *noun* number of which a given number is the square

squash squashes squashing squashed *verb* **1** to crush (something) flat **2** to stop (a difficult or troubling situation) often by force; suppress **3** to push into a confined space **4** to humiliate (someone) with a crushing reply ▷ *noun* **5** sweet fruit drink diluted with water **6** crowd of people in a confined space **7** game played in an enclosed court with a rubber ball and long-handled rackets **8** marrow-like vegetable

squat squats squatting squatted; squatter squattest *verb* **1** to crouch with your knees bent and your weight on your feet **2** to live in unused premises without any legal right to do so ▷ *noun* **3** place where squatters live ▷ *adjective* **4** short and broad

squatter *noun* **1** person who lives in unused premises without permission and without paying rent **2** *Aust, NZ* **a** someone who owns a large amount of land for sheep or cattle farming **b** *History* someone who rented land from the King or Queen

squawk *noun* **1** (of a bird) loud harsh cry ▷ *verb* **2** (of a bird) to make a squawking noise

squeak *verb* **1** to give a short, high-pitched sound or cry ▷ *noun* **2** short, high-pitched cry or sound > **squeaky** *adjective*: *squeaky floorboards*

squeal *verb* **1** to give a long, high-pitched cry or sound **2** *informal* to inform on someone to the police ▷ *noun* **3** long high-pitched cry or sound

squeamish *adjective* easily upset by unpleasant sights or situations

squeeze *verb* **1** to grip or press firmly **2** to crush or press to extract liquid **3** to push into a confined space **4** to get (something out of someone) by force or great effort ▷ *noun* **5** act of squeezing **6** tight fit

squelch *verb* **1** to make a wet, sucking sound, as when walking through mud ▷ *noun* **2** wet, sucking sound

squid *noun* sea creature with a long soft body and ten tentacles

squiggle *noun* wavy line > **squiggly** *adjective*: *a squiggly line*

squint *verb* **1** to look at something with your eyes screwed up **2** to have eyes that look in different or slightly different directions ▷ *noun* **3** eye condition in which your eyes look in different or slightly different directions

squire *noun* **1** country gentleman, usually the main landowner in a community **2** *History* knight's apprentice

squirm *verb* **1** to wriggle, writhe **2** to feel embarrassed

squirrel *noun* small furry animal with a bushy tail that lives in trees

squirt *verb* **1** to force (a liquid) out of a narrow opening **2** (of a liquid) to be forced out of a narrow opening ▷ *noun* **3** jet of liquid

Sri Lankan *adjective* **1** belonging or relating to Sri Lanka ▷ *noun* **2** someone from Sri Lanka

stab stabs stabbing stabbed *verb* **1** to push a knife or something pointed into the body of (someone) **2** to jab (at) **3** **stab in the back** to behave treacherously towards (someone) ▷ *noun* **4** act of stabbing **5** sudden unpleasant sensation **6** *informal* attempt

stable noun **1** building in which horses are kept **2** establishment that breeds and trains racehorses **3** establishment that manages or trains several entertainers or athletes ▷ *adjective* **4** firmly fixed or established **5** firm in character **6** *Science* not subject to decay or decomposition > **stability** noun: *a time of political stability*

staccato adjective consisting of short abrupt sounds

stack noun **1** pile **2** stacks large amount ▷ *verb* **3** to pile in a stack

stadium stadiums or stadia noun sports ground surrounded by rows of tiered seats

staff noun **1** people employed in an organization ▷ *verb* **2** to provide the personnel for (an organization)

stag noun adult male deer

stage noun **1** step or period of development **2** portion of a journey **3** platform in a theatre where actors or entertainers perform **4** the stage theatre as a profession ▷ *verb* **5** to put (a play) on stage **6** to organize and carry out (an event)

stagecoach noun large horse-drawn vehicle formerly used to carry passengers and mail

stagger verb **1** to walk unsteadily **2** to astound (someone) **3** to set (events) apart to avoid them happening at the same time > **staggered** adjective: *I was absolutely staggered and amazed* > **staggering** adjective: *The results have been quite staggering*

stagnant adjective (of water or air)

stale from not moving

stag night noun party for a man who is about to get married, which only men go to

staid adjective serious and rather dull

stain noun **1** mark that is difficult to remove ▷ *verb* **2** to mark; discolour **3** to colour with a special kind of dye

stained glass noun coloured pieces of glass held together with strips of lead

stainless steel noun metal made from steel and chromium that does not rust

stair noun one of a flight of steps between floors

staircase noun flight of stairs with a handrail or banisters

stairway noun flight of stairs with a handrail or banisters

stake noun **1** pointed wooden post that can be hammered into the ground as a support or marker **2** money wagered **3** interest, usually financial, held in something **4** at stake being risked ▷ *verb* **5** to support or mark out with stakes **6** to risk; wager **7** stake a claim to to claim a right to > **stake out** verb informal (of police) to keep (a place) under surveillance

stale adjective **1** (of food, air) not fresh **2** (of a person) lacking energy or ideas through overwork or monotony

stalemate noun **1** situation in which neither side in an argument or contest can win; deadlock **2** Chess position in which any of a player's moves would put his king in check and which results in a draw

stalk noun **1** plant's stem ▷ verb **2** to follow or approach stealthily **3** to pursue persistently and, sometimes, attack (a person with whom one is obsessed) **4** to walk in a stiff or haughty manner

stall noun **1** large table for the display and sale of goods ▷ plural noun **2** stalls ground-floor seats in a theatre or cinema ▷ verb **3** (of a motor vehicle or engine) to stop accidentally **4** to employ delaying tactics

stallion noun adult male horse that can be used for breeding

stamina noun enduring energy and strength

stammer verb **1** to speak or say with involuntary pauses or repetition of syllables ▷ noun **2** tendency to stammer

stamp noun **1** (also postage stamp) piece of gummed paper stuck to an envelope or parcel to show that the postage has been paid **2** small block with a pattern cut into it, which you press onto an inky pad to print a pattern or mark; also the mark made by the stamp **3** characteristic feature **4** act of bringing your foot down hard on the ground ▷ verb **5** to bring (your foot) down hard on the ground **6** to walk with heavy footsteps **7** to impress (a pattern or mark) on (something) or to mark (something) with (a pattern or mark) **8** to stick a postage stamp on >**stamp out** verb to put an end to (something)

stampede noun **1** sudden rush of frightened animals or of a crowd ▷ verb **2** to run or to cause to run in a wild, uncontrolled way

stance noun **1** attitude **2** manner of standing

stand stands standing stood verb **1** to be upright or to rise to an upright position **2** to be situated **3** to place (something) in an upright position **4** to be in a specified state or position **5** to remain unchanged or valid **6** to tolerate or bear **7** to offer oneself as a candidate **8** informal to treat (someone) to (something) **9** stand trial to be tried in a court of law ▷ noun **10** stall for the sale of goods **11** structure for spectators at a sports ground **12** firmly held opinion **13** US, Aust witness box **14** rack or piece of furniture on which things may be placed >**stand by** verb **1** to support (someone) **2** to remain with or stick to (a decision, promise) **3** to be ready and available (to do something) **4** to look on without taking any action >**stand down** verb to resign (from your job or position) >**stand for** verb **1** to represent or mean **2** informal to tolerate or put up with >**stand in** verb (usually followed by for) to act as a temporary replacement or substitute (for someone) >**stand out** verb to be very noticeable or to be better or more important than other similar things or people >**stand up for** verb to support or defend (someone) >**stand up to** verb **1** to remain undamaged in (rough treatment); withstand **2** to confront or challenge (a bully)

standard noun **1** level of quality **2** example against which things are judged or measured **3** moral principle **4** distinctive flag

5 upright pole ▷ adjective **6** usual, regular or average **7** accepted as correct

standard English noun form of English taught in schools, used in text books and broadsheet newspapers, and spoken and written by most educated people

standardize verb to cause to conform to a standard > **standardization** noun

stand-by noun **1** something available for use when you need it: *a useful stand-by* ▷ adjective **2** (of a ticket) made available at the last minute if there are any seats left

stand-in noun substitute

standing adjective **1** permanent or regular ▷ noun **2** reputation or status **3** duration: *a friend of 20 years' standing*

standpoint noun point of view

standstill noun complete stop

stanza noun verse of a poem

staple noun **1** small, thin piece of wire or metal bent so that the two ends form prongs capable of piercing papers, carpets and other materials, and fired into place using a stapler or staplegun ▷ verb **2** to fasten with staples ▷ adjective **3** (of a food) forming a regular and basic part of someone's everyday diet

star stars starring starred noun **1** large ball of burning gas in space that appears as a point of light in the sky at night **2** shape with four, five, six or more points sticking out in a regular pattern **3** asterisk **4** famous actor, sports player or musician **5** stars astrological forecast, horoscope ▷ verb **6** (of an actor, entertainer)

to be a star (in a film or show) **7** (of a film, show) to have (someone) as a star ▷ adjective **8** leading, famous

starboard noun **1** right-hand side of a ship, when facing forward ▷ adjective **2** of or on this side

starch noun **1** substance used for stiffening fabric such as cotton or linen **2** carbohydrate found in foods such as bread or potatoes ▷ verb **3** to stiffen (fabric) with starch

stare verb **1** to look or gaze fixedly (at someone or something) ▷ noun **2** fixed gaze

starfish starfishes or starfish noun a flat, star-shaped sea creature with five limbs

stark adjective **1** harsh, unpleasant and plain **2** absolute ▷ adverb **3** stark naked completely naked

starling noun songbird with glossy dark speckled feathers

start verb **1** to begin **2** to set (something) in motion or to be set in motion **3** to make a sudden involuntary movement from fright **4** to establish or set up ▷ noun **5** first part of something; beginning **6** place or time of starting **7** advantage or lead in a competitive activity **8** sudden movement made from fright

starter noun **1** first course of a meal **2** device for starting a car's engine

startle verb to surprise or frighten a little ▷ **startled** adjective: *a startled rabbit* > **startling** adjective: *a startling revelation*

starve verb **1** to die or suffer as a result of hunger **2** to prevent (a person or animal) from having any food **3** to deprive (someone) of something needed **4** *informal* to be hungry **5** **to be starved of** to suffer through lack of (money, affection, etc) ▷ **starvation** *noun*: *people dying from starvation*

stash *informal verb* **1** to store (something) in a secret place ▷ *noun* **2** secret store

state *noun* **1** condition of a person or thing **2** country **3** region with its own government **4** the government **5** **in a state** *informal* in an excited or agitated condition ▷ *adjective* **6** of or concerning the government **7** (of a ceremony) involving the ruler or leader of the country ▷ *verb* **8** to express in words

state house *noun* NZ publicly-owned house rented to a low-income tenant

stately home *noun Brit* very large old house which belongs or once belonged to an upper-class family

statement *noun* **1** something you say or write when you give facts or information in a formal way **2** printed financial account

state school *noun* school maintained and funded by the government or a local authority providing free education

statesman *statesmen noun* experienced and respected political leader

static *adjective* **1** never moving or changing: *The temperature remained fairly static* ▷ *noun* **2** electrical charge caused by friction. It builds up in metal objects

station *noun* **1** place where trains stop for passengers **2** **bus station, coach station**

place where some buses start their journeys **3** headquarters or local offices of the police or a fire brigade **4** building with special equipment for a particular purpose: *power station* **5** television or radio channel **6** *old-fashioned* position in society **7** large Australian sheep or cattle property ▷ *verb* **8** to send (someone) to a particular place to work or do a particular job

stationary *adjective* not moving

stationery *noun* writing materials such as paper and pens

statistic *noun* fact obtained by analysing numerical information > **statistical** *adjective*: *statistical information* > **statistically** *adverb*

statistician *noun* person who compiles and studies statistics

statue *noun* large sculpture of a human or animal figure

stature *noun* **1** person's height **2** reputation of a person or their achievements

status *statuses noun* **1** social position **2** importance given to something; prestige **3** official classification given to someone or something: *marital status*

status quo *noun* existing state of affairs

statute *noun* written law > **statutory** *adjective* required or authorized by law

staunch *adjective* loyal, firm ▷ *verb* to stop (a flow of blood)

stave *staves staving staved noun Music* the five lines that music is written on > **stave off** *verb* to delay or prevent (something)

stay *verb* **1** to remain in a place or condition **2** to be living temporarily, often as a guest or visitor **3** *Scot, S Afr* to live permanently: *where do you stay?* ▷ *noun* **4** short time spent somewhere

stead *noun* **stand someone in good stead** to be useful to someone

steadfast *adjective* firm and determined >**steadfastly** *adverb*

steady steadier steadiest; steadies steadying steadied *adjective* **1** regular or continuous **2** not shaky or wavering; firm **3** (of a voice, gaze) calm and controlled **4** sensible and dependable ▷ *verb* **5** to make (something, someone or yourself) steady >**steadily** *adverb*

steak *noun* **1** thick slice of meat, especially beef **2** large piece of fish

steal steals stealing stole stolen *verb* **1** to take (something) unlawfully or without permission **2** to move quietly and secretively

stealth *noun* quietness and secrecy

steam *noun* **1** hot vapour formed when water boils ▷ *adjective* **2** (of an engine) operated using steam as a means of power ▷ *verb* **3** to give off steam **4** (of a vehicle) to move by steam power **5** to cook or treat with steam >**steamy** *adjective*: *a steamy atmosphere*

steam engine *noun* engine worked by steam

steamer *noun* **1** ship powered by steam **2** container used to cook food in steam

steed *noun* *lit* horse

steel *noun* **1** very strong metal containing mainly iron with a small amount of carbon ▷ *verb* **2** to prepare (yourself) for something unpleasant

steel band *noun* a group of people who play music on special metal drums

steep *adjective* **1** sloping sharply **2** *informal* (of a price) unreasonably high ▷ *verb* **3** to soak (something) thoroughly in liquid >**steeply** *adverb*

steeped *adjective* **steeped in** deeply affected by: *an industry steeped in tradition*

steeple *noun* a tall pointed structure on top of a church tower

steeplechase *noun* **1** horse race with obstacles to jump **2** track race with hurdles and a water jump

steer *verb* **1** to control the direction of (a vehicle or ship) **2** to influence the course or direction of (a person or conversation) ▷ *noun* **3** castrated male ox

stem stems stemming stemmed *noun* **1** long thin central part of a plant **2** long slender part, as of a wineglass **3** part of a word to which endings are added ▷ *verb* **4** to restrict or stop (the flow of something): *to stem the flow of refugees* **5 stem from** to originate from

stench *noun* foul smell

stencil stencils stencilling stencilled *noun* **1** thin sheet with cut-out pattern through which ink or paint passes to form the pattern on the surface below **2** pattern made thus ▷ *verb* **3** to make (a pattern) with a stencil

step steps stepping stepped *noun* **1** act of moving and setting

down your foot, as when walking
2 distance covered by a step
3 sound made by stepping **4** foot
movement in a dance **5** one of a
series of actions taken in order
to achieve a goal **6** degree in
a series or scale **7** raised flat
surface, usually one of a series
that you can walk up or down
8 steps stepladder ▷ *verb* **9** to
move and set down the foot,
as when walking **10** to walk a
short distance > **step down** or
step aside *verb* to resign from an
important position > **step in** *verb*
to become involved in something
in order to help; intervene > **step
up** *verb* to increase (the rate of
something) by stages

step- *prefix* denoting a relationship
created by the remarriage of a
parent: *stepmother; stepson*

steppes *plural noun* wide grassy
treeless plains in Russia and
Ukraine

stepping stone *noun* **1** one of a
series of stones for stepping on
in crossing a stream **2** means of
making progress towards a goal

stereo stereos *adjective* **1** (of a
recording, music system) having
the sound directed through
two speakers ▷ *noun* **2** a piece
of equipment that reproduces
sound from records, tapes or CDs
directing the sound through two
speakers

stereotype *noun* **1** fixed image or
set of characteristics that people
consider to represent a particular
type of person or thing ▷ *verb*
2 to make assumptions about
what sort of person someone
is and how they will behave,
based on beliefs about group

characteristics

sterile *adjective* **1** free from germs
2 unable to produce offspring or
seeds **3** lacking in new ideas and
enthusiasm > **sterility** *noun*: *an
infection that can cause permanent
sterility*

sterilize *verb* **1** to make
(something) completely clean
and free from germs, usually
by boiling or treating with
antiseptic **2** to give (a person or
animal) an operation to make
them unable to have offspring

sterling *noun* **1** British money
system ▷ *adjective* **2** excellent
in quality

stern *adjective* **1** severe, strict
▷ *noun* **2** rear part of a ship
> **sternly** *adverb*

steroid *noun* chemical that
occurring naturally in your
body and made artificially as a
medicine. Sometimes sportsmen
illegally take them as drugs to
improve their performance

stethoscope *noun* medical
instrument for listening to
sounds made inside the body

stew *noun* **1** dish of small pieces
of savoury food cooked together
slowly in a liquid ▷ *verb* **2** to cook
(meat, vegetables or fruit) slowly
in a closed pot

steward *noun* **1** person who looks
after passengers on a ship or
aircraft **2** official who helps at a
public event such as a race

stewardess *noun* woman who
works on a ship or plane looking
after passengers and serving
meals

stick sticks sticking stuck *noun*
1 long thin piece of wood **2** such a

piece of wood shaped for a special purpose: *hockey stick* **3** something like a stick: *stick of celery* **4** *informal* verbal abuse, criticism ▷ *verb* **5** to push (a pointed object) into (something) **6** to attach (something to something else) with glue or sticky tape **7** to become attached (to something) **8** (of a movable part) to become fixed in position and difficult to move **9** *informal* to put **10** to remain for a long time > **stick by** *verb* to continue to help and support (someone) > **stick out** *verb* **1** to extend or project beyond something else; protrude **2** to be very noticeable > **stick to** *verb* to keep to (something) rather than changing to something else > **stick together** *verb* to stay together and support one another > **stick up** *verb* to point upwards from a surface > **stick up for** *verb informal* to support or defend

sticker *noun* adhesive label or sign

sticking plaster *noun* small piece of fabric that you stick over a cut or sore to protect it

stick insect *noun* insect with a long cylindrical body and long legs, which looks like a twig

sticky stickier stickiest *adjective* **1** covered with a substance that can stick to other things **2** (of paper, tape) with glue on one side so that you can stick it to a surface **3** *informal* difficult, unpleasant **4** (of weather) warm and humid

stiff *adjective* **1** not easily bent or moved **2** difficult or severe: *stiff competition for places* **3** unrelaxed or awkward **4** firm in consistency **5** containing a lot of alcohol; strong: *a stiff drink* **6** (of a breeze, wind) blowing strongly ▷ *adverb* **7** *informal* utterly: *bored stiff* > **stiffly** *adverb* > **stiffness** *noun*

stiffen *verb* **1** to become stiff **2** to make (a fabric) stiff

stifle *verb* **1** to prevent something from happening or continuing; suppress **2** to suffocate > **stifling** *adjective*: *the stifling heat*

stigma stigmas *noun* **1** mark of social disgrace **2** part of a plant that receives pollen

stile *noun* a set of steps allowing people to climb a fence

stiletto stilettos *noun* woman's shoe with a high narrow heel

still *adverb* **1** now as before or in the future as before **2** up to this or that time **3** even or yet: *still more insults* **4** quietly or without movement ▷ *adjective* **5** motionless **6** silent and calm, undisturbed **7** (of a drink) not fizzy ▷ *noun* **8** photograph from a film scene ▷ *verb* **9** to make (something) still > **stillness** *noun*

stillborn *adjective* born dead

stilt *noun* **1** one of the long upright poles on which some buildings are built, for example on wet land **2** one of a pair of poles with footrests on them for walking on above the ground

stilted *adjective* (of conversation, writing, speech) formal, unnatural and rather awkward

stimulant *noun* drug or other substance that makes your body work faster, increasing your heart rate and making it difficult to sleep

stimulate *verb* **1** to encourage (something) to begin or develop:

to stimulate discussion **2** to give (someone) new ideas and enthusiasm ▷ **stimulating** *adjective: a stimulating environment* ▷ **stimulation** *noun*

stimulus **stimuli** *noun* something that causes a process or event to begin or develop

sting **stings** **stinging** **stung** *verb* **1** (of certain animals or plants) to wound by injecting with poison **2** (of a part of your body) to be a source of sharp tingling pain **3** (of a comment, remark) to cause (someone) to feel upset ▷ *noun* **4** sharp pointed organ of certain animals or plants by which poison can be injected

stink **stinks** **stinking** **stank** **stunk** *verb* **1** to give off a strong unpleasant smell ▷ *noun* **2** strong unpleasant smell

stint *noun* **1** period of time spent doing a particular job ▷ *verb* **2** **stint on** to be mean or miserly with

stipulate *verb formal* to specify as a condition of an agreement ▷ **stipulation** *noun*

stir **stirs** **stirring** **stirred** *verb* **1** to mix (a liquid) by moving a spoon etc around in it **2** to move slightly **3** to make (someone) feel strong emotions ▷ *noun* **4** excitement or shock

stirring *adjective* causing excitement, emotion and enthusiasm

stirrup *noun* one of a pair of metal loops attached to a saddle in which a rider places his or her feet

stitch *verb* **1** to sew or repair by sewing ▷ *noun* **2** one of the loops of thread that can be seen where material or a wound has been sewn **3** loop of yarn formed round a needle or hook in knitting or crochet **4** sharp pain in the side

stoat *noun* small wild animal of the weasel family, with brown fur that turns white in winter

stock *noun* **1** total amount of goods available for sale in a shop **2** supply stored for future use **3** financial shares in, or capital of, a company **4** liquid produced by boiling meat, fish, bones or vegetables **5** farm animals **6** ancestry **7** *History* **stocks** instrument of punishment consisting of a wooden frame with holes into which the hands and feet of the victim were locked ▷ *verb* **8** (of a shop) to keep (goods) for sale **9** to fill (a cupboard or shelf) with goods **10** to supply (a farm) with livestock or (a lake etc) with fish ▷ *adjective* **11** (of a phrase) clichéd or hackneyed ▷ **stock up** *verb* (often followed by *with, on*) to buy in a supply (of something)

stockbroker *noun* person who buys and sells stocks and shares for customers

stock exchange *noun* institution for the buying and selling of shares

stocking *noun* close-fitting covering for the foot and leg

stockman **stockmen** *noun* man who looks after sheep or cattle on a farm

stock market *noun* organization and activity involved in buying and selling stocks and shares

stockpile *verb* **1** to store a large quantity of (something) for future use ▷ *noun* **2** large store of something

stocktaking noun counting, checking and valuing of the goods in a shop

stocky stockier stockiest adjective (of a person) broad and sturdy

stoke verb to keep (a fire or furnace) burning by moving or adding fuel

stomach noun 1 organ in your body which digests food 2 front part of your body below the waist; abdomen ▷ verb 3 to put up with

stone stones stoning stoned noun 1 material of which rocks are made 2 a small piece of rock 3 gem; jewel 4 hard central part of some fruits 5 unit of weight equal to 14 pounds or 6.350 kilograms 6 hard deposit formed in the kidney or bladder ▷ verb 7 to throw stones at 8 to remove stones from (a fruit)

stoned adjective informal under the influence of drugs

stony stonier stoniest adjective 1 containing stones or like stone 2 unfeeling or hard

stool noun 1 seat with legs but without arms or a back 2 lump of excrement or faeces

stoop verb 1 to bend (the body) forward and downward 2 to walk with your body bent forward and downward 3 to degrade oneself ▷ noun 4 stooping posture

stop stops stopping stopped verb 1 to cease from doing (something) 2 to bring to or come to a halt 3 to prevent or restrain 4 to withhold 5 to block or plug 6 to stay or rest ▷ noun 7 stopping or being stopped 8 place where a bus, train or other vehicle stops 9 full stop 10 put a stop to to prevent (something) from happening or continuing 11 come to a stop to come to a halt

stoppage noun, noun mass stopping of work on account of a disagreement with an employer

stopper noun piece of glass or cork that fits into the neck of a jar or bottle

stopwatch noun watch which can be stopped instantly for exact timing of a sporting event

storage noun 1 storing 2 space for storing

store noun 1 shop 2 supply kept for future use 3 storage place, such as a warehouse 4 in store about to happen 5 stores stock of provisions ▷ verb 6 to collect and keep (things) for future use 7 to put (furniture etc) in a warehouse for safekeeping

storeroom noun room where things are kept until they are needed

storey storeys noun floor or level of a building

stork noun very large white and black wading bird with long red legs and a long bill

storm noun 1 violent weather with wind, rain or snow and often thunder and lightning 2 angry or excited reaction ▷ verb 3 (often followed by out) to rush violently or angrily 4 to shout angrily 5 to attack or capture (a place) suddenly >**stormy** adjective 1 characterized by storms 2 involving violent emotions

story stories noun 1 description of a series of events told or written for entertainment 2 plot of a book or film 3 news report

4 *informal* lie

stout *adjective* **1** fat **2** thick, strong and sturdy **3** determined, firm and strong ▷ *noun* **4** strong dark beer >**stoutly** *adverb*

stove *noun* apparatus for cooking or heating

stow *verb* to store or pack >**stow away** *verb* to hide on a ship or aircraft in order to travel free

straddle *verb* **1** to have one leg or part on each side of (something) **2** to be positioned across and on two sides of (something), linking the two parts: *The town straddles a river*

straight *adjective* **1** not curved or crooked **2** level or upright **3** honest or frank **4** (of spirits) undiluted **5** neat and tidy ▷ *adverb* **6** in a straight line **7** immediately **8** in a level or upright position ▷ *noun* **9** straight part, especially of a racetrack

straightaway *adverb* immediately

straighten *verb* **1** to remove any bends or curves from **2** to make (something) neat and tidy **3** to organize and sort out (a confused situation)

straightforward *adjective* **1** (of a task) easy and involving no problems **2** honest, frank

strain *noun* **1** worry and nervous tension **2** force exerted by straining **3** injury from overexertion **4** great demand on strength or resources **5** melody or theme **6** breed or variety ▷ *verb* **7** to cause (something) to be used or tested beyond its limits **8** to injure (yourself or a muscle) by overexertion **9** to make an

intense effort **10** to sieve

strained *adjective* **1** not relaxed, tense **2** not natural, forced

strait *noun* narrow channel connecting two areas of sea

straitjacket *noun* special strong jacket used to tie the arms of a violent person tightly around their body

strait-laced *adjective* prudish or puritanical

strand *noun* **1** single thread of string, wire, etc **2** element or part **3** *literary* shore

stranded *adjective* stuck somewhere with no means of leaving

strange *adjective* **1** odd or unusual **2** not familiar >**strangely** *adverb* >**strangeness** *noun*

stranger *noun* **1** person you have never met before **2** (followed by *to*) someone who is inexperienced in or unaccustomed to something

strangle *verb* to kill (someone) by squeezing their throat >**strangulation** *noun* strangling

strangled *adjective* (of a sound, cry) unclear and muffled

stranglehold *noun* complete power or control over someone or something

strap straps strapping strapped *noun* **1** strip of flexible material for lifting, fastening or holding something in place ▷ *verb* **2** to fasten (something) with a strap or straps

strapping *adjective* tall, strong and healthy-looking

strata *noun* plural of **stratum**

strategic *adjective* **1** advantageous **2** (of weapons) aimed at an enemy's homeland

strategically adverb

strategy strategies noun **1** overall plan **2** art of planning, especially in war > **strategist** noun

stratum strata noun **1** layer, especially of rock **2** social class

straw noun **1** dried stalks of grain **2** single stalk of straw **3** long thin tube used to suck up liquid into the mouth **4 the last straw** the latest in a series of bad events which makes you feel you cannot stand any more

strawberry strawberries noun sweet fleshy red fruit with small seeds on the outside

stray verb **1** to wander away **2** (of thoughts, the mind) to move on to other topics **3** to deviate from certain moral standards ▷ adjective **4** having strayed **5** scattered, random ▷ noun **5** stray animal

streak noun **1** long band of contrasting colour or substance **2** quality or characteristic **3** short stretch (of good or bad luck) ▷ verb **4** to mark (something) with streaks **5** to move rapidly **6** informal to run naked in public > **streaky** adjective

stream noun **1** small river **2** steady flow of something **3** schoolchildren grouped together by age and ability ▷ verb **4** to flow steadily **5** to float in the air **6** to group (pupils) in streams

streamer noun **1** strip of coloured paper that unrolls when tossed **2** long narrow flag

streamline verb **1** to give (a car, plane, etc) a smooth even shape to offer least resistance to the flow of air or water **2** to make (an organization or process) more efficient by removing parts of it

street noun public road, usually lined with buildings

strength noun **1** quality of being strong **2** quality or ability considered an advantage **3** how strong or weak something is **4** total number of people in a group **5 on the strength of** on the basis of

strengthen verb **1** to give (something) more power, influence or support and make it more likely to succeed **2** to improve (an object) or add to its structure so that it can withstand rough treatment; reinforce

strenuous adjective involving a lot of effort or energy > **strenuously** adverb

stress noun **1** worry and nervous tension **2** emphasis **3** stronger sound in saying a word or syllable **4** Physics force producing strain ▷ verb **5** to emphasize **6** to put stress on (a word or syllable) > **stressful** adjective: a stressful time

stretch verb **1** to extend or be extended **2** to be able to be stretched **3** to hold out your legs or arms as far as you can **4** to pull (something soft or elastic) so that it becomes longer or bigger **5** to strain (resources or abilities) to the utmost ▷ noun **6** act of stretching **7** continuous expanse of land or water **8** period of time

stretcher noun frame covered with canvas, on which an injured person is carried

strewn adjective untidily scattered: The costumes were strewn all over the floor

stricken adjective seriously

affected by disease, grief or pain, etc

strict *adjective* **1** stern or severe **2** sticking closely to specified rules **3** (of a meaning, sense, etc) complete, absolute

strictly *adverb* **1** only: *I was in it strictly for the money* **2 strictly speaking** in fact; really

stride *strides striding strode stridden verb* **1** to walk with long steps ▷ *noun* **2** long step **3** regular pace **4 strides** progress

strident *adjective* loud and harsh

strife *noun formal* conflict, quarrelling

strike *strikes striking struck noun* **1** stoppage of work as a protest **2** a military attack: *the threat of air strikes* ▷ *verb* **3** to hit **4** (of an illness, disaster or enemy) to attack suddenly **5** to light (a match) by rubbing the head against something **6** (of a clock) to indicate (a time) by sounding a bell **7** (of a thought, idea) to enter the mind of (someone) **8** to discover (gold, oil, etc) **9** to agree (a bargain, deal) **10** to stop work as a protest **11 be struck by** to be impressed by ▷ **strike off** *verb* to remove (someone) from the official register of those allowed to practise in their profession ▷ **strike out** *verb* to cross (something) out ▷ **strike up** *verb* **1** to begin (a conversation or friendship) **2** (of a band, orchestra) to begin to play

striker *noun* **1** striking worker **2** (in soccer) a player whose function is to attack and score goals

striking *adjective* impressive or very noticeable ▷ **strikingly**

adverb

string *strings stringing strung noun* **1** thin cord used for tying **2** set of objects threaded on a string **3** series of things or events **4** stretched wire or cord on a musical instrument that produces sound when vibrated **5 strings a** restrictions or conditions **b** section of an orchestra consisting of stringed instruments **6 pull strings** to use your influence ▷ *verb* **7** to provide with a string or strings **8** to thread (objects, beads) on a string ▷ **string along** *verb* to deceive (someone) over a period of time ▷ **string out** *verb* to make (something) last longer than necessary ▷ **string up** *verb informal* to kill (someone) by hanging

stringed *adjective* (of a musical instrument) having strings that are plucked or played with a bow

stringent *adjective* (of rules and conditions) strictly controlled or enforced

stringy-bark *noun* any Australian eucalypt that has bark that peels off in long, tough strands

strip *strips stripping stripped noun* **1** long narrow piece **2** *Brit, Aust, NZ* clothes a sports team plays in ▷ *verb* **3** to take your clothes off **4** to remove the covering from the surface of **5** to **strip someone of** to take (a title or possession) away from someone **6** to dismantle (an engine)

stripe *noun* **1** long narrow band of contrasting colour or substance **2** narrow band of material worn on a uniform to show someone's rank >**striped** or**stripy** or**stripey** adjective with a pattern of stripes

stripper noun entertainer who performs a striptease

striptease noun entertainment in which a performer undresses to music

strive strives striving strove striven verb to make a great effort (to do something)

stroke verb 1 to touch or caress (something) lightly with your hand ▷ noun 2 light touch or caress with the hand 3 serious medical condition involving a blockage or a rupture of a blood vessel in the brain 4 blow 5 chime of a clock 6 mark made by a pen or paintbrush 7 style or method of swimming 8 **stroke of luck** piece of luck; lucky break

stroll verb 1 to walk in a leisurely manner; amble ▷ noun 2 leisurely walk

stroller noun Aust pushchair

strong adjective 1 having powerful muscles 2 not easily broken 3 great in degree or intensity 4 determined 5 (of an argument) supported by evidence 6 having a specified number: twenty strong 7 good: a strong candidate 8 (of an economy, currency, relationship) stable and successful ▷ adverb 9 **still going strong** still healthy or doing well after a long time >**strongly** adverb

stronghold noun 1 place that is held and defended by an army 2 place where an attitude or belief is strongly held

structure noun 1 something that has been built or constructed; construction 2 the way something is made, built or organized 3 quality of being well planned and organized: The days have no real structure ▷ verb 4 to arrange (something) into an organized pattern or system >**structural** adjective >**structurally** adverb

struggle verb 1 to try hard (to do something) but with difficulty or in difficult circumstances 2 to move about violently in an attempt to get free 3 to fight (with someone) ▷ noun 4 something requiring a lot of effort 5 fight

strum strums strumming strummed verb to play (a guitar or banjo) by sweeping the thumb or a plectrum across the strings

strut struts strutting strutted verb 1 to walk pompously; swagger ▷ noun 2 piece of wood or metal which strengthens or supports part of a building or structure

Stuart noun family name of the monarchs who ruled Scotland from 1371 to 1714 and England from 1603 to 1714

stub stubs stubbing stubbed noun 1 short piece (of a pencil, cigarette) left after use 2 part of a cheque or ticket that you keep; counterfoil ▷ verb 3 to strike (your toe) painfully against an object >**stub out** verb to put out (a cigarette) by pressing the end against a surface

stubble noun 1 short stalks of grain left in a field after reaping 2 short growth of hair on the chin of a man who has not shaved recently >**stubbly** adjective

stubborn adjective 1 refusing to agree or give in;

obstinate **2** difficult to deal with > **stubbornly** adverb > **stubbornness** noun

stuck verb **1** past of **stick** ▷ adjective **2** fixed or jammed and unable to move **3** unable to get away **4** unable to continue

stuck-up adjective informal conceited or snobbish

stud noun **1** small piece of metal attached to a surface for decoration **2** disc-like removable fastener for clothes **3** one of several small round objects fixed to the sole of a football boot to give better grip **4** male animal, especially a stallion, kept for breeding **5** (also **stud farm**) place where horses are bred

studded adjective decorated with small pieces of metal or precious stones

student noun person who studies a subject, especially at university

studied adjective (of an action or response) carefully practised or planned

studio studios noun **1** workroom of an artist or photographer **2** place containing special equipment where records, films or radio or television programmes are made

studious adjective inclined to spend a lot of time studying

studiously adverb carefully and deliberately

study studies studying studied verb **1** to spend time learning (a subject) **2** to investigate (something) by observation and research **3** to look at (something) carefully ▷ noun **4** activity of studying **5** piece of research on a

particular subject **6** sketch done as practice or preparation **7** room for studying in

stuff noun **1** substance or material **2** collection of unnamed things ▷ verb **3** to push (something) somewhere quickly and roughly **4** to fill (something) with a substance or objects **5** to fill (food) with a seasoned mixture **6** to fill (an animal's skin) with material to restore the shape of the live animal

stuffing noun **1** seasoned mixture used to stuff poultry or vegetables **2** padding

stuffy stuffier stuffiest adjective **1** lacking fresh air; airless **2** very formal and old-fashioned

stumble verb **1** to trip and nearly fall **2** to walk in an unsure way **3** to make frequent mistakes in speech > **stumble across** or **on** verb to discover (something) accidentally

stump noun **1** base of a tree left when the main trunk has been cut away **2** part of a thing left after a larger part has been removed **3** Cricket one of the three upright sticks forming the wicket ▷ verb **4** to baffle > **stump up** verb informal to provide (the money required)

stun stuns stunning stunned verb **1** to shock or overwhelm (someone) **2** to knock (a person or animal) unconscious with a blow to the head

stunning adjective very attractive or impressive

stunt noun **1** acrobatic or dangerous action **2** anything spectacular done to gain publicity ▷ verb **3** to prevent or impede the growth or development of something

stupendous adjective very large or impressive ▷ **stupendously** adverb

stupid adjective 1 lacking intelligence 2 silly or lacking in good judgment > **stupidity** noun > **stupidly** adverb

sturdy sturdier sturdiest adjective strong and firm and unlikely to be damaged or injured > **sturdily** adverb

sturgeon noun fish from which caviar is obtained

stutter noun 1 difficulty in speaking characterized by a tendency to repeat sounds at the beginning of words and a problem completing words ▷ verb 2 to hesitate or repeat sounds when speaking

sty sties noun pen for pigs; pigsty

stye styes noun infection at the base of an eyelash

style noun 1 manner of writing, speaking or doing something 2 shape or design 3 elegance and smartness 4 current fashion ▷ verb 5 to shape or design (something)

stylish adjective smart, elegant and fashionable; chic; smart > **stylishly** adverb

suave adjective smooth and sophisticated in manner > **suavely** adverb

sub- prefix used with many main words to mean: 1 under or beneath: submarine 2 subordinate: sublieutenant 3 falling short of: subnormal 4 forming a subdivision: subheading

subconscious noun 1 Psychoanalysis part of your mind that can influence you without your being aware of it ▷ adjective 2 happening or existing in someone's subconscious and therefore not directly realized or understood by them: a subconscious fear of rejection > **subconsciously** adverb

subcontinent noun large land mass that is a distinct part of a continent

subdue subdues subduing subdued verb 1 to overcome and bring under control 2 to make (a colour, light or emotion) less strong

subdued adjective 1 rather quiet and sad 2 not very noticeable or bright

subject noun 1 person or thing being discussed, dealt with or studied 2 Grammar word or phrase that represents the person or thing performing the action of the verb in a sentence. For example, in the sentence My cat catches birds, my cat is the subject 3 area of study 4 person living under the rule of a monarch or government ▷ verb 5 to **subject someone to** to cause someone to undergo or experience (something unpleasant) ▷ adjective 6 **subject to a** affected by; liable to **b** conditional upon

subjective adjective based on personal feelings and prejudices rather than on fact and rational thought

subjunctive Grammar noun 1 form of the verb sometimes used when expressing doubt, supposition or wishes ▷ *adjective* **2** in or of that mood

sublime *adjective* **1** awe-inspiring and uplifting **2** unparalleled; supreme > **sublimely** *adverb*

submarine *noun* ship that can travel beneath the surface of the sea

submerge *verb* to go below or to put (something) below the surface of a liquid

submission *noun* **1** state of being submissive and under someone's control **2** act of submitting **3** something submitted for consideration

submissive *adjective* quiet and obedient

submit **submits** **submitting** **submitted** *verb* **1** (often followed by *to*) to surrender yourself or agree (to something) because you are not powerful enough to resist it **2** to send in (an application or proposal) for consideration

subordinate *noun* **1** person under the authority of another ▷ *adjective* **2** of lesser rank or importance ▷ *verb* **3** to treat (something) as less important

subordinate clause *noun* *Grammar* clause which adds details to the main clause of a sentence

subscribe *verb* **1** to pay (a subscription) **2** to give support or approval (to a theory, belief, etc) > **subscriber** *noun*

subscription *noun* sum of money that you pay regularly to belong to an organization or to receive regular copies of a magazine

subsequent *adjective* occurring or coming into existence after

something else: *the December uprising and the subsequent political violence* > **subsequently** *adverb*

subservient *adjective* submissive, servile > **subservience** *noun*

subside *verb* **1** to become less intense **2** to sink to a lower level

subsidence *noun* act or process of subsiding

subsidiary **subsidiaries** *noun* **1** company which is part of a larger company ▷ *adjective* **2** of lesser importance

subsidize *verb* **1** to provide part of the cost of (something) **2** to help (someone) financially > **subsidized** *adjective*

subsidy **subsidies** *noun* financial aid

substance *noun* **1** solid, powder, liquid or paste **2** essential meaning of something **3** solid or meaningful quality **4** physical composition of something **5** wealth

substantial *adjective* **1** of considerable size or value **2** (of food or a meal) sufficient and nourishing **3** solid or strong

substantially *adverb* generally, essentially or mostly

substitute *verb* **1** to take the place of (something or someone) or to put (something or someone) in the place of another ▷ *noun* **2** person or thing taking the place of (another) > **substitution** *noun*: *the substitution of margarine for butter*

subterfuge *noun* the use of tricks or deceitful methods to achieve an objective

subtitle *noun* **1** secondary title of a book **2** **subtitles** printed

a b c d e f g h i j k l m n o p q r s t u v w x y z

translation or transcript that appears at the bottom of the screen for some films and television programmes ▷ *verb* **3** to provide with a subtitle or subtitles

subtle *adjective* **1** very fine, delicate or small in degree **2** using indirect methods to achieve something > **subtlety** *noun* > **subtly** *adverb*

subtract *verb* to take (one number or quantity) from another

subtraction *noun* subtracting of one number from another, or a sum in which you do this

suburb *noun* residential area on the outskirts of a city

suburban *adjective* **1** relating to a suburb or suburbs **2** dull and conventional

suburbia *noun* suburbs and their inhabitants

subversive *adjective* **1** intended to destroy or weaken a political system: *subversive activities* ▷ *noun* **2** person who tries to destroy or weaken a political system > **subversion** *noun*

subvert *verb* formal to cause (something) to weaken or fail

subway *noun* **1** passage under a road or railway **2** underground railway

succeed *verb* **1** to achieve the intended result **2** to turn out satisfactorily **3** to come next in order after **4** to take over a position from > **succeeding** *adjective*

success *noun* **1** achievement of something attempted **2** attainment of wealth, fame or position **3** successful person

or thing

successful *adjective* having success > **successfully** *adverb*

succession *noun* **1** series of people or things following one another in order **2** act of succeeding someone to an important position **3** right by which someone succeeds to an important position **4 in succession** without a break

successive *adjective* occurring one after the other without a break; consecutive

successor *noun* person who succeeds someone in a position

succinct *adjective* brief and clear > **succinctly** *adverb*

succulent *adjective* juicy and delicious > **succulence** *noun*

succumb *verb* **1** (followed by *to*) to give way (to something overpowering) **2** to die of (an illness)

such *adjective* **1** of the kind specified **2** so, so great or so much: *I have such a terrible sense of guilt* ▷ *pronoun* **3** such things **4 such and such** something specific but not known or named **5 such as** like

suchlike *pronoun* such or similar things: *shampoos, talcs, toothbrushes and suchlike*

suck *verb* **1** to draw (liquid or air) into the mouth **2** to take (something) into your mouth and lick, dissolve or roll it around with your tongue **3** (followed by *in*) to draw (something or someone) in by irresistible force > **suck up to** *verb* informal to do things to please (someone) in order to obtain praise or approval

sucker noun **1** informal person who is easily fooled or cheated **2** pad, organ or device which sticks to something using suction

suckle verb **1** (of a mother) to feed (a baby) at the breast **2** (of a baby) to feed at its mother's breast >**suckling** noun unweaned baby or young animal

sucrose noun chemical name for sugar

suction noun **1** force involved when a substance is drawn or sucked from one place to another **2** process by which two surfaces stick together when the air between them is removed: *They stay there by suction*

Sudanese adjective **1** belonging or relating to the Sudan ▷ noun **2** someone from the Sudan

sudden adjective happening quickly and unexpectedly >**suddenly** adverb >**suddenness** noun

sudoku noun puzzle in which a player enters numbers in a square made up of nine three-by-three grids, so that every column, row, and grid contains the numbers one to nine

sue sues suing sued verb to start legal proceedings against

suede noun thin, soft leather with a velvety finish on one side

suffer verb **1** to experience pain or misery **2** to deteriorate in condition or quality **3** to undergo or be subjected to (pain, injury) **4** to tolerate >**sufferer** noun >**suffer from** verb to be affected by (a condition) >**suffering** noun

suffice verb formal to be enough for a purpose

sufficient adjective enough, adequate >**sufficiently** adverb

suffix noun letter or letters added to the end of a word to form another word, for example -ly and -ness in smartly and softness

suffocate verb **1** to be killed or to kill (someone) by deprivation of oxygen **2** to feel uncomfortable from heat and lack of air >**suffocation** noun

suffrage noun right to vote in political elections

suffragette noun (in Britain in the early 20th century) a woman who campaigned militantly for the right to vote

suffused adjective literary **suffused with** flooded with (light or colour)

sugar noun sweet substance used to sweeten food and drinks

suggest verb **1** to propose (an idea, plan) **2** to bring (something) to mind or indicate

suggestion noun **1** thing suggested **2** hint or indication

suggestive adjective **1** suggesting something indecent or sexual in nature **2** suggestive of conveying a hint of >**suggestively** adverb

suicidal adjective **1** liable to commit suicide **2** having potentially fatal consequences; very dangerous >**suicidally** adverb

suicide noun **1** killing oneself intentionally **2** person who kills himself or herself intentionally **3** self-inflicted ruin of someone's own prospects or interests: *political suicide*

suicide bomber noun terrorist who carries out a bomb attack, knowing that he or she will be killed in the explosion

suit noun 1 set of clothes designed to be worn together 2 outfit worn for a specific purpose 3 one of the four sets into which a pack of cards is divided 4 lawsuit ▷ verb 5 to be acceptable to or convenient for 6 (of a colour, piece of clothing) to cause (someone) to look good

suitable adjective appropriate or proper > **suitability** noun: his suitability for the role > **suitably** adverb: a lack of suitably qualified applicants

suitcase noun case in which you carry your clothes when you are travelling

suite noun 1 set of connected rooms in a hotel 2 set of matching furniture or bathroom fittings 3 set of musical pieces in the same key

suited adjective right or appropriate for a particular purpose or person: He is well suited to be minister for the arts

suitor noun old-fashioned man who is courting a woman

sulk verb 1 to be silent and sullen because of resentment or bad temper ▷ noun 2 resentful or sullen mood > **sulky** adjective

sullen adjective disagreeably silent and unwilling to be sociable > **sullenly** adverb

sulphur noun Chemistry pale yellow nonmetallic element which burns with a very unpleasant smell

sultan noun (of certain Muslim countries) ruler or sovereign

sultana noun 1 dried grape 2 the wife of a sultan

sum sums summing summed noun 1 amount of money 2 problem in arithmetic; calculation 3 total > **sum up** verb 1 to summarize 2 to form a quick opinion of

summarize verb to give a short account of the main points of

summary summaries noun 1 brief account giving the main points of something; précis; résumé ▷ adjective 2 done quickly, without formalities: Summary executions are common > **summarily** adverb: He was summarily dismissed

summer noun warmest season of the year, between spring and autumn

summit noun 1 top of a mountain or hill 2 highest point 3 meeting between heads of state or other high officials to discuss particular issues

summon verb 1 to order (someone) to come 2 (often followed by up) to gather (one's courage, strength, etc)

summons summonses summonsing summonsed noun 1 official order requiring someone to appear in court 2 an order to go to someone ▷ verb 3 to order (someone) to appear in court

sumptuous adjective lavish, magnificent

sum total noun complete or final total

sun suns sunning sunned noun 1 star around which the earth and other planets revolve 2 any star around which planets revolve 3 heat and light from the sun ▷ verb 4 to expose (yourself) to the sun's rays

sunbathe verb to lie in the sunshine in order to get a suntan

sunburn noun painful reddening of the skin caused by overexposure to the sun > **sunburnt** or **sunburned** adjective

sundae noun ice cream topped with fruit etc

Sunday noun day between Saturday and Monday

Sunday school noun special class held on Sundays to teach children about Christianity

sundial noun device showing the time by means of a pointer that casts a shadow on a marked dial

sundry adjective **1** several, various **2 all and sundry** everybody

sunflower noun tall plant with large golden flowers

sunglasses plural noun spectacles with dark lenses that you wear to protect your eyes from the sun

sunken verb **1** a past participle of **sink** ▷ adjective **2** having sunk to the bottom of the sea, a river or lake **3** constructed below the level of the surrounding area **4** curving inwards: Her cheeks were sunken

sunlight noun bright light produced when the sun is shining > **sunlit** adjective

sunny sunnier sunniest adjective full of or exposed to sunlight

sunrise noun **1** daily appearance of the sun above the horizon **2** time of this

sunset noun **1** daily disappearance of the sun below the horizon **2** time of this

sunshine noun light and warmth from the sun

sunstroke noun illness caused by spending too much time in hot sunshine

suntan noun browning of the skin caused by exposure to the sun > **suntanned** adjective

super adjective informal very nice or very good; excellent

super- prefix used with many main words to mean: **1** above or over: superimpose **2** outstanding: superstar **3** of greater size or extent: supermarket

superb adjective excellent, impressive or splendid > **superbly** adverb

supercilious adjective showing arrogant pride or scorn

superego superegos noun psychology part of your mind that acts as a conscience

superficial adjective **1** not careful or thorough **2** (of a person) without depth of character, shallow **3** of or on the surface > **superficially** adverb

superfluous adjective formal unnecessary or no longer needed

superhuman adjective beyond normal human ability or experience

superimpose verb to place (something) on or over something else

superintendent noun **1** senior police officer **2** supervisor

superior adjective **1** greater in quality, quantity or merit **2** higher in position or rank **3** believing oneself to be better than others ▷ noun **4** person of greater rank or status > **superiority** noun

superlative adjective **1** of outstanding quality ▷ noun

a b c d e f g h i j k l m n o p q r s t u v w x y z

2 *Grammar* the form of an adjective or adverb that indicates the greatest degree of it: *quickest*; *best*; *easiest*

supermarket *noun* large self-service store selling food and household goods

supernatural *adjective* **1** of or relating to things beyond the laws of nature ▷ *noun* **2 the supernatural** supernatural forces, occurrences and beings collectively

superpower *noun* extremely powerful nation

supersede *verb* to replace or supplant on account of being more modern

supersize or **supersized** *adjective* larger than standard size

supersonic *adjective* of or travelling at a speed greater than the speed of sound

superstar *noun* very famous entertainer or sports player

superstition *noun* **1** irrational beliefs founded on ignorance or fear **2** idea or practice based on the belief that certain things bring good or bad luck >**superstitious** *adjective*

supervise *verb* to watch over (an activity) in order to check that it is carried out correctly or safely >**supervision** *noun* >**supervisor** *noun*

supper *noun* light evening meal

supplant *verb* to take the place of (someone or something); oust

supple *adjective* able to bend and move easily

supplement *verb* **1** to add something to (something) in order to improve it **2** to add to

(something) ▷ *noun* **3** thing added to complete something or make up for a lack **4** magazine inserted into a newspaper

supplementary *adjective* added to something else to improve it

supplier *noun* firm that provides particular goods

supply supplies supplying supplied *verb* **1** to provide (someone) with something **2** to provide or send (something) ▷ *noun* **3** amount available **4** supplying **5** *Economics* willingness and ability to provide goods and services: *All food prices are based on supply and demand* **6 supplies** food or equipment

support *verb* **1** to take an active interest in and hope for the success of (a sports team, political principle, etc) **2** to bear the weight of; hold up **3** to give practical or emotional help to **4** to provide (someone) with money for the necessities of life **5** to help to prove (a theory etc) ▷ *noun* **6** supporting **7** means of support **8** encouragement and help **9** money >**supporter** *noun* person who supports a team, principle, etc

supportive *adjective* (of a person) encouraging and helpful in troubled times

suppose *verb* **1** to presume to be true **2** to consider as a proposal for the sake of discussion **3 be supposed to a** to be expected or required to: *You were supposed to phone me* **b** to be permitted to: *We're not supposed to swim here* >**supposing** or **suppose** *conjunction* what if

supposed *adjective* presumed to

be true without proof; alleged
> **supposedly** adverb: a supposedly
safe investment

supposition noun 1 something
supposed 2 supposing

suppress verb 1 to put an end
to 2 to prevent publication
of (information) 3 to restrain
(an emotion or response)
> **suppression** noun

supremacy noun 1 supreme
power 2 state of being supreme

supreme adjective highest
in authority, rank or degree
> **supremely** adverb extremely

surcharge noun additional charge

sure adjective 1 free from
uncertainty or doubt 2 reliable or
accurate 3 inevitable or certain
4 **sure of** confident about
▷ adverb, interjection 5 informal
certainly > **surely** adverb it must
be true that

surf noun 1 foam caused by waves
breaking on the shore ▷ verb 2 to
go surfing 3 **surf the Internet**
to go from website to website
reading the information > **surfer**
noun

surface noun 1 outside or top of an
object 2 superficial appearance
▷ verb 3 to come up from under
the water

surfboard noun long smooth
board used in surfing

surf club noun Aust organization of
lifesavers in charge of safety on a
particular beach, and which often
provides leisure facilities

surfeit noun excessive amount;
too much

surfing noun sport of riding
towards the shore on a surfboard
on the crest of a wave

surge noun 1 sudden powerful
increase. ▷ verb 2 to increase
suddenly 3 to move forward
strongly

surgeon noun doctor who
performs operations

surgery surgeries noun
1 treatment involving cutting
open part of the patient's body
to treat the affected part 2 place
where a doctor, dentist, etc can
be consulted 3 occasion when
a doctor or dentist is available
for consultation 4 Brit occasion
when an elected politician is
available for consultation

surgical adjective used in or
involving a medical operation
> **surgically** adverb

surly surlier surliest adjective
ill-tempered and rude > **surliness**
noun

surmise verb, noun (to) guess;
conjecture

surmount verb to overcome
(a problem) > **surmountable**
adjective: He see any hurdles as
surmountable.

surname noun family name; last
name

surpass verb formal to be greater
than or superior to

surplus surpluses noun amount
left over in excess of what is
required

surprise noun 1 unexpected
event 2 amazement and wonder
▷ verb 3 to cause (someone)
to feel amazement or wonder
4 to come upon, attack or
catch (someone) suddenly
and unexpectedly > **surprised**
adjective: I was surprised to see him
there > **surprising** adjective: a

surprising choice

surreal adjective very strange and dreamlike; bizarre

surrender verb 1 to stop fighting and give oneself up 2 to give away (to a temptation or influence) 3 to give (something) up to another ▷ noun 4 surrendering

surreptitious adjective done secretly or stealthily > **surreptitiously** adverb I found myself surreptitiously looking through her diary

surrogate adjective 1 acting as a substitute for someone or something ▷ noun 2 substitute

surround verb 1 to be or come all around (a person or thing) 2 to encircle or enclose (something or someone) with something ▷ noun 3 border or edging

surrounding adjective (of an area) all around: the surrounding countryside

surveillance noun close observation

survey verb 1 to look at or consider (something or someone) as a whole 2 to inspect (a building) to find out what condition it is in and assess its value 3 to examine and measure (an area), often to make a map 4 to find out the opinions or habits of (a group of people) ▷ noun 5 detailed examination of something, often in the form of a report

surveyor noun person whose job is to survey buildings or land

survival noun managing to go on living or existing in spite of great danger or difficulties

survive verb 1 to continue to live or exist after (a difficult experience) 2 to live on after the death of (another) > **survivor** noun

sus- prefix another form of **sub-**

susceptible adjective (often followed by to) liable to be influenced or affected by > **susceptibility** noun: a person's susceptibility to illness

suspect verb 1 to believe (someone) to be guilty of something without having any proof: They suspected her of being a witch 2 to think (something) to be false or questionable: He suspected her motives 3 to believe (something) to be the case: She suspected he was right ▷ noun 4 person who is suspected ▷ adjective 5 not to be trusted

suspend verb 1 to hang (something or someone) from a high place 2 to delay or stop (something) 3 to remove (someone) temporarily from a job or team

suspender noun 1 strap for holding up stockings 2 **suspenders** US braces

suspense noun state of uncertainty while awaiting news, an event, etc

suspension noun 1 delaying or stopping of something 2 temporary removal of someone from their job 3 system of springs and shock absorbers supporting the body of a vehicle 4 liquid mixture in which very small bits of a solid material are contained and are not dissolved

suspicion noun 1 feeling of not trusting a person or thing 2 belief that something is true or likely to happen without definite proof

3 slight trace

suspicious *adjective* **1** (of a person) feeling suspicion **2** (of a thing or person) causing suspicion > **suspiciously** *adverb*

sustain *verb* **1** to keep up, maintain or prolong **2** to give (someone) the energy, strength and nourishment needed to keep them going **3** to suffer (an injury or loss)

sustainable *adjective* **1** capable of being sustained **2** (of development, a resource) capable of being maintained at a steady level without exhausting natural resources or causing ecological damage

sustenance *noun* formal food

swab swabs swabbing swabbed *noun* **1** small swab of cotton wool used to apply medication, clean a wound, etc ▷ *verb* **2** to clean (something) with a mop and a lot of water **3** to clean or take specimens of (a wound) with a swab

swag *noun* **1** informal stolen property **2** swags of *Aust, NZ* informal lots of

swagger *verb* **1** to walk or behave arrogantly ▷ *noun* **2** arrogant walk or manner

swagman swagmen *noun Aust & NZ* history tramp who carried his belongings in a bundle on his back

swallow *verb* **1** to make (something) go down your throat and into your stomach **2** to make a gulping movement in the throat, as when nervous **3** informal to believe (something) gullibly **4** to refrain from showing (a feeling) **5** to engulf or absorb ▷ *noun* **6** small bird with long pointed wings and a forked tail **7** swallowing

swamp *noun* **1** watery area of land; bog ▷ *verb* **2** to cause (something) to fill or be covered with water **3** to overwhelm (something or someone) > **swampy** *adjective*

swan *noun* large usually white water bird with a long graceful neck

swap swaps swapping swapped *verb* **1** to exchange (something) for something else ▷ *noun* **2** exchange

swarm *noun* **1** large group of bees or other insects flying together ▷ *verb* **2** (of bees, insects) to fly together in a large group **3** (of people) to go somewhere quickly and at the same time **4** (of a place) to be crowded or overrun

swarthy swarthier swarthiest *adjective* dark-complexioned

swashbuckling *adjective* having the exciting behaviour of pirates, especially those depicted in films

swastika *noun* symbol in the shape of a cross with the arms bent over at right angles. It was the official symbol of the Nazis in Germany, but in India it is a good luck sign

swat swats swatting swatted *verb* to hit (an insect) sharply in order to kill it

swathe *noun* **1** long strip of cloth wrapped around something **2** long strip of land ▷ *verb* **3** to wrap (someone or something) in bandages or layers of cloth

swathed *adjective* swathed in wrapped in

sway verb 1 to swing to and fro or from side to side or to cause (someone) to waver in opinion ▷ noun 3 power or influence 4 swaying motion

swear swears swearing swore sworn verb 1 to use obscene or blasphemous language 2 to state or promise on oath 3 to state earnestly > **swear by** verb to have complete confidence in > **swear in** verb to cause (someone new to a position) promising to fulfil their duties

swearword noun word considered obscene or blasphemous which some people use when they are angry

sweat noun 1 salty liquid given off through the pores of the skin when you are hot or afraid ▷ verb 2 to have sweat coming through the pores 3 to be anxious

sweater noun (woollen) garment for the upper part of the body

sweatshirt noun long-sleeved cotton jersey

sweaty sweatier sweatiest adjective covered or soaked with sweat

swede noun large round root vegetable with yellow flesh and a brownish-purple skin

Swede noun someone from Sweden

Swedish adjective 1 belonging or relating to Sweden ▷ noun 2 main language spoken in Sweden

sweep sweeping sweeps swept verb 1 to remove dirt from (a floor) with a broom 2 to move smoothly and quickly 3 to spread rapidly 4 to move majestically 5 to carry (something or someone) away

suddenly or forcefully 6 to stretch in a long wide curve ▷ noun 7 sweeping 8 sweeping motion 9 wide expanse 10 sweepstake 11 chimney sweep

sweeping adjective 1 (of a curve or movement) long and wide 2 affecting a lot of people to a great extent; wide-ranging 3 (of a statement) based on a general assumption rather than on careful thought; indiscriminate

sweet adjective 1 tasting of or like sugar 2 kind and charming 3 attractive and delightful 4 (of wine) with a high sugar content 5 pleasant and satisfying ▷ noun 6 things such as toffees, chocolates and mints 7 dessert > **sweetly** adverb > **sweetness** noun

sweet corn noun type of maize with sweet yellow kernels, eaten as a vegetable

sweeten verb to add sugar or another sweet substance to (a food or drink)

sweetener noun sweet, artificial substance that can be used instead of sugar

sweetheart noun 1 form of address for someone you are very fond of 2 boyfriend or girlfriend

sweet pea noun climbing plant with bright fragrant flowers

sweet tooth noun strong liking for sweet foods

swell swells swelling swelled swollen verb 1 to become larger and rounder 2 to increase in number 3 (of a sound) to become gradually louder ▷ noun 4 regular up and down movement of waves in the sea ▷ adjective 5 US informal excellent or fine

swelling noun **1** enlargement of part of the body, caused by injury or infection **2** increase in size

sweltering adjective uncomfortably hot

swerve verb to change direction suddenly to avoid colliding with something

swift adjective **1** moving or able to move quickly ▷ noun **2** fast-flying bird with narrow crescent-shaped wings > **swiftly** adverb > **swiftness** noun

swig swigs swigging swigged verb **1** to drink (something) in large mouthfuls, usually from a bottle ▷ noun **2** large mouthful of drink

swill verb **1** to rinse (something) in large amounts of water **2** to drink (something) greedily ▷ noun **3** sloppy mixture containing waste food, fed to pigs

swim swims swimming swam swum verb **1** to move through water, using your arms and legs to help you **2** to be covered or flooded with liquid **3** to reel: *Her head was swimming* ▷ noun **4** act or period of swimming > **swimmer** noun

swimming noun activity of moving through water using your arms and legs

swimming bath noun public swimming pool

swimming costume noun clothing worn by a woman when she goes swimming

swimming pool noun (building containing) an artificial pond for swimming in

swimming trunks plural noun shorts or briefs worn by a man when he goes swimming

swimsuit noun swimming costume

swindle verb **1** to cheat (someone) out of money or property ▷ noun **2** trick in which someone is cheated out of money or property > **swindler** noun

swine noun **1** pig **2** nasty and unpleasant person

- The plural of *swine* is always *swine* when it refers to pigs.
- Both *swine* and *swines* are possible when it means people

swing swings swinging swung verb **1** to move to and fro from a fixed point **2** to move (something) or to move in a curve **3** (of an opinion or mood) to change sharply **4** informal to be hanged ▷ noun **5** seat hanging from a frame or a branch, which moves backwards and forwards when you sit on it **6** sudden or extreme change **7** instance of swinging

swipe verb **1** to strike (at something) with a sweeping blow **2** informal to steal **3** to pass (a credit card or debit card) through a machine that electronically reads information stored in the card ▷ noun **4** sweeping blow

swirl verb **1** to move quickly in circles ▷ noun **2** whirling motion **3** twisting shape

swish verb **1** to move with a soft whistling or hissing sound ▷ noun **2** whistling or hissing sound ▷ adjective **3** informal fashionable, smart

Swiss adjective **1** belonging or relating to Switzerland ▷ noun

2 person from Switzerland
● The plural of *Swiss* is *Swiss*

switch *noun* **1** small control for an electrical device or machine **2** abrupt change **3** exchange or swap ▷ *verb* **4** to change abruptly (to something) **5** to replace (something) with something else >**switch off** *verb* **1** to turn (a light or machine) off by means of a switch **2** to stop paying attention >**switch on** *verb* to turn (a light or machine) on by means of a switch

switchboard *noun* place in an office where telephone calls are received and connected to the appropriate people

swivel swivels swivelling swivelled *verb* **1** to turn round on a central point ▷ *adjective* **2** (of a chair, stool) revolving

swollen *verb* a past participle of swell ▷ *adjective* **2** having swelled up; enlarged or puffed up

swoon *verb* **1** to faint ▷ *noun* **2** faint

swoop *verb* to sweep down or pounce suddenly

swop same as **swap**

sword *noun* weapon with a long sharp blade and a short handle

swordfish swordfishes or **swordfish** *noun* large fish with a very long upper jaw

sworn *verb* past participle of swear ▷ *adjective* **2** bound by or as if by an oath: *sworn enemies*

swot swots swotting swotted *informal verb* **1** to study or revise hard ▷ *noun* **2** someone who spends too much time studying >**swot up** *verb* to find out as much about a subject as possible in a short time

sycamore *noun* tree that has large leaves with five points

syllable *noun* part of a word pronounced as a unit

syllabus syllabuses or **syllabi** *noun* list of subjects for a particular course or examination

symbol *noun* shape, design or idea that is used to represent something

symbolic *adjective* having a special meaning that is considered to represent something else

symbolize *verb* **1** (of a shape, design or idea) to be a symbol of **2** to represent (something) with a symbol >**symbolism** *noun* **1** representation of something by symbols **2** movement in art and literature using symbols to express abstract and mystical ideas

symmetrical *adjective* having two halves that are mirror images of each other >**symmetrically** *adverb*

symmetry *noun* state of having two halves that are mirror images of each other

sympathetic *adjective* **1** feeling or showing kindness and understanding to other people **2** likeable or appealing **3** (followed by *to, towards*) agreeable or favourably disposed (to something) >**sympathetically** *adverb*

sympathize *verb* **1** to feel or express understanding and concern **2** to have similar feelings

sympathizer or **sympathiser** *noun* supporter of a particular cause

sympathy sympathies *noun*

tab | 539

1 compassion for someone's pain or distress **2** agreement with someone's feelings or interests

symphony symphonies *noun* composition for orchestra, with several movements

symptom *noun* **1** something wrong with your body that is a sign of an illness **2** sign that something is wrong
> **symptomatic** *adjective*: *The price dispute was symptomatic of other problems*

synagogue *noun* place of worship and religious instruction for Jewish people

synchronize *verb* **1** (of two or more people) to perform (an action) at the same time **2** to set (watches) to show the same time **3** to match (the soundtrack and action of a film) precisely
> **synchronization** *noun*

syncopation *noun* *Music* stressing of weak beats instead of the usual strong ones

syndicate *noun* group of people or firms undertaking a joint project

syndrome *noun* **1** medical condition characterized by a particular set of symptoms **2** set of characteristics indicating a particular problem

synod *noun* church council

synonym *noun* word with the same meaning as or a similar meaning to another

synonymous *adjective* **1** having the same or a very similar meaning **2** (followed by *with*) closely associated: *the Statue of Liberty is synonymous with New York*

synopsis synopses *noun* summary or outline of a book,

play or film

syntax *noun* *Grammar* way in which words are arranged to form phrases and sentences

synthetic *adjective* **1** (of a substance) made artificially rather than naturally **2** not genuine; insincere

syphon same as **siphon**

Syrian *adjective* **1** belonging or relating to Syria ▷ *noun* **2** someone from Syria

syringe *noun* **1** hollow tube with a part inside that can be raised or pushed down to draw up or squirt down liquid **2** similar device, with a fine hollow needle at one end, for giving injections and taking blood samples ▷ *verb* **3** to clean (part of the body) using a syringe

syrup *noun* **1** solution of sugar in water **2** thick sweet liquid
> **syrupy** *adjective*

system *noun* **1** method or set of methods for doing something **2** set of interconnected pieces of equipment **3** *Biology* set of organs that together perform a function: *the immune system* **4** scheme of classification or arrangement

systematic *adjective* following a fixed plan and done in an efficient way > **systematically** *adverb*

t

tab *noun* small flap or projecting label

tabby tabbies noun cat with dark stripes on a lighter background

tabernacle noun 1 portable shrine of the Israelites 2 Christian place of worship not called a church 3 Jewish temple

table noun 1 piece of furniture with a flat top supported by legs 2 arrangement of information in columns ▷ verb 3 to submit (a motion) for discussion by a meeting

tablecloth noun a cloth used to cover a table and keep it clean

table football noun game like soccer played on a table with sets of miniature figures on rods allowing them to be moved to hit a ball

tablespoon noun large spoon for serving food

tablet noun 1 pill of compressed medicinal substance 2 inscribed slab of stone etc

table tennis noun game like tennis played on a table with small bats and a light ball

tabloid noun small-sized newspaper with many photographs and a concise, usually sensational style

taboo taboos noun 1 social custom that some words, subjects or actions must be avoided because embarrassing or offensive 2 religious custom that forbids people to do something ▷ adjective 3 forbidden by a taboo

tacit adjective implied but not spoken > **tacitly** adverb

taciturn adjective habitually not talking very much

tack noun 1 short nail with a large head 2 course of action: in desperation I changed tack ▷ verb 3 to fasten (something to a surface) with tacks 4 to stitch (a piece of fabric) with tacks

tackies or **takkies** plural noun S Afr informal tennis shoes or plimsolls

tackle verb 1 to deal with (a task) 2 to confront (an opponent) 3 Sport to attempt to get the ball from (an opposing player) ▷ noun 4 Sport act of tackling an opposing player 5 equipment for fishing

tacky tackier tackiest adjective 1 slightly sticky 2 informal vulgar and tasteless

tact noun skill in avoiding giving offence; diplomacy ▷ **tactful** adjective careful not to offend people > **tactfully** adverb: He tactfully refrained from further comment > **tactless** adjective: tactless remarks > **tactlessly** adverb in a tactless manner

tactic noun method or plan to achieve an end > **tactical** adjective: a tactical move > **tactically** adverb: to vote tactically > **tactics** noun plural art of directing military forces in battle

tactile adjective of or having the sense of touch

tadpole noun black long-tailed larva of a frog or toad

taffeta noun stiff shiny silk or rayon fabric

tag tags tagging tagged noun 1 small label made of cloth, paper or plastic 2 children's game where the person being chased becomes the chaser upon being touched ▷ verb 3 to attach a tag to > **tag along with** verb to accompany (someone), especially if uninvited

tail noun **1** part extending beyond the end of the body of an animal, bird, or fish **2** rear or last part or parts of something ▷ verb **3** informal to follow (someone) secretly >**tail off** verb to become gradually less >**tails** plural noun **1** informal man's coat with a long back split into two below the waist ▷ adjective, adverb **2** with the side of a coin uppermost that does not have a portrait of a head on it

tailback noun Brit queue of traffic stretching back from an obstruction

tailor noun **1** person who makes men's clothes ▷ verb **2** to adapt (something) to suit a purpose

tailor-made adjective perfect for a purpose

taint verb **1** to spoil (something) with a small amount of decay, contamination or other bad quality ▷ noun **2** something that taints

taipan noun Aust large poisonous Australian snake

take takes taking took taken verb **1** to remove (something) from a place **2** to accompany (someone) somewhere **3** to use (a mode of transport or a road) to go from one place to another **4** to steal **5** to swallow (medicine) **6** to bear (something painful): We can't take much more of this **7** to measure (someone's temperature or pulse) **8** to require (time, resources or ability) **9** to accept >**take after** verb to look or behave like (a parent etc) >**take down** verb to write down (what someone is saying)

>**take in** verb **1** to understand **2** to deceive or swindle >**take off** verb (of an aircraft) to leave the ground >**take over** verb to start controlling >**take to** verb to like (someone or something) immediately

takeaway noun shop or restaurant selling meals for eating elsewhere

takings plural noun money received by a shop, theatre or cinema, etc

talc noun talcum powder

talcum powder noun powder, usually scented, used to dry or perfume the body

tale noun story

talent noun natural ability; gift >**talented** adjective: a talented pianist

talisman noun object believed to have magic power

talk verb **1** to express ideas or feelings by means of speech **2** to gossip **3** to make an informal speech about something ▷ noun **4** discussion or gossip **5** speech or lecture >**talkative** adjective fond of talking; chatty >**talk down to** verb to talk to (someone) as if you are more important or clever than him or her

tall adjective **1** higher than average **2** of a specified height: a wall ten metres tall

tally tallies tallying tallied verb **1** (of numbers or statements) to be exactly the same or give the same results or conclusions ▷ noun **2** record of a debt or score

Talmud noun books containing the ancient Jewish ceremonies and civil laws

talon noun bird's hooked claw

tambourine noun percussion instrument like a small drum with jingling metal discs attached

tame adjective **1** (of animals) brought under human control **2** (of animals) not afraid of people **3** uninteresting and unexciting ▷ verb **4** to make (a wild animal) tame

tamper verb (followed by with) to interfere with (something)

tampon noun firm piece of cotton wool inserted into the vagina to absorb the blood during menstruation

tan tans tanning tanned noun **1** brown coloration of the skin from exposure to sunlight ▷ verb **2** (of skin) to go brown from exposure to sunlight **3** to convert (an animal's hide) into leather ▷ adjective **4** yellowish-brown

tandem noun bicycle for two riders, one behind the other

tang noun strong sharp taste or smell ▷ **tangy** adjective having a strong sharp taste or smell

tangata whenua plural noun NZ original Polynesian settlers in New Zealand

tangent noun **1** line that touches a curve without intersecting it **2 go off at a tangent** to move to an unrelated and completely different line of thought or action

tangerine noun **1** small orange-like fruit of an Asian citrus tree **2** reddish orange ▷ adjective **3** reddish-orange

tangible adjective clear or definite enough to be easily seen or felt: tangible proof

tangle noun **1** confused mass or situation ▷ verb **2** to catch or trap (someone) in wires or ropes so that it is difficult to get free

tango tangos noun S American dance

taniwha noun NZ mythical Maori monster that lives in water

tank noun **1** container for liquids or gases **2** armoured fighting vehicle moving on tracks

tankard noun large beer-mug, often with a hinged lid

tanker noun ship or truck for carrying liquid in bulk

tannin noun vegetable substance used in tanning

tantalizing or **tantalising** adjective excitingly and tormentingly desirable but difficult or impossible to get: a tantalizing glimpse of riches to come

tantamount adjective **tantamount** to equivalent in effect to

tantrum noun childish outburst of temper

Tanzanian adjective **1** of Tanzania ▷ noun **2** person from Tanzania

tap taps tapping tapped verb **1** to hit (something) lightly **2** to fit a device to (a telephone) in order to listen secretly to the calls ▷ noun **3** light knock **4** valve to control the flow of liquid from a pipe or cask

tap dancing noun style of dancing in which the dancers wear shoes with metal toe caps and heels that click against the floor

tape noun **1** long thin strip of fabric used for binding or fastening **2** strip of sticky plastic used for sticking things together **3** (recording made on) a cassette containing magnetic tape ▷ *verb* **4** to record (sounds or television pictures) using a tape recorder or a video recorder **5** to attach (things) with sticky tape

tape measure *noun* tape marked off in centimetres or inches for measuring

taper *verb* **1** to become narrower towards one end ▷ *noun* **2** long thin candle

tape recorder *noun* device for recording and reproducing sound on magnetic tape

tapestry tapestries *noun* fabric decorated with coloured woven designs

tar *noun* thick, black, sticky substance used in making roads

tarantula *noun* large hairy spider with a poisonous bite

target *noun* **1** something you aim at when firing weapons **2** goal or objective **3** person or thing at which an action or remark is directed: *a target for our hatred*

tariff *noun* **1** tax that a government collects on imported goods **2** list of fixed prices

Tarmac® *noun* mixture of tar, bitumen and crushed stones used for roads etc

tarnish *verb* **1** to become stained or less bright **2** to damage or taint (someone's reputation)

tarot card *noun* card in a special pack used mainly in fortune-telling

tarpaulin *noun* sheet of heavy waterproof fabric

tarragon *noun* herb with narrow green leaves used in cooking

tarry tarries tarrying tarried *verb old-fashioned* **1** to linger or delay

2 to stay somewhere briefly

tar-seal *noun NZ* tarred road surface

tart *noun* **1** pie or flan with a sweet filling ▷ *adjective* **2** sour or sharp to taste **3** (of a remark) unpleasant and cruel

tartan *noun* **1** design of straight lines crossing at right angles, especially one associated with a Scottish clan **2** cloth with such a pattern

tartar *noun* hard deposit on the teeth

tarwhine *noun* edible Australian sea fish, especially a sea bream

task *noun* (difficult or unpleasant) piece of work to be done; duty

Tasmanian devil *noun* black-and-white marsupial of Tasmania that eats flesh

tassel *noun* decorative fringed knot of threads

taste *noun* **1** sense by which the flavour of a substance is distinguished in the mouth **2** distinctive flavour **3** small amount tasted **4** brief experience of something **5** liking **6** ability to appreciate what is beautiful or excellent ▷ *verb* **7** to distinguish the taste of (a substance) **8** to take a small amount of (something) into the mouth **9** to have a specific taste: *it tastes like chocolate* > **tasteful** *adjective* having or showing good taste > **tastefully** *adverb*: *a tastefully decorated home* > **tasteless** *adjective* **1** vulgar and unattractive **2** (of a remark or joke) offensive **3** (of food) having very little flavour

taste bud *noun* small organ on the

tongue which perceives flavours

tasty tastier tastiest *adjective* pleasantly flavoured

tatters *plural noun* **in tatters** badly torn >**tattered** *adjective* ragged or torn

tattoo tattoos tattooing tattooed *noun* **1** pattern made on the body by pricking the skin and staining it with indelible inks **2** military display or pageant ▷ *verb* **3** to make a pattern on the body of (someone) by pricking the skin and staining it with indelible inks

tatty tattier tattiest *adjective* shabby or worn out

taught *verb* past of **teach**

taunt *verb* **1** to tease (someone) with jeers ▷ *noun* **2** jeering remark

Taurus *noun* second sign of the zodiac, represented by a bull

taut *adjective* drawn tight

tavern *noun* old-fashioned pub

tawdry tawdrier tawdriest *adjective* cheap, showy and of poor quality

tawny *adjective* yellowish-brown

tax *noun* **1** amount of money that people have to pay to the government so that it can provide public services ▷ *verb* **2** to levy a tax on (something) **3** to make heavy demands on (someone) >**taxation** *noun* levying of taxes

taxi taxis taxiing taxied *noun* **1** (also **taxicab**) car with a driver that may be hired to take people to any specified destination ▷ *verb* **2** (of an aircraft) to run along the ground before taking off or after landing

tea *noun* **1** drink made from

infusing the dried leaves of an Asian bush in boiling water **2** cup of this drink **3** leaves used to make this drink **4** *Brit, Aust, NZ* main evening meal **5** *Chiefly Brit* light afternoon meal of tea, cakes, etc **6** drink like tea, made from other plants; infusion

tea bag *noun* small porous bag of tea leaves, placed in boiling water to make tea

teach teaches teaching taught *verb* **1** to tell or show (someone) how to do something **2** to give lessons in (a subject) **3** to cause (someone) to learn or understand >**teacher** *noun* person who teaches, especially in a school >**teaching** *noun: the teaching of English in schools*

teak *noun* very hard wood of a large Asian tree

team *noun* **1** group of people forming one side in a game **2** group of people or animals working together >**team up with** *verb* to join (someone) to work together

teamwork *noun* cooperative work by a team

teapot *noun* container with a lid, spout and handle for making and serving tea

tear tears tearing tore torn *noun* **1** (also **teardrop**) drop of fluid appearing in and falling from the eye **2** hole or split ▷ *verb* **3** to rip a hole in (soemthing) **4** to rush somewhere >**tearful** *adjective* weeping or about to weep >**tearfully** *adverb: She smiled tearfully*

tearaway *noun* wild or unruly person

tease *verb* **1** to make fun of

(someone) in a provoking or playful way ▷ noun **2** person who teases

teaspoon noun small spoon for stirring tea

teat noun **1** nipple of a breast or udder **2** rubber nipple of a feeding bottle

tea tree noun Aust, NZ tree found in Australia and New Zealand with leaves containing tannin, like tea leaves

tech noun informal technical college

technical adjective **1** of or specializing in industrial, practical or mechanical arts and applied sciences **2** skilled in technical subjects **3** relating to a particular field ▷ **technically** adverb according to a strict interpretation of the rules: technically illegal

technical college noun college with courses in subjects like technology and secretarial skills

technicality technicalities noun **1** petty point based on a strict application of rules **2** technicalities detailed methods used for a process or activity

technician noun person skilled in a particular technical field

technique noun **1** method or skill used for a particular task **2** skill and ability developed through training and practice

techno- prefix craft or art: technology

technology technologies noun **1** application of practical or mechanical sciences to industry or commerce **2** area of activity

requiring scientific methods and knowledge: computer technology ▷ **technological** adjective: an era of rapid technological change ▷ **technologically** adverb: technologically advanced

teddy teddies noun soft toy bear; (also **teddy bear**)

tedious adjective causing fatigue or boredom

tedium noun quality of being boring and lasting for a long time

tee tees teeing teed noun **1** small peg from which a golf ball can be played at the start of each hole **2** area of a golf course from which the first stroke of a hole is made ▷ **tee off** verb to make the first stroke of a hole in golf

teem verb **1** (followed by with) to be full of (people or things) **2** to rain heavily

teenager noun person aged between 13 and 19 ▷ **teenage** adjective **1** aged between 13 and 19 **2** typical of people aged between 13 and 19: teenage fashion

teens plural noun period of being a teenager

teeter verb to wobble or move unsteadily

teeth noun plural of **tooth**

teethe verb (of a baby) to grow his or her first teeth

teetotal adjective drinking no alcohol ▷ **teetotaller** noun person who never drinks alcohol

tele- prefix distance: telecommunications

telecommunications noun communications using telephone, radio, television, etc

telegram noun formerly, a message sent by telegraph

telegraph noun formerly, a system for sending messages over a distance along a cable

telepathy noun direct communication between people's minds >**telepathic** adjective able to communicate with other people's minds

telephone noun 1 device for transmitting sound over a distance along wires ▷ verb 2 to call or talk to (someone) by telephone

telephone box noun small shelter in the street containing a public telephone

telescope noun long instrument shaped like a tube with lenses that make distant objects appear larger and nearer

Teletext® noun electronic system that broadcasts pages of information onto a television set

televise verb to broadcast (an event) on television

television noun 1 system of producing a moving image and accompanying sound on a distant screen 2 device for receiving broadcast signals and converting them into pictures and sound

tell tells telling told verb 1 to make (something) known to (someone) in words 2 to order or instruct (someone) to do something 3 to judge correctly (what is happening or what the situation is) 4 (of an unpleasant or tiring experience) to have a serious effect >**teller** noun bank cashier >**telling** adjective having a marked effect

telltale noun 1 person who reveals secrets ▷ adjective 2 revealing

telly tellies noun informal television

temerity noun boldness

temp noun Brit informal temporary employee, especially a secretary

temper noun 1 outburst of anger 2 calm mental condition: I lost my temper 3 frame of mind ▷ verb 4 to make (something) less extreme

temperament noun person's character or disposition

temperamental adjective having changeable moods

temperate adjective (of climate) not extreme

temperature noun 1 degree of heat or cold 2 informal abnormally high body temperature

tempest noun literary violent storm

tempestuous adjective violent or strongly emotional

template noun pattern used to cut out shapes accurately

temple noun 1 building for worship 2 region on either side of the forehead

tempo tempos or tempi noun 1 rate or pace 2 speed of a piece of music

temporary adjective lasting only for a short time >**temporarily** adverb: the peace agreement has temporarily halted the civil war

tempt verb 1 to entice (someone) to do something 2 **be tempted to do something** to want to do something you think might be wrong or harmful

temptation noun 1 state of being tempted 2 tempting thing

ten adjective, noun the number 10

tenacious adjective determined

and not giving up easily
> **tenaciously** adverb: In spite of his illness, he clung tenaciously to his job
> **tenacity** noun determination

tenant noun person who rents land or a building > **tenancy** noun: He took over the tenancy of the farm

tend verb **1** to be inclined (to do something) **2** to take care of (someone or something)

tendency tendencies noun inclination to act in a certain way

tender adjective **1** (of meat) easy to cut or chew **2** (of a person) gentle and affectionate **3** (of a body part) painful and sore **4 at a tender age** young and inexperienced > verb **5** to offer (an apology or your resignation) > noun **6** a formal offer to supply goods or services at a stated cost

tendon noun strong tissue attaching a muscle to a bone

tendril noun slender stem by which a climbing plant clings

tenement noun (especially in Scotland or the US) building divided into several flats

tenet noun doctrine or belief

tenner noun Brit informal ten-pound note

tennis noun game in which players use rackets to hit a ball back and forth over a net

tenor noun **1** (singer with) the second highest male voice **2** general meaning > adjective **3** (of a voice or instrument) between alto and baritone

tense adjective **1** emotionally strained; anxious **2** (of a situation or period of time) causing nervousness and worry

3 stretched tight > verb **4** to become tense > noun **5** Grammar form of a verb showing the time of action

tension noun **1** emotional strain; anxiety **2** degree of stretching

tent noun portable canvas shelter

tentacle noun long thin parts of an animal such as an octopus that it uses to feel and hold things

tentative adjective cautious or hesitant > **tentatively** adverb cautiously or hesitantly

tenterhooks plural noun **on tenterhooks** in anxious suspense

tenuous adjective slight or flimsy

tenure noun **1** legal right to live in a place or to use land or buildings for a period of time **2** period of the holding of an office or position

tepee noun cone-shaped tent, formerly used by Native Americans

tepid adjective slightly warm

term noun **1** word or expression **2** fixed period **3** period of the year when a school etc is open or a law court holds sessions **4** terms conditions of an agreement **5** type of language: The young priest spoke of her in glowing terms **6 come to terms with** to learn to accept (something difficult or unpleasant) > verb **7** to give a name to or describe (something)

terminal adjective **1** (of an illness) ending in death > noun **2** place where people or vehicles begin or end a journey **3** point where current enters or leaves an electrical device **4** keyboard and VDU having input and output links with a computer

> terminally *adverb*: terminally ill

terminate *verb* to come to an end or bring (something) to an end **> termination** *noun*: the termination of trade

terminology terminologies *noun* set of technical terms relating to a subject

terminus terminuses *noun* railway or bus station at the end of a line

termite *noun* white antlike insect that destroys timber

tern *noun* gull-like sea bird with a forked tail and pointed wings

ternary *adjective* consisting of three parts

terrace *noun* **1** row of houses built as one block **2** paved area next to a building

terracotta *noun* brownish-red unglazed pottery

terrain *noun* area of ground, especially with reference to its physical character

terrapin *noun* small turtle-like reptile

terrestrial *adjective* of the earth or land

terrible *adjective* **1** very serious **2** *informal* very bad **> terribly** *adverb* very or very much: terribly upset

terrier *noun* a small short-bodied dog

terrific *adjective* **1** great or intense **2** *informal* excellent **> terrifically** *adverb*: terrifically repressed

terrify terrifies terrifying terrified *verb* to fill (someone) with fear

territory territories *noun* **1** area under the control of a particular government **2** area inhabited

and defended by an animal **> territorial** *adjective* of the ownership of a particular area of land or water: a territorial dispute

terror *noun* **1** great fear **2** terrifying person or thing

terrorism *noun* use of violence and intimidation to achieve political ends **> terrorist** *noun, adjective*: terrorist attacks

terrorize *verb* to force or oppress (someone) by fear or violence

terse *adjective* (of a statement) short and rather unfriendly

tertiary *adjective* **1** third in degree, order, etc **2** (of education) at university or college level

test *verb* **1** to try out (something) to ascertain its worth, capability or endurance **2** to ask (someone) questions to find out how much he or she knows **>** *noun* **3** deliberate action or experiment to find out whether something works or how well it works **4** set of questions or tasks given to someone to find out what he or she knows **> testing** *adjective* (of a situation or problem) very difficult to deal with: a testing time

testament *noun* *Law* will

test case *noun* lawsuit that establishes a precedent

testicle *noun* either of the two male reproductive glands

testify testifies testifying testified *verb* **1** to give evidence under oath **2 testify to** to be evidence of

testimony testimonies *noun* formal statement, especially in a court of law **> testimonial** *noun* statement saying how good someone or something is

testis testes *noun* testicle

test match *noun* one of a series of international cricket or rugby matches

testosterone *noun* male hormone that produces male characteristics

test tube *noun* narrow round-bottomed glass tube used in scientific experiments

tetanus *noun* painful infectious disease caused by germs getting into wounds

tether *noun* 1 rope or chain for tying an animal to a spot 2 **at the end of your tether** at the limit of your endurance ▷ *verb* 3 to tie (an animal) up with rope

Teutonic *adjective* of or like the (ancient) Germans

text *noun* 1 main written part of a book, rather than the pictures or index 2 any written material 3 novel or play studied for a course 4 text message ▷ *verb* to send a text message to (someone) >**textual** *adjective*: *textual analysis of Shakespeare*

textbook *noun* book about a particular subject for students to use

textile *noun* fabric or cloth, especially woven

text message *noun* message sent in text form, especially by means of a mobile phone

texture *noun* structure, feel or consistency

Thai Thais *adjective* 1 of Thailand ▷ *noun* 2 person from Thailand 3 main language spoken in Thailand

than *conjunction, preposition* used to introduce the second element

of a comparison

thank *verb* to express gratitude to (someone)

thankful *adjective* grateful >**thankfully** *adverb*: *Thankfully, she was not injured*

thankless *adjective* unrewarding or unappreciated

thanks *plural noun* 1 words of gratitude 2 **thanks to** because of (someone or something): *I'm as prepared as I can be, thanks to you* ▷ *interjection* 3 polite expression of gratitude

thanksgiving *noun* 1 act of thanking God, especially in prayer or in a religious ceremony 2 US, Canada public holiday in the autumn

thank you *interjection* expression of gratitude

that *adjective, pronoun* 1 used to refer to someone or something already mentioned, familiar or at a distance ▷ *conjunction* 2 used to introduce a clause ▷ *pronoun* 3 used to introduce a relative clause

thatch *noun* 1 roofing material of reeds or straw ▷ *verb* 2 to roof (a house) with reeds or straw

thaw *verb* 1 to make or become unfrozen 2 to become more relaxed or friendly ▷ *noun* 3 warmer weather causing snow or ice to melt

the *adjective* the definite article, used before a noun

theatre *noun* 1 place where plays etc are performed 2 hospital operating room 3 drama and acting in general

theatrical *adjective* 1 involving or performed in the theatre

2 exaggerated or affected > **theatrically** adverb

thee pronoun old-fashioned objective form of **thou**

theft noun act or an instance of stealing

their adjective of or associated with them > **theirs** pronoun (thing or person) belonging to them

● Be careful not to confuse *their* with *there*

them pronoun refers to people or things other than the speaker or those addressed

theme noun **1** main idea or subject being discussed **2** tune, especially one played at the beginning and end of a television or radio programme

themselves pronoun emphatic and reflexive form of **they** or **them**

then adverb **1** at that time **2** that being so

theology noun study of religions and religious beliefs > **theologian** noun person who studies religion and the nature of God > **theological** adjective: *theological books*

theoretical adjective **1** based on theory rather than practice or fact **2** not proved to exist or be true > **theoretically** adverb in theory

theory theories noun **1** set of ideas to explain something **2** idea or opinion **3 in theory** in an ideal or hypothetical situation

therapeutic adjective **1** causing you to feel happier and more relaxed **2** *Medicine* (of treatment) designed to treat a disease or improve a person's health

therapy therapies noun curing

treatment > **therapist** noun person skilled in a particular type of therapy

there adverb **1** in or to that point or that place ▷ pronoun **2** used to say that something exists or does not exist or to draw attention to something: *There are flowers on the table*

● Be careful not to confuse
● *there* with *their*. A good way
● to remember that *there* is
● connected to the idea of
● place is by remembering the
● spelling of two other place
● words, *here* and *where*

thereby adverb formal by that means

therefore adverb consequently, that being so

thermal adjective **1** of heat **2** (of clothing) retaining heat

thermometer noun instrument for measuring temperature

thermostat noun device for controlling temperature, e.g. on a central-heating system

thesaurus thesauruses noun reference book in which words with similar meanings are grouped together

these adjective, pronoun plural of **this**

thesis theses noun written work submitted for a university degree

they pronoun refers to: **1** people or things other than the speaker or people addressed **2** people in general **3** *informal* he or she

thick adjective **1** of great or specified extent from one side to the other **2** measuring a certain amount from one side to the other **3** having a dense

consistency 4 *informal* stupid or insensitive

thicken *verb* to become thick or thicker

thicket *noun* dense growth of small trees

thief thieves *noun* person who steals

thieving *noun* act of stealing

thigh *noun* upper part of the human leg

thimble *noun* cap protecting the end of the finger when sewing

thin thinner thinnest; thins thinning thinned *adjective* **1** not thick **2** slim or lean **3** (of a liquid) containing a lot of water: *thin soup* ▷ *verb* **4** to make (something such as paint or soup) thinner by adding liquid

thing *noun* **1** an object rather than a plant, animal or human being **2** **things** possessions, clothes, etc

think thinking thought *verb* **1** to consider, judge or believe (something) **2** to make use of the mind **3** to be considerate enough or remember (to do something)

third *adjective, noun* **1** (coming as) number three in a series ▷ *noun* **2** one of three equal parts

Third World *noun* developing countries of Africa, Asia and Latin America

thirst *noun* **1** desire to drink **2** craving or yearning > **thirstily** *adverb*: *drinking her milk thirstily* > **thirsty** *adjective*: *Drink when you feel thirsty during exercise*

thirteen *adjective, noun* the number 13 > **thirteenth** *adjective, noun*

thirty thirties *adjective, noun* the number 30 > **thirtieth** *adjective,*

noun

this *adjective, pronoun* **1** used to refer to a thing or person nearby, just mentioned or about to be mentioned ▷ *adjective* **2** used to refer to the present time: *this morning*

thistle *noun* prickly plant with purple flowers

thong *noun* **1** thin strip of leather etc **2** skimpy article of underwear or beachwear that covers the genitals while leaving the buttocks bare

thorn *noun* prickle on a plant > **thorny** *adjective* **1** covered with thorns **2** (of a subject or question) difficult to discuss or answer

thorough *adjective* **1** complete **2** (of a person) careful or methodical > **thoroughly** *adverb*: *I thoroughly enjoy your programme*

thoroughbred *noun* animal of pure breed

thoroughfare *noun* main road in a town

those *adjective, pronoun* plural of **that**

thou *pronoun obsolete* singular form of **you**

though *conjunction* **1** despite the fact that ▷ *adverb* **2** nevertheless

thought *verb* **1** past of **think** ▷ *noun* **2** thinking; reflection **3** concept or idea **4** ideas typical of a time or place > **thoughtful** *adjective* **1** kind and considerate **2** quiet and serious because thinking about something > **thoughtfully** *adverb* > **thoughtless** *adjective* inconsiderate > **thoughtlessly** *adverb*

thousand *adjective, noun*

1 the number 1000 ▷ *noun*
2 thousands large but
unspecified number; lots
>**thousandth** *adjective, noun*

thrash *verb* **1** to beat (someone),
especially with a stick or whip
2 to defeat (someone)
completely >**thrash out** *verb* to solve (a
problem) by thorough argument

thread *noun* **1** fine strand or yarn
2 idea or theme connecting the
different parts of an argument or
story **3** spiral ridge on a screw,
nut or bolt ▷ *verb* **4** to pass
thread, tape or cord through
(something) **5** to carefully make
(your way) somewhere

threadbare *adjective* (of clothing)
old and thin

threat *noun* **1** declaration of intent
to harm **2** dangerous person or
thing **3** possibility of something
unpleasant happening

threaten *verb* **1** to make or be a
threat to (someone) **2** to be
likely to harm (someone or
something)

three *adjective, noun* the number 3

three-dimensional *adjective*
having height or depth as well as
length and width

threesome *noun* group of three

threshold *noun* **1** bar forming the
bottom of a doorway **2** entrance
3 point at which something
begins to take effect

thrice *adverb* old-fashioned three
times

thrift *noun* wisdom and caution
with money >**thrifty** *adjective*
inclined to save money and not
waste things

thrill *noun* **1** sudden feeling of
excitement **2** something causing

a sudden feeling of excitement
▷ *verb* **3** to cause (someone)
to feel a thrill **4** (followed by
to) to feel a thrill because of
(something) >**thrilled** *adjective*
extremely pleased >**thrilling**
adjective very exciting and
enjoyable

thriller *noun* book, film, etc with
an atmosphere of mystery or
suspense

thrive *thrives thriving thrived* or
throve verb **1** to be healthy, happy
or successful >**thriving** *adjective*:
*the river's thriving population of
kingfishers*

throat *noun* **1** passage from the
mouth and nose to the stomach
and lungs **2** front of the neck

throb *throbs throbbing
throbbed verb* **1** (of a body part) to
produce a series of strong beats or
dull pains **2** to vibrate with a loud
rhythmic noise

throes *plural noun* **1** violent
pangs or pains **2 in the throes
of** struggling to cope with
(something)

thrombosis *thromboses noun*
forming of a clot in a blood vessel
or the heart

throne *noun* **1** ceremonial seat of a
monarch or bishop **2** position of
being king or queen

throng *noun* **1** large crowd
▷ *verb* **2** to go to (a place) in large
numbers

throttle *noun* **1** device controlling
the amount of fuel entering
an engine ▷ *verb* **2** to strangle
(someone)

through *preposition* **1** from end to
end or side to side of **2** because of
3 during ▷ *adjective* **4** finished: I'm

through with the explaining

- Do not confuse the spellings of *through* and *threw*, the past tense of *throw*

throughout *preposition, adverb* in every part (of)

thrive *verb* a past tense of **thrive**

throw throws throwing threw thrown *verb* **1** to hurl (something) through the air **2** to move (yourself) suddenly or with force **3** to bring (someone) into a specified state, especially suddenly: *It threw them into a panic* **4** **throw a tantrum** to suddenly begin behaving in an uncontrolled way **5** **throw light on** to make (something) have light on it **6** **throw yourself into** to become enthusiastically involved in (an activity)

throwback *noun* something that has the characteristics of something that existed a long time ago: *a throwback to the fifties*

thrush *noun* **1** brown songbird **2** fungal disease of the mouth or vagina

thrust thrusts thrusting thrust *verb* **1** to push (something) somewhere forcefully **2** to make (your way) somewhere by pushing between people or things ▷ *noun* **3** sudden forceful movement **4** most important part of an activity, idea or argument

thud thuds thudding thudded *noun* **1** dull heavy sound ▷ *verb* **2** to make such a sound

thug *noun* violent man, especially a criminal

thumb *noun* **1** short thick finger set apart from the others ▷ *verb*

2 to signal with the thumb for (a lift in a vehicle)

thump *noun* **1** (sound of) a dull heavy blow ▷ *verb* **2** to strike (someone or something) heavily **3** to make a fairly loud, dull sound, as of something falling **4** (of your heart) to beat strongly and quickly

thunder *noun* **1** loud noise accompanying lightning **2** any loud rumbling noise ▷ *verb* **3** to rumble with thunder **4** to make a loud continuous noise

thunderbolt *noun* lightning flash

thunderous *adjective* very loud

Thursday *noun* day between Wednesday and Friday

thus *adverb formal* **1** therefore **2** in this way

thwart *verb* to foil or frustrate (someone or his or her plans)

thy *adjective old-fashioned* of or associated with you (thou)

thyme *noun* bushy herb with very small leaves

thyroid *adjective, noun* (of) a gland in the neck controlling body growth

tiara *noun* woman's semicircular jewelled headdress

Tibetan *adjective* **1** of Tibet ▷ *noun* **2** person from Tibet

tic *noun* twitching of a group of muscles, especially in the face

tick *noun* **1** mark (✓) used to check off or indicate the correctness of something **2** recurrent tapping sound, as of a clock **3** tiny bloodsucking parasitic animal ▷ *verb* **4** to mark (something) with a tick **5** (of a clock) to make a ticking sound > **ticking** *noun* > **tick off** *verb informal* to speak angrily to (someone) who has done something wrong

ticket noun card or paper entitling the holder to admission, travel, etc

tickle verb **1** to touch or stroke (someone) to produce laughter **2** to please or amuse (someone)

tidal adjective of or relating to tides

tidal wave noun very large destructive wave

tide noun **1** rise and fall of the sea caused by the gravitational pull of the sun and moon **2** current caused by this **3** widespread feeling or tendency >**tide over** verb to help (someone) through a difficult period of time

tidings plural noun formal news

tidy tidier tidiest; tidies tidying tidied adjective **1** neat and orderly **2** Brit, Aust, NZ informal (of a sum of money) fairly large ▷ verb **3** to put (a place) in order

tie ties tying tied verb **1** to fasten (one thing to another) with string, rope, etc **2** to make (a knot or bow) in (something) **3** to link (one thing with another) closely **4** (followed by with) to score the same as (another competitor) ▷ noun **5** long narrow piece of material worn knotted round the neck **6** connection or feeling that links you with a person, place or organization: I had very close ties with the family

tied up adjective busy

tier noun one of a set of layers or rows that has other layers or rows above or below it

tiff noun petty quarrel

tiger noun large orange-and-black striped Asian cat

tiger snake noun fierce, very poisonous Australian snake with dark stripes across its back

tight adjective **1** stretched or drawn taut **2** closely fitting **3** secure or firm **4** (of a plan or arrangement) allowing only the minimum time or money needed to do something ▷ adverb **5** held firmly and securely: he held me tight >**tightly** adverb: he buttoned his collar tightly >**tightness** noun: a feeling of tightness in the chest

tighten verb **1** to stretch or pull (a rope or chain) until it is straight **2** to make (a rule or system) stricter or more efficient **3 tighten your hold on** to hold (something) more firmly

tightrope noun rope stretched taut on which acrobats perform

tights plural noun one-piece clinging garment covering the body from the waist to the feet

tiki tikis noun NZ small carving of an ancestor worn as a pendant in some Maori cultures

tile noun **1** flat piece of ceramic, plastic, etc used to cover a roof, floor or wall ▷ verb **2** to cover (a surface) with tiles >**tiled** adjective covered with tiles

till conjunction, preposition **1** until ▷ verb **2** to plough (ground) for raising crops ▷ noun **3** drawer for money, usually in a cash register

tiller noun lever to move a rudder of a boat

tilt verb **1** to slant (something) at an angle ▷ noun **2** slope

timber noun **1** wood as a building material **2** wooden beam in the frame of a house, boat, etc >**timbered** adjective

time *noun* **1** past, present and future as a continuous whole **2** specific point in time **3** unspecified interval **4** instance or occasion **5** period with specific features ▷ *verb* **6** to note the time taken by (an activity or action) **7** to choose a time for (something) > **timer** *noun* device that measures time, especially one that is part of a machine > **timing** *noun* **1** skill in judging the right moment to do something **2** when an event actually happens

timeless *adjective* not affected by the passing of time or by changes in fashion

timely timelier timeliest *adjective* happening at the appropriate time

timescale *noun* length of time during which an event takes place

timetable *noun* plan showing the times when something takes place, the departure and arrival times of trains or buses, etc

timid *adjective* **1** easily frightened **2** shy, not bold > **timidity** *noun* > **timidly** *adverb*

timpani *plural noun* set of kettledrums

tin *noun* **1** soft metallic element **2** (airtight) metal container

tinder *noun* dry easily-burning material used to start a fire

tinge *noun* trace: *a tinge of envy* > **tinged** *adjective*: *Her homecoming was tinged with sadness*

tingle *verb, noun* (to feel) a prickling or stinging sensation > **tingling** *noun* **1** prickling or stinging sensation ▷ *adjective* **2** prickling or stinging

tinker *noun* **1** travelling mender of

pots and pans ▷ *verb* **2** (followed by *with*) to fiddle with (an engine etc) in an attempt to repair it

tinkle *verb* **1** to ring with a high tinny sound like a small bell ▷ *noun* **2** this sound or action

tinned *adjective* (of food) preserved by being sealed in a tin

tinsel *noun* long threads with strips of shiny paper attached, used as a decoration at Christmas

tint *noun* **1** small amount of a particular colour **2** weak dye for the hair ▷ *verb* **3** to give a tint to (one's hair) > **tinted** *adjective* having a small amount of a particular colour

tiny tinier tiniest *adjective* very small

tip tips tipping tipped *noun* **1** narrow or pointed end of anything **2** money given in return for service **3** useful piece of advice or information **4** rubbish dump ▷ *verb* **5** to tilt or overturn (something) **6** to pour (something) somewhere quickly or carelessly > **tipped** *adjective*: *tipped for success*

tipple *noun* alcoholic drink that someone usually drinks

tipsy tipsier tipsiest *adjective* slightly drunk

tiptoe tiptoes tiptoeing tiptoed *verb* to walk quietly with the heels off the ground

tirade *noun* long angry speech

tire *verb* **1** to reduce the energy of (someone), as by exertion; exhaust (someone) **2** (followed by *of*) to become weary or bored with > **tired** *adjective* exhausted > **tiredness** *noun* > **tiring** *adjective* causing tiredness

a
b
c
d
e
f
g
h
i
j
k
l
m
n
o
p
q
r
s
t
u
v
w
x
y
z

tireless adjective energetic and determined

tiresome adjective boring and irritating

tissue noun **1** substance of an animal body or plant **2** piece of thin soft paper used as a handkerchief etc

tit noun any of various small songbirds

titanic adjective huge or very important

titillate verb to excite or stimulate (someone) pleasurably > **titillation** noun act of exciting or stimulating

title noun **1** name of a book, film, etc **2** name signifying rank or position **3** Sport championship > **titled** adjective having a high social rank with a title such as Lord, Lady or Sir

titter verb to laugh in a nervous or embarrassed way

TNT noun trinitrotoluene, a powerful explosive

to preposition **1** indicating movement towards, equality or comparison, etc: walking to school; forty miles to the gallon **2** used to mark the indirect object or infinitive of a verb > adverb **3** to a closed position: pull the door to

- The preposition to is spelt with one o, the adverb too has two os, and the number two is spelt with wo

toad noun animal like a large frog

toadstool noun poisonous fungus like a mushroom

toast noun **1** sliced bread browned by heat **2** drink a toast to **3** to drink an alcoholic drink in honour of (someone) > verb

3 to brown (bread) by heat **4** to warm (oneself) in front of a fire **5** to drink a toast to (someone) > **toaster** noun electrical device for toasting bread

tobacco noun dried leaves of the tobacco plant, which many people smoke in pipes, cigarettes and cigars

tobacconist noun person or shop selling tobacco, cigarettes, etc

toboggan noun narrow sledge for sliding over snow

today noun **1** this day **2** the present age > adverb **3** on this day **4** nowadays

toddler noun young child beginning to walk > **toddle** verb to walk with short unsteady steps

to-do to-dos noun Brit, Aust, NZ fuss or commotion

toe toes noun **1** movable part of your foot resembling a finger **2** part of a shoe or sock covering your toes

toff noun Brit informal rich or aristocratic person

toffee noun chewy sweet made of boiled sugar

toga noun garment worn by citizens of ancient Rome

together adverb **1** with each other; jointly **2** at the same time **3** so as to be joined or fixed to each other: She clasped her hands together **4** very near to each other > adjective **5** informal organized > **togetherness** noun feeling of closeness and friendship

- Two nouns joined by together with do not make a plural subject, so the following verb is not plural: Jones, together with his partner, has had great success

toil noun **1** hard work ▷ verb **2** to work hard

toilet noun (room with) a bowl connected to a drain for receiving and disposing of urine and faeces

toiletries plural noun cosmetics used for cleaning or grooming

token noun **1** sign or symbol: *as a token of goodwill* **2** voucher exchangeable for goods of a specified value **3** disc used as money in a slot machine ▷ adjective **4** not being treated as important: *a token contribution to your fees*

told verb past of **tell**

tolerable adjective **1** bearable **2** informal quite good

tolerance noun **1** acceptance of other people's rights to their own opinions or actions **2** ability to endure something ▷ **tolerant** adjective: *tolerant of different points of view*

tolerate verb **1** to allow (something) to exist or happen **2** to endure (something) patiently ▷ **toleration** noun act of tolerating something

toll verb **1** to ring (a bell) slowly and regularly, especially to announce a death ▷ noun **2** charge for the use of a bridge or road **3** total loss or damage from a disaster

tom noun male cat

tomahawk noun fighting axe of the Native Americans

tomato tomatoes noun red fruit used in salads and as a vegetable

tomb noun large grave for one or more corpses

tomboy noun girl who acts or dresses like a boy

tome noun large heavy book

tomorrow adverb, noun **1** (on) the day after today **2** (in) the future

ton noun **1** unit of weight equal to 2240 pounds or 1016 kilograms (**long ton**) or, in the US, 2000 pounds or 907 kilograms (**short ton**) **2 tons** informal a lot

tone noun **1** sound with reference to its pitch, volume, etc **2** quality of a sound or colour **3** style of a piece of writing and the ideas or opinions expressed in it ▷ verb **4** to harmonize (with) **5** to give tone to **6** give more firmness or strength to (the body or a part of the body) ▷ **tonal** adjective involving the quality or pitch of a sound or of music ▷ **tone down** verb to make (something) more moderate

tone-deaf adjective unable to perceive subtle differences in pitch

tongs plural noun large pincers for grasping and lifting

tongue noun **1** muscular organ in the mouth, used in speaking and tasting **2** language **3** cooked tongue of an ox **4** flap of leather on a shoe

tonic noun **1** medicine that makes you feel stronger, healthier and less tired **2** anything that makes you feel stronger or more cheerful

tonight adverb, noun (in or during) the night or evening of this day

tonne noun unit of weight equal to 1000 kilograms

tonsil noun small gland in the throat

tonsillitis noun painful swelling of the tonsils caused by an infection

too adverb **1** also, as well **2** to excess

● The adverb too has two os,
● the preposition to is spelt with one o, and the number
● two is spelt with wo

tool noun **1** implement used by hand **2** object, skill or idea needed for a particular purpose: *a bargaining tool*

toot verb (of a car horn) to make a short hooting sound

tooth teeth noun **1** bonelike projection in the jaws for biting and chewing **2** toothlike prong or point

toothpaste noun paste used to clean the teeth

top tops topping topped noun **1** highest point or part **2** lid or cap **3** highest rank **4** garment for the upper part of the body **5** toy that spins on a pointed base ▷ adjective **6** at or of the top ▷ verb **7** to be at the top of (a poll or chart) **8** to be greater than (a specified amount)

top hat noun man's tall cylindrical hat

topic noun subject of a conversation, book, etc > **topical** adjective relating to current events

topping noun sauce or garnish for food

topple verb to become unsteady and fall over

top-secret adjective meant to be kept completely secret

top-up card noun card used to add credit to a mobile phone

topsy-turvy adjective in confusion

Torah noun Jewish law and teaching

torch noun **1** small portable battery-powered lamp **2** long stick with burning material wrapped round one end

torment verb **1** to cause (someone) great suffering ▷ noun **2** great suffering **3** source of suffering

torn verb **1** past participle of **tear** ▷ adjective **2** unable to decide between two or more things

tornado tornadoes or **tornados** noun violent whirlwind

torpedo torpedoes torpedoing **torpedoed** noun **1** self-propelled underwater missile ▷ verb **2** to attack or destroy (a ship) with torpedoes

torrent noun **1** rushing stream **2** rapid flow of questions, abuse, etc

torrential adjective (of rain) very heavy

torrid adjective **1** very hot and dry **2** highly emotional

torso torsos noun trunk of the human body

tortoise noun slow-moving land reptile with a dome-shaped shell

tortuous adjective **1** winding or twisting **2** not straightforward

torture verb **1** to cause (someone) severe pain or mental anguish ▷ noun **2** severe physical or mental pain **3** torturing > **torturer** noun person who tortures people

Tory Tories noun member of the Conservative Party in Great Britain or Canada

toss verb **1** to throw (something) lightly **2** to throw up (a coin) to decide between alternatives by guessing which side will land uppermost **3** to move (the head) suddenly backwards, esp. when angry **4** to move repeatedly from side to side

tot tots totting totted noun **1** small child **2** small amount of strong alcohol such as whisky ▷ verb **3** tot up to add (numbers) together

total totals totalling totalled noun **1** whole, especially a sum of parts ▷ adjective **2** complete **3** of or being a total ▷ verb **4** to amount to (a certain figure) **5** to add together (a set of numbers or objects) ▷ **totally** adverb: something totally different

totalitarian adjective of a dictatorial one-party government ▷ **totalitarianism** noun principles of a totalitarian system

tote verb to carry (a gun)

totem pole noun post carved or painted with symbols and pictures by Native Americans

totter verb to move unsteadily

toucan noun tropical American bird with a large bill

touch verb **1** to come into contact with **2** to tap, feel or stroke **3** to move (someone) emotionally ▷ noun **4** sense by which an object's qualities are perceived when they come into contact with part of the body **5** gentle tap, push or caress **6** small amount: a touch of mustard **7** detail: finishing touches **8** touch and go risky or critical

touchdown noun landing of an aircraft

touching adjective emotionally moving

touchy touchier touchiest adjective easily offended

tough adjective **1** (of a person) strong and independent and able to put up with hardship **2** (of a substance) difficult to break **3** (of a task, problem or way of life) difficult or full of hardship **4** (of policies or actions) strict and firm ▷ **toughen** verb to become stronger or make (something) stronger ▷ **toughness** noun: a reputation for toughness and determination

toupee noun small wig worn to cover a bald patch

tour noun **1** long journey during which you visit several places **2** short trip round a place such as a city or famous building ▷ verb **3** to make a tour of (a place)

tourism noun tourist travel as an industry

tourist noun person travelling for pleasure

tournament noun sporting competition with several stages to decide the overall winner

tourniquet noun strip of cloth tied tightly round a limb to stop bleeding

tousled adjective (of hair) ruffled and untidy

tout verb **1** to seek business in a persistent manner **2** to try to sell (something) ▷ noun **3** person who sells tickets for a popular event at inflated prices

tow verb **1** (of a vehicle) to drag (another vehicle), especially by means of a rope ▷ noun **2** towing **3** in tow following closely behind

towards or **toward** preposition **1** in the direction of **2** with regard to **3** as a contribution to **4** near to

towel noun piece of thick soft cloth

for drying yourself

towelling noun material used for making towels

tower noun tall structure, often forming part of a larger building
>**towering** adjective: towering cliffs
>**tower over** verb to be much taller than

town noun 1 group of buildings larger than a village 2 central part of this

township noun SAfr urban settlement formerly for Black or Coloured people only

towpath noun path beside a canal or river

toxic adjective poisonous

toxin noun poison of bacterial origin

toy noun something designed to be played with >**toy with** verb 1 to consider (an idea) without being very serious about it 2 to play or fiddle with (an object)

toyi-toyi or **toy-toy** noun SAfr dance of political protest

trace verb 1 to track down and find 2 to follow the course of 3 to copy (a drawing or a map) exactly by drawing on a thin sheet of transparent paper set on top of the original > noun 4 track left by someone or something 5 very small amount

track noun 1 rough road or path 2 mark or trail left by the passage of anything 3 railway line 4 course for racing 5 separate section on a record, tape or CD > verb 6 to follow the trail or path of (animals or people) >**track down** verb to hunt for and find (someone or something)

track record noun past

accomplishments of a person or organization

tracksuit noun warm loose-fitting suit worn by athletes etc, especially during training

tract noun 1 wide area 2 pamphlet, especially a religious one 3 Anatomy system of organs with a particular function: the digestive tract

traction noun Medicine application of a steady pull on an injured limb by weights and pulleys

tractor noun motor vehicle with large rear wheels for pulling farm machinery

trade noun 1 buying, selling or exchange of goods 2 person's job or craft > verb 3 to buy and sell (goods) 4 to exchange (things) >**trader** noun person who trades in goods

trademark noun (legally registered) name or symbol used by a firm to distinguish its goods

tradesman tradesmen noun 1 skilled worker 2 shopkeeper

trade union noun society of workers formed to protect their interests

tradition noun custom or practice of long standing; convention >**traditional** adjective 1 (of customs or beliefs) having existed for a long time without changing 2 (of an organization or institution) using older methods rather than modern ones >**traditionalist** noun person who supports the established customs and beliefs of his or her society >**traditionally** adverb

traffic traffics trafficking trafficked noun 1 vehicles

coming and going on a road **2** illegal trade in something such as drugs ▷ *verb* **3** (followed by *in*) to buy and sell (drugs or other goods) illegally

traffic lights *plural noun* set of coloured lights at a junction to control the traffic flow

traffic warden *noun* Brit person employed to control the movement and parking of traffic

tragedy tragedies *noun* **1** shocking or sad event **2** serious play, film, etc in which the hero is destroyed by a personal failing or adverse circumstances

tragic *adjective* **1** very sad, often involving death, suffering or disaster **2** (of a film, play or book) sad and serious > **tragically** *adverb*: *Tragically, she died before the project was finished*

trail *noun* **1** path, track or road **2** tracks left by a person, animal or object ▷ *verb* **3** to drag (something) along the ground **4** to hang down loosely **5** to move slowly, without energy or enthusiasm > **trail off** *verb* (of a voice) to gradually become more hesitant until it stops completely

trailer *noun* **1** vehicle designed to be towed by another vehicle **2** extract from a film or programme used to advertise it

train *verb* **1** to instruct in a skill **2** to learn the skills needed to do a particular job or activity **3** to prepare for a sports event etc **4** to aim (a gun etc) **5** to cause (an animal) to perform or (a plant) to grow in a particular way ▷ *noun* **6** line of railway coaches or wagons drawn by an engine **7** sequence or series

8 long trailing back section of a dress **9** line or group of vehicles or people following behind something or someone

trainee *noun* person being trained

trainers *plural noun* sports shoes

trait *noun* characteristic feature

traitor *noun* person who betrays his or her country or group

trajectory trajectories *noun* curving path followed by an object moving through the air

tram *noun* public transport vehicle powered by an overhead wire and running on rails laid in the road

tramp *verb* **1** to walk heavily ▷ *noun* **2** homeless person who travels on foot **3** long country walk

trample *verb* (followed by *on*) **1** to tread heavily on and damage **2** to show no consideration for (someone or his or her rights or feelings)

trampoline *noun* tough canvas sheet attached to a frame by springs, used by acrobats, etc

trance *noun* unconscious or dazed state

tranquil *adjective* calm and quiet > **tranquillity** *noun*: *a haven of peace and tranquillity*

tranquillizer or **tranquilliser** *noun* drug that reduces anxiety or tension

trans- *prefix* across, through or beyond

transaction *noun* business deal that involves buying and selling something

transcend *verb* to go beyond or be superior to (something)

transcribe *verb* to write down (something said)

transcript noun written copy of something spoken

transfer transfers transferring transferred verb 1 to move (something) from one place to another: *They transferred the money to the Swiss account* 2 to move (someone) to a different place or job within the same organization ▷ noun 3 movement of something from one place to another 4 design that can be transferred from one surface to another >**transferable** adjective: *Your Railcard is not transferable to anyone else*

transfixed adjective so impressed or frightened by something that you cannot move

transform verb to change the shape and character of >**transformation** noun: *He's undergone a personal transformation*

transfusion noun injection of blood into the blood vessels of a patient

transient adjective lasting only for a short time >**transience** noun: *the transience of the club scene*

transistor noun
1 semiconducting device used to amplify electric currents 2 small portable radio using transistors

transit noun 1 carrying of goods or people by vehicle from one place to another 2 **in transit** travelling or being taken from one place to another: *damaged in transit*

transition noun change from one state to another >**transitional** adjective (of a period or stage) during which something changes from one form or state to another

transitive adjective Grammar (of a verb) requiring a direct object

transitory adjective not lasting long

translate verb to turn (something from one language into another >**translation** noun: *an English translation of Faust* >**translator** noun person who translates from one language into another

translucent adjective letting light pass through, but not transparent

transmission noun 1 passing or sending of something to a different place or person 2 broadcasting of television or radio programmes 3 broadcast

transmit transmits transmitting transmitted verb 1 to pass (something) from one person or place to another 2 to send out (signals) by radio waves 3 to broadcast (a radio or television programme) >**transmitter** noun piece of equipment used to broadcast radio or television programmes

transparency transparencies noun 1 transparent quality 2 colour photograph on transparent film that can be viewed by means of a projector

transparent adjective 1 able to be seen through, clear 2 easily understood or recognized >**transparently** adverb in a transparent manner

transpire verb 1 formal to become known 2 informal to happen
- Some people think that it
- is wrong to use *transpire* to
- mean 'happen'. However, it
- is very widely used in this
- sense, especially in spoken
- English

transplant verb 1 to transfer (an organ or tissue) surgically from one part or body to another **2** to remove and transfer (a plant) to another place ▷ noun **3** surgical transplanting **4** thing transplanted

transport verb **1** to convey (goods or people) from one place to another **2** to enrapture ▷ noun **3** business or system of transporting **4** vehicles used in transport > **transportation** noun transporting of people and things from one place to another

transvestite noun person who enjoys wearing clothes normally worn by people of the opposite sex

trap traps trapping trapped noun **1** device for catching animals **2** plan for tricking or catching someone ▷ verb **3** to catch (animals) in a trap **4** to trick (someone) into something > **trapper** noun person who traps animals for their fur

trapdoor noun door in a floor or roof

trapeze noun horizontal bar suspended from two ropes, used by circus acrobats

trapezium trapeziums or **trapezia** noun four-sided shape with two parallel sides of unequal length

trappings plural noun accessories that symbolize an office or position

trash noun **1** anything worthless **2** US, SAfr rubbish

trauma noun emotional shock

traumatic adjective very upsetting

travel travels travelling travelled verb **1** to go from one place to another, through an area

or for a specified distance ▷ noun **2** travelling, especially as a tourist > **traveller** noun: air travellers > **travelling** adjective: travelling entertainers > **travels** plural noun journeys to distant places

traveller's cheque noun cheque bought at home and then exchanged abroad for foreign currency

traverse verb to move over or back and forth over (an area)

travesty travesties noun grotesque imitation or mockery

trawl noun **1** net dragged at deep levels behind a fishing boat ▷ verb **2** to fish with such a net

trawler noun trawling boat

tray noun flat board, usually with a rim, for carrying food or drinks

treachery noun wilful betrayal > **treacherous** adjective **1** disloyal or untrustworthy **2** unreliable or dangerous > **treacherously** adverb in a treacherous manner

treacle noun thick dark syrup produced when sugar is refined

tread treads treading trod trodden verb **1** to set your foot (on something) **2** to crush (something) by walking on it ▷ noun **3** way of walking or dancing **4** part of a tyre or shoe that touches the ground

treadmill noun **1** cylinder turned by treading on steps projecting from it **2** dreary routine

treason noun **1** betrayal of one's sovereign or country **2** treachery or disloyalty

treasure noun **1** collection of wealth, especially gold or jewels **2** valued person or thing ▷ verb **3** to prize or cherish (something)

> **treasured** adjective: my most treasured possessions

treasurer noun official in charge of funds

Treasury noun government department in charge of finance

treat verb **1** to deal with or regard (someone or something) in a certain manner **2** to give medical treatment to (a patient or an illness) **3** to subject (something such as wood or fabric) to a chemical or industrial process **4** to provide (someone) with something as a treat ▷ noun **5** pleasure, entertainment, etc given or paid for by someone else
> **treatment** noun **1** medical care **2** way of treating a person or thing

treatise noun formal piece of writing on a particular subject

treaty treaties noun signed contract between states

treble adjective **1** triple ▷ noun **2** (singer with or part for) a soprano voice ▷ verb **3** to increase (something) three times

tree noun large perennial plant with a woody trunk

trek treks trekking trekked noun **1** long difficult journey, especially on foot ▷ verb **2** to make such a journey

trellis noun framework of horizontal and vertical strips of wood

tremble verb **1** to shake or quiver **2** to feel fear or anxiety ▷ noun **3** trembling > **trembling** adjective: with trembling fingers

tremendous adjective **1** huge **2** informal great in quality or amount > **tremendously** adverb

tremor noun **1** involuntary shaking **2** unsteady quality in the voice, e.g. when upset **3** minor earthquake

trench noun long narrow ditch, especially one used as a shelter in war

trenchant adjective (of writing or comments) bold and firmly expressed

trend noun general tendency or direction

trendy trendier trendiest adjective informal consciously fashionable

trepidation noun fear or anxiety

trespass verb to go onto another's property without permission > **trespasser** noun: Trespassers will be prosecuted

tresses plural noun long flowing hair

trestle noun board fixed on pairs of spreading legs, used as a support

trevally trevallies noun Aust, NZ any of various food and game fishes

tri- prefix three

triad noun **1** group of three **2** chord of three notes consisting of the tonic and the third and fifth above it

trial noun **1** Law investigation of a case before a judge **2** trying or testing

triangle noun **1** geometric figure with three sides **2** triangular percussion instrument > **triangular** adjective having three sides

triathlon noun sports contest in which athletes compete in three different events

tribe noun group of clans or families believed to have a common ancestor >**tribal** *adjective* of tribes

tribulation *noun* great distress

tribunal *noun* board appointed to inquire into a specific matter

tributary tributaries *noun* stream or river flowing into a larger one

tribute *noun* **1** sign of respect or admiration **2** **a tribute to** positive result of (something): *His success is a tribute to hard work*

trice *noun* **in a trice** instantly

triceps *noun* muscle at the back of the upper arm

• The plural of *triceps* is *triceps*

trick *noun* **1** deceitful or cunning action or plan **2** feat of skill or cunning done in order to entertain >**verb 3** to cheat or deceive (someone)

trickery trickeries *noun* deception

trickle *verb* **1** to flow in a thin stream or drops **2** to move gradually >*noun* **3** thin stream of liquid **4** small number or quantity of things or people

tricky trickier trickiest *adjective* difficult to do or deal with

tricycle *noun* three-wheeled cycle

trifle *noun* **1** something that is not very important or valuable **2** dessert of sponge cake, fruit, custard and cream **3** **a trifle** a little >**trifle with** *verb* to toy with (someone or something)

trifling *adjective* insignificant

trigger *noun* **1** small lever releasing a catch on a gun or machine **2** action that sets off a course of events >*verb* **3** (usually followed by *off*) to set (an action or process) in motion

trigonometry *noun* branch of mathematics dealing with relations of the sides and angles of triangles

trill *noun* **1** shrill warbling sound made by some birds >*verb* **2** (of a bird) to sing with short high-pitched repeated notes

trillion *noun* **1** one million million; 1,000,000,000,000 **2** formerly, one million million million, 10^{18} **3** **trillions** large but unspecified number; lots

trilogy trilogies *noun* series of three related books, plays, etc

trim trimmer trimmest; trims trimming trimmed *adjective* **1** neat and smart >*verb* **2** to cut or prune (something) into good shape **3** *noun* **4** decoration **4** haircut that neatens the existing style >**trimmed** *adjective*: *trimmed with flowers*

trimmings *plural noun* extra parts added to something for decoration or as a luxury

Trimurti *noun Hinduism* three deities Brahma, Vishnu and Siva

Trinity *noun Christianity* union of God the Father, God the Son and God the Holy Spirit in one God

trinket *noun* small or worthless ornament or piece of jewellery

trio trios *noun* **1** group of three musicians who sing or play together **2** piece of music for three performers **3** any group of three

trip trips tripping tripped *noun* **1** journey to a place and back, especially for pleasure >*verb* **2** to stumble or cause (someone) to stumble

tripe *noun* stomach of a cow used as food

triple adjective **1** having three parts ▷ verb **2** to increase (something) three times

triplet noun one of three babies born at one birth

tripod noun three-legged stand, stool, etc

tripper noun tourist

trite adjective (of a remark or idea) commonplace and unoriginal

triumph noun **1** (happiness caused by) victory or success ▷ verb **2** to be victorious or successful

triumphal adjective celebrating a triumph

triumphant adjective feeling or showing triumph

trivia plural noun trivial things or details

trivial adjective to make (something) seem less important or complex than it is

troll noun giant or dwarf in Scandinavian folklore

trolley noun **1** small wheeled table for food and drink **2** wheeled cart for moving goods

trombone noun brass musical instrument with a sliding tube

troop noun **1** large group **2 troops** soldiers ▷ verb **3** to move in a crowd

trooper noun low-ranking cavalry soldier

trophy trophies noun **1** cup, shield, etc given as a prize **2** memento of success

tropic noun **1** either of two lines of latitude at 23½° N (**tropic of Cancer**) or 23½° S (**tropic of Capricorn**) **2** the tropics part of the earth's surface between these lines

tropical adjective of or in the tropics

trot trots trotting trotted verb **1** (of a horse) to move at a medium pace, lifting the feet in diagonal pairs **2** (of a person) to move at a steady brisk pace ▷ noun **3** trotting

trotter noun pig's foot

trouble noun **1** (cause of) distress or anxiety **2** care or effort **3 in trouble** likely to be punished for doing something wrong ▷ verb **4** to cause (someone) to worry **5** to cause inconvenience to or bother (someone) > **troubled** adjective: She was deeply troubled > **troubling** adjective worrying

troublesome adjective causing problems or difficulties

trough noun long open container, especially for animals' food or water

trounce verb to defeat (someone) utterly

troupe noun group of performers who work together and often travel around together

trousers plural noun two-legged outer garment with legs reaching usually to the ankles

trout noun game fish related to the salmon

● The plural of trout is trout

trowel noun hand tool with a wide blade for spreading mortar, lifting plants, etc

truant noun **1** pupil who stays away from school without permission **2 play truant** to stay away from school without permission > **truancy** noun staying away from school without permission

truce noun temporary agreement to stop fighting

truck noun 1 railway goods wagon 2 large vehicle for transporting loads by road > **trucker** noun truck driver

truculent adjective aggressively defiant > **truculence** noun aggressive defiance

trudge verb 1 to walk heavily or wearily ▷ noun 2 long tiring walk

true truer truest adjective 1 in accordance with facts; accurate 2 genuine 3 **come true** to actually happen > **truly** adverb very

truffle noun 1 edible underground fungus 2 sweet flavoured with chocolate

trump noun 1 card of the suit outranking the others 2 **trumps** suit outranking the others

trumpet noun 1 valved brass instrument with a flared tube ▷ verb 2 (of an elephant) to cry loudly

truncated adjective made shorter

truncheon noun club carried by a policeman

trundle verb to move (something) heavily on wheels

trunk noun 1 main stem of a tree 2 large case or box for clothes etc 3 person's body excluding the head and limbs 4 elephant's long nose

truss verb 1 to tie (someone) up ▷ noun 2 supporting belt with a pad for holding a hernia in place

trust verb 1 to believe in and rely on (someone or something) 2 to consign (something) to someone's care 3 to believe that (someone) will do something successfully or properly ▷ noun 4 confidence in the truth, reliability, etc of a person or thing 5 obligation arising from responsibility 6 arrangement in which one person administers property, money, etc on another's behalf > **trusting** adjective inclined to trust others

trustee noun person holding property on another's behalf

trustworthy adjective reliable or honest

trusty trustier trustiest adjective faithful or reliable

truth noun 1 state of being true; reality 2 something true

truthful adjective honest > **truthfully** adverb: I answered all their questions truthfully

try tries trying tried verb 1 to make an effort or attempt (to do something) 2 to test or sample (something) 3 to subject (a person) to a legal process involving the hearing of evidence to decide whether or not they are guilty of a crime ▷ noun 4 attempt or effort 5 test of something: You gave it a try 6 Rugby score gained by touching the ball down over the opponent's goal line

- You can use try to in speech and writing: try to get here on time for once. Try and is very common is speech, but you should avoid it in written work: just try and stop me!

trying adjective informal difficult or annoying

tryst noun arrangement to meet

tsar or **czar** noun History Russian emperor > **tsarina** or **czarina**

noun History female tsar or the wife of a tsar

tsetse fly noun bloodsucking African fly whose bite transmits disease, especially sleeping sickness

T-shirt noun simple short-sleeved cotton shirt with no collar

tsunami noun large, often destructive sea wave, caused by an earthquake or volcanic eruption under the sea

tuatara noun large lizard-like New Zealand reptile

tub noun open, usually round container

tuba noun valved low-pitched brass instrument

tubby tubbier tubbiest adjective (of a person) short and fat

tube noun 1 hollow cylinder 2 flexible cylinder with a cap to hold pastes >**tubing** noun 1 length of tube 2 system of tubes

tuberculosis noun serious infectious disease affecting the lungs

tubular adjective of or shaped like a tube

TUC abbreviation (in Britain and S Africa) Trades Union Congress

tuck verb 1 to push or fold (something) into a small space 2 to push the loose ends of (a piece of fabric) inside or under something to make it tidy >noun 3 stitched fold >**tuck away** verb 1 to eat (a large amount of food) 2 to locate (something) in a quiet place where few people go

tucker noun Aust, NZ informal food

Tudor noun family name of the English monarchs who reigned from 1485 to 1603

Tuesday noun day between Monday and Wednesday

tuft noun bunch of feathers, grass, hair, etc held or growing together at the base

tug tugs tugging tugged verb 1 to pull (something) hard >noun 2 hard pull 3 (also**tugboat**) small ship used to tow other vessels

tug of war noun contest in which two teams pull against one another on a rope

tuition noun instruction, especially received individually or in a small group

tulip noun brightly coloured spring flower

tumble verb 1 to fall, especially awkwardly or violently >noun 2 fall

tumbler noun stemless drinking glass

tummy tummies noun informal stomach

tumour noun abnormal growth in or on the body

tumultuous adjective (of an event or welcome) very noisy and excited

tuna noun large marine food fish

● The plural of tuna is tuna

tundra noun vast treeless Arctic region

tune noun 1 (pleasing) sequence of musical notes 2 correct musical pitch: She sang out of tune >verb 3 to adjust (a musical instrument) so that it is in tune 4 to adjust (a machine) to obtain the desired performance 5 (followed by to) to turn or press the controls of a radio or television set to select (a particular station)

tuneful adjective having a pleasant

and easily remembered tune

tuner noun person who tunes pianos

tunic noun piece of clothing, often sleeveless and rather shapeless, covering the top part of the body and reaching to the hips, thighs or knees

Tunisian adjective **1** of Tunisia ▷ noun **2** person from Tunisia

tunnel tunnels tunnelling tunnelled noun **1** underground passage ▷ verb **2** to make a tunnel

turban noun Muslim, Hindu or Sikh man's head covering, made by winding cloth round the head

turbine noun machine or generator driven by gas, water, etc turning blades

turbot noun large European flat fish that is caught for food
● The plural of turbot is turbot

turbulence noun **1** confusion, movement or agitation **2** atmospheric instability causing gusty air currents ▷ **turbulent** adjective **1** (of a period of history) involving much uncertainty and possibly violent change **2** (of air or water currents) making sudden changes of direction

tureen noun serving dish for soup

turf turves; turfs turfing turfed noun short thick even grass ▷ **turf out** verb informal to throw (someone) out

turgid adjective (of language) pompous

Turk noun person from Turkey

turkey turkeys noun **1** large bird bred for food **2** meat of this bird

Turkish adjective **1** of Turkey ▷ noun **2** Turkish language

turmoil noun agitation or confusion

turn verb **1** to change position or direction **2** to change the position or direction of (something) **3** to move or cause (something) to move round an axis; rotate **4** to direct (one's attention or thoughts) to someone or something **5** (usually followed by into) to change (something) into (something else) ▷ noun **6** turning **7** opportunity to do something as part of an agreed succession **8** change in the way something is happening or being done: a turn for the worse **9 in turn** in sequence one after the other ▷ **turn down** verb **1** to reduce the volume or brightness of (a radio or heater) **2** to refuse or reject (a request or an offer) ▷ **turn up** verb **1** to arrive or appear **2** to be found **3** to increase the volume or brightness of (a radio or heater)

turncoat noun person who deserts one party or cause to join another

turning noun road or path leading off a main route

turning point noun moment when a decisive change occurs

turnip noun root vegetable with orange or white flesh

turnout noun number of people appearing at a gathering

turnover noun **1** total sales made by a business over a certain period **2** rate at which staff leave and are replaced

turnstile noun revolving gate for admitting one person at a time

turpentine noun strong-smelling colourless liquid used for cleaning and for thinning paint

turps noun turpentine oil

turquoise adjective **1** blue-green ▷ noun **2** blue-green precious stone

turret noun small tower

turtle noun sea tortoise

tusk noun long pointed tooth of an elephant, walrus, etc

tussle noun fight or scuffle

tutor noun **1** person teaching individuals or small groups ▷ verb **2** to act as a tutor to (someone)

tutorial noun period of instruction with a tutor

tutu noun short stiff skirt worn by ballerinas

TV abbreviation **1** television **2** television set

twang noun **1** sharp ringing sound **2** nasal speech **3** verb to make a twang or cause (something) to make a twang

tweak verb **1** to pinch or twist (something) sharply ▷ noun **2** tweaking

twee adjective informal too sentimental, sweet or pretty

tweed noun thick woollen cloth

tweet noun, verb (to) chirp

tweezers plural noun small pincer-like tool for pulling out hairs or picking up small objects

twelve adjective, noun the number 12 >**twelfth** adjective, noun

twenty noun the number 20 >**twentieth** adjective, noun

twice adverb two times

twiddle verb to fiddle or twirl (something) in an idle way

twig noun small branch or shoot

twilight noun **1** soft dim light just after sunset **2** final stages of something: *the twilight of his career*

twin noun **1** one of a pair, especially of two children born at one birth ▷ adjective **2** denoting one of two similar things that are close together or happen together

twine noun **1** string or cord ▷ verb **2** to twist or coil round (something)

twinge noun sudden sharp pain or emotional pang

twinkle verb **1** to shine brightly but intermittently ▷ noun **2** flickering brightness

twirl verb to cause (something) to spin or twist round and round

twist verb **1** to turn (something) out of the natural position **2** to distort or pervert (something) **3** to wind or twine (something) **4** to injure (a body part) by turning it too sharply or in an unusual direction **5** to change the meaning of or distort (someone's words) slightly ▷ noun **6** twisting **7** unexpected development in the plot of a film, book, etc

twisted adjective **1** bent **2** (of a person, mind, behaviour) unpleasantly abnormal

twit noun informal foolish person

twitch verb **1** to move spasmodically **2** to pull (something) sharply ▷ noun **3** little jerky movement

twitter verb (of birds) to utter chirping sounds

two adjective, noun the number 2

- Do not confuse the spelling
- of the preposition *to*, the
- adverb *too* and the number
- *two*

two-faced adjective deceitful, hypocritical

twofold *adjective* having two equally important parts or reasons

twosome *noun* two people or things that are usually seen together

two-time *verb informal* to deceive (a lover) by having an affair with someone else

two-up *noun Aust, NZ* popular gambling game in which two coins are tossed and bets are placed on whether they land heads or tails

tycoon *noun* powerful wealthy businessman

type *noun* **1** class or category **2** printed text ▷ *verb* **3** to write (something) with a typewriter or word processor > **typing** *noun* work or activity of producing something on a typewriter or word processor

typewriter *noun* machine that prints a character when the appropriate key is pressed

typhoid *noun* (also **typhoid fever**) acute infectious feverish disease

typhoon *noun* violent tropical storm

typhus *noun* infectious feverish disease

typical *adjective* true to type; characteristic > **typically** *adverb*

typify typifies typifying typified *verb* to be typical of (a situation or thing)

typist *noun* person who types with a typewriter or word processor

tyrannosaurus *noun* very large meat-eating dinosaur that walked upright on its hind legs

tyranny tyrannies *noun* tyrannical rule

tyrant *noun* person who treats the people he or she has authority over cruelly and unjustly

tyre *noun* rubber ring, usually inflated, over the rim of a vehicle's wheel to grip the road

u

ubiquitous *adjective* being or seeming to be everywhere at once

udder *noun* the baglike organ that hangs below a cow's body and produces milk

UFO *abbreviation* unidentified flying object

Ugandan *adjective* **1** belonging or relating to Uganda ▷ *noun* **2** someone from Uganda

ugly uglier ugliest *adjective* of unpleasant appearance > **ugliness** *noun*

UK *abbreviation* United Kingdom

ulcer *noun* **1** open sore on the surface of the skin which takes a long time to heal **2** something similar inside the body > **ulcerous** *adjective* of, like or characterized by ulcers

ulterior *adjective* (of a motive, aim, etc) apart from or beyond what is obvious

ultimate *adjective* **1** final in a series or process **2** highest or supreme ▷ *noun* **3** best or most advanced example of something: *the ultimate in luxury* > **ultimately** *adverb*: *Ultimately, the film is more* concerned with making money than reflecting reality

ultimatum noun final warning stating that action will be taken unless certain conditions are met

ultra- prefix **1** used to form adjectives describing extreme degrees of a quality; extremely: ultramodern **2** also used to describe qualities that go beyond a specified extent, range or limit ultrasonic; ultraviolet

ultramarine adjective vivid, deep blue

ultrasonic adjective of or producing sound waves with a higher frequency than the human ear can hear

ultrasound noun sound which cannot be heard by the human ear because its frequency is too high

ultraviolet adjective **1** (of light) beyond the violet end of the spectrum and invisible to the human eye. It is a form of radiation that causes your skin to darken after being exposed to the sun ▷ noun **2** light like this

umbilical cord noun long flexible tube of blood vessels that connects an unborn baby with its mother and through which the baby receives nutrients and oxygen

umbrella noun device used for protection against rain, consisting of a folding frame covered in material attached to a central rod

umpire noun **1** Cricket, Tennis official who makes sure that the game is played according to the rules and who makes a decision if there is a dispute ▷ verb **2** to act as umpire in (a game)

umpteen adjective informal very many ▷ **umpteenth** adjective: He checked his watch for the umpteenth time

un- prefix **1** not: unidentified **2** denoting reversal of an action: untie **3** denoting removal from: unthrone

unabashed adjective not embarrassed or discouraged by something

unabated adjective, adverb without any reduction in intensity or amount

unable adjective **unable to** lacking the necessary power, ability or authority to (do something)

unacceptable adjective **1** not satisfactory **2** intolerable

unaccompanied adjective alone

unaccustomed adjective not used (to something)

unaffected adjective **1** not changed in any way by a particular thing **2** genuinely natural; unpretentious

unaided adverb, adjective without help

unambiguous adjective having only one possible meaning; clear

unanimous adjective **1** in complete agreement **2** agreed by all ▷ **unanimity** noun ▷ **unanimously** adverb

unannounced adjective happening unexpectedly and without warning

unarmed adjective without weapons

unassuming adjective modest or unpretentious

unattached adjective neither married nor in a steady relationship

unattended *adjective* left alone or not being cared for

unauthorized or **unauthorised** *adjective* done without official permission

unavoidable *adjective* unable to be prevented or avoided

unaware *adjective* not aware or conscious

unawares *adverb* **1** by surprise: *caught unawares* **2** without knowing

unbalanced *adjective* **1** biased, one-sided or not organized in such a way that each part receives the right amount of emphasis **2** mentally disturbed **3** unequal

unbearable *adjective* not able to be endured > **unbearably** *adverb*

unbeatable *adjective* unable to be beaten

unbelievable *adjective* **1** hard to believe or imagine **2** very great or surprising > **unbelievably** *adverb*

unborn *adjective* not yet born

unbroken *adjective* continuous or complete

uncanny *adjective* strange and difficult to explain > **uncannily** *adverb*

uncertain *adjective* **1** not knowing what to do **2** doubtful or not known > **uncertainty** *noun*

unchallenged *adjective* accepted without any questions being asked

uncharacteristic *adjective* not typical or usual

uncivilized or **uncivilised** *adjective* unacceptable, for example by being very cruel or rude

uncle *noun* **1** brother of your father or mother **2** husband of your aunt

unclear *adjective* confusing and not obvious

uncomfortable *adjective* **1** not physically relaxed **2** anxious or uneasy > **uncomfortably** *adverb*

uncommon *adjective* **1** not happening or seen often **2** unusually great > **uncommonly** *adverb*

uncompromising *adjective* not prepared to compromise > **uncompromisingly** *adverb*

unconcerned *adjective* lacking in concern or involvement

unconditional *adjective* without conditions or limitations > **unconditionally** *adverb*

unconscious *adjective* **1** not conscious, as a result of shock, accident or injury **2** unaware **3** (of a feeling, attitude) not understood by or in the conscious awareness of the person who has it > *noun* **4** part of the mind containing instincts and ideas that exist without your awareness > **unconsciously** *adverb*

uncontrollable *adjective* not able to be controlled or stopped > **uncontrollably** *adverb*

unconventional *adjective* not behaving in the same way as most other people

unconvinced *adjective* not at all certain that something is true or right

uncouth *adjective* lacking in good manners and refinement

uncover *verb* **1** to find out (something secret or hidden) **2** to remove the cover, top or lid from (something)

undaunted *adjective* not put off or

discouraged

undecided adjective 1 not having made up your mind 2 (of an issue or problem) not agreed or decided upon

undemanding adjective not difficult to do or deal with

undeniable adjective unquestionably true
> **undeniably** adverb

under preposition 1 below or beneath 2 subject to or affected by 3 supervised by 4 less than 5 **under way** being carried out; in process

under- prefix 1 below: underground 2 insufficient or insufficiently: underrate

underarm adjective 1 Sport denoting a style of throwing, bowling or serving in which the hand is swung below shoulder level ▷ adverb 2 Sport in an underarm style

undercarriage noun 1 the part of an aircraft, including the wheels, that supports it when it is on the ground 2 framework supporting the body of a vehicle

underclass noun social group consisting of those who are poorest and whose situation is unlikely to improve

underclothes plural noun clothes that you wear under your other clothes and next to your skin

undercover adjective done or acting in secret

undercurrent noun underlying opinion or emotion that may become stronger

undercut undercuts undercutting undercut verb to charge less than (a competitor) to

obtain trade

underdeveloped adjective (of a country) without modern industries and having a low standard of living

underdog noun person or team in a weak or underprivileged position

underestimate verb to fail to realize how large, great or capable something or someone is

underfoot adverb under the feet

undergo undergoes undergoing underwent undergone verb to experience or have (something)

underground adjective 1 below the surface of the ground 2 secret, unofficial and usually illegal ▷ noun 3 railway system in which trains travel in tunnels below ground 4 movement dedicated to overthrowing a government or forces of occupation

undergrowth noun small trees and bushes growing beneath taller trees in a wood or forest

underhand adjective sly, deceitful and secretive

underlie underlies underlying underlay underlain verb to be the foundation, cause or basis of > **underlying** adjective fundamental or basic

underline verb 1 to draw a line under 2 to emphasize

underling noun person of lesser rank; subordinate

undermine verb to weaken (something or someone) gradually

underneath preposition, adverb 1 below or beneath ▷ adjective 2 lower ▷ noun 3 lower part or surface

underpants plural noun piece of clothing worn by men and boys under their trousers; briefs

underpass noun section of a road that passes under another road or a railway line

underpin underpins underpinning underpinned verb to give strength or support to

underprivileged adjective lacking the rights and advantages of other members of society

underrate verb not to recognize the full value or worth of (someone or something) ▷ **underrated** adjective

understand understands understanding understood verb 1 to know or grasp the meaning or nature of (something or someone) 2 to interpret (something or someone) correctly 3 to assume, gather or believe

understandable adjective able to be understood; comprehensible ▷ **understandably** adverb

understanding noun 1 ability to learn, judge or make decisions 2 personal interpretation of a subject 3 mutual agreement, usually an informal or private one ▷ adjective 4 kind and sympathetic

understatement noun a statement that does not say fully how true something is

understudy understudies understudying understudied noun 1 actor who studies a part in order to be able to replace the usual actor if necessary ▷ verb 2 to act as an understudy for (someone with an important part)

undertake undertakes undertaking undertook undertaken verb to agree to (something) or to do (something)

undertaker noun person whose job is to prepare bodies for burial or cremation and arrange funerals

undertaking noun 1 task or enterprise 2 agreement to do something

undertone noun 1 quiet tone of voice 2 underlying quality or feeling

undervalue undervalues undervaluing undervalued verb to rate (something) as less important or valuable than it really is

underwater adverb, adjective 1 beneath the surface of the sea, a river or a lake ▷ adjective 2 designed to work in water: an underwater camera

underwear noun clothing that you wear under your other clothes and next to your skin

underwent past tense of undergo

undesirable adjective not desirable or pleasant, objectionable

undid past tense of undo

undisputed adjective definite and without any doubt: the undisputed champion

undivided adjective (of attention) complete

undo undoes undoing undid undone verb 1 to open, unwrap or untie 2 to reverse the effects of

undoing noun cause of someone's downfall

undoubted adjective certain or

indisputable >**undoubtedly** adverb

undress verb to take off your clothes

undue adjective greater than is reasonable; excessive >**unduly** adverb

undulating adjective formal moving gently up and down

undying adjective never ending; eternal

unearth verb to reveal or discover (something) by searching

unearthly adjective 1 strange and unnatural 2 (of a time, hour) ridiculous or unreasonable

uneasy adjective (of a person) worried, anxious or apprehensive >**unease** noun 1 feeling of anxiety 2 state of dissatisfaction >**uneasily** adverb >**uneasiness** noun

unemployed adjective 1 out of work ▷ plural noun 2 people without a job

unemployment noun state of being without a job

unending adjective having lasted for a long time and seeming as if it will never stop

unenviable adjective not to be envied

unequal adjective 1 (of society) not offering the same opportunities and privileges to all people 2 different in size, strength or ability

uneven adjective 1 (of a surface) not level or smooth 2 not the same or consistent >**unevenly** adverb

uneventful adjective (of a period of time) without any interesting happenings

unexpected adjective surprising; not expected >**unexpectedly** adverb

unfailing adjective continuous or reliable >**unfailingly** adverb

unfair adjective not right, fair or just >**unfairly** adverb >**unfairness** noun

unfaithful adjective having sex with someone other than one's regular partner >**unfaithfulness** noun

unfamiliar adjective 1 (often followed by to) not known (to) 2 (followed by with) not acquainted (with)

unfashionable adjective not popular or no longer used by many people

unfavourable adjective not encouraging or promising, or not providing any advantage

unfit adjective 1 in poor physical condition 2 unsuitable

unfold verb 1 to open or spread (something) out from a folded state 2 (of a situation) to develop and become known

unforeseen adjective happening unexpectedly

unforgettable adjective impossible to forget; memorable >**unforgettably** adverb

unforgivable adjective bad or cruel to such an extent that it can never be forgiven or justified >**unforgivably** adverb

unfortunate adjective 1 unlucky, unsuccessful or unhappy 2 regrettable or unsuitable >**unfortunately** adverb

unfounded adjective without any truth; groundless

unfriendly unfriendlier

unfriendliest *adjective* cold and unpleasant or unwelcoming

ungainly ungainlier ungainliest *adjective* moving in an awkward or clumsy way

ungrateful *adjective* not grateful or thankful

unhappy unhappier unhappiest *adjective* **1** sad and depressed **2** not pleased or satisfied **3** unfortunate or wretched >**unhappily** *adverb* >**unhappiness** *noun*

unhealthy unhealthier unhealthiest *adjective* **1** likely to cause illness **2** not fit or well

unheard-of *adjective* never having happened before and therefore surprising or shocking

unhinged *adjective* mentally ill

unhurried *adjective* slow and relaxed

unicorn *noun* imaginary animal that looks like a white horse with a straight horn growing from its forehead

unidentified *adjective* of which the name or nature is not known

uniform *noun* **1** special set of clothes worn by people at work or school ▷ *adjective* **2** regular and even throughout; unvarying **3** alike or like >**uniformity** *noun* >**uniformly** *adverb*

unify unifies unifying unified *verb* to make (something) one or to become one by joining together different elements >**unification** *noun: the unification of Italy*

unilateral *adjective* (of decision, action) made or done by only one person or group >**unilaterally** *adverb*

unimaginable *adjective*

impossible to imagine or understand properly

unimportant *adjective* having very little significance or importance

uninhabited *adjective* without anyone living there

uninhibited *adjective* behaving freely and naturally, showing your feelings

unintelligible *adjective formal* impossible to understand

uninterested *adjective* having or showing no interest in someone or something

uninterrupted *adjective* continuing without breaks or interruptions

union *noun* **1** organization of workers that aims to improve the working conditions, pay and benefits of its members **2** uniting or being united

unique *adjective* **1** being the only one of a particular type **2** without equal or like **3 unique to** belonging or relating only to (a particular person or thing) >**uniquely** *adverb* >**uniqueness** *noun*

unisex *adjective* designed for use by both sexes

unison *noun* **in unison 1** doing the same thing together at the same time **2** in complete agreement

unit *noun* **1** single complete thing **2** group or individual regarded as a basic element of a larger whole **3** fixed quantity etc, used as a standard of measurement **4** piece of furniture designed to be fitted with other similar pieces

unite *verb* **1** to join together to act as a group **2** to cause (people or things) to enter into an association or alliance

United Kingdom noun Great Britain together with Northern Ireland

United Nations noun international organization that tries to encourage peace, cooperation and friendship between countries

unity unities noun 1 state of being one 2 mutual agreement

universal adjective 1 concerning or relating to everyone in the world or every part of the universe 2 existing everywhere > **universally** adverb

universe noun the whole of space, including all the stars and planets

university universities noun place where students study for degrees

unjust adjective not fair or reasonable > **unjustly** adverb

unjustified adjective (of a belief or action) without reason or basis

unkempt adjective untidy and not looked after properly

unkind adjective unpleasant and rather cruel > **unkindly** adverb > **unkindness** noun

unknown adjective 1 not known 2 not famous ▷ noun 3 unknown person, quantity or thing

unlawful adjective not legal

unleaded adjective (of petrol) containing less lead, in order to reduce environmental pollution

unleash verb to release (a powerful or violent force)

unless conjunction except under the circumstances that

unlike adjective 1 dissimilar or different ▷ preposition 2 not like

or typical of

unlikely adjective improbable

unlimited adjective (of a supply) not limited or restricted

unload verb to remove (cargo) from (a ship, truck or plane)

unlock verb to turn the key in (a door or container) so that it can be opened

unlucky adjective having or causing bad luck > **unluckily** adverb

unmarked adjective 1 with no marks of damage or injury 2 with no signs or marks of identification

unmistakable or **unmistakeable** adjective not ambiguous; clear > **unmistakably** or **unmistakeably** adverb

unmitigated adjective 1 not reduced or lessened in severity etc 2 total and complete

unmoved adjective not affected by emotion; indifferent

unnatural adjective 1 strange and frightening because not usual 2 artificial and not typical > **unnaturally** adverb

unnecessary adjective not necessary or required > **unnecessarily** adverb

unnerve verb to cause (someone) to lose courage, confidence or self-control > **unnerving** adjective

unobtrusive adjective not very noticeable

unoccupied adjective without anybody living there

unofficial adjective without the approval or permission of a person in authority > **unofficially** adverb

unorthodox *adjective* unconventional and not generally accepted

unpack *verb* 1 to remove the contents of (a suitcase, trunk, etc) 2 to take (something) out of a packed container

unpaid *adjective* 1 without pay 2 not yet paid

unpalatable *adjective* very unpleasant and hard to eat or accept

unparalleled *adjective* not equalled; supreme

unpleasant *adjective* not pleasant or agreeable > **unpleasantly** *adverb* > **unpleasantness** *noun*

unpopular *adjective* disliked by most people

unprecedented *adjective* formal that has never happened before or is the best of its kind so far

unpredictable *adjective* having behaviour that is impossible to predict

unprepared *adjective* not ready

unproductive *adjective* not producing anything useful

unqualified *adjective* 1 lacking the necessary qualifications 2 total or complete

unquestionable *adjective* so obviously true or real that nobody can doubt it > **unquestionably** *adverb*

unravel unravels unravelling unravelled *verb* 1 to unwind, disentangle or undo (something) 2 to become unravelled 3 to explain or solve (a mystery)

unreal *adjective* so strange that you find it difficult to believe

unrealistic *adjective* 1 not facing up to reality or the practicalities of a situation 2 not true to life

unreasonable *adjective* unfair and difficult to deal with or justify > **unreasonably** *adverb*

unrelated *adjective* not connected

unrelenting *adjective* continuing in a determined way without caring about any hurt that is caused

unreliable *adjective* that cannot be relied upon

unremitting *adjective* continuing without stopping

unrest *noun* anger and dissatisfaction among the people

unrivalled *adjective* better than anything else of its kind

unroll *verb* 1 to open out or unwind (something rolled or coiled) 2 (of something rolled or coiled) to become opened out or unwound

unruly unrulier unruliest *adjective* difficult to control or organize

unsatisfactory *adjective* not good enough

unsaturated *adjective* (of an oil, fat) made mainly from vegetable fats and considered healthier than saturated

unscathed *adjective* not harmed or injured

unscrew *verb* to remove (something) by turning it or by removing the screws holding it

unscrupulous *adjective* prepared to act dishonestly; unprincipled

unseemly *adjective* (of behaviour) not suitable for a particular situation and showing a lack of control and good manners

unseen *adjective* not seen

unsettle *verb* to make (someone) restless or worried

unshakable or **unshakeable** *adjective* (of a belief, faith, etc) so strong that it cannot be destroyed

unsightly *adjective* unpleasant to look at

unskilled *adjective* (of work) not requiring any special training

unsolicited *adjective* given or happening without being asked for

unsound *adjective* **1** not based on truth or fact **2** unstable

unspeakable *adjective* very unpleasant

unspecified *adjective* not stated specifically

unspoilt or **unspoiled** *adjective* unchanged and still as at a previous time

unspoken *adjective* not talked about

unstable *adjective* **1** likely to change suddenly and create difficulty or danger **2** not firm or fixed properly and likely to wobble or fall

unsteady *adjective* **1** having difficulty in controlling the movement of your legs or hands **2** not held or fixed securely and likely to fall over > **unsteadily** *adverb*

unstuck *adjective* **come unstuck** to become separated from something

unsuccessful *adjective* not having success at something > **unsuccessfully** *adverb*

unsuitable *adjective* not right or appropriate for a particular purpose > **unsuitably** *adverb*

unsuited *adjective* not appropriate for a particular task or situation

unsung *adjective* not appreciated

or praised enough

unsure *adjective* uncertain or doubtful

unsuspecting *adjective* having no idea of what is happening or going to happen

untangle *verb* to undo, removing any twists or knots

untenable *adjective* formal (of a theory, argument or position) that cannot be successfully defended

unthinkable *adjective* out of the question; inconceivable

untidy untidier untidiest *adjective* messy and disordered > **untidily** *adverb* > **untidiness** *noun*

untie unties untying untied *verb* to open or free (something that is tied)

until *conjunction* **1** up to the time that ▷ *preposition* **2** in or throughout the period before **3** **not until** not before (a time or event)

untimely *adjective* occurring before the expected or normal time

unto *preposition* old-fashioned to

untold *adjective* incalculably great in number or quantity

untouched *adjective* **1** not changed, moved or damaged **2** not eaten

untoward *adjective* unexpected and causing difficulties

untrue *adjective* **1** not true, incorrect or false **2** disloyal or unfaithful

unused *adjective* **1** not yet used **2** **unused to** not accustomed to

unusual *adjective* uncommon or extraordinary > **unusually** *adverb*

unveil *verb* to reveal (a statue or painting) officially, by drawing back a curtain

unwanted *adjective* not wanted or desired

unwarranted *adjective formal* not justified or not deserved

unwelcome *adjective* not welcome or wanted

unwell *adjective* not well; ill

unwieldy *adjective* too heavy, large or awkward to be easily handled

unwilling *adjective* not willing or prepared (to do something) > **unwillingly** *adverb*

unwind unwinds unwinding unwound *verb* **1** to relax after a busy or tense time **2** to undo or unravel (something)

unwise *adjective* foolish or not sensible

unwitting *adjective* **1** not intentional **2** not knowing or conscious > **unwittingly** *adverb*

unworthy *adjective formal* not deserving or worthy

unwrap unwraps unwrapping unwrapped *verb* to remove the wrapping from

unwritten *adjective* **1** not printed or in writing **2** operating only through custom

up *adverb, preposition* **1** indicating movement to or position at a higher place ▷ *preposition* **2** along (a road or river) ▷ *adverb* **3** towards or in the north: *I'm flying up to Darwin* **4** **go up** to increase ▷ *adjective* **5** of a high or higher position **6** out of bed

up-and-coming *adjective* likely to be successful

upbringing *noun* education of a person during the formative years

update *verb* to bring (something or someone) up to date

upgrade *verb* **1** to improve (equipment) **2** to promote (a person or job) to a higher rank

upheaval *noun* big change that causes a lot of trouble

uphill *adjective* **1** sloping or leading upwards **2** requiring a great deal of effort ▷ *adverb* **3** up a slope

uphold upholds upholding upheld *verb* to support and maintain (a law or decision) > **upholder** *noun*

upholstery *noun* soft covering on a chair or sofa

upkeep *noun* act, process or cost of keeping something in good repair

upland *adjective* (of an area) high or relatively high > **uplands** *plural noun* area of high or relatively high ground

uplifting *adjective* making you feel happy

upload *verb* to transfer a computer file or program from your computer into the memory of another computer

up-market *adjective* sophisticated and expensive

upon *preposition* **1** on **2** up and on **3** in the course of or immediately after

upper *adjective* **1** higher in physical position, wealth, rank or status ▷ *noun* **2** part of a shoe above the sole

upper class *noun* highest social class > **upper-class** *adjective*

uppermost *adjective* **1** highest in position, power or importance ▷ *adverb* **2** in or into the highest place or position

upright *adjective* **1** vertical or erect **2** honest or just ▷ *adverb* **3** vertically or in an erect position

▷ *noun* **4** vertical support, such as a post

uprising *noun* rebellion or revolt

uproar *noun* disturbance characterized by loud noise and confusion

uproot *verb* **1** to displace (a person or people) from their native or usual surroundings **2** to pull (a tree or plant) out of the ground together with its roots

upset upsets upsetting upset *adjective* **1** unhappy or distressed ▷ *verb* **2** to sadden, distress or worry (someone) **3** to disturb the normal state or stability of (something) **4** to tip over or spill (something) **5** to make (someone) physically ill ▷ *noun* **6 stomach upset** slight stomach illness caused by an infection or by something you have eaten > **upsetting** *adjective*

upshot *noun* final result or conclusion

upside down *adjective, adverb* the wrong way up

upstage *verb informal* to draw attention away from (someone) by being more attractive or interesting

upstairs *adverb* **1** to or on an upper floor of a building ▷ *noun* **2** upper floor ▷ *adjective* **3** situated on an upper floor

upstart *noun* person who has risen suddenly to a position of power and behaves arrogantly

upstream *adverb, adjective* in or towards the higher part of a stream

upsurge *noun* rapid rise or swell

uptake *noun* **quick, slow on the uptake** *informal* quick or slow to understand or learn

uptight *adjective informal* nervously tense, irritable or angry

up-to-date *adjective* **1** modern or fashionable **2** having the latest information

up-to-the-minute *adjective* latest and newest possible

upturn *noun* improvement

upturned *adjective* **1** facing upwards **2** upside down

upward *adjective* **1** towards a higher place, level or condition ▷ *adverb* **2** (also **upwards**) from a lower to a higher place, level or condition

uranium *noun* radioactive silvery-white metallic element, used to produce nuclear energy and weapons

Uranus *noun* seventh planet from the sun in the solar system

urban *adjective* relating to a town or city

urbane *adjective* well-mannered and comfortable in social situations

Urdu *noun* official language of Pakistan; also spoken by many people in India

urge *noun* **1** strong impulse, inner drive or wish ▷ *verb* **2** to press or try to persuade (someone to do something)

urgent *adjective* requiring speedy action or attention > **urgency** *noun* > **urgently** *adverb*

urinal *noun* a bowl or trough fixed to the wall in a men's public toilet for men to urinate in

urinate *verb* to get rid of urine from your body

urine *noun* pale yellow fluid excreted by the kidneys to the bladder and passed as waste from the body >**urinary** adjective

urn noun **1** vase used as a container for the ashes of the dead **2** large metal container with a tap, used for making and holding tea or coffee

us pronoun used by a speaker or writer to refer to himself or herself and at least one other person; used as the object of a verb or preposition

US or **USA** abbreviation United States (of America)

usage noun **1** way in which a word is used in a language **2** the degree to which something is used, or the way in which it is used

USB abbreviation Universal Serial Bus: standard for connecting sockets on computers

USB drive noun Computers small data storage device that plugs into a computer

use verb **1** to do something with (something) in order to do a job or achieve a purpose **2** to take advantage of (someone); exploit **3** to consume or expend (energy, resources, etc) **4** **used to do something** previously did or previously had the habit of doing something: I used to live there; He used not to like milk; He didn't use to like milk ▷ noun **5** act of using something or being used **6** ability or permission to use something **7** usefulness or advantage **8** purpose for which something is used >**usable** adjective able to be used >**user** noun

used adjective **1** second-hand **2** **used to something** accustomed to something

useful adjective helpful >**usefully** adverb >**usefulness** noun

useless adjective **1** of no use or

help **2** in vain **3** informal very poor or bad at something; hopeless >**uselessly** adverb >**uselessness** noun

username noun Computers name entered into a computer for identification purposes

usher noun **1** official who shows people to their seats, as in a church ▷ verb **2** to conduct or escort (someone somewhere)

USSR abbreviation Union of Soviet Socialist Republics, a country which was made up of a lot of smaller countries including Russia, but which is now broken up

usual adjective happening, done or used most often >**usually** adverb most often, in most cases

usurp verb to seize (a position or power) without authority >**usurper** noun

ute noun Aust, NZ informal utility truck

utensil noun tool for practical use: cooking utensils

uterus uteri noun womb

utility utilities noun **1** usefulness **2** public service, such as electricity

utility truck noun Aust, NZ small truck with an open body and low sides

utilize verb formal to make practical use of >**utilization** noun

utmost adjective extreme or greatest

utter verb **1** to express (something) in sounds or words ▷ adjective **2** total or absolute >**utterly** adverb

utterance noun something said or uttered

V

v. abbreviation 1 versus 2 very

vacant adjective 1 (of a toilet, room, position, etc) unoccupied 2 (of an expression, look) without interest or understanding > **vacantly** adverb

vacate verb formal 1 to leave (a room) 2 to give up (a job or position)

vacation noun 1 time when universities and law courts are closed 2 Chiefly US holiday

vaccinate verb to inject (a person or animal) with a vaccine > **vaccination** noun

vaccine noun substance designed to cause a mild form of a disease to make a person immune to the disease itself

vacuum noun 1 space containing no air, gases or other matter ▷ verb 2 to clean (a room, carpet, etc) with a vacuum cleaner

vacuum cleaner noun electrical appliance which sucks up dust and dirt from carpets and upholstery

vagina noun (in female mammals) passage from the womb to the external genitals

vagrant noun person with no settled home; tramp > **vagrancy** noun: You'll get arrested for vagrancy

vague adjective 1 not clearly explained 2 unable to be seen or heard clearly 3 absent-minded > **vaguely** adverb > **vagueness** noun

vain adjective 1 excessively proud, especially of your appearance 2 bound to fail; futile ▷ noun 3 **in vain** unsuccessfully > **vainly** adverb

vale noun literary valley

valentine noun 1 person to whom you send a romantic card on Saint Valentine's Day, 14th February 2 (also **valentine card**) a card sent on Saint Valentine's Day

valet noun man's personal male servant

valiant adjective brave or courageous > **valiantly** adverb

valid adjective 1 soundly reasoned 2 officially accepted > **validity** noun

validate verb to prove (something) to be true > **validation** noun

valley noun low area between hills, often with a river running through it

valour noun literary bravery

valuable adjective having great value or worth

valuation noun assessment of how much something is worth

value values valuing valued noun 1 importance, usefulness 2 monetary worth 3 **values** moral principles ▷ verb 4 to think (something) is important; appreciate 5 to assess the value of > **valued** adjective > **valuer** noun

valve noun 1 device to control the movement of gas or liquid through a pipe 2 small flap in your heart or in a vein which controls the flow and direction of blood

vampire noun (in folklore) corpse that rises at night to drink the blood of the living

van noun **1** motor vehicle larger than a car but smaller than a lorry, used for carrying goods **2** railway carriage for goods, luggage or mail

vandal noun person who deliberately damages property >**vandalism** noun >**vandalize** or **vandalise** verb

vane noun flat blade on a rotary device such as a weathercock or propeller

vanguard noun most advanced group or position in a movement or activity

vanilla noun seed pod of a tropical plant, used for flavouring

vanish verb **1** to disappear suddenly or mysteriously **2** to cease to exist

vanity noun feeling of excessive pride about your looks or abilities

vanquish verb literary to defeat (someone) completely

vapour noun **1** moisture suspended in air as steam or mist **2** gaseous form of something that is liquid or solid at room temperature

variable adjective **1** not always the same; changeable ▷ noun **2** something that can change **3** Maths symbol such as x which can represent any value or any one of a set of values >**variability** noun

variance noun **at variance** at odds or not in agreement (with)

variant noun **1** something that differs from a standard or type ▷ adjective **2** differing from a standard or type

variation noun **1** change from the normal or usual pattern

2 difference in level, amount or quantity

varicose veins plural noun knotted and swollen veins, especially in the legs

varied adjective of different types, quantities or sizes: Eat a healthy and varied diet

variety varieties noun **1** state of being diverse or various **2** different things of the same kind; assortment **3** particular type **4** light entertainment composed of unrelated acts

various adjective **1** several **2** of several kinds >**variously** adverb

varnish noun **1** liquid which when painted onto a surface gives it a hard clear shiny finish ▷ verb **2** to apply varnish to

vary varies varying varied verb **1** to change **2** to make changes in

vascular adjective Biology relating to tubes or ducts that carry fluids within animals or plants

vase noun ornamental jar, especially for flowers

vasectomy vasectomies noun operation to sterilize a man by cutting the tube that carries the sperm

Vaseline® noun thick oily cream made from petroleum, used in skin care

vast adjective extremely large >**vastly** adverb >**vastness** noun

vat noun large container for liquids

VAT abbreviation (in Britain) value-added tax, a tax which is added to the costs of making or providing goods and services

vault noun **1** secure room for storing valuables **2** underground burial chamber **3** an arched roof, often found in churches ▷ *verb* **4** to jump over (something) by resting your hand(s) on it > **vaulted** *adjective* having an arched roof

VCD *abbreviation* video compact disc: an optical disc used to store computer, audio or video data

VCR *abbreviation* video cassette recorder

VDU *abbreviation* visual display unit: monitor screen attached to a computer or word processor

veal *noun* calf meat

Veda *noun* ancient Hindu sacred text; also these texts as a collection > **Vedic** *adjective*

veer *verb* to change direction suddenly

vegan *noun* person who eats no meat, fish, eggs or dairy products

vegetable *noun* **1** edible roots or leaves such as carrots or cabbage ▷ *adjective* **2** relating to plants or vegetables

vegetarian *noun* **1** person who does not eat meat, poultry or fish ▷ *adjective* **2** suitable for a vegetarian > **vegetarianism** *noun*

vegetation *noun* plant life in a particular area

vehement *adjective* expressing strong feelings > **vehemence** *noun* > **vehemently** *adverb*

vehicle *noun* **1** machine, especially with an engine and wheels, for carrying people or objects **2** something used to achieve a particular purpose or as a means of expression > **vehicular** *adjective*

veil *noun* piece of thin cloth covering the head or face > **veiled** *adjective*

vein *noun* **1** tube that takes blood to the heart **2** line on a leaf or an insect's wing **3** layer of ore or mineral in rock **4** streak in marble, wood or cheese **5** feature of someone's writing or speech: *a vein of humour* **6** mood or style: *in a lighter vein* > **veined** *adjective*

veld or **veldt** *noun* high grassland in southern Africa

veldskoen or **velskoen** *noun* S Afr tough ankle-length boot

velocity velocities *noun technical* speed at which something is moving in a particular direction

velvet *noun* fabric with a thick soft pile > **velvety** *adjective* soft and smooth

vendetta *noun* long-lasting bitter quarrel which results in people trying to harm each other

vending machine *noun* machine that dispenses goods such as sweets or drinks when you put money in it

vendor *noun* person who sells something

veneer *noun* **1** superficial appearance: *a veneer of sophistication* **2** thin layer of wood etc covering a cheaper material

venerable *adjective* worthy of great respect

venerate *verb formal* to feel great respect for > **veneration** *noun*

vengeance *noun* **1** act of harming someone because they have harmed you; revenge **2** with **a vengeance** very forcefully or strongly

venison *noun* deer meat

venom *noun* **1** poison produced by snakes, scorpions and spiders, etc **2** malice or spite > **venomous** *adjective*

vent noun 1 outlet , hole or slit through which fumes or fluid can escape and fresh air can enter 2 **give vent to** to release (a strong feeling) in an outburst ▷ verb 3 to express (a strong feeling) in an outburst

ventilate verb 1 to let fresh air into (a room or building) 2 to discuss (ideas or feelings) openly > **ventilated** adjective > **ventilation** noun

ventilator noun machine that helps people breathe when they cannot breathe naturally, for example if they are very il

ventriloquist noun entertainer who can speak without moving his or her lips, so that the words appear to come from a dummy > **ventriloquism** noun

venture noun 1 risky undertaking, especially in business ▷ verb 2 to go to an unknown and possibly risky place 3 to dare to express (an opinion) 4 to dare (to do something)

venue noun place where an event is held

Venus noun second planet from the sun in the solar system

veranda or **verandah** noun platform with a roof that is attached to an outside wall of a house at ground level

verb noun word that expresses the idea of action, happening or being, e.g. run; take; become; to be

verbal adjective 1 spoken 2 relating to verbs > **verbally** adverb

verdict noun 1 decision that states whether a prisoner is guilty or not guilty 2 opinion formed after examining the facts

verge noun 1 grass border along a road 2 **on the verge of** having almost reached (a point or condition) > **verge on** verb to be near to (a condition)

verify verifies verifying verified verb to check the truth or accuracy of > **verifiable** adjective > **verification** noun: The winning card will be subject to verification

veritable adjective rightly called; without exaggeration: a veritable feast > **veritably** adverb

vermin plural noun animals, especially insects and rodents, that spread disease or cause damage

vernacular noun most widely spoken language of a particular people or place

verruca noun wart, usually on the foot

versatile adjective having many skills or uses > **versatility** noun

verse noun 1 poetry 2 one part of a song, poem or chapter of the Bible

versed adjective **versed in** knowledgeable about

version noun 1 form of something, such as a piece of writing, with some differences from other forms 2 account of an event from a particular person's point of view

versus preposition 1 in opposition to or in contrast with 2 Sport, Law against

vertebra vertebrae noun one of the bones that form the spine

vertebrate noun any animal that has a spine

vertex vertexes or vertices noun highest point of a triangle or pyramid

vertical adjective straight up and down ▷ **vertically** adverb

vertigo noun dizziness, usually when looking down from a high place

verve noun enthusiasm or liveliness

very adverb **1** more than usually, extremely ▷ adjective **2** absolute or exact: the very top; the very man

vessel noun **1** ship or large boat **2** literary container, especially for liquids **3** Biology thin tube along which liquids such as blood or sap move in animals and plants

vest noun **1** piece of underwear worn for warmth on the top half of the body **2** US waistcoat

vestige noun formal small amount or trace

vestry vestries noun part of the church building where a priest or minister changes into their official clothes

vet vets vetting vetted noun **1** medical specialist who treats sick animals; veterinary surgeon **2** US, Aust, NZ military veteran ▷ verb **3** to check the suitability of something

veteran noun **1** someone who has served in the armed forces, particularly during a war **2** someone who has been involved in a particular activity for a long time

veterinary adjective concerning animal health

veterinary surgeon noun medical specialist who treats sick animals

veto vetoes vetoing vetoed verb **1** (of a person in authority) to say no to ▷ noun **2** right of someone in authority to say no to something

vexed adjective annoyed, worried or puzzled

VHF abbreviation very high frequency: a range of high radio frequencies

via preposition by way of

viable adjective **1** able to be put into practice **2** Biology able to live and grow independently > **viability** noun

viaduct noun long high bridge that carries a road or railway across a valley

vibrant adjective **1** full of life, energy and enthusiasm **2** (of a colour) strong and bright > **vibrancy** noun > **vibrantly** adverb

vibrate verb to move back and forth rapidly by a tiny amount > **vibration** noun

vicar noun priest in the Church of England

vicarage noun house where a vicar lives

vice noun **1** serious moral fault in someone's character, such as greed, or a weakness, such as smoking **2** criminal activities connected with prostitution and pornography **3** tool with a pair of jaws for holding an object while working on it

vice- prefix deputy or assistant to: vice-president

viceregal adjective **1** of or concerning a viceroy **2** (in Australia and New Zealand) of or concerning a governor or governor-general

viceroy noun governor of a colony who represents the monarch

vice versa adverb Latin the other

way round: *Wives criticize their husbands, and vice versa*

vicinity vicinities *noun* surrounding area

vicious *adjective* cruel and violent > **viciously** *adverb* > **viciousness** *noun*

victim *noun* someone who has been harmed or injured by someone or something

victor *noun* person who has defeated an opponent, especially in war or sport; winner

Victorian *adjective* 1 of or in the reign of Queen Victoria (1837–1901) 2 of or relating to the Australian state of Victoria

victory victories *noun* winning of a battle or contest > **victorious** *adjective*

video videos videoing videoed *noun* 1 short for video cassette, video cassette recorder, video tape ▷ *verb* 2 to record (a TV programme, film or event) on video ▷ *adjective* 3 relating to or used in producing sound and pictures

video recorder *or* **video cassette recorder** *noun* tape recorder for recording and playing back TV programmes and films

vie vies vying vied *verb* to compete (with someone)

Vietnamese *adjective* 1 belonging or relating to Vietnam ▷ *noun* 2 someone from Vietnam 3 main language spoken in Vietnam

view *noun* 1 opinion or belief 2 everything that can be seen from a given place 3 picture of this 4 in view of taking into consideration 5 on view available to be seen by the public;

on show ▷ *verb* 6 to think of (something) in a particular way

viewer *noun* person who watches television

viewpoint *noun* 1 opinion or way of thinking about something 2 place from which you get a good view of an area or event

vigil *noun* night-time period of staying awake to look after a sick person, pray, make a protest etc

vigilant *adjective* watchful in case of danger

vigilante *noun* person, especially one of an unofficial group, who takes it upon himself or herself to protect the community and catch and punish criminals

vigorous *adjective* energetic or enthusiastic > **vigorously** *adverb* > **vigour** *noun* physical or mental energy

Viking *noun* History seafaring raider and settler from Scandinavia from the 8th to the 11th centuries

vile *adjective* very unpleasant or disgusting

villa *noun* 1 large house with gardens 2 holiday home, usually in the Mediterranean

village *noun* 1 small group of houses and other buildings in a country area 2 rural community > **villager** *noun*

villain *noun* 1 someone who harms others or breaks the law 2 main wicked character in a play > **villainous** *adjective* > **villainy** *noun*

vindicate *verb* to prove (someone) right or to prove (their actions or ideas) to have been justified > **vindication** *noun*

vindictive adjective maliciously seeking revenge > **vindictiveness** noun

vine noun trailing or climbing plant, especially one producing grapes

vinegar noun sharp-tasting liquid made from sour wine, beer or cider > **vinegary** adjective

vineyard noun area of land where grapes are grown

vintage adjective 1 (of wine) of a good quality and stored for a number of years to improve 2 best and most typical ▷ noun 3 wine from a particular harvest of grapes

vinyl noun type of plastic, used to make things such as floor coverings and furniture

viola noun stringed instrument lower in pitch than a violin

violate verb 1 to break (a law or agreement) 2 to disturb (someone's peace or privacy) 3 to treat (a sacred place) disrespectfully > **violation** noun

violence noun 1 use of physical force, usually intended to cause injury or destruction 2 great force or strength in action, feeling or expression

violent adjective 1 (of a person) making use of physical force or weapons in a way that may cause injury or death 2 (of n event) happening unexpectedly and with great force 3 (of an act, feeling, pain etc) very forceful > **violently** adverb

violet noun 1 plant with bluish-purple flowers ▷ adjective, noun 2 bluish-purple

violin noun four-stringed musical instrument played with a bow > **violinist** noun

VIP abbreviation very important person

viper noun type of poisonous snake

virgin noun 1 person, especially a woman, who has not had sexual intercourse ▷ adjective 2 not yet used or explored; fresh > **virginity** noun

virginal adjective 1 looking young and innocent 2 looking fresh, clean and unused ▷ noun 3 keyboard instrument popular in the 16th and 17th centuries

Virgo noun sixth sign of the zodiac, represented by a girl

virile adjective having the traditional male characteristics of physical strength and a high sex drive > **virility** noun

virtual adjective 1 having the characteristics of something without being formally recognized as being that thing 2 of or relating to virtual reality > **virtually** adverb practically, almost

virtual reality noun computer-generated environment that seems real to the user

virtue noun 1 moral goodness 2 positive moral quality 3 advantage, merit 4 **by virtue of** formal by reason of > **virtuously** adverb

virtuoso virtuosos or virtuosi noun person with impressive skill at something, especially music > **virtuosity** noun

virtuous adjective morally good

virus viruses noun 1 microorganism that can cause disease 2 Computers program that alters or damages the information stored in a computer system

visa *noun* permission to enter a country, granted by its government and shown by a stamp on your passport

viscount *noun* British nobleman ranking between an earl and a baron

Vishnu *proper noun* a Hindu god and one of the Trimurti

visibility *noun* range or clarity of vision

visible *adjective* **1** able to be seen **2** noticeable or evident >**visibly** *adverb*

vision *noun* **1** ability to see **2** mental image of something **3** foresight **4** unusual experience, in which you see things not seen by others, as a result of a mental disorder, divine inspiration or taking drugs >**visionary** *adjective* **1** showing foresight **2** idealistic but impractical ▷ *noun* **3** visionary person

visit *verb* **1** to go or come to see (someone or something) ▷ *noun* **2** instance of visiting >**visitor** *noun*

visor *noun* transparent part of a helmet that you pull down to protect your eyes or face

visual *adjective* **1** relating to sight **2** designed to be looked at

visualize *verb* to form a mental image of

vital *adjective* **1** essential or very important **2** energetic, exciting and full of life **3** necessary to maintain life >**vitality** *noun* physical or mental energy >**vitally** *adverb*

vitamin *noun* one of a group of substances that you need to stay healthy. They occur naturally in food

vivacious *adjective* full of energy and enthusiasm >**vivacity** *noun*

vivid *adjective* very bright in colour or clear in detail >**vividly** *adverb* >**vividness** *noun*

vivisection *noun* the act of cutting open and experimenting on living animals for medical research >**vivisectionist** *noun*

vixen *noun* female fox

v-mail *noun* video message sent by e-mail

vocabulary vocabularies *noun* **1** all the words that a person knows in a particular language **2** all the words in a language **3** specialist terms used in a given subject **4** list of words in another language with their translation

vocal *adjective* **1** relating to the voice **2** outspoken >**vocally** *adverb*

vocation *noun* **1** strong wish to do a particular job, especially one which involves serving other people **2** occupation that someone feels called to; calling **3** profession or trade

vocational *adjective* (of skills, training) directed towards a particular profession or trade

vociferous *adjective* formal outspoken or strident >**vociferously** *adverb*

VOD *abbreviation* video on demand: TV system allowing users to watch programmes at a time of their own choosing

vodka *noun* (Russian) spirit distilled from potatoes or grain

vogue noun fashion

voice noun sounds produced by your vocal cords as when speaking, shouting or singing, or the ability to make such sounds ▷ verb to express (an opinion or emotion)

void noun empty space or feeling

volatile adjective 1 liable to sudden change, especially in behaviour 2 evaporating quickly > **volatility** noun

volcanic adjective (of a region) having many volcanoes or created by volcanoes

volcano volcanoes noun mountain with an opening through which lava, gas and ash are ejected

vole noun small mouse-like rodent

volition noun formal **of your own volition** out of your own choice rather than because persuaded to do something

volley noun 1 simultaneous firing of a lot of shots 2 burst of questions or critical comments 3 Sport stroke or kick at a moving ball before it hits the ground

volleyball noun team game where a ball is hit with the hands over a high net

volt noun unit used to measure the force of an electric current

voltage noun force of an electric current measured in volts

volume noun 1 amount of space occupied or contained by something 2 amount 3 loudness of sound 4 book or one of a series of books

voluminous adjective 1 (of clothes) large and roomy 2 (of writings) extensive

voluntary adjective 1 done by choice 2 done without payment > **voluntarily** adverb

volunteer noun 1 person who offers voluntarily to do something 2 person who voluntarily undertakes military service ▷ verb 3 to offer (to do something) 4 to give (information) willingly

voluptuous adjective 1 (of a woman) having a plump and sexually exciting figure 2 sensually pleasurable > **voluptuously** adverb > **voluptuousness** noun

vomit verb 1 to be sick or to bring up (the contents your stomach) ▷ noun 2 partly digested food and drink that has come back up from someone's stomach

voodoo noun form of magic practised in the Caribbean, especially in Haiti

vote noun 1 expression of choice made in an election or at a meeting where decisions are taken 2 right to make this choice 3 total number of votes cast 4 collective voting power of a given group: the Black vote ▷ verb 5 to indicate your choice by writing on a piece of paper or by raising your hand 6 to propose (that something should happen) > **voter** noun

vouch verb **vouch for** 1 to provide evidence for 2 to give your personal assurance about the good behaviour or support of (someone)

voucher noun ticket used instead of money to buy specified goods

vow verb 1 to promise (something) solemnly ▷ noun 2 solemn and binding promise 3 **vows** formal promises made when marrying or entering a religious order

vowel noun sound made without your tongue touching the roof of your mouth or your teeth, or one of the letters a, e, i, o, u, which represent such sounds

voyage noun long journey by sea or in space >**voyager** noun

vulgar adjective **1** socially unacceptable or offensive: vulgar language **2** showing a lack of good taste or refinement >**vulgarity** noun >**vulgarly** adverb

vulnerable adjective liable to be physically or emotionally hurt >**vulnerability** noun >**vulnerably** adverb

vulture noun large bird that lives in hot countries and feeds on the flesh of dead animals

vying verb present participle of **vie**

W

wacky wackier wackiest adjective informal eccentric or funny

wad noun **1** small mass of soft material **2** roll or bundle, especially of banknotes

waddle verb **1** to walk with short swaying steps ▷ noun **2** swaying walk

waddy waddies noun Aust heavy wooden club used by Australian Aborigines

wade verb **1** to walk with difficulty through water or mud **2** to

proceed with difficulty

wader noun **1** long-legged water bird **2** waders angler's long waterproof boots

wafer noun **1** thin crisp biscuit **2** thin disc of special bread used at Communion

waffle verb **1** informal to speak or write in a vague wordy way ▷ noun **2** informal vague wordy talk or writing **3** square crisp pancake with a gridlike pattern

waft verb to drift or carry gently through the air

wag wags wagging wagged verb **1** to move rapidly from side to side ▷ noun **2** wagging movement **3** old-fashioned humorous witty person

wage noun **1** (often plural) payment for work done, especially when paid weekly ▷ verb **2** to engage in (war)

wager noun **1** bet on the outcome of something ▷ verb **2** to bet (money) on the outcome of something

wagon or **waggon** noun **1** four-wheeled vehicle for heavy loads **2** railway freight truck

waif noun young person who is, or seems, homeless or neglected

wail verb **1** to cry out in pain or misery ▷ noun **2** long unhappy cry

waist noun part of the body between the ribs and hips

waistcoat noun sleeveless garment that buttons up the front, usually worn over a shirt and under a jacket

wait verb **1** to do little or nothing until something happens **2** to be ready (for something) **3** to be delayed **4** to serve food and drink in a restaurant ▷ noun **5** act or period of waiting

waiter noun man who serves food and drink in a restaurant

waiting list noun list of people waiting for medical treatment, etc

waitress noun woman who serves food and drink in a restaurant

waive verb not to enforce (a law, right, etc)

wake wakes waking woke woken verb **1** to rouse (someone) from sleep ▷ noun **2** gathering to mourn someone's death **3** track left by a moving ship **4** **in the wake of** following, often as a result > **wake up** verb to stop being asleep or to rouse (someone) from sleep > **wake up to** verb to become aware of

waken verb to wake (someone)

walk verb **1** to move on foot with at least one foot always on the ground **2** to pass through or over (a distance) on foot **3** to accompany (someone) on foot ▷ noun **4** act or instance of walking **5** distance walked **6** manner of walking **7** place or route for walking > **walker** noun person who walks > **walk into** verb to get into (a difficult situation) unexpectedly

walkabout noun **1** informal walk among the public by royalty or other famous people **2** period when an Australian Aborigine goes off to live and wander in the bush

walking stick noun wooden stick for leaning on while walking

Walkman® noun small portable cassette player with headphones

walk of life noun social position or profession

walkover noun easy victory in a competition or contest

walkway noun often raised passage or path for walking along

wall noun **1** structure of brick, stone, etc used to enclose, divide or support **2** something having the function or effect of a wall ▷ verb **3** to enclose (someone or something) with a wall or walls

wallaby wallabies noun animal like a small kangaroo

wallaroo wallaroos noun large, stocky kangaroo that lives in rocky or mountainous regions of Australia

wallet noun small folding case for paper money, credit cards, etc

wallop informal verb **1** to hit (someone) hard ▷ noun **2** hard blow

wallow verb **1** (followed by in) to take pleasure (in an unpleasant emotion) **2** to roll (in liquid or mud) ▷ noun **3** act or instance of wallowing

wallpaper noun thick coloured or patterned paper covering the walls of rooms

walnut noun **1** edible nut with a wrinkled shell **2** tree it grows on **3** its wood, used for making furniture

walrus walruses noun large sea animal with long tusks

waltz noun **1** ballroom dance **2** music for this ▷ verb **3** to dance a waltz **4** informal to move in a relaxed confident way

wan wanner wannest adjective pale and sickly-looking

wand noun thin rod, especially one

used in performing magic tricks

wander verb **1** to walk about without a definite destination or aim **2** to go astray ▷ noun **3** act or instance of wandering ▷ **wanderer** noun person who wanders

wane verb **1** to decrease gradually in size or strength **2** (of the moon) to decrease in size ▷ noun **3** **on the wane** decreasing in size, strength or power

wangle verb informal to get (something) by crafty methods

want verb **1** to need or long for **2** to desire or wish (to do something) ▷ noun **3** act or instance of wanting **4** lack or absence (of something) ▷ **wanted** adjective searched for by the police

wanting adjective lacking or not good enough: The department was found wanting

wanton adjective without justification: wanton destruction

WAP abbreviation wireless application protocol

war wars warring warred noun **1** fighting between nations **2** contest or campaign ▷ adjective **3** of, like or caused by war ▷ verb **4** to fight a war ▷ **warring** adjective: warring husbands and wives

waratah noun Aust Australian shrub with crimson flowers

warble verb to sing in a high voice

ward noun **1** room in a hospital for patients needing a similar kind of care **2** political division of a town **3** child under the care of a guardian or court ▷ **ward off** verb to prevent (something) from harming you

-ward or **-wards** suffix -ward and -wards form adverbs or adjectives that show the way something is moving or facing: homeward; westwards

warden noun **1** person in charge of a prison or youth hostel **2** official responsible for the enforcement of laws: a traffic warden

warder noun prison officer

wardrobe noun **1** cupboard for hanging clothes in **2** person's collection of clothes **3** costumes of a theatre company

ware noun **1** articles of a specified type or material: silverware **2** wares goods for sale

warehouse noun large building for storing goods before they are sold or distributed

warfare noun activity of fighting a war

warhead noun explosive front part of a bomb or missile

warlock noun man who practises black magic

warm adjective **1** moderately hot **2** providing warmth **3** (of a colour) mainly made up of yellow or red **4** affectionate ▷ verb **5** to make (someone or something) warm ▷ **warmly** adverb: warmly dressed ▷ **warm up** verb **1** to become warmer or make (something) warmer **2** to do gentle stretching exercises before more strenuous exercise **3** to become more lively or make (someone or something) more lively

warmth noun **1** mild heat **2** friendliness

warn verb **1** to make (someone) aware of possible danger or harm **2** to advise (someone) not to do something >**warning** *noun* something said or written to warn people of a problem or danger >**warn off** *verb* to advise (someone) not to become involved

warp *verb* **1** to twist (something) out of shape **2** to damage (someone's mind) ▷ *noun* **3** state of being warped **4** lengthwise threads on a loom

warrant *noun* **1** document giving official authorization to do something ▷ *verb* **2** to make (an action) necessary

warranty warranties *noun* (document giving) a guarantee

warren *noun* **1** series of burrows in which rabbits live **2** overcrowded building or part of a town

warrigal *Aust noun* **1** dingo ▷ *adjective* **2** wild

warrior *noun* person who fights in a war

warship *noun* ship designed and equipped for fighting in wars

wart *noun* small hard growth on the skin

wartime period of time during which a country is at war

wary warier wariest *adjective* watchful or cautious >**warily** *adverb* >**wariness** *noun* state of being wary

was *verb* first and third person singular past tense of **be**

wash *verb* **1** to clean (oneself, clothes, etc) with water and usually soap **2** to be washable **3** to flow gently **4** *informal* to be believable or acceptable: *That excuse won't wash* ▷ *noun* **5** act or process of washing **6** clothes

washed at one time **7** thin coat of paint **8** disturbance in the water after a ship has passed by >**washable** *adjective* able to be washed without being damaged >**wash away** *verb* to carry (something) away by moving water >**wash up** *verb* to wash dishes and cutlery after a meal

washbasin *noun* a deep bowl, usually fixed to a wall, with taps for hot and cold water

washer *noun* ring put under a nut or bolt or in a tap as a seal

washing *noun* clothes and bedding to be washed

washing machine *noun* machine for washing clothes in

washing-up *noun* washing of dishes and cutlery after a meal

wasp *noun* stinging insect with a slender black-and-yellow striped body

wastage *noun* **1** loss by wear or waste **2** reduction in size of a workforce by not replacing people who have left

waste *verb* **1** to use (time, money, etc) carelessly or thoughtlessly **2** to fail to take advantage of (an opportunity) ▷ *noun* **3** act of wasting or state of being wasted; misuse **4** anything wasted **5** rubbish **6** wastes desert ▷ *adjective* **7** rejected as worthless or unwanted >**waste away** *verb* to become weak and ill >**waster** or **wastrel** *noun* layabout

wasted *adjective* unnecessary: *a wasted journey*

wasteful *adjective* extravagant

wasteland *noun* land that is not being used, e.g. because it is infertile

wasting *adjective* (of a disease) causing gradual and relentless weight loss and loss of strength and vitality

watch *verb* **1** to look at (someone or something) closely **2** to guard or supervise (someone or something) ▷ *noun* **3** small clock for the wrist or pocket **4** period of guarding or supervising **5** sailor's spell of duty > **watch for** *verb* to keep alert for (something) > **watch out** *verb* to be very careful > **watch out for** *verb* to keep alert for (something)

watchdog *noun* **1** dog kept to guard property **2** person or group guarding against inefficient or illegal conduct in companies

watchful *adjective* careful to notice everything that is happening

watchman *noun* man employed to guard a building or property

water *noun* **1** clear colourless tasteless liquid that falls as rain and forms rivers etc **2** body of water, such as a sea or lake **3** level of the tide **4** urine: *to pass water* ▷ *verb* **5** to put water on or into **6** (of the eyes) to fill with tears **7** (of the mouth) to fill with saliva > **water down** *verb* **1** to dilute (a drink) **2** to make (something) weaker

watercolour *noun* **1** paint thinned with water **2** painting done in watercolours

watercress *noun* edible plant growing in clear ponds and streams, whose leaves are eaten in salads

waterfall *noun* place where the waters of a river drop vertically

waterfront *noun* street or piece of land next to an area of water

watering can *noun* container with a handle and a long spout, which you use to water plants

waterlogged *adjective* (of land) soaked through, with water on the surface

watermelon *noun* large melon with green skin and red flesh

waterproof *adjective* **1** not letting water through ▷ *noun* **2** waterproof garment ▷ *verb* **3** to make (a garment) waterproof

watershed *noun* important period or event that marks a turning point

watersider *noun* NZ person employed to load and unload ships

water-skiing *noun* sport of riding over water on skis towed by a speedboat

water table *noun* level below the surface of the ground at which water can be found

watertight *adjective* **1** not letting water through **2** having no loopholes or weak points

waterway *noun* a canal, river, etc that ships or boats can sail along

waterworks *noun* building where the public water supply is stored and cleaned, and from where it is distributed

watery *adjective* (of food or drink) thin like water

watt *noun* unit of electrical power

wattle *noun* Australian acacia tree with spikes of brightly coloured flowers

wave *verb* **1** to move (the hand) from side to side as a greeting or signal **2** to move or flap (something) from side to side

▷ *noun* **3** moving ridge of water on the surface of the sea **4** curve in the hair **5** prolonged spell of something: *the crime wave* **6** gesture of waving **7** vibration carrying energy through a substance

wavelength *noun* distance between the same points of two successive waves of energy

waver *verb* **1** to hesitate or be undecided **2** to be unsteady; person who wavers

wavy wavier waviest *adjective* having waves or regular curves

wax *noun* **1** solid shiny fatty or oily substance used for sealing, making candles, etc **2** sticky yellow substance in the ear ▷ *verb* **3** to coat or polish (something) with wax **4** to increase in size or strength **5** (of the moon) to get gradually larger

way *noun* **1** manner or method **2** characteristic manner **3** route or direction **4** track or path **5** distance **6** room for movement or activity: *You're in the way* **7** passage or journey

wayside *noun* side of a road

wayward *adjective* difficult to control > **waywardness** *noun* quality of being wayward

WC *abbreviation* water closet: toilet

we *pronoun* (used as the subject of a verb) **1** the speaker or writer and one or more others **2** people in general **3** formal word for *I* used by editors and monarchs

weak *adjective* **1** lacking strength; feeble **2** likely to break **3** unconvincing **4** lacking flavour > **weaken** *verb* to become weak or make (someone or something)

weak > **weakly** *adverb* feebly

weakling *noun* feeble person

weakness *noun* **1** lack of moral or physical strength **2** great liking (for something)

wealth *noun* **1** state of being rich **2** large amount of money and valuables **3** great amount or number

wealthy wealthier wealthiest *adjective* having a large amount of money and valuables

wean *verb* **1** to accustom (a baby or young mammal) to food other than mother's milk **2** to coax (someone) to give up former habits

weapon *noun* **1** object used in fighting **2** anything used to get the better of an opponent > **weaponry** *noun* weapons collectively

wear wears wearing wore worn *verb* **1** to have (clothes or jewellery) on the body **2** to show (a particular expression) on your face **3** to deteriorate by constant use or action **4** to endure constant use (well or badly) ▷ *noun* **5** clothes suitable for a particular time or purpose: *beach wear* **6** damage caused by use > **wear down** *verb* **1** to make (something) flatter and smoother as a result of repeated rubbing **2** to cause (someone) to stop resisting and to fall in with your wishes by repeatedly doing something or asking them to do something > **wearer** *noun*: *contact lens wearers* > **wearing** *adjective* very tiring > **wear off** *verb* to gradually become less intense > **wear on** *verb* (of time) to pass slowly > **wear out** *verb* to become or make (something) worn, weak, damaged and unusable through frequent use

wear and tear *noun* damage caused to something by normal use

weary wearier weariest; wearies wearying wearied *adjective* **1** tired or exhausted **2** tiring ▷ *verb* **3** (followed by *of*) to become weary (of something) >**wearily** *adverb* in a weary manner >**weariness** *noun* state of being weary

weasel *noun* small animal with a long body and short legs

weather *noun* **1** day-to-day condition of the atmosphere of a place **2 under the weather** *informal* slightly ill ▷ *verb* **3** to be affected by the weather **4** to come safely through (a difficult time) ▷ *noun* a statement saying what the weather will be like in the immediate future

weather vane *noun* device on a roof that revolves to show the direction of the wind

weave weaves weaving wove woven *verb* **1** to make (fabric) by crossing threads on a loom **2** to make up (a story) **3** to move from side to side while going forwards >**weaver** *noun* person who weaves cloth

web *noun* **1** net spun by a spider **2** anything intricate or complex: *web of deceit* **3** skin between the toes of a duck, frog, etc **4 the Web** short for **World Wide Web** >**webbed** *adjective* (of feet) having skin between the toes

weblog *noun* same as **blog**

website *noun* group of connected pages on the World Wide Web

wed weds wedding wedded or **wed** *verb* **1** to marry **2** to unite (things) closely

wedding *noun* act or ceremony of marriage

wedge *noun* **1** piece of something such as wood, metal or rubber with one thin end and one thick end that can be used to wedge something in place ▷ *verb* **2** to fix (something) in place with a wedge **3** to squeeze (something) into a narrow space

wedlock *noun* marriage

Wednesday *noun* day between Tuesday and Thursday

wee *adjective* Brit, Aust, NZ informal small or short

weed *noun* **1** wild plant growing where undesired **2** *informal* thin feeble person ▷ *verb* **3** to clear (a garden) of weeds >**weed out** *verb* to remove or eliminate (what is unwanted)

week *noun* **1** period of seven days, especially one beginning on a Sunday **2** hours or days of work in a week

weekday *noun* any day of the week except Saturday or Sunday

weekend *noun* Saturday and Sunday

weekly weeklies *adjective, adverb* **1** happening, done, etc once a week ▷ *noun* **2** newspaper or magazine published once a week

weep weeps weeping wept *verb* **1** to shed tears **2** to ooze liquid

weevil *noun* small beetle that eats grain etc

weft *noun* cross threads in weaving

weigh *verb* **1** to have (a specified weight) **2** to measure the weight of **3** to consider (something) carefully **4 weigh anchor** to raise a ship's anchor or (of a ship) have its anchor raised > **weigh down** *verb* to stop (someone) moving easily because of added weight > **weigh up** *verb* to assess

weight *noun* **1** heaviness of an object **2** unit of measurement of weight **3** object of known mass used for weighing **4** heavy object **5** importance or influence ▷ *verb* **6** to add weight to (something)

weighted *adjective* A system that is weighted in favour of a particular person or group is organized in such a way that this person or group will have an advantage

weightlifting *noun* exercise or competitive sport in which participants lift heavy weights > **weightlifter** *noun*

weighty weightier weightiest *adjective* **1** important or serious **2** very heavy

weir *noun* river dam

weird *adjective* **1** strange or bizarre **2** unearthly or eerie

weirdo weirdos *noun informal* peculiar person

welcome *verb* **1** to greet (a guest) with pleasure **2** to receive (something) gladly ▷ *noun* **3** friendly greeting ▷ *adjective* **4** received gladly **5** freely permitted > **welcoming** *adjective*

weld *verb* **1** to join (pieces of metal or plastic) by softening with heat ▷ *noun* **2** welded joint > **welder** *noun* person who welds pieces of metal or plastic

welfare *noun* **1** wellbeing **2** help given to people in need

welfare state *noun* system in which the government takes responsibility for the wellbeing of its citizens

well better best; wells welling welled *adverb* **1** satisfactorily **2** skilfully **3** completely **4** intimately **5** considerably **6** very likely ▷ *adjective* **7** in good health ▷ *interjection* **8** exclamation of surprise, anger, etc ▷ *noun* **9** hole drilled into the earth to reach water, oil or gas ▷ *verb* **10** to flow upwards or outwards

well-advised *adjective* sensible or wise

well-balanced *adjective* sensible and without serious emotional problems

wellbeing *noun* state of being well and happy

well-earned *adjective* thoroughly deserved

well-heeled *adjective informal* wealthy

wellies *plural noun Brit, Aust informal* wellingtons

well-informed *adjective* knowing a lot about a subject or subjects

wellingtons *plural noun Brit, Aust* high waterproof rubber boots

well-meaning *adjective* having good intentions

well-off *adjective informal* quite wealthy

well-to-do *adjective* quite wealthy

well-worn *adjective* **1** (of a word or phrase) boring from overuse **2** so much used as to be shabby

Welsh *adjective* **1** of Wales ▷ *noun* **2** language of Wales

Welshman Welshmen *noun* a man from Wales

welt *noun* raised mark on the skin caused by a blow

welter noun jumbled mass

wench noun facetious young woman

wept verb past of **weep**

were verb form of the past tense of be used after we, you, they, or a plural noun

werewolf werewolves noun (in folklore) person who can turn into a wolf

Wesak noun Buddhist festival celebrating the Buddha, held in May

west noun 1 (direction towards) the part of the horizon where the sun sets 2 region lying in this direction 3 **the West** western Europe and the US ▷ adjective 4 to or in the west 5 (of a wind) from the west ▷ adverb 6 in, to or towards the west ▷ **westerly** adjective to or towards the left

western adjective 1 of or in the west ▷ noun 2 film or story about cowboys in the western US

West Indian noun person from the West Indies

westward adjective 1 towards the west 2 lying in the west ▷ adverb 3 towards the west ▷ **westwards** adverb towards the west

wet wetter wettest; wets wetting wet or wetted adjective 1 covered or soaked with water or another liquid 2 not yet dry 3 rainy 4 Brit informal (of a person) feeble or foolish ▷ noun 5 moisture or rain 6 Brit informal feeble or foolish person ▷ verb 7 to make (someone or something) wet ▷ **wetness** noun

wet suit noun close-fitting rubber suit worn by divers etc

or something) with a hard blow ▷ noun 2 such a blow 3 informal share 4 informal attempt

whale noun 1 large fish-shaped sea mammal 2 **have a whale of a time** informal to enjoy yourself very much

whaling noun hunting of whales for food and oil ▷ **whaler** noun person who hunts whales

wharf wharves or wharfs noun platform at a harbour for loading and unloading ships

what pronoun 1 which thing 2 that which 3 request for a statement to be repeated 4 **what for?** why? ▷ interjection 5 exclamation of anger, surprise, etc ▷ adverb 6 in which way, how much: what do you care?

whatever pronoun 1 everything or anything that 2 no matter what

whatsoever adverb at all

wheat noun 1 grain used in making flour, bread and pasta 2 plant producing this

wheel noun 1 disc that revolves on an axle, usually fixed under a vehicle to make it move ▷ verb 2 to push or pull (something with wheels) 3 to turn round suddenly

wheelbarrow noun shallow cart for carrying loads, with a wheel at the front and two handles

wheelchair noun chair with wheels for use by people who cannot walk

wheeze verb 1 to breathe with a hoarse whistling noise ▷ noun 2 wheezing sound 3 informal trick or plan ▷ **wheezy** adjective making a hoarse whistling noise

whelk noun edible snail-like shellfish

a
b
c
d
e
f
g
h
i
j
k
l
m
n
o
p
q
r
s
t
u
v
w
x
y
z

when adverb **1** at what time? ▷ conjunction **2** at the time that **3** although **4** considering the fact that ▷ pronoun **5** at which time

whence adverb, conjunction obsolete from what place or source

- You should not write from whence because whence already means 'from where'

whenever adverb, conjunction at whatever time

where adverb **1** in, at or to what place? ▷ pronoun **2** in, at or to which place ▷ conjunction **3** in the place at which

whereabouts noun **1** present position ▷ adverb **2** at what place

whereas conjunction but on the other hand

whereby pronoun by which

whereupon conjunction at which point

wherever conjunction, adverb at whatever place

wherewithal noun necessary funds, resources, etc

whet whets whetting whetted verb **1** to sharpen (a tool) **2** whet someone's appetite to increase someone's desire

whether conjunction used to introduce an indirect question or a clause expressing doubt or choice

whey noun watery liquid that is separated from the curds in sour milk when cheese is made

which adjective, pronoun **1** used to request or refer to a choice from different possibilities ▷ pronoun **2** used to refer to a thing already mentioned

whichever adjective, pronoun **1** any out of several **2** no matter which

whiff noun **1** slight smell **2** trace or hint

while conjunction **1** at the same time that **2** but ▷ noun **3** period of time > while away verb to pass (time) idly but pleasantly

whilst conjunction while

whim noun sudden desire; impulse

whimper verb **1** to cry in a soft whining way ▷ noun **2** soft unhappy cry

whimsical adjective unusual or playful

whine noun **1** high-pitched unhappy cry **2** annoying complaint ▷ verb **3** to make such a sound > whining noun, adjective (making) a whining sound

whinge whinges whinging or whingeing whinged Brit, Aust, NZ informal verb **1** to complain ▷ noun **2** complaint

whinny whinnies whinnying whinnied verb **1** to neigh softly ▷ noun **2** soft neigh

whip whips whipping whipped noun **1** cord attached to a handle, used for beating animals or people **2** dessert made from beaten cream or egg whites ▷ verb **3** to strike (an animal or a person) with a whip, strap or cane **4** informal to pull, remove or move (something) quickly **5** to beat (especially eggs or cream) to a froth **6** to rouse (people) into a particular condition **7** informal to steal (something) > whip up verb to cause and encourage (an emotion) in people: people who try to whip up hatred against minorities

whip bird noun Australian bird whose cry ends with a sound like the crack of a whip

whiplash injury noun neck injury caused by a sudden jerk to the head, as in a car crash

whippet noun racing dog like a small greyhound

whirl verb 1 to spin or revolve 2 to be dizzy or confused ▷ noun 3 whirling movement 4 intense activity 5 confusion or dizziness

whirlpool noun strong circular current of water

whirlwind noun 1 column of air that spins round and round very fast ▷ adjective 2 much quicker than normal

whirr noun 1 continuous soft buzz ▷ verb 2 to make a whirr

whisk verb 1 to move or remove quickly 2 to beat (especially eggs or cream) to a froth ▷ noun 3 egg-beating tool

whisker noun 1 any of the long stiff hairs on the face of a cat or other mammal 2 **by a whisker** informal only just 3 **whiskers** hair growing on a man's face

whisky whiskies noun strong alcoholic drink made from grain such as barley

whisper verb 1 to speak softly, using the breath but not the throat 2 to rustle ▷ noun 3 soft voice 4 informal rumour 5 rustling sound

whist noun card game in which one pair of players tries to win more tricks than another pair

whistle verb 1 to produce a shrill sound by forcing the breath through pursed lips 2 to signal (something) by a whistle ▷ noun 3 whistling sound 4 instrument blown to make a whistling sound

whit noun **not a whit** not the slightest amount

white adjective 1 of the colour of snow 2 pale 3 light in colour 4 (of coffee) containing milk or cream ▷ noun 5 colour of snow 6 clear fluid round the yolk of an egg 7 white part, especially of the eyeball ▷ **whiteness** noun

white-collar adjective (of a worker) working in an office rather than doing manual work

white lie noun harmless lie, told to prevent someone's feelings from being hurt

whitewash noun 1 mixture of lime and water used for painting walls white ▷ verb 2 to cover (something) with whitewash 3 to conceal or gloss over (unpleasant facts)

whither adverb obsolete to what place

whiting noun edible sea fish

whittle verb to cut or carve (wood) with a knife ▷ **whittle down, away** verb to reduce (something) or wear (it) away gradually

whizz or **whiz** whizzes whizzing whizzed verb 1 to make a loud buzzing sound 2 informal to move quickly ▷ noun 3 loud buzzing sound 4 informal person who is skilful at something

who pronoun 1 which person 2 used to refer to a person or people already mentioned

whoa interjection command to slow down or stop a horse

whoever pronoun 1 any person who 2 no matter who

whole adjective 1 containing all the elements or parts 2 uninjured or undamaged ▷ noun 3 complete thing or system 4 **on the whole**

in general > **wholeness** noun
> **wholly** adverb completely

wholehearted adjective
enthusiastic and sincere
> **wholeheartedly** adverb

wholemeal adjective **1** (of flour)
made from the whole wheat grain
2 made from wholemeal flour

wholesale adjective, adverb
1 buying goods cheaply in large
quantities and selling them to
shopkeepers **2** on a large scale
> **wholesaler** noun person who
works in the wholesale trade

wholesome adjective good for the
health or wellbeing

whom pronoun objective form
of **who**

whoop verb **1** to shout or cry in
excitement ▷ noun **2** shout or cry
of excitement

whooping cough noun infectious
disease marked by violent
coughing and noisy breathing

whore noun offensive a prostitute,
or a woman believed to act like a
prostitute

whose pronoun of whom or of
which

- Many people are confused
- about the difference
- between whose and who's.
- Whose is used to show
- possession in a question
- or when something is
- being described: whose bag
- is this? the person whose car
- is blocking the exit. Who's,
- with the apostrophe, is a
- short form of who is or who
- has: who's that girl? who's got
- my ruler?

why adverb **1** for what reason
▷ pronoun **2** because of which

wick noun cord through a lamp
or candle which carries fuel to
the flame

wicked adjective **1** morally bad;
evil **2** mischievous > **wickedly**
adverb in a wicked manner
> **wickedness** noun state of being
wicked

wicker adjective made of woven
cane

wicket noun **1** set of three cricket
stumps and two bails **2** ground
between the two wickets on a
cricket pitch

wide adjective **1** large from side to
side; broad **2** having a specified
width **3** spacious or extensive
4 far from the target **5** opened
fully ▷ adverb **6** to the full extent
7 over a wide area **8** far from the
target > **widely** adverb > **widen**
verb to make (something) wider or
to become wider

wide-awake adjective completely
awake

wide-ranging adjective covering
a variety of different things or a
large area

widespread adjective affecting
a wide area or a large number of
people; common

widow noun woman whose
husband is dead and who has not
remarried

widowed adjective whose husband
or wife has died

widower noun man whose wife is
dead and who has not remarried

width noun **1** distance from side to
side **2** quality of being wide

wield verb **1** to hold and use (a
weapon) **2** to have and use
(power)

wife wives noun woman to whom

a man is married

Wi-Fi noun system of accessing the Internet from machines such as laptop computers that are not physically connected to a network

wig noun artificial head of hair

wiggle verb **1** to move jerkily from side to side ▷ noun **2** wiggling movement

wigwam noun Native American's tent

wiki noun website (or page within one) that can be edited by anyone who looks it up on the Internet

wild adjective **1** (of an animal) not tamed or domesticated **2** (of a plant) not cultivated **3** excited and uncontrolled **4** violent or stormy **5** informal furious **6** random ▷ noun **7 the wilds** desolate or uninhabited place ▷ **wildly** adverb extremely or intensely ▷ **wildness** noun state of being wild

wilderness noun uninhabited uncultivated region

wildfire noun **spread like wildfire** to spread quickly and uncontrollably

wild-goose chase noun search that has little chance of success

wildlife noun wild animals and plants collectively

Wild West noun western part of the USA when first settled by Europeans

wiles plural noun crafty tricks

wilful adjective **1** headstrong or obstinate **2** intentional ▷ **wilfully** adverb in a wilful manner

will¹ verb (often shortened to 'll) used as an auxiliary verb to form the future tense, to indicate intention or expectation, and to express invitations and requests: *Tom and I will go shopping later; I will not let you down; Robin will be annoyed; Will you have something to drink?; Will you do me a favour?*

will² noun **1** strong determination **2** desire or wish **3** instructions written for disposal of your property after death ▷ verb **4** to use your will in an attempt to do (something): *I willed my eyes to open* **5** to wish or desire (something): *if God wills it* **6** to leave (property) to someone in a will: *The farm was willed to her*

willing adjective **1** ready or inclined (to do something) **2** keen and obliging ▷ **willingly** adverb voluntarily ▷ **willingness** noun state of being willing

willow noun **1** tree with long thin branches **2** its wood, used for making cricket bats

wilt verb to become limp or lose strength

wily wilier wiliest adjective crafty or sly

wimp noun informal feeble timid person

win wins winning won verb **1** to come first in (a competition, fight, etc) **2** to gain (a prize) in a competition **3** to get (something) by effort ▷ noun **4** victory, especially in a game ▷ **win over** verb to gain the support or consent of (someone)

wince verb **1** to draw back, as if in pain ▷ noun **2** act of wincing

winch noun **1** machine for lifting or hauling using a cable or chain wound round a drum ▷ verb **2** to lift or haul (something) using a winch

a
b
c
d
e
f
g
h
i
j
k
l
m
n
o
p
q
r
s
t
u
v
w
x
y
z

wind¹ *noun* **1** current of air **2** hint or suggestion **3** ability to breathe easily **4** gas produced in the stomach, causing discomfort ▷ *verb* **5** to render (someone) short of breath

wind² **winds winding wound** *verb* **1** to coil or wrap (something) round something else **2** to tighten the spring of (a clock or watch) **3** to move in a twisting course > **wind up** *verb* **1** to reach an end or bring (something) to an end **2** to tighten the spring of (a clock or watch) **3** *informal* to annoy or tease (someone)

windfall *noun* sum of money received unexpectedly

wind instrument *noun* musical instrument played by blowing

windmill *noun* machine for grinding grain or pumping water, driven by sails turned by the wind

window *noun* **1** opening in a wall, usually with a glass pane or panes, to let in light or air **2** display area behind the window of a shop **3** area on a computer screen that can be manipulated separately from the rest of the display area **4** period of unbooked time in a diary or schedule

window box *noun* a long, narrow container on a windowsill in which plants are grown

windowsill *noun* ledge along the bottom of a window

windpipe *noun* tube linking the throat and the lungs

windscreen *noun* front window of a motor vehicle

windsurfing *noun* sport of riding on water using a surfboard

propelled and steered by a sail

windswept *adjective* (of a place) exposed to strong winds

windy **windier windiest** *adjective* involving a lot of wind: *It was windy and cold*

wine *noun* **1** alcoholic drink made from fermented grapes **2** similar drink made from other fruits ▷ *verb* **3** **wine and dine** to entertain (someone) with fine food and drink

wing *noun* **1** one of the limbs or organs of a bird, insect or bat that are used for flying **2** one of the winglike supporting parts of an aircraft **3** side part of a building that sticks out **4** group within a political party **5** part of a car body surrounding the wheels **6** *Sport* (player on) either side of the pitch **7** **wings** sides of a stage ▷ *verb* **8** to fly **9** to wound (a bird) slightly in the wing or (a person) slightly in the arm > **winged** *adjective* having wings

wink *verb* **1** to close and open (an eye) quickly as a signal **2** (of a light) to twinkle ▷ *noun* **3** winking **4** smallest amount of sleep

winkle *noun* shellfish with a spiral shell > **winkle out** *verb informal* to get (information) from someone

winner *noun* person who wins a prize, race or competition

winning *adjective* **1** gaining victory **2** charming

winter *noun* **1** coldest season ▷ *verb* **2** to spend the winter

wintry **wintrier wintriest** *adjective* **1** of or like winter **2** cold or unfriendly

wipe *verb* **1** to clean or dry

(something) by rubbing **2** to erase (a tape) ▷ noun **3** wiping ▸**wipe out** verb to destroy (people or a place) completely

wire noun **1** thin flexible strand of metal **2** length of this used to carry electric current ▷ verb **3** to equip (a place) with wires

wireless noun old-fashioned same as **radio**

wireless application protocol see **WAP**

wiring noun system of wires

wiry wirier wiriest adjective **1** lean but strong **2** (of hair) stiff and rough

wisdom noun **1** good sense and judgment **2** knowledge collected over time

wisdom tooth noun any of the four large molar teeth that come through usually after the age of twenty

wise adjective having wisdom; sensible ▸**wisely** adverb

wisecrack informal noun clever, sometimes unkind

wish verb **1** to want or desire (something) **2** to feel or express a hope about someone's wellbeing, success, etc ▷ noun **3** expression of a desire **4** thing desired

wishbone noun V-shaped bone above the breastbone of most birds

wishful thinking noun hope or wish that is unlikely to come true

wishy-washy adjective informal not firm or clear

wisp noun **1** light delicate streak **2** twisted bundle or tuft ▸**wispy** adjective (of hair) thin and untidy

wistful adjective sadly longing ▸**wistfully** adverb sadly and longingly

wit noun **1** ability to use words or ideas in a clever and amusing way **2** person with this ability **3** (sometimes plural) practical intelligence

witch noun **1** person, usually female, who practises (black) magic **2** ugly or wicked woman

witchcraft noun use of magic

witch doctor noun (in certain societies) a man appearing to cure or cause injury or disease by magic

witchetty grub noun Aust large Australian caterpillar, eaten by Aborigines

with preposition indicating presence alongside, possession, means of performance, characteristic manner, etc: *walking with his dog; a man with two cars; hit with a hammer; playing with skill*

withdraw withdraws withdrawing withdrew withdrawn verb to take (something) out or away or to move out or away

withdrawal noun **1** taking something away **2** changing or denying a statement **3** taking money from a bank account

withdrawal symptoms plural noun unpleasant effects suffered by an addict who has suddenly stopped taking a drug

withdrawn adjective unusually shy or quiet

wither verb to wilt or dry up

withering adjective (of a look or remark) scornful

withhold withholds withholding withheld verb not to give

a
b
c
d
e
f
g
h
i
j
k
l
m
n
o
p
q
r
s
t
u
v
w
x
y
z

(something)

within preposition, adverb in or inside

without preposition not accompanied by, using or having

withstand withstands withstanding withstood verb to oppose or resist (something) successfully

witness noun 1 person who has seen something happen 2 person giving evidence in court ▷ verb 3 to see (an incident) at first hand 4 to sign (a document) to confirm that it is genuine

witticism noun witty remark

witty wittier wittiest adjective clever and amusing > **wittily** adverb in a clever and amusing manner

wives noun plural of **wife**

wizard noun 1 magician 2 person with outstanding skill in a particular field > **wizardry** noun something that is very cleverly done

wizened adjective wrinkled

wobbegong noun Aust Australian shark with brown-and-white skin

wobble verb 1 to move unsteadily 2 to tremble or shake ▷ noun 3 wobbling movement or sound

wobbly wobblier wobbliest adjective unsteady

woe noun grief

wok noun bowl-shaped Chinese cooking pan, used for stir-frying

woke verb past tense of **wake**

woken verb past participle of **wake**

wolf wolves; wolfs wolfing wolfed noun 1 wild hunting animal related to the dog 2 cry **wolf** to raise a false alarm ▷ verb

3 to eat (food) quickly and greedily

woman women noun 1 adult human female 2 women collectively

womanhood noun state of being a woman

womb noun hollow organ in female mammals where unborn babies grow

wombat noun Aust small heavily-built burrowing Australian animal

wonder verb 1 to be curious (about something) 2 to be amazed (at something) ▷ noun 3 wonderful thing; marvel 4 emotion caused by an amazing or unusual thing ▷ adjective 5 spectacularly successful: a wonder drug

wonderful adjective 1 very fine 2 magnificent or remarkable > **wonderfully** adverb

wondrous adjective old-fashioned wonderful

wont adjective 1 accustomed or inclined (to do something) ▷ noun 2 custom

woo verb 1 to try to persuade (someone) 2 old-fashioned to try to gain the love of (a woman)

wood noun 1 substance trees are made of, used in carpentry and as fuel 2 area where trees grow

wooded adjective covered with trees

wooden adjective 1 made of wood 2 stiff and without expression

woodland noun forest

woodpecker noun bird that drills holes into trees with its beak to find insects

woodwind adjective, noun (of) a type of wind instrument made of wood, played by being blown into

woodwork noun 1 parts of a house that are made of wood, e.g. doors and window frames 2 making things out of wood

woodworm or **woodworms** noun insect larva that bores into wood

woody woodier woodiest adjective 1 (of a plant) having a hard tough stem 2 (of an area) covered with trees

woof noun 1 barking noise made by a dog 2 cross threads in weaving

wool noun 1 soft hair of sheep, goats, etc 2 yarn spun from this

woollen adjective made from wool >**woollens** plural noun clothes made from wool

woolly woollier woolliest; woollies adjective 1 of or like wool 2 vague or muddled ▷ noun 3 knitted woollen garment

woolshed noun Aust, NZ large building in which sheep are sheared

woomera noun Aust notched stick used by Australian Aborigines when throwing a spear

word noun 1 single unit of speech or writing 2 brief remark, chat or discussion 3 message 4 promise 5 command ▷ verb 6 to express (something) in words

wording noun choice and arrangement of words

word processor noun machine with a keyboard, microprocessor and VDU for electronic organization and storage of text

work noun 1 physical or mental effort directed to making or doing something 2 paid employment 3 duty or task

4 something made or done 5 works a factory b total of a writer's or artist's achievements c activities relating to building and construction d mechanism of a machine ▷ adjective 6 of or for work ▷ verb 7 to do work 8 to be employed 9 to operate (something) 10 (of a plan etc) to be successful 11 to cultivate (land) 12 to manipulate, shape or process 13 to cause (someone) to reach a specified condition >**work out** verb 1 to find (the solution to a problem) by using your reasoning 2 to happen or progress >**work up** verb 1 to make (yourself) very upset or angry about something 2 to develop >**work up to** verb to progress towards (something) gradually >**worked up** adjective

workable adjective able to operate successfully; practical

workaholic noun person obsessed with work

worker noun a person employed in a particular industry or business

workforce noun people who work in a particular place

workhouse noun (in England, formerly) building where poor people were given food and lodgings in return for work

working class noun social class consisting of manual workers >**working-class** adjective: a working-class background

workload noun amount of work to be done

workman workmen noun a man whose job involves physical skills

workmanship noun skill with which an object is made

workmate noun fellow worker

workout noun session of physical exercise

workshop noun room or building with equipment for making or repairing things

world noun 1 planet earth 2 people in general 3 society of a particular area or period 4 a person's life and experiences ▷ adjective 5 of the whole world

worldly worldlier worldliest adjective 1 not spiritual 2 wise in the ways of the world

world war noun war that involves countries all over the world

worldwide adjective throughout the world

World Wide Web noun worldwide communication system which people use through computers; the Internet

worm noun 1 small thin animal with no bones or legs 2 Computers type of virus 3 **worms** illness caused by parasites in the intestines ▷ verb 4 to rid (an animal) of worms > **worm out** verb to extract (information) from someone craftily

worn verb past participle of **wear**

worn-out adjective 1 used until too thin or too damaged to be of further use 2 extremely tired

worried adjective unhappy and anxious; troubled

worry worries worrying worried verb 1 to be anxious or uneasy or to cause (someone) to be anxious or uneasy 2 to annoy or bother (someone) 3 (of a dog) to chase and try to bite (sheep etc) ▷ noun 4 (cause of) anxiety or concern > **worrying** adjective: a worrying report about smoking

worse adjective, adverb comparative of **bad** or **badly**

worsen verb to grow worse or make (something) worse

worse off adjective having less money or being in a more unpleasant situation than before

worship worships worshipping worshipped verb 1 to show religious devotion to (a god) 2 to love and admire (someone) ▷ noun 3 act or instance of worshipping 4 **Worship** title for a mayor or magistrate > **worshipper** noun person who worships

worst adjective, adverb superlative of **bad** or **badly** ▷ noun 2 worst thing

worth preposition 1 having a value of 2 deserving or justifying ▷ noun 3 value or price 4 excellence 5 amount to be had for a given sum

worthless adjective having no real value or use

worthwhile adjective worth the time or effort involved

worthy worthier worthiest; worthies adjective 1 deserving admiration or respect ▷ noun 2 informal notable person

would verb (often shortened to 'd) used as an auxiliary verb to express invitations and requests, to talk about hypothetical situations, to describe habitual past actions and to replace will in reported speech: Would you like some tea?; We'd like two tickets, please; I'd write to him if I were you; I wouldn't have come if I'd known; She would always watch the late news;

He said he would call back

would-be *adjective* wanting to be or claiming to be: *a would-be pop singer*

wound¹ *noun* **1** physical injury, especially a cut **2** injury to the feelings ▷ *verb* **3** to cause a wound to (someone) > **wounded** *adjective*

wound² *verb* past of **wind²**

wow *interjection* **1** exclamation of astonishment ▷ *noun* **2** *informal* astonishing person or thing

WPC *abbreviation* woman police constable

wrangle *verb* **1** to argue noisily ▷ *noun* **2** noisy argument

wrap wraps wrapping wrapped *verb* **1** to fold (something) round (a person or thing) so as to cover ▷ *noun* **2** garment wrapped round the shoulders **3** sandwich made by wrapping a filling in a tortilla > **wrap up** *verb* **1** to fold paper round **2** to put warm clothes on **3** *informal* to finish or settle (a matter)

wrapped up *adjective informal* (followed by in) giving all your attention (to someone or something)

wrapper *noun* cover for a product

wrapping *noun* material used to wrap

wrath *noun* intense anger

wreak *verb* **wreak havoc** to cause chaos

wreath *noun* twisted ring or band of flowers or leaves used as a memorial or tribute

wreck *verb* **1** to destroy ▷ *noun* **2** remains of something that has been destroyed or badly damaged, especially a vehicle **3** person in

very poor condition > **wrecked** *adjective*

wreckage *noun* wrecked remains

wren *noun* small brown songbird

wrench *verb* **1** to twist or pull (something) violently **2** to sprain (a joint) ▷ *noun* **3** violent twist or pull **4** sprain **5** difficult or painful parting **6** adjustable spanner

wrest *verb* to take (something) by force

wrestle *verb* **1** to fight, especially as a sport, by struggling with and trying to throw down (an opponent) **2** to struggle hard (with a problem) > **wrestler** *noun* person who wrestles

wrestling *noun* sport of struggling with and trying to throw down an opponent

wretch *noun* wicked or unfortunate person

wretched *adjective* **1** unhappy or unfortunate **2** worthless > **wretchedly** *adverb* in a wretched manner > **wretchedness** *noun* state of being wretched

wriggle *verb* **1** to move (the body) with a twisting action ▷ *noun* **2** wriggling movement > **wriggle out of** *verb* to manage to avoid (doing something) > **wriggly** *adjective*

wring wrings wringing wrung *verb* **1** to twist, especially to squeeze liquid out of (a wet cloth) **2** to clasp and twist (the hands)

wrinkle *noun* **1** slight crease, especially one in the skin due to age ▷ *verb* **2** to become slightly creased or make (something) slightly creased > **wrinkled** *adjective* > **wrinkly** *adjective*: *wrinkly stockings*

wrist *noun* joint between the hand and the arm

writ *noun* legal document that orders a person to do something

write **writes** **writing** **wrote** **written** *verb* **1** to mark paper etc with (letters, words or numbers) **2** to set (something) down in words **3** to communicate with someone by (letter) **4** to create (a book, piece of music, etc) > **write down** to record (something) on a piece of paper > **write up** *verb* to write a full account of (something), often from notes

writer *noun* **1** author **2** person who has written something specified

writhe *verb* to twist or squirm in or as if in pain

writing *noun* **1** something that has been written **2** person's style of writing **3** piece of written work

written *verb* past participle of **write**

wrong *adjective* **1** incorrect or mistaken **2** immoral or bad **3** not intended or suitable **4** not working properly ▷ *adverb* **5** in a wrong manner ▷ *noun* **6** something immoral or unjust ▷ *verb* **7** to treat (someone) unfairly or unjustly > **wrongly** *adverb* in a wrong manner

wrongful *adjective* illegal, unfair or immoral > **wrongfully** *adverb*

wrought iron *noun* pure form of iron formed into decorative shapes

wry *adjective* **1** drily humorous **2** (of a facial expression) twisted > **wryly** *adverb* in a wry manner

X

X or **x** *noun* **1** indicating an error, a choice, or a kiss **2** indicating an unknown, unspecified, or variable factor, number, person, or thing

xenophobia *noun* fear or hatred of people from other countries > **xenophobic** *adjective*: *xenophobic attitudes*

Xerox® *noun* **1** machine for copying printed material **2** copy made by a Xerox machine ▷ *verb* **3** to copy (a document) using such a machine

Xmas *noun informal* Christmas

XML *abbreviation* extensible markup language: a computer language used in text formatting

X-ray or **x-ray** *noun* **1** stream of radiation that can pass through some solid materials **2** picture made by sending X-rays through someone's body to examine the inside of it ▷ *verb* **3** to photograph or examine (someone or something) using X-rays

xylem *noun technical* plant tissue that conducts water and minerals from the roots to all other parts. It forms the wood in trees and shrubs

xylophone *noun* musical instrument made of a row of wooden bars of different lengths played with hammers

y

-y *suffix* used to form nouns: *anarchy*

yabby yabbies *noun* small edible Australian crayfish

yacht *noun* boat with sails or an engine, used for racing or for pleasure trips

yachting *noun* sport or activity of sailing a yacht

yachtsman yachtsmen *noun* man who sails a yacht
> **yachtswoman** *noun*

yak *noun* Tibetan ox with long shaggy hair

yakka or **yacker** *noun* Aust, NZ informal work

yam *noun* tropical root vegetable

yank *verb* **1** to pull or jerk (something) suddenly ▷ *noun* **2** sudden pull or jerk

Yankee or **Yank** *noun* informal person from the United States

yap yaps yapping yapped *verb* to bark with a high-pitched sound

yard *noun* **1** unit of length equal to 36 inches or about 91.4 centimetres **2** enclosed area, usually next to a building and often used for a particular purpose: *builder's yard*

yardstick *noun* standard against which to judge other people or things

yarn *noun* **1** thread used for knitting or making cloth **2** informal long involved story, often with invented details to make it more interesting or exciting

yashmak *noun* veil worn by some Muslim women over their faces when they are in public

yawn *verb* **1** to open your mouth wide and take in more air than usual, often when tired or bored ▷ *noun* **2** act of yawning

yawning *adjective* (of a gap or opening) very wide

ye *pronoun* **1** archaic or dialect you **2** in language intended to appear old) the

yeah *interjection* informal yes

year *noun* **1** period of twelve months or 365 days (366 days in a leap year), which is the time taken for the earth to travel once around the sun **2** period of twelve consecutive months, not always January to December, on which administration or organization is based: *the current financial year*

yearling *noun* animal between one and two years old

yearn *verb* to long (for something or to do something) very much
> **yearning** *noun*

yeast *noun* fungus used to make bread rise and to ferment alcoholic drinks

yell *verb* **1** to shout or scream loudly ▷ *noun* **2** loud shout or cry of pain, anger or fear

yellow *noun, adjective* **1** the colour of buttercups, egg yolks or lemons ▷ *adjective* **2** informal cowardly ▷ *verb* **3** to become or make (something) yellow, often with age > **yellowish** *adjective*

yellow box *noun* a large Australian eucalyptus tree

yellow fever *noun* serious infectious tropical disease

yelp verb 1 to give a sudden, short cry ▷ noun 2 sudden, short cry

yen noun 1 monetary unit of Japan 2 informal longing or desire
● The plural of yen in sense 1 is yen

yes interjection expresses agreement, acceptance or approval or acknowledges facts

yesterday adverb 1 on the day before today 2 in the recent past ▷ noun 3 the day before today 4 the recent past

yet adverb 1 up until then or now 2 now or until later 3 still 4 used for emphasis: She'd changed her mind yet again ▷ conjunction 5 nevertheless or still

yeti noun same as **abominable snowman**

yew noun evergreen tree with needle-like leaves and red berries

Yiddish noun language of German origin spoken by many Jewish people of European origin

yield verb 1 to give in 2 to give up control of or surrender (something) 3 to break or give way 4 to produce or bear (a crop or profit) ▷ noun 5 amount of food, money or profit produced from a given area of land or from an investment

yippee interjection exclamation of happiness or excitement

yob noun informal bad-mannered or aggressive youth

yodel yodels yodelling yodelled verb to sing normal notes with high quick notes in between

yoga noun Hindu method of exercise and discipline aiming at spiritual, mental and physical wellbeing

yogurt or **yoghurt** noun slightly sour thick liquid food made from milk that has had bacteria added to it, often sweetened and flavoured with fruit

yoke noun 1 wooden bar put across the necks of two animals to hold them together, and to which a plough or other tool may be attached 2 literary oppressive force: the yoke of the tyrant 3 fitted part of a garment to which a fuller part is attached

yokel noun person who lives in the country and is regarded as being rather stupid and old-fashioned

yolk noun yellow part of an egg

Yom Kippur noun annual Jewish religious holiday; Day of Atonement

yonder adjective, adverb old-fashioned or dialect (situated) over there

yore noun of yore literary a long time ago

Yorkshire pudding noun baked batter made from flour, milk and eggs and usually eaten with roast beef

you pronoun (refers to) 1 the person or people addressed 2 people in general

young adjective 1 in an early stage of life or growth ▷ plural noun 2 young people in general 3 babies or offspring, especially referring to young animals

youngster noun young person

your adjective 1 of, belonging to or associated with you 2 of, belonging to or associated with people in general

yours pronoun something belonging to you